UNIVERSITY OF CONNECTICUT — GROTON, CONN. — SOUTHEASTERN BRANCH LIBRARY —
JUN 22 1970

The Civilization of the West

THE Civilization OF THE West

A Brief Interpretation

BY JAMES M. POWELL

THE MACMILLAN COMPANY, NEW YORK
COLLIER-MACMILLAN LIMITED, LONDON

First Printing

Library of Congress catalog card number: 67-18126

THE MACMILLAN COMPANY, NEW YORK
COLLIER-MACMILLAN CANADA, LTD., TORONTO, ONTARIO

Printed in the United States of America

TO

MATTHEW AND LORETTA POWELL,

MY PARENTS

Preface

At a time when the non-Western World has begun to challenge the hegemony of the West, the study of Western civilization is no mere exercise in nostalgia for a lost past. Rather, the civilization of the West has been the catalytic agent in the shaping of our age of crisis and change. We must study Western civilization to understand the basic forces shaping the new world toward which we are moving.

The present book, whatever its shortcomings, has tried to emphasize the unfolding of Western civilization from its origins in the great river valleys and in Greece and Rome to its role in re-fashioning the whole earth. It does not try to minimize the importance of other civilizations to exalt the West, but rather to place the contributions of Western man in a world context looking to a future world that will be neither of East nor West and yet of both.

No historian possesses the detailed knowledge needed to write so broadly conceived a work. He must rely on the studies of others who have interpreted their periods from a more intimate foundation than most scholars can hope to develop save in one field. Yet, I must confess, the literature of synthesis is so great that my own acquaintance with it leaves many vistas unexplored. I can only hope that my efforts will aid the young college students for whom this book is primarily intended.

My primary debts are to my teachers and to my students; their inspiration is the basis for this book. But I must personally thank several persons who have played a special role in the making of this book. Lawrence McCaffrey and I taught a course in the history of Western civilization at the

University of Illinois. Many features of this work arose from our efforts there. Over the years, I have "picked many brains" for ideas. My colleague, A. R. Schoyen of Syracuse, contributed much to my thinking in our long conversations. Also, Father John Bush, S.J., of LeMoyne College, proved himself a kind friend and intelligent companion while I was writing. I also owe a special word of thanks to those who helped me collect illustrations. Mr. Terry Bender, Director of the Rare Book Room at Syracuse University, and Dean Lawrence Schmeckebier of the School of Art, were especially helpful. The museum staffs at the University of Michigan were very co-operative. My typists, Mrs. Joan Cassidy, Mrs. James Coyne, and Mrs. Robert Foster, responded to my appeals, sometimes to the detriment of other work on their schedules. I thank them and apologize to anyone I may have inconvenienced. I deeply appreciate the aid and advice of Robert J. Patterson, History Editor, and Joseph Falzone, Production Editor, of The Macmillan Company. Finally, I wish to acknowledge the continuing and inspiring assistance I have ever received from my wife, Judith. No critic has had better judgment. If there are defects in this book, they are chiefly due to my failure or inability to follow her suggestions. If there is merit, much of the credit is hers.

J. M. P

Contents

Part III
THE AGE OF WESTERN LEADERSHIP 291

Part IV
CRISIS, CHANGE, AND A NEW WORLD 449

MAPS

Introduction

"Clio gesta canens transactis tempora reddit."
"Clio, singing of famous deeds, restores the past to life."

The Historian Writes History

History is an adventure. It embodies man's most serious attempts to govern himself wisely, to secure adequate means of livelihood, to understand his relationship to other men, and to reach creatively beyond the mask of reality to grasp its hidden meanings.

History is an act. The past is not a frozen instant but a continuum. The single fact possesses no dimension; its existence has meaning only in relation to other facts, some causal, some dependent, some merely contemporary but related through a complex of causes. Christmas day of the year 800 A.D. becomes more meaningful if we add the fact of the coronation of Charlemagne. The coronation is understandable in light of Charlemagne's invasion of Italy and his destruction of the Lombards, of his vast campaigns to extend his territories at the expense of Avars, Saxons, and Moslems, of the charges against the Pope which Charlemagne came to Rome to investigate, of the persistence of the imperial dream, and many other events. Christmas day, 800 A.D., has many aspects; the events of that day present many problems needing explanation. Simplicity gives way to complexity. It is not possible to grasp the meaning of this day by a simple apprehension of a single fact. The quest for full understanding, or for as complete an understanding as is possible with the evidence available, demands interpretation.

The task of the historian is to supply an interpretation consistent with the evidence. Unlike the poet and novelist, he cannot allow his imagination freedom to create new evidence; his world is already peopled and his characters have already done their deeds. Homer, in writing of the Trojan

War, created the epic conflict between Agamemnon and Achilles to portray better the character of these two great heroes. Vergil twisted legend with reality to celebrate the glory and give greater meaning to the history of Rome in the Augustan age. Alessandro Manzoni chose humble characters, a girl and boy in love, in *The Betrothed* to heighten the contrast between the beloved Archbishop of Milan and a tyrannical noble attempting to prevent a wedding to further his own designs. Charles Dickens exposed the evils of debtors' prisons in *Oliver Twist* and wrote feelingly of the excesses of the French Revolution in *A Tale of Two Cities*. Each of these writers employed history in a work of imagination, but they did not write history. They refused to fetter their creative genius. Although their works contain much evidence of value to the historian, their contribution is not the result of conscious effort to interpret the past as accurately as possible.

Of course, historians also create the books they write. They use their imagination to reconstruct the past. To them, imagination is a tool of inquiry applied to the existing fabric of evidence. If an historian were to tamper even slightly with his data, his interpretation would be suspect. Error at some critical point in his discussion would almost certainly destroy his interpretation. The past is scattered with the debris of the works of authors who have failed to substantiate their positions. Yet, such is the nature of historical writing that their ideas must be continually reconsidered lest a summary rejection overlook some insight that would be lost. Edward Gibbon's explanation of the decline and fall of the Roman Empire has few supporters today, but no historian of that period can afford to neglect his work. For Gibbon's contribution lay in much more than his attempt to show that Christianity had played the leading role in the fall of the empire; few men have attained his grasp of Roman civilization in the broad sweep. Moreover, his was a happy inspiration for those who followed him and who, less influenced by eighteenth-century rationalism, saw in his thesis the budding of another view: Christianity, which in so many ways was incompatible with pagan Rome, was a significant force in the creation of Medieval civilization. In the search for meaning, the historian must explore imaginatively if he hopes for even modest success in his attempt to reconstruct past reality. His failures, however, ought not be judged too harshly; the task of baring the truth of the past and making it evident to man in the present presents greater challenges than almost any other man faces.

The first challenge stems from our conception of truth. The existence and nature of truth have posed problems for philosophers of all periods.

Merely to list their arguments would require more time than we can devote to this topic. Yet the nature of historical truth is fundamental to an understanding of history. Therefore, we must attempt at least to reconcile the ideal of absolute certainty to the limitations of historical investigation.

Historians have long been fond of contrasting historical truth with the certainty that results from scientific experiment. H_2O signifies that two hydrogen atoms combine with one oxygen atom to form water. The concrete certainty, verifiable time after time, of this statement appears much more absolute than an historian's argument that economic factors played a significant role as a cause of the French Revolution of 1789. Yet appearances can be deceptive. The mere operational verifiability of a scientific experiment does not ensure the truth of the complete hypothesis. To put the matter more simply, behavior has no meaning without scientific interpretation. Isaac Newton's description of the universe stood the test of scientific observation for almost two centuries before Albert Einstein's relativity theory provided a more inclusive explanation of the same phenomena. Yet Einstein's theory can not be called *true.* The relative paucity of our knowledge of the world around us makes the ideal of truth a goal still to be attained. The contrast between truth in history and truth in the natural sciences is unreal because both disciplines represent efforts by man to understand external reality. It does not matter that an experiment may be repeated, while the past may not. Repetition offers some advantages to the observer, but none great enough to cover his greatest disadvantage: the fact that he is an observer rather than a participant. The historian and the scientist inescapably share that role.

Nevertheless, truth is man's greatest quest. It becomes all the more important as man comes to understand that no branch of knowledge holds a monopoly to the complete truth or even to the right road. For then the search for truth demands that man explore the totality of his heritage as well as his present environment. A major element in the quest for truth is man's attempt to arrive at a fuller understanding of himself.

Historians observe the past. What do they hope to find? The answer to this question involves understanding the changing role of history as a branch of literature and as a discipline.

Through most of the past, the study of history has been regarded as a branch of literature and, indeed, this tradition has never been totally absent. However, those historians who have cast their history in the mold of literature have tended to study the great moments of the past to the neglect of the lesser and to emphasize political events over social and economic changes. From Herodotus to Gibbon, they were caught up in the drama of titanic struggles and momentous decline. Consciousness of this drama as well as fidelity to literary craft tended to shape their writing according to the principles of aesthetics, a fact which accounts to a significant extent for their tendency to see past reality in terms of abrupt and dramatic changes rather than as a product of slow and gradual development.

However, these historians also had a didactic purpose in their art; they aimed to create a useful work. Thucydides, the Greek general who wrote of the Peloponnesian War, and whose art is concealed in his disciplined style, summed up his role in this way. ". . . if it be judged useful by those inquirers who desire an exact knowledge of the past as an aid to the interpretation of the future . . . I shall be content." Thucydides did not accept the notion that the past would repeat itself in the future, but he did believe that human acts tended to spring from similar circumstances. He thought men could learn to avoid past mistakes but they must study the causes of those mistakes. Therefore, Thucydides stressed these causes throughout his work. He sought to reach behind the events themselves and to grasp the real grounds on which men acted; he refused to be satisfied with the reasons given by the principals. His view was that of the rational humanist offering men a hope of improvement in an age of despair. His art was one with that of Sophocles the dramatist. In both cases tragedy was the great teacher.

For the humanist historians of the ancient period, the end of their study was never distant. The image of man was constantly before their eyes. Christian writers, on the other hand, contemplated history as the working out of a divine plan. St. Augustine of Hippo's *City of God,* composed just as the Roman world was cracking under pressure of the barbarian Germanic tribes, did not pause to lament the destruction of the empire or the imperial city, for this was part of God's plan. Augustine did not write to assure men that they could learn from the past to build better nor to promise them hope based on faith in rational man, but rather to tell them that hope must be joined to faith in the designs of the Christian God. Augustine believed man's purpose was not to be found in Rome but in Jerusalem, not in the city of men, but in the city of God. During all the centuries in which men were striving to erect a new civilization on the ruins of Rome, the vision of the city of God remained a tantalizing but ever-receding goal, a dream never fully understood even by those most ardent in its pursuit. The attempt to transform earth into the vestibule of heaven caused men of the Middle Ages deep anguish, for it forced them to attempt a reconciliation between their earthly ambitions and the divine plan. The tensions produced by these efforts generated some of the most important thoughts in history, especially in the realm of political theory.

Augustine had attempted to see human history in terms of the purpose ordained for mankind by God. He believed history was simply the working out of Divine Providence and it revealed the glory of the plan and thereby glorified the planner, God. Within the Augustinian view of history there was little room left for human responsibility. Man might violate the design; he could never hope to create a design for a good society himself. At best, human history was the story of man's search for and conformity to a preexisting order; at worst it was the story of frailty and failure. The task of the historian was to keep the role of Divine Providence ever before men's eyes. This task inspired the world chronicles of the Middle Ages and Early Modern period; it was never far from the minds of most writers in these eras.

The transition from Medieval to Modern, however, saw more and more historians taking pride in human accomplishments. Although many of these authors continued to plan their histories as universal chronicles of civilization, a new monographic history was also rising which left the role of Providence to the background and concentrated more on explaining the causes of human glory. Pope Pius II's *Historia Bohemica* was limited to one country and concentrated on the Hussite Wars. It was basically a work of literary exposition, although the author had taken pains to visit the country and to study the original sources.

The new age was ardently dedicated to a belief in the relevance of history. In general, the Middle Ages had accepted or rejected historical documents with little effort to examine their merits. Forgeries were perpetrated in the papal chancery itself. Lorenzo Valla was the key figure in fashioning the tools of a new criticism. He proved that the Donation of Constantine, which purported to establish the claim of the Popes to a virtual overlordship of Western Europe, was a forgery. Though he was not the first to reject the document nor even the first to show it was a forgery, the method of internal criticism which he employed placed in the hands of succeeding historians and philologists a basic key for determining the authenticity of past writings. In a sense, we might say that Valla was the founder of the historical method.

Under the influence of the religious revolutions of the sixteenth century, history became a polemic weapon. The publication of the *Magdeburg Centuries* of Mathias Flacius Illyricus in 1559 was an attempt to view the past history of Christianity from the Lutheran position. Marred by its biased selection of materials, it drew a response from the Catholic historian, Cardinal Caesar Baronius. His *Annales Ecclesiastici* was begun in 1588 and manifested the defensive tone of Catholic historical and religious writing following the Council of Trent. In the hands of polemicists history was a weapon. They subordinated historical truth to partisan prejudice, very often without a full awareness that this was happening. However, the polemicists did make an important contribution to historical studies. They made men more aware of the importance of history. Their present was never long separated from their past. Moreover, they dominated the writing of ecclesiastical history until the early twentieth century. During this long period, they rendered important service to history as they developed new tools for research and became more aware of the importance of critical preparation of their works, if only to avoid the ridicule of their enemies.

The growth of a critical consciousness of the past received further impetus in the seventeenth century from the studies of the famous Jesuit editors of the *Acta Sanctorum* (Lives of the Saints), begun by Jean Bollandus. The Bollandists undertook to prepare critical editions of the early writings on the lives of the saints. Their zeal for revealing the past led them to reject many of the tales accepted as true for centuries and brought them into conflict even within the Catholic Church. One of the most famous of these controversies, involving the foundation of the famous French abbey of St. Denis outside Paris led to a conflict with Benedictine scholars and to the publication of one of the great works in the history of textual criticism, the *De Re Diplomatica* by the Benedictine monk, Jean Mabillon. This work systematized the knowledge gained in previous centuries about the falsity of historical documents. It enabled scholars to know with greater certainty whether they were dealing with a genuine document or a forgery. The seventeenth century equipped the historian with better tools than he had ever before possessed in his quest for historical actuality. It gave to his discipline some claim to a scientific methodology just at the time when the English philosopher, Francis Bacon, was proclaiming in the *Novum Organum* the superiority of induction over deduction in scientific enquiry. As the eighteenth century unfolded, the French *philosophes*, champions of reason, armed with this spirit of criticism, used history to attack organized religion and the institutions which had grown up in Europe during the Middle Ages. Harkening to Voltaire's cry to destroy that infamous institution the Church, the editors of the great French *Encyclopedia* devoted their best efforts to revealing its shortcomings and proving it an anachronism in an age of enlightenment.

With similar fervor, they attacked the vestiges of feudalism, which held France in a vice-grip of conservatism. They called for reform, the wiping away of all traces of the reactionary past. Their movement attracted historians from other countries, among whom Edward Gibbon justly has obtained a leading place. His *Decline and Fall of the Roman Empire* stood for the triumph of "reason" over a superstitious and obscurantist past. The historians of the eighteenth century who wrote under the influence of these attitudes—and not all did—generally possessed a deep sense of mission which colored all their historical writing. They wrote from a lofty moral pinnacle overlooking the whole of mankind's past. As a matter of fact, they were more the judges of men than historians.

But the ideals of these rationalists were also productive. In the early nineteenth century, their criticisms focused on the Bible. They drew their techniques largely from Friedrich August Wolf's attack on the authenticity of Homer as author of the *Iliad* published in 1795. Wolf had argued on the basis of the text that the *Iliad* was the work of many separate authors. He had pointed to apparent inconsistencies in plot and style to support this position. The nineteenth-century critics of the Bible used similar arguments to deny the authenticity of certain books and to change the dates traditionally assigned to some. They challenged the Gospel of St. John largely on the grounds that its conception revealed a deeper understanding of Greek philosophical ideas than was believed possible at the time of its composition. Therefore, the Higher Critics, as these savants of the Bible were called, dated it much later than the other gospels. They also posited the existence of an original version, the so-called Ur-Mark, on which the synoptic gospels were based. Although many of their positions have been modified, the influence of the Higher Critics played an important part in determining the direction of later scripture studies. Moreover, they profoundly influenced the growth of the nineteenth-century scientific school of history, represented by historicism.

Historicism set before those who pursued history as a science the ideal of presenting the past *wie es eigentlich gewesen ist*, that is, exactly as it had been. Nor was this an empty goal, for the historicists believed that they had at hand the knowledge and tools to accomplish this noble aim. They advocated a rigorous objectivity based on close contact with the sources and they rigorously trained themselves and their students to examine the historical evidence critically, using the methods developed in the seventeenth and eighteenth centuries and perfected by themselves. This methodology was enshrined in works such as Bernheim's *Lehrbuch der Historischen Methode* (Textbook of Historical Method).

Historicism offered a view of history as the key to understanding all human experience. Its adherents saw in it those qualities which had lifted the natural sciences from their origins in magic and alchemy and brought them the verifiability of experimental truth. Even Karl Marx, the father of modern Communism, could not escape the grasp of historicism. His deterministic interpretation of history based on the dialectics of materialism sprang from roots deep in Historicist thinking. Marx accepted the "scientific" methodology and the ideal of objective reality of the historicists as the basis of his economic determinism.

Under the historicists, the writing of history enjoyed a golden age. Convinced of the value and even the utility of their task, they worked unstintingly to collect documents from all historical periods. They made governments conscious of the need for carefully preserved and well-ordered public archives and they demanded access to these records in the name of historical truth. The nineteenth century saw the beginnings of the *Monumenta Germaniae Historica,* initiated by Gustav Pertz, of the *Rolls Series* containing the writings of English medieval authors, and many other great collections of documents. Leopold von Ranke wrote the history of the Popes; Treitschke studied the rise of Prussia. Bishop William Stubbs devoted a lifetime to English Constitutional history. George Bancroft poured his efforts into a multivolumed history of the United States, while Hubert Howe Bancroft collected vast amounts of materials for his histories of Pacific North America.

The confidence of the historicists dominated the writing of history well into the twentieth century. Only the disillusionment of the period following World War I succeeded in gradually bringing historicism into disrepute. A world which had lost its optimism could not bring itself to accept the notion that historical truth was absolute. Bitter experience of man's ability to devise weapons for use against other men, brought home to the postwar world the reality of retrogression in history and undermined the facile optimism of the historicists. But the virtual destruction of historicism left a major problem for the historians. Previously they had almost unanimously accepted the scientific conception of their discipline. Now they found themselves divided. The generation of historians who survived World War II has spent a considerable part of its effort in groping for a clearer understanding of its craft (See bibliography for the Introduction). The writings of Marc Bloch, W. H. Walsh, R. C. Collingwood, Herbert Butterfield, V. H .Galbraith, and E. H. Carr have all appeared in print since the close of the war and each in his own manner lines up the strongest defenses he can muster in behalf of history. Why does history

Leopold von Ranke. One of the leading German historians of the nineteenth century. His desire was an objective history. (Rare Book Room, Syracuse University Library)

need these defenses? The chief answer is that historians have not yet recovered from their shock at the decline and fall of history as an absolute. Nor have they yet found a substitute for historicism.

Herein lies the challenge of history. It is not as Carl Becker once maintained that every generation must be its own historian; it is rather that the first half of the twentieth century saw the destruction of that consensus about the nature and role of history which was historicism. The task for the historian in the second half of the twentieth century is that set forth at the beginning of this chapter: to reconcile the ideal of absolute certainty to the limitations of historical investigation and interpretation. The long highway already traveled in the growth of history as a discipline reveals how difficult and yet how important a task this is.

All disciplines, whether in the natural sciences, the social sciences, or the humanities are seeking a deeper understanding of man and the universe. Each discipline has its limitations imposed by the nature of the investigation. All are limited by the fact that human vision comprehends only a part of the total vision that is reality. The mere fact that it is possible to weigh and analyze air does not give the chemist or the physicist any great advantage over the historian for the simple reason that weighing and analyzing are useless unless the chemist and physicist can draw conclusions from the evidence they obtain. As they draw conclusions they participate in an intellectual process similar to that of the historian when he attempts to interpret evidence; they share his shortcomings. Just as he is certain that the evidence before him does not represent all that happened at a given moment in history, they are certain that they can reach more deeply into matter to unlock its secrets. It is from this fact that students of history should take heart. There is a better hope than that offered by the historicists. Their hope and their optimism were based largely on a smug satisfaction with their own intellectual success. The hope for the future of history lies in a clearer grasp of the essential problems facing the historian; the problem of historical truth, the limitations of evidence, and the limitations of the historian. From this starting point, the quest must continue.

PART I

"Carmina Calliope libris heroica mandat."
"Calliope commits heroic songs to writing."

1 The Eastern Basis: Patterns and Variety

Every historian who attempts to understand a particular society or civilization must face the problem of its origins. For the audacious soul who wishes to learn more about Western civilization, those origins reach beyond history into the ages when tribes of men first made those decisions that have had such an important role in the shaping of the West. Unhappily, no historian can ever hope to penetrate to that period to learn why men migrated to one place rather than another, why they organized themselves in the ways they did, or how they learned the basic skills which enabled them to found the first civilizations. Our best answers to these questions must always have a great element of guessing in them despite the advances made by anthropologists and archaeologists.

We begin with a few bits of information. Early men did not settle evenly over the face of the earth. Some men remained nomadic until well into historic times, some even to the present, while others settled and began to plant and reap in the cycle of nature. Some men provided evidence of greater skill and artistic ability than others at a very early date. This information is valuable for it explains to some extent the wide cultural variations found in early civilizations, the instability of some of them, and the relative advancement of some societies over others in creative achievement. While it is certainly not true that prehistoric people lived in isolation from one another, it is true that the amount of contact between widely separated peoples was manifestly less than during the period of recorded history. This was especially true after a group of people had settled in a certain area and begun to engage in agricultural activities. Some may even have sought out a relative isolation to avoid clashes with other bands of men. At any rate, the possibility for such isolation existed in the uneven scattering of peoples over the earth. Those who did settle tended to choose places of natural fertility suitable to the raising of grains, which formed the staple of their diet. Some chose rich river valleys where annual flooding replenished the soil and reduced or even removed the need for continual movement in search of newer and more fertile fields when present soil became exhausted.

The rich flood plains created in Mesopotamia by the Tigris and Euphrates Rivers and the valley of the Nile River in Egypt were the centers of two of the earliest civilizations. But from these valleys, and especially from the great plain of Mesopotamia, early civilization spread over the Near East and Asia Minor. Mesopotamia and Egypt became seats of empires, centers of great cultures, and important influences on the development of other civilizations. The recorded history of Western civilization has its most significant beginnings in these valleys.

Mesopotamia and Her Invaders

The fertile valley created by the Tigris and Euphrates had early attracted a settled population. Indeed, the accessibility of this region, at the head of the Persian Gulf and beckoning to the peoples of the mountain, hill, and desert country all around, determined already in the Neolithic age that its population was to be made up of differing racial stocks. When the Sumerians arrived somewhat after 4000 B.C., they found a Neolithic population engaged in agriculture already dwelling on the fertile plain. The Sumerians, probably an amalgam of peoples from the East, laid the foundations for a city-state system about 3000 B.C. Within these cities, which were largely agricultural communities, the temple served as focal point for both religious and political life. The *ensi* or king was merely a servant of the god of the city, whose duty it was to carry out his will. Within this framework, there is evidence for a kind of primitive democracy. A council of elders and an assembly of warriors met with the *ensi* to decide important questions affecting the life of the community. The loyalties of the Sumerians were local, to the god of the town, to its *ensi*, and to their temple and its priests.

The first attempt to impose any kind of unity over this region was made by Sargon I of Akkad. His Akkadian Empire (2400 B.C.) reached from the Persian Gulf to northern Babylonia and was therefore limited almost entirely to the land between the rivers. The Akkadians were a Semitic peo-

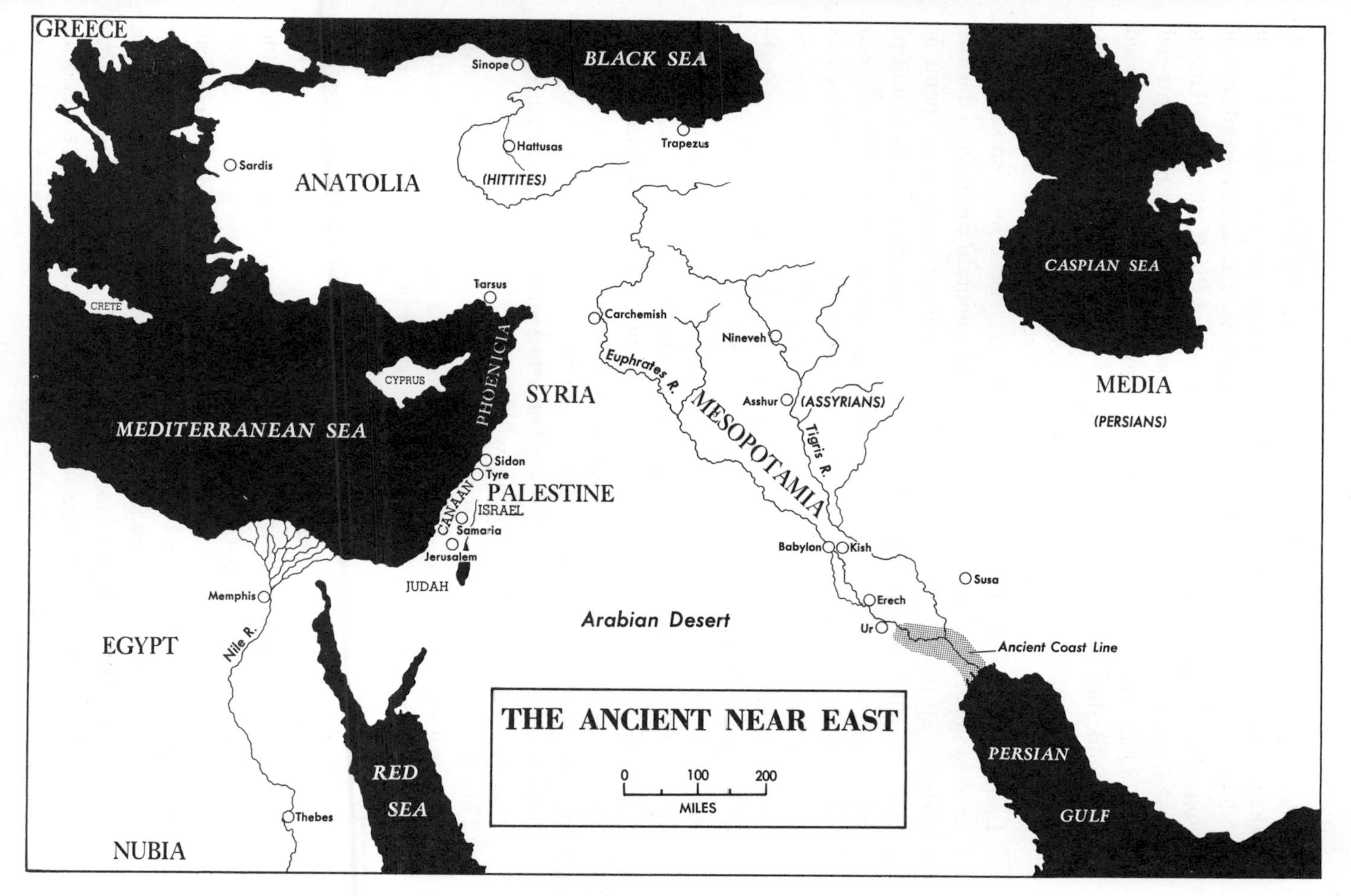
THE ANCIENT NEAR EAST
0
100
200
MILES
GREECE
BLACK SEA
Sinope
Trapezus
Hattusas
(HITTITES)
Sardis
ANATOLIA
CRETE
Tarsus
CYPRUS
MEDITERRANEAN SEA
PHOENICIA
SYRIA
Sidon
Tyre
PALESTINE
CANAAN
ISRAEL
Samaria
Jerusalem
JUDAH
Carchemish
Euphrates R.
MESOPOTAMIA
Nineveh
Asshur
(ASSYRIANS)
Tigris R.
Babylon
Kish
Erech
Ur
Susa
Ancient Coast Line
CASPIAN SEA
MEDIA
(PERSIANS)
Arabian Desert
PERSIAN
GULF
Memphis
Nile R.
EGYPT
Thebes
RED
SEA
NUBIA

ple, who made no great effort to change the culture they found in this region. However, their coming did lead to the adoption of Akkadian by the people and the relegation of the Sumerian language to the status of a "classic" tongue, used chiefly for official records. The achievement of Sargon lasted for more than three centuries before the Guti, a little known barbarous people, swept down from the mountains and destroyed his empire. Once more the Mesopotamian tendency toward localism reasserted itself and, during this period, Ur and Lagash, two of the major cities, enjoyed an almost golden age.

The invasion of the Amorites, who had gradually extended their power from Babylon in the period following 1800 B.C., once more subordinated local to imperial interests. We know that Hammurabi promulgated a law code for all the peoples of his kingdom. From a constitutional point of view, the chief significance of this code was the creation of a more unified system of justice. Though it would be unwise to say that local legal institutions perished as a result, certainly the jurisdiction of local judges was controlled and even limited by the code. But Hammurabi's attempt at centralization was doomed to failure. His empire fell before the new wave of barbarian invasions which swept across Mesopotamia and Asia Minor and which brought in its wake new peoples of an Indo-European stock. Among these peoples the Hittites rapidly rose to prominence.

The Hittites had established themselves in central Asia Minor about 1900 B.C. From their capital at Hattushash near the Halys River, they expanded eastward and southward in the fifteenth century. By the thirteenth century, they dominated most of Asia Minor and Mesopotamia and were engaged in a titanic struggle with the Egyptians for control of Syria. They came into contact with the sea peoples, especially the Ahhijava (Achaeans), who were probably Mycenaean Greeks. The vastness of the Hittite Empire marked it in two ways. It was chiefly the result of conquest and therefore lacked basic political stability and its size operated to weaken it in time of peril. The long struggle with Egypt wore out the Hittites without bringing more than an indecisive peace (1269 B.C.). Thus the close of the thirteenth century saw the overthrow of their power and the collapse of their imperial system.

The destruction of Hittite power created a vacuum in the political structure of the Middle and Near East. Although this led to a temporary resurgence of local rule and the establishment of Kassite hegemony from Babylonia over some regions formerly controlled by the Hittites, the long-range effect was to invite the formation of a new imperialist authority bent on military conquest. The rise of the militaristic Assyrians, a hitherto quiescent force, to the role of dominance comes, therefore, as no surprise. They pushed their frontiers from Babylon outward to encompass part of Asia Minor and Syria as well as Egypt. No enemy was able to withstand their iron weapons. As true military rulers, they sought tribute more than the instruments of government and therefore made little attempt to change the city-state organization of the East. It was this preservation of local institutions which worked to their undoing; it provided a political base for those who became dissatisfied with Assyrian rule. As long as the conquerors remained in control and did not overreach themselves, these local disaffections were of little moment. But the growth of the empire caused a loosening of their grasp and the unhappy subject peoples found support among the Medes and Persians to the East for their plan to overthrow the Assyrians. In 612 B.C., a coalition of Chaldeans of Babylon and Medes destroyed Nineveh, the Assyrian capital, and the empire fell as rapidly as it had risen. But the rule of the Chaldeans proved to be merely a prologue to the introduction of the Persians into Mesopotamia, although for a brief moment it had looked otherwise. Under Nebuchadrezzar II (604–562 B.C.) the Chaldeans expanded into Palestine and took the city of Jerusalem (586 B.C.), carrying the inhabitants to Babylon. That city became a wonder of the ancient world with its hanging gardens and its beautiful streets and avenues. But, while much of the glory remained, the city fell to the Persians in 539 B.C.

The Medes had held the Perisans as a tributary people. Forced to fight beside the Medes, they were therefore spectators at the overthrow of the Assyrian Empire. What effect this may have had upon their aspirations for independence, it is impossible to say, but they overthrew the rule of the Medes and embarked on a program of expansion that was to create for them the greatest empire in history to that time. Under the leadership of Cyrus, the "great king," Babylon fell to the Persians without a fight; a new empire was born.

The Persian conquests engulfed Mesopotamia, Syria, Asia Minor, and Egypt. With their military prowess, the Persians revealed a considerable talent for civil administration. They connected far-flung outposts by a military post system and built a great highway from Sardis in Asia Minor to the royal capital at Susa. The satraps, or provincial governors, served during the king's pleasure and could be removed without notice; their administration was subject to review without any advance warning. The Persians retained considerable autonomy for many different parts of their empire, following here the example of previous Near Eastern empires. Greek city-states on the coast of western Asia Minor continued to enjoy not merely commercial prosperity stemming from their position in the empire, but also considerable political autonomy in the conduct of their local affairs. But the Persians also had to face the problems of their predecessors in governing so broad a domain. Communications, although rapid by previous standards, were too slow to permit effective use of the army. Moreover, the many different elements in the population of the empire never completely accepted Persian rule and served in the armies only reluctantly. Though overawed by the power of Persia, they could not be counted on in time of crisis. That time came in the fourth century B.C. when the disciplined Macedonian and Greek army of Alexander the Great crushed the empire of the "great king" like a hollow shell.

The civilization of Mesopotamia and the East was constantly changing under the various conquerors of these regions, yet it retained, at least until the Persian conquest, a cultural unity that enables scholars to speak of it as a single civilization. Even after the Persian conquest, many features remained as they had been during preceding millennia.

Community life centered on the city-state, which might best be defined as an urban center and its surrounding agricultural dependencies. As we have seen, even the formation of more centralized governments did not put an end to the local autonomy of the city-state. No doubt, for the average person, this community commanded a loyalty far greater than any he might give to a distant and almost unknown emperor. The city-state was not merely the center of political authority for the region; it was also a cultural and religious center. Here were the temple and the priests who wrote down the great religious myths of the past in the wedge-shaped cuneiform writing common to this whole region. Although this art of writing was not limited to the priests—merchants and scribes possessed it, too—theirs was a special charge because they were the intellectual leaders of the community.

The imperialist conquerors of Mesopotamia attempted again and again to gather up the strands of localism and unify them. Hammurabi promulgated his great code partially to this end. He drew on the common legal experience of the region and yet attempted to find a principle of unity that would provide for his code a validity greater than that of local custom. He claimed not to act in the name of the Amorites or on the authority he possessed by right of his victories, but by the divine power conferred on him by the gods to promote the welfare of the people. In claiming to act for the gods, Hammurabi did not establish himself as a god-king in the way that the Pharaohs of Egypt did, but attempted to establish his role as a mediator or interpreter of the gods for mankind. The

Babylonian cuneiform tablet. Among the earliest forms of writing, these tablets record much of the history, law, and business records of Mesopotamian civilization. (Rare Book Room, Syracuse University Library)

importance of this concept cannot be exaggerated. Through the Hebrew tradition, which had its roots in Mesopotamia, it entered Western political thought where it survived well into modern times.

What had made Hammurabi's appeal to a divine sanction for his laws more valid was the existence of a more or less common religious tradition among the people of the great river plain. Environment played an important role in the shaping of religious mythology. The land of Mesopotamia has an unstable climate. Storm, heat, flood, and drought threatened those who desired to live from its soil. Man's efforts to ward off these evils played an important part in forming his mythology. Moreover, the stresses of nature and the influx of ideas introduced by new peoples entering the region operated against the idea of beneficent deities. The people believed Mesopotamian divinities acted arbitrarily and often vindictively, sending floods to destroy the labors of man in the fields and scorching heat to parch the crops. They felt hope lay in placating them, in discovering their desires in advance and meeting their demands. The theology of the Mesopotamian peoples posited a continuing tension between the various gods and goddesses representing earth and sun and water in which man's role was that of the victim. The myth of creation reveals the conflict between earth and water. But it also shows how these elements united to bring forth life. Given the nature of this tension, the king, the law-giver, had as his chief duty to ward off the anger of the gods.

The literature of Mesopotamia reflected this tension. In the Gilgamesh Epic, the hero faced almost insurmountable tasks in his quest for the secret of immortality. Hindered at every turn by the gods, he succeeded in finding the plant of life only to suffer defeat in his attempt to bring his gift to others of his race. A strong note of pessimism permeates this story and the whole of Mesopotamian literature. Man could never hope for freedom and justice in a world under the influence of arbitrary divinities.

It is against this background that one must view the social life of these peoples. Man, though created from divinity, was a creature of a lower order than the gods who ruled, for he had been born of divinity dethroned from its high seat and condemned to the slime below. All men, from kings to peasants, shared this unfortunate state. All were subject to a common fate, all might lose in the never-ending game of placating the gods. This fact explains the importance of the priests in Mesopotamian society. The temples and the lands which they controlled dominated the agricultural economy of the region. No king dared to venture into war with an enemy without first consulting the priests to determine the mind of the gods. Next in importance were the warriors, on whom rested the responsibility to protect this land which was under constant threat of invasion. Environment also played a part in making society more fluid. Contacts were not limited to the narrow river valley and a few points beyond. Mesopotamia stood at the juncture of the great paths of migration from East to West. Thus the merchant class, which had played a minor role in Egypt and was there closely controlled by the state, was relatively large and prosperous. The advent of the various empires promoted a unity beneficial to commerce. From Greece to India and the Far East, merchants carried spices, metals, pottery, wine, and oil. Abundant business records preserved on clay tablets reveal the existence of a class of people with interests broader than those of the peasants and possessing a position in society higher on the social ladder. This "middle class"—to borrow a modern term—had not only a better standard of living but also a higher level of education than most farmers and herdsmen. Concentrated in cities, this class formed the nucleus for a genuine urban and non-noble society with far-ranging contacts and curiosities. It, together with environmental factors and the influence of new peoples, must receive partial credit for the dynamic qualities of Mesopotamian culture. But the mass of men were engaged in agriculture and pastoral pursuits. Their life kept them tied to a soil which was seldom their own, but which they tilled for the god to whose temple it belonged. The farmers of the plain irrigated their lands with the waters of the Tigris and Euphrates and prayed that the gods would not bring flood or earth-cracking heat to destroy the fruits of their labors. The uncertainty of their existence gave little cause for hope and lent encouragement to the pessimistic strain in Near Eastern thought.

Mesopotamia was the heartland of the conquerors. Its tribute furnished them the wealth to finance their victories over the surrounding regions and the weakness of one empire provided the motivation for other peoples to attempt to establish a new one. But it would be a mistake to view its history merely in terms of a succession of empires. To do so would be to ignore the factors which had a continuing development and, in some cases, important influences beyond the region itself. In politics, the structure of the city-state in its primitive forms developed there. The appeal to a higher authority as a sanction for human laws found expression in the code of Hammurabi. Scientific achievements in mathematics and astronomy had a direct influence on the later contributions of the Greeks. Their religious ideas, while far from the monotheism of the Jews, possessed a strong ethical content that was passed on. Finally, the tenor of economic life passed on to subsequent peoples their broad experience in commerce. It is not surprising that many historians have called this region a "cradle of civilization."

Egypt: The Narrow Land

The Nile River, rising in Central Africa and fed by several great tributaries on its long and determined meandering to the Mediterranean Sea, forms a fertile valley about twelve miles wide and five hundred miles long and then spreads out over a great delta before entering the sea. This narrow land is Egypt.

During the paleolithic age, when the valley was uninhabitable, a nomadic people eked out their existence among the forbidding rocks while, in the delta, another group built homes on high ground amid the marshy land. From these inauspicious beginnings two kingdoms developed during the neolithic period. For more than a millenium the two kingdoms, the White Kingdom of the south and the Red of the delta maintained their separated existence. Toward the end of this age, the Egyptians began to create the complicated system of canals and dikes needed to take best advantage of the annual flooding of the river with its soil-renewing deposit of rich silt. About 3100 B.C. they were united through the efforts of the White King, Narmer, traditionally known as Menes, the traditional founder of the first dynasty. According to the Egyptian priest, Manetho, thirty dynasties ruled in Egypt until the overthrow of native Egyptian rule by the Persians in 523 B.C.

The Old Kingdom (3100–2200 B.C.), with its capital at Memphis, led Egypt out of its period of isolation. The strong leadership of the Pharaoh, a god-king with absolute power, no doubt played an important role in the commercial contacts which the Egyptians established with Crete, Syria, and Nubia in this era. Egyptian merchants established colonies and traded for copper and lumber as far north as Lebanon in the period following 2500 B.C. The Pharaoh was sole owner of all the land; all Egyptians, from the humblest peasant to the mightiest noble, owed him rent in kind or service for the right to use it. A whole army of officials, necessary in so highly centralized a government, answered to him. This bureaucracy kept careful records of all transactions and filed them for future reference. Egypt was not, however, a mere bureaucratic despotism; the government of the Pharaoh was the object of an intense loyalty, best witnessed in the voluntary construction of the great pyramids as tombs for the god-kings.

Near the end of the third millennium B.C.—about 2200—the Old Kingdom lost its vigor and the Pharaohs came more and more under the control of the great nobles and aristocrats whom they had appointed to rule various nomes or provinces and to serve in the priesthoods. The nobility took advantage of the weakness of the kings to make their offices hereditary and to convert to their own use the lands and revenues which had formerly belonged to the kings. Their rivalries for power led to internal warfare and division of the great kingdom until, about 2000 B.C., the ruler of Thebes in upper Egypt succeeded in gaining recognition of himself as god-king and Pharaoh.

The Middle Kingdom lasted for approximately three hundred years, until 1730 B.C. It began with the efforts of the Pharaohs of the eleventh dynasty to reestablish the royal power. These men seem to have been political realists. They did not attempt an immediate return to the absolutism of the Old Kingdom, but worked within the framework of aristocratic rule which had characterized the two centuries prior to 2000 B.C. Their efforts to win the obedience and loyalty of the nobility met with success. Moreover, they were able to gain the support of the masses by permitting them to share in the privileges of the nobility, particularly by allowing them to bequeath their land to their families at death. In general, the

Middle Kingdom seems to have brought greater dignity and even freedom to more Egyptians before its destruction by the Hyksos.

The Hyksos were an Indo-European people who swept down on Egypt in the eighteenth century B.C. and succeeded in conquering them. Their major advantages over the Egyptians in warfare were their use of iron weapons and the horse. The rule of the Hyksos was a profound traumatic experience for the Egyptians, who made every effort not merely to erase it from their memories, but also to destroy all evidence that it ever occurred. The Egyptians deeply resented these foreigners, who worshipped alien deities and ruled them through the agency of armies imported from Asia. Egyptian resentment broke out into successful rebellion under the leadership of Ahmose I (1570–1545 B.C.), the founder of the eighteenth dynasty.

The restoration of native rule ushered in one of the most glorious ages in the whole of Egyptian history. Ahmose I and his successors carried their war against the Hyksos into Asia Minor and Syria, where they succeeded in subjecting the island of Cyprus, parts of Asia Minor and even struck northward as far as the Euphrates River. Thutmose III devoted his efforts, after he had escaped the tutelage of a hated stepmother, to further extension of the Egyptian Empire. Under his rule, Egypt was the dominant power in the Near East.

In the years following the death of Thutmose III, however, various subject peoples showed a greater and greater tendency to renew their old feuds and to ignore the Pharaoh. Amenhotep III (c. 1411–1375 B.C.) spent part of his reign in Syria attempting to deal with the recalcitrants to little avail. The reign of Amenhotep IV led tragically to the collapse of the empire and civil war in Egypt. This ruler, whom some historians have considered to be the most enlightened spirit in Egyptian history, was more deeply concerned about philosophy than conquest. He desired to bring all peoples to a great unity and the means he chose to this end was religion. He raised the god Aton to the pinnacle of Egyptian theology because this deity was also reverenced by the subject peoples of Asia. Amenhotep changed his name from Amon-is-satisfied to Ikhnaton (Serviceable-to-Aton). He moved his capital from Thebes, where the priesthood of Amon-Ra, the Egyptian god of the sun predominated, to a new site at Tell al-Amarna. There in the nineteenth century scholars discovered the archives from the period, which told in vivid detail the dismal tale of intrigue and rebellion against a dreamer-king. Ikhnaton's great ambition to mold his subjects into a unity under Aton disappeared in face of their rivalries. His death gave the signal for a civil war which wiped out virtually all traces of his movement. While his noblest monument is the beautiful *Hymn to the Sun,* which he composed and which praises his god Aton, the radiant and beneficent influence of the sun, he must also be charged with at least part of the blame for the decline of the Egyptian Empire.

Under Ramses II, Egypt made an attempt to recover the position she had lost in Syria. But she found her efforts checked by the power of the Hittites, who had taken advantage of her weakness to strengthen the position of their own empire. From their capital in Asia Minor, they controlled a vast force of allies and mercenaries whom they were prepared to send against the invading Egyptians. In 1286 B.C. at Kadesh they succeeded in ambushing Ramses' army. While the result was not a victory for either side, it forced Egypt to agree to peace. In the still-preserved treaty, the two sides agreed to keep peace and to render mutual aid to one another in case of internal strife. Ramses, to seal the bargain, took a Hittite princess as his chief wife. But the treaty proved of little value for the Hittite Empire fell suddenly before a new Indo-European invasion of Asia Minor and, after the death of Ramses, Egypt also declined. The power of the pharaohs fell into the hands of the priestly caste in upper Egypt, while the delta fell prey to Libyan invaders, who had long cast covetous eyes from their forbidding waste on the rich bottom land of the Nile.

The Ramesids were the last great pharaohs of Egypt. The Assyrians, who had overrun the rich plain of Mesopotamia had fiercely extended their sway throughout Asia Minor and Syria. Egypt's turn came when the conquerors took Thebes in 661 B.C. The Assyrian conquest was short-lived, but so was Egypt's attempt to maintain her independence under Psamtik (663–609 B.C.). Though his twenty-sixth dynasty brought a temporary prosperity and political stability, the heyday of Egyptian power was passed. The end of independence came when the Persians, successors of the Assyrians in their control of Mesopotamia, descended on Egypt in 523 B.C. and conquered it without difficulty. The Persian king of kings assumed the title of Pharaoh. Henceforward the history of Egypt was almost completely intertwined with the fate of the Persian Empire until it fell to Alexander the Great of Macedon in 332 B.C.

The political life of Egypt was for the ancients an unparalleled example of the durability of one way of life. Amid the instability of political arrangements throughout the eastern Mediterranean world, the Pharaohs continued to rule the narrow land for century after century in almost monotonous procession. During this period of more than two millennia, the

Egyptians built up a rich cultural heritage, the remains of which remind the traveler in their land today of their accomplishment.

The long span of Egyptian history presents a unity, but not a uniformity, of cultural experience. In part this may be attributed to the relative isolation in which Egyptian civilization developed, but this factor operated more in a negative than in a positive manner. It minimized the influence of non-Egyptian elements in the formative period of the culture, but did not provide an active unifying force for it. This force came rather from the deep and continuing influence of religion in Egyptian life.

The religion of the Egyptians reflected their experience in the narrow land. The constant presence of sun and river dominated their thinking. On the one hand, a beneficent sun nurtured life along the river; on the other, an angry sun parched the land and scorched the crops. The river, the Nile, annually brought new life to the valley. Tons of rich silt from the highlands of the south swept northward in its annual torrent forming a rich ooze over the floor of the valley. The precious waters, gathered in canals, sustained and nourished the fields of grain planted in the fertile soil until the harvest. Thus Egyptian life adapted itself to an annual cycle in which man and nature cooperated. This annual cycle of life and death was a drama of fertility, destruction, and new hope integral to Egyptian religion. Nowhere is this theme more poignantly illustrated than in the beautiful myth of Isis and Osiris.

Isis, goddess of the land, was the wife of Osiris, god of the river. Her love for him was so great that when he drowned in the river she called upon Anubis, the Jackal god, to restore his life. Anubis did her bidding and Osiris once more brought life to the land. The meaning of the river was a theme worked deep into the fiber of religion in Egypt. But Osiris was also the god of death. These twin themes of life and death played the most important part in Egyptian religious thought.

Egyptian preoccupation with death was not morbid. On the contrary, they were not given to deep philosophical speculation and tended to accept each day for the joys that it might bring. The strong concern with death was merely one aspect of their belief in immortality. They prepared for life after death in a most elaborate way. The kings of the Old Kingdom built the pyramids to house their remains, their treasures, and food for immortality. The discovery of the tomb of Tutankhamen in 1921 revealed for the first time the care lavished by the Egyptians on their dead kings. In the stone chambers of this eighteen-year-old monarch's grave were exquisite vessels of gold and wood. His head was encased in a

Isis and Harpocrates. This wall painting from Karanis, Egypt, illustrates the persistence of the cult of Isis into the Roman period and shows the continuing influence of Egyptian art in the later period. (The Kelsey Museum of Archaeology, University of Michigan)

painted-gold likeness. Such care also extended to the bodies of the dead, which from a very early period were embalmed and wrapped with cloth. All these preparations were made that the *ka*, the character or individuality of the dead person, might live on. Though immortality was first reserved only to the monarch and those specially designated by him, it gradually became the expectation of every Egyptian.

Religion permeated every aspect of life in the narrow land. The priesthoods sheltered men of education and culture. Very early in their history, the priests had applied themselves to practical problems affecting the day-to-day tasks of the people. Perhaps, and one can almost be certain, it was from one of the temples that the first calendar came, for the Egyptians had a year divided into twelve months and 365 days from a time before the union of the Red and White Kingdoms. The priests also studied astronomy, though they do not seem to have gone far beyond some basic observations. They also developed the study of mathematics using the decimal system. Their system of computation was unwieldy, but it is most certainly one of the major ancestors of our complex advanced mathematical studies. In medicine, experience played the most important role in their discovery of cures, but medications were surrounded by religious rites. They developed considerable skill as surgeons, especially in their ability to set broken bones, but often they had to admit—as in the case of a broken neck—that they had no treatment. Egyptian medicine made great strides from a very early period, but it gradually fell under the spell of a basic conservatism which stifled efforts to find new cures or to try new surgical techniques. In their view, it was better to permit a patient to die than to prescribe a treatment not sanctioned by tradition. This conservatism promoted the unity of Egyptian culture by preserving the influences and forms of the past, but it tended to stifle creativity.

The influence of religion in art and literature tied their development to tradition. Although the Egyptians revealed great craftsmanship, only occasionally did their creative talents break out of these limits to attempt bold experimentation. The great pyramids, tombs of the Pharaohs of the Old Kingdom, once rich depositories of Egyptian art, though they were

Fragment from the Book of the Dead. A beautiful example of Egyptian hieroglyphic writing. The Book of the Dead is a major work in Egyptian religious literature. (*Rare Book Room, University of Michigan*)

despoiled by grave robbers centuries ago, reveal their concern with life after death. The Valley of the Kings also concealed the tombs of many monarchs. But the richest legacy of Egyptian art is to be found in their temples. Beautiful columns decorated often with the flower of the papyrus reed support in massively rigid dignity the great stone vaults. Statues of the god-kings and their queens loom above the desert and against the rock of the valley walls or rise on islands in the sacred river. Painting, vibrant with activity especially during the age of the Egyptian Empire, reveals much about the tenor of life along the Nile. The literature of the Egyptians, however, is their greatest legacy to aid our understanding. Through it we learn how deeply religion permeated the atmosphere of the Old Kingdom but how, under the empire, it no longer gripped the hearts and minds of a sophisticated aristocracy, who even dared to satirize the Pharaoh himself. This age produced erotic love lyrics, mocked at the gods, and created a more naturalistic style, but it also saw Ikhnaton author his beautiful hymn in honor of Aton, an almost revolutionary departure from the traditional polytheism of Egypt:

> Beautiful is thine appearing in the horizon of heaven,
> Thou living Sun, the first who lived!
> Thou risest in the eastern horizon,
> And fillest every land with thy beauty.
> Thou art beautiful and great and glistenest,
> And art high above every land.
> Thy rays, they encompass the lands,
> So far as all that thou hast created.
> Thou art Rē, and thou reachest unto their end,
> And subduest them for thy dear son (Ikhnaton).*

The Egyptian masses may well have never heard these words, for they lived as peasants on the lands of the Pharaoh. They tended the irrigation canals, tilled the soil, planted and reaped the grain, lived and died—all in the hope of immortality. A few became craftsmen and fashioned the tools or shaped the pottery which served the needs of every class and which was carried over the sea in ships by the small merchant class, who visited such far off lands as Knossos in Crete, Mycenae in Greece, and who roamed the markets of Asia Minor, Mesopotamia, Lebanon, and Syria. It was from the labor of these classes that the wealth sprang to create the civilization of Egypt.

Egyptian society was highly stratified; her cultural and intellectual life

* From: *The Literature of the Ancient Egyptians* by Adolph Erman, translated by Aylward M. Blackman (London: Methuen & Co., 1927), p. 289. Used with Permission.

Ruins of Karanis, Egypt, a great town built on the edge of the desert. (Kelsey Museum of Archaeology, University of Michigan)

were enjoyed by only a few. There was greater emphasis on preservation than on creativity. Nevertheless, influence on the world of the eastern Mediterranean was great. Her hieroglyphic writing, gradually evolved from picture-symbols to an alphabetical system of notation, influenced the writing of the Minoan civilization of Crete and that of the Mycenaean Greeks, who learned to write through their contact with the Minoans. The style of Egyptian pottery and other art objects, including painting, can be seen in the work of many Near Eastern people during antiquity. Her architecture anticipated many of the advances—the use of columns and pilasters—we associate with the Greeks and Romans. Perhaps the role of Egypt in the building of ancient civilization was not so direct as that of Mesopotamia, but recent scholarship has pointed to much closer bonds between the Egyptians and the other peoples of the eastern Mediterranean than earlier evidence suggested. Egypt's isolation has been overstressed, while her contacts have been minimized. Yet similarities in Near

Eastern and Egyptian mythology as well as evidence of Egyptian colonization in Syria and the islands indicate that, for much of its history, Egypt had a vital role in the shaping of ancient civilization.

Syria and Her Peoples

The region lying along the Mediterranean shore between Mesopotamia and Egypt was frequently in contention between the major powers of these areas. Yet these struggles for the control of this strategic and even rich land do not begin to tell the entire story of Syria. That story cannot be told apart from the peoples who inhabited the land and gave it a distinctive character. These peoples were often pawns in the politics of greater powers, yet they managed to preserve their identity and to play a significant role in the shaping of the civilization of the West. Of first importance were the Hebrews, who had settled in the hill country of Palestine about 1800 B.C. This small group decisively formed the religious thought of most of the West through its gradual acceptance of the idea of one God and its concept of the ethical relationships between that God and man. The other peoples of the regions were of lesser importance, although the Phoenicians carried the civilization of the Near East with them as they traded throughout the Mediterranean basin and the Aramaeans both collected and disseminated the culture of this area by their expeditions to the East. What makes the story of these peoples even more exciting is the rapid increase of our knowledge of this area thanks to the work of archaeologists like Kathleen Kenyon and Nelson Glueck. Miss Kenyon's excavations at Jericho have pushed the history of Palestine back into the neolithic age, while shedding considerable light on Biblical times. The evidence of archaeology has been of considerable importance in revising the Biblical account of the history of this region.

In the history of the Hebrews, the Old Testament stands as the remarkable account of the spiritual struggles of this people. This collection of writings is not history in the modern sense at all. During the past thirty to forty years, scripture scholars have steadily added to our understanding of the language, meaning, and the theological significance of the Bible. They have coined the term "salvation history" to describe the intent of its authors and editors. This term refers to the consciousness of the divine presence and the emphasis on God's role in giving meaning to human existence that permeates the Old Testament. Of course, the conception of the Bible as "salvation history" does not destroy its value to the modern historian of Hebrew civilization. It merely places the text in its historical setting so that the scholar can better judge the meaning of this most important source. The Old Testament remains, along with archaeology and various other aids, the chief source of our knowledge of the ancient Hebrews.

The Hebrews were a group of various peoples rather than a single nation. Scholars suggest that the word *Habiru,* found in Mesopotamian texts, refers to them. These *Habiru* were herdsmen and artisans dwelling in the hills around Mesopotamia. They were nomads who sometimes came down into the cities of the plain, but who did not settle there. Probably shortly after the second millennium B.C., some of the *Habiru* traveled southwest to Syria. The leader, or patriarch, of one of the family units that made this trek was Abraham. In the Biblical account he was the "father" of the Hebrews.

The society of the Hebrews in the time of Abraham followed the pattern of many other migratory peoples through history. The basic unit was the family, consisting not merely of parents and children, but of a larger group tracing its origins to a common ancestor. In addition, this family unit possessed retainers and slaves. The Old Testament account of life in this period receives confirmation from an Egyptian source, the story of Sinuhe, who had been an official of the Pharaoh but had to go into exile to escape death. He found refuge with a pastoral people and married the daughter of the partriarchal leader. Eventually, he succeeded to the position of leader himself. The story describes vividly the treatment of those who threatened the flocks that were the livelihood of his people. The raiding of flocks was the most important offense against the group. However, although these nomads were inhospitable to strangers, they were fond of receiving their friends with elaborate feasts as a sign of their regard and to demonstrate their willingness to give up the best for the sake of friendship. The importance of allies against other marauders was one factor in the development of ties outside the family unit. These alliances were most often sealed by intermarriage and lasted through many generations.

The Hebrews who migrated to Syria came into contact with a Canaanite culture far superior to their own. The Canaanites dwelt in cities and engaged in commerce as well as agriculture. Some of the Hebrews adopted the Canaanite mode of living, but many remained true to their ancestral way of life. However, the hill country of Syria was arid and the newcomers found it difficult to find enough forage for their flocks. Some of them moved on to the south and entered Egypt. There, one of their leaders gained considerable influence at the court of the Pharaoh. For some time after Joseph's death, the Hebrews remained in Egypt. Gradually, however, their position weakened and many suffered oppression. At this critical hour, a new Hebrew leader arose to lead them out of Egypt.

In the history of the Hebrews as related in the Old Testament, certain leaders appear in a providential role to interpret the will of God to man. Their position is in keeping with the Hebrew view of history as the story of God's effort to preserve his people and of their special place as the chosen people of God. In keeping with this view of history, the ancient Hebrew authors saw Moses as an instrument of Divine Providence to lead the Hebrews out of bondage in Egypt and to strengthen in them the concept of the worship of Yahweh, the one true God.

Moses was a Hebrew who had been reared by an Egyptian princess. Only after entering adulthood did he come to realize his identity as one of the oppressed Hebrews. He believed that God had chosen him to lead his people out of Egypt. Relying on this sense of a divine mission, he worked to convince the Pharaoh that he should release them from their slavery. However, the liberation of the Hebrews was merely one aspect of Moses' mission. His chief task was to bring to his people the belief that Yahweh was their special deity, who demanded their submission and laid down commandments for them. In the continuing controversies surrounding the evolution of the Hebrew conception of monotheism, the belief in one supreme and unique God, it has become increasingly apparent that Moses regarded Yahweh not as the only god but rather as the special and all-powerful protector of the Hebrews, to whom they owed a complete allegiance.

The practice of choosing a particular deity as a special protector was general throughout Mesopotamia. The use of the term "God of Abraham" in the Old Testament has parallels in other literature of the Near East. The early Hebrews had been polytheists; Yahweh was only one of the deities they had worshipped. Moreover, polytheistic tendencies remained strong even in the time of Moses. Recent scholarship on the Old Testament has revealed the existence of these early beliefs along with the efforts of later editors of the various books to recast them in a monotheistic style. All of this evidence argues for a gradual evolution of monotheistic ideas among the Hebrews rather than a sudden acceptance of them as a result of Moses' teaching.

The chief contribution of Moses as the instrument of Yahweh in history was his role as the arranger of the covenant between that deity and the Hebrews and his emphasis on the ethical aspect of that covenant. He believed the Hebrews must worship Yahweh alone and, in return for that worship, Yahweh would protect them. God laid down the manner in which they should worship. Not merely were they required to offer sacrifice but they also had to obey His law, contained in the Ten Commandments. These laws, which bear some resemblance to earlier Near Eastern codes of legislation, were unique in that they contained no provision for human enforcement. The sanction was divine. Moral force exerted by the power of Yahweh rather than physical compulsion was the basis for compelling obedience to the law. As Moses led the Hebrews through the wilderness in search of their "promised land," these religious ideas triumphed over the former traditions of this people to lay the foundation for a nation united by religion.

Moses led the Hebrews out of Egypt and to the "promised land" of Canaan, where in modern times their spiritual descendants have founded the state of Israel. In the period of the Judges, the Hebrews gradually conquered the numerically superior Canaanites and laid the foundation for their monarchy. Their chief center was at Jerusalem and it was there that they set up their religious headquarters and later established the capital of their kingdom.

The establishment of the monarchy caused considerable disagreement among the religious and political leaders of the nation. The prophet Samuel opposed granting the power to rule to any one man on the ground that Yahweh alone was the ruler of the Hebrew people. Only the necessity for strong leadership against external enemies caused Samuel and the leaders of the opposition to accept the monarchy. Samuel anointed Saul, thus ushering in the "golden age" of the Hebrew nation. Under his successors, David and Solomon, the power of the kingdom extended beyond the borders of Palestine. Jerusalem became a great capital, the home of the temple built by Solomon to contain the "Holy of Holies." The building of this temple marked the triumph of Yahweh over all other deities and the complete establishment of his worship among the Hebrews. The priesthoods of the temple directed the religious life of the nation.

The Hebrew concept of kingship differed, however, from that of neighboring peoples. In their view, the ruler was bound by law and might be deposed for failure to observe it. Saul, the first king, incurred the opposition of the religious leaders, who deposed him in favor of David. Because the divine law was superior to the king, the Hebrew ruler was limited in his power. In the Christian era, this concept of law placing limitations on kingship played an important role in establishing the relationship of the medieval kings to the Church. This theory was also one of the important influences shaping Western thought about the limitations of governmental power down to the modern period.

The glory of the monarchy proved a crushing economic burden to the Hebrew nation, whose resources were limited by the fact that most of the population was composed of poor farmers and herdsmen. Although Solomon had exploited the mines on the Sinai Peninsula for copper, the effort to sustain a monarchy amid the rivalries of the great Near Eastern powers put the kingdom under a constant threat. Its golden age corresponded to that precise period after the decline of Hittite and Egyptian hegemony in Syria and Palestine when various smaller powers were able to assert their temporary independence. The decline of the Hebrew Kingdom was not, however, entirely the result of external forces. Conflict within led to the division of the kingdom just as the rising power of Assyria engulfed Syria in the late eighth century B.C.

But political decline did not halt the process of theological development that formed the unique contribution of Hebrew civilization. Under the Prophets (ninth to fifth centuries B.C.), the definitive statement of monotheistic belief occurred. They proclaimed that Yahweh was not merely the God of the Hebrews but the sole real God and they attempted to remove the last vestiges of Yahweh as a god of nature by revealing Him as a Being apart from all nature, which was His creation. The Prophets set forth the Hebrew view of history in which Yahweh causes all things according to a providential pattern. This view was to play an important role in later Western thinking through both Jewish and Christian writers.

The Hebrew nation was only one of the lesser states that flourished between the thirteenth and seventh centuries B.C. Its unique position in Western civilization overshadows the contribution of peoples like the Phoenicians and the Aramaeans. Their influence was more on their contemporaries and less on the broad currents of civilization. Nevertheless, the Phoenicians deserve some consideration for two reasons. First, they perfected an alphabet and carried it from the Near East to Greece, probably in the eighth century. This alphabet was the basis for Roman writing and also for the later scripts used throughout Europe. The spread of this alphabet greatly reduced the number of symbols necessary for writing languages that had formerly relied on syllabic or word notation systems. The alphabet was of great value in making literacy more common—the Phoenician traders were aware of its advantages in commerce. From these beginnings, the first steps toward a more broadly based educated group of citizens was possible. The second reason for discussing the Phoenicians lies in their wide-ranging commerce on the Mediterranean Sea and even in the Atlantic Ocean. They traded for tin in Britain and copper in Spain.

They established the city of Carthage in North Africa, which became the center of a vast commercial empire in the western Mediterranean after the eighth century. The trade of the Phoenicians not only laid the foundation for the economic unity of the Mediterranean world but also transmitted the advances made in one culture to others. The Aramaeans, whose lands lay in the northeast of Syria, played a similar role with regard to peoples lying to the east. These merchant powers acquired great wealth and influence far beyond their actual political importance because of their strategic role in the ancient economy. Their position points to the continuing role of trading nations in the history of civilization.

The size of these small states excluded them from the center of the stage in the power struggles of the great empires of the Near East. Yet history must recognize their importance in the growth of civilization for their contributions to religion, political theory, ethics, literature, and commerce. Certainly the Hebrews have had the greatest and most enduring influence. Spiritually, Western man has never lost contact with that legacy of moral and doctrinal content enshrined in the concept of one God. Two of the most pervasive notions of Western thought, sin and salvation, are part of that heritage. Through the teachings of Jesus Christ, the Hebrew influence has affected the course of Western civilization. But it has not stopped at that point. Islam incorporated many Hebrew concepts, especially the strict monotheism of the Jews, and carried these to the East. Thus, the Hebrew influence has crossed the cultural boundaries of East and West.

2 The Greek Ferment

In the long history of the development of Western man, Greek civilization was the school of the West. During several centuries, Greek philosophers like Socrates and Greek writers like Sophocles posed essential questions regarding man. What was more important, they tried to answer these questions not by an appeal to divine intervention but by attempting to reason about human experience. The Greek outlook was essentially rational; its concern with cause and effect led to major advances in philosophy and the beginnings of scientific methodology. When Thucydides wrote about the Peloponnesian War, he attempted to give his readers an understanding of its causes. In contrast with the providential view of history accepted by the Hebrews, the Greeks saw the past as the result of internal and proximate causes. They did not deny the existence of supernatural forces, but neither did they try to interpret the great problems of man and nature in terms of them. Throughout the twenty-three centuries since the decline of Athens, Western man has continued to study the great works created by Greek writers and artists. It is in this sense that the West has gone to school under Greek masters.

Yet the political and social development of Greece was not a placid pool suitable for contemplation. On the contrary, part of the secret of the Greek genius may well lie in the constant tensions and continuing crises that beset the Greeks. What gives to these ideas their sense of urgency and universality is the extent to which great thinkers and writers involved themselves in all aspects of human life and behavior.

The Formation of the Greek Character

No civilization springs suddenly into full flower without a long period of evolution. The formation of a peculiarly Greek civilization was the work of hundreds of years, of which many periods are known only very sketchily. Thanks to the work of numerous scholars during the past century, our knowledge of the over-all pattern of Greek development is much clearer than it was to students living in the first half of the nineteenth century. They lived before Heinrich Schliemann had realized his dream of rediscovering the lost world of Homer's *Iliad* and *Odyssey.* They did not know of the complex and powerful Minoan civilization that preceded the Greeks on the island of Crete. Yet it would be a mistake to dwell only on how much historians and archaeologists have added to our knowledge. For much of the history of Greece still remains in shadow despite such astounding accomplishments as the feat of the young architect, Michael Ventris, in deciphering the Linear "B" tablets of Mycenae and providing proof that the Greeks had built a great civilization in southern Greece centuries before the great writers and thinkers of fifth century Athens were born. New chapters are constantly being added to the story of the formation of the Greek character.

The discovery of the Minoan civilization, which flourished on the island of Crete from about the fourth millennium B.C. until about 1500 B.C., raised important questions about the origins of the Greeks and of Greek civilization. For the population which created Minoan culture was certainly not Greek. It had come to Crete probably from southwestern Asia Minor and its culture showed continued influences from Asia Minor and, to a lesser extent, from Egypt, a land with which the Minoans had considerable direct contact.

The heyday of Cretan culture was reached between 1750 and 1500 B.C., an age which saw the completion of the great palace complex at Knossos on the northern shore of the island. From Knossos the rulers of the island carried on an extensive trade in olive oil, a staple of life in the Mediterranean, as well as pottery, wine, and honey. Through their pottery archaeologists have been able to trace the routes followed by their ships around the coasts of Asia Minor and Egypt.

This complex urban civilization developed a system of writing involving the use of symbols to identify the various syllables of words. Although scholars have not yet arrived at a satisfactory solution that would enable them to translate this "Linear A," continued research will hopefully provide not merely this key but will also thereby reveal more about the identity and origins of the Cretans. Cretan art, revealed in beautiful fresco work, depicting scenes from daily life and nature, points to a highly sophisticated people. The famous paintings, showing young men and women leaping over the heads and backs of bulls in a gymnastic exercise that may have had religious connotations, recapture the realism of the moment. Among the Greeks, the legend of Theseus and the Minotaur (Bull of Minos) may have preserved the memory of young Mycenaean hostages forced to perform this risky feat as a tribute to the gods of their Minoan lords. Cretan frescoes also revealed the close communication of their civilization with nature by depicting fish and animals in a lifelike manner. But chiefly the art of the Cretans mirrors the life and interests of the nobility and upper class. The prominent role given women in this art may well indicate their importance in the ruling class of society. Indeed, the presence of numerous statuettes of the Potnia Theron (Earth Mother) goddess, whose cult was common throughout Asia Minor, not only supports this view but also throws light on the probable place of origin of the Cretans.

About 1500 B.C., this flourishing civilization met with disaster. Invaders from Mycenae, on the mainland of Greece, captured the great palace at Knossos and subjected the Cretans to their rule. But the Mycenaeans did not destroy the island culture; rather they participated in it. Cretan art forms found their way to the mainland and from these and other elements the Mycenaeans built their own great center of civilization, whose influence reached across the eastern Mediterranean in the period following 1500 B.C. The Mycenaeans also benefited from the Cretan system of writing. Using characters from Linear A, they developed a new script, Linear B, which spread from the island to the mainland and was discovered chiefly at Pylos and Mycenae. Its preservation was, like that of Linear A, accidental, for the characters were scratched on clay tablets, which were generally destroyed through the action of nature. By chance, however, some were baked in fires that destroyed their storage places, thus causing them to endure. It was to these that archaeologists and linguists turned their attention in the hope of unlocking the secret of the language in which they were written. Michael Ventris, a young English architect and amateur student of languages, announced in 1952 that Linear B script had been deciphered as an archaic form of the Greek language, and he and Professor John Chadwick began to prepare translations of the documents. Decipherment of Linear B unlocked the secret that Mycenaean civilization was Greek.

The decipherment of Linear B provided a tangible link between the classical Greeks and the age of the Homeric Epics. Homer, the poet of the *Iliad* and the *Odyssey* wrote of a Mycenaean age when Achaeans had crossed the foaming Aegean Sea to attack the great walled city of Troy in northwest Asia Minor. Homer had written of the mighty Achilles, greatest of the Achaean warriors, of King Agamemnon of Mycenae, and Nestor, whose voice was like the melodic rhythm of cicadas and who ruled in Pylos. The Achaeans who set forth from Greece to sack the Troy of King Priam spoke the Greek tongue. What is more, they had built a vast sea empire that dominated Crete and possessed colonies around the shores of the eastern Mediterranean. Traces of their colonies have been found on the island of Cyprus and along the coast of Syria at Ras Shamra.

Unfortunately, the absence of chronicles or historical inscriptions from the Mycenaean age makes it very difficult to reconstruct the narrative of their past. Hittite records mention the Ahhijava (Homer's Achaeans?) in tones of respect indicating that these people were a power to be reckoned with, and Egyptian documents from the thirteenth century B.C. include the Akkaiwasha among the sea peoples invading the Delta region and causing considerable damage. If, as many scholars believe, these are the Mycenaeans, their power was far-ranging.

Further evidence of this strength comes from an examination of the ruins of their cities. The greatest of these was Mycenae, situated in the southern part of the Peloponnesian Peninsula of Greece not far from the sea and dominating a fertile plain. This city, according to Homer, was the seat of King Agamemnon, leader of the Achaean forces before the city of Troy. Its massive walls required tremendous labor; the great lion gate demanded great skill and artistic talent. The Mycenaeans were masters in working gold, as we can see from the beautiful cup of Nestor found at Pylos. The translation of Linear B has revealed their ability to organize and administer their warehouses, in which wine, oil, and grain were stored. It was on this agricultural base that their trade with other areas developed. Thus, the wedding of agriculture to commerce increased the wealth and power of the Mycenaeans.

From the Linear B tablets we learn that the Mycenaeans did not worship the same gods as the Cretans. Although they had come into contact with fertility rites centered on a female goddess and adopted them, their major divinities were gods of the sky, among whom Zeus, father of all the gods, was chief. Homer depicted their sacrifices of heifers and their libations of wine poured on the ground to invoke the favor of the gods. Human sacrifice, although not absent, was rare. The gods were partisans in the affairs of men. Their jealousies and angers mirrored human qualities, yet they were also above men and capable of greater nobility. The highest end of man was to become immortal and godlike. Generally, however, the Greeks of Homer's epics saw man's end in pessimistic terms. Hades offered little that would tempt the earthbound man to leave this life for another. It was misty and gloomy, presided over by Cheron, who rowed the shades of men across the sluggish river that formed its borders. Only the greatest heroes escaped this existence; they alone might cavort with the gods. Although the religion described by Homer in the *Iliad* and *Odyssey* belonged to a period later than the Mycenaean age, there was no doubt much in common between the two periods.

Who were these Greeks who had built so brilliant a civilization at Mycenae? What was their relationship to the later Greeks? Archaeological evidence reveals that Greeks had settled in the peninsula shortly after the beginning of the second millennium B.C. They had come down from the north, but, in doing so, they had passed over most of the northern part of the peninsula in favor of more intensive settlement in the south. Where were they before 1900 B.C.? The best recent evidence indicates that they dwelt in north central Asia Minor, that they were displaced by the Hittite invasions and forced westward toward the region of Troy. From there, they crossed into Europe and divided into two groups, one of which traveled northwest toward the basin of the Danube River while the other, probably the group we call Mycenaean, turned southward into Greece, where they built the flourishing civilization we have described.

The great crisis of Mycenaean civilization occurred about 1200 B.C. At that time, fire destroyed the great citadel of Mycenae. Throughout the Mediterranean other Mycenaean centers met similar fates. Certainly no single cause could have produced destruction on so wide a scale. In Greece itself, the chief cause of this disaster was an invasion from the north by a Greek-speaking people whom later Greeks called the Dorians. These Dorians overran the Peloponnesus and were probably the ancestors of Spartans. Yet, we may wonder at the way in which the relatively rude Dorians could conquer the advanced and mighty Mycenaean civilization so easily. Homer's poetry describes in vivid detail the unsettled conditions of the early period of Greek history. Perhaps the victory of the Achaeans over Troy, a battle whose traditional date is 1184 B.C., was purchased at the expense of exhausting the resources of the Mycenaeans and made them easy prey to the aggressive Dorians. Perhaps such a protracted war also caused the withdrawal of forces from other colonies, the

THE GREEK WORLD
0 20 40 60 80 100
MILES
BLACK SEA
THRACE
MACEDONIA
LYDIA
IONIA
Hebrus R.
Agrianes R.
Axius R.
Peneus R.
Caicus R.
Hermus R.
Mecestus R.
Rhyndacus R.
Maeander R.
Byzantium
Bosporus
Troy
Hellespont
Mt. Olympus
Mt. Mycale
Ephesus
Miletus
SAMOTHRACE
THRACIAN SEA
LEMNOS
LESBOS
CHIOS
SAMOS
AEGEAN SEA
SPORADES
CYCLADES
DELOS
MELOS
RHODES
CARPATHOS
CYPRUS
Thermopylae
Delphi
Thebes
Plataea
Marathon
Athens
SALAMIS
Corinth
Mycenae
Sparta
MYRTOAN SEA
PELOPONNESUS
IONIAN SEA
CRETAN SEA
Knossos
CRETE
MEDITERRANEAN SEA

neglect of trade, and paved the way for their fall at the hands of various local forces. At any rate, with the fall of Mycenae, Greece receded into an age of darkness which lasted from about 1100 to 750 B.C.

The "Dark Ages" (1100–750 B.C.) were a period of rebuilding following the collapse of Mycenaean civilization. The foundation for this process was partly Mycenaean, but so much of that culture was lost that inevitably many new institutions and patterns had to be created. Gradually new powers began to evolve. The monarchical government which characterized the earlier period gave way to city-states ruled by aristocratic cliques. Trade recovered slowly, achieving some of its former vitality only near the end of the period. Toward the end of this period, the Homeric Epics were composed. They drew on the Mycenaean age for their stories of Achilles the warrior, Hector the horse-tamer, and Odysseus the wily, but much of the background and many of the experiences related to the ninth and eighth centuries rather than the twelfth century B.C.

Musician, from a Greek bowl. Simplicity and grace are characteristics of Greek art in the classical period. (Kelsey Museum of Archaeology, University of Michigan)

The end of the Dark Ages found Greece a country of populous city-states, each with its distinctive form of government. The country grew crowded and men began to turn their attention in new directions in search of homes. Thus, from the middle of the eighth century, Greece entered a period of colonization which carried men from the shores of the peninsula into the Black Sea, along the western coast of Asia Minor, to North Africa, and to Sicily and southern Italy. New cities sprang up. Such important centers as Cyrene in Africa, Syracuse on the east coast of Sicily, Naples in Italy, and Marseilles in southern France owed their foundation to these Greek colonizers. Although politically independent, the colonies continued to have close commercial and cultural ties with those cities on the Greek mainland that had furnished their first settlers. Through them, Greek culture and Greek political experience influenced a large part of the Mediterranean world.

Unity and Rivalry: City–State and Empire

The city-state was the most characteristic institution of Greek political life, although its development showed wide variations from city to city. In all probability, the nature of Greek geography played an important role in bringing about these differences. Numerous valleys separated from one another by mountains which were difficult to traverse encouraged isolated growth along distinct lines. Moreover, this isolation discouraged the development of more centralized forms of government. Gradually, however, some cities rose to greater prominence. Sparta dominated the Peloponnesus in southern Greece; Corinth grew rich in trade with southern Italy from its post on the isthmus that bears its name; Athens, greatest of all, became mistress of the Aegean Sea and carried on extensive commerce through its islands and with the Greek colonies on the Black Sea and in Asia Minor.

The Spartans had entered the Peloponnesus from the north and subjected the native population to their rule gradually over the course of several centuries. Since they were relatively few in number compared to the conquered peoples, they had constant concern lest revolution destroy their power and deprive them of their position as a kind of noble class. For this reason the Spartan constitution was rather conservative. The Spartans determined from an early date that they could not afford the luxury of violent disagreement among themselves and proceeded along the path of political compromise. They preserved the kingship after other Greek cities abandoned it. But, because of grave internal strife that threatened to disrupt the state, the Spartans established five Ephors, who exercised wide power and might even depose a king. The Gerusia or Council of Elders and the popular assembly possessed limited legislative power, but the leaders could decide to ignore these bodies and to pursue another course than that which they had supported. Thus, the Spartan constitution combined features which we associate with monarchy with others that we associate with democratic forms of government. But it was in fact rule by an oligarchy, for a small group of leaders kept power concentrated in their hands.

The existence of a large subject population influenced the structure and goals of Spartan society. The Spartans stressed the importance of military training. From early youth, Spartan boys lived in common and trained in the arts of war. The Spartan code of morality was designed to inculcate in them a rigid loyalty to the state and a willingness to serve it in whatever ways it might command. From their ranks came the crypteia or secret police, whose task it was to prevent conspiracies from developing among the subject peoples. These subjects were of two kinds. The perioeci, or dwellers-around, were those conquered peoples who continued to live in their own towns under the dominance of the Spartans. Technically allied to the Spartans, their freedom was entirely dependent on their continued submission to them. However, their lot was immeasurably better than that of the helots, who were virtually agricultural slaves, condemned to till the soil for the Spartans. Thus the Spartans formed a closed hereditary noble military caste. Yet this military strength did not make the Spartans an aggressive power. Fear of revolution by the helots was the major factor in persuading them to remain aloof from military ventures outside their own land. Not until the fifth century, and then reluctantly, did Sparta employ her unmatched army to dominate Greece.

The growth of Athens offers much in striking contrast to that of Sparta. Indeed, at first one might wonder how two such different cities could both be Greek. But the secret lies in the strikingly different way in which these two cities developed. Where Sparta had conquered the native population of Laconia, the Athenians appear to have gradually created a united people by absorbing the native elements. Athenian culture was the result of a long development with roots in the Mycenaean age. The government of Athens moved very gradually in the direction of democracy. Overthrow of the monarchy by aristocratic elements paved the way for control of the government by the nobility. Their rule became oppressive as they attempted to maintain their position during the economic and social upheavals of the sixth century. Small farmers and the poorer citizens living within the city found little hope for justice in courts run by members of the aristocracy. The lack of a written law code left interpretation of the law in the hands of those who administered it and stood to profit from that administration. Consequently, small farmers, whose lands were burdened by debt found little recourse save to sell themselves into slavery. Major reform was necessary and an attempt in this direction was made under the leadership of Solon, whose policies aimed at redressing the chief grievances of the farmers without destroying political control by the aristocracy. A major feature was the "seisachtheia" or lifting off of burdens, which prevented any Athenian citizen from being reduced to slavery to satisfy his debtors. But Solon's reforms failed to meet an increasing demand for broader participation in political life. The aristocracy continued to maintain its preponderant role in the state and the Athenians turned toward more drastic solutions. The tyranny established in Athens by Pisistratus had the support of the city poor and the farmers and appears to have been popular with them. But it did not provide a permanent solution to the political imbalance among the various groups hoping to attain power. In 510 B.C., the nobility succeeded in overthrowing the tyranny and Athens entered a brief period of chaos. Its emergence from this period came as a result of the brilliant reforms of Cleisthenes, who remodeled the constitution to prevent dominance of the state by one political faction. By 502 B.C., he had put into practice a new organization of the city tribes aimed at bringing together into each tribe representatives of all major factions—the rural small farmers, the merchants and tradesmen, and the old aristocracy. Cleisthenes thus laid the basis for Athenian democracy by assuring the popular assembly a dominant voice in public affairs.

The sixth century also witnessed the gradual expansion of Athenian hegemony over surrounding territories. Megara and Salamis, islands controlling the sea approaches to the city, fell into her hands. Moreover, Athens' ties with the Greek cities of Asia Minor grew closer because of her trade. These cities had been conquered by the Persians during the sixth century. Although Persian rule was far from harsh and even drew support from the aristocratic elements in the Greek cities of Asia Minor, there were also periodic attempts at revolt. Democratic Athens proved more receptive than conservative Sparta to requests for assistance and thus earned the enmity of the Persian kings. According to one story, the Persian king Darius ordered his servants to repeat "Sire, remember the Athenians" lest he forget the manner in which they had aided his enemies.

In 493 B.C., a great Persian fleet crossed the Aegean and landed an army at the bay of Marathon across a narrow neck of land from Athens. Greece was unprepared. The Spartans promised aid, but held back because of religious scruples until it was too late. Only a small force from Plataea joined nine thousand Athenians on the plain of Marathon. Outnumbered almost two to one, the Greeks were nevertheless victorious. The Persians, unwilling to risk a siege of Athens, sailed away.

But victory at Marathon won only a respite for the Greeks, as they were well aware. Athens took the lead in arousing the other Greek cities to the danger of a renewed Persian attack. Under the inspired leadership of Themistocles, the Athenians began the construction of a great fleet. On the Persian side, Darius' son Xerxes began long preparations for a massive invasion of Greece. In 480 B.C., this great army crossed the Hellespont and descended on the peninsula while a fleet sailed along the coast. This time the Greeks were prepared. A small band of Spartans led a detachment northward to meet the Persian army while the Athenians completed their preparations for meeting the main force at sea. Leonidas, King of Sparta, and his handful of troops put up a gallant stand against the "Immortals," the best of the Persians. They chose for a battleground the narrow pass at Thermopylae, where the mountains press close to the sea. Greatly outnumbered, the Greeks were betrayed by one of their own, who led the Persians around to their rear by another route. Leonidas and three hundred Spartans fell in battle. Thermopylae became a proud badge of courage in the ancient world. Yet, like many other battles in which the courage of brave men won the plaudits of those who remained, Thermopylae was futile. The Greeks would have accomplished more by a strategic withdrawal and continued harassment of the Persian army. As it was, Greece now lay open to the invaders.

The Spartans and their allies, fearful of the results of a Persian invasion of their homeland, fell back to defend the Peloponnesian peninsula leaving Athens and her allies to fend for themselves. Because the Athenians realized they could not defend their city they crossed to the island of Salamis and watched the burning of their city by the advancing Persians. Meanwhile, Themistocles made preparations to meet the Persian fleet. He divided the Greek fleet into two parts and, using half as a decoy, concealed the other half around the headland of the island of Salamis. As the Persian king watched from his throne, his fleet pursued the seemingly fearful Athenians through the narrow waters between Salamis and the mainland. Then, when the Persian fleet had entered the channel, the Greeks closed the opening. Aeschylus the playwright has described the destruction of the Persians: "The jutting shores and rocks were piled with dead, and every Persian ship that still survived rowed hard for refuge in disordered flight." Broken by the defeat, Xerxes hastened in retreat, spurred on by fear of further Greek attacks and news of uprisings among the Greeks of Asia Minor. But the danger to Greece was far from over, for Persian troops continued to hold the north of Greece and the mainland, including Athens. The Athenians managed to persuade the Spartans to assist them in ridding Greece of this danger. At Plataea (479 B.C.), the Greek allies administered a crushing defeat to the Persian army and forced the remaining Persians to withdraw from Greece.

Although the Greeks had succeeded in driving the foreigners from their soil, they realized that Persia still remained a great power that might decide to launch further attacks on Greek soil. Even after they had wrested control of the Hellespont from the Persians, they remained concerned about the possibility of a renewed attack. This was especially true of the Athenians, who took the initiative in the formation of the Delian League in 478 B.C.

This league was chiefly a naval alliance of the Aegean powers, with Athens as the dominant partner. It drew its name from the fact that the treasury of the league was located on the sacred island of Delos. The purpose of the league was to enable the members to carry on joint naval operations against the Persians in the Aegean, but very quickly it took on the character of a commercial alliance. In the beginning, each member city was expected to contribute men and ships for the fleet, according to a prescribed rate. Smaller cities paid sums of money rather than men or ships and this soon became the usual manner of raising the levy. Thus the Athenians controlled the fleet of the entire league and reaped the advantage in her greatly strengthened naval power. As the danger from Persia subsided, Athens had to apply pressure to keep the alliance together and to maintain the fleet. Consequently, the character of the league gradually changed from a voluntary alliance against the Persians to a commercial league with Athens as the leader. This has led historians to speak of "The Athenian Empire," even though Athens was never able to exercise the kinds of controls generally associated with the term.

The empire was not without advantages to its members. The powerful Athenian navy, strengthened by contributions of the members, defended their trade from the attacks of the Persians as well as from the pirates who infested the waters of the Aegean Sea. Moreover, the alliance encouraged commercial exchanges within its framework. Of course, Athens became the metropolis, but all members shared in the prosperity. On the other hand, wealth came at the expense of freedom. The obligation to pay tribute and furnish rowers for the navy was probably not as onerous as Athens' interference in the internal government of the cities of the empire.

Athenian coin with head of Athena on the obverse. (Kelsey Museum of Archaeology, University of Michigan)

In each city, the Athenians supported those elements most inclined to back their policy. Thus, they attempted to ensure that a "democratic" regime rather than an "oligarchic" or Spartan-sympathizing government ruled in these cities. There were also restrictions on the individual citizens of the "allies." In lawsuits where an Athenian was involved, the cases had to be tried in Athens. Obviously, the old equality of the Delian League had given way to a new equality of which the Athenians possessed a greater share than the citizens of their allies.

The Persian Wars had a considerable impact on Athens. The rise of the empire made her a great center and, under the leadership of Pericles (461–429 B.C.), the Athenians rebuilt it as a marble capital crowned by the Parthenon on the Acropolis. To do this, they used funds from the treasury of the Delian League. The historian Thucydides has Pericles call his city "the School of Greece." In the same speech, Pericles praises Athens for its democratic traditions, contrasting it to Spartan regimentation of social life. Yet in a very real sense, Periclean Athens was less democratic than it had been prior to the Persian Wars. True, the lower classes were a major element in the political life of the city by reason of their control of the popular assembly, but they lacked a sense of direction on their own and could only find this through leaders able to hold their loyalty. Periclean democracy, therefore, was based on control of the popular assembly and was demagogic. Pericles used the demand of the lower classes for a share in the government as the base on which to build his power. In return for support, they received employment in the fleet or in the law courts. The results of this demagogic government in the realm of foreign policy were especially serious. As long as Pericles lived, he was able to control the masses; after his death, Athenian government lacked stability. The popular assembly vented its will for good or bad on those who attempted to lead; leadership became a function of pleasing the mob. These conditions proved disastrous for Athens in the Peloponnesian War.

The causes of this struggle between Athens and Sparta are complex. Thucydides believed that the major cause of the war was the overweening pride of Athens. Sparta was a vehicle for punishing the Athenians for their immoderate policies.

But the causes of the war go far deeper than the pride of the Athenians. The growth of the Athenian Empire had altered the political structure of

Athenian coin, owl of Athens on the reverse. Athenian coins are found throughout the eastern Mediterranean area. They were almost an international currency for trade. (Kelsey Museum of Archaeology, University of Michigan)

Greece and threatened the independence not only of the members of the empire but also of any states which might attempt to pursue goals in competition with the Athenians. Corinth, which had long held a preponderant position in the trade with Sicily and southern Italy, feared expansion of Athenian interests in that area. While Sparta had no great commercial interests, she was concerned about the effect of the expansion of Athenian power on her position as leader of the Peloponnesian League. Moreover, some of the members of the Athenian Empire had grown restive under the constant pressure of its demands and looked to Sparta to furnish leadership to an opposition. It was against this background that the Spartans decided to go to war against Athens.

On the surface, Athens had a considerable advantage. She had a full treasury and the finest fleet in Greece. Sparta, on the other hand, was supreme on land, but lacked strong economic support. Athens, however, had to be concerned about the loyalty of her allies. She was reluctant to commit her entire resources to an all-out effort for victory. Consequently, the opening years of the war saw the Spartans invade Attica and ravage her fields while Athenian farmers looked out angrily from atop city walls; Athens sent her fleet against Sparta without daring an invasion. A major break came in 430 B.C. when plague swept Athens. Pericles himself succumbed in 429. The loss of his leadership further hampered the Athenian hope for victory. The war continued its ruinous course without decisive advantage to Spartans or Athenians until 421 B.C., when a temporary truce gave the Athenians a respite to whip their allies back into line and recover somewhat from the devastation.

But in 415 B.C., Athens, persuaded by the brilliant young general Alcibiades, renewed the attack by attemping to take Syracuse in Sicily. The plan failed and the Athenians condemned Alcibiades as a traitor. The sudden rise and fall of Alcibiades is symptomatic of the political turmoil within Athens after the death of Pericles had unleashed the masses, who quickly fell prey to one demagogue after another. Without leadership, the Athenians lost the initiative in the war even as Sparta gained substantially from the defection of Alcibiades. The growing strength of the oligarchic faction, which favored peace with Sparta, further weakened the city. Despite a number of impressive naval victories, the internal problems within the city continued to hamper effective prosecution of the war. The chief blow came when the Spartan naval commander Lysander decisively defeated the Athenian fleet at Aegospotami in 405 B.C. Athens without a fleet was unable to withstand a prolonged siege and had to accept terms. The scepter had passed from Athens to Sparta.

The Peloponnesian War did more, however, than substitute Spartan for Athenian; it severely weakened the independence of the Greek city-states and made them seek safety in alliances with one another. The age of the city-state was rapidly drawing to a close. Sparta proved even less capable of effective leadership than Athens. When, in 371, the Thebans overthrew the harsh dominance of Sparta, Greece was unwittingly moving into the orbit of a new power that would attempt to weld the various leagues of Greek cities into a unified force. This new power was centered in the north, in Macedonia.

Philip II, King of Macedon, had been a student of military tactics at Thebes and an astute observer of Greek politics. Returning to Macedonia, he had consolidated his power and reduced the troublesome barbarian tribes of the northwest of his kingdom. His success on these fronts allowed him to turn ambitious attention toward Greece. Although Macedonia shared a common language with the Greeks, most Greeks regarded the northerners as barbarians. But common cultural ties had strengthened Macedonian interest in Greece itself. With wealth in his hands from control of the gold and silver mines in the north of Greece and an army seasoned in campaigns against the barbarians, Philip stepped into the power vacuum created in Greece by the defeat of Thebes. By 337 B.C., he had defeated the Athenians and Thebans and established an Hellenic League with himself as president. But he was cut down by an assassin before he could follow up the fruits of his victories or launch his dreamed-of invasion of Persia. The kingship fell to his eighteen-year-old son Alexander, who vigorously set out to further his father's goals.

The immediate result of Philip's assassination was a rebellion in Macedonia and among the Greek cities. But Alexander, with the support of his father's generals, rapidly moved against his enemies and destroyed the city of Thebes as an example to the other Greek cities. The lesson was sufficient. Alexander was now free to turn his attention to the conquest of Persia.

Throughout the fifth century the threat of Persian interference in Greek affairs had remained in the background. After the Peloponnesian War, however, the Greeks themselves had encouraged Persian intervention by their attempts to gain advantage over one another. In 387 the Spartans appealed to King Artaxerxes for aid against the Athenians. The result was a treaty imposed upon the Greeks by the great king. In 371 B.C., awareness of the Persian threat led Athenian delegates to a peace conference held at Sparta to urge those in attendance to scrap their differences to invade Persia. Thus, Alexander's proposal for an invasion of Persia was no

Coin: head of Philip II of Macedon. This coin reflects the strong Greek influence on Macedon under the rule of the father of Alexander the Great. (Kelsey Museum of Archaeology, University of Michigan)

mere grandiose dream but a policy that might aid him in unifying the Greek cities behind him. It identified him with the Panhellenic cause.

Alexander's success as a conqueror was phenomonal. By 331 B.C., he was master of the entire western portion of the Persian Empire, including Asia Minor, Syria, and Egypt, where he was saluted as a god. He defeated Darius III and captured the royal treasure of the Persians and then continued eastward to the River Indus. Everywhere he went he left garrisons and established cities named for himself, the most famous being Alexandria in Egypt. These became centers for the Hellenization of the surrounding area. Still, he needed some unifying force to hold this vast empire together. He dreamed of a vast empire where all men were united in the bonds of a common brotherhood and a Hellenized civilization. By securing divine honors for himself, he desired to create a bond of unity that would transcend the differences between Greek and Persian. But the value of this effort was never proven because Alexander died in 323 B.C., worn out from his strenuous campaigning. The empire which he created failed and fell into the hands of his generals, who established dynasties that were to control the future of Greece, Asia Minor, Persia, and Egypt. The most enduring aspect of Alexander's conquest was his spread of Greek culture throughout the East. He ushered in a Hellenistic age, in which Greek language and learning became the chief elements of the culture of the educated classes throughout the eastern Mediterranean world.

Greek Culture: Climax and Decline

Volumes of words in praise of Greek culture have been written from the time of the Romans to the present. Nor is this praise unwarranted. For the influence of Greek thought has been a quickening influence in every phase of Western civilization and has so permeated our thought that, in a very true sense, Western man is Greek. For this reason it is manifestly important for us to learn the pathways of the Greek mind.

Religion, as we have already seen, was fundamental in the thought of most peoples of the ancient world. Most knowledge was associated in one way or another with supernatural powers and the beings that exercised them. Among the Greeks, religion was enveloped in an elaborate mythology, in which manlike gods influenced the plans of men. Zeus, the father of the gods, was theoretically supreme, but his power was sometimes challenged by lesser deities. In the *Theogony,* composed in the eighth century, the author attempted to order these religious traditions into a connected story, beginning with a primordial chaos and continuing through the rise of Zeus to supreme authority. But, in a way that contrasts with the development of religious thought in the Near East and Egypt, the Greeks did not devote their major intellectual efforts to theological speculation. This is not to say that the Greeks did not owe much to Near Eastern thought. Their scientific and mathematical learning was directly related to that of the East through the Greeks of Asia Minor. Greek mythology also was indebted to the East, but the Greeks did not follow the Eastern tendency of rationalizing nature in myth; rather they sought for explanations of natural phenomena in nature herself.

Early Greek thinkers attempted to find the basic elements in nature. Thus, their thought combined both scientific and philosophical aspects. In the late seventh century, Thales of Miletus attempted to explain how change takes place. The problem is subtle. When a boy grows up, he *becomes* a man. He has changed. The boy has ceased to exist. Yet the man is the same person as the boy. Something has not changed. The process is similar with other changes. Thales concluded that there must be one unchanging element underlying all nature. He believed that this element was water. Of course, from the view of modern science it is easy to ridicule this belief, but to do so would be to ignore the great advance implicit in Thales' thought: *natural rather than supernatural forces are basic to nature.* Anaximander, a contemporary of Thales, posed a different solution to the problem of change. For him, the essence of all things was without limits. Anaximander could not define this essence any more clearly, because, as soon as he gave it any character of its own, it would be something subject to change.

Not all early Greeks believed that it was possible to find one element or essence underlying all matter. Democritus, for example, believed that the universe was made up of seeds. There are some resemblances between this view and modern atomic theory. The seed theory avoided the necessity of finding a single element in all matter; change could be explained in terms of different seeds.

These thinkers set the pattern for the development of Greek philosophy. The philosophers of the fifth and fourth centuries, especially Socrates, Plato, and Aristotle, were perhaps more concerned with human problems than their predecessors; but their solutions were the result of reasoned questioning rather then answers sought in the fabric of ancient myths. Socrates' conception of justice was human rather than divine.

The figure of Socrates is one of the noblest in history. He spent his life asking men to think about "the good," "the true," "the beautiful." As a teacher, he won his pupils by his penetrating questions, which pointed up fallacies in their views and encouraged them to think further. His thought owed much to the sophists, professional teachers who prided themselves in their ability as debaters. But he rejected the label of professional and looked down on the sophists because they took pay for something that could not be purchased: wisdom. After the Peloponnesian War, he became very unpopular with the democratic politicians of Athens, who accused him of atheism and corrupting the youth of the city by his ideas. In his famous defense, Socrates showed the absurdity of the charges, but submitted to the judgment of the court that he should drink the poison hemlock. For the modern mind, his unwillingness to accept the easy way out, such as escape to exile, is hard to understand. But the student of Greek thought must keep in mind the primacy which the Greeks assigned to the city-state over the individual. The Greek found his fullest development as a citizen of the *Polis.* Socrates, therefore, chose to die a citizen rather than to live an exile.

Plato, a pupil of Socrates, whose thought is closely bound up with that of his master, ranged widely over all human experience. In his greatest work, *The Republic,* he set forth the outline of a utopian society in which philosophers would rule. His ideal state was strictly regimented, resembling Sparta much more than Athens in this respect. The aim of the state was to secure justice for its citizens. Plato did not appear to have a very high regard for democratic government and no strong belief that such a government could provide justice. Perhaps his observations of Athens in the period after the Peloponnesian War provided some basis for this attitude. One of his major contributions to future thought was his theory of knowledge. This is one of the most difficult problems faced by man. How do we know? In the seventh book of the *Republic,* he tells the famous parable of the cave. His purpose is to describe the process whereby men know things outside themselves. For Plato, the real world is not the world of the eyes but the world of the mind. Our ideas have their reality in various prototypes existing as a universal mind. Here, we should note that Plato follows those early Greek thinkers who attempted to find a single element or force that underlay all nature. For him, however, this force was not material but ideal. Plato's approach to the problem of knowledge has had a continuing influence on philosophers down to the twentieth century.

Although Aristotle was a student in Plato's Academy, his thought differed on essential points from that of his teacher. His interest in natural science—he was the author of treatises on biology—and his inductive approach to learning stood in stark contrast to Plato's theory of ideas. Although not sympathetic to democracy, his study of the constitutions of the Greek city-states shows that he was not utopian in his ideas of government. Rather, he attempted to examine and compare the various constitutions to determine their strengths and weaknesses. His *Metaphysics* attacked the problem of the nature of things. His approach was a compromise between those who posited a single element and those who proposed the seed theory. In Aristotle's view, all beings have essence and existence. The essence is individual and determines what this being is; existence is indeterminate and simply asserts that something "is." Change occurs not in the essence but in the "accidents," which depend on the being and have no existence without it. Thus, Aristotle provides for change that does not alter the essence of a being. In his studies on logic, he fashioned the basic rules of reason that dominated this discipline until modern times. His approach, although deductive, showed the influence of his scientific interest in his attempt to establish logical categories of beings. Much more than Plato, he was an heir of the early Greek thinkers and his influence on medieval and modern thought stimulated an empirical approach to knowledge.

With the advent of Alexander the Great and the Hellenistic age, Greek philosophy became more concerned with ethical problems. Cynics, like

Aristotle. The Hellenistic artist has given us a realistic sculpture of the philosopher. Note the careful detail in face and hands. (The Bettmann Archive)

the famous Diogenes who carried a lamp in search of an honest man, rejected the world. Epicurus, near the end of the fourth century, taught that happiness was the goal of man's existence. He believed the fullest realization of this goal could be found in intellectual pursuits, but his views were perverted into a philosophy of hedonism in which pleasure of the senses became the only good for man. The most pervasive and influential of the Hellenistic philosophies was Stoicism, whose founder Zeno envisioned a great world-state in which all men would serve as brothers. Stoicism placed heavy emphasis on the practical virtues of the public man. It believed that men ought to cooperate in the divine plan for the universe and should find in a natural law the guidelines for a better life. Stoicism became especially influential in Rome and many of its ideas found a sympathetic audience with the rise of Christianity.

For the most part, Greek philosophers accepted the world as ordered by divinity, but they did not attempt to found their ideas of the universe and man on that base. They did not go to the font of mythology for inspiration. Rather, they raised up the ideal of the man of reason seeking to know more about himself, his society, and the world around him. In reason, they found the key to human nobility and foundation of their humanism.

For a fuller understanding of Greek humanism, we must study not merely philosophy, but also art, literature, and science. In these areas, their achievement set a standard for other civilizations to emulate. The restraint of their sculpture, the discipline of their literary forms, and their advances in various sciences, especially medicine, reveal characteristics which we have already discussed in connection with their philosophy. They did not coldly reject mythology but subordinated it to reason so that it might provide a framework for art and literature more universal than individual experiences. But this ideal of moderation came as the climax to a long development which began before the eighth century B.C.

In the *Iliad* and the *Odyssey*, the Greeks possessed two of the greatest epic poems ever written. These poems were probably the work of Homer and were composed during the eighth century. The setting of the *Iliad* is the Trojan War, which saw the Mycenaen Greeks sail off to battle against Troy in northwestern Asia Minor. The theme is the anger of the great Greek warrior Achilles at being deprived of his war prize by King Agamemnon and his refusal to participate further in the war. The greatness of the poem lies in the poet's development of his theme. Homer sets a contrast between excess and moderation. The flaw in Achilles' character is his pride, or *hubris,* his lack of moderation in controlling his anger.

Homer thus reveals his concern for fundamental human values. However, his work is less restrained than that of later writers. Brutality, less common in later writing, abounds in the *Iliad.* The *Odyssey* reveals in this same embryonic way the Greek concern about the relation between passion and reason. It relates the adventure of Odysseus on his return from the Trojan War. Its wild tales of Cyclops and Sirens make it a model of romantic adventure. But the unifying theme centers on the cunning of Odysseus in achieving his goal. Both the *Iliad* and the *Odyssey* accept popular mythology and incorporate the gods into their action in a very complete way. The gods play a major role in shaping human affairs and determining success or failure, certainly a greater role than in later writing. But the Greeks were unwilling to make men the mere playthings of the deities. Man's fate was in the hands of the gods, but his reason made him a worthy contender against them.

Greek poetry in the sixth century revealed the existence of erotic aspects of the Hellenic character that owed much to the rites of the fertility cults of Asia Minor. As might be expected in lyric verse, the restraint that came to typify the Greek character was present to a much less degree than in the earlier epics. The outstanding poets of the period were Sappho, who lived in the Ionian Islands off Asia Minor, and Pindar, a Spartan who spent a large part of his life in Athens. But their work is overshadowed by that of the tragedians of the fifth century: Aeschylus, Sophocles, and Euripides.

For more than a century, the dramatic works of these authors dominated the Athenian stage. Aeschylus was the founder and molder of tragedy. He introduced a second character into the play and made dramatic dialogue possible. He drew his plots both from mythology and from historical experiences. In his *Prometheus,* his hero stands as the defender of human liberty from the arbitrary will of the gods. Despite his acceptance of traditional mythology as part of the motive force to his drama, Aeschylus focused on the human struggle and suffered with man in his defeat. In his work we may see a continuing growth of the Greek effort to view man apart from divine intervention. This effort was further advanced in the plays of Sophocles. The dramas of Sophocles did not draw as much on mythology as on legend, the tales of Greek heroes and heroines whose exploits were well known to his audience. In *Antigone,* for example, he used the story of the desire of Antigone, daughter of King Oedipus of Thebes, to provide honorable funeral rites for her brothers, who rebelled against their uncle, King Creon, to point out the conflict between the law of the state and a "higher law." Traditional myth played almost no role in this play. In Euripides' work, drama criticized the *mores* of society. *Medea,* the barbarian wife of Jason, was a woman of passion intent on avenging her husband's desertion of her for a royal bride. Contrary to Greek standards, the author developed a sympathy for this foreign woman, who was driven even to the murder of her own sons. Euripides has made of this play a major criticism of Greek life, holding up a foreigner as a mirror to his audience. Jason, symbol of Greece, was the tragic figure. Stripped of all he loved, he was left to contemplate the results of his actions. The human element has usurped the role of the divine in the work of Euripides. *Hubris* brought the hero to his tragic end. Prometheus, Creon, Jason, all suffered from this flaw.

The fourth century was the beginning of the decline of Greek literature. The great work was in the comedies of Aristophanes, which made fun of the leading figures and foibles of the age. Historical writing declined from the clear and reasoned account of the Peloponnesian War by Thucydides to the romantic adventure told by Xenophon in the Anabasis about the hardship of a Greek army attempting to escape from Persia. His *Cyropaideia* or education of Cyrus is close to being a novel. Although this century witnessed the climax of Greek philosophical speculation, its literature no longer captured the spirit of moderation that characterized Greek humanism in its intense concern for the nature of man's strivings. The Hellenistic age that followed produced little that was original save some pastoral poetry that expressed the yearning of the urbanite for a romantic rural environment. Hellenistic authors were chiefly critics and encyclopedists. Their coming marked the end of the creative humanism that sought to understand man in his wholeness and to measure him against the yardstick of restraint.

Greek art and architecture trace their origins from Mycenae. The "Dark Ages" had seen a decline from the pinnacle of Mycenaean craftsmanship. Only gradually did new forms of similar quality to the old evolve. Athenian red and black figure pottery certainly marked the climax of a long artistic development in this area. In sculpture, the high point was reached in the fifth century, especially in the work of Phidias, commissioned by Pericles to sculpt the beautiful statue of Athena in the Parthenon atop the Acropolis. Greek sculptors were able to give human warmth to the marble in which they worked and to capture the grace and rhythm of movement. The Doric and Ionic styles of architecture typify the restraint of Greek architects and their abhorrence of the flamboyant in the classical period. Even the more elaborate Corinthian with columns crowned by acanthus leaves was not overly ornate and did not detract from the clean lines of the buildings. But in the Hellenistic age, the tendency toward ornamentation reveals the loss of the ideal.

The science of the Greeks became the foundation for that of Western man until the beginning of the modern era and even then remained as a monument to their achievement. Aristotle's method of classification in biology, although inadequate by the standards of modern science, provided the first systematic basis for the study of animal and plant life. The work of Archimedes in physics established the principle that a body displaces its weight in water. He discovered the relationship between the volume of a sphere and a cylinder and also invented a machine for raising water for irrigation purposes. The Greeks knew the principle of steam power and had invented an elementary form of the steam engine. However, they did not attempt to apply the knowledge of the many principles they had learned to create machines to work for them, save in a few instances chiefly connected with warfare. Scientific theory became divorced from applied science to the detriment of both.

The Greeks were essentially humanists. Their literature and art reveal their deep concern with human attainment and the perfection of human form. Their love of beauty led them to surround themselves with works of

Euclid, the mathematician. The Greeks especially excelled in mathematics, which they regarded as a branch of philosophy. (*Rare Book Room, Syracuse University Library*)

art in their statuary and public buildings. But to fail to discuss their limitations would be to work them an injustice and to destroy the real image of their humanism. Their society possessed the institution of slavery and even Aristotle found reluctant justification for it in a doctrine that held that some men are naturally destined for that role. Their sense of moderation did not always save them from excess; the best example is the execution of Socrates. Although they set up noble goals, they did not always achieve them. When Thucydides accused the Athenians of overweening pride, he was thinking of their attempt to build power excessively. If so, Pericles' oration in praise of Athens is an irony that warns of the danger in too much confidence in man's success. *Hubris,* overweening pride, was in the mind of the Greeks the most dangerous sin of the humanist.

3 Rome the Builder

The contribution of the Romans to the development of Western civilization must be seen in two lights. First, they established an empire based in Italy and from that seat dominated the Mediterranean world for more than five hundred years. Second, their political, social, and economic institutions and the fruit of their thought influenced directly those people who founded Europe in the early Middle Ages. The Romans moved the seat of power to the West and founded cities in the lands west of the Rhine and south of the Danube. Prior to their rise, the East had held the lead. Now Egypt, Mesopotamia, and Greece could not match this Western giant. The Romans built the greatest empire of antiquity. They founded cities which became centers for the dissemination of their culture. But they also built institutions, including one of the most outstanding legal systems ever devised by man. This system took root throughout their empire and influenced the growth of law codes in both East and West.

The Romans were a practical people, more given to the tasks of ruling than to speculations about the nature of justice, more concerned about the use of their public works than their artistic worth. Not that they did not consider philosophy, literature, art, and architecture important; they did. But their scheme of values did not place these attainments on the same level as the great deeds of the statesman and soldier. The real heritage of Rome is not found in fallen cities or aqueducts, but in the continuing influence of their political institutions and legal thought. A common cliché refers to Rome as eternal. In a true sense it will live as long as we continue to dwell in its shadow.

Groping Toward an Empire

"From the beginning Rome was ruled by Kings. . . ." But it was not as a monarchy that Rome was destined to rise to a position of power. The small town on the Tiber River in central Italy had as its chief importance in the sixth century B.C. the fact that it controlled a major route between the north and the south of Italy. The Romans had a strong tradition that their early history was marked by a period of Etruscan domination of the city and the overthrow of a monarchy.

The Etruscans had settled along the coast and in the hills of north central Italy, perhaps after migrating westward from Asia Minor. They built cities and began to trade, especially, after the eighth century, with the Greeks of southern Italy. It was probably as a result of this commerce that they subjected Rome to their rule, for it was the gateway to the south. If we accept Roman legends, the last king of Rome was Etruscan. In 509 B.C., the native Roman nobility, called the Patricians, led a revolution that expelled the Etruscans and established a republic controlled by the nobles. The mass of citizens, the Plebeians, were excluded from the magistracies and their voting power was limited. This aristocratic government was cleverly designed to prevent power from becoming concentrated in the hands of a single individual. There were two consuls, elected for only one year and each acting as a check on the other. The Senate was composed of Patricians who had held the consulate. Other offices leading to the consulate were reserved for Patricians. In this way, the republic remained an aristocratic institution.

Very early in the history of the republic, however, the Plebeians began to agitate for a greater voice in government. They were not without power. Some were men of wealth and influence; most served as infantry in the army. They used their position to negotiate with the Patricians, threatening to secede from the city if their demands were not met. In the long struggle that ensued, they gradually won the right to hold the consulship and to marry into Patrician families. They secured recognition for the office of tribune, whose person was inviolate and who possessed the right of veto over acts of the Senate and the assemblies, as well as over the consuls. Plebeian demands resulted in the creation of the Decemviri, or Board of Ten, who drew up the Law of the XII Tables, the basis of Roman law. This collection of laws aimed at preventing arbitrary interpretation of the law by the Patrician magistrates, who had had no restrictions before this time because there was no written collection to which the

Plebeians could appeal. Though the Law of the XII Tables was not a complete code of public and private law, later Romans saw in it the foundation of their legal system. These reforms led to a shift in the control of the Roman Republic from the Patricians to the Plebeians by the early third century.

As early as the fifth century, the Romans had begun to expand their rule outward from the city, gradually gaining control of surrounding Latin peoples and then conquering the Etruscans to the north. Soon Rome was the dominant power on the peninsula. But this expansion of Roman power brought her into conflict with Carthage, the other major power in the western Mediterranean.

Carthage had been founded by the far-ranging Phoenicians on the coast of North Africa in the seventh century B.C. The Carthaginians had long carried on extensive trade in oil, copper, silver, ivory, gold, precious stones, and many other commodities, ranging from Syria and Egypt to Spain and Britain. The Carthaginians ruled not only in North Africa, but also possessed colonies in Spain and the Balearic Islands and the western part of Sicily. Their navy was the greatest in the western Mediterranean. But their rule was harsh and aroused deep resentments among their foreign subjects. As a result, this empire often faced revolts, especially in Spain.

Rome and Carthage came into conflict at Messina in the north of Sicily. A band of Italian mercenaries seized Messina from the Greek tyrant of Syracuse and appealed to Carthage for aid, but they turned to Rome when it appeared that the Carthaginians might prove an even greater threat. The Romans were reluctant; they had no great concern about the mercenaries, but they did fear Carthaginian control of the strait of Messina. Moreover, these two powers had long been wary of one another. Only Rome's almost total commitment to the Italian peninsula and her lack of interest in foreign trade had kept them from becoming embroiled earlier. Now that the Romans found themselves in a confrontation, they decided they had to act.

The first Punic War lasted from 264 to 241 B.C. Rome soon found that her strong army would avail her little against the Carthaginians without a fleet. She therefore strove to remedy this defect, while forcing the Greek ruler of Syracuse to desert the Carthaginians and provide financial aid for her own effort. Still, the war did not go easily for the Romans. After initial victories, they were unable to defeat the Carthaginians in Africa. Instead, they met a series of disastrous defeats. Indeed, only a change of government at Carthage, which brought to power a party more interested in retrenchment than prosecution of the war, enabled the Romans to deliver the telling blow in a sea battle off western Sicily. The Carthaginians were forced to accept terms depriving them of Sicily and islands off Africa and requiring that they pay the Romans an indemnity of 3200 talents ($3, 480,000). Both sides had suffered greatly. But Rome quickly turned her attention to organizing her new Sicilian possessions and to her pressing domestic problems; Carthage began rebuilding her shattered maritime empire.

The following decades saw continued Roman expansion in northern Italy and efforts to rid the Adriatic Sea of pirates, who found shelter along the Illyrian coast. Rome was drawn from these activities by the outbreak of the second Punic War in 218. The war broke out in Spain, where the Carthaginian general Hannibal had attacked Saguntum, a city allied to Rome. It was the bloodiest and most devastating war ever fought by the Romans, for it took place to a large extent on Italian soil. The brilliant Hannibal brought his army to Italy, where he remained through most of the war. His presence forced the Romans to take shelter behind city walls. The Roman army reeled under the shock of defeats at Trebia, Lake Trasimene, and Cannae. But Rome refused to give up. She raised new armies and found a capable general in Scipio Africanus. Under his leadership, the army conquered Spain. The defeat of Hannibal's brothers, Hasdrubal and Mago, cleared the way for Scipio's invasion of Africa in 204. Two years later, at Zama, Scipio crushed Carthage. It was the end. Carthage had to surrender her entire empire; she was left a powerless city-state in North Africa. The war indemnity was set so high that Carthage could never recover. Rome was now mistress of the western Mediterranean.

But the second Punic War had left deep scars on Italy. Hannibal's long sojourn had forced the farmers to seek refuge in the cities. Others, serving in the army, had to sell their lands to sustain their families. Rome herself became the capital of a great empire, but her walls could hardly contain the population who had left the countryside. Thus, the second Punic War bequeathed to posterity the problem of a large urban population without means to support themselves. They, in the meantime, found aid among wealthy patrons in return for their political support. The war also had enriched many members of the Senate, who had invested in huge estates which they could best work with gangs of enslaved captives rather than with more expensive free labor. The latifundia, or industrial farms, made it more difficult for the small free farmer, long regarded as the backbone of the Roman state and army, to sustain himself and his family. Thus war had transformed the social and economic structure of Italy.

Rome had now become a major Mediterranean power and was more and more drawn into the disputes of the Hellenistic states to the East. When Philip V of Macedon attempted to conquer the kingdom of Pergamum and the mighty commercial power of Rhodes, they appealed to Rome, arguing that Philip's plans were aimed at Rome herself. Despite opposition from the people, the Senate decided to lead Rome into war against Macedonia. The defeat of Philip V brought the Romans into the very center of affairs in Greece and Asia Minor. In a series of wars fought during the first half of the third century, Roman control of Greece and Asia Minor tightened. Moreover, during this same period, the Romans completed the work of Scipio Africanus in Spain.

The city on the Tiber was now ruler of a vast empire stretching from the Strait of Gibraltar to Syria and including a large part of North Africa. Its administration of these lands followed no single pattern. In Spain, direct rule through provincial governors prevailed; in North Africa, the kingdom of Numidia was nominally a Roman ally. Generally, Roman rule proved no worse than its predecessors and, indeed, often was a decided improvement. The Romans did not attempt to alter local religious customs and seem to have laid fairly mild terms on most of the peoples they conquered. Finally, the Romans made such an example of rebels as to discourage neighboring states from attempting revolution.

But some Romans demanded the complete destruction of Carthage. Their motive was chiefly fear of economic competition, for Carthage possessed neither army nor navy. Moreover, the treaty with Rome prevented her from defending herself against attacks by Numidia. Rome refused to help. Carthage had to declare war. The war was a blot on Rome's character; Numidia and Rome defeated the Carthaginian army easily. The Romans destroyed Carthage and sowed the site with salt to prevent resettlement. The Carthaginians had done nothing sufficient to provoke such vengeance, but the year 146 B.C. marked their end.

The unsolved problems rising from the economic and social impact of the Punic Wars, from the increased dominance of Roman political life by the Senate, and from the acquisition of an empire troubled Rome increasingly after 146 B.C. The Gracchi brothers, Tiberius and Gaius, were the first Roman statesmen to attempt a reform program. They proposed measures to ease the burden of the small farmer, to establish colonies for landless Roman citizens, to grant citizenship to all Latins, and to provide grain for the city populace to make it more independent of the wealthy senatorial patrons who controlled its vote. The Gracchi were not radicals. They represented the moderates, who desired to head off a major conflict. The opposition to their reforms by the intransigent element in the Senate nearly drove the state into civil war and resulted in the violent death of both brothers. But the problems remained and the Senate was too shortsighted to take effective action. The way was open for a dictator.

The last century of the Roman republic saw the efforts of a succession of military leaders to gain control of Rome. Both the *Populares,* the reform party, and the *Optimates,* the senatorial party, turned to this source for the power needed to rule. Increasingly, the reform program was lost in the personal ambitions of dictators who claimed to speak for the *Populares,* while the Senate found it increasingly difficult to control its champions. In desperation, some tried to halt the process. Marcus Tullius Cicero, consul, senator, and Rome's greatest orator, proposed a harmony of the senators and leading business interests, in order to bring peace. But it was already too late. In 59 B.C., Julius Caesar, backed by Crassus, one of the wealthiest men in Rome, became consul. Caesar allied himself with the *Populares* in his bid for power. With Crassus and Pompey, another general, he joined in the First Triumvirate to promote the common interests of the three. After his consulship, Caesar continued to keep a close eye on affairs in Rome, while he led campaigns against the Gauls resulting in the subjection of the Gauls to Rome. When Crassus was killed in a campaign against Persia, Pompey's control of Rome increased. Caesar de-

Julius Caesar. The victorious Roman dictator appears in all his power and ruthlessness. (Rare Book Room, Syracuse University Library)

cided to act. He marched on Rome and forced Pompey to flee to Egypt for refuge. But it was a short-lived refuge, for Pompey was murdered. Caesar, having conquered Egypt, had become master of the Roman Empire. But he was a ruler without any real program. Because he came to power at the head of his army, he had not needed to develop one. His chief efforts were directed toward restricting the power of the Senate and preventing his enemies from gaining advantage over him by the same means he had used to gain power. For example, he abolished political clubs and increased the Senate to nine hundred members. His increasing power, especially his effort to create around himself the aura of a god, caused the senatorial conservatives to conspire against him. On the Ides of March (March 15), 44 B.C., he was assassinated.

Immediately, the struggle for power broke out between Caesar's nephew and adopted heir, Octavian, and Marcus Antonius, Caesar's closest associate. Because of the threat posed to their power by the senatorial party, they joined with Lepidus, Caesar's commander of cavalry, in the Second Triumvirate in 43 B.C. until Antonius and Octavian, having defeated the conspirators against Caesar, divided the spoils between themselves. Octavian took the west and Antonius the east. But friction between the two rulers increased. Octavian was particularly angered when Antonius divorced his sister to marry Cleopatra, Queen of Egypt. Finally, Octavian declared war on Antonius and Cleopatra and defeated their forces decisively at Actium in 31 B.C. He was now the master of Rome.

The victory of Octavian marked the end of the Roman Republic. The causes of its passing were complex. The failure to broaden participation in public life led to a polarization of political opposition in the Senate and the *Populares.* It proved impossible thereafter for either side to work within the framework of the constitution. The task of ruling the vast territories conquered by the Romans taxed the resources of a government and administration built to direct a city-state. The maintenance of a large army posed a threat to continued civilian rule. The existence of a large urban populace in Rome played into the hands of demagogues and dictators. Octavian's proclamation of peace in 29 B.C. seemed to many Romans to hold promise of an end to these problems.

The Empire: Strengths and Weaknesses

On his return to Rome in 27 B.C., Octavian proclaimed the restoration of the republic, but this was only a façade. He was a military dictator. He was the conqueror and had behind him the support of the army plus

The Colosseum. This vast arena was the scene of numerous spectacles, including mock sea battles. Here it is shown in the eighteenth century. (Rare Book Room, Syracuse University Library)

the enormous wealth of Egypt, which he kept as his personal property. He also had enormous personal prestige and support within Rome because of his gifts to the poor. He had broken the power of the Senate by his defeat of the conspirators responsible for the murder of Julius Caesar and by filling that body with his own supporters. But Octavian was also a conservative, who genuinely desired to restore peace and stable government. He worked with the Senate. He restored the forms of republican government. He remained the power, however, in order to preserve peace. He contented himself with the role of *Princeps*, or first citizen, employing his enormous power and prestige to ensure the maintenance of this façade by influencing elections to the various offices and controlling the actions of those who owed their election to his support.

Augustus had succeeded in bringing peace to the empire. His reign, and the term is not inappropriate, which lasted until 14 A.D., was a golden

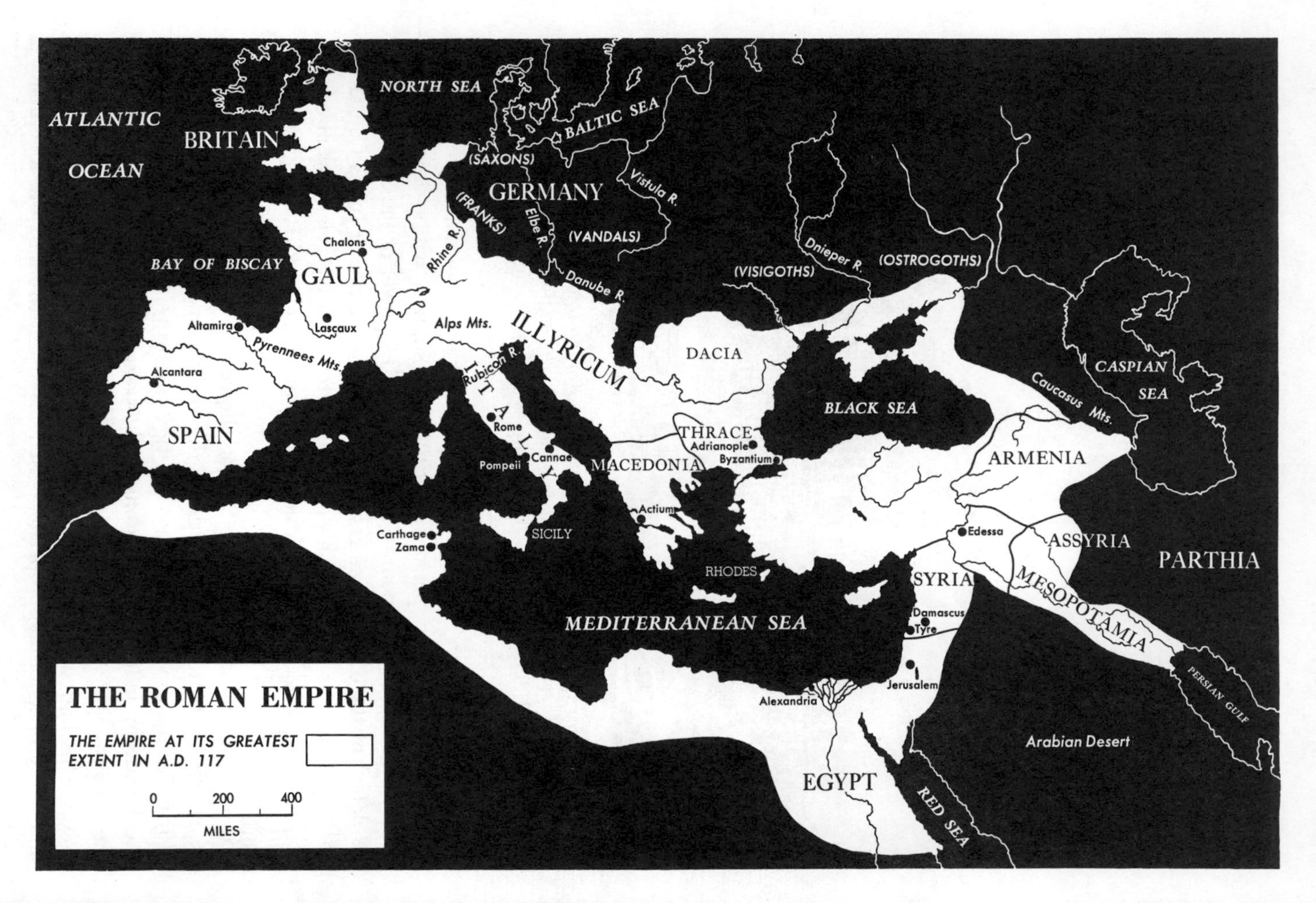
THE ROMAN EMPIRE
THE EMPIRE AT ITS GREATEST EXTENT IN A.D. 117
0
200
400
MILES
ATLANTIC OCEAN
BRITAIN
NORTH SEA
BALTIC SEA
(SAXONS)
GERMANY
(FRANKS)
Elbe R.
Vistula R.
(VANDALS)
Danube R.
Dnieper R.
(VISIGOTHS)
(OSTROGOTHS)
BAY OF BISCAY
Chalons
GAUL
Rhine R.
Lascaux
Altamira
Pyrennees Mts.
Alcantara
SPAIN
Alps Mts.
ILLYRICUM
Rubicon R.
ITALY
Rome
Pompeii
Cannae
SICILY
Carthage
Zama
DACIA
BLACK SEA
CASPIAN SEA
Caucasus Mts.
THRACE
Adrianople
Byzantium
MACEDONIA
Actium
RHODES
MEDITERRANEAN SEA
ARMENIA
Edessa
ASSYRIA
PARTHIA
SYRIA
MESOPOTAMIA
Damascus
Tyre
Jerusalem
Alexandria
PERSIAN GULF
Arabian Desert
EGYPT
RED SEA

age in art and literature, an era of prosperity. He did not attempt to expand the frontiers of the empire, though some territory was added, but directed most of his efforts to building an efficient corps of administrators to rule what had been conquered. He restored the confidence of the Romans, which was badly shattered during the civil wars. He was very conscious of his own public image and constantly employed propaganda to put himself before the people in the best light. There could be no doubt who the real ruler of Rome was.

As long as Augustus ruled, Rome enjoyed an almost unparalleled sense of security and well-being. But like many strong men, he had never settled on a definite successor for very long and had never specified a means of succession. His own vacillations had ended with his death and the election of his last choice, his son-in-law, Tiberius, as Princeps. But the problem remained to plague the empire under his successors and became a major source of internal disorders.

The reign of Tiberius (14–37 A.D.) saw significant changes in the government. The Roman historian Tacitus charged him with despotism, but Tacitus was probably too harsh in his judgment. Tiberius was suspicious and aloof. He distrusted even the members of his own family. But he made an effort to rule effectively and was generally successful. He strengthened Roman civil administration in the provinces and established the boundaries of the empire in Germany. He tried to also cut expenses, although his reduction in money for entertainment of the Roman populace injured his popularity. But the most significant change in the government arose from Tiberius' distrust of the Senate. He did not attempt to keep up the pretense of joint rule. He also discontinued the practice of summoning the assemblies to elect candidates for the consulate and other offices. In these departures from Octavian's practice, his rule forecast the growing tendency toward monarchy in imperial government.

The unfortunate choice of Gaius Caligula (37–41) as a successor to Tiberius ushered in a period of political turmoil during which the influence of the Praetorian Guard over the choice of the emperor ceased. It was an officer of this body that assassinated Caligula and forced the Guard's candidate, Claudius, on the Senate. He proved an able ruler, spending most of his efforts in building up the bureaucracy and in embarking on an extensive program of public works. His relations with the Senate were better than under Tiberius and he apparently attempted to restore the principle of cooperation. But he fell victim to a palace intrigue led by his second wife, Agrippina, who wished to put her son Nero on the throne. This ruler has long suffered unjustly at the hands of historians. The first five years of his reign were among the most serene in the history of the Principate. He promoted trade between East and West by his reform of the Roman coinage and acted vigorously against dishonesty in government. His chief advisor was the Roman philosopher Seneca, who composed his speeches for him. But, as Nero attempted to rule independently of his mother Agrippina, they grew more and more estranged. The resultant plots and murders put a blot on what had been, until then, a peaceful rule. During the later years of his reign, Nero turned against Seneca and embarked on a savage policy of reprisal against supposed plots on his life. Finally, deserted by the Senate and faced with a rebellion by the Praetorian Guard, he committed suicide. He was the last of the Julio-Claudians, the descendants of Augustus, and with him passed any pretense of orderly succession to the Principate.

Gradually, the Praetorian Guard had come to play an increasingly larger role in the selection of the emperor. But the armies in the provinces began to advance their candidates for the throne. It was only because he commanded the support of the army as well as the Senate that Vespasian was able to end the chaos following the death of Nero and restore good government. He was a very able man, who had served extensively both as a civil administrator and a military commander. He worked assiduously to balance the budget, but his major program lay in his effort to broaden the base of Roman government. He reformed the army by opening its officers' ranks to the provincial aristocracy and he brought them into the civil service. Vespasian's sons, Titus (79–81) and Domitian (81–96), continued the record of good administration set by their father. Domitian was an able administrator and carried out an extensive program of road building as well as increasing the pay of soldiers without levying new taxes. However, he ran afoul of the Senate and was murdered in 96 A.D.

From Nerva (96–98) to Marcus Aurelius (161–180), the empire enjoyed good government; during this period, too, the empire reached its broadest extent and achieved its greatest prosperity. In part, the credit of this "golden age" belongs to the previous rulers, who had gradually reformed the army and the civil service, inproved the methods of taxation, and maintained the value of the coinage. Hadrian attempted to consolidate Roman holdings, building the vast walls aimed at preventing the barbarians from entering Roman territory. He improved the bureaucracy further by taking it out of the hands of freedmen and putting it in charge of experienced equestrians, members of the Roman middle class. Antoninus Pius (138–161) and Marcus Aurelius maintained the policies of their predecessors in preserving prosperity. But Marcus Aurelius, whose *Medi-*

tations mark him as one of the greatest Stoic philosophers, was forced to defend the empire against the Parthians in the East, who were a constant threat to Roman rule in Asia Minor, Mesopotamia, and Syria, and the barbarian German tribes who forced their way across the Danubian frontier in 167 and into northeastern Italy. He died at Vienna in 180, while campaigning against the Germans.

The first two centuries of the Roman Empire were, on the whole, an age of peace and prosperity. With the exception of Caligula and the later reign of Nero, the level of government was high. Under these circumstances, it would seem out of place to speak of a decline. Yet the failure of the Romans to find a workable system for the selection of the Princeps was a basic flaw that would threaten stability and order in less settled and prosperous times. Moreover, the influence of the Praetorian Guard and of the armies in the provinces over the choice of the ruler constituted a real danger to peaceful transfer of power. As long as the empire was able to repel outside enemies and to maintain prosperous trade within its borders, these problems did not present insurmountable obstacles to continued good government. But, as perils increased from without and as economic and social unrest was aggravated within, this political flaw in the structure of the empire made it too responsive to the pressures that resulted.

But these problems were still in the future to the Romans of this period. They could still look back over the centuries since the accession of Octavian without feeling deep apprehension for the future. True, Tacitus had written in a somewhat pessimistic vein of the decline of Roman virtue and others had taken up the theme, but Rome was still mistress of the world. She still had a glorious future. But even more, she had a rich past, which had seen her language, Latin, spread throughout her western domains and bear fruit in a vital literature. Her contact with the East and especially Greece made her not merely the heir of that tradition, but its guardian in East and West.

Greco–Roman Civilization

The Roman Empire reached from Britain to Persia and from the mouth of the Rhine to the Sahara Desert. It had been won by conquest over a period of more than five hundred years. It encompassed hundreds of different peoples from the Latins of Rome, the Greeks of Sicily, the Berbers of Africa, the Gauls of France, and the Britains, to Syrians, Jews, Egyptians, and Greeks throughout the East. While the peoples of the West found Roman culture superior to their own and tended to adopt the

Latin tongue and Roman institutions, the Easterners already possessed highly developed cultures and institutions of their own. Moreover, the conquests of Alexander the Great in the late fourth century B.C. had spread Greek culture throughout the East and North Africa. Greek had come into general use as the language of the business classes and men of culture. Therefore, Roman conquest did not result in a full-scale adoption of Roman culture in the East.

On the contrary, Roman contact with the East and particularly with the Greeks wrought significant changes in many areas of Roman life. The period following the Second Punic War saw the rise of a strong group of Grecophiles in Rome itself. The great family of the Scipios were patrons of the new movement. On the other hand, some Romans felt that Greek culture was effete and would result in the weakening of the homespun virtues of Rome. Cato the Elder denounced Greek influence for undermining the stern customs of the Roman farmer-soldiers who had defeated Carthage and made Rome the mistress of the West. But the attraction of the Greeks was too great. Their influence dominated the comedies of Plautus and Terence in the third and second centuries B.C. Plautus borrowed his plots from earlier Athenian comedies, while Terence, whose patron was Aemilianus Scipio, followed Greek models even more closely. It became customary for Roman youth of the upper classes to finish their educations in Greece. Thus, by the end of the second century, educated Romans were fully familiar with Greek literature, philosophy, and art. As Rome continued her conquest of the West, the civilization which she founded reflected her assimilation of Greek culture.

The Romans, however, did not possess the Greek bent toward speculative studies; their interests were more practical. Their philosophical writings concentrated on man's moral behavior and were especially influenced by Stoicism and Epicureanism. Marcus Tullius Cicero, the greatest Roman orator, wrote essays on duty, old age, and friendship, which reflected his debt to the Stoics. The poet, Lucretius Carus, writing in the first century B.C., summed up the Epicurean view of man in *De Rerum Natura,* "On the Nature of Things." Creation resulted from the chance formations of atoms. The soul is material. Above all, man should avoid pain and find his pleasure in the contentment that springs from the absence of desire. He condemned the sensuous pleasures of the idle and praised the life of those who live close to nature. The *De Rerum Natura* obtained its originality from the beauty of its poetry rather than from its ideas, which were borrowed from Greek sources. Its philosophy is almost one of *ennui,* of boredom with a purposeless existence, but it is saved

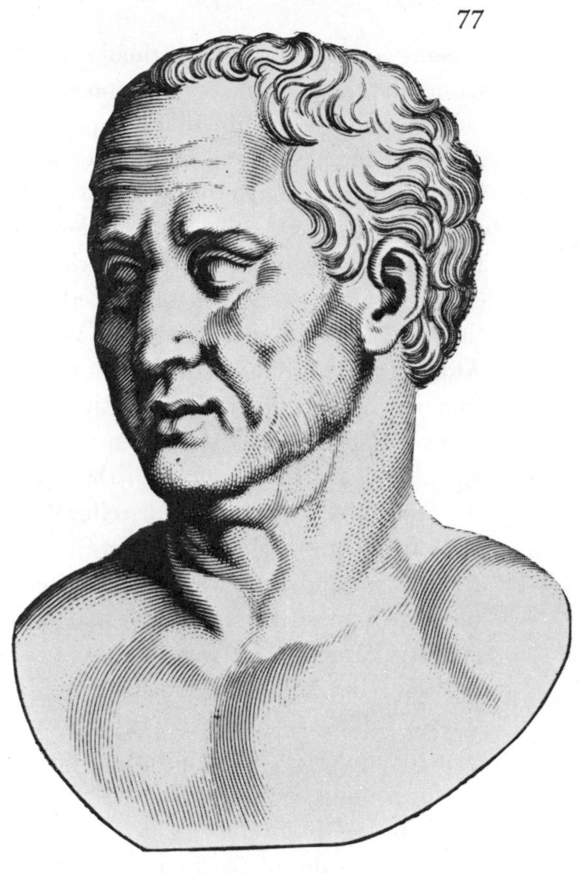

Marcus Tullius Cicero. Rome's greatest orator and defender of the Roman Republic. (Rare Book Room, Syracuse University Library)

from that by the author's love of nature. The essays of Seneca and the *Meditations* of Marcus Aurelius were the chief philosophical works from the Imperial period. Both authors were Stoic in their outlook. Seneca held a lofty idea of world brotherhood and came close to monotheism in his religious views. Marcus Aurelius wrote his reflections in Greek, attempting to find in Stoicism some consolation for the vicissitudes of life and death. His work was intensely personal. Of all of these writers, only Lucretius presented his readers with a philosophy that attempted to answer the basic questions about the origins of things. Yet even his work was dominated by his practical concern about the ethical life. Evidently the Romans were so absorbed by problems of human conduct, by the outward forms of living, that they had little inclination to seek answers to the secrets of being.

Roman philosophy was little influenced by religious ideas, save for the general concepts of natural theology, which were basic to Stoicism. Consequently, the influence of religion was more apparent in the formal channels of public worship than in private devotion. While the traditional deities of the hearth and home, the Lares and Penates, received a place of honor in every Roman house, worship became more external, formalized, and identified with the state under the later republic and the empire. Roman gods were equated with their Greek counterparts and much of Greek mythology was incorporated without significant change. Jupiter, the head of the Roman Pantheon, was identified with Zeus, Minerva with Athena, and Mercury with Hermes. Public worship of the gods became a function of patriotism. During the later republic, many upper-class Romans began to embrace Eastern mystery religions, such as the cult of the Egyptian Isis. They sought in these mysteries the key to salvation from the atmosphere of the secular religion of the state. Although many sophisticated Roman thinkers like Lucretius and Marcus Aurelius turned toward rationalism and even atheism, religion remained a much more important force in Roman culture than it had been among the Greeks of the fourth century. However, it was not the traditional deities who captured this position, but the new gods of the East, especially the Christian God, whose followers increased rapidly among the lower classes and even gained supporters of high rank in the first two centuries of the empire. By the beginning of the third century Christianity was one of the major religions of the empire.

The literature of the republic and early empire reflected the views and interests of the educated Roman aristocracy; indeed, much of it was closely identified with government or the court of the Princeps.

Roman historical writers owed much to the Greeks. Polybius, who composed a history of Rome during the Punic Wars, wrote in Greek, which was his native tongue. His work enjoyed a high reputation for accuracy. He attended the siege of Carthage in 146 B.C. with Publius Scipio. His work is full of admiration for the Romans but does not descend to the level of flattery; the same cannot be said for the *Roman History* of Titus Livius. Livy wrote during the Augustan age. He was an excellent Latin stylist and approached history from the viewpoint of literature. Though he realized the importance of accurate sources, he did not hesitate to employ literary devices in order to fill in gaps in the story of Rome's early development. His major purpose was to celebrate the grandeur of the Principate and, in a very flattering fashion, he sometimes exaggerated the importance in Rome's past of the great families of his own day. Despite these shortcomings, however, his work preserved many important elements of Roman history that would otherwise have perished and, as literature, enjoys an enduring reputation. During the early empire, historical writers neglected general history in favor of a monographic approach. The leading figure of this period was Cornelius Tacitus. His *Annals* dealt with the reign of Tiberius, whose suspicious mind and shabby treatment of the Senate, caused Tacitus to criticize him severely. The *Histories* cover the period from Galba to Domitian. Tacitus was a stern moralist. In the *Germania* he contrasted the vices of contemporary Rome with the purity of the German barbarians. Although critical of the empire and a lover of the republic, he made some effort to be impartial. However, he could not overcome his bias. The Greek biographer Plutarch was a contemporary of Tacitus. His *Lives* were among the most popular literature of the age. From the standpoint of the historian, they leave much to be desired. But their lively style and interesting treatment of great Greeks and Romans has ensured them a continuing audience. As a genre of literature, history celebrated the great deeds and great men of the past. Though sometimes uncritical, it served to remind Romans of their heritage.

Roman literature was most often didactic and practical in its aims. The ideal of Roman education was the public man. The major literary figure of the late republic was the orator and statesman, Marcus Tullius Cicero. Consul and senator, he was also one of the great lawyers of his day. His prosecution of Verres, the crooked governor of Sicily, his defense of his former teacher, Aulus Licinius Archias the poet, and his speeches in behalf of the politician Milo all reveal his tremendous skill with words. But most famous is the series of attacks he made in the Senate unmasking the conspiracy of Cataline against the republic. In them he combined mastery of language with a great cause, the defense of the state. His Latin style was so highly regarded by later ages that the major compliment one could pay to a medieval or renaissance author was to call his work Ciceronian. Cicero summed up in his life the career for which Roman education aimed to prepare the scions of the great Roman houses.

Latin poetry owed much to Greek forms, but did achieve a beauty of its own. The greatest poet was Publius Vergilius Maro, whose *Aeneid* celebrated the grandeur of Rome in the fabled adventures of Aeneas as he traveled from Troy westward to Italy where his descendants would found Rome. Although the debt to the Homeric Epic is everywhere evident, Vergil adds a quality of Roman patriotism that colors the entire work. In his *Odes and Epodes* and in the *Satires,* Horace has created some of the most beautiful poetry of any age. He writes of the charms of the simple life and of the country, of the pleasures of his Sabine farm. His satires are gentle stories well told, like that of the city mouse and the country mouse. He was a friend of Vergil and shared his dream of Rome immortal. On the other hand, the *Satires* of Juvenal are vitriolic attacks on the vices of his fellow Romans. While Horace reflected the serenity of the Augustan age, Juvenal mirrors a popular concern about life under the second-century Principate. The later age longed for a return to a romanticized republican era in which private and public virtue had been greater than it was under the emperors of the second century.

While Roman art was heavily dependent on Greek for its technical perfection, it was not strictly imitative. The Romans excelled in depicting their military leaders, statesmen, and emperors as individuals and in capturing in marble many of their dominant personality traits. Triumphal arches, such as the Arch of Titus in Rome, were richly carved with scenes celebrating victory. The Romans also excelled in frescoes, some of the best of which were found in the excavation of Pompei, which was buried by an eruption of Mount Vesuvius near Naples. These reveal their love of vivid colors, especially reds. This art was natural and realistic, fully in keeping with the practical bent of the Roman mind.

The genius of Roman architects and engineers created the most extensive and impressive work of all antiquity. Here the Roman talent for the useful found its outlet. The forum or open square was the center of the Roman city. About it were the various public buildings. These were high-vaulted and supported by columns, which enabled the architects to break the arch of the roof to add a clerestory whose windows would furnish additional light. The streets were well paved as were the major highways connecting the various parts of the empire. Rome and some of the provincial cities received their water supplies from the mountains many miles away through a system of aqueducts. These bridged gorges with their high arches cut through hills on their way to the cities. Rome also had an excellent sewage system, which carried waste into the Tiber to be swept out to sea. Of course, such accomplishments presuppose a fairly high degree of mathematical knowledge, but this appears to have been limited to that which was needed for practical ends. The Romans had no great interest in any other science outside of medicine and their chief contribution in that area was in compiling encyclopedias, such as that of Pliny the Elder, which collected geographical, etymological, and scientific lore from earlier sources in a rather uncritical manner.

The pattern of life across the broad expanse of the Roman Empire cannot be described in terms of uniformity. Life in the fertile crescent differed markedly from that in Gaul or North Africa. Nevertheless, it is

Roman Forum. Here the major business of the empire was transacted. Augustus had a small house in the Forum. (The Bettmann Archive)

The Pantheon. Now a Christian church, this temple illustrates the genius of Roman architects in building so large a dome. (The Bettmann Archive)

possible to speak of the unity of the empire in more than a political sense. The Mediterranean Sea did not separate the various parts of the empire so much as it bound them together. It was a natural highway for communication and trade. Roman cities grew up around its shores. Many different parts of the empire complemented or served others. Corn from Egypt, North Africa, and Sicily provided food to feed the masses in Rome dependent on the corn dole. The wine of Marseilles added sparkle to Roman tables. Tin from Britain furnished a basic ingredient for bronze. The riches of the East, silks, precious stones, and ivory, adorned Romans of wealth. In Italy, gangs of slaves worked the latifundia to produce the olive oil which was one of the major commodities for export. The prosperity of the Empire hung on the continuance of growth of this interaction. This unity was essential to the maintenance of the empire. It was this unified civilization that was Rome's greatest contribution to the West. For the unity of Roman culture provided one of the chief elements in European civilization. Europe was, in part, the result of the transformation of Rome in the West.

But the beginning of the third century did not see any cataclysmic changes in the Roman Empire. The pattern of life did not alter markedly. Yet it is in this period that we may find the beginnings of the transformation of that empire in the increasing strength of Christianity and the first great movements of the barbarians against the empire.

4 Forces Reshaping the Empire

The idea of a cataclysmic fall of the Roman Empire has gradually been superseded by the notion of decline. In the view of most recent scholars, the empire entered a period of gradually increasing senility after the beginning of the third century and was unable to cope effectively with internal or external problems. As a result, the efforts of the strong rulers of the late third and early fourth century were directed to consolidation and retrenchment. The empire lost control of its ancient heritage in Rome and became Byzantine. In this process, internal decline produced by adverse economic and social conditions was more important than the external force of the barbarians. However, it would be a mistake to play down the role of the barbarians in transforming the empire. A new Europe was beginning to form even as the unity of Rome was being weakened.

In the East, this period witnessed the gradual consolidation of Roman rule; in the West, the breakdown of Roman political control presaged the formation of the first efforts of the Germanic peoples to rule the former imperial territory. What began to emerge were the beginnings of Christian Europe.

It was Christianity that was to try to create in the new Europe the unity of Rome. It preserved Roman culture and the Roman ideal of universalism, transmitting these to the barbarians while preserving them among the last of the Romans. Thus, in the new Europe, three elements dominated—Christian, Roman, and barbarian.

Christianity and Rome

Among the Eastern cults which became popular during the later republic and the early empire, Christianity showed the greatest zeal in gaining adherents. Its origins were in Palestine among the Jews. Judaism had enjoyed a privileged status in line with the Roman policy of toleration, despite periodic unrest in the country. It was ruled partly by a native king and partly by a Roman procurator with headquarters in Jerusalem. The Romans looked upon Christianity as a Jewish sect during its early period and, indeed, there was some justification for this view because it had gained its early followers within the Jewish communities dispersed through the cities of the empire and at Rome itself. Its founder, Jesus, had been Jewish as had most if not all of his early followers. Jesus, however, had come into conflict with some of the Jewish leaders and had been accused by them of blasphemy. He was condemned and crucified outside the city of Jerusalem in 29 A.D. His followers first scattered but later began to meet in secret and then more openly. They proclaimed that Jesus had risen from the dead and had walked in their midst, that he had strengthened their faith and commissioned them to teach his doctrines. However, they did not break with traditional Jewish rites immediately, but continued to worship in synagogues and in the temple at Jerusalem. Despite continued friction, they considered themselves Jews.

The chief teachings of Jesus are contained in the New Testament, a collection of writings by various early Christian writers from the first and second century. The four gospels are almost but not quite biographical; although they stress many of the events in the life of Jesus, they emphasize his teachings. The acts of the Apostles and the epistles record the events in the history of the very early Christian community and contain advice written by various of Jesus' followers to groups of Christians throughout the Roman world.

The heart of Jesus' teaching was his doctrine of love. Jesus' crucifixion was a sacrifice of love to God the Father to atone for the sins of men and to lead them to eternal salvation. The Last Supper, in which Jesus celebrated the Passover with his Apostles for the last time and offered them bread and wine with the words "this is my body" and "this is my blood," was celebrated among the early Christians as the "Agape" or love-feast. Jesus condemned formalism and advocated humility and simplicity. His parable of the Publican and the Pharisee stressed the point that humility and purity of heart not external piety were the marks of the virtuous man.

He often spoke of peace, using the term not merely to denote peace among peoples but also inner contentment. He emphasized that he was the Son of God and depicted Him not only as the judge of man's life and the rewarder of his good deeds, but also as a forgiving father. Jesus did not couch his teaching in speculative terms, but in the concrete language of parables. He did not formulate doctrines into a theological system, but contented himself with pointing out lessons and illustrating them by stories. Although he seems to have been familiar with the prescriptions of the Jewish law, he did not parade his knowledge. Nevertheless, he did come into conflict with some of the Jewish leaders, especially among the Pharisees. The major cause for this disagreement was his rejection of their interpretation of the laws of ritual purity, which he regarded as narrow and legalistic and his condemnation of the hypocrisy of inner vices behind the mask of virtue. His term "whited sepulchres" struck at the root of this difference. His supporters were largely people from the villages, though he did attract some from the upper classes.

The most important conflict to break out among the early Christians was over the admission of non-Jews. Since most of them were Jewish, they had followed essential Jewish practices, including circumcision and dietary laws. Many believed that all who wished to become Christian should first accept these requirements before receiving baptism, which was symbolic of the cleansing of the soul from the results of Adam and Eve's sin of disobedience which had descended to all other human beings. On the other hand, Paul, who had been converted to Christianity after the death of Christ, was filled with a desire to preach to non-Jews and saw these requirements as a stumbling block to non-Jewish converts. He argued that Christ had established a new law supplanting the old, that the prescriptions of the old law did not apply to Christians, and that the rite of baptism was the only necessary requirement to becoming a Christian. His view met with considerable opposition. The Apostle, Peter, who had acted on several occasions as a spokesman for the views of the Apostles during Jesus' lifetime, led the opposition; he saw Christianity continuing within the framework of Judaism. Jesus was the Jewish Messiah come to fulfill the expectations of the Jews. However, Paul continued to press for his view and gained the support of the others. With the victory of the Pauline view, Christianity began an intensive missionary program among the gentiles, in which Paul and his followers played a leading part. Within a very short time there were Christian communities composed of Jews and gentiles throughout the Roman world.

The spread of Christianity naturally brought it to the attention of

Roman authorities and even the emperors themselves. Judging from mentions found in the letters of Pliny the Younger, in Tacitus, and in the writings of some of the emperors, knowledge of this new sect was sketchy and often inaccurate. Pliny wrote to the Emperor Trajan that he found it difficult to learn anything about them. However, popular gossip labeled the Christians as "cannibal," judged them guilty of serious immorality and of disloyalty to the state. For these reasons, the emperors from Nero onward through Nerva ordered that those discovered to be Christians should be put to death. This law was not enforced rigidly by all the emperors. According to Christian tradition, both Peter and Paul met death in Rome during Nero's persecution. Paul, as a Roman citizen, was beheaded. Peter was crucified upside down. Recent excavations beneath the Basilica of St. Peter in Rome have confirmed the existence of a Christian cemetery and the practice of early Christians coming as pilgrims to ask these holy men to intercede for them. Early Christian writers, men like Justin Martyr (ca. 100–166), confirm the evidence of persecutions by the emperors, but do not reveal very much about how extensive or well organized they were. Although the later records mention the names of many martyrs who suffered death under the Romans, we know that some of these did not exist. They were invented later to please local desires to have a martyr-patron to venerate. Some, like Philomena, were invented as late as the nineteenth century. The persecutions were real, but it is difficult to determine how severe they were.

As Christianity moved into closer contact with Greco-Roman civilization and began to make converts among the educated classes, some Christian thinkers attempted to synthesize its teachings with what they regarded to be the better elements of that thought. Men like Justin Martyr and Tertullian were concerned with attempts to explain its teachings to those embued with Greek philosophy. Some wished to retain the simplicity of Jesus' teachings while others saw similarity between his views and those of the philosophers. Some condemned the study of pagan classics on the ground that they would pervert Christians; others recommended them because of the truths which they contained. As early as the time of Paul, who seems to have had some contact with Greek philosophy, there had been attempts to formulate the basic Christian message in a body of doctrine. By the beginning of the third century, both Stoicism and Neoplatonism had had considerable influence on Christian writings. The appeal of Stoicism lay in its lofty moral ideas and its conception of all men as brothers, as well as in its almost religious approach to philosophical questions. Neoplatonism offered a framework that proved most compatible with Christianity for the formulation of doctrine. Neoplatonic concepts of the soul and the role of reason were especially influential.

The organization of early Christianity developed along various lines. The Apostolic age had little time for the development of complex organization. Most communities in this period had an almost autonomous existence, although there is evidence from the Epistles and some other sources of communication between them and of attempts to preserve standards of behavior and belief. In certain major centers direction of the Church was entrusted to one man, who came to be known as the bishop (Greek: *Episcopos*, overseer). During the course of the second century, the bishop became more prominent. Men like Irenaeus, Bishop of Lyons, were powerful advocates of the rights of the episcopacy and worked for greater centralization within the Church to prevent the development of heretical ideas. At Rome, the episcopacy appears to have achieved prominence quite early. Clement, one of the earliest bishops, wrote to the Corinthians suggesting ways in which they might improve their church and their lives.

A major problem for the early Church was the growth of heresy. Almost from the beginning, there were serious differences among Christians over points of belief. Attempts to combine Christian teaching and Greek philosophical concepts led to differences over the nature of Christ and the doctrine of the Virgin-birth. The influence of other Eastern religions was also important, especially in the rise of Manichaeanism, which taught that evil was a positive principle struggling with God, the principle of good. It also held that all matter is intrinsically evil. In the fourth century, the Arian heresy denied that Jesus possessed a divine nature. Its formulation of Christian teaching consistent with Greek philosophy captivated the minds of large segments of Christians especially in the East. Many of the Germanic peoples converted to Christianity accepted Arianism.

The spread of Christianity within the Roman Empire was due to various factors. The zeal of its missionaries combined with a strong sense of divine mission was a mighty force against the official paganism of Rome, which had no interest in converts. Christianity preached a doctrine of salvation that promised the individual that he would receive an eternal reward for his virtuous life in heaven. It taught men that God had a special concern for their souls. It emphasized a message of love and brotherhood. In an age of oversophistication, it raised an ideal of simplicity. To those who suffered, it offered hope and a reason for suffering, as well as the example of the savior. The appeal of Christianity was broad, not aimed at one class or group but at all men.

Christ in majesty, tenth century. The theme of Jesus as judge and ruler developed in the period following the acceptance of Christianity as the official Roman religion in the practice of depicting Him as a monarch. (Metropolitan Museum of Art, Gift of George Blumenthal, 1941)

By the fourth century, Christianity had spread throughout the empire and reached into all ranks of society. True, the third century had witnessed, if anything, an intensification rather than abatement of the persecutions. Decius was the first emperor to attempt a systematic persecution of Christians throughout the empire. However, even the Stoic philosopher Marcus Aurelius had enforced measures against them. But, as they grew in numbers and influence, it was becoming more apparent that they were a vital force within the empire, that persecution would not destroy them, and that some other means must be found to deal with them. By the end of the third century, after Diocletian's persecutions, the empire began to turn toward more tolerance.

During these early centuries, Christianity had proved itself a force greater than the Roman Empire. Despite attempts to stop its spread, it had permeated Roman society. Its detractors argued that it sapped the energies of the state. Its supporters maintained that Christianity brought new vitality to a decadent society. Between these views is the position that Christianity drastically changed the Roman Empire. The pagan empire became Christian. But it also retained much of its ancient heritage from the past. Henceforth, this fusion of Greco-Roman and Christian elements shaped the Western mind to a very large degree. Christianity, with Judaism, provided not merely an ethical foundation, but for many centuries offered man's chief hope for the realization of his dream of the good society in a future life.

Rome and the Barbarians in the West

Beyond the boundaries of the Roman Empire to the north and east lived the barbarians. Julius Caesar had fought against the Allemanni and other Germans during the first century B.C. Marcus Aurelius had died at Vienna after defeating a German attempt to breach the Danube and invade northern Italy. But between these dates Roman legions on the frontiers had controlled the movement of the Germans effectively. During the third century almost every emperor was concerned with the increasing pressure of the barbarians against the frontiers of the empire.

The Germans were composed of numerous different tribes. At the time of Rome's expansion into Gaul in the time of Caesar, the Allemanni and their confederates were settled along both banks of the Rhine. Further east were the Marcomanni, Burgundians, Franks, and the Goths. Historians have long disputed about the level of culture among the Germans. Among ancient writers, Tacitus praised them for their courage and their freedom from the civilized vices of the Romans, but he portrayed them as rude and nomadic people, much given to fighting and drunkenness. Ammianus Marcellinus, writing in the late fourth century, maintained that they abhorred towns as pits of their freedom. Tacitus describes how each chief had about him a group of companions who owed him their allegiance and would fight for him until death if necessary. We do not have to look far to see in this statement a glimmer of the later institution of feudalism as it developed in the early Middle Ages.

Modern scholars, however, have not been unanimous in accepting the Roman view of the Germans. They point out that some of the German tribes had been in contact with the empire for more than two centuries and had no doubt learned much about Roman customs. Moreover, archaeological evidence indicates that some Germans were settled in villages and were engaged in agriculture. They traded both among themselves and with Roman merchants who traveled through their lands. Public business was carried out in the tribal assembly, composed of the warriors, who clashed their shields against their spears to signify approval of the course recommended to them by their chief. Their legal system culminated in the assembly, which delegated power to the chiefs, who held court in the villages. Most crimes were punishable by a fine, which differed in amount depending on the ranks of the criminal and his victim. But some crimes like treason demanded the death penalty. Fines were divided between the injured parties and the king, thus ensuring the preservation of the concept that all justice was in some sense "royal" justice. It would be a mistake to think of the Germans at the end of the fourth century as the crude and uncouth barbarians described by Tacitus, though it would be an even greater mistake to compare the level of their culture with that of the civilized Roman of the day.

The causes of the German threat to the empire are to be found in an increase of population, the attractiveness of imperial lands, and the pressures exerted on them by the movement of peoples farther east, especially the Huns, who after 372 had reached the Volga River and dislodged the eastern or Ostro-Goths. In all probability, the fact that large numbers of Germans had turned from their nomadic existence to agriculture was a major fact in the growth of their population. The increasing tendency of Romans to permit Germans to serve in the Roman army not only increased their contact with Roman civilization, but also encouraged them to seek a future for themselves and their families within the empire. Finally, the movement of other tribes pressed on by the Huns caused larger bodies of Germans to seek protection within the empire and even to force their way in. All of these factors operating after the death of Marcus Aurelius in 180 A.D. contributed to a mounting sense of crisis during the third and fourth centuries.

However, the Roman emperors might have been better able to meet the onslaughts of the barbarians had they not been faced in the third century by a resurgent Persia on their eastern frontiers. The Persians, or Parthians, had remained unconquered in the eastward advance of the empire. They disputed with Rome for control of upper Mesopotamia and Armenia. This frontier was never pacified. As early as the mid-first century, Crassus had fallen in a disastrous defeat administered by the Parthians. During the first two centuries of the empire, Rome was generally successful in maintaining her eastern frontier, but the first quarter of the third century brought a new and vigorous dynasty to the Persian throne. Throughout the third and fourth centuries, the emperors had to commit large numbers of men and quantities of money to the defense of the East, thus weakening their ability to resist the Germans.

Moreover, the third century was one of serious internal crisis within the empire. In the century between the death of Marcus Aurelius and the accession of Diocletian (285), no fewer than twenty emperors reigned. Although the strong rule of Septimius Severus (193–211) restored order after the disastrous government of Commodus, the tyrannical and incompetent son of Marcus Aurelius, and the revolts of the Praetorian Guard, there were too few rulers with his ability and decisiveness. A low point was the reign of Heliogabalus, who was installed on the throne by the Empress Julia Maesa. He arrived in Rome from the East dressed in purple silk, with rouged cheeks, and surrounded by the devotees of his special religious cult to the sun. During the three years of his rule, he devoted his time chiefly to pleasure and service of his god. It is little wonder that he lost popularity and was murdered by the Praetorians abetted by Julia Maesa herself. The Emperor Gallienus (253–268) devoted a large part of his reign to campaigns in the East, as did Aurelian (270–275). Although both embarked on major reform programs aimed at restricting the power of the army in politics and curbing inflation, it remained for Diocletian (293–312) to take drastic steps aimed at arresting the political, social, and economic decline of the empire.

The third century proved the need for action to ensure the stability of government and to provide for orderly succession. Political instability and the wars against the Persians and Germans were very expensive. To raise sufficient money to meet these costs, the emperors had increasingly resorted to the device of reducing the value of the coinage. As a result, prices had gotten out of hand. Between 267 and 274 prices had risen eight hundred per cent and it required a whole sackful of money to carry out ordinary purchases. Aurelian attempted to meet this problem by issuing a new coin and by severely restricting the right to coin money. He also placed the colleges—the guilds of merchants—that controlled the transport and processing of grain and other foods under government regulation. These measures, however, failed to arrest inflation and to remove the burdens of the poor in securing food at reasonable prices. They did, on the other hand, point in the direction of future reforms: namely, tighter government control, which was carried out under Diocletian.

Diocletian was born in Illyria (modern Yugoslavia) and was a soldier by profession. He rose to power at the head of his army and relied on it to maintain him there. But once in power, he became convinced that the empire was simply too big to be ruled by any one man. He devised a system for preserving the unity of the empire by dividing it into four administrative areas. Two of these were to be ruled by Augusti, one senior, the other junior; two were to be ruled by Caesars, adopted by the Augusti as their successors. The purpose of this plan was to provide an orderly method for succession and to establish a government easier to direct. The vastness of the empire was a telling factor against its survival as the barbarians and the Persians required the emperors to meet threats on several fronts. Diocletian's reform was, therefore, an attempt to consolidate Rome's position without surrendering territory.

Indeed, consolidation was a major theme of all of the reforms of this period. Following guidelines laid down by Gallienus and Aurelian, but moving far beyond their measures, Diocletian propelled Rome along the road toward oriental autocracy. He instituted an entirely new court ceremonial in which officials knelt before the emperor, who became a more remote and awesome figure. By emphasizing the divine character of the imperial office, he may well have hoped to place it above the reach of the ambitious adventurer and secure for it a greater stability. But his action had even broader implications. For he laid the foundation for increased Eastern influence and thus contributed to that process which historians call "Byzantinization," that is, the transformation of the Roman Empire from a Western to an Eastern state. Diocletian's preference for his residence in Nicomedia in Asia Minor, was no doubt another factor in this change. It was, moreover, along Eastern lines that Diocletian sought to reform the empire's economic and social structure.

These reforms did not spring from a concern for the prosperity of the citizens but from the necessity to ensure continued fiscal soundness of the state. Until modern times, few rulers grasped the concept that economic legislation should take primary account of the broad economic needs of people and should be drawn up to promote their welfare. Most assumed that the welfare of the individual citizen was secondary to the needs of the community as a whole. Consequently, most legislation proceeded from the premise that by curing the ills of the state, one might heal the economic ills of the body politic as well. Diocletian's reforms reveal the weakness in this view. The Roman system of taxation had evolved as the empire grew without reference to the future needs of the empire. Its foundation in tributes from provinces and in the personal income of the emperor reflected the manner in which Rome had built the empire. Diocletian created a system based on a capitation tax, which was aimed at tapping the resources of the wealthier provinces more than the poorer. In theory, this system was good. Certainly, it provided a better foundation for the state's fiscal system, one that was more flexible and more dependable as well as one that could raise larger sums of money. But it served only the needs of the state. The curials, the members of the urban middle class who were leaders in the provincial cities, were made responsible for the collection of the capitation tax. They had once taken a leading role in enriching the life of the cities; now they sought to escape the tremendous burden placed on them. Frustrated from collecting the taxes from wealthy provincial senators, they shifted as much of the load as they could to the small farmers and the poor. Finally, they had to sacrifice their own wealth to raise the needed money. The burden was too great and many sought to escape, so that later emperors bound them to their position by law. The result was a serious decline of the provincial cities, the seats of Roman culture. Moreover, small farmers were also seriously affected by these taxes. Many simply deserted their farms but others turned to robbery to avoid the taxation. As a result, Constantine issued a law in 322 binding them to the soil. These *coloni* were the foundation for an agricultural system built on labor that was tied to the land. The colonate was one of the foundations of the medieval institution of serfdom. Though Diocletian's reform of the tax structure improved the immediate fiscal position of the empire, it accentuated existing tendencies toward regimentation and helped to undermine the social classes that had been the backbone of the empire.

His attempt to regulate prices and wages also failed because farmers and estate owners refused to raise the grain needed to feed the masses at the prices stipulated by the decrees. Black market practices were widespread. The basic problem of securing food at reasonable prices for the working class remained unsolved and was even aggravated by the ensuing shortages. The Roman Empire did not possess the sophisticated governmental machinery and the economic know-how needed to make the Edict of Prices of 301 work.

Still, Diocletian's reign was far from a failure. He laid the foundation on which Constantine and his successors were to build in creating a strong Roman state in the East, where Rome was to survive for more than a thousand years as the Byzantine Empire. Diocletian's preference for the East, his great palace in Nicomedia, his conviction of the importance of the East in Roman strategy, and the greater success of his and his successors' reforms in the East all contributed to that survival. Already present in Diocletian's policies there is a hint of the road to be followed by those emperors who were to concentrate on the East to the neglect of the West.

By the early fourth century, the Roman emperors had embarked on policies that would ensure the continuity of Roman rule in the East but would result in the gradual loss of Roman political control in the West. The hallmark of the era lay in the direction of consolidation and greater intervention of the state in the economic and social spheres. Rome was being transformed by these processes working from within. Moreover, the religious revolution wrought by Christianity also transformed Rome. As the empire became more Christian, it lost much of its worldly sophistication. Men looked more to the after-life than to the vain grandeur of the empire. Their ideals were creating the religious and moral foundations of a new civilization. In the East, Christianity played an important role in the making of the Byzantine Empire; in the West, it became the basis for unity in the new world dominated by the barbarians. These "heirs of the Roman Empire" played a leading part in the making of Europe.

5 The East: Byzantium and Islam

While the Western part of the Empire struggled to maintain itself against the barbarians, the process of consolidation was transforming the Eastern part into a centralized Roman state. Barbarian rulers in the West still sought to legitimatize their power by gaining recognition from Eastern emperors, but this practice more and more was losing its meaning as it became obvious that the East could no longer effectively participate in Western politics. Gradually, the East was becoming separated from the West; an old Rome was being displaced by a new Rome, whose center was at Constantine's great city on the Bosporus, which he called Constantinople but which also retained its ancient name of Byzantium. The new Rome assumed more and more a Greek and Eastern character. It developed a distinctive art and architecture. Yet it was the heir of Rome. Roman law and government were the foundation on which it rested. Its *Basileus* was successor of Augustus and Diocletian. Until 1453, it remained a vital testimony to the enduring qualities of the Roman Empire.

Through much of its history, Byzantium was itself threatened by the rise of a new force from the Arabian peninsula in the seventh century in Islam. Yet Islam, the religion of Mohammed and his followers, should not be judged in such a negative fashion, nor even for its contributions to Western civilization. As a result of its spread, the Mediterranean world was enriched by ideas and products from India and Indonesia, from Persia and Africa. The great storehouse of Greek learning, so much of which was lost to the West by its separation from the Eastern Roman Empire, became part of the Arab heritage to be transmitted to all the people with whom they came into contact and, among these, Latin Europeans. But we must not ignore either the flourishing Arab civilization which eventually stretched from the Pyrenees of Spain to the Philippines, an empire whose common bond was not political but cultural and religious and within whose boundaries flourished thinkers of great originality and writers of splendid ability. Although we may emphasize the interrelationship between East and West, we must never lose sight of the unique qualities of Eastern culture.

From Rome to Byzantium

The period from the accession of Constantine in 306 to the death of Justinian in 565 is critical in the transition of the empire from Latin to Byzantine. Constantine was the Latin-speaking ruler of a united empire, the Western half of which spoke Latin; Justinian, despite his efforts to restore Roman rule in the West, was primarily the Latin ruler of a Greek-speaking East. Constantine had granted tolerance and favored the growth of Christianity; Justinian inherited a Christian empire and worked to purge it of any last traces of Roman paganism. Between these two reigns the major elements of Byzantine civilization began to form and to dominate the East.

Diocletian's decision to abdicate the imperial purple in May, 305, opened the door to a test of his provisions for the imperial succession. At first, all seemed to go well. Both he and his fellow Augustus, Maximian, resigned and were replaced by their Caesars, Maximian by Constantius Chlorus and Diocletian by Galerius. Constantius was to rule the West with his Caesar and was also to be the senior of the Augusti. But the ambitious Galerius had no intention of playing the second role. With Constantius's son Constantine as a hostage, he hoped to dominate the empire. After the death of his father, the youthful Constantine revealed his intention of gaining control of the imperial throne. By 306, he had won the title of Augustus and turned his attention toward his rivals. After victorious campaigns in Spain, Constantine invaded Italy, defeating Maxentius, the son of Maximian, in the Battle of Milvian Bridge in 312. Significantly, the banners of his troops bore the ☧ sign, made up of the first two Greek letters of *Christos* (Christ), and the words "in this sign conquer." Whether motivated by a religious experience or by political expediency, Constantine had cast in his lot with the Christians. He became their patron and protector. In 313, at Milan, he joined with his co-emperor Licinius in an agreement to extend religious toleration to Christians throughout the empire. Though probably never promulgated in that form, this agreement has come down as the "Edict of Milan." It was not the first instance of an emperor extending protection to the Christians and their property, but it was a turning point in the history of Roman relations with the religion of Christ. From Constantine onward, the Roman Empire must increasingly be regarded as a Christian empire.

The reign of Constantine the Great is, on the one hand, the logical climax of the work of reform begun by Diocletian and, on the other, the period in which the foundation for the Christian Byzantine Empire was laid in the East. His great reform of the currency resulted in the creation of the gold solidus which was to become the basic unit in international commerce until the high Middle Ages. Its stability promoted the prosperity of the Eastern and, to some extent, of the Western part of the empire over the next two centuries, and enabled his successors to collect taxes in gold and to finance their wars against the barbarians and the Persians. But Constantine also moved further along the already well-charted road of regimentation by binding tenants of large landed estates—the *coloni*—to the land. Thus the foundation for the medieval institution of serfdom was laid during this late Roman period. Constantine also required many skilled workers of the towns—bakers, carpenters, shoemakers—to remain at their trades throughout their lives and to train their sons for the same craft. This hereditary guild system, whose foundation was in the Roman *collegia* or guilds, survived under the Byzantine Empire and Islam in those areas conquered from the Byzantine Empire. It may also have had some influence on the structure of the medieval guilds in Italy and throughout Western Europe, though there is no direct evidence confirming this view. But Constantine's position as one of the architects of the Byzantine Empire depends chiefly on his founding of the city of Constantinople on the site of the ancient city of Byzantium and the removal of the capital of the empire to this new seat. Constantinople became a Christian city, dominated by its numerous churches. Its location on the great trade route between the Black Sea, Asia Minor, and the Aegean Sea made it the center of a lucrative commerce between the Orient and the West, between Northern Europe and the Mediterranean world. Moreover, the removal of the capital to a Greek city paved the way for the creation of a Greek empire. But this process took almost two centuries following Constantine's death in 337 A.D.

Constantine's immediate successors continued to control both the Eastern and Western parts of the empire. Under his sons, Constantius and Constans, the division of rule as established by Diocletian was maintained. But the Emperor Julian succeeded to the whole empire. His was a brief and stormy reign. Despite his recognized ability as an administrator, he lacked many qualities needed for the imperial office, and the chief of these was good judgment. Moreover, he had rejected Christianity and now attempted to establish a new religion, which incorporated most of the elements of ancient Greek and Roman religion in a new theological synthesis. From a political point of view, this move cost him the support of the largest element in the empire. Moreover, it is doubtful whether it was possible to carry out a successful revival of paganism in the empire. His own religious synthesis was highly intellectualized and somewhat artificial and had little in the way of popular appeal even to those who still clung to the old traditions. The fact that Julian persecuted Christianity served only to further undermine his position. He was killed, perhaps by a Christian soldier in his own army, while engaged in a campaign against the Persians. With his death, the army acclaimed a Christian general, as emperor.

Perhaps the greatest of the fourth-century emperors was Theodosius (379–395). Called to the throne from a military post, he provided the empire with strong leadership during a time of crisis. The attacks of the Goths on the Danubian frontier were threatening the heartland of the empire. The West was far from secure. He made a temporary settlement by giving the Goths a place to settle along the Danube in 382, but this measure was to cause serious problems for his successors. In the field of religion, he revealed his staunch support of orthodox Christianity against the Arians and, in 395, he proclaimed it the official religion of the empire. However, the old Roman religion continued to enjoy some official tolerance.

The fifth century, which witnessed smashing attacks by barbarians, which saw the emperors finally lose all control of the Western provinces to barbarian kings who styled themselves "Patricians" of the Romans, brought the fruits of the policy of consolidation in the East initiated under Diocletian and Constantine. Under Theodosius II, an effort was made to collect all imperial legislation still in force to make it more available for study in the Theodosian Code (438). This emperor was also a patron of higher education; he reformed the school founded in Constantinople by Constantine and endowed it with ten chairs in Latin and Greek grammar, five in Greek and three in Latin rhetoric, as well as chairs in law and philosophy. As is evident from the number of chairs, Greek studies flourished alongside Latin in the new capital, but already they had something of a preponderance. The reign of the Emperor Leo I (457–

474) was troubled by barbarian attacks on the Eastern part of the empire, while the emperor himself was the tool of Aspar, a powerful Dacian general, who controlled the Gothic elements in the army. Under Zeno (474–491), the struggle against the revolting Goths continued. Zeno was able to do little when Odoacer, who was the chief power in Italy at this time, deposed the youthful puppet, Romulus Augustulus, Emperor in the West, and sent the imperial regalia to the East. He was simply too busy with the intrigues and revolts among the Gothic mercenaries to pay much serious attention to events in the West. The empire was moving further along the road of consolidation of imperial power in the East. The climax was reached in the reign of Justinian (527–565).

Although Justinian was not the last Latin-speaking emperor to hold the throne of Constantinople-Byzantium, he was the last to attempt seriously to regain the provinces in the West lost to the empire. His successors were to content themselves with a policy of trying to keep those portions of Italy they had inherited and playing Western politics to their own advantage at opportune times. Justinian also improved relations with the Western Church during his reign by his favoring of the Orthodox Christians in the East over the followers of the Monophysite heresy. But his greater fame rests on the codification of Roman law which he ordered. It was both more thorough and more scholarly than the Theodosian Code and served as the foundation for the future law of the empire of the East and for the spread of Roman law throughout the barbarian West in the Middle Ages.

The loss of the Western provinces during the reign of Zeno came as the culmination of more than a hundred years of concentration by the emperors on consolidation of their position in the East. In several cases they had deliberately diverted barbarian tribes from the East with promises of opportunity in the West or simply the freedom to pillage without serious opposition. In this way the Visigothic threat was turned against Rome, which was sacked by Alaric in 410. The Visigoths then made their way across southern France and through the Pyrenees into Spain. The full fury of the Huns was directed against Gaul and Italy rather than the East by this policy during the mid-fifth century. Although Roman emperors continued to sit on a Western throne, the real power was more and more concentrated in the hands of barbarian generals like Stilicho and Ricimer, who controlled the mercenary soldiers of the Roman army and used their power to dominate puppet emperors like Honorius. The overthrow of Romulus Augustulus in 476 by Odoacer, another of these generals, was therefore an act without any great dramatic significance for historical developments in the West. In fact, the coming of the Ostrogoths to Italy, encouraged by the Eastern emperor, established the first peace and prosperity in that devastated land in almost seventy years. Theodoric the Ostrogoth was both a capable ruler and a proponent of Roman culture. But his kingdom lacked real stability and declined quickly after his death. The Vandals entered Gaul along the Rhine frontier and passed through Spain, establishing their rule in North Africa under Genseric. He became the scourge of the central Mediterranean, attacking Italy and Sicily, even sacking the city of Rome in 455. But the Vandal Kingdom of North Africa was not merely a haven for pirates; it was a strongly centralized monarchy whose wealth was firmly based on the traditional agricultural riches of North Africa. Thus, the fifth century saw the gradual loss of the West. Justinian determined to recoup these losses and restore the lost grandeur of Rome.

Taking advantage of whatever pretexts presented themselves, Justinian sent his armies successfully into North Africa and Italy to overthrow the heirs of both Genseric and Theodoric. His generals, Belisarius and Narses, were far more able than their opponents. Yet there is a real question as to the wisdom of Justinian's policy. Although he was actually able to reconquer both North Africa and Italy and even part of Spain, he did so only by departing from the policy of consolidation in the East. He had to hold back the threat of a Persian attack on the Eastern empire by bribes. His efforts on both fronts constituted a serious drain on the imperial treasury and unduly jeopardized the prosperity and security of the East. Moreover, in the long run, the gains in the West were illusory. They could not be maintained against the rising power of the barbarians and the new force of Moslem expansion in North Africa in the seventh century.

Justinian's religious policy also met with considerable opposition. The Monophysites, who taught that Christ had only one nature, which was divine, had flourished in Egypt and Syria, where their adherents had become identified with popular movements for greater local autonomy within the empire and freedom from dominance by the Orthodox Byzantines. Justinian's Empress, Theodora, a strong-willed influence on his early reign, favored the Monophysites, but after her death Justinian embarked on a policy aimed at creating doctrinal unity throughout the empire. This program had especially strong support from Pope Agapitus. However, it mainly served to alienate the peoples of the Eastern provinces and Egypt. Consequently, they put up little opposition to the seventh-century attacks of the Moslems. Indeed, they looked upon the followers of the prophet as possible emancipators from the tyranny of the Byzantine Empire.

Byzantine casket with mythological and other scenes, ninth to tenth centuries. These scenes are not typical of the formal and distant quality of much Byzantine art, but reflect the naturalism achieved by artists in the great age of Byzantine culture. (Metropolitan Museum of Art, Gift of J. P. Morgan, 1917)

Only in his code of laws did Justinian create an enduring monument to which later generations looked with the greatest admiration. He brought together the finest legal minds of his age and asked them to edit the works of the great jurists and to compile all imperial legislation still in effect. He also had them prepare an introductory text for the law. They carried out their work admirably. The *Institutes* made it possible for the beginner to study the basic principles of Roman public and private law. The *Digest* contained the opinions of earlier legal experts arranged in a manner that made their work accessible and made possible the comparison of their views. This point was important because their authority was not equal and in cases of conflict the views of one jurist took precedence over those of others. The *Code* was an organized compilation of the actual legislation to which was added the *Novels,* those laws promulgated by Justinian himself. The work was in Latin, but was later translated into Greek. In these two languages, its use rapidly spread throughout the territories of the empire, including those regions newly conquered by Justinian's armies in the West. However, it did not replace the Theodosian Code in Italy nor did it spread into Gaul or Northern Europe. It was not until the eleventh century, with the revival of legal studies at Bologna, that there began that movement called the "revival" of Roman law. That "revival" referred chiefly to the reintroduction of Justinian's legal work into the development of law in Western Europe.

With the passing of Justinian, the empire in the East made the decisive turn in the direction of a Greek rather than a Latin culture as the dominant influence shaping its civilization. By the end of his reign the chief characteristics of Byzantine civilization had taken form in government, social life, and in art and architecture. What remained was for the cleavage between East and West to become wider and for Byzantium to become the leader in civilizing and Christianizing the Slavs of Southeastern Europe and Russia. But Byzantium met opposition from Islam in her pursuit of these goals after the middle of the seventh century.

The World of Islam

While to the Christian world of East and West and all those civilizations which touched its borders or felt its power, the rise of the empire of Islam in the seventh century posed a threat to the peoples of the Arabian Peninsula and to all who adopted the faith of the Prophet Mohammed it represented the opportunity for fulfillment. Islam brought a new vitality to the Near and Middle East and spread across North Africa into Spain and through India to the East Indies and Philippines. But the land of its origin was the unlikely Arabian Peninsula and its founder was a merchant and religious thinker named Mohammed.

Dish: Islamic. The intricate arabesques of this Iranian dish from the twelfth century are the triumph of the designer's art. (*Collection of the University of Michigan Museum of Art*)

In the long history of the Near East, the Arabian Peninsula had played no important role before the seventh century of the Christian era. Surrounded on three sides by the waters of the Persian Gulf, the Indian Ocean, and the Red Sea and separated by rugged terrain from the fertile valley of Mesopotamia, the Peninsula was largely a desert area inhabited partly by Bedouin herdsmen and partly by a small population of merchants and city-dwellers, who profited from the trade between India and the West along the caravan route through Mecca and Medina. The Bedouins were a tough and fearsome lot, much given to feuding among themselves and raiding caravans. Their religious beliefs were simple, consisting chiefly of a primitive totemism that assigned divine qualities to natural objects. The city-dwellers were mixed. Some were Jews and Christians; others followed some form of paganism. Prior to the preaching of Mohammed, religion does not seem to have played a major role in their lives.

Mohammed (570?–632) was born in Mecca and was a member of the influential Kuraish clan, which played an important role in the politics of the city. However, he was orphaned at an early age and did not profit from these connections. He became a camel driver and merchant, leading his caravans across the desert even as far as Damascus in Syria, a city whose beauty and lush green gardens caused him to see it as a paradise. He married a wealthy widow and thereafter devoted his leisure to his interest in religion. After devoting considerable time to his speculation, he began his career as a religious teacher in Mecca. But the ruling class of Mecca was little interested in religion. Moreover, they feared that Mohammed would create dissension and injure the commercial prosperity of the town. Therefore the prophet had to flee with his followers to Medina. This was the famous Hegira of 622.

In Medina, Mohammed's teaching underwent further development and met with greater success. Mohammed accepted and taught a purely monotheistic concept of God, largely based on the Hebrew concept of the deity. He rejected the Christian doctrine of the trinity—three persons in one God—as blasphemous. Five times a day the devout Moslem was to bow and pray. He was enjoined to give alms to the poor and to fast from sunup to sundown during the month of Ramadan, the ninth of the lunar year. In the arid heat of the East, this fast was very rigorous. He was forbidden to eat pork or drink wine. No Moslem man could marry more than four wives, although he was permitted an unlimited number of concubines. However, the injunction that he treat all with the same kindness and affection put a real limit on the number most men could care for. In addition to these direct injunctions contained in the Koran, the Islamic bible, numerous other regulations were compiled in the sacred law of Islam and interpreted by the *Ulema,* the professional teachers of the law who constituted an educated aristocracy throughout Islam.

Mohammed owed much to both Judaism and Christianity for his religious thought and he did not attempt to conceal this from his followers. Among the prophets recognized in the Koran are Abraham and Jesus. Jews and Christians received special designation as "peoples of the book" and were not subject to forced conversion. Islamic monotheism, which insisted on the basic simplicity and unity of the Divine Being, owed more to Judaism than to Christianity. But Mohammed was much more than a religious eclectic; he preached a doctrine, which had a direct and magnetic appeal to the peoples of the desert and which transcended theology to create a political unity and the foundations for the theocratic state. Islam created a tie binding the Arab peoples together stronger than the local forces of tribalism and petty feuding. The appeal of Islam was not based on its relationship with Christianity and Judaism but on its own value in the eyes of the Arab Bedouins. Though some Christians and Jews swelled the numbers of early Moslem converts at Medina, their numbers did not make them a significant influence in the early history of the movement.

The rapid spread of Islam beyond the confines of the Arabian Peninsula is a phenomenon requiring some consideration. The pattern for its expansion was already laid out in the lifetime of the prophet. Its main instrument was the Jihad, or holy war. This use of war as an instrument in religious policy, while not unique, was of greater importance in ensuring the success of Mohammedanism than any other type of missionary effort. It appealed to the fighting instincts of the Bedouins and provided an outlet for their desire to gain wealth by booty won in raiding their neighbors. Moreover, those who fell in the Jihad were ensured a place in paradise. However, the Moslems never attempted to convert all those whom they conquered. They permitted large minorities to live according to their own beliefs in the lands they overcame. This policy was partly dictated by the practical consideration that only non-Moslems paid the capitation tax and partly by a sincere tolerance for other religious views. The Islamic world was seldom disturbed by major persecutions of minority religious groups. However, only Moslems could rise to positions of power and influence during the early period and this factor encouraged many of the former ruling classes in conquered lands to embrace Islam.

Within the lifetime of the prophet, the Arabs broke out of the Peninsula and carried out raids against villages in Syria. When Mohammed died in 632, Abu Bakr, his chief lieutenant, succeeded as caliph or commander of the faithful. But the spell of the prophet was broken; internal strife and rivalry between the legitimists, who sought to keep the succession in the family of the prophet, and those who desired a fully elective caliphate marred the next three reigns. Finally, with the death of Ali, Mohammed's son-in-law in 661, Muawiya, governor of Syria, seized control of the caliphate and established the Umayyad dynasty at Damascus. Nevertheless, the expansion of Islam continued without significant interruption. Moslem armies pushed across North Africa snatching up Egypt and destroying the last vestiges of Byzantine power there. They met with stubborn resistance from the Berbers, but succeeded in winning them to Islam. In 711, they crossed into Spain, pushing northward across the Pyrenees until they met their first major defeat in the Battle of Tours-Poitiers (732) at the hands of the Frankish mayor of the palace, Charles Martel. Meanwhile, in the East, they toppled the Persian Empire and drove eastward across the Indus River. The empire they created was larger than any before in history and it brought together peoples of many different cultures. The Umayyads laid the foundation for a golden age of

Astrolabe, thirteenth century. This important advance in the technology of navigation was introduced into the West by Arab sailors. (The Metropolitan Museum of Art, Gift of Edward C. Moore, 1891)

Islam lasting from the eighth through the middle of the thirteenth century.

Arab culture has sometimes been praised with extravagance and, at other times, has been condemned as sterile. There is no denying that the greatest creation of the Arabs was the empire; they did not produce the outstanding literary, artistic, and scientific work emanating from their domains. Nor were they noted for great originality; they borrowed freely wherever they conquered. But this judgment does not begin to do justice to the rich culture which they inherited and which flourished within their domains.

The Arabs were the heirs of Hellenistic culture, which had spread throughout the Near East, the Persian Empire, and Egypt. Moreover, they came into direct contact with Indian civilization and through it that of the Far East. Under the Abbassids, who held the caliphate from 750 to 1258, leading Islamic scholars not only translated many of the works of Aristotle and other Greek authors into Arabic, but also undertook the major task of harmonizing this learning with the Koran. Averroes (Ibn Rushd, 1126–1198) and Avicenna (980–1037?) wrote commentaries on the works of Aristotle; their work had a profound effect on Western scholars in the thirteenth century. Moslem scholars were especially interested in science and medicine. Medical treatises and encyclopedias by such learned physicians as Al-Razi (ca. 860–925) and Avicenna went beyond the treatments recommended by the Greeks, from whom they learned the foundations of their art. Not content with preserving the work of Galen and Hippocrates, they made careful observations of numerous diseases and set down the results along with recommendations for treatment. Although Islamic law frowned on the study of anatomy, their knowledge of drugs and their experimental attitude made them the leading physicians of the Middle Ages. At the eleventh-century court of the Norman King Roger II in Sicily, Arab physicians prescribed for the king and his family. Their astronomy was based on thorough and accurate observation, although, like most peoples of the period, they mixed it with astrology in the hope of finding the answers about their future in the stars. Likewise, chemistry was diverted from its course because the chemists spent a large part of their effort seeking the philosopher's stone, which would change lead and other common metals into gold. Needless to say, the effort met no great reward. But it was not entirely wasted, for their experiments sometimes resulted unexpectedly and happily in the discovery of new drugs and chemicals. In mathematics, the pioneering work of the Moslems in algebra must be added to their transmission of the Hindu numbers and the invention of the zero. They were able to work both quadratic and cubic equations. As many historians have observed, their knowledge of science far surpassed their contemporaries in the West. Indeed, in most fields of science they were the teachers of later Western scholars through those of their writings that were translated from Arabic into Latin. Ironically, the West seized leadership and laid the foundations for a scientific and technological revolution that found no counterpart in the East.

The language of the Koran was Arabic, the language of the rude bedouins of the desert, seemingly unsuited to the creation of a great world literature. Yet the Koran itself proved the poetic qualities of the language and the necessity that all the faithful read that holy book in the original tongue led to widespread use of Arabic throughout the Islamic world. It became the language of the ruling classes and therefore the language of literature. This does not mean, however, that the authors were Arabs. Most often they were not. Among the greatest of them was Omar Khayyám, a Persian, whose *Rubaiyat* advocated a "take the cash and let the credit go" philosophy of life. It was a view but little suited to the devout Moslem and reflected instead the pleasure-loving influence of the

Persian casket, Islamic. Although Islam was hostile to the depiction of the human figure in art, this casket reveals how local artistic traditions could survive the Islamic conquests for a long period. (*Collection of the University of Michigan Museum of Art*)

East. The *Thousand and One Nights,* ostensibly tales told the caliph of Bagdad by the slave girl Sharazad to stave off her execution, is a collection of adventures long familiar to Western readers as the Arabian Nights.

The art and architecture of Islam owed its greatest debts to the conquered peoples. Both Persian and Byzantine influence played an important role. The strong prejudice of the Moslems against depiction of the human figure militated against the development of portrait painting and sculpture, while the preference for geometrical designs resulted in the striking arabesque decorations that are a feature of colorful Islamic tapestries and of architectural decoration. In general, however, Islamic art did not break out of traditional forms. While its beauty is very often unquestioned, it seems lacking in the creative spirit. Much the same might be said of architecture. Since Arabia itself had had little in the way of distinctive architecture, the Arabs borrowed extensively from the Persians. Many features of their architecture found their way to Western Europe where they may have influenced the Gothic of the Middle Ages.

But, while Islam retained a cultural unity throughout the medieval period, it was unable to prevent the forces of disintegration which led to the rise of independent caliphates in Egypt and Spain. Abbassid control of the East was weakened by the presence of a rival caliphate at Bagdad, thus enabling a resurgent Byzantine Empire to join forces with Frankish crusaders in the eleventh century in the reconquest of Asia Minor and the establishment of the Latin Kingdom of Jerusalem.

6 The Barbarians and the Imperial Dream

The fifth century saw the end of Roman political dominance in the West. The brief successes of Justinian in restoring Roman rule in Italy and North Africa during the sixth century merely served to illustrate the impossibility of recreating the empire of ancient Rome in the West. But Roman culture did not die. True, the invasions of the barbarians wrought serious devastation on many regions of the West and destroyed or weakened many of those institutions which had played the most important role in the continuance of learning and the arts. However, this decline was partially compensated for by the flourishing state of Christian art and letters during this crucial age. We must never forget that the great North African bishop, Augustine of Hippo, lay dying as the Vandals were besieging his diocesan city. Great Roman writers like Boethius and Cassiodorus served at barbarian courts. Certainly all was not lost.

The pessimism of many earlier historians at the decline of the Roman Empire in the West into barbarism must now be tempered by the realization that this age also saw vital elements of a new civilization struggling to achieve their identity. The period from the fifth through the ninth century must be understood not only from the view of a great empire in its agonies, but also from the vision of the new society beginning to take shape. This new civilization drew much from Roman culture, but it was fundamentally the creation of the barbarian peoples and the religion they gradually adopted as their own: Christianity. From these elements rose not a bastardization of antiquity but a dynamic new culture founded on many significantly new institutions.

The building of this new civilization was not without its failures and false starts. In one sense, the entire period from the decline of Rome to the collapse of the Empire of Charlemagne might be called a false start, but for the fact that this very same period saw much of the political, social, economic, and cultural foundations for the new civilization laid firmly in place. Perhaps the history of this period would have been significantly different if the long shadow of the Roman Empire had not so haunted the dreams of the barbarians who had so important a role in the new political forms that were to dominate Europe. Perhaps, since we must speculate, the stubborn memory of the empire prevented the Germanic invaders from confidently turning to the task of making their own political institutions serve new ends in ruling these vast lands. But the facts of history decreed otherwise. Rome as a dream was a potent force shaping the direction of history in the period when Rome as political reality had ceased to be effective.

The Search for Stability

The chief impression gained by the student reading the literature of the fifth century is of the lack of stability throughout most of the West. The regular channels of government still functioned in many areas of the empire until mid-century and even later, but lines of communication with the central authority were frequently interrupted or broken off entirely. The result was, of course, a tendency for many regions to look to local leaders and even to powerful barbarian chieftains in their area rather than to the impotent imperial authority. Regionalism and particularism thus were characteristic of the age. Lack of strong central authority gave the initiative to opportunists as well as to responsible local officials and opened the way for further erosion of imperial control and the eventual supplanting of it by Germanic invaders.

At the center, the fifth century witnessed twice the sack of Rome, by the Visigoths in 410 and the Vandals in 455, as well as the devastation of northern Italy by the Huns. Still, for the first three-quarters of the century, the façade of Roman imperial rule was retained. Increasingly, however, the emperors were mere puppets under the control of the powerful Germanic chieftains who controlled the army. Finally, in 476, Odoacer, the Visigothic power behind the throne, deposed the infant emperor Romulus Augustulus and sent the imperial regalia to the Emperor Zeno in Constantinople. This action did not mark the end of the empire in the West, but it did bear effective testimony to the power in the hands of the

Germans. The distant Eastern emperor could not act very forcefully in affairs in the West; he had to entrust his theoretical power to the leader of the Germanic troops there. Odoacer had taken a significant step in removing part of the mask from the actuality of Roman weakness in the West.

The disintegration of Roman political power in the West proceeded at a rapid pace during the late fifth and early sixth centuries. The Ostrogoths entered Italy under the leadership of their king Theodoric (454?–526), who had lived as a hostage and had received part of his education at the imperial court in Constantinople. Buffeted by the Huns as they swept across Southeastern Europe, the Ostrogoths had sought asylum within the empire. But, miserable with the treatment they had received from the imperial officials, they broke into open rebellion. For this reason the emperor turned their attention to Italy so that they might work their violence against the pretensions of Odoacer rather than the walls of Constantinople. Theodoric's invasion was successful and the Ostrogoths took possession of the former seat of the empire.

Theodoric preserved many Roman elements in his rule besides keeping up the pretense of acting in behalf of the emperor in the East. His Ostrogoths claimed lands and property for themselves, but generally did not dispossess the Romans; rather, they contented themselves with the booty and lands of the defeated Odoacer and his troops. Influential Romans served at the Ostrogothic court. The noble Boethius (480?–524?), a senator, renowned for his literary and philosophic studies, and Cassiodorus the historian lent their prestige to the regime. Though the Ostrogoths had been converted to Arianism rather than orthodox Christianity, Theodoric worked to maintain proper relations with the Roman Church and attempted to prevent the spread of friction between the two groups. His own appreciation of Roman culture appears to have been high for he supported the Roman element in the population even against the seeming interests of his own people. Perhaps his consciousness that the Ostrogoths were a minority in a strange land dictated this caution, although they held the only effective military power in Italy. Theodoric allowed the Romans to retain their own legal system and he administered his kingdom through Roman officials, who continued to hold the old offices. He contented himself with holding the actual reins of power in his own hands.

With the death of Theodoric, however, the Ostrogothic Kingdom of Italy lacked the leadership to maintain itself against Justinian's army in Italy. (See Chapter 5.) But the Roman reconquest was short-lived. It lasted only until a new wave of Germanic invaders swept into Italy and pushed the imperial forces out of northern Italy. These Lombards founded their kingdom in 568; it endured until it was overthrown by the Franks in the eighth century.

Neither the Ostrogoths nor the Lombards succeeded in establishing a lasting regime. Yet their attempt must be viewed against a broader background in which the Germanic peoples were searching for political stability. In part, they were building on the old order, maintaining at least the fiction of ties with the empire to lend legitimacy to their efforts; but they were also pointing the direction for the development of the more successful barbarian kingdoms, especially that of the Franks. In this search for stability, a very important part was played by Christianity.

The Christian Church in the West did not escape the effects of Roman decline and the barbarian invasions. During the fourth and fifth centuries the Church had become closely identified with the Roman state. Beyond a doubt this factor was important in increasing the prestige of the Roman bishop. With the waning of imperial power in the West and the moving of the administrative capital from Rome to Ravenna, the prestige of the Popes, as the Roman bishops came to be called, increased further. Another important factor lending greater authority to the Papacy in this period was the number of distinguished and able bishops of the Roman See. In the tremendous struggle between the orthodox and Arians, the Papacy led the fight for the preservation of orthodoxy in the West and served as the voice of this position in all relations with the bishops of the East. Gradually, the Popes began to articulate their claim to leadership over the whole Church. Pope Damasus (366–384) asserted that the Roman Church was above all others because Christ had said to Peter: "Thou are Peter and upon this rock I will build my Church." The outstanding leadership of Pope Leo I in the mid-fifth century in extending the authority of Rome over other bishops in the West was significant in the development on the administrative level of this claim to primacy. In the late fifth century, Pope Gelasius I (492–496) formulated a major position on the relation of the religious to temporal authority, maintaining that priests were superior to secular rulers because they were responsible to God even for the souls of kings.

Side by side with the development of these papal claims rose monasticism, which, in the West, proved an effective instrument in spreading and strengthening Christianity among the barbarians. Monasticism had its origins in the East. Its roots preceded the rise of Christianity. During the first years of the Church's existence men had gone out into the desert regions to seek their salvation in lonely contemplation away from the temptations and distractions of the cities. Some remained hermits, like the famous Egyptian St. Anthony, while others formed small communities to practice together a rigorous life of spiritual and physical asceticism. The triumph of Christianity in the Roman Empire and the accompanying decline in the original fervor of its followers stimulated the development of these communities. In the East, St. Basil of Cappadocia wrote a rule, which stressed communal life and moderation in the search for salvation. In the West, Benedict of Nursia (480–543) became the father of Latin monasticism, founding a community of monks on Monte Cassino in southern Italy and providing them with a rule which has endured to the present day among the various Benedictine communities. Benedict set up the motto: *Ora et Labora* (pray and work). He particularly stressed communal prayer in the singing of the Psalms from the Old Testament, which became the divine office, recited by the clergy every day. His monks also performed manual labor in the fields. They lived together, ate together, and prayed together. He warned them about excessive penances and put them under the leadership of an elected abbot (father) to serve as their spiritual guide. Moderation was the guideline of the rule. Although meat was forbidden, it was believed that it should be given to those who were ill so that they might recover their strength. Wine was permitted in a small measure. This Benedictine way of life attracted followers quickly and spread throughout Western Europe with the encouragement of the Papacy, which found the monks a useful instrument in the missionary work of the Church.

The fifth and sixth centuries saw an intensive effort by the Church to convert the barbarians. Although some, like the Visigoths and the Ostrogoths, had accepted Arianism and had thus come into conflict with orthodox Christians in the West, many remained pagans, adhering to their tribal deities. In 432, Patrick, a Britain, who had been captive of the Irish in his youth, returned to Ireland as a bishop to convert them. He received papal support from Pope Leo the Great and succeeded in building a strong native Church, founded largely on a monastic clergy, who followed a rule which he devised for them. These Irish monks played an important part in the conversion of northern England and Scotland, as well as working among the Germans on the continent. Their monastic foundations at St. Gall and Bobbio in Switzerland and Italy carried Irish art and poetic traditions onto the continent. Another great missionary, Augustine, inspired by Pope Gregory the Great in the early sixth century, began the systematic conversion of the Anglo-Saxons in England. By the seventh century, the English Church flourished and great centers of culture could be found in this formerly barbarian land.

The spread of the Church among the barbarian peoples was an essential part of the making of medieval society. Winning their souls to Christianity also served to introduce them to those elements of Roman civilization which were preserved within the Church. Of course, the change from pagan barbarian to baptized Roman was not sudden or dramatic. Baptism itself did not induce the Germans to give up their love of fighting and to settle down to peaceful tasks. In fact, the transition from lusty warrior to peaceful ruler took centuries during which the turbulence of the nobility frequently disrupted the quiet of the land. During the fifth and sixth centuries, however, the first tentative steps were made in this direction. This point is well illustrated in the rise of the Franks.

Clovis, King of the Franks. Later medieval tradition softened and ennobled the barbarian founder of the Frankish monarchy. (*The Metropolitan Muesum of Art, The Cloisters Collection, Purchase, 1940*)

In the last quarter of the fifth century, this Germanic people, whose lands were astride the northern Rhine, grew restive and began to raid neighboring Roman territory under the leadership of one of their kings, Clovis (465?–511). The Romans of northern Gaul were cut off from aid, and despite a stubborn resistance organized by local nobility, succumbed to the Franks. In this way the Frankish kingdom had its beginnings. Clovis was a powerful and unscrupulous leader; he did away with all possible rivals and directed his efforts to subduing the neighboring German tribes. While he was engaged in war against the Allemanni, he heeded the advice of his Catholic wife, a Burgundian princess, and sought the assistance of the Christian God to bring him victory. Having won, he embraced the Catholic faith with three thousand of his warriors. While conversion did not transform the morals of Clovis and his followers, it opened the way for their cooperation with the Church and the Roman populace. Since most of the other Germans were either Arians or pagans, it gave the Franks considerable advantage by making their rule more appealing to the Roman populace.

Under Clovis, the expansion of the Frankish kingdom pushed southward toward the Pyrenees and the Mediterranean Sea. When he died in 511, this vast kingdom was divided, according to the Germanic custom, among his four sons. The Germans did not regard the kingdom as a state but as a patrimony and treated it accordingly. In the long run, this view was to work to the detriment of the Frankish kingdom, but Clovis' immediate successors continued his expansionist program until the reign of King Dagobert (629–639). Thereafter, the Merovingians, as Clovis' dynasty was called, ceased to take an active part in the actual government of the kingdom. These "do-nothing kings" were mere puppets in the hands of the powerful nobility and especially, the mayors of the palace, who came to control the affairs of the kingdom. Of course, with the division of the kingdom on the death of the king, the kingdom was frequently not united and the royal brothers often quarrelled over the division of the patrimony. Gregory of Tours, in his *History of the Franks,* has left a vivid picture of the turbulent and barbarous Merovingian courts.

The decline of the Merovingians must, however, be told in connection with the rise to power of a powerful noble house that gained control of the office of mayor of the palace in the Frankish kingdom of Austrasia. It was a scion of this house, Pepin of Heristal, who succeeded in making himself mayor for the whole Frankish kingdom by his victory over the Neustrian mayor in 687. From this position, he worked to increase first the position of his own family and then to strengthen the control of the Frankish kingdom over the nobility. For now the interests of the kingdom were closely identified with those of his family. He also returned to the expansionist program of Clovis and his immediate successors, warring on the Burgundians, the Frisians of Holland north of the Rhine, and crossing the Rhine into Bavaria and the lands of the Allemanni. His successor was the brilliant Charles Martel (690–741), his illegitimate son. Charles not merely met the threat of Islamic invasion by defeating the Moslems in the Battle of Tours-Poitiers in 732, but closely identified his regime with the Church to make use of its wealth and lands to support his army. His use of mounted warriors may well foreshadow the rise of the knights of the Middle Ages, especially since he used the lands of the Church as benefices to support them. Charles Martel also was victorious against the other Germanic peoples, further strengthening the positions of the Franks in Central Europe. His support of the missionary efforts of men like Boniface among the Germans was motivated not merely by his devotion to the Church but also by the realization that conversion to the Church would probably dispose the Germans to join the Frankish kingdom.

Charles Martel, despite the great power in his hands, was still mayor of the palace. His son, Pepin the Short (?–768), was not content with that role. When Charles died, he divided the realm between his two sons as mayors of the palace for Austrasia and Neustria. But Carlman, the elder of the sons, withdrew to a monastery, leaving the entire kingdom to his brother. Pepin determined to become king in name as well as in fact. To legitimate his position, he sought recognition of the kingship from the Papacy. The Pope, as much because he needed support himself as because his decision was the only one that could be made under the circumstances, authorized the assumption of the crown by Pepin the Short. Thus, the last of the Merovingians had his head shaved and was carried off in a cart to the monastery; a new dynasty ruled the Kingdom of the Franks.

The descendants of Pepin of Heristal had already shown their strength. The kingship was more in the way of a reward for their success than anything else. By the death of Pepin the Short, they had expanded the Frankish kingdom southward to Aquitaine and the Mediterranean and eastward into the lands beyond the Rhine. They had won the staunch support of the Papacy, in return for which, they lent their own aid to the Popes when it was needed. Pepin the Short campaigned against the Lombards in northern Italy on behalf of the Pope and confirmed Papal control of the so-called patrimony of St. Peter in central Italy. This region had been effectively under the rule of the Popes for only brief periods following the reign of Gregory the Great, but the Popes had long claimed the right to rule it. In particular, their fear of Lombard dominance of Rome increased their desire to create a bulwark against Lombard expansion southward. Pepin was thus rendering a signal service by recognizing the papal claims and putting his army at the side of the Pope. This alliance became even closer under Pepin's son Charles.

The Carolingian Empire

Pepin the Short died in 768 and the kingdom was divided between his two sons, Charles and Carloman. But this arrangement did not last. When Carloman died in 771, Charles (768–814) ignored the claims of his heir and united the entire kingdom in his own hands. He was free to continue the policy of his family by expanding the Frankish realm both southward and eastward. Moreover, he was admirably equipped for the task. He stood over six feet and was every inch the warrior. Although lame, he was an excellent athelete and he practiced the abstemiousness characteristic of many men of athletic bent. He could not read or write, but he could understand Latin and even Greek. He was deeply interested in almost every aspect of life and surrounded himself with men of learning, although he himself was less an intellectual than a restless man of action. First and foremost, he was a German warrior.

It was as a fighter that he most distinguished himself. In a reign of more than forty-five years, he engaged in fifty-four separate campaigns. Seldom was there a year in which he did not travel with his army. But he did not fight without purpose. His wars were directed against enemies who stood in the way of his chief purpose: the Saxons, powerful bulwark against further expansion beyond the Rhine; the Lombards, a threat to the Papacy and hence to the Frankish monarchy; the Moslems in Spain, against whom he fought not so much in the cause of religion as to ensure the frontier at the Pyrenees.

Charles' relations with the Church were generally excellent. He conquered the Lombards and united their kingdom to his own, thus removing the chief thorn in the side of the Papacy. He took a considerable interest in the affairs of the Roman Church, even to the point of arbitrating disputes between the various factions vieing for the papal office. In the year 800, he journeyed to Rome to investigate charges made against Pope Leo III. Leo, however, met the Frankish king outside of Rome and swore his innocence; he also invited Charles to accompany him to Rome for the celebration of the feast of Christmas.

Christmas, 800, became the day of Charles' coronation as emperor. The Pope placed the crown on his head and the assembled populace saluted him as "King of the Romans." An empire was born. But what empire? Certainly, not the ancient Roman Empire, whose rule in the West had long since disappeared save for the small territories in Italy still controlled by the Byzantine emperor? Perhaps the Pope and the Roman populace were merely recognizing *de facto* the success of Charles in welding together a great Germanic empire in Western and Central Europe. But that does not explain the reason for conferring on him the title of emperor. The choice of that title must have had a meaning of its own apart from Charles' conquests.

Charles was saluted as Emperor of the Romans. He was proclaimed by the Roman populace. But his empire was scarcely Roman. This fact, however, meant little to a people in search of stability and who were looking for that order in the only place they had any memory of it before: in the restoration of imperial power. The conferring of the title of emperor of the Romans had significance, therefore, not in a territorial sense nor even as a restoration of Roman rule, but rather as the hoped-for fulfillment of a dream that this ruler would restore to the West that order which it had enjoyed under the protection of the Roman Empire. The title of emperor placed the West under the protection of the king of the Franks, Charles the Great, to whom men now looked as the builder of a new imperial order. Thus the title was symbolic. It represented the dream of empire that dominated still the thinking of man in the West. It also symbolized the completion of the first stage in the making of Europe in the founding of the new European empire of the Franks.

Between 800 and 814, Charlemagne, as the French historians called him, played out the role of emperor which he had accepted. He continued to expand his realm. Empire or kingdom made no difference in his pursuit of the policies of his house. Nor did the title of emperor basically alter his relations with the Church. The coronation by the Pope was not a conferral of power and Charlemagne did not take it as such. He continued to play a leading role in ecclesiastical affairs. He regarded himself as anointed by God in a way that his predecessors would not have. Perhaps the influence of his favorite book, the *City of God* by St. Augustine of Hippo, formed in his consciousness a sense of historical purpose or destiny that his more barbarian ancestors could never have had. But these differences were hardly essential. He was still the Germanic king in all that he did to build the Frankish realm. But he was aware that he was something more. Was it idle policy in pursuit of vain grandeur that caused him to negotiate with the empress of Byzantium for recognition of his claim to be emperor? More likely, it was calculated policy to win the

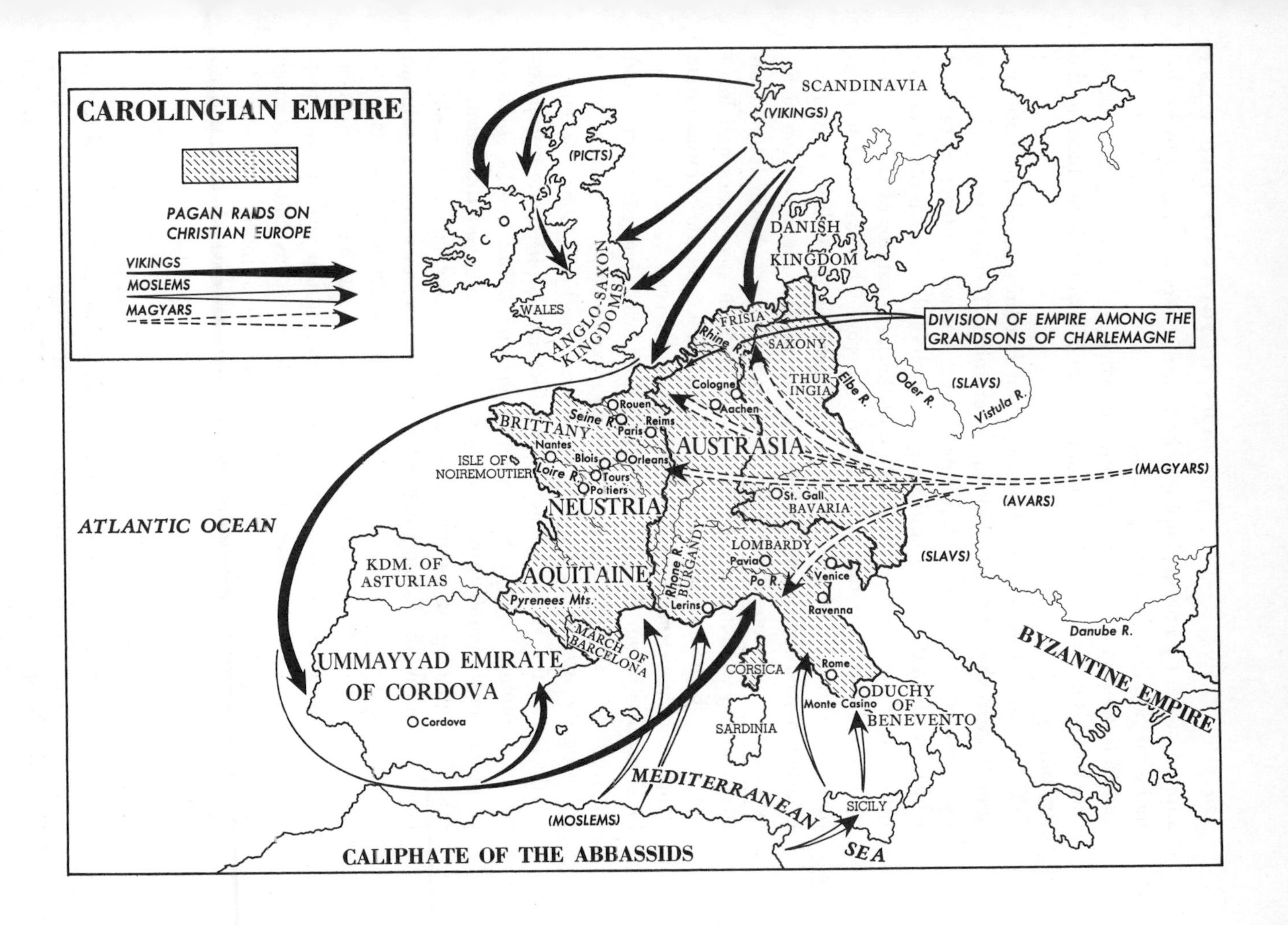

CAROLINGIAN EMPIRE
PAGAN RAIDS ON CHRISTIAN EUROPE
VIKINGS
MOSLEMS
MAGYARS
SCANDINAVIA
(VIKINGS)
(PICTS)
SCOTS
WALES
ANGLO-SAXON KINGDOMS
DANISH KINGDOM
DIVISION OF EMPIRE AMONG THE GRANDSONS OF CHARLEMAGNE
FRISIA
Rhine R.
SAXONY
THURINGIA
Elbe R.
Oder R.
(SLAVS)
Vistula R.
Cologne
Aachen
Rouen
Seine R.
Paris
Reims
BRITTANY
Nantes
Blois
Orleans
ISLE OF NOIREMOUTIER
Loire R.
Tours
Poitiers
AUSTRASIA
(MAGYARS)
(AVARS)
St. Gall
BAVARIA
NEUSTRIA
ATLANTIC OCEAN
KDM. OF ASTURIAS
AQUITAINE
Pyrenees Mts.
Rhone R.
BURGANDY
LOMBARDY
Pavia
Po R.
Venice
Ravenna
Lerins
(SLAVS)
Danube R.
BYZANTINE EMPIRE
MARCH OF BARCELONA
UMMAYYAD EMIRATE OF CORDOVA
Cordova
CORSICA
SARDINIA
Rome
Monte Casino
DUCHY OF BENEVENTO
MEDITERRANEAN SEA
SICILY
(MOSLEMS)
CALIPHATE OF THE ABBASSIDS

support of the Byzantine Empire as he moved closer and closer to its domains in Southeastern Europe and Italy. At any rate, by 812, he had gained the recognition from the Emperor Michael I in return for a clarification of his interest in Dalmatia and Venice. He would leave them to the Byzantines.

That Charles the Great's empire was not Roman is nowhere more evident than in the administration of government. The industry and commerce which had been so vital a part of the economic life of Rome and which had furnished the foundation for much of the Roman tax structure were gone. The growth of colonate and the large estates of the late Roman period had continued to the Frankish period. They were the foundation of the wealth of the Frankish monarchy and nobility. Therefore, Charles showed the deepest concern for the proper administration of his estates in the famous *Capitulare de villis,* which set down detailed instructions on wine-making, planting, tools, and the necessities and luxuries of life in the country. Gone, too, with Rome was the administrative structure of government with its trained civil service. Charles relied on local counts, whom he appointed to collect taxes, judge disputes, and carry out his instructions. He sent out the *missi dominici* from his court to check on the manner in which these things were being done. Moreover, the decline of the money economy of the Roman Empire made it impossible to continue to collect sufficient sums for public works, military purposes, and administrative expenses. Charles followed the Germanic practice of placing his counts on estates from whose income (usually in kind) they drew the support needed for their sustenance and to maintain their place in society. Public works suffered greatly under this system, for road repairs and construction were now in the hands of the local peasantry, who had to render some service during the year for this purpose, but who were usually as reluctant to do so as those in charge of them were to coerce them. Their labor was more necessary to the operation of the estate than to building roads which they had no great use for. Already in the Empire of Charlemagne, the essential features of medieval government and social life were beginning to take shape as local interests began to overshadow those of the realm.

The hope signified in the imperial title that Charlemagne would restore a vital political order in the West was vain. Although he, as a great leader, succeeded briefly in holding the forces of decentralization in check, he did not succeed in harnessing them to the task of creating a lasting government. Charles was too much tied to the traditions of his ancestors, too much the Germanic barbarian prince to be the creator of new political forms needed for this task. Thus, when he died in 814, he bequeathed his son, Louis the Pious, a Germanic kingdom but little different from that which he had inherited from his father. What was different was the fact that Western Europe was defined by its borders.

Louis the Pious (814–840) lacked the qualities which had enabled Charles to work against the centrifugal forces of the age. He was indecisive and hesitant. His vigorous sons, Lothair, Ludwig, and Pepin, forced their father to grant each of them his own kingdom, thus fragmenting the empire within Louis' own lifetime. Efforts by leading churchmen of the time like Jonas of Orleans to inculcate a feeling of filial piety were of no avail. Louis himself could not cope with the ambitions and rivalries of his offspring. Yet his failure was not so much personal as it was related to the nature of Frankish kingship. The strong rule of Charlemagne had merely interrupted and had not destroyed the decentralizing tendencies implicit in the division of the kingdom and the growth of local authority.

One of the most important developments in the period following the death of Charlemagne was the growing power of the nobility. Neither Louis nor his successors were able to prevent them from gathering effective political control of local affairs into their own hands. Indeed, the events of the ninth century encouraged this tendency. After the death of Louis the Pious, the nobles profited from the turmoil as his sons continued to quarrel over the division of the empire. Angilbert of Fontenay wrote:

> Hell laughed at broken trust, brother from brother torn
> And war cried out upon the fearful battle fray;
> And brother brother killed, and kindred slew their kin,
> And fathers to their sons no mercy dared to pray.*

The conclusion of the Treaty of Verdun in 843 divided the imperial patrimony and brought an end to the intense fighting between the sons of Louis the Pious. The Frankish concept of the kingdom as a patrimony had triumphed for the time being. The forces of disintegration had won over the effort to create a unified empire.

But internal strife was not the only factor in the decline of Carolingian rule. During the first half of the ninth century, Norsemen began to raid along the coasts of Western Europe from their homeland in Scandinavia. By the middle of the century, their summer raids turned into more permanent invasions as they began to spend the winter along the coast and to travel up the rich river valleys, pillaging especially the monasteries. In 845, they attacked Paris for the first time, and in 853, they burned Nantes.

* From P. S. Allen, *The Romanesque Lyric* (Chapel Hill: University of North Carolina Press, 1928), p. 228. Reprinted with permission.

The kings were powerless to deal with this situation. The nobility refused to support their efforts to defeat the Norsemen in the field, because they did not want to strengthen the power of the kings. As a result, the monarchy resorted to bribery, to the payment of the Danegeld, a tribute to the Norsemen in return for their promise to look elsewhere for booty. But these solutions were only temporary as the Norsemen were more and more becoming permanent settlers in parts of the kingdom and especially in the northwest along the coast of the North Sea. In 911, Charles the Simple granted the Vikings the whole region along this coast, which thereby became the Norman duchy. This grant gave this group of Norsemen a vested interest in turning away from their depredations and encouraged them to oppose their fellow Vikings who attempted to raid along the coast. In fact, the Normans, as they may now be called, built a powerful duchy, which played an important part in the making of the new Europe. A Norman Duke, William, conquered England in 1066, and Norman adventurers established a kingdom in southern Italy and Sicily.

The ninth and tenth centuries were also troubled by continued incursions of the Moslems along the coasts of Southern Europe and raids by the Magyars from the East. From Africa and Spain Moslem pirates raided along the coast of southern France. One group even seized control of a major Alpine pass and interfered with communication between France and Italy. Their raids in Italy were carried out within sight of Rome, but their greatest achievement in this quarter was the conquest of the island of Sicily and its thriving ports of Palermo, Messina, and Syracuse. Scarcely less important was their control of Sardinia, by which they dominated the Tyrrhenian Sea and interfered with the coastal trade of both Italy and southern France. Well might one of their writers have declared that no one dared to float even a plank on the Mediterranean without the permission of Allah. No doubt, such unsettled conditions adversely affected the trade of the West with Byzantium and the great Eastern markets, although it certainly did not result in its complete disruption. But Europe had also to face the westward sweep of the Magyar horsemen from the steppe lands of South Central Asia. Through most of the tenth century, Central Europe lived in fear of their attacks.

The ninth and tenth centuries saw the process of fragmentation of the remains of the Carolingian Empire carried almost to absurd lengths, until the imperial title was tossed about by petty nobility. The weakness of central authority was marked by its inability to prevent the nobles from usurping judicial and fiscal rights which had formerly belonged to the crown. Some who had served as counts within the framework of Carolingian administration used their positions to benefit their families and to ensure the security of their heirs. Men of humble origins—Baldwin I, Count of Flanders, is an example—were sometimes able to overcome this handicap and rise to high estate partly because of their ability in war and partly because of their shrewdness. Ecclesiastics also sought to increase their own power at the expense of the crown. They used the grants of immunity from royal courts and taxes as a basis for claiming independence from the counts, thus effectively removing themselves from both royal and noble control. But not all were so fortunate. Many found themselves caught up in one or another fragment of territory and thus drawn within the orbit of some ambitious noble. Then, whether these were noble or peasant, churchly or secular, they lost their independence. It was out of this anarchy—for we can hardly term it anything else—that feudalism rose. It was an attempt on the part of a fragmented society to find those points of contact which would unify it once again. Feudalism was founded on the conception of personal contractual relationships: the binding of one man to another.

The collapse of the Carolingian Empire was inevitable. It represented a false start along the road in search of stability. The dream on which it was based was the hope that the Germanic king of the Franks could restore the integrity of the West. That hope was vain. But out of the ashes of the Carolingian Empire and perhaps within those ashes were forged the connecting links which would bind society together in the feudal bond, the foundation of Europe in the West.

The Quality of Early Medieval Civilization

When St. Augustine of Hippo died with the Vandals at his gates, the majority of his contemporaries still regarded themselves as Romans living within the shelter, now somewhat weakened, of the Roman Empire. But Augustine himself had a vision that carried him beyond his own age; he saw the city of God. This vision was to have a profound effect on the molding of early medieval civilization by setting up a tension between man's secular aspirations and the goal of the heavenly city. This tension was formed in the reaction of Christianity to the ideals of the Roman Empire.

The culture of the fifth and sixth centuries combined many elements of a declining Roman civilization with new elements that were Christian and barbarian. It was the age of the last lingering romanticists of old Rome and of the fathers of the Church, but it was also the age of the barbarian invasions. Roman paganism had retreated from the seats of power; the gods had lost their place in the senate house. Its last strength was in the provinces. Almost the last gasp of paganism came from the pen of that literate defender of tolerance, Symmachus. The real possessors of the age were Christian writers. It was their task to provide a rationale for Christian society and to justify the new religion to the peoples of the empire. The real herald of the age was St. Augustine.

Augustine Aurelius (354–430) belonged as much to the fourth as to the fifth century so far as the span of his life is marked out on the calendar, but his spirit looked to the future. Born of Christian parents, he was not baptized until later life and then, only after deep soul-searching. In his *Confessions,* he recounted his spiritual wanderings. For a while he became a Manichaean, perhaps seeking there for some rationale to understand his own attraction to bodily pleasure. He did not find it. Finally, through the prayerful efforts of his mother, Monica, and the instruction of Ambrose, Bishop of Milan, he was converted to orthodox Christianity. To his religious experience, he brought the soul of the new Christian, the feelings of the zealous convert, and the mind of a great Roman intellectual. In all that he wrote, these qualities were present. His *City of God* was at the same time a vision born of Christian innocence and a synthesis of the human past, both in the service of his ardent desire to show that the Rome of the pagans suffered not because Christianity had triumphed but because the age of Rome had passed. The new age was not to be found in an earthly city of human creation but in the city of God. But this city was no mere dream. To the men of the early Middle Ages it took on a concrete reality as an empire of peace which they hoped to found. It was thus that its spirit moved Charlemagne.

Not all men were imbued with Augustine's vision of the future. Some, even among the Christians, feared the results of the decay of cultural values in this transitional age. Boethius and Cassiodorus, both Romans intimately connected with the court of Theodoric in Italy, seem to have been similarly moved by their environment to attempt to preserve the great works of antiquity. Boethius translated works of Aristotle and Plato into Latin. It was from these translations that men of the Middle Ages knew something of Aristotle's logic and Plato's *Timaeus.* Cassiodorus retired from public life and dedicated himself to scholarship at his country home in Vivarium, which he turned into a monastery, where monks copied manuscripts of the ancient classics. Boethius, unfortunately, was accused of plotting against Theodoric and was condemned to death. While in prison, he wrote the *Consolations of Philosophy,* a crown for the value he placed on Greek and Roman thought. Beyond a doubt, the efforts of men of this type played an important role in preserving Roman cultural elements during the Middle Ages and reinforced the hope for a rebirth of Rome.

But the great Roman tradition had lost most of its vitality by this period. It was an age of compilers. Among the most influential was the Spanish bishop, Isidore of Seville (died 636 A.D.), author of the *Etymologies.* This fantastic work owes much to the Roman encyclopedist Pliny for its descriptions of foreign lands. The good bishop was no doubt gullible in his acceptance of Pliny's tales of strange creatures on the bottom of the earth, but he did preserve a considerable amount of useful knowledge that became an essential element in medieval education. His work was cited constantly by later authors, showing how well they knew it.

Christian literature was dominated by churchmen. Pope Gregory I (590–604), the last of the Latin fathers of the Church, wrote the *Pastoral Rule,* as a guide to the clergy. He was also the author of Biblical commentaries on the Book of Job as well as sermons on the Old and New Testament. Much of the poetry of the period was based on religious themes and was also the work of ecclesiastics. The fifth century had produced Paulinus of Nola, who revealed considerable skill in the use of traditional Latin meters in composing his panegyric in honor of St. John the Baptist and other poems in honor of St. Felix of Nola.

The writing of history was also largely in the hands of the clergy after the late fifth century. Gregory of Tours (538?–593) composed his *History of the Franks* partly from legends and hearsay and partly from his own observations. The work is as good as was his evidence. In the main, he reveals himself as an honest, if sometimes gullible historian. But the most important historical work of the period was written in England by the Venerable Bede (673–735), a monk at Jarrow. His work belongs to a later period than Gregory's; it was written after 731, more than a century after Gregory had died. Moreover, Bede was more deeply learned. Where Gregory's Latin leaves much to be desired and his knowledge of the classics scarcely goes beyond Virgil, Bede had a fine sense of style and a wide-ranging mind. His *Ecclesiastical History of the English People* stands as the high point of early medieval historiography.

The age of transition from the decline of Roman power to the rise of the Middle Ages was far from a barren waste. In some respects it was a continuation of trends which had developed under the late empire in the work of encyclopedists. The new elements were largely Christian and it was in this area that new literary forms came into being. In poetry the abandonment of Roman metrical schemes in favor of accented and rhymed verse was a major change. Biblical commentaries and sermons became an important element in the new writing along with devotional and moral literature. History largely broke with classical models and tended to follow an annalistic approach, though the influence of Augustine's *City of God* gave men a sense of the working out of the will of God in time. This attitude had an important influence on historical thought throughout the Middle Ages.

But, while learned men continued to produce at least some work of value, the main attention of this age was elsewhere, on the problems of creating a stable political and social order. In the turbulence of the fifth, sixth, and seventh centuries, there was a general decline in the level of education because of the influx of the uneducated barbarians and the decay and closing of many schools. True enough, Ireland and the north of England enjoyed what amounted to a renaissance of learning toward the end of this period, with great monastic schools and scholars like Theodore of Tarsus, the Greek-speaking Archbishop of Canterbury, Benedict Biscop, a great collector of manuscripts, and the Venerable Bede. Nor was this movement entirely isolated from the continent. Irish monks, in particular, spread their learning abroad through their missionary efforts and their continental monastic foundations. Moreover, it was to this source that Charlemagne turned in his efforts to restore education on the continent.

The restoration of education had to wait for the reestablishment of some measure of political stability. As long as the leaders of society were more concerned about mere survival than the things of the intellect, it was inevitable that the decline would continue. Moreover, the commitment of men like Charles Martel and Pepin the Short to expanding the Frankish kingdom and building the place of their dynasty seems to have occupied their entire vision and left little room for thoughts about education and learning. It remained for the imperial figure of Charlemagne to devote his energies to this matter. In 789, a decade before his imperial coronation in Rome, Charles issued a capitulary commanding that schools be organized in conjunction with every monastery and bishopric in his kingdom. Nor did he leave the matter here. He recruited some of the most outstanding scholars of the age, among them Alcuin, the Englishman who directed the school at Tours, and surrounded himself with learned men in his palace school. The king himself spent part of his time in the school and even, according to the story told by his biographer, tried hard to learn to read and write. Alas, it was of no avail! Though he slept with the tablet beneath his pillow, the letters would not remain fixed in his memory.

But whether Charles could read and write was of little importance, since he possessed two great advantages to overcome the handicap. He had secretaries to perform the task and a great and imaginative mind full of curiosity that never allowed him to be content with the state of his knowledge. When he discovered, for example, the difficulties in reading the old Merovingian script, he ordered all public documents written in the plain but beautiful letters of the Carolingian minuscule.

But the impetus given intellectual life in the Frankish kingdom by Charles went beyond the restoration of the schools. At centers like Tours, Ferrieres, and the great Benedictine Abbey of Fulda, scholars collected and copied ancient manuscripts, produced textbooks for the schools, wrote poetry and commentaries on sacred scriptures, theological treatises, and discussed the duties of rulers. Rabanus Maurus, called the "first teacher of Germany," was born at Mainz in 782. He headed the monastic school at Fulda and later became its abbot, all the time writing texts for use in the schools. His pupil, Walafrid Strabo, wrote commentaries on the Old and New Testaments and composed the *Visio Wettini,* a poem that anticipates the *Inferno* of Dante Alighieri. Sedulius Scotus composed the "Book of Christian Governors" at Liège in the mid-ninth century. At Ferrieres, the Abbot, Servatus Lupus, spent a large part of his effort in collecting and collating manuscripts for his library, in which were represented such authors as Cicero, Virgil, Livy, Caesar, Sallust, Suetonius, the Latin of Josephus' History, and the *De Arithmetica* of Boethius. There was even some writing in the vernacular. The *Heiland* was a life of Christ in the alliterative verse of the Old Saxon. Another writer prepared a prose digest of the Gospels in Frankish.

Probably the most brilliant and original mind of the day belonged to John Scotus Erigena. He knew the Greek language and had read extensively in Greek and Roman philosophy, especially in the writings of the Neoplatonics. It was from them that he drew his conception of the eternity of ideas in the mind of God. He maintained that they were both eternal and created. His *Peri Physeon* was an attempt to synthesize all the Greek and Latin sources on the origins and causes of the universe. In addition to his original studies, he also translated works from Greek into Latin. His influence on later medieval thinkers was probably lessened by his espousal of Neoplatonism, whose influence declined in the later Middle Ages.

Historians have generally used the term "Carolingian Renaissance" to refer to the vigor of intellectual life at this time. Yet, what is witnessed was not so much rebirth as it was a new birth. The Carolingian age witnessed briefly the first flickerings of medieval intellectualism, the first original fruits of the Christian European cultural synthesis in the West. Perhaps, we should clarify. Certainly, the classical and Roman element played an important educational role in this period. It was beginning to take the position that it would maintain in medieval schooling until the rise of the universities at the end of the twelfth century. But, we should not speak of this as a revival, for the grammars of Priscian and Donatus, used by the schools, had always demanded this classical foundation. The Carolingians did not revive the classics so much as they restored the schools. The quality of intellectual life in the early Middle Ages was, on the other hand, very different from that of the classical world. Men had moved far along the way of creating a Christian framework for their society, although many pagan elements remained, as we may see from Charlemagne's condemnation of these practices in 789. Whereas the emphasis of the fifth century was still for the most part Roman Christian, that of the ninth century was much more European Christian. It was not alone that classical models were debased in the hands of inadequate craftsmen, as was certainly true in the realm of art and architecture; the whole spirit of society was different. Though John Scotus Erigena reveals the revival of Neoplatonism in the Carolingian period, the most remarkable point about him is that he was not typical of his age. He is a lonely mountain top in his concern for the speculative philosophies of Greece and Rome; his contemporaries were largely practical men concerned with the problems of education first and more speculative matters only secondarily. Their classicism was practical. Their poetry was most often didactic. They were teachers. Like Charles himself to whom men looked to restore political order and on whom they conferred the imperial title as a seal to that task, the Carolingian teachers were builders of order, practitioners of the peaceful arts that Charlemagne hoped to foster. The collapse of his empire inevitably imperiled the success of their task. Yet so much had been done, that all was not lost. In the Carolingian age, the educational foundations of Western Europe were relaid along the lines that they would develop for the next several hundred years.

PART II
Europe as the West

"Signat cuncta manu loquiturque Polymnia gestu."
"Polyhymnia expresses all things with her hands and speaks by gesture."

7 From Feudalism to Feudal Monarchy

There is a strong tendency to stress the chaotic conditions that existed in Western Europe in the aftermath of the collapse of the Carolingian Empire. Certainly, no historian should minimize the effects of internal and external disorder, weakened central authority, and the fragmentation of political, economic, and social life in that period. But neither should we ignore those factors operating to create a unified society. Through the greatest turmoil, the institution of monarchy remained as a focal point. Though the power of the kings was often weak virtually to the point of nonexistence, the figure of the king remained. Moreover, the feudal system cannot be regarded as the cause of the breakdown of the central authority, but as the product of it. While it is, no doubt, true that the ambitions of the nobility to concentrate effective power over local affairs in their own hands frustrated efforts to build the royal authority, the main feature of feudal society was a system of personal contracts which attempted to tie an already fragmented society together, a system we recognize as feudalism. Ultimately, the role of feudalism was in the direction of unifying medieval political and social life in Western Europe. For the monarchies created in the twelfth century and even earlier were feudal in their foundation and character. The position of the king was founded on his role as lord over his vassals.

Viewed from this position, the feudal age is most important for the development of Western Europe; this importance lies chiefly in the process of state-building which had its origins here. The feudal age climaxed in the creation of a stable society, that stability for which men had sought since the fall of Roman government in the West. No longer may we regard these as "Dark Ages." Rather, in the feudal age, we may discover the foundations of Western European society as it moves toward its most significant achievement: the creation of the national state.

Feudalism as a Political System

The nobles, who gained most by the decline of the Carolingian Empire, were the foundation of feudalism. Many of them had held positions of authority within the empire and, as the monarchy found it more difficult to enforce its will in local matters, these nobles usurped its authority. The offices which they held during their lives, they tried to hand on to their sons to provide security for their families. Thus, in some cases, the office of count, which had been under the direct control of the crown and granted at the royal pleasure, became hereditary. The attacks of the Norsemen on the coastal regions and up the river valleys placed the burden of defense on local authorities, who thereby came to dominate the political life of the districts under their protection. These attacks also led lesser nobles and freemen to seek protection of the more powerful. Moreover, the unsettled conditions of the time encouraged the rise of adventurers; some of these sought to legitimate the positions they snatched, while others drove men to seek protection from them. In the history of the rise of the feudal system, the key to understanding the historical force operating in this period is to be found in the need men had for protection for themselves, their property, and their families.

The essence of the feudal oath of fealty is found in the act of homage, by which one man promises to serve another. Homage—the term means to become the man of another—consisted of a ceremony in which the prospective vassal placed his hands in those of his lord and swore to render him service, usually military, in return for protection. The lord, on his side, granted his vassal a fief, usually land with tenants or serfs to till it, which would support the vassal in his status as a military retainer. Thus, feudalism was based first of all on a personal contract uniting vassal and lord. This was, in the chaotic conditions of the age, the most elemental social tie, that of one man to another.

The origins of this feudal tie are not easily to be found. The Roman relationship between patron and client offers some similarities to the feudal bond in the way in which the client depended on his patron for support. However, Roman practice had not developed the military aspect of this relationship to the extent that it is found in early feudalism. Many

Roman clients rendered personal service or agricultural labor in return for protection. Among the Celtic peoples, where the term *vassus* had its origin, each chieftain had a group of companions who fought at his side and acted as his lieutenants in the government of the clan. But neither Roman nor Celt had developed the concept of feudalism as a system of political control, whereby the authority to rule fell into the hands of local powers. The Romans also had the institution of the *precarium,* in which a landholder granted a part of his land to another, who "prayed" to him for it. During the later empire, a small landowner might turn to the *precarium* as a means of securing protection, by beseeching a large holder to take his land and himself under his protection. The land then became technically part of the large estate, but was granted back to the original holder. These practices indicate the deep roots of personal contractual relationship among both the Romans and the barbarians and indicate some of the sources for the feudal relationship.

Although earlier practice no doubt provided the climate and pointed some direction for feudal development, the main outlines of feudalism did not appear until approximately the time of Charles Martel in the eighth century. In his war against the Moslems, culminating in the Battle of Tours-Poitiers in 732, Charles relied heavily on armed and mounted troops. To support them, he turned to the estates of the Church, part of which he confiscated and used for the support of the cavalry. The creation of a mounted force radically altered the complexion of warfare in the early Middle Ages by reducing the importance of light-armed infantry. The greater wealth required to support a knight made entry into this group impossible without considerable wealth. Since the number of knights who could be supported within the household of a great landholder was relatively small, the practice of conferring benefices in the form of land was almost the only solution to the problem of securing military help in an age when land was the chief form of wealth.

After the mid-ninth century the weak later Carolingians were forced to recognize the right of vassals to pass their holdings to their heirs. By that time, the power of the nobles in local affairs was already well entrenched and the main features of feudalism had appeared in a fairly complete form. The concentration of public power in local hands during the weakness of the monarchy made the feudal nobility the real rulers of the land.

Since the feudal system developed not as an ideal from a rational plan for organizing society but rather out of the experience of the age, it is a mistake to expect complete order. Indeed, the surprising element is the degree of similarity found in the feudal practices of regions well removed from one another. No doubt, the fact that the Carolingian Empire had spread over almost entire Western and Central Europe, as well as into Italy, contributed to the growth of the feudal regime along many of the same lines from northwestern France to northern Italy and from the Pyrenees to the lands beyond the Rhine. But the pattern followed different lines of development in southern Italy and in England, which was conquered by the Normans under William the Conqueror in 1066. Especially would it be a mistake to assume that the presence of feudal institutions signified a similarity of political and social development; their existence was only one of many factors influencing the direction of these changes.

Yet, throughout the entire region described it is possible to speak of certain common elements in the feudal structure, particularly where French or Norman influence played some part in its development. Certainly, the major features of feudalism as a system of private government based on a military landholding class tied to one another by oaths of fealty are to be observed generally. Around this relationship developed various obligations encumbent on both lord and vassal. Fundamental was the military service owed the lord by the vassal. Usually, the vassal had to spend forty days in service each year. He was obliged to come to the defense of the lord in case of attack and to support him against rebellious vassals. Since, as the feudal regime evolved, one vassal sometimes owed fealty to several lords, there was the problem of his primary allegiance. In Normandy and England, all vassals swore their first loyalty to the Duke of Normandy or the King of England. In France, the kings worked assiduously to obtain a direct hold on the vassals of their great dukes and counts, but the policy was only gradually successful in a process that continued into the early modern period. In connection with the military obligation, the vassal gradually accepted certain customs aimed at protecting this service for the lord. The lord possessed the right of wardship over the heirs of his vassals and they were forbidden to marry without his permission and the payment of a fine. These and like customs were aimed at protecting the integrity of the fief, that is, the income which supported the individual vassal or knight, and of ensuring the lord always received the military service due from the fief. The vassal also rendered service at his lord's court. After the middle of the tenth century, the principle of hereditability of fiefs was established and the vassal could, on his death, pass the fief on to his heirs, who paid the relief to the lord. If a vassal broke his feudal oath, he forfeited his fief, although this usually meant there would be a struggle to enforce the decision.

The fief, or benefice, became a more and more important feature of feudalism from the mid-tenth century on. Usually, as we have seen, it consisted of land, which would be tilled by peasants who would pay a part of their produce, usually in kind or produce, to their lord. However, some fiefs were incomes from rents or dues on fairs and other commercial enterprises controlled by the monarchy or the nobility. Nor did all knights have fiefs. As a matter of fact, during the earlier period, only the wealthier and more powerful possessed fiefs of land; many received their support within the households of their lords. The growing hunger for land and the security it ensured for one's heirs, however, caused the number of landless knights to decrease considerably in the eleventh and twelfth centuries until their role was insignificant. It is in this sense that we can speak of the intimate connection between feudalism and the soil.

In a later chapter, we shall deal with the agricultural organization of medieval society in greater detail. Here it is only important to note the intimate relationship between the peasantry and the nobility in their mutual interest in the soil. During the early Middle Ages probably most peasants were bound to the land they tilled as serfs. They were not slaves, however, and they shared in the goods they produced. Their lot was probably not so bad as it is often pictured. They formed the economic foundation of the feudal system; that system, on the other hand, even granted its shortcomings, provided them the protection and order they needed to carry out their task and to live their lives. Inadequate though this was, it was all that they knew. Without it, they would have suffered more.

Feudalism had an important impact on the social history of the Middle Ages. The concept of lordship was not born in the Middle Ages, but it certainly was characteristic of the period. The presence and importance of a military aristocracy shaped the manners and customs of early Europe to a large extent. The development of chivalry under the aegis of the Church as a civilizing influence on the crudity of knightly manners and morals profoundly influenced the European idea of courtesy. Moreover, the aristocratic class-consciousness developed within feudal society persisted into modern times—perhaps, there are still more traces of it than we acknowledge. Finally, feudalism was most important in molding the division of social classes in the Middle Ages; it constituted an active force especially in the shaping of the peasant regime.

The most important role of feudalism in the early Middle Ages was political. The feudal regime was founded on the relationship between individuals and, as such, touched on the basic element in the creation of the social order. It was from this foundation that the Middle Ages began the building of a new society. The task of that society was to build a new form of political institution and its goal was accomplished in the feudal monarchy.

Building States in France and England

Feudalism had developed in a monarchical society and, in some respects, was built on the idea of monarchy. Although the last Carolingians had been weak and ineffective, they theoretically retained their position at the top of the feudal hierarchy. In France, the kings were hardly able to control the activities of great lords like the dukes of Normandy and Aquitaine, but these men were their vassals. In England, the situation was different. Although there is some evidence of an incipient feudalism prior to the Norman conquest of 1066, the Anglo-Saxon kingdom was much more than the continuation of the old Germanic traditions of kingship, in which the king was the war-leader and the nobles, or *thegns,* constituted his companions and advisors. It was, therefore, the Norman conquest, which introduced continental feudalism into England. Moreover, the Norman kings of England were able to command the allegiance of the subvassals in the same way as the Dukes of Normandy. For this reason, English feudalism was more centralized than that in France. This difference explains much that is dissimilar in the development of the feudal monarchies of these two countries.

With the death of the last Carolingian king in France in 987, the nobility elected one of their own number, Hugh Capet, the Great Count, whose lands were centered about Paris and the Seine River, as their king. Hugh and his ancestors had gradually built their power in this region to the point where they were among the most powerful nobles in northern France, yet they possessed no special claim to the monarchy and had no greater opportunity to build a strong kingship than others. Indeed, the early history of the Capetian house was not spectacularly different from the later history of the Carolingians. The process of degeneration of royal power was not arrested. In fact, within the domains of the monarchy, the feudal nobility succeeded in gaining control of vast estates and even in making the offices of the monarchy into hereditary sinecures. It was not until the reign of Louis VI (1108–1137) that France found a monarch able to reverse this trend. When Louis ascended the throne, he was unable to journey from Paris to Rheims for his coronation because the roads were unsafe. By the end of his reign, the entire region was firmly in his control. Louis, with the aid of his able minister, the Abbot Suger of the

Paris monastery of St. Denis, had succeeded in curbing the power of the nobility within the royal domain and breaking their hereditary hold on royal offices. He had destroyed the robber barons who infested the highways. Moreover, he had defended the kingdom against the attack of the Holy Roman Emperor. As a result, Louis laid foundations for a strong French kingdom on which his successors might build.

But France in the twelfth century was still largely confined to the region of the Île de France, the homeland of the Capetians. It was only with the accession of Philip Augustus (1180–1223) that substantial gains were made at the expense of the great feudal nobility who ruled virtually independent of the king in western and southern France, most importantly the King of England, who since the time of Henry II had created a vast empire in France. Philip was an astute diplomat and an aggressive builder of the French monarchy. In 1185, he gained control of part of southern Flanders at the expense of his uncle-in-law, the Count of Flanders. He used his wife's claims to a dowry as the basis for his activities. But his chief efforts were against the English. Henry II and his successors controlled Normandy, Anjou, Poitou, Brittany, and Aquitaine. Technically, however, the English king was the vassal of Philip for these lands, and Philip used every advantage and pretext the feudal law gave him to deprive the English of them. Nor did he hestitate at promoting rebellion. He employed agents to subvert the English king's vassals. When King John of England ran afoul of one of his vassals in France by marrying his betrothed, Philip used the pretext to summon John to his court. Of course, John refused and Philip seized the opportunity to declare the English lands forfeit. At the Battle of Bouvines (1214), Philip defeated John's nephew and ally, the Emperor Otto of Brunswick, and made good on most of his claims. He had greatly increased the size of the realm he had inherited, confining the English to small territories in the southwest and even expanding in the south.

Major additions to the French realm in the reign of Louis VIII came as a result of the Albigensian Crusade. Pope Innocent III called on northern French barons to fight against these heretics, whose stronghold was in Languedoc. The crusade not only destroyed the Albigensians and much of the flourishing civilization of southern France, but also aided in bringing this territory under the control of the French monarchy.

The vast lands added to the realm in the late twelfth and early thirteenth century put a heavy burden on the mechanism of government. Consequently, the reign of Louis IX (1226–1270) was deeply concerned with reorganizing royal administration and consolidating the gains made in the previous century. One of the most important acts of the reign was the Treaty of Paris (December 4, 1259), which saw legal recognition granted to the conquests of Philip Augustus. In return, Henry III of England became vassal of Louis IX for Aquitaine and Poitou. Among the most important administrative improvements of the reign was the reorganization of the *Chambre de Comptes,* which had charge of public finance, to make it a more efficient agency. Louis also promoted the use of uniform weights and measures against the chaotic conditions which had existed earlier and imposed a uniform coinage system. He also introduced gold into the Frankish monetary structure for the first time. He was deeply concerned about the honesty of royal administration and created the *enquêteurs* to check on local officials. His biographer and friend, the Sire de Joinville, paints him as a sober and hard-working monarch and a just judge. The Catholic Church recognized these qualities in pronouncing him one of its saints. Yet to the French monarchy of the Middle Ages, his lasting importance was as the king who consolidated and strengthened the position which had been won by his grandfather Philip Augustus and his father Louis VIII.

When Philip IV ascended the throne of France in 1285, he inherited a strong kingdom, but one whose needs sorely taxed the resources of the monarchy. The history of his reign is the story of attempts to secure adequate taxation and revenues to carry out the ambitious policies he had inherited from his predecessors. This problem brought him into conflict with Pope Boniface VIII when he attempted to levy taxes on the French clergy. Boniface responded with the Papal Bull "Clericos laicos" in which he forbade the king to collect these taxes and argued for the complete independence of the clergy from secular rule. Philip refused to heed the Pope's commands and entreaties; instead he summoned a meeting of the *Estates General*—composed of representatives of the nobility, clergy, and the towns—and obtained its support. When Boniface excommunicated him in 1302 in the Papal Bull *Unam Sanctam,* he called for a general council of the Church to judge the worthiness of the Pope for his office. Beyond doubt, Philip was willing to go to great lengths to defend the competence of secular rulers against what he regarded as the unwarranted invasion of the Papacy.

The power of the French feudal monarchy climaxed in the reign of Philip the Fair. The king finally triumphed over the forces of feudal decentralization represented by the Kings of England; his challenge to the Church also ended in apparent victory. When Boniface VIII died at Anagni in 1303—in part because of the harsh handling dealt him by

Philip's agents—the Papacy came under French influence and even moved the seat of its administration to Avignon, which, although located in the south of France, was technically papal territory. There the Popes remained during most of the fourteenth century. But the French monarchy still faced its greatest challenge in the Hundred Years' War, which broke out between France and England in 1337.

The causes of the war are to be found partly in the attempts of the French to exercise greater control over the towns of Flanders, with whom the English carried on an extensive trade in wool, and partly in the traditional enmity between the two kingdoms rising from the French conquest of the English possessions on the continent. When Louis X of France died without heir in 1318, Edward III of England put forward his own claim to the throne. However, the French refused to consider an Englishman as their king. Edward took no immediate action to secure the throne but bided his time until 1337, when he launched the war.

The Hundred Years' War revealed major changes in military tactics that influenced the future of warfare profoundly. The English use of longbowmen proved very effective against mounted cavalry. The introduction of cannon during the late phases of the war made siege warfare more practicable. The day of the medieval knight was drawing to a close. Greater emphasis was put on the ranks of disciplined infantry who could even withstand a cavalry charge. In the long run, the decline of the feudal army based on the knights meant also the further weakening of the political power of the aristocracy and the additional strengthening of the central authority.

Through much of its length, the war favored the English. At Poitiers in 1347, King John of France himself was captured and forced to sign the Treaty of Bretigny. The English were again victorious under Henry V, the victor at Agincourt in 1415, who forced the mad Charles VI of France to recognize his claim to the throne of France. Only Henry's premature death (1422) prevented the successful pressing of this claim. Still England managed to hold the northern part of the realm, while the *Dauphin,* heir to the French throne, vacillated in the south. It was at this juncture that the youthful and romantic figure of Joan of Arc (Jeanne d'Arc) appeared to reinspire and reinvigorate the fading French hopes. Of course, the French army had learned its lessons in military tactics; Joan provided the will to win. She led the army to victory and the Dauphin Charles to Rheims, where he was crowned king. Despite her capture and condemnation as a witch by an English-dominated ecclesiastical court, her spirit had infused in the French a sense of patriotism and pride that changed the course of the war. From 1436, the year in which Charles VII retook the city of Paris until 1450, when the English were pushed out of Aquitaine, the history of the war is a tale of French victories.

The results of the Hundred Years' War for France are best summed up in her future history. The war so weakened or destroyed the French nobility that it was no real match for the power of the monarchy. To this extent, the war ended any possibility that the Estates General of France would develop into a truly representative institution through which French barons and the middle class might have a voice in government. France had moved away from the feudal monarchy and toward the territorial state. In that state the power of the French king would be absolute. Moreover, the war settled forever the question of English lands on the continent; England began her history as an island nation. Finally, in both countries, the war stimulated feelings of patriotism that tied men in the future more closely to their own countries in a way the men of the Middle Ages had never been.

Thus, the history of France in the Middle Ages saw the gradual increase of royal authority at the expense of the feudal aristocracy until the kings were strong enough to assert their power in the late twelfth and thirteenth centuries. From that point, the feudal monarchy had as its chief aim to destroy the power of England on the continent, chiefly because the English king represented a threat not to France but to the French king within the feudal system. When this threat was removed by Philip Augustus, France was free to develop internally under Louis IX and Philip the Fair. But the outbreak of the Hundred Years' War brought a renewal of the English threat, this time aimed at a France closely identified with its monarchy. The war witnessed the beginnings of the transformation of the feudal monarchy into a territorial state in which centralized government virtually triumphed over feudal decentralization.

In England, although many features are similar to those in France, the lines of development are somewhat different. There, the feudal monarchy sprang into existence, if not full-blown at least in robust youth, as a result of the Norman conquest in 1066. William (1066–1087), Duke of Normandy, claimed the English throne vacated by the death of Edward the Confessor, last of the Anglo-Saxon line; the English nobility raised up Harold, one of their own number, to be king. The defeat of Harold and his Anglo-Saxon allies at Hastings delivered England into the hands of William and a handful of Norman barons and knights who had followed him from the continent. But William was far removed from his Viking ancestors, who had raided along those shores. He was the product of the strong Norman duchy and he transferred to England some of the principles which had given the dukes of Normandy so much power in their mainland domains. Although he rewarded those who had aided him in his conquest with grants of land to be held as fiefs, he reserved for himself the allegiance of their subvassals. The English king was thus to be the liege lord of all vassals in England. Naturally this fact greatly increased his power. But perhaps more important was the act of conquest itself, which made all English land immediately subject to the king. As heir to the Anglo-Saxons, William did not hesitate to retain the old English militia as an addition to his feudal levies to strengthen the power of the crown. Finally, he embarked on a thorough reorganization of the kingdom. He ordered the collection of data about the wealth of the conquered land compiled in the great Domesday book to obtain a more thorough picture of his conquests. He entrusted the reform of the English Church to the Norman Abbot, Lanfranc of Bec, who not only brought it more closely under the supervision of Rome, but rooted out many of the peculiarly English practices which had separated it from the Church on the continent. In sum, William showed himself a determined builder of a strong feudal monarchy, which he bequeathed to his heirs.

The successors of the conqueror were, for the most part, able, though this view would scarcely hold for his son William Rufus (1087–1100), who succeeded in alienating many of the nobility and Anselm, Archbishop of Canterbury, by his cruelty and caprice. Although the twelfth century witnessed the disastrous interregnum and struggle for the crown following the death of Henry I in 1135, it also saw the growing tendency of the monarchy to reach further into the affairs of its subjects. In particular, the development of the royal judicial system under Henry I and especially under his grandson, Henry II (1154–1189), signaled the spread of royal authority at the expense of the feudal aristocracy. The establishment of justices in Eyre to travel through the various shires giving justice in the king's name, the use of the sheriff—an old Saxon official—as a royal representative, and the rapid enumeration of various royal writs as remedies in various types of cases were signs of the king's interest in government on the lowest levels.

The rise of the royal courts, interpreters of the Anglo-Saxon common law, was accompanied by a greater specialization and centralization within the king's council. As in France, the council had been a large body of important magnates who frequently traveled with and advised the king on public matters. Under Henry II, greater importance was attached to a smaller body, the *Curia Regis,* within which the exchequer, concerned with fiscal matters, gained special importance. In the one hundred and twenty-five years after the conquest, the English kings succeeded in creating a strong feudal monarchy with most of the effective authority of the kingdom in their own hands.

But this process was not carried out, as in the case of France, to its conclusion in the creation of a completely centralized monarchy. The history of the thirteenth and fourteenth centuries in England must be told against the background of the successful efforts of the feudal nobility and its allies to regain some measure of the control it had lost to the royal courts. The instrument fashioned for this control was parliament and it rose slowly out of the old royal council in the course of the following centuries. Henry II's sons, Richard the Lion-Hearted and John, proved incapable of carrying the tradition of aggressive royal authority established under their father. In part, their problems were a reaction to the rule of Henry II. He had alienated both nobility and church by his policies; only his power protected him from them. Aside from his encroachments on the authority of the feudal aristocracy, his running conflict with Thomas à Becket, Archbishop of Canterbury, had a bad end. Thomas was murdered before the altar of his cathedral by known sympathizers with the royal cause. Although Henry disclaimed responsibility, he had to accept part of the guilt. In addition, Henry had vigorously opposed French attempts to weaken his power on the continent, where his own inheritance and that of his wife, Eleanor of Aquitaine, stretched the length of western France. He bequeathed to his sons the struggle with the wily Philip Augustus. Against these challenges from so many fronts, abler men than Richard and John might have failed. As it was, Richard devoted himself chiefly to military exploits of little moment and emerged a romantic but ineffective ruler, while John roused the opposition of the nobility, the Church, and the French king without being able to cope successfully with any of them.

The reign of King John (1199–1216) opened with his disastrous loss of his continental dominions to Philip Augustus of France. By 1204, Normandy was gone and most of Anjou and Aquitaine quickly followed. During the next decade John planned the reconquest of these domains, only to witness the dashing of all his plans against the shields of French knights with the defeat of his ally, the Emperor Otto, at Bouvines in 1214. At home, his success was no greater. After alienating much of the nobility by his attempts to increase the power of the crown and by his heavy taxes, he triggered an uprising of the barons in 1215. Defeated by them, he had to accede to their demands for redress of grievances and for recognition of their privileges contained in the *Magna Carta*. This great charter aimed primarily at securing the position of the feudal nobility and its allies, especially the town of London. But its impact was much greater. It became, indeed, a frame of reference against which the English nobility judged their monarchs in the future and it nudged England further along the road to constitutional government by ensuring a limited voice for the nobility in the political life of the kingdom. To this extent, *Magna Carta* was an expression of those forces operating to create representative government in the form of a parliament in England. These tendencies were to be further developed during the reign of John's son, Henry III.

The long reign of Henry III (1216–1272) was marked by the weakness of the king and the restiveness of the nobility. As discontent with the failure of Henry to follow the advice of his feudal council increased, the focal point came to be his employment of the Great Council chiefly to secure additional grants of taxation rather than to seek aid in settling the affairs of the realm. In 1264, opposition crystallized around Simon de Montfort, who summoned the nobility and led them against the king. In 1265, he called a parliament, which contained representatives not only from the barons, but also two knights from every shire and two burghers from every town. Although Simon was defeated that same year, his work had provided another impetus to the development of the English Parliament.

The reign of Henry's able son, Edward I (1272–1307), saw that king employ Parliament regularly, chiefly to raise taxes, but also for other purposes. His codification of the English common law climaxed the efforts of his predecessors in their attempts to improve the English administrative and legal structure. For this great work, he has been hailed as the "English Justinian."

The Hundred Years' War played an important role in shaping the constitutional development of England. Although, as described above, the basic elements of English government had already begun to take shape prior to the outbreak of the war, it was the continuing need of the English kings for support in their French campaigns and particularly for funds for the wars that caused them to call frequent parliaments, thus giving that institution no chance to fall into disuse. Beyond doubt, the war also stimulated a feeling of loyalty to the English crown. England became more aware of its identity as a result of the long struggle with France. The loss of the continental possessions, although hardly recognized as irrevocable by contemporaries, caused Englishmen to focus more on the island and its people and to see about themselves certain characteristics that set them apart from the French across the English Channel. But most importantly, the war ended in defeat for England. This fact meant much more than the loss of foreign domains of the English king. It signified a turning point in English history. After the mid-fifteenth century, England no longer concentrated its attention on the continent to the extent that it had in the Middle Ages; rather it began to look westward into the Atlantic. It began, tentatively, to move in the direction of Europe's future, toward the formation of an Atlantic community.

By the end of the Hundred Years' War France and England had passed beyond the feudal monarchy and laid the foundations for the territorial state, whose major characteristics were: (1) a greater centralization of governmental authority in both the political and economic spheres, and (2) the weakening of the power of the nobility in local political life. The territorial state was dynastic rather than feudal, based more upon control of land than upon the people who inhabited it. Nevertheless, it generally possessed a certain national cohesiveness at least in the main core of its territories and hence was the beginning of the formation of the national state. But it also turned back to the age of feudalism, for the dynastic principles of the early modern period were not far removed from those that had motivated the kings and barons of the Middle Ages.

The Persistence of the Imperial Dream

The Empire of Charlemagne had been based more in Western than in Central Europe. Indeed, of the first five great duchies of Germany: Franconia, Bavaria, Swabia, Saxony, Thuringia, the first two alone had been amalgamated completely into the Frankish kingdom before the reign of Charlemagne and Saxony held out through most of his reign. Nevertheless, it was in these Eastern lands that the medieval empire came into being, not as a successor of the Carolingian or Roman Empire so much as an expression of the persistence of the dream of empire in Italy. For the German kings became emperors not as the result of their creation of a strong German monarchy but rather because of their involvement in Italian affairs.

The early history of the German monarchy following the death of the last Carolingian to rule in Germany does not differ markedly from the events following the establishment of the Capetians in France. The nobles chose one of their own number, Conrad, Duke of Franconia, to be king. Having done so, they proceeded to pay little heed and less respect to his attempt to strengthen the monarchy. When Conrad died, he urged the nobles to elect the Duke of Saxony as his successor, for he felt that the Saxon duke possessed greater power than his own Franconian successor and would be better able to control the decentralizing tendencies among the great dukes. In this his judgment proved correct. For the German king had little control over the dukes save that which he could exercise as a result of superior arms. The German duchies had not been integrated into a feudal system in the same manner as the lands of the French nobility. Therefore, the German king could not command feudal allegiance nor enforce feudal obligation on the dukes. Saxony was the strongest of the duchies and her warriors were well known for their bravery and ability in battle. The result was the choice of Henry the Fowler, Duke of Saxony, as king by the Franconian and Saxon nobility.

Henry devoted his chief efforts to strengthening his own duchy internally and warding off the attacks of more barbarous peoples from the East, especially the Magyars, who posed the greatest threat to the security of all of Central Europe in the tenth century. His major acquisition was the Duchy of Lorraine, which had recognized the Frankish Carolingians. This rich and strategic land centered on the lower Rhine Valley. It attracted the cupidity of the German king, who felt that it should be a German duchy.

The choice of Henry's son Otto (936–973) as his successor marked the beginning of the effort of the Saxon kings to rule the whole of Germany. Otto conceived of the dukes as his feudal vassals and servants and worked to make this conception a reality. The early part of his reign was devoted to putting down rebellions and deposing the dukes. He replaced them first with members of his own family, but this proved no effective solution, for his own son and son-in-law rebelled against him. Otto therefore had to find some stable and dependable force upon which he could rely for assistance in ruling his kingdom. He found this in the Church. He relied on the bishops and archbishops as advisors and administrators and as a counterbalance to ducal power. On their side, the great clerics supported the monarchy against the forces of ducal decentralization, which threatened to absorb the lands and offices of the Church. Thus, Otto strengthened the practice, already in existence, of the king investing the bishops and abbots with the signs of their spiritual authority. The episcopacy was therefore a royal as well as an ecclesiastical office.

Besides the attention which he devoted to the reorganization of the administration of the kingdom, Otto also led the defense of Central Europe against the Magyars, defeating them decisively in 955 at Lechfeld. In doing so, he brought together an army from all the German duchies. Beyond doubt, the nature of the emergency caused the dukes to forget momentarily their differences, but credit must also go to the ability of Otto in planning the campaign and securing their support. His reign saw the beginnings of German eastward expansion to lands which had been settled earlier by the Slavic peoples. This *Drang-nach-Osten* (drive to the East), as German scholars call it, was a reversal of the direction of previous German movement and must be regarded as an example of the expansionist tendencies inherent in the establishment of a strong German monarchy.

Otto was also attracted to affairs in Italy, where the last claimant of the Carolingian imperial title, Berengar of Ivrea, King of Lombardy, was attempting to extend his domains beyond Italy. Otto defeated Berengar and took the iron crown of the Lombards for himself. In 962, he was crowned as Emperor by Pope John XII. Thus, the Holy Roman Empire of the Middle Ages was born among the Germans. The reasons for its creation are difficult to discover. The tendency among the Italians and the Papacy to regard the empire as the form of government uniquely suited to a Christian society stemmed from their Augustinian concept of the medieval world. To some of them, at least, Augustine's *City of God* was a plan for the harmony of emperor and pope which they desired to create. The heritage of imperial Rome was far from dead. Indeed, both through historical tradition and the reality of Byzantine power, Rome remained the image of government that dominated the thinking of many medieval writers and thinkers from Augustine to Dante. But it would be a mistake to look further back than the Carolingian Empire for the chief motive in establishing the Holy Roman Empire.

In the eleventh century, the attempt of the German emperors to continue the policies of Otto the Great culminated in the reign of the Salian Emperor Henry III. Otto's immediate successors were able to do little more than maintain their inheritance. When Henry III (1039–1056) ascended the throne, the German emperors were well established in Germany and the German kingdom was well on its way to becoming a model in the building of a strongly centralized feudal government. But the German kings had accomplished these significant gains neither within the structure of the feudal system nor by destroying the power of the great duchies. Rather, they had posed against the forces of decentralization the support which they gained from the bishops of the empire and from the lesser nobility. Ironically, the very policies which had favored the growth of the monarchy under earlier rulers and which enabled Henry III to exercise a control within Germany and over the Papacy greater than any ruler since Charlemagne, played a leading role in the disruption of the monarchy and the unleashing of the forces of decentralization in the reign of his son, Henry IV (1056–1106).

The development of the German monarchy in the eleventh century was caught up in a great political and religious crisis between Pope and emperor. The seed of their difference was contained in the practice of lay investiture, whereby the emperor conferred on the bishops the symbols of their spiritual authority, their mitre and crosier. But lay investiture was merely the external manifestation of conflicting goals rooted deeply in the parallel growth of Church and monarchy during the previous three-quarters of a century or more. On the one hand, Pope Gregory VII stood at the head of a vigorous reform movement, aimed at rooting out the unworthy pastors and strengthening the control of the Roman Pontiff over the administration of Church discipline. On the other hand, Henry IV was the heir of Otto the Great and the German emperors who had built the strength of the German monarchy partly on the bishops of the Church, whom they appointed and who were their counterpoise to the power of the dukes. Both of these leaders, Gregory and Henry, were the products of established historical movements to restore the fabric of Church and empire. The essence of their conflict lay in the fact that each attempted to gain control of the bishops for his own purposes and to hold it.

Gregory drew support from the Cluniac reform movement, which had its origins in France at the monastery of Cluny, founded in 911. The Cluniac monks, by the terms of their founding, owed allegiance to no feudal lord, but only to the Pope. As their movement spread, especially through the establishment of new branches of the order and the reform of older Benedictine communities, they carried with them their conception of independence from the feudal regime and their ideals of religious life. In particular, they decried the widespread abuse of simony—the buying and selling of ecclesiastical offices—and the neglect of the clerical celibacy—an ideal held up for the clergy of the Western Church from early Roman times, but frequently violated. The movement had received considerable support from the Emperor Henry III, who had selected a number of popes from the ranks of its leaders and supporters. In doing so, he had unwittingly lent strength to the movement that was to produce the great crisis between Church and empire in the eleventh century.

Gregory VII, who had served as a major official of the Roman Church under several of his predecessors, was a man of indomitable will and ardent conviction. Certain that the abuse of lay investiture prevented the triumph of the reform movement as he conceived it, he did not hesitate from action. He maintained in the *Dictatus Papae* of 1075 that only he, as Pope, had the right to appoint and depose bishops. When Henry IV countered, he excommunicated him. This act was aimed directly at the weakness of the German monarch, the potential disloyalty of the nobility to the crown. Henry, faced with the possibility of rebellion, journeyed south to Italy to forestall Gregory, already on the road to Germany to launch further proceedings against the emperor. The meeting at Canossa in Tuscany ended in a temporary reconciliation, but did nothing to settle the basic problem they were facing. Consequently, the conflict broke out again within a short time. But the war that ensued settled nothing. Henry's brief moment of victory following the death of Gregory was cut short by the rebellion of his own son, who seized the throne as Henry V. The real settlement of the investiture struggle came out of the protracted negotiations culminating in the Concordat of Worms in 1122.

The settlement at Worms was a compromise in which the Church conceded to the emperor the right to confirm bishops in their feudal lands prior to their receiving the symbols of their spiritual authority. It did not radically alter the position of the German bishops in their relationship to the monarchy; they continued to be deeply involved in the administration of the empire. It did not deprive the king of his influence in their selection. Implicitly, he obtained recognition of his role in their election. But it did distinguish between the temporal and spiritual role of the bishop and thus provided a measure of control over the episcopacy for the Pope. Lay investiture never again arose as an issue between Pope and emperor, but it loomed as a major sign of the difficulty of these two great medieval powers in finding a *modus vivendi* in the community of the Middle Ages.

The accession of a new dynasty, the Hohenstaufen, in the twelfth century marked a decisive attempt on the part of the German rulers to rebuild the power they had lost during the investiture struggle. The effort of Frederick I Barbarossa (1152–1190) to consolidate his position in Germany by strengthening his Swabian Duchy was of little avail, since he became deeply involved in the restoration of imperial authority in northern Italy. There, the weakness of preceding emperors had encouraged the independent development of cities like Milan, the mistress of the plain of Lombardy. The resources that Frederick committed to his Italian campaigns did not win him victory; rather his policies roused the fear of the Papacy and caused the Milanese to take the lead in the formation of the Lombard League to oppose him. Frederick's effort to impose imperial podesta as his representatives in the cities failed. However, he passed on to his son, Henry VI, not merely his imperial conception of the role of the German monarchy—which had received considerable impetus through the revival of studies of Roman law—but also a claim to the Norman kingdom of Sicily as the basis for future action.

The imperial vision of Henry VI was grandiose and short-lived. Although he succeeded in 1194 in his conquest of the Norman kingdom, his death three years later prevented him from realizing his ambitions to create a Mediterranean empire and to lead a crusade to incorporate the holy places in the East into his empire. His infant son, Frederick Roger, the later Emperor Frederick II, became a pawn in the struggle to control both the empire and the kingdom of Sicily.

The thirteenth century witnessed a brief moment of light and glory for the medieval empire before its decline. The reign of Frederick II (1220–1250) brought no respite in the conflict between empire and Papacy, but it did give the Middle Ages an opportunity to realize the full implication of strong imperial rule in Central Europe and Italy. The basis for Frederick's power was not the German kingdom, but his Sicilian state, which he conceived as an imperial domain that would provide the resources needed for carrying out his design to unite Germany and Italy under a single ruler. Heir to Henry VI, he was raised to the imperial throne with the aid of Pope Innocent III, who was bent on thwarting the ambitions of Otto of Brunswick to gain control of Italy. Although Otto lost the support of the Papacy because of his invasion of Italy, Frederick succeeded in defeating Otto and his allies with the aid of King Philip Augustus of France in 1214. Upon his return to Italy, he devoted the early years of his reign to restoring his rule in the kingdom of Sicily. In 1231, he issued the Constitutions of Melfi, a codification of the law of the kingdom, which revealed his concern for the strength of the monarchy and his determination to curb the power of the nobility in political life. Though he spent but little time in Germany, his concern for the empire was great. He attempted to placate the nobles and bishops in the north by granting them broad privileges in order to give himself time to secure his position in Italy. This policy failed because of his defeat in Italy. The alliance of the Papacy and the Lombard cities deprived him of final victory. Yet his conception of the medieval empire had a profound influence on his contemporaries. German poets sang of his conflict with the Pope in almost nationalist tones. And no one realized more fully the significance of Frederick's goal than Pope Innocent IV, who dedicated his every fiber to the destruction of the Hohenstaufen house lest the dream live on. Some historians have seen in Frederick the harbinger of secular monarchy determined to destroy the too pervasive power of the Papacy in temporal affairs; perhaps a better judgment is that he was the genuine heir of the medieval dream of empire, which, when recognized by his contemporaries for all of its possibilities, caused the Papacy and the northern Italian cities to unite in fear of his threat to their independence.

The death of Frederick II led to the interregnum, during which no claimant was able to make good his claim to the imperial throne. When in 1274, the crown fell to Rudolf of Habsburg, whose chief concern was his Duchy of Austria, it signaled the transformation of the Holy Roman Empire into a wholly German institution. The brief excursion of the Emperor Henry VII into Italy seemed to some, especially Dante, to bode the revival of the medieval dream. But the thought was doomed to disappointment. The increasing role played by the house of Habsburg in imperial politics and their success gaining control of the imperial crown was an important factor in the growing autonomy of the German nobility. For the policy of the Habsburgs was not imperial or even monarchic; its aims were chiefly dynastic and concentrated on the consolidation of its rule in southeastern Germany and the neighboring lands.

While England and France succeeded in creating centralized states in the course of the later Middle Ages, the German monarchs, fascinated by the medieval dream of empire, turned from their task of state-building to the creation of the empire. Perhaps it would be better to say that they made this turn because it appeared to them the best way to build a state. The failure of the monarchy in the investiture controversy and the imperial involvement in Italy distracted the German monarchs from the task of creating a German state. But, in the age of the Hohenstaufen, especially in the reign of Frederick II, there was a brief moment in which the emperors glimpsed Italy as the key to the building of a unified Holy Roman Empire. The failure of this attempt paved the way for a Germany disunited under the rule of the nobles and for the development of French hegemony on the continent in the years after 1450.

8 Manor and Town

The process of state-building which consumed so much of the political energies of medieval man represents only one facet in the development of civilization in the European Middle Ages. Side by side with it went the economic transformation of society. The foundation of economic life after the collapse of Roman rule in the West was almost entirely agricultural. By the later Middle Ages, an entire new urban society had sprung up. Put in these terms, it becomes immediately evident that this period witnessed significant changes in the economic history of Europe.

Manor and town therefore symbolize the polarity of two periods in economic development. It would be a mistake to reduce this symbol to an overly simple explanation of the direction of the economy. In fact, there is both an agricultural and urban society growing side by side throughout the Middle Ages and significant changes occurred in both. Moreover, agriculture remained the major occupation of men at the end of the period as at the beginning and many men in the towns earned their living by dealing in the products of the land. The change was in the ratio of urban to rural population, in the increase of industrial and commercial wealth accompanied by the growth of a money economy, and the growing realization of this change and its impact on the thinking of the men of this age. Indeed, if it has now become a truism to state that the Middle Ages were not static, it still remains for us to point out that the men of that period realized that their age was not static. The study of economic history reveals the growing sense of awareness, even among churchmen, of the changing nature of their society.

The Agricultural Basis of Medieval Civilization

All early civilizations developed in societies that were chiefly agricultural in nature, although there were considerable differences in the degree of reliance on farming as against other sources of wealth. Thus, when we speak of the vibrant commercial life of the Roman Empire, which extended well into the fourth and even the fifth centuries, the tendency is to forget that many of the products that were traded had an agricultural origin. Moreover, far more people gained their livelihood from the soil than lived by commercial or industrial pursuits. On the other hand, there has probably never existed an agricultural society in which there was not a certain modicum of trade and industry, even if these aspects were purely local and limited to handicraft goods. It is well to keep in mind that the labeling of an age as agricultural or urban is a matter of degree of emphasis rather than an absolute.

The collapse of the Roman political authority in the West does not appear to have swept away the long-established organization of agricultural life in the former lands of the empire. True enough, the introduction of German auxiliaries to the Roman army and the later practice of rewarding their service with grants of land may have had bad effects on those areas along the frontier which bore the burden of these settlements. Moreover, the mass invasions of Gaul, Italy, and Spain by the barbarians had major consequences on the customary ways of owning and holding land, although these effects were somewhat mitigated by the relatively small numbers of invaders who reached certain areas in Southern Europe. Therefore, in agriculture as in other spheres of activity, Roman practices and customs continued to exist along side of those customs introduced by the new peoples.

In the late Roman Empire, probably the most characteristic institutions of the agricultural regime were the latifundia—the large estates worked by slaves or peasants of servile status—and the colonate, whereby peasantry were bound to the land they tilled under the dominance of a wealthy landowner. The decline of slavery in the late imperial and early medieval period had gradually increased dependence of landholders on tenant farmers. Some of these were freemen, who paid a rent for the land they farmed; others, the majority, were *coloni,* who surrendered a portion of the harvest and were required by law to remain on the land. From the time of Diocletian onward, the position of the peasantry appears to have become more precarious.

Generally, the Germanic invaders did not substantially alter the position of the peasantry whom they found on the lands they took over. As *domini terrae,* lords of the land in the truest sense, they very often assumed the position of the former Roman landholders without fuss. However, the process varied considerably in those regions where Roman traditions were less well established. In Italy, for example, where Romans were numerous, agricultural leases used in accordance with Roman law persisted through the Middle Ages; in France north of the Loire River, where Roman influence was not as pronounced, the Roman system of leasing was either unknown or had disappeared. Perhaps in these northern regions, the institution of serfdom found in the early Middle Ages owed less to the colonate than to the Germanic precedent. The evidence of the presence of agricultural serfs prior to German entry into the empire is slight, but the possibility of such serfs suggests an agricultural organization already existing before the invasions.

Many historians have argued that the barbarian invasions destroyed the commercial economy of the West and forced on it a purely local subsistance-level agriculture. This house economy, they believed, was the economic handmaiden of feudalism insofar as both were the result of the fragmentation of a larger framework. The great Belgian historian, Henri Pirenne, who argued for a continuity of Roman trade patterns in the Mediterranean basin until the time of the Islamic invasions of the West in the late eighth century, caused many historians to reject these views. Pirenne argued that evidence of continued trade in Merovingian Gaul proved that the decline of commerce in the late imperial age had not been fatal to international trade. Rather, he maintained, the control of the Mediterranean by the Moslems in the eighth century turned that sea into a Moslem lake on which not even a board could float "without the permission of Allah." Pirenne's critics have attacked this view from numerous positions, with the general effect that discussions of the disappearance of all commerce and the existence of a house economy in either the late imperial or Carolingian ages have given way to the recognition of a continuing, although limited, commerce through the early Middle Ages.

Nevertheless, the predominantly agricultural character of the early medieval period is the major economic influence on the development of that age. For this reason, it is important to understand as much as we can about changes in organization and technology affecting farming.

Under the Romans, the practice of planting one field while permitting another to lie fallow was usual. The soil of Southern Europe is generally lighter and does not hold moisture as well as that of Northern Europe.

Moreover, the climate of the South favors the two-field system, because the amount of rainfall is considerably below the average for the North. Finally, the two-field system rested the land and made the use of fertilizers, which were never common and were therefore not feasible, less necessary. These conditions also probably gave rise to the development of the Roman plow, the *aratrum*, a scratch plow, which did not dig deep and turn the soil, thereby wasting the precious top soil. But both the two-field system and the Roman plow spread into Northern Europe in the Roman period and remained the customary method and tool of the peasants there into the early Middle Ages. Although, the heavy plow, the *carucca,* was

The wheeled plow. One of the most important technological innovations of the early Middle Ages. (*The Bettmann Archive*)

known probably in Roman times, it came into its own only in a few regions—as in the Po Valley—in that period and did not come into common use in Northern Europe until after the sixth century. Its suitability to the heavier moist soils of the North was due to its ability to dig deep and turn the soil, while the addition of wheels made it more efficient. Besides this major technological change, the early Middle Ages also saw the introduction of the three-field system, so that approximately sixteen per cent more land came under cultivation. Under this system, which rotated wheat, rye, and other grains, with legumes, the individual peasant was able to dramatically increase his production and therefore created a greater agricultural surplus.

Beyond doubt, these and other improvements in the technology and organization of agriculture permitted a substantial increase of the population of Europe, indeed, encouraged such a growth.

As the discussion of feudalism in the previous chapter has shown, this agricultural system was fundamental to the support of the feudal aristocracy. The fief, or benefice, was in the vast majority of cases, a grant of a large or small portion of land along with the peasantry who worked it. Although the agricultural unit granted was sometimes the manor, this type of organization was far from universal. Therefore, in Italy, we find members of the feudal nobility holding fiefs of land, where the agricultural unit was the free village, which paid a rent. We also find instances of land held by money lease, by sharecropper lease, and by hereditary lease. At some time, labor services were required from the peasantry, at other times not. Nor was the manor itself a uniform type of organization where it was found.

The classic divisions of the manor are into the lands of the lord (Demesne), the lands of the peasants, the common, the forest—over which the lord has exclusive rights, and the manse or manor house, with its mill and ovens. But many manors had only a few of these. Moreover, although the court of the lord was the ordinary place for settling disputes among the peasants of the village, control of legal matters was heavily concentrated in the hands of the leading families of the village itself. These constituted a village aristocracy, a kind of select group from whom came those who had their pledge to support fellow peasants having suits in court and who served as jurors. Nor was the manor a stable unit. Individuals came and went in the course of following specialized skills they had acquired. The leading families disappeared and their place was taken by others. There is considerable evidence of mobility. Although the rights of the feudal lord received special protection in law, it was sometimes to his

Medieval agriculture, ca. 1500. Peasants labored in the shadow of Church and manor house. (*The Bettmann Archive*)

interest to make special agreements with his peasants that changed their obligations.

In the course of the Middle Ages, increasing demand for agricultural products combined with the needs of feudal lords for additional income wrought important changes in the agricultural regime. In particular, the gradual movement toward an economy in which money rather than goods played a leading role led many lords to sell charters to agricultural villages granting them extensive control over their internal affairs. Among the burdens the peasants wished most to escape were labor services owed to the lord and the payments in kind. Therefore, they were willing to pay a fixed rent, called in France the *cens,* to avoid these obligations. In the twelfth century, both ecclesiastical and lay property holders began to see ways to increase the cultivated land under their control. In France, attractive terms were set for those who would clear woodland and farm it. In the Netherlands, monasteries and the Counts of Flanders took the lead in reclamation of additional land from the sea by diking and draining. In Eastern Europe, with the expansion of German power into Prussia, successful attempts were made to persuade peasants from the Low Countries and Germany to move east. All of these efforts to expand land under cultivation also resulted in considerable improvement in the lot of those peasants who participated in them.

The connection between agriculture and feudal society was basically the relationship between the producer and a military aristocracy. Land was a form of income used to support the knights and lords. John of Salisbury, writing in the twelfth century, reflected the medieval tendency to

Harvesting. The peasants never worked far from the village and often were within sight of it. While men cut, the women bound the grain into sheaves. (*The Bettmann Archive*)

view social relationships in terms of an organic whole and to see the peasants as the feet in a society where the feudal nobility were the arms. Both were necessary to the welfare of the body. Conflict between the members of this body was not only unthinkable, but also were injurious to the functioning of the body as a whole. The views of this medieval theorist reveal not merely the extent to which men in the Middle Ages were committed to a hierarchic and organic theory of society, but also stressed the intimacy of the dependence of the feudal class on the agricultural regime.

Significant changes in agricultural organization and technology also played a role in the growth of cities. The invention of the horse collar in the early Middle Ages made possible the gradual introduction of the horse-drawn plow during the tenth and eleventh century. Since the horse had greater speed than oxen, the peasant with a horse-drawn plow could produce more than his neighbor still forced to use his team of oxen. Application of this advantage was slow but steady; inevitably it led to increased surpluses of farm goods. The use of the windmill and the water mill were early instances of machine technology; both had applications to the processing of grain. The growing importance of regional trade in the early Middle Ages was largely due to an increase in the commerce of foodstuffs. Of course, it is difficult to estimate the over-all role of the rise of local markets in the development of urban centers, but it must have been considerable. Thus, while the rise of cities was the result of many complex factors, it owed much to the firm foundation furnished by the agricultural regime.

The Growth of an Urban Economy

Of all the significant elements introduced into Western civilization or receiving a distinctive cast in the Middle Ages, hardly any was more important than the city. As is well known, the city is not the creation of the medieval period. It flourished in antiquity and was, indeed, the characteristic unit of society in the Roman Empire. These Roman cities were administrative and military centers, the focal point of culture, and the economic centers of the region in which they were located. Their decline in the West following the collapse of Roman political authority and the barbarian invasions was a tragic consequence of economic dislocation and political impotence. Attempts by the Roman emperors of the late fourth and fifth centuries to force the members of the town curias or councils to assume burdens of taxation beyond their capacity was only one factor illustrating the failure of imperial authorities to correctly diagnose the economic ills of the late empire. The decline of urban government inevitably followed. Yet it would be a mistake to see Europe in the period from the sixth through the tenth century as completely rural. Cities continued to flourish wherever their essential functions were important to society. Rome, no longer the center of the empire and therefore but a shadow of her former self, survived as the city of the Popes, who assumed an increasing importance as administrators in the Western Church. In southern Italy and in Venice, economic ties with the Mediterranean East pumped the health-giving blood of wealth into urban centers. Even in Northern Europe, where the effects of the barbarian invasions were most thorough, there is ample evidence of the continuance of cities and towns. Along the Rhine and the Rhone, the Loire and the Seine, towns grew alongside monasteries. Wherever there was a bishop, one could expect to find some concentration of population and the same could often be said of markets. These places were not cities, at least not often. They were too small, too much a part of the surrounding countryside, too lacking in specialized crafts, too little centers of culture. Yet it would be unwise to deny completely their urban character, sometimes a heritage of a more flourishing past, more often a harbinger of a prosperous future.

Perhaps the tendency among historians to regard the decline of the cities of antiquity as a great tragedy has blinded us to the creative contribution of the Middle Ages in providing a new ground in which cities might grow. For it was a new ground; the medieval city was related to but radically different from the city of antiquity. For example, by some seemingly ironic quirk, the medieval town began its period of expansion about or somewhat before the year one thousand, in an age when feudal decentralization was at its height. That the first stirrings of the towns predated the major increase in international trade during the eleventh century seems certain. Under these circumstances, the first bloom of urban centers was probably stimulated not by trade with the East but by changes within Europe itself and most significantly the growth of the population. Other factors also played some part. Within a few generations following the year one thousand, kings in France, Germany, and England were making their first efforts to reassert royal authority and to impose royal order. Stability, even that created within relatively small areas by baronial control, aided in the carrying on of regional trade. Of course, the gradual imposition of royal authority over larger areas promoted not merely regional and interregional trade, but also encouraged the growth of international trade. Finally, an increase in wealth, expressed partly in larger agricultural surpluses used to feed a larger population and partly the result of dues on market rights and rents, made possible larger markets near the castles of great nobles and in episcopal towns.

Certainly there was no single catalyst in the medieval environment that determined the rise of the towns. The origins of cities followed patterns traced under the peculiar circumstances which brought each into existence. In some, the political factors played a larger role; in others, the economic factor was more significant. But whatever furnished the primary impetus for the establishment of cities, their future growth and even survival was influenced to a large extent by economic considerations.

The most flourishing urban centers of the Middle Ages developed along the major highways of trade or where, for one reason or another, regional trade was concentrated. In Italy, Venice on the Adriatic Sea and Genoa on the Tyrrhenian Sea were gateways into northern Italy and Northern and Western Europe for the trade from the East and from North Africa. Pisa, despite her position in central Italy, was also an important market for goods from the East and the major rival of Genoa, because she had both access to the sea and to a north-south trade route. Along the Southern European littoral, Marseilles, Narbonne, and Barcelona had fine harbors and controlled access routes inland. In Northwestern Europe, the towns of the Low Countries—Bruges, Utrecht, Ypres, to name but a few —grew rich in the profitable trade in English woolens which they processed and sold to Italian merchants at the fairs in Champagne.

The thirteenth century witnessed the most startling increase in population. Although the records on which studies of medieval population are based do not permit absolute statements about the numbers of persons involved, the sharp line of increase is evident. Paris, with about 25,000 at the beginning of the thirteenth century, more than doubled her population within one hundred years. In that same century, her position as administrative center of France was confirmed. Naturally, this role greatly increased the attractiveness of the city to merchants, tradesmen, and those engaged in various crafts. The important industrial and commercial centers of Italy also grew in this period. Between 1139 and 1250, Pisa, Florence, Lucca, Bologna, Mantua, and Parma built new and more extensive walls. This construction was necessary because of the large increase in townspeople.

Behind this tremendous growth lay the gradually increasing importance of commerce in the medieval economy. Although, as described above, there was not a complete absence of international trade at any time during the Middle Ages, the quantity of goods involved in trade between

The Medieval town. The city of Carcassone, view from the air of the most perfect walled city in the world. (The Bettmann Archive)

East and West on the Mediterranean and between Western Europe and Northeastern Europe in the period before 1100 did not begin to compare with the volume of trade in these areas that developed after that time. The major factors changing the commercial picture were a new aggressive policy on the part of some European cities in their attempt to secure the seas about them for their own ships and a greater security for internal trade in Europe. In the late eleventh century, Pisa and Genoa cooperated in driving the Moslems from Sardinia and the Tyrrhenian Sea. The Pisans also aided the Norman invaders of southern Italy in their effort to conquer the island of Sicily from the Arabs in the eleventh century. At the beginning of the first crusade in 1095, the Genoese provided ships to carry the crusaders to the East. Within Europe, political consolidation under the German, English, and even the French monarchy in this period, along with relatively large and stable political units like the Duchies of Normany and Aquitaine, created more favorable conditions for trade. Trading privileges gained abroad, especially in the East, and markets at home were the essential ingredients for the growth of commerce in the thirteenth century.

In this trade, the important commodities were foodstuffs to feed the larger urban populations, spices and luxury goods to provide the needs of a society whose tastes demanded more than the tainted meats and rough clothing of the early Middle Ages, and cloth—especially wool, which was the staple in the trade from Europe to the Orient. Wines from southwestern France went to England. Wool from England was processed in the Low Countries, but might end up in Acre or Alexandria. Cheese from Sicily appeared on tables in Genoa. Grain from Apulia in southern Italy fed Moslems in Tunis. Spices, like pepper and currants came from the Far East by camel train and ship to season food on lords' tables. Silks, damask, and muslins adorned the homes and persons of the wealthy. The sharp and bitter features of life in the early Middle Ages were softened under the impact of the influx of luxury goods.

In the more important commercial cities, the merchants and those who chiefly profited from trade became the most important element in political life. From the twelfth century onward, they and their families began to gain an increasingly larger share of the political offices and consequently to influence the direction of town policies. They took the lead in working to preserve the independence of the cities from kings and feudal lords and to win greater concessions of privileges from those lords who still controlled some aspects of their political life. In the twelfth century, the north Italian communes, led by Milan, united in the Lombard League to oppose the attempts of Frederick Barbarossa to bring them under imperial control. The towns of the Low Countries fought the Counts of Flanders and later the French kings to remain independent. At times, the burghers made alliances with the monarchy to thwart the designs of local feudal lords against them. The kings found such alliances to their benefit because the towns were more and more an important source of income to the crown. The townsmen were frequently willing to pay for their liberties. No doubt, it was in these conflicts that the leading men of the towns emerged with a distinctive identity. They preserved this distinctive quality as townmen in their whole outlook. Since they were very often involved in trade, they tended to shape the policies of the town to promote commerce by securing privileges, by attempting to crush their competitors, or by regulating the sale of goods in their communes. Thus, in the course of the Middle Ages, a whole body of regulation developed, governing economic life. Along with these laws came an attitude that it was the duty of the commune to promote trade to increase its power and that of its citizens. The basic concepts of mercantilism grew out of the economic regulations of the medieval towns.

The towns had a great power of attraction over the surrounding country. They provided opportunity for those with special skills to improve their position. The shoemaker no longer was restricted to a role as a part-time craftsman but could pursue his occupation through the whole year to his greater profit because he no longer had to spend part of the year tilling his fields. Moreover, the towns also developed industries which gave even those without skill a chance to improve their position. Although, throughout the Middle Ages, most manufacturing was organized as household industry in the countryside around the town, there were some industries, like the dyeing of cloth or the making of glass, which encouraged the greater concentration of labor. Besides the skilled dyers and glass-blowers, there was need for men and boys to perform menial tasks and for carters to haul the goods to market. As industrial centers, the towns had a great need for labor and attempted to attract it by granting advantageous terms to those who would come to settle. If a serf succeeded in spending a year and a day within the confines of the town, he was free of his servile obligations. From this practice arose the old saying: "City air makes a man free."

The towns offered opportunity, but not to all on an equal basis. Those men who came to the town with some wealth or training fared better than the untrained peasants. They might rise eventually to become members of the ruling class, rich merchants and landowners. Their homes were luxurious palaces with great central courts. Decorated with tapestries and paintings and filled with fine furniture, dinnerware and silver, these houses reflected the increasingly sophisticated tastes of the rich. But the less fortunate found themselves crowded into tenements built side by side across narrow streets, where the stench was often overpowering and where filth and disease were prevalent. With the outbreak of the bubonic plague in the mid-fourteenth century—the so-called Black Death—the rich fled to the relative safety of the country while the poor died as they had lived. Disease was a much greater factor limiting the growth of population in the Middle Ages than it has been in the more recent period. The Black Death may well have swept away as many as one-third of the people of Western Europe. Such a disaster had violent effects on the economy. Wage levels were forced upward, but they lagged behind prices. Neglect of fields and trade compounded the problems by creating shortages. Thus, those who had sought their future in the towns did not always find there an easy path to wealth nor even to a modest security.

In the fourteenth century, Western Europe was definitely more urban in character than it had been three hundred years earlier. It had reestablished and strengthened the old ties that had once united the eastern and western Mediterranean in commerce during the Greek and Roman periods. Moreover, it had begun to strike out into new directions. The cities of Northern Europe created a vast trading network from London to Novgorod in the famed Hanseatic League. The merchants of the Hanse dealt in naval stores and furs from Scandinavia and Russia and wool from England and the Low Countries. Fishermen sailed into the Atlantic and the North Sea. In 1282, the Vivaldi brothers sailed from Genoa into the Atlantic never to return, forerunners of that later Genoese who was to land at San Salvador in 1492. All of these activities were signs of the increased vitality of European cities in the later Middle Ages. But they should not cause us to forget the fact that the largest part of the European population was still rural in character. That rural element was, in fact, basic to the continued growth of the European economy.

Beyond the West: Europe in the Age of the Crusades

The dynamism of the age between the eleventh and the thirteenth centuries was evident not merely in the building of the feudal monarchies and the growth of the towns; it also had its effects in turning Europeans toward new ventures in distant lands, the most significant of which was the Crusades.

In 1095, Pope Urban II, exiled from Rome by internal disorders, called a meeting of clergy and lay nobility to meet him at Clermont in southern France. There he summoned them to the noble task of freeing the Holy Land from the domination of the Moslems. His ringing "God Wills It!" launched a movement that was to consume the energies of thousands of Western knights during the following centuries. Urban's purpose was primarily religious, though he was not unaware of the importance of aid to the Byzantine Empire, which had suffered a disastrous loss of Asia Minor as the result of the Battle of Manzikert some years earlier. Nor was he a mere idealistic dreamer. He was not interested in haphazard and disorganized efforts, but in a well-led and directed military campaign. He acted because he believed that the Moslem Turks had become too aggressive and were harassing Christian pilgrims on their trips to visit the scenes of Jesus' life and death.

The nobility who took up the crusade were no doubt motivated by many factors other than religious considerations. Ambition was a primary element in the decision of some, who had little prospect of securing estates in Europe. Adventure drew others. The importance of this motive should not be underestimated in an age when knights were accustomed to creating their adventure in the tournaments during the intermittent recesses of warfare. Greed for booty was no small factor; the knights certainly would not eschew on the crusade a custom so strong as pillaging camps and battlefields after the battle. Yet religion furnished the chief motive for uniting them and turning them in the direction of the East.

The First Crusade was composed of lesser nobility for the most part, although men like Duke Robert of Normandy, son of William the Conqueror, were indeed powerful. But no crowned head joined the movement. Instead, Raymond of Saint-Gilles, Count of Toulouse, and Bishop Adhemar of Puy took the lead in organizing the expedition. Most of the nobles came from France, although there was a Norman-Italian contingent from southern Italy. They traveled by land and sea, meeting at Constantinople, where a conflict over cooperation with the Byzantine Empire threatened the success of the entire mission. It was only the diplomatic ability of Raymond Saint-Gilles that saved it. They crossed the Hellespont into Asia Minor, and with Byzantine aid, scored several major victories that freed this province for the empire. When the combined armies arrived at Antioch, however, the spirit of cooperation had virtually disappeared. The Byzantines and the crusaders went their separate ways. The ill-feeling between Latin and Greek engendered by these encounters did nothing to dispel the mistrust caused by differences in religious rites, language, and culture. The Byzantines looked on the crusaders as land-hungry despoilers of imperial domains; the crusaders carried back to the West tales of harassment. Anti-Byzantine propaganda in the West played an important role in shaping the future of the crusades.

After the Latin conquest of Antioch and the establishment of the first of the crusader states in the East by the Norman-Italian Bohemond, the army moved on to Jerusalem. Divisions within the Moslem ranks prevented them from uniting to prevent the capture of the Holy City in 1098. With this conquest, the crusaders elected Godfrey of Boulogne as king. Although Godfrey refused the title out of deference to the religious significance of Jerusalem, he laid the foundations for the Latin Kingdom of Jerusalem.

The Latin Kingdom transplanted Western feudalism to the East. Despite the need for unity to oppose Moslem attacks, each of the great barons sought first his own interests and security for his own territories. Only a major threat could force them to join together temporarily and then their councils were scenes of serious disputes. The kings were sometimes able, but too weak and dependent on help from Western Europe to do more than prolong a tenuous existence for the kingdom. Added to the disunity caused by feudalism and the weakness of the monarchy was the intense rivalry of Venice, Genoa, and Pisa, each attempting to strengthen its commercial position at the expense of the other in the infant kingdom. The kings had granted them extensive trading privileges in major cities like Acre in return for aid. Finally, each new group of crusaders arriving at the East felt little hesitation about embarking on its independent course without much pretence of cooperation with the ruler of the Latin Kingdom of Jerusalem, or even the great nobility. At the core of these problems was the fact that feudalism was little suited to a military outpost far removed from the West.

The history of the Latin Kingdom of Jerusalem reveals its basic lack of stability. No sooner was the conquest accomplished than Moslem counterattacks threatened to topple it. Only the timely arrival of additional reinforcements from the West in the early twelfth century prevented this disaster. But the presence of the crusaders was again threatened in the 1130's by the increasing power of Zangi, Atabeg of Mosul, and his son and successor, Nur-ed-Din. In 1144, Zangi turned from his effort to conquer the Moslem ruler of Damascus in order to take the crusader state of Edessa, the key to control of northern Syria. The fall of Edessa roused the West and led Pope Eugenius III to issue a call for a new crusade. St. Bernard of Clairvaux, the greatest preacher of the time, traveled through Europe to second the Papal plea.

The Second Crusade was led by Conrad III, King of Germany, and Louis VII, King of France. From the first, there was little coordination of efforts between the forces of the two kings. They decided to travel separately through the Byzantine Empire, rather than follow the sea route recommended by King Roger II of Sicily. The Germans went first and, after serious differences with the Byzantines, met disaster at the hands of the Islamic Turks in Asia Minor. The French fared somewhat better, though not much. They fought the Byzantines, who were still disturbed by the recent German passage. When they arrived in Asia Minor, they gathered up the remnants of Conrad's army and made their way to a port from which they secured transport for Antioch. Unfortunately, a

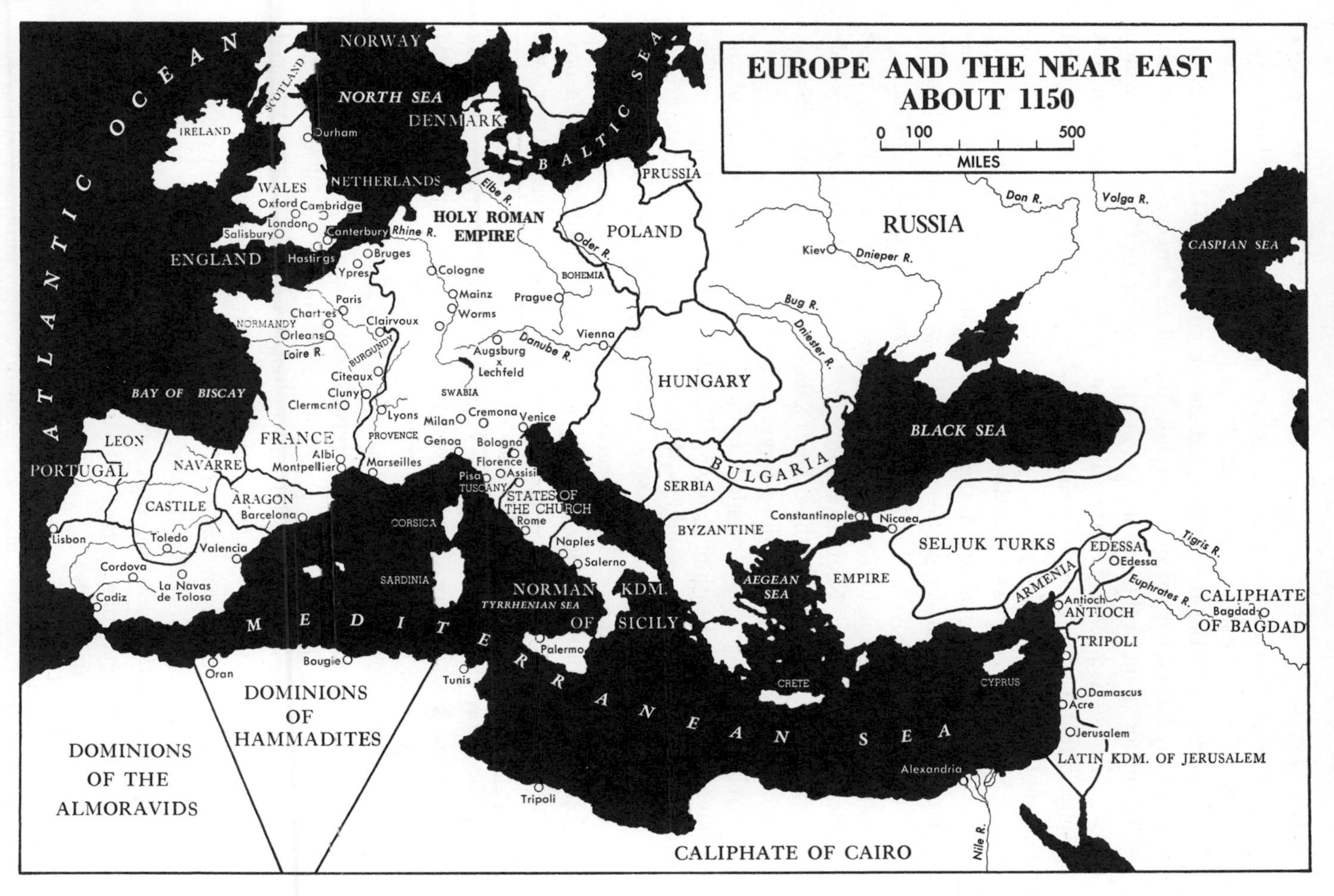
EUROPE AND THE NEAR EAST
ABOUT 1150
0 100 500
MILES
ATLANTIC OCEAN
NORWAY
NORTH SEA
DENMARK
BALTIC SEA
IRELAND
SCOTLAND
Durham
WALES
NETHERLANDS
Oxford
Cambridge
London
Salisbury
Canterbury
Hastings
ENGLAND
Rhine R.
Elbe R.
HOLY ROMAN
EMPIRE
PRUSSIA
POLAND
Oder R.
BOHEMIA
Bruges
Ypres
Cologne
Mainz
Worms
Prague
Paris
Chartres
NORMANDY
Orleans
Loire R.
Clairvoux
BURGUNDY
Citeaux
Cluny
Clermont
Vienna
Danube R.
Augsburg
x
Lechfeld
SWABIA
BAY OF BISCAY
LEON
PORTUGAL
NAVARRE
CASTILE
ARAGON
Barcelona
Lisbon
Toledo
Valencia
Cordova
La Navas
de Tolosa
Cadiz
FRANCE
Albi
Montpellier
Lyons
PROVENCE
Marseilles
Milan
Cremona
Venice
Genoa
Bologna
Florence
Assisi
Pisa
TUSCANY
STATES OF
THE CHURCH
Rome
Naples
Salerno
CORSICA
SARDINIA
NORMAN
KDM.
OF
SICILY
TYRRHENIAN SEA
Palermo
MEDITERRANEAN SEA
Oran
Bougie
Tunis
Tripoli
DOMINIONS
OF
HAMMADITES
DOMINIONS
OF THE
ALMORAVIDS
RUSSIA
Kiev
Dnieper R.
Don R.
Volga R.
CASPIAN SEA
Bug R.
Dniester R.
HUNGARY
BLACK SEA
BULGARIA
SERBIA
BYZANTINE
EMPIRE
Constantinople
Nicaea
AEGEAN
SEA
CRETE
CYPRUS
SELJUK TURKS
ARMENIA
EDESSA
Edessa
Tigris R.
Euphrates R.
Antioch
ANTIOCH
CALIPHATE
OF BAGDAD
Bagdad
TRIPOLI
Damascus
Acre
Jerusalem
LATIN KDM. OF JERUSALEM
Alexandria
Nile R.
CALIPHATE OF CAIRO

shortage of ships forced Louis VII to leave part of his army behind to become Moslem prisoners. Once at Antioch, the crusaders turned their attention not to the formidable and dangerous Nur-ed-Din, but to the relatively harmless ruler of Damascus, himself the enemy of Nur-ed-Din. The major result of their effort was not the conquest of Damascus, which would have had some military value, but the further weakening of that city so that it was unable to resist Nur-ed-Din. Well might Saint Bernard term this crusade an "abyss."

Though the vigorous leadership of King Baldwin III of Jerusalem resulted in some expansion of the crusader state at the expense of the Fatimite dynasty in Egypt, the results were very temporary. Baldwin IV was a leper; moreover, he lacked the ability to unite the various factions into which the kingdom was divided. Islam, on the other hand, came close to unity in the Near East, through the efforts of Nur-ed-Din's able nephew and successor, Salah-ed-Din (Saladin). He not only inherited his uncle's position, but also added Egypt to his domains.

While the crusaders struggled among themselves for control of the kingdom after the death of Baldwin IV, Saladin consolidated his position. When th infamous Reynauld du Chatillon, who had gained control of the great fortresses of Krak des Chevalliers and Montreal, broke the truce with Saladin by raiding Moslem caravans, he sealed the fate of the kingdom in the twelfth century. On July 4, 1187, Saladin defeated the crusader army at Hittin and on October 2, Jerusalem surrendered. Only Tyre survived as an outpost of the crusaders in the Holy Land.

The effort of the Third Crusade to regain the lost territory met only slight success. Frederick Barbarossa led his German army across Asia Minor, only to drown in the River Saleph in Cilicia on June 10, 1190. Richard the Lion-hearted of England and Philip II (Augustus) of France had ostensibly put aside their quarrels in the interest of the crusade, but neither trusted the other. Philip did little fighting; he was ill most of the time he was in the Holy Land and returned to France early. Richard alone, fascinated by the romance of the crusade, continued the war. His conquests opened the approach to Jerusalem, but he found himself unable to attempt a siege of that great city. Instead, he entered into a truce with Saladin, whom he had come to respect, and gained thereby the right for Christians to make pilgrimages to Jerusalem. The Third Crusade was the last of the great crusades to be directed against the Moslems in the Holy Land; in the thirteenth century, the crusaders turned their attention more to the conquest of Egypt and were even diverted from this goal to other and more selfish ends on occasions.

In 1204, the Venetians turned the Fourth Crusade against the Byzantine Empire despite the weak protests of Pope Innocent III. On the pretence that they were supporting the legitimate claimant to the imperial throne, the crusaders took and sacked Constantinople. Their leaders divided the empire with the Venetians. This Latin Empire attempted to impose Latin Christianity on the Greeks, who since 1054 had refused to accept the Westerners in full communion and had rejected the claims of the Papacy to primacy over the whole Church. The unfortunate effort of the Latin Empire of Constantinople to force the Greeks to accept a Latin Patriarch and to follow the lead of the Western Church further alienated the peoples of the East and widened the cleavage in religious matters. Nor did the Fourth Crusade succeed in aiding the cause of the Holy Land even indirectly. Although the possession of Constantinople might have proved of strategic value to the Westerners in their war against the Moslems, there is little evidence to indicate that it became more than an outpost of Venetian commercial expansion.

The later crusading efforts of the thirteenth century were under the direction of two very different figures. Frederick II, the Holy Roman Emperor (1220–1250), was an ardent opponent of Papal policies in Italy. Louis IX of France (1226–1280) was famed for his humility and his religious spirit. Frederick's Crusade (1228–1229) could hardly be given the name. Taken up after many delays—the last had caused Pope Gregory IX to excommunicate him—it resembled more a pilgrimage than a crusade for Frederick took very few troops with him. Moreover, he negotiated with the sultan rather than fighting him to secure the return of Jerusalem to the Latin kingdom. For his unorthodox approach to crusading, Frederick was roundly denounced by his enemies. In point of fact, he had done much to strengthen the faltering cause of the crusade by regaining Jerusalem. By contrast, Louis IX attempted to carry through the strategy of gaining control of the Holy Land through the conquest of Egypt. The plan had much to commend it, including force of historical precedent set by earlier conquerors, but Louis' crusaders were unequal to the task and his effort met disaster. Louis was a persistent crusader. He finally died near Tunis in North Africa, fighting Moslems far removed from the Holy Places because he had been convinced of the importance of gaining a foothold in North Africa by his ambitious brother Charles of Anjou. Charles, who had gained control of the Kingdom of Sicily, did not look at North Africa through the eyes of a crusader; he saw there the key to Mediterranean dominance for his southern kingdom.

With the fall of Acre to the Moslems in 1291, the crusaders were deprived of their last foothold on the Near Eastern mainland and retired to the island of Cyprus and to Rhodes, which came under the control of the Knights of the Hospital, one of the quasi-religious military orders to rise out of the crusading movement. The loss of the mainland put the dream of recovering the lands of the Bible into the limbo of unrealized ambitions. Although later efforts to defeat Turkish expansion in Southeastern Europe and to control Moslem sea power on the Mediterranean were called crusades, the term had a hollow usage. Those efforts were part of European defense; the crusade had disappeared as reality and found existence only in the visions of dreamers after the end of the thirteenth century.

The judgment of historians on the Crusades has often been harsh. Indeed, if one sets their admitted goal alongside their accomplishments, it is hard to see where they succeeded at all. A brief history of Latin dominance along the shores of the Near East was scant accomplishment for the effort expended. Moreover, such episodes as the Fourth Crusade worked to the injury of East-West relations. The animosities created by the crusader conquest of Constantinople in 1204 have remained to plague every effort to increase understanding between Latins and Greeks until the present. Yet, against a broader canvas, the Crusades were an important aspect of the expansion of the Western European horizon. Europe and the East met first in battle and then in commerce. The civilization of the West was richer for that meeting. Europe moved beyond the West to meet the Moslems; perhaps the effort played a more important role in moving Western thinkers out of the traditional patterns of thought they had followed since the early Middle Ages. Nor can it be a coincidence that the great age of European expansion and discovery follows the Crusades by less than a century and without a significant break; the role of the Italians in European expansion owed much to their experience gained in trade and war during the Crusades. When Frankish knights made their way through alien lands at the end of the eleventh century, they little dreamed that they were the precursors of Cortez and Pizarro. Yet they were.

9 Intellect and Art in the Middle Ages

From the decline of Roman civilization to the dawn of the modern age, Europe was involved in the building of a new culture. The components of that culture were Roman, Christian, barbarian, Islamic, Greek, and Byzantine—to name only the more important. But these varied elements combined in the unity of medieval culture to form one of the most important stages in the development of Western thought.

Because the medieval intellect represented a stage in European intellectual development, it must be viewed as part of the whole pattern of that growth and not as an isolated phenomenon. The importance of medieval thought to the West lies in its direct relationship to the rise of new ideas and institutions that would play a major role in shaping the thinking of modern men. In the pages that follow, we shall attempt to point up some areas in which that influence has been greatest, while providing an understanding of the nature of medieval culture itself. Certainly no age in the history of mankind has been unimportant, but certain periods do have a special importance in light of their contribution to some future age or trend. The Middle Ages witnessed the birth of a distinctly European culture.

Ideas and Institutions

Between the eleventh and the fourteenth centuries the Middle Ages witnessed the making of scholasticism, the revival of Roman law, and the founding of the universities. Scholasticism, the method of the schoolmen, was the first systematized approach to knowledge since the age of Aristotle, to whom it owed so much for its logical framework. The revival of Roman law was much more than a rediscovery of the *Corpus Juris Civilis* (Body of Civil Law) of Justinian; the commentators of the eleventh and twelfth centuries—called glossators—breathed new life into the Roman legal principles while applying them to current problems. The founding of the universities provided European civilization with an adaptable institution uniquely suited to preserving and enlarging the bounds of traditional wisdom.

The early Middle Ages had lived under the long shadow cast by the authority of antiquity. The men of that period had, for the most part, sought truth among the works of those whose learning they respected. As late as the twelfth century, Bernard of Chartres challenged his contemporaries to see that their accomplishments were made possible by the fact that they were "pygmies standing on the shoulders of giants." This attitude represented the conviction of most thinkers that they could do no better than to rely on the great writers of antiquity and the Fathers of the Church. It is not surprising that this tradition produced largely encyclopedias, compendia, and commentaries.

Although the figure of John Scotus Erigena looms over the Carolingians who were his contemporaries, it is not to him that we look to find some traces of a rejection of the sterile traditions of that age. The first author to exhibit not merely independence of thought but also concern about how one could be certain of the truths he had discovered was Anselm, Archbishop of Canterbury (1033–1109). His watchwords were "fides quaerens intellectum," faith seeking understanding, which meant not only that learning could confirm doctrine, but more that the mind has an obligation to seek to understand better even the mysteries of faith. It was this latter spirit that informed Anselm's own investigations of the mystery of the Incarnation, according to which God became man in the person of Jesus, in his *Cur Deus Homo?* (Why God became man.)

If any individual could claim the title of founder of Scholasticism, it would be Peter Abelard (1079–1142), the brilliant but erratic and vain master of logic, whose teaching in Paris on the Monte Ste. Geneviève brought him fame. Abelard was a cleric in minor orders, but not a priest. His forte was dialectic, or argumentation based on logic, rather than theology. In the *Sic et Non* (Yes and No), he set forth opposing views of the Fathers and other non-Biblical authorities and attempted to resolve their differences by logic. Abelard recognized that it was not always possible to resolve differences and continued to rely on the greater authority of one writer over another as a determinant in these cases. He was far from being a rebel in his thought, though some of his views were called heretical by Bernard of Clairvaux. His method, in part, had been developed by lawyers to resolve problems in the presentation of evidence. His great originality lay in pointing the direction for future thinkers through his applications of the method to theological questions.

Abelard's student, Peter Lombard (d., 1160) composed the famous *Four Books of Opinions* (*Libri Sententiae IV*). The great advantage of his work was that it systematized the teaching of medieval theology. The contribution of the Lombard moved theological learning further from the positive theology of the early Middle Ages, which had emphasized the authority of the Church Fathers, in the direction of a logical science, which might be understood more clearly as a result of reason. It also favored the ordering of theological study into a reasoned pattern of development, an approach that found its fullest expression in the *Summa Theologica* of Thomas Aquinas (1225?–1274?).

Thomas was born in southern Italy and studied at Frederick II's University of Naples. He was a member of the Dominican Order and a student of the famed Dominican scholar, Albertus Magnus of Cologne, the foremost student of Aristotelian philosophy of the day. The intense intellectual climate of the twelfth century, which had spawned Abelard, had also led to a revival of Aristotelian studies and the rediscovery of the unknown treatises of Aristotle on logic. In the thirteenth century, a number of Aristotle's scientific writings had become available through translations from the Arabic. Albert and Thomas both profited from these writings in their own work.

Aquinas attempted, through his study of Aristotle, to steer a course through the Scylla and Charybdis of medieval philosophy: nominalism and realism. The advocates of realism maintained that the only true reality existed in universal concepts, a view taught by Plato in his *Republic*. The nominalists asserted that universals were merely "names," that only individuals existed. Thomas followed Aristotle in rejecting the Platonic statement of realism and presenting the view that each individual being has an essence or determining factor that makes it distinctive from other kinds of beings and defines what it is. It also has existence in common with all other beings. Aquinas defined God as a being whose essence is "to Be," that is, His essence puts no limitations on His existence. A man is a rational animal; his ability to reason distinguishes him from other animals. The essence, rational animal, belongs to a particular kind of being. In this way, Aquinas attempted to preserve the concept of universals, while maintaining the existence of individual beings.

In his debates with the Averroists—like Siger of Brabant—who had been influenced by the great Arab philosopher's teaching that there were two truths, one in philosophy and another in theology, Thomas argued for the unity of all knowledge. In his view, reason could ultimately surmount the problems arising from seeming contradictions between matters of faith and the discoveries of the philosophers. He himself endeavored to show that Aristotle was incorrect in trying to prove that the universe had existed from all eternity and that, therefore, there was no real contradiction between the philosophical view of the origin of the universe and the Christian concept of Creation.

His *Summa Theologica* opened with a discussion of theology as a science and discussed, in question form, the whole range of natural and revealed religion. Each question was aimed at a particular point: "Whether or not God Exists?" Thomas quoted authorities on each side of the question in the fashion of Abelard, but spent the body of the question in stating a rational argument to prove his point. His method was based on the logic of Aristotle, and he often invoked the authority of the Philosopher, as he called him, in the course of his argument, but he relied chiefly on the gradual formation of his viewpoint in the mind of his reader through the cumulative effect of his evidence and argument. The greatness of the *Summa Theologica* rests not so much on its solution of individual questions as on its presentation of a vast synthesis of medieval thought in the field of theology, one that is at the same time largely consistent and all-encompassing.

Along with the development of Scholasticism went a more professional and disciplined attitude toward learning. Thomas himself employed William of Marboecke as a translator to ensure the quality of his Aristotelian studies. Roger Bacon (1214?–1294), generally viewed as a figure well in advance of his age, stated well the motivation of a scholar like Thomas in doing this by insisting that only translations made by experts in the various fields could have any real value. The empirical attitude usually associated with Roger Bacon may also be found, though to a lesser degree, in Thomas Aquinas.

The vigorous development of Scholasticism did not mean that there was anything like unanimity of thought in the Middle Ages, even on major questions. In the later thirteenth century, Duns Scotus attacked

Aquinas' attempts to prove the existence of God by reason and maintained the essential mystery of the central articles of faith. The followers of William of Ockham (?–1349?) in the fourteenth century denied the possibility of finding absolute proofs in philosophy or theology. The Church was generally more tolerant to these differences than has been suspected, and charges of heresy were more often the result of accusations made by opposing scholars than of the independent investigations of the inquisition.

The decline of Scholasticism in the fourteenth and fifteenth centuries, as theologians and philosophers lost the vision of the synthesis and turned more to disputation for its own sake, should not obscure the deep impact that Scholasticism as a method had already had in giving European thought a systematic framework within which to work.

The revival of Roman law in the eleventh and twelfth centuries reveals yet another aspect of medieval thought. For, although the tradition of Roman law had persisted in some parts of Europe, and especially Italy, throughout the Middle Ages, knowledge of Justinian's codification in the sixth century was scant. Most Roman law was based on the Theodosian Code made in the fourth century or on the Roman legal traditions which had remained strong in some areas. Yet the rediscovery of Justinian's Code did not turn the medieval jurists into antiquarians; the major interest of the glossators was in the application of the law to their own day. In pursuing these efforts, men from Irnerius (ca. 1100) on, made Justinian's Code once more living law; Roman ideas about property, sovereignty, marriage, and inheritance influenced current practices. From Italy, knowledge of the law spread into France and even Germany by the end of the Middle Ages. Important centers for legal study sprang up first in Bologna and Pavia, and later at Montpellier in southern France. Study of the Roman law was also introduced at Oxford and Cambridge, though royal patronage of the English common law prevented the acceptance of Roman law in the courts. The law had a major influence on the development of political theory on the continent, especially since it put in the hands of kings the Roman concept of centralized authority and the Roman view that the monarch is supreme and has no limit on his power.

Perhaps the greatest influence of the Middle Ages on subsequent history is to be found in the institutions which it created for itself and which have survived. In political and social life, the debt to the Middle Ages is immediately apparent if we study the origins of modern representative government or the organization of the family. In education, our most characteristic institution, the university, originated during the late twelfth and early thirteenth centuries. One of the most noteworthy marks of medieval institutions is their ability to survive and adapt; the university has shown more than ordinary capability to do both. It is difficult to imagine the relationship between the twentieth century "multiversity" and the schools of the Middle Ages, but study soon reveals that the latter had much in common with the complex educational institutions of this period. The medieval university was flexible; since it was composed of various schools or faculties—law, medicine, theology, and the arts were the usual—it was always possible to add new faculties. Since the university had come into existence to meet the educational needs of the early thirteenth century, a period of great specialization and interest in practical sciences, it did not oppose the presence of practical schools within its community. Since it was generally in conflict with authority to preserve its privileges, it did not become as closely identified with Church or government as it might and more easily escaped their influence in the modern period; indeed, its intellectual independence is as much medieval as modern.

The creation of the first universities was the work of students and scholars rather than kings or Popes. Need rather than desire dictated the where and when of their founding. The school of glossators at Bologna who followed in the wake of Irnerius gathered students interested in law. When the students came into conflict with the city of Bologna, they sought the

Paris, the Seine River, and Notre Dame. In this area, the University of Paris had its beginnings in the twelfth century. (*Author*)

support of the emperor and received a charter of privileges. This document was the beginning of the university. At Paris, scholars had long gathered on the left bank of the Seine and on the Monte Sainte Geneviève to conduct lessons. The attempt of the chancellor of the Paris diocese to assert his control led them to seek aid from the Pope. Innocent III granted them the privilege of forming a separate corporation of masters —or university—near the end of the twelfth century. Other universities were founded as the result of migrations of students or masters to other and more attractive centers. Oxford, which had long possessed a grammar school received a group of Paris scholars; later, Oxford itself furnished the nucleus of students and masters at Cambridge. The Emperor Frederick II founded the University of Naples in 1224 to train administrators and lawyers for the royal service in the Kingdom of Sicily. Between the thirteenth and sixteenth centuries, universities came into existence at Louvain in the Low Countries, Salamanca in Spain, Prague in Bohemia, Wittenberg in Germany, and numerous other centers.

Although clerics predominated at the medieval universities, the training was not merely an education for the service of the Church. Many of these clerics took no more than minor orders and were, therefore, not members of the priesthood. Some entered the service of the Church as secretaries, lawyers, or theologians, but many served kings or great feudal aristocrats in similar capacities. The growing towns sought and obtained the services of men trained in the universities to staff their chancelleries and to represent them at royal and feudal courts. University education opened the doors to many different opportunities.

Student life was hard, although there were also pleasurable pastimes. After the thirteenth century, colleges established by wealthy donors to provide lodging and board for deserving students were more common, but during the early period most students lived wherever their means permitted. The universities possessed no buildings and classes were held in rented quarters. The lecturer carefully read the text under discussion and commented on it, while the students took careful notes on wax tablets, later transcribing the corrected work to parchment. Libraries were small; books were expensive. Students worked under very difficult conditions of damp and cold. Yet there were lighter moments. Taverns abounded and both students and masters sought their firesides as often as they could. At times, fights broke out between town and gown, sometimes leading to serious riots. Then the students might threaten to secede from the town and find a more hospitable place. Usually, the differences were settled.

Matriculation and examinations were essentially the same, so that it was possible to spend a few years in one university and then pass to one or two others before submitting to an examination for a degree. Many students, although not the majority, appear to have yielded to the temptation to adopt this wandering life as their own. It is due to their efforts that we have some of the finest student songs and poems of the Middle Ages, the verse of the Goliards, the wandering scholars. Wine, women, and song were their themes; education their avocation.

The medieval university more closely resembled the modern graduate or professional school than the college of liberal arts. In fact, the teaching of the arts within the university generally came after the establishment of schools of law, medicine, or theology. Perhaps this fact explains why the institution has survived so long. The different interests of the various faculties enabled the university to change by including those with new interests and specialties without the need for the individual faculties to make a major adjustment. Thus the almost innate conservatism of existing curricula merely slowed and did not halt the process of change.

The contribution of the Middle Ages by its development of the scholastic method, its revival of legal learning, and its founding of the universities ranks with the greatest in the history of human development. Although medieval intellectuals were sometimes obscurantists, although their methods never led them to trust experience and observation to the extent that moderns have found valuable and necessary in learning about this universe, the balance sheet must indicate that they were truly creative innovators.

Literature, Art, and Architecture

In a society in which religion and the Church played such a leading role, one expects to find that literature and the arts reflected this dominance. Certainly our experience with Egyptian civilization has borne this out. In medieval society, the strength of the clergy as the literate class of the early Middle Ages goes far to account for the small amount of nonreligious writing from that period. After the rise of towns, however, one would expect to find more secular literature; although the amount does increase somewhat, it is still rather small before the early fourteenth century. The simple fact is that the literate layman of the high Middle Ages did not compose literature and was still pretty much content with the traditional fare provided by clerics and traveling minstrels. He was more likely involved in business or served at the court of a lay or ecclesiastical lord. He was more common in Italy than in Northern Europe, and it is there that we witness the bulk of his literary output, in the letters written in his official capacity and in town chronicles. There is also some poetry from southern France and Italy. The total is by no means impressive, especially when compared with the output of the clergy.

The major language of medieval literature was Latin, not the language of Cicero and Vergil, but the Latin of the Church, which had its origins in the Latin speech of the Roman masses. The continual study of Latin grammar in the Middle Ages did produce a few outstanding stylists like John of Salisbury in the twelfth century, but most writers adopted a utilitarian view toward the learning of the language and made little conscious effort to improve their writing. There was, in fact, a rather strong anti-intellectual strain running through that society and influenced by a Christian renunciation of learning that frowned on such things.

The vernacular languages, both Romance and Germanic, possessed some literature of their own. Romance tongues, descendants of the vulgar Latin of the classical period but much corrupted by the process of barbarization, developed in the area where Roman influence had been greatest—in France, Italy, Spain, and Portugal, although Roumanian provides an example of a Romance language in Southeastern Europe. The Germanic languages flourished to the North, in Germany, the Low Countries, Scandinavia, and those regions where Germanic influence made inroads into the Romance regions, especially along the Rhine-Danube frontier. In the Middle Ages, the literatures in these tongues can be divided into the traditional epic and saga of the early folk and poetry and tales composed during the Middle Ages itself.

Latin literature was largely in the service of the Church. Indeed, the mass of it is of little interest to the modern reader because of its narrow ecclesiastical bent and its poor quality. Yet some works possess the character of great literature. Especially is this true of the poetry. Prose literature was generally didactic: sermons, theological treatises, commentaries on sacred scripture and the writings of the Fathers of the Church, chronicles and annals, and educational manuals.

Much of the finest poetry produced during the Middle Ages found its way into the ceremonials of the Church. The beautiful *Dies Irae*, composed by Thomas of Celano in the thirteenth century, became the sequence of the mass for the dead. Drawing its theme from the Last Judgment and inspiration from both Old Testament and classical sources, it presented the Christian with an image of the peace to be found by the soul in the presence of God. The figure of God the Judge finds its counterpart in the "Pious Jesus Lord," whom the soul implores for rest. Thomas Aquinas composed the *Panis Angelicus* in honor of the sacrament of the Eucharist, commemorating the Last Supper. In simple language, disciplined by the mind of the trained theologian, the poem states not merely the theology but also the imagery of the sacrament. Jacapone da Todi's *Stabat Mater,* also incorporated into the liturgy, paints a vivid word picture of the last scenes of Jesus' passion. The sorrowful mother was standing tearful near the cross, while her son was hanging there.

Stabat Mater Dolorosa
  Iuxta crucem lacrimosa
Dum pendebat filius.

In prose literature, the sermons of St. Bernard of Clairvaux, the great Cistercian preacher of the twelfth century were marked by intense depth of feeling. Perhaps Pope Innocent III's *De Miseria Humanae Conditionis* illustrates best the tone of much devotional literature. Written prior to his accession to the Papacy, it gives the appearance of a scholastic exercise. Most of it has been culled from previous authors, yet here and there the person of the author intrudes. Although it paints man in all his frailties, Innocent maintains that he might as easily have written a work that would have dwelt on man's virtues and strengths. Perhaps, it is revealing that he chose instead to think of man on the lower plain, a creature essentially vile. Ecclesiastical writing was usually heavily laden with Biblical quotations and salted with the words of the Fathers. It offered little that was original, save in the treatises on theological questions developed within the schools.

Medieval chronicles and annals are of many varieties and values. A monk at Ursberg composed a much-used annal of no literary value in the thirteenth century that is typical of most, with its short statements about major events and its lack of any attempt to judge the relative importance of materials. The coronation of an emperor and a local drought receive similar treatment. On the other hand, the chronicles of Matthew Paris and Roger of Wendover attempt a view of universal history and are especially valuable for their own times. The careful, if somewhat pedestrian, Richard of San Germano, a layman learned in law, wrote his chronicle of events in southern Italy during the reign of Frederick II with considerable effort to present original materials. The results are not the most readable history, but they are fairly reliable. On the other hand, the gossipy Franciscan friar from Parma, Salimbene de Adam, picked up tales both true and fantastic to incorporate in his chronicle. Here and there, one finds evidence of the development of a critical spirit.

Modern scholars studying the Middle Ages have singled out the twelfth century as a period of renaissance. They point to the great interest in classical studies at the Cathedral school of Chartres, about seventy miles southwest of Paris. There, Bernard of Chartres inculcated in his young pupils a deep appreciation for the style of the ancients, not sparing the rod when he found a laggard. His method was based on memorization of selected passages, drill in grammar, and imitation of styles. His great student John of Salisbury paid tribute to the results of the system in his own works.

John of Salisbury was the greatest prose author of the twelfth century. His *Metalogicon* is more than a recounting of his education or even the educational problems of his day. It is more than a treatise on the logic of Aristotle. Yet it is all of these. John attacks the educational faddists of his time, the Cornificians as he calls them after an infamous critic of Vergil, for their desire to short cut their way to learning. He holds up to them the model of his own education at Chartres under Bernard, at Paris under Abelard, and elsewhere under some of the great masters of the day. In the *Policraticus,* John reveals himself as an able political thinker, a major source for the understanding of the nature of medieval society. In the *Historia Pontificalis,* his work stands above that of his contemporaries for his breadth of understanding and for his care in presenting detail. His great ability combined with his sense of style raised him to the pinnacle of medieval prose authors.

The twelfth century also produced Hugh of St. Victor, whose educational manual, the *Didascalicon Eruditia,* was one of the most influential of the age. Hugh was not a humanist, at least not in the sense that John of Salisbury was, but he had a deep concern about the organization of education. He attempted to present his readers with an orderly approach to the various branches of learning. His advice was sound. But the work was not really original; Hugh was content with drawing on the best sources available to him.

No discussion of the twelfth century should fail to mention the anti-intellectualism of men like Abbot Peter of Celle. For Peter, there was only one school, that in which the soul learned the way of the true Christian. He had little use for books and masters and praised, instead, that school in which Christ teaches the hearts of men. This same strain may be found in St. Bernard of Clairvaux and other medieval mystics. It characterized those, who, impatient with learning, sought the purpose of man's existence in direct communion with God. In the thirteenth century, the Franciscan theologians, Duns Scotus and Bonaventure, were the major proponents of this view. In his *Mind's Road to God* (*Itinerarium Mentis ad Deum*), Bonaventure set down basic rules for mysticism.

Not all Latin literature was serious. The poetry of the Goliards, the wandering scholars of the universities, was often a parody on religious verse. The light blasphemies of these poems, which invoke the Trinity in jest, are not serious questioning of the Church's authority as much as expressions of youthful rebellion. Nor do the celebration of the charms of women, wine, and song necessarily indicate that these pursuits were major occupations. Perhaps, after much study, the desire to drink oneself to death in a tavern comes naturally. Certainly the scholar who expressed that wish also desired the angels to ask God to grant him "grace and absolution." The lighthearted humor of the students reveals to us much about the human qualities of the men of the Middle Ages we would not otherwise know.

At no time during the Middle Ages can we say that vernacular literature was nonexistent. In fact, the types of literature found in the common tongues go far to prove that the vernacular enjoyed as widespread a popularity as any work composed in Latin. This writing sprang from the popular imagination and drew its inspiration from those currents which had their deepest roots in the popular mind.

The *chanson de geste* of the twelfth and thirteenth centuries was heir to an epic tradition, which had its origins in a nonliterary past. The Scandinavian saga literature, incorporating the deeds of mighty heroes, and epics like the Anglo-Saxon *Beowulf* belong to this genre. But the chanson had developed within the framework of feudal society and therefore incorporated the ideals of that society to a large extent. Its hero was the Christian knight, represented in a Roland or Charlemagne, rather than the barely Christian Beowulf, whose baptism was due to the work of a monastic editor. The *Song of Roland* stirred in its hearers the romance of the crusade and excited admiration for a folk-hero, whose classical prototype can be found in Hercules. In the *Parzival,* Wolfram von Eschenbach drew on the medieval legend of the knightly quest for the Holy Grail—the chalice used by Jesus at the Last Supper—in recounting the qualities of pure chivalry found in the perfect knight. The *Niebelungenlied,* the song of the Niebelungs, recreated the world of Attila the Hun and

Theodoric the Ostrogoth, but made these barbarians heroric figures. These romances depicted a world of men, in which the civilizing influence of woman was not felt very strongly.

Lyric poetry grew and flourished in the twelfth century in the south of France until the Albigensian Crusade of Innocent III cut it at the root. The poet-duke, William IX of Aquitaine, was the best known of those nobles who patronized and participated in the art of the troubadours. The Provençal lyric, named for the region in which it flourished, developed from several sources. Count William of Poitiers, the first of the troubadours, must have been acquainted with the Latin poetry of Fortunatus and with Ovid's *Art of Love,* for his work reveals influence from both. The proximity of Arab Spain, with its own poetic tradition, was also important. Moreover, there is an apparent debt to the religious Latin poetry of the Middle Ages. The theme of most of the poems is unrequited love. The poet loves one whom he cannot possess because she is already married or is above him in station. Therefore, he worships from afar. Love rests in the heart and finds its expression more in words and sighs than in bodily union. This poetry was partly inspired by and also gave additional impetus to the cult of the Virgin Mary, the Mother of Jesus. In its exaltation of the position of womanhood, it contributed a notable element to medieval life.

With the destruction of Provençal culture by the Albigensian Crusade, the troubadours were scattered. Some found refuge in southern Italy at the Court of Frederick II, who may himself have composed lyric verse. In time, a Sicilian style developed and obtained an audience in northern Italy through the poetry of the pathetic figure, King Enzio, Frederick II's son, who whiled away his time in a Bolognese prison writing poems. The influence of the troubadours also spread into Germany, where it gave rise to the Minnesingers, the poets of love. Walther von der Vogelweide, who deserves a place among the greatest poets, did not, however, confine his themes to love. He was deeply concerned with the political and social issues of his day. His cry for brotherhood and understanding marks him as one of the greatest figures in the long quest for freedom:

> Who fears not, God, Thy gifts to take,
> And then Thy ten commandments break,
> Lacks that true love which should be his Salvation.
> For many call Thee father, who
> Will not own me as brother too:
> They speak deep words from shallow meditation.
> Mankind arises from one origin;
> We are alike both outward and within;

Our mouths are sated with the selfsame fare.
And when their bones into confusion fall,
Say ye, who knew the living man by sight,
Which is the villain now and which the knight,
That worms have gnawed their carcasses so bare?
Christians, Jews, and heathens serve Him all,
And God has all creation in His care.[1]

There is a continuous line of development from the troubadours of Provence to the figure of Dante Alighieri, last poet of the Middle Ages and morning bird of the Renaissance. In this development, medieval literature reveals the trend away from a society in which the clergy formed the only literate group and the feudal aristocracy almost the only lay audience. With the development of a more urban society, tastes changed. The feudal epic gave way to the lyric, the monastic chronicle had to make way for the annals and chronicles of the towns. In content, the tone of the new literature was more secular, pointing to the greater concern of this age with this world than that to come. The Augustinian conception of society as a "kingdom of God" no longer attracted most thinkers and writers of the fourteenth century.

The art of the Middle Ages had its roots in classical antiquity. Early Christian Churches were formerly Roman temples and the favored architecture in the late imperial period was the so-called basilican style, characterized by its arched roof and double colonnade with clerestory. From the basilica, the early medieval architects developed the Romanesque, which remained dominant in Southern Europe throughout the Middle Ages, but gave way to the Gothic in the North. The thick walls of Romanesque churches, needed to support the weight of their great roofs, made it difficult to provide sufficient windows for adequate lighting. The total impression of the Romanesque architecture is one of dignity and stateliness, with major emphasis on the heavy side. The early twelfth century saw builders in Northern Europe begin to utilize the pointed arch and exterior buttressing to create buildings that were higher and lighter than the Romanesque. The delicate balance between thrust from the roof and buttressing permitted a widespread use of windows. Indeed, at Chartres and the Sainte Chapelle, windows cover most of the wall space with tremendous effect, for the artists in stained glass had an opportunity to display their work to its greatest benefit. The glass of Chartres has excited the artistic admiration of men in every age.

To contrast Gothic and Romanesque styles, however, is puerile. Each has a beauty and value all its own. The strength of Romanesque accords

[1] From *I Saw the World,* trans., I. G. Colvin (London: Edward Arnold, 1938).

with the long-enduring Roman traditions of the South and rises as a symbol of stability against the bright countryside of Italy. The gray mass of Gothic floats above the green fields of the North, lifting the eyes upward to blue cloud-massed skies. From a structural point of view, the Gothic provided greater scope to artists to decorate its exterior, while the Romanesque offered the greatest challenge to the artists in its interior. In the Gothic, the focal point was usually the great main entrance with its scenes from the Last Judgment or other Biblical themes. The interior was more simple, with emphasis on the vari-colored glass. In the Romanesque, the exteriors were usually more plain, the lines more sharp, but the interiors were lavishly covered with paintings and mosaics.

Sculpture and painting of a religious nature predominated in the Middle Ages. The rise of Gothic encouraged the use of statuary in conjunction with the structure itself, while the Romanesque favored the free-standing techniques of antiquity. However, no firm line can be drawn between

Interior of an ancient basilica, Vatican. This plan reveals the basic features incorporated in the Romanesque style. (*The Bettmann Archive*)

Detail of the flying buttresses, St. Étienne of Bourges. These supports counter the outward thrust of the roof, enabling the builders to raise it to great heights without thick walls. (*Author*)

them in this matter. There was a considerable amount of free-standing sculpture, especially in wood, done in the North in the twelfth and thirteenth centuries. Most popular were figures of the Madonna and Child, the Virgin Mary alone, and the saints. Painting had existed in classical antiquity, but the loss of the art meant that its revival followed the lines laid down by sculpture and mosaic during the twelfth and thirteenth centuries. During the thirteenth century, the influence of Byzantine and Gothic models was most important. There was a lack of perspective in the figures portrayed and little attention was given to natural groupings of individuals in the composition. It was not until the time of Giotto, who died in 1336, that the first advances were made in securing a three-dimensional effect in painting. Despite these technical problems, however, the later Middle Ages saw the foundation for the blossoming of art in the Renaissance.

Historians seeking the meaning of medieval literature and art have often spent much time in discussing the relationships between this period and antiquity as well as its connections with the Renaissance. The results of these discussions have been very fruitful to a better understanding of the Middle Ages by revealing that this era was not a gap or hyphen between two great ages in the history of human culture, but rather was an age that played an important role by preserving and transforming its ancient heritage and by providing the foundation for the creative age that followed. But it has not been sufficiently stressed that the processes whereby the men of the Middle Ages worked to accomplish these ends were not automatic or determined. Their efforts were creative in the fullest sense of the word. They did not merely transmit what they had received from the past to the future; they created a new synthesis, uniquely their own, that deserves to be understood because of its important role in the shaping of Western civilization.

The Triumph of the Church

Wherever one turns in his investigation of the Middle Ages he finds the Church. It is not alone that the monks were the literate class nor that the vast majority of Western Europeans belonged to the Church. These facts were evident to all and accepted by all. But the Church was more than the communion of the faithful; it was an integral part of the structure of society, taking its place alongside or even above the developing feudal monarchies and the empire. Above all, the Church came to mean the Papacy and the hierarchy, the visible signs of the internal control which the Church attempted to exercise in the affairs of men. In a very important sense, the medieval Church was a government and, in the course of time, had developed to a high degree the machinery of government. But the process of creating the medieval Church of the thirteenth century, with its strong Papacy and mighty administrative machinery, had its roots far earlier in the Middle Ages.

The brilliance of the Papacy in the fifth and sixth centuries under leadership furnished by men like Leo the Great and Gregory I the Great had not lasted. More and more the papal office fell under the control of the ambitious and unruly members of the Roman nobility, families like the Orsini and the Colonna, who attempted to secure the office for members of their own clan. The protection of the Carolingian monarchy had, it is true, rescued the Popes from these chaotic conditions for a time, but the very strength of the Carolingians precluded the development of strong Popes. After the collapse of the Carolingian power in Italy, the Popes once more found themselves pawns in local political strife. In the tenth century, the force of feudal disintegration seemed about to sweep away the very office itself, as it was making significant inroads into the organization of the Church on the local level by securing control of bishoprics and abbacies. Popes of this period turned to the only source of authority available, the rising German monarchy, represented by the able and resolute Otto I.

The alliance of the Church and the German monarchy was based on a common interest. The Church was simply too weak to resist the encroachments of the local nobility by itself. The monarchy needed a loyal and well-trained corps of leaders to serve it. Under Otto and his successors, the practice of utilizing bishops in the administration of the government grew apace. They were the king's men, chosen by him for the qualities that he needed, often without reference to their spiritual preparation or clerical vocation. Under the Saxon emperors, however, the Papacy itself was hardly in a position to protest.

Despite the interference of German emperors directly in Italian affairs and their support of the Popes on numerous occasions, the position of these bishops in Rome was tenuous to say the least. The Emperor Henry III was certainly the most aggressive of the German rulers in his attempt to aid the Papacy and support the cause of Church reform. He interfered directly in the selection of Popes, bringing to the papal chair men who were devoted to the reform movement.

Within the Church itself, concern over the growing control of ecclesiastical offices by laymen, over the laxity of the clergy in the observance of celibacy, and over the open buying and selling of Church offices had brought together a nucleus of churchmen like St. Peter Damian to work and preach against these evils. One of the major focal points of the reform movement was to be found in the Cluniac monasteries, which had spread through France, Germany, and Italy in the tenth and eleventh centuries. The Cluniacs, drawing their name from the French monastery of Cluny, had a tradition of freedom from lay control. Cluny itself, founded in 911, was under the direct lordship of the Pope. Its daughter houses jealously guarded their position to prevent any authority over their affairs save that of the Pope himself. Naturally, the spread of the Cluniac houses and the rise of monks trained within the order to positions of influence in the Church brought this conviction into the leading circles of the Church. The Cluniacs thus spearheaded the movement for reform in the eleventh century. They furnished much of the personnel from which Henry III's Popes drew their supporters.

Ironically, Henry's support of the Papacy so strengthened it that the

Popes could turn their attention to the problems of the relations between the bishops and the crown in Germany. When Henry died, his son, Henry IV, was too young to assume the throne and his mother acted as regent. The nobles took advantage of the situation to advance their own position. Therefore, when Henry IV reached his majority, he was faced with a considerable task of rebuilding the royal power. His major support was the German episcopacy. But the renewed Papacy under the vigorous leadership of the determined and reform-minded Gregory VII (1073–1085) was anxious to bring an end to the practice whereby the German kings invested the bishops with the signs of the spiritual office and controlled them from the moment of their selection on. In 1075, Gregory stated his position in the *Dictatus Papae* that only the Pope had the power to appoint and depose bishops. The challenge to the German monarchy was too great to be ignored. The investiture struggle, so-named from the custom of placing mitre and sceptre in the bishop's hands, destroyed the co-operation which had become almost traditional under previous emperors and Popes.

The conflict between emperor and Pope opened up many questions. Within Germany, it invited the rebellious nobility to ally with the Papacy against a too-strong monarchy. On the personal level, it summoned forth the strongest passions of two great-willed leaders. On the theoretical level, it called into question the traditional conceptions of relations between temporal and spiritual powers and led to serious political polemic. Breaking through the bonds of words, it was fought out on the field of battle. Gregory himself betrayed the depth of commitment that was his by his unyielding adherence to his original demands. Henry IV, forced to vacillate for fear of rebellion, nevertheless stood as strongly for his right to appoint the German bishops. Only the departure of these two antagonists from the scene laid the foundations for a compromise settlement.

The Concordat of Worms concluded in 1122 between Henry V and Pope Calixtus II was more of a victory for the German bishops than for either the monarchy or the Papacy. The German emperor surrendered on the question of investing the bishops with the signs of their spiritual authority, while the Popes granted the royal representatives the right to be present during the election of the bishop by the cathedral chapter. Since the influence of the king over the choice of the bishop remained, the Papacy had gained little. But the monarchy had been forced to compromise. Moreover, the long internal struggle had weakened it. The bishops gained the most because they now were in a position to seek the protection of the Papacy against the king, knowing that papal power was a considerable factor in any contest.

The investiture struggle must not distract us from the changes taking place in the organization of the Church and in its discipline. The Cluniac attack on simony and the failure of the clergy to observe chastity resulted in increased attention of bishops and Pope to clerical life. In order to carry out these tasks, additional machinery was needed. During the twelfth century, the system and jurisdiction of clerical courts was expanded. The systematization of appeals to the Pope made necessary reforms in the structure of the Roman Curia, the ruling body of the Church. Gregory VII and his successors drew heavily on the experience of contemporary monarchs in improving the operation of papal government.

The election of Lothar di Segni as Pope Innocent III in 1198 brought to the papal throne a youthful and vigorous exponent of the new concepts of ecclesiastical administration. A product of the reform movement, Innocent paid tremendous attention to all of the details of his office. His relations with the monarchs of his day pointed up his conception of the papal office. He forced Philip Augustus of France to restore the wife he had put away to her rightful position. He openly supported Otto of Brunswick against Philip of Swabia for the imperial crown following the death of Henry VI. But, when Otto showed signs of asserting his independence of the papal tutelage, he summoned the youthful Hohenstaufen Frederick II from the Kingdom of Sicily to take the imperial crown. When John of England refused to accept the chapter's choice as Archbishop of Canterbury, Innocent rescinded the matter to Rome and chose the Roman Cardinal, Stephen Langton, as Archbishop. When John refused to allow Stephen to enter England, Innocent excommunicated and deposed him, and called on Philip Augustus of France to carry out the sentence. John capitulated. But Innocent was also deeply concerned about religious matters. He summoned the Lateran Council of 1215, which dealt with problems of heresy. He ordered the crusade against the Albigensian heretics in Provence. He heard numerous cases involving erring priests and sinning bishops. He wrote countless letters of advice and instruction. He waged the papal office in a way that had never been done before. No wonder that his reign has been called the pinnacle of papal power.

Yet the creation of the strongly centralized and bureaucratic papal office during the twelfth century transformed the Papacy by placing greater emphasis on the externals of power than on spiritual leadership. Innocent III seems to have recognized this fact toward the end of his life when he lamented how busy he had been in the details of administration to the detriment of his spiritual mission. However, his successors scarcely wasted any thought on this problem. When we note that probably the major achievement of Pope Gregory IX was the codification of canon law carried out by Raymond of Penafort, the direction of the development of papal authority is obvious. Added to this concern was the long struggle with the Emperor Frederick II. Here, the substantive question was no longer concern over control of spiritual authority by the emperor, but fear of the growth of a powerful empire that might dominate Italy and the Papacy. In the minds of the supporters of a strong papal government, the growth of the empire under the Hohenstaufen must have threatened to turn back the clock to the time of Henry III or Charlemagne. What was at stake was not, in a sense, a secular versus a hierocratic conception of government, but the whole secular administration of government created by the reformed Papacy since the eleventh century. The Church was a state not too different in a sense from other states of the period. Although its special area of competence was over the souls of men, its machinery reached out broadly into many areas. Conflict with the empire and the monarchies of Western Europe was inevitable wherever the expanding royal power was attempting to define its own powers and to create its own channels of administrative and judicial authority. The presence of Frederick II in Italy gave his efforts a special urgency, but his attempts in themselves were hardly different in quality to those made by Henry II of England or Philip Augustus of France. In fact, the great royal Saint of France, Louis IX, came into conflict with the Papacy to a lesser degree in these same areas of disputed jurisdiction.

The final conflicts between the medieval Church and the temporal powers were fought out in an ideological arena that does much to obscure the essential practicality of the problems. As the thirteenth century drew to a close, pressures increased. Wars demanded more money. Kings needed greater powers to maintain the positions they had made for themselves during the Middle Ages. King Philip IV the Fair of France needed funds desperately to continue his war against Edward I of England. He attempted to raise money by taxing the clergy of France. His action brought him immediately into conflict with Pope Boniface VIII. The assertions of Boniface to the independence of the clergy were the logical extension of the policies and programs developed in the time of Innocent III and even earlier. That Boniface pushed these further in the direction of maintaining that the Church was almost a state within a state, there is no doubt. But his logic was faultless. The pamphleteers of the period, who couched their discussion in terms of the spheres of secular or spiritual authority have largely obscured the problem forced on both monarchy and Papacy by the logic of history. Without a major shift in the development of one or the other, they had to meet in conflict over just such questions as this one. The Church had gone too far in developing the apparatus of the state to turn willingly from that path. The state had developed along similar lines. Not even the shattering defeat of Boniface VIII at the hands of Philip the Fair and his subsequent death at Anagni were sufficient to change this direction. The French Popes who took the papal office to Avignon attempted to build there the type of government they had witnessed in Rome.

The medieval Church was not, however, a monolithic state. It remained throughout its existence a vibrant organism pulsing with change. While the forces of centralization were strongest, the work of reform continued under the direction of the Papacy in the hands of new religious orders admirably suited to bring the message of religion to the men of the town. Francis of Assisi (1182–1226), one of the most admired figures of the Middle Ages, founded his order of begging, or mendicant, friars with the approval of Pope Innocent III. Francis rebelled against the increasing materialism of his age. Himself the son of a merchant, he rejected the attitudes of the rising urban middle class and called on all to embrace the poverty which Christ had enjoined upon his followers in the gospels. His call electrified the age and attracted men and women from every walk of life to his two foundations for men and women. Unfortunately, his own inability to realize the difficulties of translating his dream into institutional reality led to disillusionment within his lifetime and the gradual transformation of the Franciscan order into a more traditional organization. Nevertheless, many of Francis' ideals informed their work and preaching; they carried them throughout the cities of Europe and into the universities.

The founding of the Dominicans in the early thirteenth century by the Spanish clergyman, Dominic Guzman (1170–1221), was of great importance in the theological development of the Church. It was this order which nurtured such thinkers as Thomas Aquinas and Albertus Magnus. The concern of the Dominicans for doctrinal purity and their involvement in the papal inquisition in southern France marked them as militants in their religious outlook. Although Dominic himself had opposed force in the conversion of heretics and had attempted to safeguard their consciences, his views were drowned out in the demand to extirpate heresy. The inquisition, although not the instrument of sadism so often pictured, was an attempt to destroy ideas by force. Its failure must stand as a naked reminder to all who attempt such means.

Within medieval Europe, heresy became an increasingly serious problem after the early twelfth century. The attempt to destroy the Albigensian heretics, who professed a kind of Manichaean dualism and frowned on bodily pleasure, was successful only to the extent that it destroyed their major centers and forced them to flee. Their followers found refuge in the towns of northern Italy, where they continued to preach their doctrines throughout the late medieval period. Another important group, the Waldensians, followers of a merchant of Lyons, embraced apostolic poverty and traveled about preaching the message of the gospels. They ran afoul of ecclesiastical authority and were condemned as heretics. Most of these groups, with the exception of the Albigensians, flourished in the towns. Beyond a doubt, their message was not merely theological but also social. In fact, their major problems seem to have arisen from their rejection of the social teachings of their age and their attempt overthrow them. In the later period, their successors embraced theories justifying the violent overthrow of existing institutions, including the destruction of both Church and monarchy. These ideas persisted to form a very important element in the developing of early fundamentalist Protestantism.

The importance of the Church in medieval society has led historians to attempt to contrast the medieval and modern periods by the gradual decline in the power of the Papacy and the Church it represented. There is much to be said for this manner of portrayal, for the age following the death of Boniface VIII does usher in a decline. But the Church still remained a viable and influential element in the new society that was created. The Church did not end with the Middle Ages; it survived not as a relic but as a continuing force.

10 The Age of Transition

In the last stages of medieval civilization, the tempo of life quickened. Novelty, individualism, new approaches to learning and the arts, a revived classicism, all of these elements wrought a change in the character of this period. Historians apply the term "Renaissance" to this age. Indeed, the idea of these centuries as an era of "rebirth" captured the minds of some contemporaries. But this age was both medieval and modern. The similarities to the Middle Ages are sometimes so striking as to cause one to wonder whether this era represents anything more than a continuation of medieval culture; but the contrast reveals that the difference between the Middle Ages and the Renaissance is to be found not merely in the intensity of the change, but also in its essential nature. It is not just that the Renaissance rejected elements from medieval life. It is rather that the Renaissance struck off in new directions, emphasizing man as the center of history, exalting his achievements, and stressing the importance of the world around man. Although there is much that is medieval in the Renaissance, there is much also that is not. This fact alone marks the period as one of transition.

Between 1300 and 1500, the great shift from medieval to modern civilization occurred. In many respects, the modern age fulfilled the work of the Middle Ages. That work was, first and most important, the creation of Europe as the seat of Western civilization. The age of transition began the last stage in that process: the development of a secular Western culture.

The Age of Humanism: The Origins

The fourteenth century was the first age of humanism. This century opened with a severe setback to the pretensions of the Papacy in the French defeat of Boniface VIII and the subsequent removal of the Popes to Avignon in southern France. It was, to a large extent, the century of Dante Alighieri, Francesco Petrarch, and Giovanni Boccaccio, the great triumvirate of Italian literature in the early Renaissance. It witnessed the rise of Florence to preeminence in Tuscany and the growth of humanism there and elsewhere in Italy. With Giotto and Massacio, the fourteenth century was the first great age in the history of Italian painting. As it drew to a close, the first great tyrants of Renaissance Italy were establishing their power and consolidating their positions. All of these aspects reveal the vitality and the rapidity of change in this period.

The problem of the origins of humanism has long captivated the minds of historians. In the nineteenth century, Jacob Burkhardt's *Civilization of the Renaissance in Italy* attempted to describe the birth of humanism in terms of a new individualism, which fed on the spirit of the ancient classics of Greece and Rome. More recent scholars have found its first traces in the rise of a civic spirit in the city-states of fourteenth-century Italy, especially in Florence, or in the education in Latin rhetoric given laymen in Italy, which laid the basis for an approach to learning based on philology and literary criticism. All of these approaches reveal certain aspects of the growth of the spirit of humanism in Italy. Certainly, they lend more precision to discussion of what humanism is.

Humanism arose in the fourteenth century in northern Italy, This period saw an increased interest in the ancient Roman and Greek classics and the growth of a secular view of human history. Man became the focal point of interest to the humanists. They stressed his individuality and his achievements. For the most part, the early humanists were laymen and were very often members of leading families in the cities. They reacted against medieval scholasticism. They believed that theirs was a new age. It was these humanists who coined the term "Middle Ages" to describe the period from the decline of Rome to their own day. They glorified antiquity. To the study of the ancient writers, they applied the methods of philology and literary criticism they were developing. They edited the works of the great classical authors to secure texts more faithful to the original. But their attachment to these pursuits was no sterile antiquarianism, for they found in the ancients inspiration for their own age. However, this development of humanism was gradual and did not appear to the same degree in all the great Italian literary figures of the fourteenth century.

Of the great triumvirate of Italian letters of this period, Dante Alighieri (1265–1321) not merely stands first chronologically, but also represents a figure in transition. The poet of the *Divine Comedy* drew on the rich theological and allegorical tradition of the Middle Ages to describe himself as a pilgrim through Hell, Purgatory, and Paradise. The major thrust of the poem is on the effort of the poet to understand his personal relationship to the real world. The *Divine Comedy* is centered on man the individual. In this sense, it looks toward the future rather than the past. Likewise, in the *De Monarchia* (On Monarchy), Dante's appeal to the Emperor Henry VII to come to Italy and to deliver it from factional strife, the author does not merely dredge up a dead dream. Modern commentators have frequently pointed out how anachronistic it was of Dante to call on the medieval concept of universal empire more than a half century after the death of Frederick II and after the crushing defeat of the German imperial idea at the hands of the Papacy. Yet the form of the *De Monarchia* also suggests that Dante's appeal to the medieval tradition may not have been as important in his eyes as securing the aid of the emperor. In fact, the form is that of a letter addressed to the emperor and contains therefore much that is aimed at reminding Henry of the past role of the German Empire. The style in which the letter is couched, the references to Roman antiquity, and the spirit and tone of much of the content mark it as a product of the Renaissance rather than the Middle Ages. The conception of a unified Italy reveals the beginning of national feeling. Moreover, Dante also was interested in linguistic and philological studies in a way that anticipates later humanist scholars. His *De Vulgari Eloquentia* is a treatise on the development of the Italian language and a defense of its use. On the other hand, he was not a serious classical scholar despite his wide knowledge of ancient literature. Nor does he more than hint at the kind of broad interests that characterized the later humanists.

The work of Francesco Petrarch (1304–1374) is, however, much more the product of the conscious individualist seeking to express himself. Though there is much about his sonnets to Laura that recalls the formalized conception of love made popular in the writings of the Provençal troubadours of the Middle Ages, his deeply personal commitment to his art sets him apart from earlier authors. Petrarch apparently met Laura only on one or two occasions; she was already married. She may not even have known about his devotion. He puts her on a pedestal as an ideal image of womanhood. His adoption of the narrow discipline of the sonnet form indicates perhaps a greater concern with his art than with Laura herself. Petrarch was also deeply interested in the classics. Unlike Dante, he was not content with the acquaintance that early education may have brought. On more than one occasion, he wrote friends asking their aid in locating manuscripts of ancient authors. He also tried, unsuccessfully, to learn Greek and later sought to have the Iliad of Homer translated into Latin that he might read a careful edition based on a good original text. His admiration of the classics inspired his Latin epic, the *Africa,* devoted to the conquests of the great Roman General, Scipio Africanus. He regarded this as his most important work and spent much time in improving it throughout his later years. Petrarch was a much more conscious stylist in his Latin writing than Dante. He was also more influenced by classical models. It is difficult to escape the conclusion that he wrote not merely for the laurel crown, which he persuaded the Romans to confer on him in honor of his poetic work, the *Africa,* but for a broader posterity, which he believed would celebrate his name. In sum, the egoism of Petrarch is a conscious individualism in which the recognition brought by fame played a leading role.

On first examination, the *Decameron* of Giovanni Boccaccio (1313–1375) appears to place him more in the tradition of a medieval storyteller than a Renaissance humanist. The *Decameron* is a collection of tales, many based on the medieval fabliaux, united by the fact that they are told by a group of young people who have taken refuge in a villa in the country to escape the ravages of the Black Death in Florence in 1348. They are written in the Florentine dialect used by Dante in the *Divine Comedy.* The stories are often ribald and anticlerical in tone, both elements not uncommon in medieval writing of this type. But Boccaccio's treatment is much more sophisticated and urbane than that found in medieval writings. His characters are more individuals than types. His style is aimed more at an urban than a courtly audience. Moreover, the *Decameron* represents merely one aspect of his interests. He learned Greek and imitated the finest classical style, that of Cicero, in his writing of Latin. He devoted much time and effort to compiling a vast geographical dictionary of antiquity as an aid to classical studies. Wherever he traveled, he looked for manuscripts of the ancient writers to copy and add to his collection. Like Petrarch, he frowned on the barbarism of the preceding age and looked to antiquity for his models of perfection.

The homeland of these three great writers was Florence, set in the hills of Tuscany in central Italy. This city became the major cultural center of

Giovanni Boccaccio, author of the Decameron. *The eyes are those of a penetrating observer. (The Bettmann Archive)*

Italy during the Renaissance. A growing center of the wool industry, Florence was also important in banking and commerce. Florentine families like the Bardi and the Peruzzi built international reputations in finance before the collapse of their banks in 1343. In the latter years of the fourteenth century, the Medici began their rise to prominence, lending money to the Papacy and many other European monarchs. The Florentines also obtained a favored position in commerce with the Kingdom of Sicily during the late thirteenth century and used this role to their advantage in increasing their economic activity in the south.

After 1293, the Florentines drove the nobility from political life. Thereafter, for more than a century, until the rise of Cosimo de Medici, various factions of the Guelf party controlled the republic. During this period, a civic humanism exalted the republican traditions of the city. The humanist Coluccio Salutati maintained that it owed its greatness to having been founded in the age of the Roman Republic rather than under the tyranny of Julius Caesar. His history was incorrect, but his patriotism was obvious. Civic pride also played a major part in the chronicles of the city composed by Matteo and Fillipo Villani.

Florence became a city of great beauty. Nature had provided a great valley on the banks of the Arno River; the Florentines adorned that valley with some of the most beautiful buildings of the Renaissance. Giotto designed the campanile or bell tower for their Cathedral of Santa Maria del Fiore. The Palazzo Vecchio, the city hall, dominates its piazza not far from the river. Within a century, the Florentines began to build the great palaces that remain today a testimonial to the wealth and power of her merchants and bankers, as well as to the taste of her architects and artists.

It was within this milieu and against this backdrop, that early humanism took form both in Florence and at other centers in Italy—Venice, Siena, Ravenna, and Bologna. Giovanni Boccaccio worked for the Bardi, one of the great Florentine banking houses, as their representative in

Florence and the Arno River. In the background is the Ponte Vecchio. The natural beauty of the river enhances the city. (*Author*)

Naples. Other humanists came from families of wealth and influence in the city. Salutati held an official position in the government as did many others.

The political life of the city was turbulent and, several times in the course of the fourteenth century, the possibility of revolution was imminent. Major conflicts between political factions often erupted into street fighting. Moreover, the concentration of power in the hands of a relatively small group of families caused the alienation of new men attempting to rise to a more prominent role in the city. There was social unrest, which broke into the open in 1378 in the revolt of the Ciompi, largely composed of the artisans and unskilled workers in the wool industry, who threatened briefly to take over the city.

Florence, nevertheless, had risen to a position of dominance in Tuscany. More and more towns and cities were forced to acknowledge her leadership. Pisa, which during the thirteenth century had pretensions to this position, was defeated decisively near the end of that century by the Genoese and thereafter slipped behind Florence. Siena retained her independence longer, but was unable to compete with the larger and more prosperous city. Lesser towns, like Pistoia, were early absorbed into the Florentine state.

The major threat to Florence in the late fourteenth century came from the north, where Giangaleazzo Visconti of Milan was seeking to use the strength of his city to dominate northern Italy, with an eye to the eventual unification of all Italy under his rule. The fifteenth and sixteenth centuries produced many more such men of ambition and ability. These tyrants rose to power illegally. Their periodic efforts at expanding their states roused the opposition of their neighbors, bringing momentary coalitions. After their defeat, Italy returned to normal, broken into relatively small states, each jealous of its own independence. Politically, this period witnessed the further development of the territorial state, viewed in microcosm in the Italian states.

That other great Italian institution, the Papacy, spent most of the fourteenth century in France, at Avignon. There, under the shadow of the French monarchy, a line of French Popes found themselves increasingly in difficulties with the rulers of the day. Pope John XXII came into conflict with the Emperor Louis the Bavarian. The ensuing campaign of propaganda, led by Marsiglio of Padua, attacked the foundation of papal authority by declaring that the ultimate power rests with the people. Marsiglio's *Defensor Pacis,* maintained that the emperor was the true defender of the peace. William of Ockham, a brilliant champion of the imperial position, desired a Church less intensely embroiled in the secular world and therefore desired to despoil the Church of much of the trappings of secular government and to give these to the emperor.

The prestige of the Papacy suffered greatly when the attempt of Pope Gregory XI to bring the Papacy back to Rome resulted, after his death, in the election of rival claimants to the office of Pope, one Italian and another French. The Great Schism split Christendom into two camps and led the most brilliant minds of Western Europe almost to the brink of frenzy in their efforts to find a solution. Jean Gerson, Rector of the University of Paris, joined some of the leading thinkers of the day in proposing that a general council of the Church be called to deal with the schism. He voiced the view that a council was superior to the Pope. The alternative to papal monarchy offered by this position attracted mounting support as scandal increased with the failure of the claimants to settle the dispute themselves. As each original rival died, the cardinals he had chosen selected another to replace him. Europe divided on the question of which Pope to support. On March 25, 1409, five hundred churchmen and others gathered at Pisa for a council. Their immediate concern was a solution to the schism. They deposed both the Roman and the Avignonese Popes and chose the Cardinal Archbishop of Milan, Peter Philarges, as Pope under the title Alexander V. But the attempt to effect a settlement at Pisa failed to gain the recognition of either of the rival Popes; the Great Schism became greater with the presence of a third candidate.

A new attempt at settlement was made at the Council of Constance, summoned at the behest of the Emperor Sigismund, though ratified by the rival Popes. Constance attracted many of the most brilliant leaders of the Church. It concerned itself not merely with the Great Schism, but also with the increasing need for Church reform and the rise of heresy. Indeed, the major blot on its record was the execution of the Bohemian reformer, John Hus, who had answered the summons of the Council at the promise of a safe conduct, which was violated. The council attempted to work out a program which would provide a continuing role for future councils in the government of the Church. Many of its members openly maintained the conciliarist view of the supremacy of council to Pope and wrote their views into its decrees. In its final days, the council chose Cardinal Oddone Colonna, a figure inoffensive to anyone as Pope under the title Martin V. His election was accepted by all the rival factions save that surrounding the Pisan Pope. But little heed was paid this pitiful pretence. The schism that had divided the Church was at an end.

The Great Schism weakened the Papacy at a crucial moment, depriving the Church of effective leadership just when it was entering a period of major crisis. The crying need for reform, voiced by many within the Councils of Pisa and Constance, was evident to many of the humanists of the age. But the settlement of the schism did not restore the Church's position in society. The Papacy, once more established in Rome, concerned itself chiefly with the affairs of the Papal States, which the able Spanish Cardinal Albornoz had won back and reorganized. The Popes thought like Italian princes, which they were, to the neglect of the broader problems of the Church. Interestingly enough, this tremendous shock to papal government, which had so muted its effectiveness, came not from the rising power of the territorial state but from a great internal crisis over the leadership of the papal monarchy. The Church played a lesser role in Europe in the fifteenth century.

In the fourteenth century the evidence of a new spirit informing many different elements of society mounted. This change was especially noticeable in Italy. The revival of classical scholarship—the Middle Ages had never lost interest in the classics but had tended to treat them as a warehouse of varied knowledge rather than appreciating them for their art—grew pronounced as the century progressed. The decline in the position of the Church contributed to the fact that society took on a more secular outlook. Religion still remained an important factor in the life of the time, but it loomed less and less as the dominant theme. The courtly nobility, the Popes, and the aristocratic men of wealth in the towns took an interest in this new movement, which placed so much value on human achievement. Indeed, the heart of this new spirit was ultimately to be found in the rise of humanism. Man was the center of interest. The humanists had discovered him as a new world in need of exploration.

The Renaissance in Italy and Beyond

The Renaissance reached its climax in the fifteenth and early sixteenth centuries. Wealthy patrons supported artists and writers. A cult of courtly manners sprang up. Painters and sculptors attempted to recapture the spirit of classical art. The development of classical scholarship provided the basis for more critical methods in the preparation of editions of ancient writers and for the writing of history. Renaissance men tried to view the world and society more as it was than as they wished it to be. Finally, the humanist movement spread outside of Italy to Germany, France, England, and even into Eastern Europe. For a short time, the Renaissance caught the imagination of the European elite and caused them to reexamine their world.

Beyond doubt, the greatest patrons of the Renaissance were the Popes. Julius II, himself no great spiritual leader, attempted to attract the most brilliant artists of the day to Rome. He commissioned Michelangelo to paint the frescoes on the wall of the Sistine Chapel; the result was the majestic *Last Judgment*. In Florence, the Medici, who gained control of the government during the fifteenth century, surrounded themselves with brilliance. Lorenzo the Magnificent, as much a humanist as a patron of the arts, founded the Platonic Academy in Florence. Among its most outstanding members was Marsilio Ficino, who translated the works of Plato and the Neoplatonists into Latin. He was also the author of works of theology in which he tried to show that Platonism was a true precursor of Christianity. Another member of the academy, Pico della Mirandola, urged the canonization of Plato. His *Oration on the Dignity of Man* expressed the essential concern of Renaissance humanism for a world in

Lorenzo the Magnificent. Patron of the arts and founder of the Academy, Il Magnifico was greatest of the Medici. (The Metropolitan Museum of Art, Ann and George Blumenthal Fund, 1950)

which man could attain the full development of his nature. Throughout Italy, the nobility and princes attracted humanists to their courts. The Este of Ferrara, the Gonzaga at Mantua, the King of Náples, and the wealthy oligarchs of Venice sought to glorify themselves in the art of their age.

Although dominant themes in Renaissance art continued to be religious, the treatment contrasted strongly with the Gothic styles of the late Middle Ages and more works had secular topics. Petrarch had called the Gothic barbarous; his successors seem to have followed him in rejecting most of its canons. Yet the Gothic had furnished much that was of value in the development of the new art, especially in the realm of technical advance. From Giotto to Masaccio (1400–1428?), there is an apparent mastery of perspective, of the use of light and shadow to create depth, and a greater ability to portray images in the round. Without these skills, Renaissance painters would never have been able to achieve the high degree of naturalism characteristic of their art. The classic influence itself would have remained sterile and flat without improvements in the kinds of paints and colors used. As it was, Renaissance masters like Fra Angelico worked closely within the tradition of the earlier masters, while allowing themselves greater freedom in composition to capture the mood of their age. Fra Angelico's *Annunciation* depicts the maiden qualities of the Madonna at the moment when the Angel Gabriel tells her she is to become the mother of Jesus. She is the graceful daughter of the noble Italian tradition portrayed against the simplicity of a classic background. Gabriel appears as a medieval intruder in fifteenth-century Florence. The master experimenter and the greatest of all the Florentine painters was Leonardo da Vinci. The mysterious smile of his *Mona Lisa* sums up his ability to capture the individuality of his subject. He was not a slavish imitator of ancient Greece or Rome, yet the classic influence is revealed in the simplicity and directness of his work. He was particularly skilled in composition; his *Last Supper* focuses on the figure of Jesus the Master without destroying the interest and personalities of each of the Apostles for the viewer.

The models of antiquity had a more direct influence on the painting of Botticelli and Raphael. The *Birth of Venus,* painted about 1488, drew its inspiration from the Platonic ideals of the Florentine Academy. Venus stands for the unity of both the Christian and classical traditions. That Botticelli chose a pagan goddess to express this desire for unity indicates the power of antiquity in forming his artistic inspiration. The Madonnas

"La Primavera" by Sandro Botticelli. The influence of classic forms is evident in the figures of the maidens as well as in the cupid. (*The Bettmann Archive*)

of Raphael surrounded by cherubs hearken not to the medieval Christian tradition but rather to the Roman for the ideal concept of maternity.

Overt classicism in much more evident in sculpture. Here the presence of statues surviving from Greek and Roman times furnished a direct opportunity for the artists to study the meaning of ancient art and to attempt to understand the aesthetics of antiquity. Donatello's statue of Gattemalata, portraying that mercenary captain mounted on a charger, was Roman. Michelangelo's David looked not to the Old Testament, but to the Roman conception of the god Mercury. Michelangelo concentrated on the human David, the lithe and well-formed youth who combined perfection of figure with grace of motion to express the achievement of man. The Biblical David, the rude shepherd, was therefore submerged in the Renaissance-classical ideal of human attainment.

The interest of humanists in classical scholarship was already strong in the late fourteenth century. While the Middle Ages had known the works of many of the Latin authors and had a particular fondness for Vergil and Cicero, the men of the Renaissance reflected not merely a broader interest in Roman literature but also a real fascination with Greek letters, something that had barely existed in the earlier period. The humanists and their patrons were constantly searching for books and manuscripts to add to their collections. Among the more important of these begun in this period were the Vatican Library and the Laurentian Library, based on the collection gathered by Lorenzo the Magnificent. But the efforts of the humanists only began with the collecting of books; they were never completely satisfied with the defective editions of the classics available. The invention of printing in Germany in the mid-fifteenth century and its subsequent spread to Italy encouraged further the preparation of new and more scholarly editions of the great works of the past, which now could be printed and circulated widely at costs far below those for the preparation of a manuscript. Aldus Minuccius of Venice, whose dolphin colophon was itself a classic symbol, began publication of a series of classical authors prepared under the care of leading humanist scholars. He was only one of the most famous of the many printers who sprang up and turned their attention to the new learning in the second half of the fifteenth century.

The critical spirit also inspired scholars like Lorenzo Valla, a former papal secretary in the employ of the King of Naples, to investigate historical questions more critically. Valla questioned the genuineness of the famed Donation of Constantine. This document, purportedly granted by Constantine the Great to Pope Sylvester in gratitude for a cure, stated that the Pope was to receive the imperial control of the entire Western Empire. It had been cited on numerous occasions through the Middle Ages to justify papal superiority to the temporal powers of Western Europe. However, numerous writers had shown that it was manifestly a forgery, chiefly on the ground that it contained historical information contrary to the evidence given by Constantine's friend and biographer, Eusebius. The chief contribution of Lorenzo Valla was not, therefore, in proving the falsity of the document, although his arguments made further discussion on the question pointless, but in his application of the philological methods of the humanistic classical scholars to documentary criticism. This technique, further developed by later scholars, was the foundation of the historical science of diplomatics, which provided historians with a tool to examine the genuineness of documents, thus advancing the study of history toward greater accuracy.

Although humanists chiefly sharpened the acuteness of their critical method in literary studies, the spirit on which their movement was founded and which it helped further to nurture was of tremendous importance in the rise of modern natural science. Leonardo da Vinci, great painter that he was, was also interested in engineering. He designed many different types of machines, including a model for one that flew. As an artist, the study of anatomy attracted him. His notebooks reveal a careful study of both human and animal anatomy, including the results of some autopsies. Leonardo's studies had no direct influence on his age, because he did not publish the results, but they are typical of the spirit that was leading others into the same and similar paths.

In Niccolò Machiavelli (1469–1527), the Renaissance produced a man burning with the desire to set forth the basic principles of statecraft. He drew his inspiration both from the classics and his observations of Italian history. He took a clinical view to his task of describing the road to successful tyranny in *The Prince.* His work was in the tradition of humanistic scholarship. Written in a clear and lucid style, it set forth the basic elements of supreme power. That Machiavelli did not desire to recommend this road to tyranny we may gather from his *Discourses on the First Ten Books of Titus Livy* and from his *History of Florence,* where he praised the republican form of government and civic virtue in a manner befitting a Florentine. There is no evidence that Machiavelli ever intended his small treatise on Renaissance tyranny to become a handbook for unscrupulous rulers or a guide to dictatorship. Its influence in that direction was accidental to his main purpose: to provide a critical and dispassionate understanding of a particular form of the state.

The cultural revival that swept through Italy in this period was carried northward by Italian painters and poets and humanists as well as by non-Italians who had come to Italy to study and had imbibed the spirit of the new learning there. In the north, it found a climate which contrasted greatly from that in Italy. The major influences were still those of the Middle Ages. Although the Church had suffered a great loss of prestige a a result of the Great Schism and was under serious attack because of the low state of morals among the clergy and especially the monks, the sophisticated secular attitudes common among many urban Italians had not yet developed. However, there were some indications that the pattern of life was breaking up. The writings of Geoffrey Chaucer in the fourteenth century are significant in pointing the direction toward greater realism in northern literature. Chaucer's *Canterbury Tales* drew on the fable material of the Middle Ages but reflected contemporary attitudes in its presentation. He was critical of the monastic clergy and nuns, for their failure to maintain the ideals of their vocations. His characterizations of the various characters who relate his tales show how deep was his insight into human foibles and how genuine was his realism. Similar trends were visible in painting, especially in the Low Countries, where a flourishing school of Flemish masters pointed the way in the fifteenth century.

Generally, as the Renaissance moved into Northern Europe, it became less secular. Humanism entered the service of religious reform. The outstanding figure of the Northern Renaissance was Desiderius Erasmus of Rotterdam (1466?–1536), whose major work was a translation of the New Testament in the humanistic tradition of scholarship. He is more famed,

Desiderius Erasmus of Rotterdam by Albrecht Dürer. The great humanist surrounded by his books. The artist has captured the depth of his feeling in his meditative face. (Rare Book Room, Syracuse University Library)

Sir Thomas More, after the portrait by Hans Holbein. More appears in his robes as Lord Chancellor of England, but his face is that of a quiet man of peace. (*Rare Book Room, Syracuse University Library*)

however, for his *Praise of Folly* (*Encomium Moriae*), dedicated to his good friend, the English humanist Thomas More. Erasmus had a sharp pen and a bitter tongue reserved for the monks, but his genuine concern for the reform of the Church blunted the edge of many of his criticisms. Thomas More (1478–1535), author of the *Utopia,* the most famous fabrication of an imaginary and ideal society, was trained in the law and served for a time as Chancellor of England. Like Erasmus, he was deeply concerned about the need for religious reform, but was not so outspoken in his criticisms. His later refusal to assent to Henry VIII's assumption of the position of supreme head of the Church in England led to his execution. The most important figure in the German humanist movement and the leader of the revival of Hebrew studies was Johann Reuchlin. He defended the Jews and their writings against a zealous anti-intellectual, a converted Jew by the name of Pfefferkorn. For more than ten years, he was engaged in controversy attempting to answer the attacks made on him. His writings were suppressed by the Church. In the end, he won some recognition from the Church that his position was correct.

The art of Northern Europe was much more a development from medieval forms; there was no real break with the Gothic, only a gradual change of emphasis and a tendency toward portrait art and landscapes not common in the Middle Ages. Though not typical of the period, the realism of Peter Breughel has long been admired. He depicted scenes from the daily lives of the peasants, catching them at work in the fields. dancing under the sky, or drinking with pleasure. He did not ignore the crudity of his subjects, but made it an essential part of his artistic message. Yet he made no effort to caricature what he saw. Others in the Flemish school, including Petrus Christus, remained within the framework of religious art, although there was a flourishing school of portraitists. Some of the finest of this type of painting came from the brush of Jan Van Eyck, one of the earliest, if not the first painter, to use oils. The last great figure of the pre-Reformation period was Albrecht Dürer, especially known for his woodcuts and engravings. His *Praying Hands* has been frequently reproduced. The religious upheavals of the sixteenth century were the major influence on artistic development in that age.

After the early sixteenth century, the great bloom of the Renaissance was lost in Italy to a growing mannerist style, which led to artificial and contrived expression in art and literature. In the North, the coming of the Protestant Reformation so absorbed energies that it left little strength to the Humanist movement. But the influence of the Renaissance was not destroyed utterly. In England, Shakespeare, in France, Rabelais, carried its finest expression into the seventeenth century.

The Renaissance was a "reaching out" to find the limits of man and the world in which he lived. It was also an age of transition between the Middle Ages and the modern period. Both of these aspects are evident in the great movement of expansion beyond Europe which had its climax in the late fifteenth and early sixteenth centuries.

The Expansion of Europe

Even historians are sometimes prone to forget, although Jacob Burckhardt did not, that the "Age of Reconnaissance" was intimately related to the Renaissance. The superficial observation that Columbus was an Italian contains no grounds for arguing that the discovery of America was therefore a product of the Italian Renaissance, yet, in a very important sense, the intellectual discovery of the New World was closely related to the Renaissance. It was part of a much broader movement of discovery, one not limited to explorations of distant and strange lands, where scarcely a Westerner had ever walked before, but encompassing also the whole process of learning about and assimilating masses of knowledge about the universe and this planet. This latter task was admirably suited to the men of the Renaissance.

The "distant" sea was never distant from at least some Europeans and the beginnings of geographical discovery extend far back into the Middle Ages. The legends of St. Brendan's Isles may mask the voyage of eighth-century Irishmen into the Western Sea; the Norse sagas certainly reveal the discovery of the North American coast by Vikings from Iceland and Greenland about the year 1000 A.D. The Crusades gave impetus to further exploration of the Asian land mass. In the thirteenth century, missionaries had penetrated to China and there was a bishop at Peking. At the end of that century, in the age of Dante, a Venetian prisoner named Marco Polo, lanquishing in a Genoese prison, composed the story of his travels to China. The Portuguese began the explorations of the Western coast of Africa shortly after, and, having learned the difficult skill of sailing against the wind, succeeded in pushing past the Ivory Coast in the fifteenth century. A Portuguese prince, Henry the Navigator, established a school for navigation. The discovery of the compass and the astrolabe took some of the hazard out of sailing far from the sight of land. In the fifteenth century, sailors from Bristol, England, ventured far out into the Atlantic, even to Iceland, in their pursuit of fish. The tales of dread sea monsters and even the popular misconceptions about the flatness of the earth do not appear to have deterred these mariners.

Geographical knowledge in the fifteenth century was based largely on the theories of the Greeks and the experience of the Middle Ages. Both confirmed the fact that the earth was spherical. In fact, the Greek mathematician and astronomer, Eratosthenes, had attempted to measure the circumference of the earth. His figures were available at the time of Co-

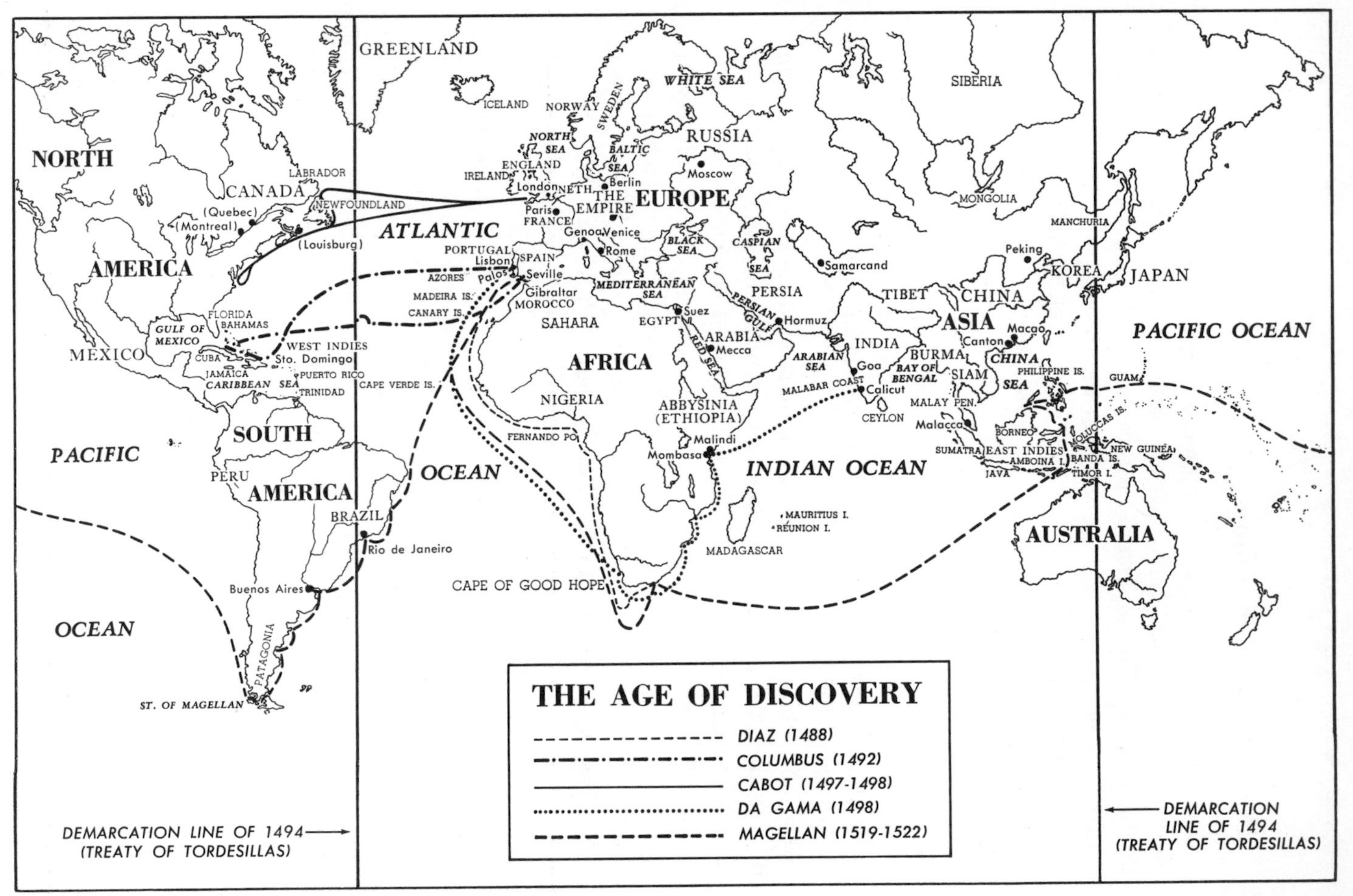
THE AGE OF DISCOVERY
DIAZ (1488)
COLUMBUS (1492)
CABOT (1497-1498)
DA GAMA (1498)
MAGELLAN (1519-1522)
DEMARCATION LINE OF 1494
(TREATY OF TORDESILLAS)
DEMARCATION
LINE OF 1494
(TREATY OF TORDESILLAS)
NORTH
AMERICA
CANADA
LABRADOR
NEWFOUNDLAND
(Quebec)
(Montreal)
(Louisburg)
GULF OF MEXICO
MEXICO
FLORIDA
BAHAMAS
CUBA
JAMAICA
WEST INDIES
Sto. Domingo
PUERTO RICO
CARIBBEAN SEA
TRINIDAD
SOUTH
AMERICA
PERU
BRAZIL
Rio de Janeiro
Buenos Aires
PATAGONIA
ST. OF MAGELLAN
PACIFIC
OCEAN
GREENLAND
ICELAND
ATLANTIC
OCEAN
AZORES
MADEIRA IS.
CANARY IS.
CAPE VERDE IS.
IRELAND
ENGLAND
London
NORTH SEA
NORWAY
SWEDEN
BALTIC SEA
WHITE SEA
RUSSIA
Moscow
NETH.
Berlin
THE EMPIRE
EUROPE
Paris
FRANCE
Genoa
Venice
Rome
PORTUGAL
Lisbon
Palos
SPAIN
Seville
Gibraltar
MOROCCO
MEDITERRANEAN SEA
BLACK SEA
CASPIAN SEA
SAHARA
AFRICA
NIGERIA
FERNANDO PO
CAPE OF GOOD HOPE
EGYPT
Suez
RED SEA
ARABIA
Mecca
ABYSSINIA
(ETHIOPIA)
Malindi
Mombasa
MADAGASCAR
MAURITIUS I.
RÉUNION I.
INDIAN OCEAN
PERSIA
PERSIAN GULF
Hormuz
Samarcand
ARABIAN SEA
INDIA
Goa
MALABAR COAST
Calicut
CEYLON
TIBET
SIBERIA
MONGOLIA
MANCHURIA
Peking
KOREA
JAPAN
CHINA
ASIA
Canton
Macao
CHINA SEA
BURMA
BAY OF BENGAL
SIAM
MALAY PEN.
Malacca
SUMATRA
JAVA
BORNEO
EAST INDIES
AMBOINA I.
PHILIPPINE IS.
MOLUCCAS IS.
BANDA IS.
TIMOR I.
NEW GUINEA
GUAM
PACIFIC OCEAN
AUSTRALIA

lumbus. Medieval explorations had carried men over land and sea from China to Iceland. There is a high probability that Columbus knew about the existence of Iceland; such knowledge was available on existing charts. Although the task of mapping the seas and continents was far from complete even where these were well known, some cartographers had placed information about unknown lands and islands lying to the west of Europe on their maps. Popular superstition may still have aroused the fears of the ignorant, but considerable evidence existed to show that new lands and new roads over the sea were a real possibility.

Indeed, the Portuguese had continued to push southward during this century, seeking a route around Africa to the rich spice islands of the Indies and hoping also to find the legendary land of Prester John, the Christian king who ruled in Africa, to join forces with him in a new crusade against the Moslems. There seemed more urgency about making such an alliance because the rise to power of the Ottoman Turks had led to a resurgence of Islamic aggression in the eastern Mediterranean. The Ottomans took Constantinople in 1453 and began the long push that would carry them far into Southeastern Europe. The Portuguese were not concerned about Ottoman threats to trade as much as they were about the possibility of discovering a feasible alternative that would provide them with an opening to the lucrative commerce with the East, which had heretofore been in Italian hands. They were among the first of the European powers to signal a basic change in the direction Europeans would look in the future. No longer would the Mediterranean basin confine them. They would look out over the Atlantic. In a very real sense, when this shift occurred, Europe had reached the new stage in its development. It had escaped forever the limitation of Mediterranean civilization; it had moved out of the *Orbis terrarum,* the Roman world, beyond Western Europe, and laid the foundations for a European community based on the Atlantic.

The importance of Christopher Columbus (1446?–1506), Genoese sailor in the service of a reluctant Spain, lies not in his discovery of America but in the fact that he was the instrument through which the men of the Renaissance discovered a new world and Europe found a new outlook. It was the spirit of the Renaissance, as well as greed for gold, missionary zeal, or the dream of empire, that moved men to exploit the New World. Columbus, by being born in the fifteenth century and by sailing west from Palos, Spain, with the Nina, the Pinta, and the Santa Maria, had founded the Atlantic community.

Discovery of a few islands off the coast of North America in 1492 or

Spanish galleon. In ships such as this, the Spaniards pioneered routes across the Atlantic and around the world. (The Bettmann Archive)

further explorations in the following years, which resulted in the discovery of both North and South America was not important in itself. Colonists and conquistadors were most important. The settlement at Hispaniola in New Spain was the first beachhead of Europe in America. The conquest of the Aztecs by Cortez was the prelude to European dominance in the New World. The coming of the Europeans brought suffering to the native peoples and destruction to their civilizations. Europeans were slow to attempt any compromises with the cultures of the natives. Only seldom did any voices raise the question of protecting the natives. Bartolomé de Las Casas waged such a campaign in Spain during the early sixteenth century and was able to win support from the Spanish crown. But the distant decrees of the Spanish government could not prevent the abuse of Indians in mines in the mountains of Mexico and Peru. The long arm of the state was frequently not long enough to cope with any problem that did not result in a major disorder that required soldiers. Certainly, the

Spaniards were not unique in their poor treatment of the natives; their actions were fairly typical of the invading Europeans.

The late fifteenth and early sixteenth centuries were not merely the age of discovery for the American continents, but for the discovery of the world. The importance of Ferdinand Magellan's circumnavigation of the earth lay not in its proof that the world was round, but in proving the possibility of exploring the whole of this planet. Sir Francis Drake soon confirmed this evidence. For more than three hundred years after, Europeans were intensely involved in the business of completing the work of exploration opened up by the daring of Magellan and Drake.

The relatively small population of the Americas, the favorable climate, the technological advantage of the Europeans, and the lack of adequate opportunities at home united to make these lands particularly attractive to European settlement. The Spaniards and Portuguese came first to Central and South America. They modeled their great *encomiendas* on the estates of their native land. At first dependent on native labor, they found it unsatisfactory and turned to the importation of large numbers of Negro slaves from West Africa. The Portuguese next began settlements along the coast of Brazil, following a pattern that did not differ significantly from that of Spain. Only when the peoples of Northern Europe, especially the English and the French, entered the race for control of the New World in the later sixteenth century did another pattern emerge. They chose the temperate regions of North America, sparsely populated by Indians, and came largely as small proprietors. Only gradually, with the cultivation of tobacco and cotton on a large scale did some of these colonies develop the plantation system and introduce Negro slavery. The Dutch, who settled the Hudson Valley, imported their seignorial patroon system from the Netherlands, but relied, as there, on the tenant labor of landless Dutch farmers. Throughout the New World, the Europeans established theirs as the dominant culture, even impressing it upon the natives where possible. In the sixteenth century, the Americas were gradually being tied to Europe, while the Atlantic was becoming a European lake.

Few other parts of the earth attracted colonization in this period. Asia was already well settled, with flourishing civilizations. Although technologically somewhat behind the Europeans, any serious attempt at large-scale colonization would have brought war. At any rate, the importance of the East lay in its trade. The Portuguese reached the East Indies and the Indian subcontinent first, but the Dutch early entered the competition for control of the Spice Islands of the East Indies. Ultimately, the Dutch were the more successful in monopolizing the rich Eastern spice trade.

Dutch ship, by Peter Brueghel the elder. In the sixteenth century, the Dutch were already laying the foundation for their later maritime empire. (The Metropolitan Museum of Art, Rogers Fund, 1921).

Africa, which provided the bulk of slaves for the new world, discouraged settlement because of its unhospitable climate and its early reputation as the graveyard of the white man. Slaves, gold, and ivory drew traders to its coasts, but the interiors remained unexplored until the nineteenth century.

This age also saw man look beyond this planet and, for the first time since antiquity, offer a new theory on the motion of the heavenly bodies. Nicolaus Copernicus (1473–1543), educated at Cracow and Bologna, a canon of the Cathedral of Frauenberg, advanced the theory that the earth and the other planetary bodies move about the sun. This view was contradictory to the long-held theory invented by the Graeco-Egyptian astronomer Ptolemy. Copernicus incorporated his ideas in his work on *The Revolutions of the Celestial Spheres,* dedicated to Pope Paul III and published shortly before his death. Where Columbus and Magellan had sailed far in search of distant lands, Copernicus had found whole worlds while remaining at home. His discovery was ultimately to open yet another dimension in the age of discovery.

The Renaissance was also the first age of modern science. In part, the discoveries of new lands stimulated an interest in various scientific areas. Geography, of course, underwent profound changes as new lands were added to maps. Exploration of these lands added details about rivers and mountains; climatic changes were noted by travelers in the tropics and the southern hemisphere. Flora and fauna were often far different from those found in Europe. Not only were new fruits and vegetables introduced to European tables, but scientists also began the first attempts since antiquity to catalog and describe the plant life they found. These were no longer the medieval herbals, listing various drugs of value to specific diseases, but attempts at classification. The scientists drew pictures of the plants. The University of Padua had the first botanical garden, but others soon followed. In all of this work, the stimulus from the discoveries made beyond the seas was important. In the transition from medieval to modern science, man was finding a new world to explore.

In the sixteenth century Europe was definitely entering the modern age. The Renaissance had provided a new spirit in humanism. This emphasis involved some rejection of the medieval conceptions of the world order. But it would be superficial to overlook also the underlying currents in political, economic, social, and intellectual life that swept through the Renaissance from the Middle Ages and into the modern period. These currents were fundamental to the formation of Europe as we know it. Although the Renaissance rejected the Augustinian conception of man's role in this life to adopt a secular view of history, the institutions through which modern society continued to operate had been formed in the Middle Ages. The growth of secular government must be seen against the whole breadth of the process of state-building having its roots in the feudal age. The urban centers of Renaissance Italy cannot be understood save in context with the growth of towns in the Middle Ages. Renaissance bankers were descendants of medieval merchants. All of these elements emphasize the transitional nature of the period from 1300 to 1500.

Yet the transition was not complete even then. One more great upheaval recalled the Middle Ages: the Protestant Reformation. It was the final act in the medieval religious drama, the first act in the modern. It was the last great medieval theological debate and it also witnessed the final triumph of the state in its effort to declare its freedom of the medieval concept of the relation between spiritual and temporal authority.

11 The Age of Reform

In the sixteenth century, religion moved to the center of the stage. Under the impact of the Great Schism and the Renaissance, the Church had been changing. The rise of a secular spirit revealed a major shift away from the traditional role of the medieval Church as the leader of Western European thought. The decline of morals among the clergy evoked demands for reform. Some new religious orders, chiefly concerned with reform and missionary endeavor, came into being. The humanists added their voices to the general cry that the Church must become more spiritual in its outlook and less concerned about its vast domains. Finally, a single monk, Martin Luther, preached his own message to those who would listen. The protest had come.

The Protestant Reformation was a theological movement. Its effect, in the realm of religion, was to break the unity of the medieval Christian Church. The Church, to some extent the Catholic as well as the Protestant, adapted to the pattern of the emerging European state-system. As a consequence of disunity, in both Catholic and Protestant lands, the Church looked to the state for support against its enemies. Its role of leadership passed almost completely to secular hands in the course of the sixteenth century. In the long outlook, the religious movements of the sixteenth century conformed to the pattern of dominance for the territorial states. Within this new society, the role of the Church would be secondary. The state took the initiative in the great age of European dominance that has its beginnings in the post-Reformation era. The Reformation was another step in the European march to world leadership.

The Failure in Leadership

The Reformation was a religious revolution. Its roots lay deep in the Middle Ages, indeed, in the very essence of Christianity as a religion. Its chief manifestation was the challenge which it made to the claim of the Papacy to lead a united Christendom in the West. In this sense, therefore, the revolt was radical, for it resulted in the triumph of patterns of religious authority different from those accepted in the Middle Ages. But, in another sense, the movement was conservative, for it did not proceed in a unified manner to the destruction of the entire institutional framework of the Church. Herein, therefore, is one of the most important problems in understanding the religious revolution of the sixteenth century; although it fed on the religious radicalism of the late Middle Ages, its chief leaders broke with the aspiration of the radicals for a free community of Christians and instead retained many of the institutions of the medieval Church.

A central element in the success of the Reformation was the lack of strong leadership within the Church during the fifteenth century. The attempt of the conciliarists to subordinate the Popes to Church councils failed after the Council of Basle in the 1430's. The effort there to draw up a program for Church reform was drowned in the dissension of the various parties, while the Pope was able safely to ignore demands that councils be convoked frequently to deal with the problems of the Church. The real gainers from the conciliar movement were the kings and princes of Western Europe, who revealed themselves as the decisive force in settling the religious conflict of the Great Schism.

Throughout the remainder of the century, the Popes, restored to their position in Rome and the Papal States, took greater interest in Italian politics than in the broad religious currents of the age. Pope Sixtus IV (1471–1484) devoted his reign to the building of the temporal power of the Papacy. He placed his relatives in positions of authority, both lay and ecclesiastic, within the Papal States. His opposition to the Medici in Florence involved him in a plot to overthrow their power, which resulted in the murder of Giuliano de Medici and war with Florence. Sixtus then turned his attention to the partition of the Duchy of Ferrara. But his designs were frustrated by his own diplomatic failures. He died in a rage at the perfidy of the Venetians, whom he accused of causing his failure. But the ambitious projects of Sixtus lived on in the dreams of Cardinal Rodrigo Borgia, who became Pope Alexander VI in 1492. His ambition for himself and his children, the famed Cesare and Lucretia, left little place for concern about the religious life of the Church.

Heresy also threatened the unity of the Church in the fourteenth and fifteenth centuries. In England, John Wyclif (d. 1384), a professor of theology at Oxford University, not only attacked the growing materialism of the Church but also came to deny the Church as an institution. He taught that sacraments administered by immoral priests had no validity. Those who followed Wyclif's ideas in England were called Lollards. They attracted popular support among the peasants and condemned not only the clergy but also many of the nobles. In Bohemia, John Hus (1369–1415) spread the ideas of Wyclif until his condemnation and execution by the Emperor Sigismund. However, his followers kept the movement alive and merged with the early Protestant movement.

Throughout England and Bohemia, men asked the value of the institutions of their day. More and more they answered their own question by affirming the interiority of the Church and by denying the right of the state to rule. This anarchic strain of fifteenth century thought placed the individual at the center of society. The nominalist views of the fourteenth-century Franciscan theologian and political thinker, William of Ockham, provided an intellectual framework for the development of these ideas by denying the validity of universal concepts and emphasizing the unique qualities of every being. But these currents went far beyond William's views by denying the need for either ecclesiastical or temporal power. Ultimately, this view of the autonomy of the individual had to clash with the established order which it hoped to destroy. These heritical views reinforced the growth of individualism and worked to undermine the authority of the medieval Church.

Within a theological framework, the attacks of heretics centered on such questions as the validity of sacraments administered by priests living in sin. The attack on the priesthood led some to assert that there should be no intermediaries between man and God, that each man should be his own priest and that the relationship between God and man should be direct. In this view are contained the elements for an assault on the entire sacramental system of the medieval Church. If each man was his own priest, there was no need for special ministers to offer the mass, to ordain other clergy, to hear confessions and forgive sins, or to anoint the dying. Baptism alone served as sufficient initiation into the Christian life. The Church as an institution was no longer needed.

Yet, not all reform movements were so radical. New religious orders were springing up. Philip Neri (1515–1595) founded the Congregation of the Oratory, dedicated to preaching and the improvement of the lives of the secular clergy. The Carthusians brought new life to the monastic ideal by their rigid observance of a rule which emphasized solitude and contemplation. A young Italian woman, Angela Merici, gathered about herself a group of companions and undertook the task of educating young women; their patroness was St. Ursula. The Theatines showed special concern for clerical reform. In Spain, a young Basque nobleman, Inigo de Loyola (1491–1556), turned from his military career and began studies for the priesthood. The group who joined him formed the nucleus of the Society of Jesus. Although their first desire was to serve as missionaries, they took a special promise to follow the commands of the Pope in whatever tasks he might assign. Some bishops were also committed to the cause of reform. The great Spanish humanist, Cardinal Ximenes de Cisneros, founded the University of Alcala to provide a better training for his clergy and supervised a scholarly edition of the Old and New Testaments, which was printed on the press of the university. Humanists like Erasmus and Thomas More were also strong adherents of the cause of reform. Yet the failure of the Papacy in the years before 1517 and for some time after that date to lift up its eyes from the mundane affairs of political machinations in Italy permitted the reform movement to waste itself in the struggle against the behemoth of corruption. The infantry awaited the battle, but the general sat in his tent and plotted strategy for another war.

The structure of the medieval Church, which so closely resembled that of contemporary states, was the cause of considerable resentment. The Church had developed a financial and administrative system that was highly centralized. During the period of the Babylonian exile in Avignon, Pope John XXII had thoroughly overhauled the tax structure to make it more efficient. Much of this money went for proper purposes of ecclesiastical administration, but too much went to further the political ambitions of the Renaissance Popes. In the Middle Ages, the system of ecclesiastical courts had come under fire from the feudal monarchy but had survived and grown more encompassing in the fourteenth century. Kings and princes deeply resented the ability of many of their subjects to escape their jurisdiction by pleading membership in the clergy. Moreover, in an age when the costs of government were growing much faster than sources of revenue, both Church taxes and the revenues of ecclesiastical courts were looked upon with envy. The Church was also the greatest single landholder in Europe; this wealth formed the endowment of bishoprics, monasteries, and charitable works. However, the increasing corruption of the clergy brought this wealth into question and led many to advocate a church of poverty.

In the fifteenth century, the Church was vulnerable to attack on many fronts. At the same time, the forces desirous of correcting the most serious abuses were hampered by lack of leadership. Given time, moderate reformers might have succeeded in electing able Popes dedicated to the task of Church reform. The Papal monarchy of the Middle Ages would perhaps have survived unscathed by these attacks. But there was no more time.

Of all areas affected by the abuses and corruption of the medieval Church, none was more deeply resentful of its position than Germany. The destruction of the German monarchy in the Middle Ages had allowed the forces of disintegration full play. Each prince was virtually a king in his microcosmic state. The power of the emperor was restrained not merely by weakness but also by the policies of the House of Habsburg, which had succeeded in gaining control of the imperial throne in the fifteenth century. The Habsburgs aimed not at a restoration of the German monarchy but at the building of the power of their dynasty through well-planned marriages. The basis of their power was the Duchy of Austria. From that foundation, they strengthened their hold in southeastern Germany and the adjacent Slavic lands. But, by marriage, they gained control of the Netherlands and Spain. Their concept of Empire was based on the principle of dynastic interest. Germany, fragmented in a Europe of powerful territorial states like France and England, was weak. There was especially deep resentment at papal taxation and violent criticism of the itinerant salesmen of indulgences. The latter practice was vicious. Although technically an indulgence was a grant of the remission of the temporal punishment for sin—that suffered in the fires of purgatory—the preachers often gave the impression that a gift to the Church would immediately result in forgiveness of all sin. "When you hear the tinkle of the bell, another soul is freed from Hell," went one popular jingle of the age. Such tactics scandalized the innocent and angered those desirous of reform. The Germans felt that the Papacy, in whose name these vices spread, was an enemy of their independence and prosperity.

In the climate created by these conditions in Western Europe and particularly in Germany, it is not surprising to find some unrest. What does surprise is the relatively mild form that the early protest took. For the Reformation did not begin with a riot, nor did it sweep forward with the

The Basilica of St. Peter's, Rome. The greatest monument to the Renaissance Papacy and a symbol of a papal leadership already in decline. (The Bettmann Archive)

force of a whirlwind. This tremendous religious revolution began in a theological debate between university professors in 1517.

The Protest

The University of Wittenberg was founded in 1502 by the Elector Frederick the Wise of Saxony. It lay outside of the main currents of the humanistic movement, which had moved northward in the fifteenth century. Its theological faculty was composed of clergy of the Augustinian order. Martin Luther joined this faculty in 1512 to teach courses in the Bible, after he had completed his studies for a doctorate in theology.

Luther was a native of Saxony. His family was of humble background, but his father had achieved considerable success and planned a career in law for his son. Martin, however, moved by an early religious experience, left the University of Erfurt and joined the Augustinians. Ordained a priest in 1507, he continued studies in theology and occupied a number of positions of trust and responsibility within his order. During this period, he went to Rome on business for his order and was shocked at the condition of religious life in the papal city. From 1512 on, he was chiefly involved in his teaching. But, in 1517, his announcement of a willingness to debate ninety-five theses on the nature of the Church, the position of the Papacy, the validity of indulgences, and the means whereby a Christian might be saved catapulted him to the center of a major controversy in Germany.

Martin Luther had spent his formative years deep in study and meditation. He was deeply introspective and, from his writings, intensely concerned about his own salvation. Fear for the loss of his soul led him to read sacred scriptures carefully in search of some clues to the manner in which he might best achieve an eternal reward. Convinced of his own sinfulness, although he was generally an exemplary priest, he came to doubt the value of his priestly acts and other pious works for his salvation. When reading the passage in St. Paul's Epistle to the Romans (1:17) which states: "The Just shall live by faith," he experienced a deep peace of soul and came to the view that faith was the key to salvation. This personal conviction remained the foundation of Luther's theological position on salvation throughout his life.

Luther drew up the ninety-five theses because he was disturbed by the preaching of a Dominican friar, Johann Tetzel, an agent for the Archbishop of Mainz, who came to Wittenberg to raise money for the building of St. Peter's Basilica in Rome. Luther desired a public debate on the practices and theology involved in the granting of indulgences. Instead of a debate, Luther found himself charged with heresy by the Leipzig theologian Johann Eck. Luther attempted to answer these charges, but refused to go to Rome. Instead, he agreed to appear under imperial safe conduct at a meeting of the Imperial Diet in Augsburg. His condemnation by the papal representative, Cardinal Cajetan, was a foregone conclusion and he returned to Wittenberg to study and preach.

On January 2, 1521, Pope Leo X issued the Bull *Decet Pontificem Romanum* condemning Luther. In April, the German reformer appeared before the Emperor Charles V at Worms and refused to recant. Banned and outlawed the following month, he sought refuge in the Castle of the Wartburg under the protection of Frederick the Wise and began his translation of the Bible into German, a work whose influence on the development of the German language marks it one of the most important literary efforts of the age. Thereafter, Luther returned to active life. He continued to win supporters, especially among the German nobility. His ability as a preacher gained him a wide popular following and his message of rebellion against the Papacy was also popular. But Luther was no anarchist. He believed in authority and supported it on the ground that its source was God. For this reason, he opposed the uprising of the Peasants War in 1524–1525. To him, the peasants stood for a denial of legitimate authority. Thus he rejected most of the tradition of the radical reform movements of the later Middle Ages.

Luther's theology was strongly in the Occamist tradition in so far as it emphasized the role of the individual in the quest for God, a view which drew further strength from the mystical theology of the Middle Ages and especially from St. Bernard of Clairvaux. However, Luther rejected most of the sacraments save for baptism and holy communion. He denied holy orders, matrimony, extreme unction (the anointing of the sick), penance (confession), and confirmation, chiefly on the ground that he could find no Biblical support for some and that the priesthood was not a separate body from all Christians. While these views placed him in accord with Wyclif and Hus, he did not attack the concept of the Church as an exter-

Martin Luther. A sympathetic drawing of the great reformer, emphasizing his human warmth. (Rare Book Room, Syracuse University Library)

nal organization. Rather he and his followers preserved, almost by accident, the episcopal organization. He supported the idea that secular princes received their authority from God and that the Church owed them respect. While his views were certainly a rejection of the Church of the Papacy, some had long been held within the Church and many were far from radical. It was chiefly in three areas—salvation, sacraments, and the Papacy—that he differed from the Roman Catholic position.

The spread of Lutheranism in northern Germany was rapid. By 1555 (The Peace of Augsburg), most of the northern princes had led their territories into the Lutheran Church. The Scandinavian countries had also begun to adopt the Lutheran Confession as their official religion. Since the princes took the leading role in bringing their territories into the Lutheran fold, their voice was extremely important in matters of religion. Luther had relied upon their support to a large extent and had received it because of their opposition to the Papacy and especially to the fiscal policies of the Roman Church. In the long run, the princes counted significantly in the success of the Reformation. The adoption at the Peace of Augsburg of the principle "cuius regio eius religio," which gave the prince the right to determine the religion of his subjects, was a recognition of this fact.

Lutheranism had rejected the radical aspects of Church reform stemming from Wyclif and Hus; Ulrich Zwingli (1484–1531), the Swiss reformer, and later John Calvin (1509–1564), the founder of the Reformed Church, which spread from Switzerland to France, the Netherlands, and the British Isles, were more influenced by these men.

Where Luther had had little contact or sympathy with humanism, Zwingli had devoted his life to classical studies. His theology tended to reflect this bent in its rejection of the miraculous. He was undoubtedly the most rationalistic of the reformers. He maintained, for example, that the Lord's Supper was merely a symbolic reenactment of the First Holy Thursday, and not the real presence of Christ in the sacrament. In his teachings, he emphasized the importance of the local church as the community of the faithful. By 1523, he succeeded in winning support for his theological position throughout the Swiss canton of Zurich, which abjured its loyalty to the Pope and to its bishop. His efforts to defend his movement brought him into conflict with Luther, who disagreed strongly with his interpretation of holy communion, and with the Catholic cantons of Switzerland. He died in battle attempting to defend Zurich. His leadership, however, was not in vain. His successors continued the reform movement in Switzerland and gradually united the church in Zurich with

Ulrich Zwingli. This portrait captures something of the intellectual character of the Swiss reformer. (Rare Book Room, Syracuse University Library)

the Reformed Church founded at Geneva under the leadership of John Calvin.

Calvin was born in France and received an excellent education in theology and law at the Universities of Paris and Orleans. However, he became deeply interested in religion and was caught up in the currents of reform. Forced to flee France because of his views, he traveled while he wrote his *Institutes of the Christian Religion,* a work which has been called a *Summa Theologica* of Reformed Protestantism. Calvin finally settled at Geneva and spent the remainder of his life in organizing the city as a theocracy in which God ruled through the pastors of the Church. An austere figure, Calvin taught that God had decreed from all eternity that some men would enjoy eternal life while others must be damned. To him, this doctrine of predestination was a fundamental mystery of salvation. God was the God of justice. How, then, could man find mercy? Calvin responded that men would find mercy by leading an upright life to the glory of God, by finding in their hearts a true unity with God, and by faithful reception of the Lord's Supper. He who followed this path might have faith that he was among those chosen by God for eternal reward. Joy was the lot of the elect.

Calvin stood in awe of the divine will and worshipped before it. In his sermons and those of the pastors of the Reformed Church, men were made to realize the terrors of a hell deprived of God's presence. The elect were chosen, but they must know the awful punishments God had in store for the damned. The tendency toward intolerance implicit in such a position was not inconsistent with an age that accepted burning as a punishment for heretics.

Calvinism in Geneva set a tone that was to remain a constant element as it spread elsewhere. The authority of the state was subordinate to the will of God expressed through the elect and especially their pastors. The latter, whose influence on the Church was as great as any bishop's, rooted out sinners and demanded their punishment. They imposed a simple, unostentatious dress and manner of living that gave the Calvinists a reputation for thrift. Their emphasis on duty and industry as virtues were important in forming the consciences of their followers and promoting the prosperity of the community. In establishing ecclesiastical administration the Calvinists insisted on the autonomy of each congregation. Yet they were not democratic, even in the loosest sense of the term. God was their ruler; Him they obeyed absolutely.

Scholars, in particular Max Weber and R. H. Tawney, have argued that the Calvinist ethic significantly influenced the rise of modern capitalism. Pointing to the preponderance of middle-class businessmen who grew up in England, France, and the Low Countries in the sixteenth and seventeenth centuries and who adopted or were born into Calvinism, they made a potent argument. But it largely ignored a factor of still greater significance: the fact that the greatest development of capitalism came within the framework of the Atlantic community as a result of the age of discovery which forced businessmen to find new techniques for foreign trade and investment in precisely those areas where Calvinist influence was strong. Without ruling out entirely the importance of the influence of Calvinism, it is nevertheless difficult to assign it a greater role in the rise of capitalism than the impact of European expansion.

The success of Calvinism and Lutheranism ironically aided the more radical reform movements to which they were opposed. Since the major focus of the struggle over religion involved the major churches, sects like the Anabaptists, though often persecuted, were able to maintain their existence. The rebaptizers, so-named from their belief that infant baptism was invalid, attempted to restore a primitive form of Christianity, which had refused service to the state, especially in time of war, and had insisted on adult baptism. The Anabaptists drew heavily from the radical traditions of the later medieval reformers, to a far greater extent than either Calvin or Luther. They insisted that the Church was basically interior, that the association of Christians for services was therefore a merely voluntary meeting. They attempted to separate themselves from the state, sometimes even to the point of accepting the basic anarchist position that the state was evil. They also argued for complete freedom of conscience, a position developed largely out of late medieval teachings on the autonomy of the individual. In various forms and under many names—Amish, Mennonites, Brethren—they have survived in spite of the frequent antagonism of the major churches and the state to them.

In England, religious reform came under royal leadership. England broke with the Papacy before the intellectual currents of continental Protestantism were a major influence on the island. But once the royal decision was made, this country underwent a gradual religious revolution in the course of the sixteenth century.

The restoration of royal power with the triumph of the Tudor dynasty under Henry VII in 1485 brought an end to the baronial anarchy of the Wars of the Roses. Henry's reign created a strong monarchy, though not in an absolutist framework. For Henry was a political realist, who wisely chose to work through Parliament and thus to build his power on support from that body. By the time of his death, he had laid the foundations for a great dynasty.

The accession of his son, the youthful Henry VIII (1509–1547), was welcome to England for the new king was full of *joie de vivre,* the model of a Renaissance prince without the dark vices associated with the Italian variety. Early in his reign, he disposed of his father's more cautious advisers and placed his trust in the brilliant and rising star of Thomas Wolsey (1475?–1530), whom he later named Archbishop of York. Wolsey was an ideal royal servant. Ambitious for himself and his master, he dreamed great dreams about the glories he and his sovereign might share. His first efforts, however, were small successes and large failures as he and Henry became involved in a brief but ignominious war with France. Wolsey's attempt to secure the imperial crown for his master failed just as did his effort to get the papal throne for himself. Yet he was a brilliant administrator and he kept a tight rein on the government of both Church and state in England. He might have achieved his dream of glory for himself and his monarch but for the failure of the king's marriage to Catherine of Aragon.

Henry's desire to divorce Catherine and to marry Anne Boleyn put Wolsey, now a cardinal, in a trap between his two masters, king and Pope. Catherine had failed to produce a male heir. Henry regarded this failure as a judgment of God against him for marrying his late brother's

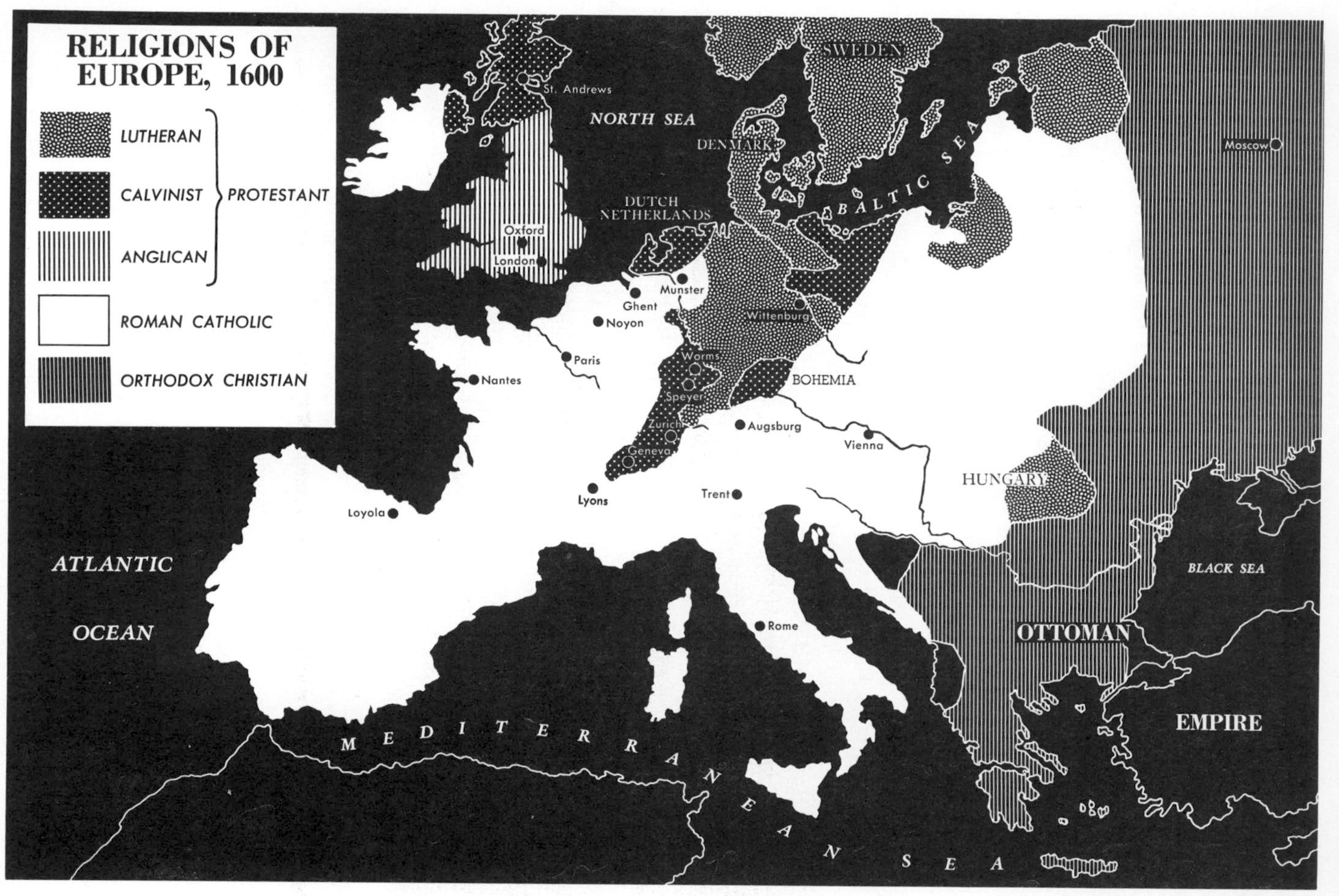
RELIGIONS OF EUROPE, 1600
LUTHERAN
CALVINIST
ANGLICAN
PROTESTANT
ROMAN CATHOLIC
ORTHODOX CHRISTIAN
St. Andrews
NORTH SEA
DENMARK
SWEDEN
BALTIC SEA
Moscow
DUTCH NETHERLANDS
Oxford
London
Munster
Ghent
Noyon
Wittenburg
Paris
Nantes
Worms
Speyer
BOHEMIA
Zurich
Geneva
Augsburg
Vienna
HUNGARY
Lyons
Trent
Loyola
ATLANTIC OCEAN
BLACK SEA
OTTOMAN EMPIRE
Rome
MEDITERRANEAN SEA

wife, for Catherine had been the wife of his brother Arthur for a few weeks prior to his death. Wolsey was unable to secure the divorce, chiefly because the Pope refused to permit him to settle the case in England. Moreover, Catherine was the aunt of the Emperor Charles V, who dominated Italy at this time Wolsey's failure cost him his position and would have cost him his life, had he not conveniently died. What he had failed to accomplish, other servants of the crown did. The passage of the Act of Supremacy in 1534 was a triumph of the territorial state over medieval universalism. Its assertion of royal control of the Church in England was the culmination of the long process by which the state had gradually assured for itself the dominant role in the Western Europe. In England, the passage of this act marked the transferral of leadership in society from the Church to the state, a transferral which was accomplished largely in the so-called Reformation Parliament, which made Henry head of the Church in England.

Henry VIII's position as head of the Church in England did not result in a basic theological upheaval. Indeed, relatively few opposed the king; those who did so revealed their commitment to the medieval ideal of a universal Christian society transcending the limits of any state. Sir Thomas More, the great English humanist, defended his refusal to swear an oath that the king was head of the Church on the ground that a king had no right to usurp the position of the Pope. The chief grounds for dispute were in the area of papal supremacy versus royal supremacy. Henry was, in fact, orthodox in his religious views; he had earlier lent his name to and published a *Defense of the Seven Sacraments* aimed at Martin Luther. This treatise earned for its author a papal commendation in the form of the title "Defender of the Faith." When the royal divorce and the act of supremacy effectively separated the English Church from Rome, the title Defender of the Faith took on a new and more important significance by asserting the unique position of the English king with respect to the Church.

But the royal break with Rome also opened England to greater influence from Protestant movements on the continent and thereby paved the way for a gradual shift in religious allegiances during the course of the sixteenth century. So long as Henry lived, this shift was slight. His choice of Thomas Cranmer (1489–1556) as Archbishop of Canterbury did bring to that See a man whose sympathies were with the Lutherans. Moreover, the influence of Thomas Cromwell, a former protégé of Wolsey raised to eminence by his ability and willingness to serve the monarchy, was in the direction of a closer alliance between England and German Protestant states. This policy, however, proved as abortive as the royal marriage with the unattractive German Protestant Princess, Anne of Cleves, which Cromwell had arranged. The fall of Cromwell pointed up Henry's determination to prevent a definitive move toward alliance with continental Protestantism and the theological implications of such a move.

When Henry VIII died in 1547, England was not aligned with the continental reform movements. The great bulk of the Anglican clergy were little influenced by Protestant ideas and continued to follow the traditional rituals as prescribed by the government. With the accession of Edward VI (1547–1553), a sickly child chiefly under the influence of relatives sympathetic to the continental reform, Protestantism got a brief opportunity to increase its influence. Cranmer's *Book of Common Prayer*, whose stately English reflected the threshold of the Shakespearian age, revealed great sympathy with continental views of the sacraments. The passage of the Forty-Two Articles in 1553 gave legal validity to Protestant theological interpretations. However, the death of the young king and the accession of his Catholic half-sister Mary, daughter of Henry VIII and Catherine of Aragon, ended Protestant growth for the time being.

Mary Tudor (1553–1558) remained loyal to the Papacy and the memory of her Spanish mother. She married Philip II, King of Spain, against the advice of the royal counselors and allowed him a major voice in English policies. Determined to root out every trace of Protestantism, she ordered the arrest and execution of more than three hundred English reformers, among them Thomas Cranmer and Hugh Latimer, Bishop of London. Her efforts were little aimed at conciliating the opposition, with the result that many moderates were driven to sympathize with the Protestant cause. Her weakness in dealing with national issues, including her loss of Calais to France, further tarnished a poor reputation. In Mary Tudor, the very qualities which had made her father strong worked against her own success, chiefly because she lacked his deep political acumen. Her death in 1558 brought no deep regrets to the mass of Englishmen. Her half-sister Elizabeth, daughter of Anne Boleyn, who succeeded to the throne, sought religious peace in conciliation while determined to maintain the power of the English crown.

Throughout Western Europe, governments played an important part in the success of the Reformation. German princes, Scandinavian kings, the English monarchy, as well as the urban burghers who supported Calvinism in Switzerland and the Low Countries pointed to the simple fact that the Reformation could not have succeeded as a religious movement without the powerful support of these elements of society. Traditionally, historians have emphasized the political gains made by the kings and princes as a result of the Reformation and have ignored the fact that these gains came in the climax of the growth of strong states in the later Middle Ages. Recently, they have not put enough stress on the Reformation as a religious movement because this obvious fact appeared less important than the lesson of political power. Yet the Reformation began in the souls of men and had its greatest influence on religious life. By raising up an alternative to the Roman Church, Protestantism broke the unity of medieval Christendom and ushered religion into the modern age.

The Later Sixteenth Century

The Reformation caught the empire and the Papacy unprepared and unable to provide effective leadership to counter its spread. Through most of the critical period of the Lutheran and Calvinist revolts in the North, France, the Holy Roman Empire, the states of northern Italy, and the Papacy struggled over Italy. The French kings after Charles VIII attempted to gain control of the Kingdom of Naples against the opposition of Spain. When Charles I of Spain became Holy Roman Emperor in 1520 under the title Charles V, France had new reasons to be disturbed, for she found herself surrounded by Habsburg domains in Germany, the Netherlands, and Spain. Naturally, the French kings sided with Charles' enemies. When the Lutheran princes formed the Schmalkaldic League (1546) to oppose the empire, they received French backing. The political balance of power played an important part in the religious struggle of the sixteenth century.

The power of Charles V also aroused the fear of the Papacy, whose major concern continued to be its control of the Papal States in central Italy. When the Pope sided with France against Charles, the emperor sent his army to Italy though he did not intend the terrible sack of Rome by his mercenary soldiers in 1527.

The deep involvement of Pope and emperor in European politics interfered with the attempts of both as well as reform-minded clergy to deal with the Protestant movements. Charles early advocated summoning a Church council at which all parties would sit down to work out their differences and undertake the reform of the Church. The Popes were strongly opposed to this course; the memory of the Conciliarist movement was too fresh. Consequently, the initiative was lost throughout the early years of. Protestant expansion. What success did accrue to the Roman Church in this period was largely due to the efforts of reformers within

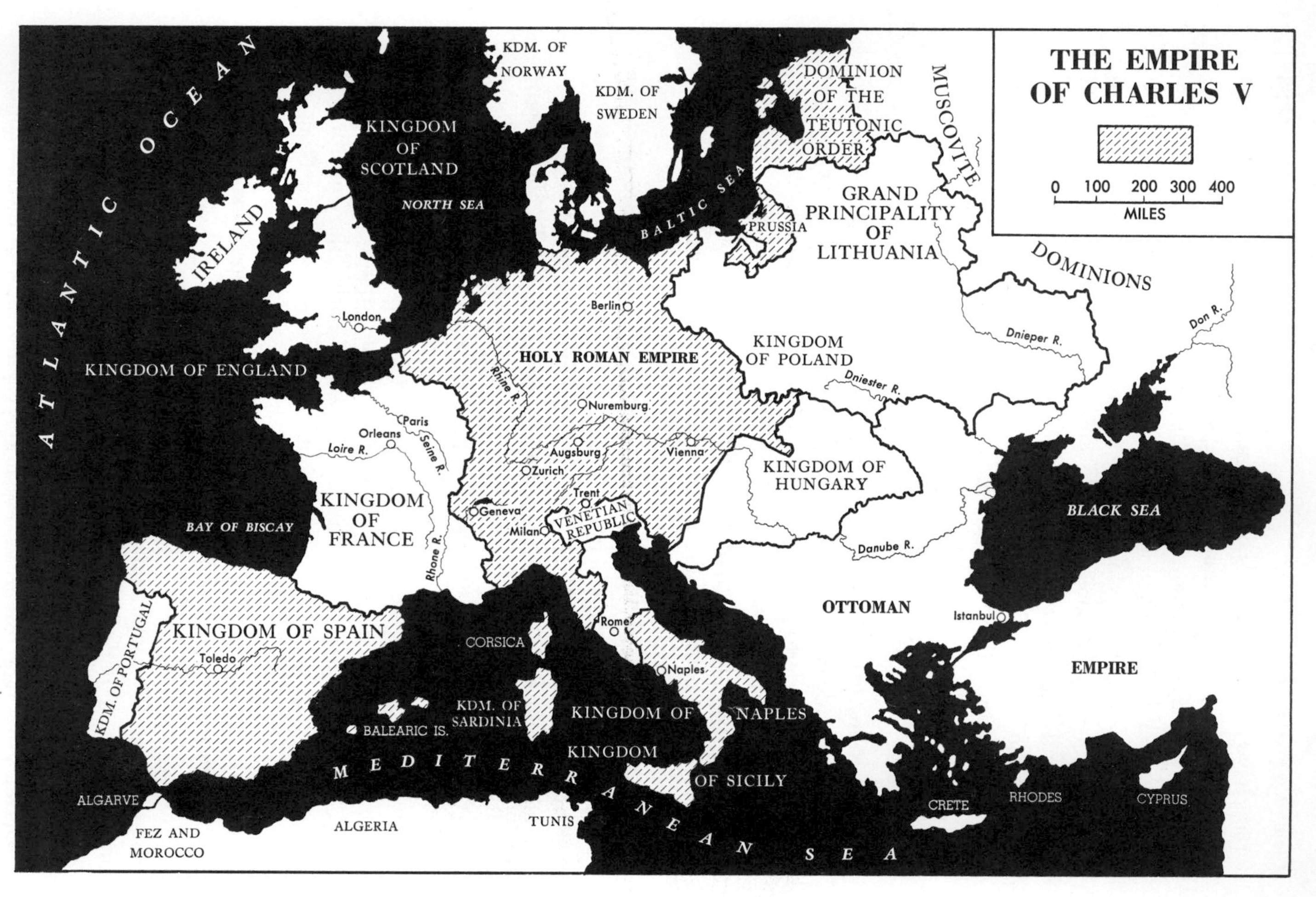

THE EMPIRE OF CHARLES V
0 100 200 300 400
MILES
ATLANTIC OCEAN
KINGDOM OF SCOTLAND
NORTH SEA
IRELAND
KINGDOM OF ENGLAND
London
KDM. OF NORWAY
KDM. OF SWEDEN
BALTIC SEA
DOMINION OF THE TEUTONIC ORDER
MUSCOVITE
DOMINIONS
PRUSSIA
GRAND PRINCIPALITY OF LITHUANIA
KINGDOM OF POLAND
Dnieper R.
Don R.
Dniester R.
HOLY ROMAN EMPIRE
Berlin
Rhine R.
Nuremburg
Augsburg
Vienna
Zurich
Trent
Geneva
Milan
VENETIAN REPUBLIC
KINGDOM OF HUNGARY
Danube R.
BLACK SEA
Paris
Orleans
Loire R.
Seine R.
KINGDOM OF FRANCE
Rhone R.
BAY OF BISCAY
KINGDOM OF SPAIN
Toledo
KDM. OF PORTUGAL
OTTOMAN
EMPIRE
Istanbul
Rome
Naples
CORSICA
KDM. OF SARDINIA
BALEARIC IS.
KINGDOM OF NAPLES
KINGDOM OF SICILY
MEDITERRANEAN SEA
CRETE
RHODES
CYPRUS
ALGARVE
FEZ AND MOROCCO
ALGERIA
TUNIS

Inigo de Loyola, Founder of the Jesuits. This famed portrait attempts to capture both Ignatius the priest and Ignatius the soldier. (*The Bettmann Archive*)

the Church. Among the most important was the recently founded Society of Jesus.

Inigo de Loyola had conceived of his order as a militia of the Papacy in missionary lands. In fact, though its importance in the mission fields in Latin America and the Far East was great, its service to the Church in Europe was probably more important. Youthful and vigorous, informed by the intellectual currents of Italian humanism, the early Jesuits were an important rallying point for the forces of reform within the Church. Loyola had attracted a number of followers of great ability during his student years at Paris. His recruits were men of high intellectual attainments. One of the early Jesuits, Peter Canisius, effectively countered Protestant popular religious propaganda in Germany through his small catechism; others worked closely in the princely courts to prevent further losses or even to win back those who had already left the Church. From an early period, they founded schools based largely on the classical traditions of the Renaissance. Not only Catholics, but Protestants as well attended, drawn by their excellent reputation.

The accession of Pope Paul III to the papal throne in 1534 finally saw the Pope give support to the growing movement for a council. But it was not until 1545, nine years after the first summons, that the council met at Trent. The Council of Trent was not the body desired by Charles V. Protestants had not been invited. Its major purpose was the reform of the Church in faith and morals rather than a rapprochement with Protestantism. Between 1545 and 1563, the council met in three widely separated sessions. It did not attempt a major definition of Catholic doctrine; its chief pronouncements concerned the Church's position on the role of faith and good works in salvation and the teaching on predestination. It asserted that man can, by the redemptive act of Christ on Calvary and by his own good works, earn an eternal reward. Concern for the vast abuses among the clergy led the council to order the establishment of seminaries as training schools of the clergy in every diocese. It forbade bishops to hold more than one diocese at once and increased the control of the bishops over all clergy in their diocese. Thus, the bishops obtained some authority over the wandering friars, who had become a scandal in the later Middle Ages. Paul III was also responsible for the reform of the Roman Curia and the introduction of new cardinals imbued with the ideals of the reform movement. These changes ensured the continuation of the work of reform under his successors. Although the Church lost considerable ground in Europe, the spiritual authority of the Papacy had managed to survive the Protestant movement.

The Council of Trent was, to a large extent, a defense of Catholicism, a consolidation of the old Church forced on it as it fell back before the rising tide of the Reformation. It was also a major instrument in reforming the Church. It stimulated an intellectual revival in Catholicism. As Protestant scholars began to write the history of the Church, it was inevitable that Catholics would respond. Cardinal Caesar Baronius composed his *Annales Ecclesiastici* as a response to the *Magdeburg Centuries,* a leading Lutheran work of the time. Numerous catechisms prepared under the auspices of the reforming clergy of the church provided for better religious education of the laity. Apologetics, that branch of theology chiefly concerned with the reasoned defense of doctrine, became more important in the life of the Church after Trent, while mystical theology, which dealt with man's personal relationship to his creator, declined. The Church increased its concern for the education of both clergy and laity, but also increased its suspicion of new ideas. One of the most important results of Trent was the *Index Librorum Prohibitorum,* a list of works forbidden to Catholic readers. The *Index* came to include not merely the works of leading Protestant authors, but also those of Catholics believed tainted with heretical views.

Protestantism found it difficult to escape the posture of rebellion against papal authority. Although the formulation of theological views by Luther and the definitive statement drawn up at the Augsburg Confession by Philip Melanchthon revealed a true point of departure for Lutheran theology, the fear of Rome inevitably permeated much of the writing of Protestants, creating a psychologically stifling atmosphere. The followers of Zwingli and Calvin, despite the latter's monumental *Institutes of the*

Philip Melanchthon, Lutheran theologian. Melanchthon provided a framework for the Augsburg Confession and worked for peaceful relations among various Protestant groups. (Rare Book Room, Syracuse University Library)

Christian Religion, were also more concerned about destroying the last traces of the old religion than about building on the theological foundations laid for them.

The period following the accession of Elizabeth I (1558) in England and the abdication of Charles V (1556) witnessed a continuation of the power struggles of the first half of the century in a new religious context. The spread of Calvinism in France gave rise to the Huguenot civil wars in that country. In Germany, the abdication of Charles left Lutherans and Calvinists for the moment without a major imperial threat. For a brief time, the resurgence of the Ottoman Turks and their rapid westward expansion forced Central and Eastern Europe to look beyond its internal differences. Under Suleiman the Magnificent, the Ottomans controlled most of Southeastern Europe, a position of power from which they were not entirely dislodged until the early nineteenth century. But, aside from these problems, the major concern of European monarchs in the last half of the century was to maintain the strength of their individual states. Only now religion played an important role in both war and diplomacy. Spain under Philip II championed the Catholic cause with the wealth of the New World. England under Elizabeth viewed Spain as a danger both to her own ambitions overseas and, more importantly, to the preservation of her religious settlement.

Elizabeth had come to the throne a Catholic, but her religious views were flexible. The unpopular efforts of Mary Tudor to force a restoration of the old religion found no support under the new queen. Her religious policies were based on political reality. She desired the support of all Englishmen for the crown. The Thirty-Nine Articles, embodying the Elizabethan religious settlement, provided a broad formula aimed at accommodating the views of both Protestant and Catholic elements in the country, as long as they were willing to accept the supremacy of the monarch in religious affairs. Those who refused—Catholic recusants and Protestant dissenters—faced legal disabilities and fines and imprisonment. Conformity was the law.

In Spain, Philip II succeeded his father Charles V in 1556; in fact, he ruled since 1540. Deeply affected by the spread of Protestantism on the continent, even in his own domains in the Netherlands, he came to regard himself as the political arm of the Catholic reform movement. His marriage to Mary Tudor had put him into close contact with English affairs. He hoped that Elizabeth would follow his lead and preserve the old faith. Her failure to do so was one of the major causes of the vigorous efforts Philip aimed at England in the second half of the century.

Emperor Charles V. Holy Roman Emperor and King of Spain, his domains included the Spanish discoveries in the new world. (Metropolitan Museum of Art, Gift of J. Pierpont Morgan, 1917)

The rise of Spain to a position of power in Europe was closely related to her leading position in the exploration of the New World. The unification of Castile and Aragon and the defeat of the Moslems at Granada had given the country a position among the major states of Europe. In 1492 the last Moslem outpost in Western Europe at Granada fell to Ferdinand and Isabella. The discovery of the new world by Columbus in that same year and the beginnings of a great flow of gold and silver into Spain from her new colonies combined with the achievement of Ferdinand and Isabella to lay the foundations for a unified state.

Spain formed part of the great empire of the Habsburgs under Charles V. Her destinies were tied to the fortunes of Germany and the Netherlands. The abdication of Charles V did not break these bonds. Although Philip II was not emperor—that post went to his uncle Ferdinand of Austria, he retained control of the Netherlands and identified himself with Habsburg interests in Italy and Germany.

Spain under Philip II was probably the wealthiest state in Europe. Her navy was certainly the strongest. Philip himself had the aid of many of the leading generals of the age, including the terrible Duke of Alva. Yet he was unable to make effective use of his power. He squandered the wealth of the New World in his wars on the continent and against England without securing any substantial return. His determination to make the Netherlands into a Spanish province and to root out the growing influence of Calvinism forced him into a long and bloody civil war. He rebuffed the attempt by moderates to prevent the outbreak of this war by gaining his promise to respect the traditional "liberties" of the estates of the Netherlands. Led by the Stadtholder of Holland, William the Silent, who employed privateers to bring war to the Spaniards, the northern provinces declared their independence. The brilliant generalship and the conciliatory policies of Alexander Farnese, Duke of Parma, who took command from the infamous Duke of Alva, succeeded in saving the Flemish and Walloon provinces for Spain, thus creating the basic division between the Republic of the Netherlands and Belgium. But, the Dutch estates had handed Philip a major defeat.

Meanwhile Philip's relations with England deteriorated. At first, he had been hopeful that he might achieve some kind of alliance, perhaps even marriage with Elizabeth, but that had come to nought. He then supported the intrigues of English Catholics, especially the supporters of Mary Queen of Scots, who was Elizabeth's rival for the throne of England and her prisoner. It was from her prison that Mary became the center of intrigues aimed at placing her upon the English throne and leading England back to Catholicism. Philip and Elizabeth played a game of cat and mouse with one another in which the Spanish monarch furnished little aid but much comfort to potentially treasonous Englishmen while Elizabeth unleashed privateers like Sir Francis Drake and John Hawkins to prey on the gold-bearing galleons of Spain enroute from Mexico and Peru to Philip's treasury.

The climax in the conflict between England and Spain arrived in 1588. Philip, convinced of the impossibility of winning the waiting war, decided on more drastic action. With characteristic ineptness, however, he chose not one enemy but two, England and France. His grand design was the elimination of all his enemies and the creation of a grand Catholic empire under the hegemony of Spain. Philip's chief strategy was based on mounting a major invasion of England. His troops under the command of the brilliant Duke of Parma waited at Dunkirk in the Netherlands, while the Great Armada under Admiral Medina Sidonia sailed to meet and escort them across the English Channel. Dutch aid played an important role in the English success that followed. The Dutch blockaded the harbor at

Dunkirk and prevented the cooperative effort of Parma and Medina Sidonia from coming off. The Armada itself, unable to accomplish its primary mission, sailed northward around Scotland and returned to Spain. Its losses, exaggerated in popular tradition, were still substantial, about one-half of the entire fleet. The English victory ended the grand design of Philip to establish a Catholic empire.

Elizabeth of England emerged as the leading figure of the age. Philip II died in defeat. France was yet too deeply involved in the conflict over Calvinism and Catholicism to cast a long shadow over Europe. Germany, slumbering for the moment, was still troubled by grave religious dissensions. Only in England did the ruling sovereign obtain the adulation of her age. Only there did she preside over the magnificent literary renaissance in which the names of Ben Jonson, William Shakespeare, and Edmund Spenser played such an important role. The Elizabethan age was the first era of English glory.

In the later sixteenth century, France was involved in a great internal struggle over religion. Calvinism had spread among the townsmen and nobles in southwestern France, though its adherents, the Huguenots, were not very numerous compared to the total population. The policy of the French monarchy was ambivalent and weak. Although anti-Protestant, the French rulers were committed to building a strong France and were unable to settle on a religious policy that would serve that objective. France produced no Elizabeth able to unite the mass of Frenchmen behind the government under a broad religious settlement. Early persecutions in the 1550's had alienated the Huguenot nobility, making it difficult for the monarchy to gain their support. The major figure of the period, Catherine de Medici, widow of Henry II, and mother of Francis II, Charles IX, and Henry III, the last of the Valois dynasty to rule France, was intent on preserving the royal line in her family. She would stop at nothing to prevent the accession of claimants from the noble houses of Guise and Bourbon unless they were allied by marriage to the Valois. Herself a politique and a religious moderate, she sided generally with the staunchly orthodox Guises against the Huguenots led by the Bourbon Henry, King of Navarre. However, she did arrange a marriage of one of her daughters to Henry in the hope of making a settlement with him. The two factions of the nobility did not hesitate to seek outside aid, the Bourbons from England, the Guises from Spain. The power of France went into eclipse because of the internal struggle. Huguenots and Catholics carried out a reign of terror. On St. Bartholomew's Day a large part of the Huguenot leaders were murdered by a Catholic mob. The Guise party

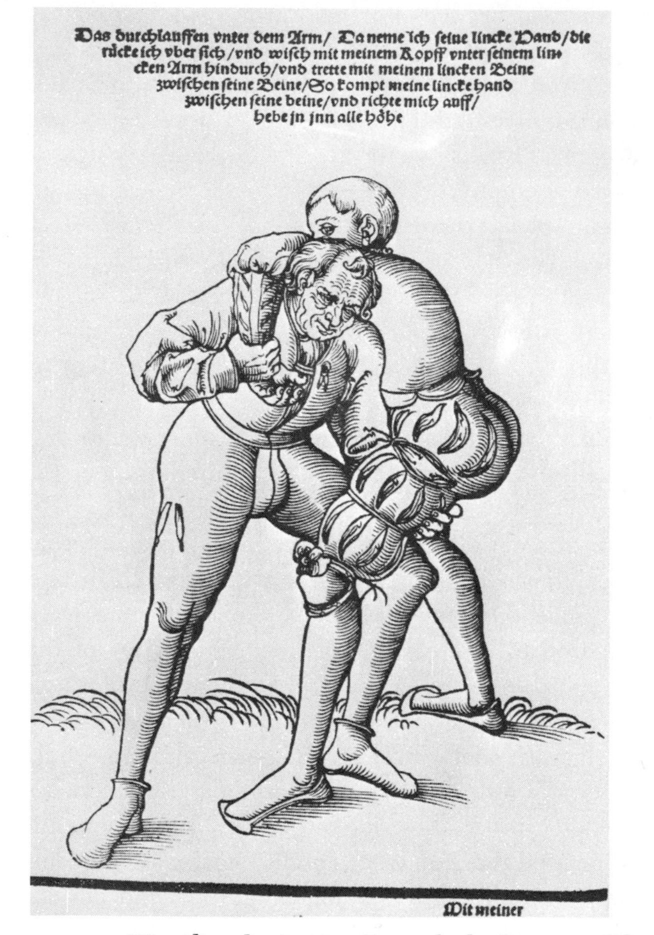

Wrestling by Lucius Cranach the Younger. The sixteenth century witnessed an increased interest in sport. Cranach, one of the great Lutheran propagandists in his art, also illustrated this technical treatise on the art of wrestling. (*Rare Book Room, Syracuse University Library*)

was more and more discredited by its alliance with Spain. Only the accession of Henry of Navarre as King of France promised the restoration of strong monarchy. But Henry was a Protestant. No Protestant could sit on the throne of Catholic France. But Henry was a politique. Realizing that only his religion stood in the way of a final solution, he became Catholic and received the crown.

The end of the sixteenth century marked no basic change in the pattern of the development of the European state-system. Religion continued to play a leading role in political life, though the Reformation had finally determined that role as one subordinate to the state. In the seventeenth century, the process of building the strong territorial state was to achieve a climax in the France of Louis XIV, whose absolutism was the final term in the struggle of the European monarchy to emancipate itself from the limitations of feudalism and to direct the resources of the entire kingdom toward goals set by the ruler.

12 The Seventeenth Century

Between the death of Elizabeth I in 1603 and the passing of Louis XIV in 1715, the territorial state reached its climax in France. The chief marks of this state were its attempt to centralize the administration of government and to establish the principle of absolute rule. These efforts did not meet with equal success throughout Europe. In fact, they achieved their fulfillment only in France. Yet the early Stuarts in England certainly hoped to imitate the French pattern and the princes of the German states entertained similar ambitions. In many ways, this territorial state was the culmination of the process of state-building begun under the feudal monarchies. Its limitations were also set in the Middle Ages by the establishment of checks on royal authority in England and the failure of kingship in Germany. The territorial state was the answer of history to the medieval desire for a universal Western European society. It spelled death to the dream of empire just as the Reformation had ended the rule of the universal church.

During this period, despite the focus on Europe, we should not lose sight of the growing European dominance of the Americas and the Far East. In the wars of the later seventeenth century, colonial rivalries began to play a more important role, pointing to the fact that the whole world was gradually becoming a European satellite.

Europe to 1648

The consolidation of the French monarchy in the seventeenth century under Cardinals Richelieu and Mazarin was achieved only because

France was able to subordinate most elements in her society to the state. This rebuilding of the monarchy began with the accession of Henry IV in 1589.

King Henry III of France was murdered by the Catholic party in 1589; his logical successor, Henry IV (1589–1610), was a Protestant, but enjoyed considerable support in France. His enemies, the Guise party, were closely allied to Philip II of Spain and their victory would certainly put France at the mercy of the Spanish king's grandiose designs for a Catholic Europe under Habsburg hegemony. Many French Catholics were unwilling to see their country become a Spanish satellite. Henry himself provided a compromise solution by his conversion to Catholicism. Henry realized that France would not tolerate a Protestant king; he believed Paris was "worth a mass."

Henry's acceptance of Catholicism paved the way for his coronation. His promulgation of the Edict of Nantes promised a solution to the religious strife. By this edict, Henry offered his former coreligionists security in certain towns of the kingdom and the opportunity to participate in political life. This edict was not, however, based on the principle of religious toleration. As a matter of fact, it gave the Huguenots certain fortified cities to guarantee their safety; it was essentially the solution of a politique, which subordinated all other questions to the needs of the state and political reality. Henry desired the support of all Frenchmen for the crown.

The reign of Henry IV was especially important for the attention it gave to the economic recovery of the kingdom. The Duc de Sully, a Calvinist, promoted road building and improved France's system of internal waterways. He was also interested in agriculture. He attempted to bring more land under cultivation and to make the marketing of farm commodities more profitable by reducing some of the internal tariffs. Also during Henry's reign, efforts were made to revive the silk industry, which had centered on the city of Lyons. Sully's wise fiscal policies combined with Henry's political sagacity to win confidence for his government. When Henry was assassinated in 1610 by a religious fanatic, the task of restoring the French monarchy was well begun.

It was a testimony to the work of Henry IV that his young son, Louis XIII (1610–1643), succeeded to the throne without major incident with his mother, Marie de Medici, as regent. Neither the king nor his mother possessed great ability to rule. Marie usually entrusted the government to her favorites at the court. Louis, when he had succeeded in throwing off his mother's domination, first appointed the Duc de Luynes as his chief minister, but, in 1624, turned to Bishop Armand Jean du Plessis de

Richelieu (1585–1642), who had come to the notice of his mother in 1618 during the meeting of the Estates General. Thereafter, Louis XIII entrusted the government entirely to Richelieu.

The success of Louis XIII was in large measure due to the decisive leadership of Cardinal Richelieu. Although a bishop and later a cardinal, his treatment of the Huguenots in France was based on his sense of the threat they posed to the strength of the French king, rather than their religious views. Their possession of fortified cities in southwestern France gave them status as an independent political power, a state within a state. Richelieu worked to destroy their role as an effective force in French politics because their power competed with that of the king. But he permitted them to retain their religious liberties. He also continued the domestic policies of Sully and increased royal support of industry, anticipating the mercantilist policies more fully developed in the later seventeenth century. He definitely viewed the economy of France as a matter of vital importance to the growth of French power. He promoted colonies, though on a small scale, partly from a belief in their strategic importance, but partly, too, for their potential economic role. His successor, Cardinal Mazarin (1602–1661), continued the tradition of strong leadership into the period of Louis XIV's minority. Richelieu and Mazarin brought France to the pinnacle of European leadership by the end of the Thirty Years' War in 1648.

While the French monarchy was moving in the direction of absolutism in the early seventeenth century, royal government in England found itself increasingly hemmed in by the growing reluctance of the English Parliament to trust the king's administration of government. Already in the last years of Elizabeth, Parliament had grown restive under royal restraint. The Virgin Queen herself, despite her enormous prestige, had had to rebuke the Commons for "meddling" in the affairs of the Crown by daring to discuss matters of religion and foreign policy long regarded as part of the royal prerogative. When she died, these problems passed to her successor, James Stuart, King of Scotland.

James I (James VI of Scotland) (1603–1625) had been reared in the stifling atmosphere of the Scottish kirk, dominated by Calvinist divines. He was intelligent, but overly sensitive. He had an exalted concept of the dignity of the royal person. He also believed that God had ordained kings to rule over their subjects and that the king was, therefore, answerable only to God. He later incorporated these ideas into a book entitled *Basilikon Doron,* which reveals him as a pedantic scholar but a convinced believer in the divine right theory of monarchy. Yet, Englishmen looked to

King James I of England. He loved the trappings of kingship. (The Bettmann Archive)

James to remedy the difficulties they had encountered during the last years of Elizabeth and his arrival in England was greeted with enthusiasm.

James I desired to be a major force in European affairs. England offered him a much broader scope for the fulfillment of these ambitions than his poor Scotland. Yet, in the long run, he was disappointed. His reign was not a continuation of the Elizabethan tradition of glory. He himself did not really know England and therefore failed to understand such basic elements as the relationship of the monarch to Parliament, the English tradition of the common law, the importance of the Elizabethan religious settlement, and the limited sources of revenue available to the Crown.

From the first years of his reign, James encountered difficulties with Parliament over religion and finance. The previous decade had witnessed the increase of Calvinist influence within the English Church. These "Puritans" objected strongly to the retention of ceremonies and teachings from the Catholic Church. They were especially strong in southeastern England and among the landed gentry who formed an important element in local political life. By the end of the century, the Puritans were a vocal minority in Parliament. Elizabeth refused, however, to grant their demands for a full-scale revision of ecclesiastical practices within the English Church. They looked to James for aid. However, the new king early revealed his antagonism to Puritanism and throughout his reign refused to permit changes in the structure of the Church that they wanted. Instead, he supported the Anglican bishops in their efforts to reduce Puritan influence. Puritans in Parliament retaliated by refusing to vote revenues desired by James and, as their strength and numbers grew, brought the machinery of that body almost to a standstill in an effort to force the king to meet their demands.

James I found his hands tied in foreign policy by the lack of support at home. His efforts to support the Protestant cause in the Thirty Years' War, first led by his son-in-law Frederick, the Elector Palatine, came to nought because he was unable to gain money to intervene directly and his attempts to secure aid from the Danish king were insufficient to be of real value. James also entered into a long and unpopular effort to marry his son Charles to a Spanish princess, a move that won little approval and aroused great opposition so soon after the war with Spain. The marriage failed to materialize and Charles later married a French princess, Henrietta Maria. In analyzing the two matches, it is apparent that the Spanish match would probably have gained more for England by bringing closer together two powers with much to fear from France. England obtained nothing substantial from the French marriage. At least in part, the vociferous opposition of anti-Spanish elements in England hindered the conclusion of a satisfactory agreement with Spain.

Parliamentary antagonism to the monarchy further impeded the efforts of James to rule England during the later years of his reign. When he died in 1625, his son Charles I (1625–1649), after a brief attempt to secure parliamentary support, attempted to avoid summoning that body for the rest of his reign. To carry out this policy successfully, Charles had to find every source of money available to the monarchy. He sold titles and enforced old legislation which required those with a substantial income to accept knighthood, save that he allowed the candidates to buy their way out of this expensive and anachronistic duty. He extended the requirement to provide money for the navy from the seaports to towns inland. This particular effort roused considerable opposition from the supporters of Parliament, culminating in the famous Hampden's Case. Hampden was tried for refusing to pay a small levy of ship money due the Crown. He was found guilty on the grounds that the Crown was within its rights to levy these dues. However, the publicity given the case served as propaganda for the parliamentary cause.

The long struggle between Parliament and the Crown broke out in open rebellion in 1642. Charles, faced with opposition in Scotland, now had to fight the parliamentary army, led by Oliver Cromwell. Defeated and taken prisoner, Charles attempted to secure help from Scotland. But, in 1649, he was tried and condemned; the charge was treason. Parliament assumed total control of England.

The English Civil War defeated the attempt of the early Stuart kings to create an absolute monarchy in England. Yet the civil war was not merely the result of the Stuart attempt to impose absolute monarchy. The identification of Anglicanism with the Crown made the king the focus of all religious opposition to the Elizabethan settlement. The genuine need of the monarchy for additional revenues in an age of rising prices was ignored by the parliamentary leaders. Once in power, they were forced to reckon with political realities they could safely ignore while they were in opposition. The civil war involved most of the energies of Englishmen during the 1640's so that their country played almost no part in the conclusion of the Thirty Years' War, which saw France emerge as the dominant power on the continent and witnessed the death rattle of the Holy Roman Empire.

In the Holy Roman Empire, the religious divisions stemming from the Reformation had permitted the fragmentation of religious loyalties along the boundaries of the territorial microcosms ruled by the individual princes. Only the dynastic interests of the Habsburg emperors and the façade of the Holy Roman Empire cloaked the fundamental disunity of

Germany. The Habsburgs had built the strength of their house not on Germany but on an alliance system which made them rulers of Southeastern Europe, in Spain, and the Netherlands in the sixteenth century. They had permitted the German princes to wield royal powers within their own territories virtually unchecked. Their control of the emperorship created a false image of government where almost no real authority existed. The Holy Roman Empire was but a long shadow cast by the Middle Ages into the modern era. So long as it persisted, it impeded rather than aided in the building of a centralized German state. But any hope, no matter how remote, that the Habsburgs might reverse this historical trend was dashed to nothing with the outbreak of the Thirty Years' War.

The causes of this war were partially religious and partially political. The Peace of Augsburg in 1555 had laid the basis for a Lutheran-Catholic settlement in the principle that each ruler should determine the religion of his territory. This arrangement made no provision for the establishment of Calvinist states. However, within Bohemia itself, there was considerable resistance not merely to rule by the Habsburgs, but even more to rule by a Catholic prince. The majority of the Bohemian nobility had embraced Protestantism, chiefly Calvinism. The dissident Protestant nobility refused to accept the Emperor Ferdinand as their king and chose Frederick, the Elector Palatine, a Protestant and a Calvinist as their ruler. Thus the lines were drawn between Catholicism and Protestantism. Yet the war also involved a dynastic struggle between the Habsburgs and the Protestant German princes.

Habsburg attempts to control Bohemia did not go unnoticed elsewhere in Germany and beyond. Frederick belonged to the League of Protestant German Princes; Ferdinand had the support of Maximilian of Bavaria, leader of the Catholic league. Frederick was the son-in-law of the English King, James I; Ferdinand could call on the Habsburgs in Spain for support. Therefore, from its beginnings, the war was more than a struggle for the Bohemian crown. It was also part of the Catholic effort to roll back Protestantism and a threat to the Protestant princes of northern Germany.

Ferdinand was able to decide the issue of the Bohemian crown rather quickly. His defeat of Frederick at the Battle of White Mountain in 1620 forced the Protestant elector to flee to the Netherlands. Bohemia, crushed by this defeat, became a mere province within the states of the Habsburgs. The defeat of Frederick, and Ferdinand's act in granting his electoral title to Maximilian of Bavaria aroused the other German Protestant princes, while Frederick himself worked to secure aid from the other

Protestant powers. English aid was not forthcoming to any great extent and a military effort by the Danish king met no success.

Imperial success appeared imminent. Ferdinand issued the Edict of Restitution in 1629, ordering that all princes must restore Church lands secularized after 1552. The aim was to regain control of those bishoprics which had gone over to the Protestant side taking their estates with them. But this move only solidified the opposition of the Protestant princes. Still, without leadership and facing a seemingly invincible imperial army, they had little hope of success. It was here that matters stood when the French minister of Louis XIII, Cardinal Richelieu became involved.

Richelieu's ambitions for the French monarchy to become the major power in Europe could succeed only if the Habsburgs were defeated. France was surrounded by their domains. But France herself was not prepared for a war; still weak from the religious wars of the sixteenth century and with the Huguenot problem unsettled, the French monarchy was just beginning to recover. Richelieu, therefore, turned northward to Gustavus Adolphus, King of Sweden, and offered him financial support for his entry into the war on the Protestant side. Gustavus Adolphus was more than willing. A staunch supporter of Swedish expansion, he had already driven to the borders of East Prussia in his effort to make the Baltic Sea a Swedish lake. Richelieu's invitation promised an opportunity to reach his objective.

As Protestant champion, the Swedish king was suspect because of his own ambitions. But the victorious course of the imperial forces did not allow the Protestant German princes the luxury of choosing their allies. Under his leadership, the tide of battle turned. The Swedish army, modernized and trained by the French, met the forces of the imperial General Wallenstein on almost equal terms. Unfortunately, Gustavus Adolphus himself was killed in battle in 1632. Although the Swedes continued to fight, the Protestant cause had suffered another serious blow. The Peace of Prague, concluded in 1635, brought an end to the Swedish phase of the war. In general, the terms were favorable to the emperor, though the Protestant princes were not required to restore the lands which they had acquired since 1552 as prescribed by the Edict of Restitution. Germany yearned for peace and this sentiment was shared by the new Emperor Ferdinand III, elected in 1637. However, Richelieu had not yet realized his war aims. In fact, the Habsburgs appeared to be stronger than ever. It was his determination that kept together the alliance against the emperor. Moreover, he had decided that the time was now opportune for direct French intervention. The final phase of the war lasted until 1648, dragged out by both sides in the hope of gaining a decisive victory. The death of Richelieu in 1642 did not weaken the French in the least; his handpicked successor, Cardinal Mazarin, brought the war to its conclusion in the Peace of Westphalia in 1648.

The Thirty Years' War destroyed much of Germany and severely weakened the last hold of the emperors over the German princes. It removed the great cloak of the Holy Roman Empire from the German states and exposed their disunity. Henceforth, the Habsburgs kept the imperial title but it meant little save as an honor conferred on the ruler of Austria. The Imperial Diet, which had been meaningless enough, now lacked even the shadow powers it once had possessed. France emerged as the leading power on the continent of Europe; the policy of Richelieu was vindicated. No other power in Europe could seriously challenge France.

In the immediate aftermath of the Thirty Years' War and the English Civil War, France emerged as the leading power in Europe. The success of the policies of Henry IV and Richelieu were partly responsible. The devastation of the Thirty Years' War left Germany disunited and in ruins, the Habsburg emperor without authority even to rebuild the weak imperial structure as it had been before the war. The English Civil War destroyed the monarchy and prevented England from playing a dominant role in continental politics before the end of the century. The road was open for a moment of glory in the history of France. The ruler who stood in that moment of history was Louis XIV.

France in the Age of Louis XIV

The age of Louis XIV was the last great era of European dynastic politics before the development of the modern nation-state succeeded in subordinating even the monarchy to the interests of the nation as a whole. It was the culmination of tendencies which had their origins in the building of the feudal monarchies of Western Europe. The king finally succeeded in dominating the feudal aristocracy in France and almost completely harnessing them to the needs of the monarchy. Louis XIV stood as a symbol of the strength of the French monarchy, of the principle of hereditary rule of one family as proprietors of the state, which had developed during the later Middle Ages.

Louis XIV came to the throne in 1642 and ruled until 1715. His was the longest reign in French history. He worked long hours with his ministers after the demands of social life had been met. He had no intention of permitting another to share in the sacred office which belonged to him alone.

Louis XIV by Rigaud. The "grand monarch" in regal apparel presents us with a splendid symbol of the grandeur of France in his age. (Syracuse University Collection)

For he was the king, chosen by God, anointed to rule by divine right. In Louis XIV, the cult of the divine-right monarchy founded its fullest expression. The absolutism of Louis XIV was founded on a high concept of duty to an office which had been conferred by God. Therefore, it did not really matter that Louis himself was not very intelligent; he was the king. Moreover, he endeavored to make up by hard work and study for some of his intellectual limitations. He was a good observer and gained a sound knowledge of European politics. But he was also prone to pass off the responsibility for failure to his ministers and other underlings, saving for himself only the credit for success. Yet he had many qualities needed for a strong monarch. He was able to choose outstanding men to serve him and to entrust major responsibilities to them. He rewarded their efforts richly with titles of nobility and pensions so that they were devoted to his service. Nor did they hesitate, on occasion, to point out to him the dangers and weaknesses of some of his policies, though they deferred to his decisions. Herein lay the key to his absolutism: ultimately all decisions were made in accordance with his will.

After 1661 and until his influence waned in the seventies, the closest advisor of the king was Jean-Baptiste Colbert (1619–1683), the shrewd and resourceful director of France's finances. This cautious scion of a middle-class business background contrasted outwardly with his ostentatious monarch. But Colbert was essentially the loyal servant of the Crown, who did not question the decisions of the king no matter what problems they raised in his own effort to secure sufficient funds to meet the expenses of government. His attempt to reorganize the fiscal system and to encourage the development of industry and agriculture met only a partial success because the mounting demands of the Crown, particularly after the king embarked on a series of wars, outpaced the revenues.

Colbert based his policies as controller general of finances and secretary of state for the navy on mercantilist ideas, which gained a wide audience in the seventeenth century through the writings of numerous authors on state fiscal policies, colonies, and similar subjects. Mercantilism did not, however, develop as a unified economic system. Although certain points of a general character may serve to indicate the nature of the mercantilist system, its chief quality was the fact that it had grown out of the practices of the later Middle Ages, largely from the economic policies of the towns, and preserved much that was contradictory in medieval economic theory. As practiced by Colbert mercantilism attempted to increase the wealth of the state and its power by ensuring the growth of industry, fostering internal trade, gaining colonies that could provide needed raw materials at lower cost and could also serve as markets, promoting a favorable balance of trade by importing less than was sold abroad, and by increasing the amount of gold and silver within the kingdom (bullionism). Colbert increased government subsidies to industry and erected high tariff walls designed to discourage imports from abroad. He favored the development of French colonies in Canada, the West Indies, and the East Indies. These enterprises were chiefly commercial. Canada supplied furs for the European market, the West Indies sugar and tobacco, and the East Indies spices, cloth, and numerous luxury items much in demand. The colonies were not permitted to trade with any other state save France. He continued earlier policies aimed at reducing internal duties which slowed and discouraged the growth of internal trade, but his success in this area was modest and a jungle of internal regulations remained in effect until the French Revolution swept away king, nobles, ecclesiastics, and the heritage of the feudal economy. But these efforts by Colbert were secondary to his primary role: to raise money to meet the royal demands. Under Louis XIV, these needs grew rapidly.

Louis desired glory for himself, the monarchy, and France. The road to glory lay through the battlefield. Louis accepted this fact and involved France in a series of wars so that half his reign was filled with war. After 1668, Colbert's influence was not so great as that of the Minister of War, the Marquis de Louvois. He increased the army from about 15,000 to about 400,000 men in less than half a century. Approximately half of these troops were mercenaries. But Louis needed a large army, for he based his strategy largely on superiority on the continent. The army was necessary to fulfill Louis' territorial ambitions. In 1667, Louis invaded the Spanish Netherlands to secure them as compensation for the fact that the dowry of his Spanish Queen had never been paid. He argued that her resignation of all claims to the Spanish throne was invalid because of the failure to pay the dowry. He pressed the war in the Low Countries on the basis of a local law which said that children of a first marriage should take precedence over the offspring of a second marriage in inheriting property. Louis' Queen, Marie Therese, was born of the first marriage of the Spanish king, while his son and heir to the throne was the child of a second. The pretext was there for Louis to utilize as justification for his march into the Low Countries. But his desire was to control the great fortresses in the Netherlands as a protection against a possible invasion of France from the territories of the Holy Roman Empire. The Spaniards were no match for the well-trained and well-led French, possessors of one of the great military minds of the age in the person of General Turenne. However, the intervention of the English and the Dutch, with the threat of Sweden's entry, gave Louis pause. Rather, he contented himself with some gains in territory along the Franco-Belgian border. The War of Devolution—so-named from the claim of Queen Marie Therese—had succeeded admirably within the limits of its cautious goals. Louis was emboldened to reach further in his quest for glory.

The Dutch had intervened at just the wrong moment to deprive Louis XIV of his full victory against the impotent forces of Spain. The French monarch decided that they posed a threat to his policy of expansion along the northern frontier. However, before moving against the formidable naval power of the Dutch, he had to make sure that England was safely in his camp. Louis accomplished this feat without difficulty by providing what the restored English King, Charles II, needed most to free himself of his reliance on Parliament: money. A subsidy purchased the Treaty of Dover in 1670 and freed Louis for his war against the Dutch. Early in 1672, the French army moved inexorably across the Netherlands; no power seemed powerful enough to prevent the loss of the Dutch republic. But the Dutch bought additional time by opening the dikes, flooding their own country. The stern demands made by Louis as a condition for peace impelled the Dutch to still further efforts to continue the war. William II, the Stadtholder, turned to diplomacy and forged a Grand Alliance with the Holy Roman Empire, Brandenburg, and Spain. Charles II of England found it impossible to remain a French ally; in 1678, Louis agreed to the Peace of Nijmegen, which brought France no significant territorial gains despite the number of her victories. Louis had lost his English ally and feared that the Dutch would force Charles into the war as their ally. Though the English king would be a reluctant ally of the Dutch, the English privateers, once unleashed, would pursue French merchantmen with full energy. Nijmegen should have proved to Louis the danger of attempting to win grandeur through war, but it only made him turn to a new direction.

It was against a changed political background that Louis made his next attempt to enlarge France to her "natural" boundaries. Charles II of England had died in 1685 and was succeeded by his brother James, the Roman Catholic Duke of York. In 1688, a group of English politicians secured the backing of James II's son-in-law, William of Holland, and forced him from the throne. From his new position on the English throne, William III accomplished what Louis most feared, a reconstitution of the Grand Alliance. The French fleet was destroyed off Normandy in 1692, but the French continued to wage a successful land war until internal discontent against the war caused the outbreak of riots within France itself. Louis accepted the Peace of Rijswick in 1697 out of necessity. His major

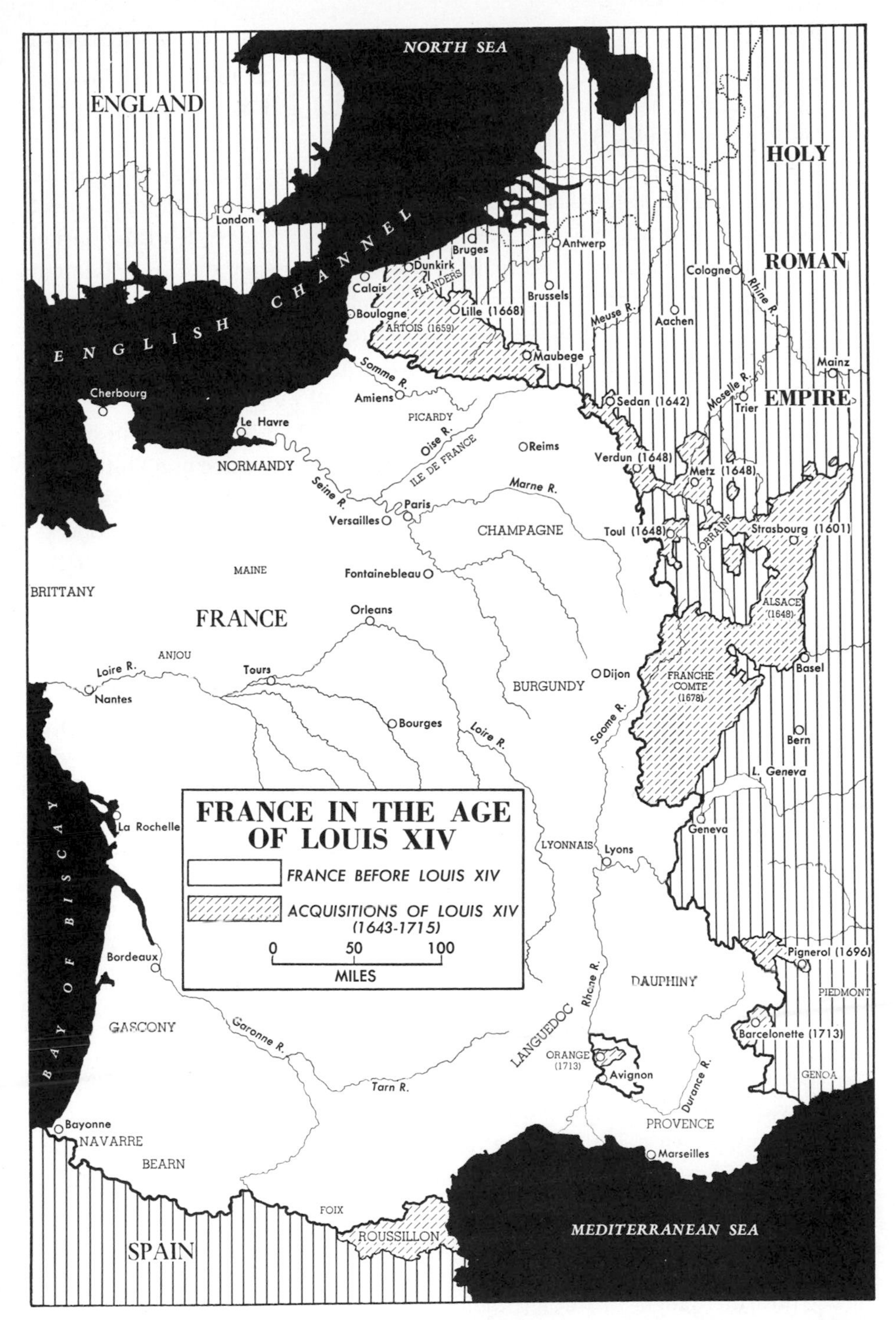

NORTH SEA
ENGLAND
HOLY
ROMAN
EMPIRE
London
ENGLISH CHANNEL
Bruges
Antwerp
Dunkirk
Calais
FLANDERS
Cologne
Rhine R.
Brussels
Boulogne
Lille (1668)
ARTOIS (1659)
Meuse R.
Aachen
Maubege
Mainz
Somme R.
Cherbourg
Amiens
Sedan (1642)
Moselle R.
Trier
PICARDY
Le Havre
Oise R.
Reims
ILE DE FRANCE
Verdun (1648)
Metz (1648)
NORMANDY
Marne R.
Seine R.
Paris
Versailles
CHAMPAGNE
Toul (1648)
LORRAINE
Strasbourg (1601)
MAINE
Fontainebleau
BRITTANY
ALSACE (1648)
FRANCE
Orleans
ANJOU
Loire R.
Tours
Dijon
Basel
FRANCHE COMTE (1678)
Nantes
BURGUNDY
Bourges
Loire R.
Saome R.
Bern
L. Geneva
FRANCE IN THE AGE OF LOUIS XIV
FRANCE BEFORE LOUIS XIV
ACQUISITIONS OF LOUIS XIV (1643-1715)
0 50 100
MILES
BAY OF BISCAY
La Rochelle
LYONNAIS
Lyons
Geneva
Bordeaux
Pignerol (1696)
DAUPHINY
Rhone R.
PIEDMONT
GASCONY
Garonne R.
LANGUEDOC
Barcelonette (1713)
ORANGE (1713)
Avignon
Durance R.
GENOA
Tarn R.
Bayonne
NAVARRE
PROVENCE
BEARN
Marseilles
FOIX
ROUSSILLON
MEDITERRANEAN SEA
SPAIN

gain was the great fortress of Strasburg in Alsace; his most bitter loss the recognition of William III as king of England and the abandonment of the claims of James II.

France was not ready for another war. The internal scars were greater than those caused by enemy armies, for the French army had yet to meet decisive defeat in the field. Louis himself was reluctant to lead the nation into war. As Charles II of Spain lay dying, he negotiated a settlement which provided for the accession of a German prince to the throne; again, in 1700, after the death of the first candidate, he negotiated another treaty with England and the Dutch to permit the Austrian archduke to succeed. But the Spanish king ignored the treaties and announced that his heir would be Philip of Anjou, grandson of Louis XIV. Louis hardly hesitated before proclaiming the acceptance of Philip, who now became Philip V of Spain. Perhaps, England and the Dutch would have accepted this situation, but Louis also insisted that Philip would be heir to the throne of France. Truly, the Pyrenees would "melt away" if this disposition of the crowns of Spain and France were permitted to stand. Louis' recognition of James III, the Old Pretender, as the legitimate successor of James II of England and his action against the Dutch fortresses in the Netherlands brought Europe into war. William III of England had died and was succeeded by his sister-in-law, Queen Anne. It was her favorite, John Churchill, Duke of Marlborough, who led a new coalition to decisive victory on the continent. The war also spread to the colonies, involving them on a larger scale than ever before. War was becoming global, breaking out of the narrower European context. French defeat now meant not merely a change in the European power structure, but also a corresponding shift throughout the colonies. The Peace of Utrecht (1713), which brought the War of Spanish Succession to a close recognized this shift by the French cession of Hudson's Bay and Acadia and the Spanish grant to England of the *Asiento,* permitting England to sell Negro slaves in Spanish America. Within Europe, the major changes gave the Holy Roman Emperor control of the Spanish Netherlands, Milan, and Naples. It was Louis XIV's last war. He had drained France of its resources, burdened it with debt, and raised doubt about the monarchy. Yet, the France of Louis XIV knew pride and glory and found for itself the beginnings of a French nation.

Frenchmen straining together against most of Europe began as fighters for the king, but ended fighting for France. They wished to defend her against the danger of foreign invasion. They found pride in their culture and their language, which more and more were capturing the minds of leading courts of Europe. The brilliance of Versailles, the great palace built by Louis as the palace of the sun, was reflected in the moons of many other European courts. The French identity was not new, but its impact on European art and literature as a national culture was new. The reign of Louis XIV saw France take a major step toward becoming a nation-state. When Louis died in 1715, that state was already forming in the consciousness of the French people. Before the century was past, France would erupt in revolutionary violence. Then, Englishmen would look across the waters of the English Channel and declaim against the French madness. For their own development of the consciousness of nationality and building of the machinery of the nation-state evolved on a very different line.

England, 1649–1715

The English Civil War, which led Charles I to the scaffold, belonged to the age of religious wars to the extent that it focused on the desires of Puritans to overturn the Anglican establishment but its political impact was in the long run as great or greater than its effect on religion in England. The military dictatorship of Oliver Cromwell (1599–1658) proved the value of strong leadership in foreign policy, but alienated Englishmen forced to live under its narrow regulation at home. When Cromwell died in 1658, the threat of a Cromwellian dynasty of "Lord Protectors" was headed off by the action of General George Monck, commander of the troops in Scotland. He secured terms from Charles II for a restoration of the Stuart monarchy and played a leading role in bringing the Stuart back from his exile to England in 1660.

Charles II (1660–1685) proved to be one of the most enigmatic monarchs ever to rule England. Faced with a very delicate situation in which monarchists desiring vengeance against the parliamentarians gathered about him while former rebels feared reprisals, Charles gave the appearance of a man torn in many directions. His major concern was the preservation of the throne for the Stuart line. To this necessity all other policy was subordinate. The king had no desire to go on his "travels" again. To this end, he attempted to build a broader base of support than the "old cavaliers," who had suffered for their king through the civil war and now expected their reward. For Charles had been restored not by cavaliers but by new men, former Cromwellians. Politically, their importance was great to any policy aimed at stabilizing the position of the monarchy. Thus Charles attempted to find support for his government among moderates.

Oliver Cromwell by Peter Lely. The artist has caught a glimpse of the soldier, while giving us an insight into the Puritan leader. (*The Bettmann Archive*)

The Restoration Parliament was dominated by cavaliers, whose chief intent was to secure the return of properties lost during the war and to redress their grievances. Charles opposed their efforts because of the threat to his position that such policies would pose. He relied on ministers committed to his views, Charles Hyde, Earl of Clarendon, the Earl of Danby, and the disparate and often mutually opposed members of the Cabal. He attempted to screen his own views behind his ministers. He played the indolent and lethargic pursuer of pleasure, surrounding himself with mistresses and favorites. Nor was this entirely a pose. After his long years of exile, he enjoyed his position as king and indulged himself in the pleasures of his court. Yet his choice of leading ministers reveals his desire to retain control of policy and to influence the direction of government. In his own way, he admired and desired to emulate Louis XIV of France, yet he dared not embark on such a course, which would surely imperil the throne.

Charles' foreign policy was cautious, but generally favorable to France. Since Parliament did not furnish adequate financial support even to meet the ordinary expenses of government, he was unable to launch an independent policy. Therefore he tried to make his foreign commitments pay some of his domestic needs. In 1668, he sold himself to the highest bidder by joining an alliance with the Dutch against Louis XIV, but in 1670, he accepted a French subsidy of £200,000 a year in the secret Treaty of Dover and pledged his aid to France. However, the alliance with France was not popular with the majority of Englishmen and roused opposition among those at home who wanted England to support Dutch Protestants against French Catholics.

Charles' preference for the French alliance was based on his admiration for Louis and on his own need. His efforts to make war pay were fruitless. In 1665, commercial competition led to involvement with the Dutch. During the protectorate, Cromwell had enacted the navigation acts, aimed at preventing trade between the English colonies and the continent except in English ships and after payment of English duties. These acts were firmly in the mercantilist tradition of the age. Under Charles II, they were strengthened by Parliament. The chief power to suffer was the Dutch republic. Cromwell had fought the Dutch successfully; Charles' efforts merely increased his expenses. Moreover plague and fire in London increased dissatisfaction with the war, while more and more Englishmen were looking to France as the real enemy. The only compensation to the English in the Peace of Breda (1667) was the cession of New Netherlands, which had been taken by a fleet under the command of the king's brother, James, Duke of York, and was therefore renamed New York. When Charles' alliance with Louis XIV drew him into war against the Dutch in 1672, his support at home was considerably weakened. He had also issued a declaration of indulgence permitting Roman Catholics and Protestant dissenters from the Church of England to worship freely in England in accordance with the aim of the Treaty of Dover to restore Catholic worship. But this action only served to increase suspicion that the king was aiming at a Catholic restoration in league with France, especially since the Duke of York became a convert to Catholicism. Parliament forced Charles to rescind this declaration and to accept the Test

Act, excluding noncommunicants of the Anglican Church from state offices. Finally, Charles was forced out of the war in 1674 and had to agree to aid the Dutch if the war did not end within four years. The policy of active alliance with France had been costly in terms of money needed for the war, the prestige and popularity of the monarchy at home, and Charles' desire to maintain the throne for his own dynasty.

The final years of Charles' rule before his death in 1685 were devoted largely to measures aimed at securing the succession for his heir and brother, James, a Roman Catholic and Duke of York. England had not had a Catholic on the throne since the reign of Mary Tudor; that experience still lived vividly in the Protestant imaginations of many Englishmen. The opposition to another Catholic was strong and found wide popular support. It was a tribute to Charles that his policy succeeded in overcoming these obstacles. When he died, his successor was James II.

The brief and stormy reign of James II (1685–1688) has given rise to mountains of historical controversy between those who believe that he was unjustly deprived of the throne and those who support the view of his contemporary opponents, the Whigs, that his reign was a threat to English Protestantism. Though the passions of scholars have cooled, agreement on the character of the king and his rule is yet to come. Perhaps the chief reason for this problem lies in the personality of James himself. He inherited and developed many of the worst traits of his Stuart ancestors. Like James I and Charles I, he tended toward a stubborn willfulness that impeded reasonable solutions to problems. Convinced that his anointing as king conferred on him a special role as a ruler responsible only to God, he ignored the advice of practical men in favor of the theoretical formulations of his spiritual advisors. Had he come to the throne with the confidence of the country, his reign, at best, would have proved difficult; without that support, it was nigh impossible.

Yet James was not the demoniac figure depicted by some earlier writers. There was little evidence to support the thesis that he desired to subvert the Anglican religious establishment. From the earliest years of his reign, he had placed the control of the established church under direction of a high commission to avoid a direct connection between it and the monarch. He was sincere in his desire to protect the rights and liberties of his subjects. Yet his favoritism in appointing Catholics to high office, despite the Test Act, and his insistence on his power to issue a declaration of indulgence aroused the fears of dissenters and Anglicans alike. James' use of Irish troops commanded by Roman Catholic officers in England recalled English fears of Cromwell's military rule. However, the final blow to his security came with the birth of his son; no longer could the Whigs argue that James would be the last Catholic ruler and that he would be succeeded by his Protestant daughter Mary, wife of William III of Holland. His Catholic second wife, Mary of Modena, gave birth to a son, who automatically became heir to the throne. Though Whig propaganda attempted to prove that the child was not legitimate, their mounting fear of a Catholic succession drove them to invite William and Mary to accept the crown. It was a "Glorious Revolution." James fled to France after dumping the great seal in the Thames River. His supporters had melted away, among them, John Churchill, later Duke of Marlborough, who had fought for James against his illegitimate nephew, the Duke of Monmouth. The arrival of William and Mary (1688–1702) was a triumphal procession.

William III had insisted that he rule jointly with his wife; in fact, he ruled while Mary only reigned. Since he had slight interest in internal English affairs, he ruled through his ministers, choosing them from the leading faction in Parliament. His government was not a party government, because these factions tended to be temporary coalitions around leading parliamentary personalities, but William's policy did further strengthen the role of Parliament in the governing of England. William's major concern lay on the continent, where he was the arch opponent of Louis XIV. With James II at the French court, the reasons for continuing his leadership of the enemies of Louis were even greater. William and Mary were rulers by parliamentary grant. They assented to the Declaration of Right (1689), which deprived the monarchy of its right to interfere in the legislative process, thus nearly completing the long task of vesting in Parliament complete control over the laws of England. But William kept a tight hand on foreign affairs. He sought and obtained the support of Parliament, including adequate financial aid, for his wars against Louis XIV.

The reign of William and Mary was made easier by the fact that Mary was the daughter of James II. The Whigs made a point of protecting the Protestant succession in the Act of Succession which excluded the infant James III from the throne and specified that William and Mary should be succeeded by James II's other daughter, Anne. The Whigs had triumphed.

Queen Anne (1702–1714) came to the throne just as war was once more breaking out between England and France. Her reign was marked by two important events, the final defeat of Louis XIV and the union of Scotland and England as the United Kingdom. In the first case, the success was due to the military genius of John Churchill (1650–1722), whom she created Duke of Marlborough; in the second case, the union was a further step in the creation of a single national state composing the whole of the British Isles, an aim that was to remain a fundamental plank of English policy into the nineteenth century and which finally foundered on the Irish question, the unsuccessful effort to make Ireland part of the United Kingdom.

The major question of the last years of Anne's reign was the future of the Stuart dynasty. Would England follow the Act of Succession and accept the German Prince, George of Hanover, descended from King James I, or would she return to the line of James II, to the Old Pretender James III. For a brief moment following the death of the queen on July 31, 1714, England wavered. The Tory Lords, sympathetic to the line of James II, hesitated. Their loyalty to the crown was based on the conviction that it represented a legitimate power to rule granted by God. Did this power pass to whomever Parliament might choose or did it remain with James III? Then the moment passed. The Viscount Bolingbroke, whose personal feelings favored James, proclaimed George of Hanover King of England by the grace of God. The question was settled. Parliament conferred the grace on the king. To Parliament had passed the task of transforming England from a dynastic state into a national state. The task was well begun in 1714.

By 1715, the territorial state that had evolved from the feudal monarchy had passed from the scene in England. For awhile longer, it survived in France, where the absolutism of the monarchy gave it a firmer hold. Yet there, too, it had received mortal blows during the very moment of its greatest glory, the rule of the sun-king, Louis XIV. No single date can ever be regarded as a watershed of history viewed internationally and in all dimensions. Yet, by 1715, the foundations had been laid for the modern era, the age of the nation-state. The major accomplishment of that state was to be the leadership of the world in the next two centuries. But this dominance was not merely political, it also embraced the economic and cultural life of the world.

The New Methods and the New Science

The seventeenth century has received various names depending on the viewpoint of the observer. From the standpoint of its architecture, it has been called the "age of the baroque." It is also the age of the "scientific revolution." Yet this century also witnessed great religious movements within Catholicism and Protestantism, particularly Jansenism and Quietism. Indeed, no term is completely adequate to describe the intellectual vitality and creativity of this century. Perhaps the most important signal of the new age was the publication in 1620 of Sir Francis Bacon's *Novum Organum,* which proclaimed the end of the dominance of Aristotelian logic and advocated an inductive approach to learning. Though Bacon's treatise was the culmination of attitudes toward learning developed during the Renaissance, it served to announce the direction in which the new century would move in its effort to bring the universe within the understanding of man. Man now possessed a new tool of learning that might unlock secrets undreamed of by his ancestors.

By the late sixteenth century, the vital contributions of the scholastic method to the development of thought were far in the past. Aristotelian logic, whose major value had been its provision of a structure for formal thought, was ill-suited to the exploration of the physical universe. The great mass of newly discovered data provided a challenge to deductive logic. Very often the results of observation countered previously held theories and even widely accepted "laws." For example, the men of the Middle Ages had accepted the Ptolemaic theory of the motion of heavenly bodies, according to which the earth was the center of the universe around which the planets and the stars revolved.

The publication of Nicholaus Copernicus' *On the Revolution of Heavenly Bodies* in the mid-sixteenth century was a major break with Ptolemy, but it rested on a mathematical rather than an experimental foundation. During the second half of the century, the Danish astronomer, Tycho Brahe (1546–1601), was able to make numerous observations of the heavens from his observatory and to provide data that could not be harmonized with the Ptolemaic system. Johannes Kepler (1571–1630) studied under Brahe. He was an excellent mathematician. It was his mathematical studies that led Kepler to theorize about the "harmonies" of the universe. Kepler espoused the position of Copernicus and advanced three laws of planetary motion, based partly on the observations of Brahe. Kepler's laws described rather than explained the behavior of planets. Each planet moved in an elliptical orbit. A line joining the center of a planet to the center of the sun (radius vector) describes equal areas of the ellipse in equal times. The square of the time required to complete a planet's revolution of the sun is proportional to the cube of its mean distance from the sun. Isaac Newton was later to explain that gravity lay behind this behavior. His debt was great both to Kepler for formulating the laws and to Brahe for making the observations on which they were based.

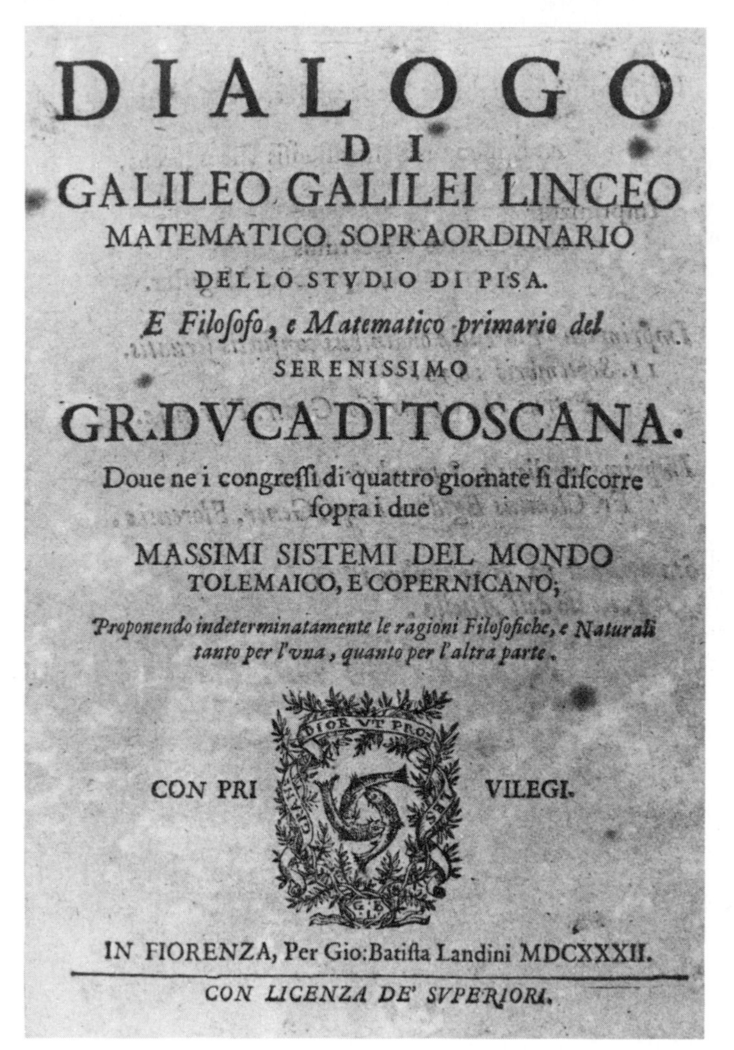

DIALOGO
DI
GALILEO GALILEI LINCEO
MATEMATICO SOPRAORDINARIO
DELLO STVDIO DI PISA.
E Filosofo, e Matematico primario del
SERENISSIMO
GR.DVCA DI TOSCANA.
Doue ne i congressi di quattro giornate si discorre
sopra i due
MASSIMI SISTEMI DEL MONDO
TOLEMAICO, E COPERNICANO;
Proponendo indeterminatamente le ragioni Filosofiche, e Naturali tanto per l'vna, quanto per l'altra parte.

CON PRI VILEGI.

IN FIORENZA, Per Gio:Batista Landini MDCXXXII.

CON LICENZA DE' SVPERIORI.

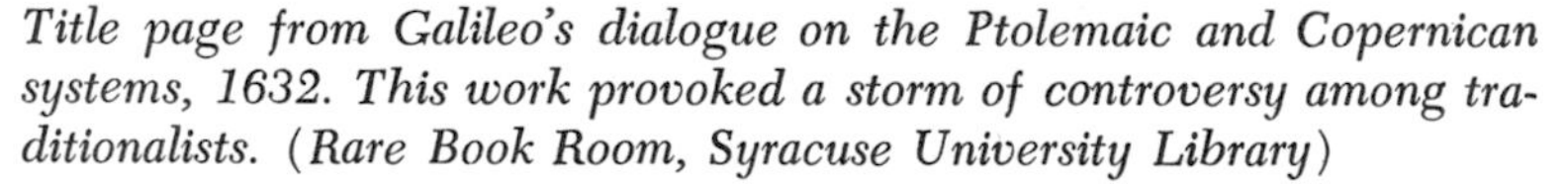

Title page from Galileo's dialogue on the Ptolemaic and Copernican systems, 1632. This work provoked a storm of controversy among traditionalists. (Rare Book Room, Syracuse University Library)

It was the telescopic observations made by Galileo Galilei (1564–1648) that finally confirmed the mathematical data of Copernicus showing that the earth revolved around the sun and revealed a whole new world for study, including the moons of Jupiter and the mountains of the moon. Galileo's defense of the Copernican theories led to his condemnation by the Church for rejecting the traditional view that the earth was the center of the universe. He was imprisoned and forced to recant. But it did not matter. Galileo was merely one of the many whose discoveries were pointing up the methodological inadequacies of any science based on deduction from general laws rather than observation. It was the work of Galileo and his predecessors that gave meaning to Bacon's *Novum Organum.*

René Descartes' *Discourse on Method* (1635) reveals another direction

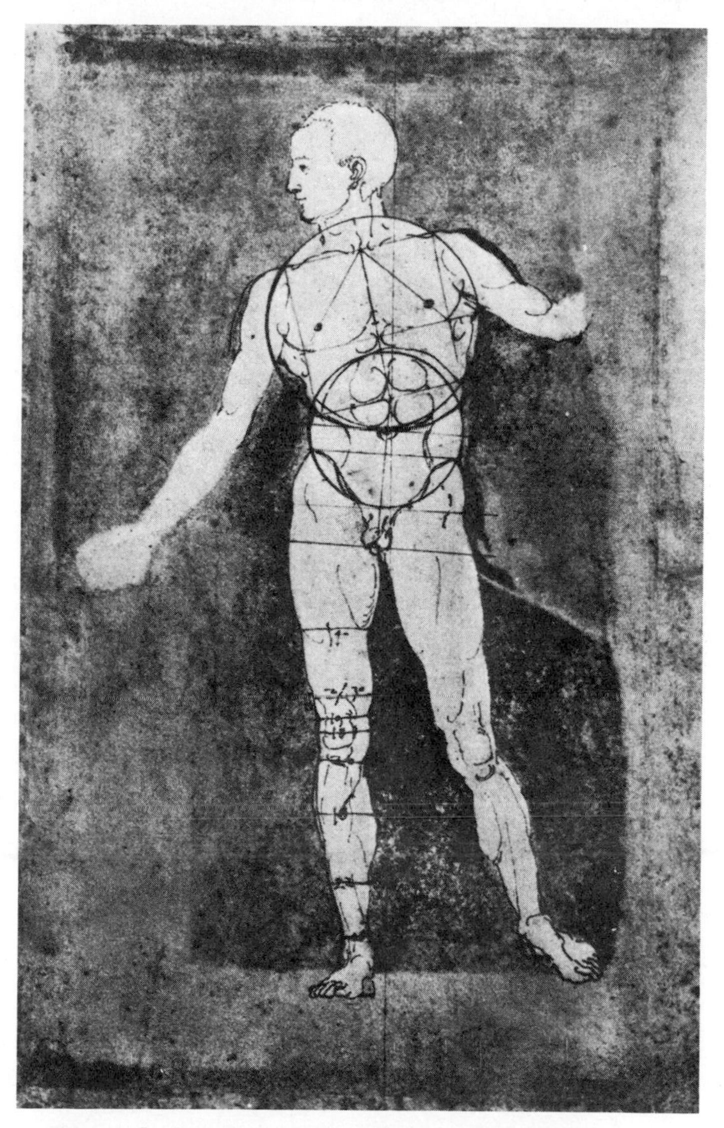

Anatomical proportions of the human body, by Albrecht Dürer. In his study of anatomy, the artist approached the scientist. (The Bettmann Archive)

of the new methodology. Descartes believed that the abstract formulas of mathematics offered the scientist the opportunity to test his hypotheses within a universal framework in which all possible cases could be encompassed. This method is not inductive despite the fact that Descartes believed that observation was essential to the understanding of nature. Its importance lay in pointing to the possibility for greater use of mathematics in the exploration of the physical universe. These methodological discoveries of the seventeenth century pointed the way for further progress in science that reached its climax in the work of Sir Isaac Newton.

In other scientific fields, too, the techniques of observation and induction proved of great significance. Medicine had relied chiefly on the work of Galen, which dated from the second century A.D. and some advances made by the Arab physicians. During the sixteenth century, anatomical studies advanced with some study of cadavers. The chief figure in this field was Andreas Vesalius (1514–1564) who taught at the University of Padua until forced into retirement. Padua also produced William Harvey (1578–1657), whose observation resulted in his discovery of the circulation of the blood. In chemistry, Robert Boyle (1627–1691) was the most significant thinker of the seventeenth century and has been called the "father of chemistry." Boyle used the technique of observation to disprove

Vesalius at the age of twenty-eight. The great physician was a young man when his epoch-making study of anatomy appeared. (Rare Book Room, Syracuse University Library)

the Greek theory that all nature is composed of four elements—earth, air, fire, and water. By defining an element as a substance not made up of other substances, he launched chemistry as a genuine experimental science, divorced from the alchemy of the Middle Ages and early modern period.

The advances in science mark the seventeenth century as one of the first ages in which observation and experimentation played a vital role in increasing human knowledge. The emphasis on science also points up the continuing growth in importance of secular over religious concerns in the culture of Europe. This emphasis on secular culture was also evident in literature and the arts.

In literature, the late sixteenth and early seventeenth centuries were the age of some of the greatest figures in world letters. This literature reflected the continued growth of individualism and a largely secular outlook on the nature of man. Michel de Montaigne's (1533–1592) essays were written in the spirit of the scientist in his criticism of his age. Miguel de Cervantes (1547–1616) wrote of *Don Quixote de la Mancha,* who longed for the return of chivalry so much that he tried to recreate that age in his own. The work is a satire on chivalric tradition, but much more. Cervantes had the ability to caricature the foibles of his age while preserving a keen sense of the character of the individual person. Don Quixote is no cardboard figure but a real person. The exaggeration of his delusions does not destroy his integrity as an individual; it serves to point up its reality. Cervantes was an acute observer of human nature, as was the great English dramatist of this age, William Shakespeare (1564–1616).

It is a truism to say that Shakespeare has no equal in English drama. Among his contemporaries, Ben Jonson has won a place in letters, but distinctly subordinate to the "Bard of Avon." The success of Shakespeare lay as much or more in his ability to create memorable characters as in his skill as a contriver of plots. The tortured Hamlet only emerges after the dramatist has shown us the sufferings of mind he had to endure. *King Lear* also reveals the artist as a close observer of human nature. Though there are types in all of the plays, perhaps more so in his comedies than the tragedies, there are few stereotypes. In the writing of Shakespeare, human experience moved across the stage.

The discoveries made at the beginning of the sixteenth century had an increasing effect on literature. Bernal Díaz del Castillo wrote a *True History of the Conquest of New Spain,* which was the forerunner of a considerable body of writing directly inspired by experiences in the new lands. Less direct influences could be found in Shakespeare's *The Tem-*

pest and Ben Jonson's *Eastward Ho.* The newly discovered lands captured the imaginations of writers and stimulated them to view the world and their characters against this changing background. As early as Thomas More's *Utopia,* some writers connected the New World with the idea of unsullied nature, a place where men lived in simplicity untouched by original sin.

During the second half of the seventeenth century, literature entered a classical phase, marked by some influence of the baroque. The writing of John Milton (1608–1674) owes much to the classic discipline of the Renaissance. Perhaps the most characteristic elements of the baroque are to be found in his *Ode on the Feast of Christ's Nativity,* whose extravagant imagery is reminiscent of the cherubs on the ceilings of the Jesuit churches. This extravagance of characterization finds its place in the theater in the creation of new heroes, whose depth of evil or height of nobility makes them caricatures of the people of the age. In music, this striving for the dramatic resulted in the opera taking on a great dramatic power. The age also witnessed the rise of numerous new forms of music.

The emphasis on sentiment and emotion had a very significant impact on religion. The teachings of Bishop Cornelius Jansen (1585–1638) denied the active role of man in salvation and reacted against the humanistic rationalism of the counter-Reformation. The Jesuits, deeply imbued with the spirit of Trent, attacked the Jansenists as heretical. Later in the seventeenth century, Quietism spread through both Catholicism and Protestantism. It advocated a passive role in man's relationship with God and appeared to its opponents to condone sin on the ground that the sinner had no real freedom. Both of these movements profoundly influenced the development of religious piety. Jansenism developed an ascetic and other worldly outlook that looked upon the pleasures of life as evil. Quietism tended to encourage emotional religious devotions that had little effect on or relation to the behavior of the individual in society.

In architecture, this period was the age of the baroque, sometimes called the "Jesuit" style because of their fondness for it in the churches they erected in Italy and Northern Europe. The Spanish influence was pronounced in Italy, but the various national cultures modified the baroque to suit their own tastes. This style was heavy, decorative, and sentimental.

As might be expected, the baroque also dominated the painting of the period. The greatest artist of the age, Rembrandt (1606–1669), captured the major elements of the style in his work. His subjects are lavishly

"Briseis Restored to Achilles," by Rubens. Here a classical scene receives a baroque treatment. (Syracuse University Collection)

dressed and reflect the fashions of the age. Gone are the sharp lines characteristic of the Renaissance artists; Rembrandt was fascinated by shadow and used it extensively to delineate features. He applied his paints thickly. To the artists of the baroque, and especially El Greco (1548–1625), realism was no longer expressed in fidelity to form, but in the artist's vision of a higher reality. They desired to paint the soul, but, failing that, they portrayed the soul within distorted limbs or agonized face or depth of expression. They captured the romantic aspect of the age.

The age of the baroque produced deep romantic feeling and emotional response. It was also an age in search of glory. Perhaps its most characteristic figure was Louis XIV. His effort to realize his dream of absolute divine right monarchy in France ultimately failed, but only after his death. His life was lived in glory in the splendor of Versailles, the palace he had built to celebrate his role as the sun-king. He fought his wars in pursuit of a greater France over which he would rule. The failure of these dreams

Santa Maria della Salute, Venice. The baroque was heavy and overornate, yet its total impression could please the eye. (*The Bettmann Archive*)

brought doom to the monarchy he cherished and worshipped. The efforts to realize them raised up forces which were to play the leading role in their destruction and in the fall of the monarchy itself. The eighteenth century reacted against the absolutism of Louis XIV and the romanticism of the age of the baroque.

13 Building the State in Northern and Eastern Europe

By the end of the seventeenth century, the territorial state had reached its climax in France. In Eastern and Central Europe, however, the evolution of the territorial state was much slower. In the Germanies and Russia, the territorial state achieved its highest form of expression only in the late eighteenth century under such rulers as Frederick the Great of Prussia, Maria Theresa of Austria, and Catherine the Great of Russia. These rulers indirectly drew much inspiration for their work of building strong states from France and especially from Louis XIV.

The pace of life in Eastern and Northern Europe lagged. There was less of an urban, more of an agricultural character to society. The cultural life of the princely courts was heavily influenced by foreign models, especially by France. The capitals of the East were no match for the splendor of Paris. Peter the Great had spent most of his efforts in building St. Petersburg. Moscow did not even begin to glitter until late in the period. Berlin was an overgrown country town at the end of the seventeenth century. Vienna, on the other hand, had charm and possessed a cosmopolitanism borne of its place as capital of a Germano-Slavic state. The slower development of political life in these regions tended to increase the importance of influences from outside on their growth. During the seventeenth and eighteenth centuries, the tempo of change quickened in these regions, telescoping the long experience of Western Europe into a relatively brief period of time.

The Rise of Prussia and the States of the North

In the aftermath of the Peace of Westphalia, which concluded the Thirty Years' War in 1648, the Germanies were badly divided and the Holy Roman Empire was shattered. The long road toward the creation of a Germany of numerous and fragmented territorial states was completed. Some leading princes even sought after and obtained the royal title, while most aped the French court in their effort to create an aura of legitimate royalty. Of the approximately two hundred German states, only a few were politically significant outside of coalition with the greater powers. The most important were Austria, whose Habsburg rulers had held the imperial crown since the fifteenth century, Brandenburg-Prussia, scattered across northern Germany and into Poland, Bavaria, the leading south German Catholic state, and Brunswick-Hanover, whose elector became King of England in 1715 as George I. Of all these states, Prussia was from an economic view least advanced in 1648. Predominantly rural and agricultural, it was not even blessed with compact frontiers, but, instead, controlled widely separated lands from Cleves in the west to East Prussia in Poland. Yet it became the leading state in north Germany.

The history of the rise of Prussia to a leading position among the German states is intimately tied to the ruling dynasty, the Hohenzollerns. During the second half of the seventeenth and through the eighteenth centuries, this family produced several outstanding rulers who overcame very real obstacles in the way of their creating a strong Prussia. The rise of the Hohenzollerns began with Frederick William IV (1640–1688), the Great Elector. He learned well the lessons of the Thirty Years' War and, on them, based a policy which was imitated and improved upon by his successors. Prussia had suffered seriously from the war, which had been fought chiefly in northern Germany. Frederick William determined to build a strong army to defend his widely scattered domains and to win respect for Prussia in international affairs. To accomplish this important end, he had to defeat the various provincial and local elements, which made the Prussian state a hodge-podge of local administrations in which the influence of the central government was slight. Characteristically, he combined both goals so that one would serve the other. He recruited his officials from the ranks of former army officers and moved them about to prevent them from building strong local attachments and to remind them of their dependency on himself. In the years after the Thirty Years' War he gradually increased his army from less than ten thousand to about fifty thousand men. To raise money to support this army, he entered into alliances with more powerful states willing to pay a subsidy for the aid of his army. However, he also used alliances to gain independence for his lands in the east from Poland and Sweden. During his reign, he worked to increase the prosperity of his domains and thereby to enlarge the financial base on which his government rested. His outlook was mercantilistic, though he did not attempt to engage in extensive trade overseas. Rather, he promoted commerce in the Baltic and encouraged the development of industry. He obtained the services of thousands of Huguenots expelled from France by the revocation of the Edict of Nantes (1685) and made them an advantageous addition to his realm by granting them special opportunities to establish themselves in business and trade. By the end of his reign, he had made Prussia a state to be respected and a coveted ally among the lesser European governments.

At the death of Frederick William, the "Great Elector," Prussia was still a conglomeration of various domains united under the central control of the Hohenzollern ruler of Brandenburg. Frederick William had not even attempted to change the status of his domains; such a move might have drawn down the enmity of one of the major powers, in particular, Austria, whose emperor was the only crowned king of a German state. True enough, the Elector of Saxony was also King of Poland. Later, George of Hanover became King of England. But their titles came from lands outside the empire. The Great Elector's son and successor, Frederick III, made acquisition of the royal title a chief aim of his reign.

Frederick III stands pale next to the towering figure of his father and the aggressive son who succeeded him. Yet he was a capable ruler, who not merely preserved his patrimony, but brought to it greater stature in new dimensions. He was a patron of the new scientific learning and gained the support of the German philosopher-mathematician, Leibnitz, as a propagandist and supporter for his regime. He founded a university at Halle. However, his chief project was the acquisition of a crown. In 1700, the Emperor Leopold I granted him the right to use the royal title "in Prussia," that is, in the lands which he held from the King of Poland. Poland was in no position to object strongly. But, by the end of his reign, Frederick was ignoring the niceties of style and calling himself King of Prussia. His aid to the emperor in the struggle against Louis XIV was too valuable for that ruler to raise a strong objection. Prussia had become a kingdom.

The accession of Frederick William I (1713–1740)—the royal title caused the adoption of a new numbering system—brought to the Prussian throne a ruler of no great intellectual attainments but with a simple dedication to strengthening the power of Prussia. It is difficult to imagine Frederick William I as the son of Frederick III (King Frederick I). He had no intellectual interests and soon sent the academics and intellectuals his father had attracted to Prussia off to other and more hospitable climes. This action certainly did no good for his reputation at other courts, but he cared little about such things. His chief interest was his army to which he devoted his personal attention and all the income that he could raise. He took greatest pride in a special regiment of Potsdam Guards who were all over six feet tall and were recruited from all over Europe. He instituted a system of compulsory military service, the first in the history of Europe since antiquity, to ensure a continuing supply of men for military service. This emphasis on the army attracted many of the best young men to a military career. In fact, the nobility (Junkers) had to furnish younger sons as officers. But the burden was not great, for the military career opened doors to advancement in all levels of government and to influence at the court. Frederick William reformed the central administration of government, setting up the General Directory for Finances, War, and Domains to control and coordinate the activities of these most important and interlocking aspects of the Prussian state.

In foreign policy, Frederick William followed a policy of extreme caution. His personal deference for Austria was genuine and prevented him from moving against imperial leadership. Moreover, he lacked real vision and had no goals beyond the limited suggestion that military power was necessary to the preservation of the Prussian state, a view he had inherited from his immediate ancestors. Perhaps too, fear of defeat and loss of his wonderful army made him afraid to test it too much in the field. At any rate, the powers of Europe felt that Prussia posed no threat so long as Frederick William I was King. When he died in 1740, Prussia was stronger than ever before in its history. His son, Frederick II (1740–1786) inherited a potentially great crown. Much depended on him for its future.

The reputation of the new king certainly gave other powers little cause to fear. He had rebelled against the military atmosphere of his father's court and even attempted to run away. He was a friend to Voltaire, the leading French savant of the day. He even played the violin. On the other hand, these reports were somewhat misleading, for he had also served with distinction in the army and was much more intelligent than his father. As king, he did not abandon his father's emphasis on the army but

Frederick the Great. Determination marks the face of the Prussian ruler, who brought his state to greatness in the eighteenth century. (The Bettmann Archive)

gave it more meaning by his own goal: to make Prussia the leading German state. He harbored the resources of the state for this purpose. He was an absolutist, devoted to duty, worn out with service of Prussia.

To a large extent, Frederick benefitted from the work of his ancestors, but he also made significant contributions of his own. He was a Prussian "Justinian." He issued a law code that attempted to protect the rights of the commoners against the infringements of the nobles, though his effort was far from successful. He was committed to the building of a sound economy and was blessed with prosperity. His treasury grew rich with increased revenues from taxation during his reign. He encouraged trade and industry on a larger scale than his predecessors and founded the Bank of Berlin to act as the state bank. His outlook was mercantilistic; he levied high tariffs aimed at keeping out foreign manufactured goods in order to increase the Prussian balance of trade.

His interest in culture was broad. In this aspect he resembled his grandfather. He refounded the Berlin academy and attracted numerous foreign intellectuals to the country. His high regard for the French led him to favor both them and their language. He made elementary education mandatory, but did little to implement the requirement. He also planned a modern curriculum for the "Realschule" with emphasis on modern languages and economics instead of the ancient classics. He favored all things he believed would strengthen and enrich the state.

However, Frederick's major accomplishment was the creation of a modern state with a solid block of territory as its basis. His major gains were at the expense of Austria. In the so-called Silesian Wars, he gradually won from Austria recognition of his right to rule the hitherto Austrian province of Silesia, thus giving him a huge connecting block of territory to the southeast of Brandenburg. He also added West Prussia and Netze connecting Brandenburg and East Prussia. The whole territory gave him command of the southern shore of the Baltic Sea over more than half its length, including a number of important commercial ports. His army made him a valued ally and enabled him to play a major role in European politics. Prussia, under Frederick the Great, was the most important power in Northern Europe at this time.

The Prussian state of Frederick the Great was built along the lines of Louis XIV's France. It was a territorial or princely state. Prussia lagged behind Western Europe in the growth of national feeling. Likewise, just as the Germanies failed to develop centralized government, Prussia failed to move in the direction of the nation-state. Her leadership to unify Germany came only slowly in the nineteenth century and from causes largely outside of the understanding of Frederick the Great.

In Scandinavia, the seventeenth and eighteenth centuries witnessed struggles between the monarchy and the aristocracy for control of the government. Royal government was in decline during this period. It was not that the monarchs were weak or incompetent; rather the whole pressure of the age was in the direction of a broader participation in political life. The need of the government for support to realize its ambitious policies of conquest made that government more responsive to indirect controls exercised by those groups of subjects possessing some measure of political and economic influence. A process similar to the Whig revolution that had overthrown James II of England played an important part in limiting the authority of monarchs in Sweden and Norway-Denmark.

The great heyday of Swedish conquest had been the early seventeenth century under the leadership of Gustavus Adolphus, who had promised to create a mighty power in Northern Europe, a territorial state that might rival France and England. But these hopes fell at the Battle of Lutzen (1632), where the great monarch perished. In the second half of the seventeenth century, aristocrats and monarch struggled over the great Swedish Empire. During the minority of King Charles XI, the nobles in control of the government overstepped themselves and became involved in war with Frederick William III of Brandenburg. Charles stepped in at the end of the war and gathered the reins of power into his own hands. He secured passage of special laws in the Riksdag (parliament) to limit the powers of the nobility and he enunciated the divine right theory of kingship. By refraining from war, he was able to maintain a sure hand on the administration of his kingdom.

Charles XII (1697–1718) spent the first decades of the eighteenth century fighting to enlarge his domains and to protect them from the increasing military might of Russia and Prussia. His father's wisdom in avoiding war provided him with the means to pursue it. But his efforts were vain. He simply was no match for the rising power of Russia and Prussia. By the time of his death, he had lost most of the Swedish possessions along the shore of the southern Baltic. But, more important, he had weakened the monarchy. His successor and her husband, King Frederick, accepted a new constitiution modeled on the English "declaration of right" signed by William and Mary in 1688. Although Gustavus III attempted to reassert the initiative of the monarch in the executive control of government, Sweden moved further along the road to constitutional monarchy.

The union of Norway and Denmark had created a powerful state. There, the nobility had played a leading part until discredited in a war against Sweden in the mid-seventeenth century. Thereafter, King Frederick III (1648–1670) moved to create an hereditary and absolute monarchy. By diluting the power of the nobles—they found many of their privileges now granted to other classes, Frederick ultimately may have weakened the power of the monarchy, but for the short run, he eliminated his major opposition. But most of the energy of the Danish kings in the later seventeenth and eighteenth centuries went into wars against Sweden and her allies aimed at recouping the losses to Gustavus Vasa and his predecessors.

The rise of Prussia combined with the decline of the other Baltic powers created a significant shift of the balance of power both in Northern Europe and in the Germanies. In Northern Europe, no longer Sweden and Denmark, but Prussia was the dominant power. In the Germanies, the traditional role of Austria, homeland of the Habsburgs, had received a challenge. The results of these shifts became important in the nineteenth and twentieth centuries. For it was Prussia rather than Austria that took the lead in creating the modern German national state, while the Scandinavian countries were forced into a secondary role by the increasing power of Germany. These events were presaged in the increasing interest of the Austrian Habsburgs in Southeastern Europe.

Austria, Italy, and Southeastern Europe

The ability of Cardinal Mazarin and the French to dictate much of the settlement of the Thirty Years' War was significant in marking out the future of the House of Habsburg in Europe. Since the early sixteenth century and before, the avowed policy of the French to reduce the power of the Habsburgs had operated as one of the touchstones of their foreign policy. The opportunity at Westphalia was the climax of these plans. The Holy Roman Emperor lost virtually all vestiges of the already shadowy authority he possesed over the German states. Whatever ambitions the Habsburgs may have entertained about the creation of a German state were now dead. To all intents and purposes the Holy Roman Emperor had become merely the ruler of Austria and some scattered domains elsewhere in Western Europe. However, his real power lay in the East, in his possession of the Kingdom of Bohemia, of Hungary—though largely in Turkish hands—and other lands in Southeastern Europe. Such diverse possessions precluded almost from the beginning the possibility of building a nation; the best the Habsburgs might hope for was a loyalty to crown and empire that would bind their disparate lands in some kind of territorial unity.

The reduction of Austrian influence in the Germanies was accompanied by a continuing growth in Southeastern Europe. Not only did the Austrians and their allies halt the Turkish advance in the late seventeenth century, but Austria made significant territorial gains in Hungary. In 1686, hard on the heels of King Jan Sobieski's defense of Vienna, the Austrians took Budapest, the Hungarian capital, and in 1687, they decisively defeated the Turks in the Battle of Mohacs. By the Treaty of Karlowitz in 1699, Austria obtained the whole of Hungary save for one district. Karlowitz increased the extent of Austria's concern about Southeastern Europe and further turned her interests away from Germany.

But Austria retained major interests in Central and Western Europe. The effort to defeat Louis XIV found Austrian armies commanded by the brilliant Prince Eugene of Savoy side by side with the forces of the Duke of Marlborough. The recognition of the Austrian role in Louis' defeat came in the Treaty of Rastadt in 1714 with the transfer of the Spanish Netherlands to Austrian control. Thus, while Austria's interests in Southeastern Europe continued to increase, she remained one of the major European powers.

The heir of the Emperor Charles VI was his daughter, Maria Theresa (1740–1780), wife of Francis, Duke of Lorraine and later Tuscany. No woman could succeed to the imperial title, but Charles was determined that his daughter should inherit the whole of his dominions intact. During the later years of his reign, he worked to gain the assent of the powers to her succession in the so-called pragmatic sanction. When he died in 1740, he had succeeded in obtaining the assent of the peoples of his own domains as well as that of the chief powers of Europe. For the first time in history, Austria had a queen, in fact if not in name.

The powers had accepted the pragmatic sanction, but not all were willing to abide by it. Frederick the Great of Prussia coveted German Silesia, one of Austria's chief possessions. Scarcely had Maria Theresa inherited her domains than Frederick, in December, 1740, led his army into Silesia. He anticipated no major problem in its conquest and was caught by surprise at the vigorous response of his opponent. Though defeated in the first major battle of the war, she entered into an alliance with Holland and England; Frederick allied with France and Bavaria. Still the Austrians met reverses in the field. Finally, Maria Theresa looked to Russia for assistance and the fear of a threat to his eastern flank caused Frederick to enter into peace talks. He deserted his imperial creation to Maria Theresa in return for her cession of most of Silesia.

Meanwhile, the coalition formed by the Austrian ruler pressed Frederick's candidate, the Emperor Charles VII, against the wall. Frederick decided once more to come to his aid. The Second Silesian War broke out in 1744.

The death of Charles VII and the election of Francis I as Emperor was the major achievement of this phase of the war. Maria Theresa's armies were no match for the coalition against her. Once more she had to confirm Frederick's title to Silesia. But Maria was not ready yet to grant her final defeat.

During the decade that followed her Chancellor, Count von Kaunitz, attempted to win for Austria the support of France in order to bring to her side the powerful land power needed for victory. His effort received considerable assistance from Frederick the Great's acceptance of a treaty with Great Britain. Louis XV of France, fearing that he would be isolated, joined Austria in what historians have labeled the diplomatic revolution. This reversal of traditional alignments illustrated the importance of a new principle in European international politics: the balance of power.

The effort of the major powers, and particularly England, to maintain their position forced them to forge an alliance system that would guarantee their strength. The balance of power simply recognized that European wars no longer involved individual states but almost inevitably drew most European states to take sides. Diplomacy, therefore, came to occupy a position of great importance as an instrument of state policy. This position was not newly won, but the diplomatic revolution shows how great a role diplomacy had come to play in the affairs of states.

With the diplomatic revolution complete, Frederick and Maria Theresa faced one another. It was the Prussian king who took the initiative; he invaded Saxony in August, 1756. The war went badly at first. Only English subsidies permitted Frederick to continue. The Austrian-French alliance was proving its value. Moreover, the Russian support of this alliance meant that Frederick was almost completely surrounded by enemies. However, the death of the Russian ruler, Elizabeth I, in 1762, and the accession of Peter III brought a major change. Peter withdrew from the war. His wife and successor, Catherine, kept Russia out of the war. Without Russian support, Maria Theresa and her allies lacked the force necessary for victory. The Treaty of Hubertusberg in 1763 did not materially alter the *status quo* in Central and Eastern Europe. Frederick kept Silesia; the Habsburgs continued to control the imperial crown. But the treaty further strengthened Austrian interests outside of Germany.

Despite the involvement of Austria in the Silesian wars, Maria Theresa did not neglect the internal development of her state. The necessity of fighting the war forced her to recognize the traditional privileges of the Hungarian aristocracy to secure their support. Nor did she proceed against the privileges of the nobility elsewhere in her domains. Nevertheless, she worked quietly and effectively to reform the confused and anachronistic government of her diverse domains. In this context, reform meant greater centralization, but a centralization accomplished slowly so as not to arouse a strong opposition. She approached those areas most in need of reform with caution. She did not raise taxes or seek new sources of income as much as she attempted to reduce her own expenditures by making the government more efficient. Her efforts to free peasants of the burdens of labor services still imposed in most parts of her domains met only a limited success. Where her power was greatest, as on her own estates, the lot of the peasants improved, but the nobles generally failed to follow her enlightened example. Her major achievement was in gathering greater control of the administration and financing of government into her own hands. When she died, in 1780, some progress had been made on the road to creation of an Austrian state. The future of the Austrian state rested with her successors. But, already, certain conditions existed which would help to shape that future. The most important of these was the fact that Austria had vast interests outside of Germany, among the Bohemians, Slavs, and Hungarians. The effort to create a state out of such diverse peoples provided the chief theme of the history of this area during the nineteenth century.

Italy in the seventeenth and eighteenth centuries was more and more the pawn of foreign rulers. Divided into a patchwork of states, which retained the fierce local loyalties of the earlier period, Italy merited Napoleon's description of it as a "geographical expression." During this period, Austrian influence mounted in the north and east with their control of Milan and the Duchy of Tuscany in the eighteenth century. The states of the Church, most of central Italy, languished under the post-Tridentine Papacy. The custom of appointing governors as a sign of papal favor encouraged a spoils system second to none in Europe. Though potentially despotic, papal rule was usually rather lax; the rule of the Church absorbed so much effort that little was left to devote to local government. A Spanish house ruled in the Kingdom of Naples and Sicily. Despite the prevalence of foreign influence, Italy managed to preserve not merely a modicum of prosperity, but also an active cultural life. If this period marked a decline from the heights of the Renaissance, there remained much of value.

The greatest power in Southeastern Europe through most of this period was not European at all. The Ottoman Empire, with its seat at Constantinople (Istanbul) after 1453, must be counted one of the major European powers in the seventeenth century. Its control of Greece, and most of the Slavic lands south of the Danube, as well as a major part of Hungary, had come as a result of aggressive expansion in the fifteenth and sixteenth centuries. In this period, the Ottomans possessed one of the most advanced states in terms of its organization of political life. Its well-trained and loyal bureaucracy was drawn not merely from the Moslem population, but, through the operation of the *Devshirme* system, from the Christian populace as well. Although the *Devshirme* meant separation from families and the sacrifice of Christian beliefs for those selected, many Christian parents looked upon it as an opportunity for advancement for their children rather than as a burden to be escaped. Moreover, not all who rose to positions of influence in the empire within the *Devshirme* gave up their family or religious ties. Many continued to practice their religion in private. For the empire, the system had the advantage of securing the services of a brilliant and devoted group of public servants. The high qual[illegible] of Ottoman government and the toleration extended to Christians [illegible] the Ottoman sultans of the early period made their subjects content and impressed on neighboring peoples the advantages they might obtain from Ottoman rule. The Magyar nobility of the early and middle seventeenth century were merely one group who found an Ottoman alliance advantageous.

The power of the Ottoman Empire gained the respect of the states of Europe. Throughout the sixteenth century, it proved its ability to meet Europeans on equal terms on the field of battle. Through most of that century, the Ottoman threat was a major cause for concern to Europe. During the seventeenth century, continued expansion of the empire proceeded until the decisive victory of Jan Sobieski, King of Poland, at the very gates of Vienna in 1683, brought an end to expansion. During the following century, Austria and her allies gradually pushed the Ottoman Empire out of Hungary and nibbled away at other Ottoman territories in Southeastern Europe.

After the seventeenth century, though still formidable, the Ottoman Empire found itself increasingly on the defensive. Within its vast frontiers, decay was gradually spreading. It was in the grips of a stagnant conservatism that refused to recognize the need for change. The army, once the equal or better than most in the West, clung to its antique weapons and tactics and refused to change. An entrenched military elite, fearful of losing their position, concealed their incompetence and grew rich from the graft they obtained from military contractors. The *Ulema,* religious leaders who controlled higher education, did not accept any changes in their traditional teachings. The empire remained an imposing but largely hollow shell of its former power. It continued to exist largely because no other power of that period actually realized the extent of its weakness.

In Southern and Southeastern Europe, though Austria showed how dynastic interest might be combined with a desire to establish a stronger and more centralized government, the majority of the powers were in decline. Of all of them, only Austria was to play a leading role in the affairs of Europe in the early nineteenth century and her role was increasingly subordinate to the rising power of Prussia in Germany. The process of state-building, which had captured the minds of European rulers and led to the establishment of the mighty powers of Western Europe had some influence in this region. But the existence of large multinational states like the Austrian and Ottoman Empires inhibited the growth of the nation-state in the nineteenth century.

Eastern Europe and the Rise of Russia

At the dawn of the modern age, the greatest state of Eastern Europe was the Kingdom of Poland-Lithuania. During the fourteenth and fifteenth centuries, the Jagellon dynasty had added considerably to the territories of the realm, which included lands from the Baltic to Austria and eastward into the Ukraine, even beyond the old Ukrainian capital of Kiev. In the sixteenth century, however, royal authority declined while the influence of the aristocracy in political life increased until it controlled not merely the Diet, but the monarchy itself. The Polish king did not possess extensive domains to pay for a large standing army and was forced to accede to the desires of the nobles in most instances. From time to time, a strong ruler, by dint of personality or determination, might succeed in restoring some hint of the royal power, but such efforts were transitory. By the seventeeth century, Poland was in decline.

The growth of Prussia in the late seventeenth century and the rise of Russia to the east pointed to Poland's greatest problems, her lack of natural and defensible frontiers and the failure of the nobles to unite behind their monarchy. By the middle of the century, the Russians had deprived Poland of most of the Ukraine; by the end of the century, German control of Prussia had led to its integration into the Prussian kingdom by Frederick William I.

Poland suffered from the anarchy of aristocratic rule. Theoretically, all members of the nobility were equal, despite wide differences in wealth. The Polish Diet, which jealously guarded all power, was itself a limited body. In theory, any member of the Diet could veto legislation and dissolve the body. Not even the ancient Athenian assembly had gone so far. The failure of the Diet to provide strong kings was amply illustrated with the election of Frederick Augustus of Saxony as the successor to Jan Sobieski in 1697. Augustus attempted to use his Saxon duchy as a basis for the creation of a strong Polish state. On his death, the rival forces contending for the throne precipitated the War of Polish Succession. As a result of the peace treaty in 1735, Augustus III, son of the former king, was allowed to succeed. But the war had made Poland's weakness apparent to all and encouraged the powers to seek a more permanent solution.

The solution was partition. In 1772, Frederick the Great invaded Poland, followed by Catherine of Russia and a far from willing Maria Theresa. Frederick and Catherine each made significant gains; Maria Theresa received Polish Galicia. But these moves were merely the beginning. At first, it appeared that the partition might arouse Polish patriotism and bring the unity that the crown had failed to achieve. But, just on the brink of success, the nobles split and a few of the leaders called on Catherine of Russia to support the old regime. Quite happily, she moved her armies into Poland. The two partitions that followed in 1793 and 1795 extinguished the Polish kingdom.

Poland had fallen before Prussia and Russia, victim to two rising giants in Europe. Of the two, Russia was potentially the greater, but she had long languished under foreign domination. In the eighteenth century, she was still not far removed from the age of Mongol domination and her nobles were still a crude and sometimes barbarously cruel lot. Yet her advance during the previous two centuries had been remarkable. From a small tributary state dominated by the Mongols, the princes of Moscow had created a vast state, whose purpose was to rule over all Russians.

The beginnings of the Muscovite state were in the efforts of the princes of Moscow to throw off the dominance of the Tartars, or Mongols. Ivan III (1462–1505) refused to continue the tribute payments to the Mongols. He desired to emancipate himself and to proclaim his state of Muscovy as the successor of the Byzantine Empire. He wed a niece of the last Byzantine ruler to strengthen his claim to the mantle of the Byzantine emperor as leader of the Orthodox Church. During his reign, the doctrine that Moscow was the "third Rome" was proclaimed. According to this theory, Moscow was heir to Constantinople, which, in turn, had inherited the position of the Rome of the West after the fall of the Western Empire. This doctrine assumed the identity of religious with political authority that was to be characteristic of the position of the Russian rulers in religious matters until the collapse of the Russian Empire in the twentieth century.

Ivan drew the conception of his powers as ruler of the Principality of Moscow not only from native Russian traditions, but also from Mongol and Byzantine sources. He was sole owner of all lands within the principality; all other landholders possessed only a limited control of the land. The Russians, like the Germanic tribes of the West, accepted this principle of patrimony as the basis for political sovereignty. But Ivan was also heir to the Byzantine tradition of the ruler as *autokrator,* an absolute ruler, divinely appointed, and responsible only to God. From the Mongols, the ruler of Moscow learned that his absolutism knew no bounds, that his subjects were utterly subject to his will, and that he might torture or destroy them if he wished.

Alongside the realities of this absolutist conception of the ruler as *autokrator* stood the reality of a powerful and unruly nobility, the Boyars, jealous of their privileges and suspicious of the prince. Ivan III broke with his predecessors by creating a new class of royal officials completely dependent on him for their incomes and their status. Since their income depended on continued service to the prince, they could not afford to resist his will. Thus, he effectively reduced the role of the Boyars in the administration of government.

One of the most powerful of the Russian rulers in this period was Ivan IV (1533–1584), called Ivan the Terrible. He took the title "Tsar," from the Byzantine *Caesar*, thus completing his grandfather's effort to stress the continuity between Constantinople and Moscow. During the ten years after his accession to full power, Ivan IV increased the judicial authority of the monarchy by putting royal justice directly into competition with that of the nobility and by restricting their power on the estates granted them for their support. The Boyars feared that this policy would result in their complete destruction and began to plot against Ivan. As news of the plots reached him, he began to fear for his life and determined on harsher policies to keep the nobles in line. His fear drove him to great excesses, including the virtual elimination of the Boyars. His foreign policy succeeded in adding the khanate of Kazan to the principality of Moscow, but he met defeat in the north at the hands of the Poles and Swedes. When Ivan died, resentment against him was deep. Only the efforts of the regent, Boris Godunov, staved off rebellion for a time and gave the principality good rule. But Boris died in 1605 and the Boyars placed thir own candidate on the throne. For the next eight years, the kingdom was plunged into a mammoth struggle for control of the crown which ended only with the election of Michael Romanov in 1613.

The seventeenth century was constantly troubled. High taxes levied by the Tsarist government were unpopular and led to riots against Michael Romanov's son Alexei. In the middle of the century, the Cossacks of the Ukraine revolted against Poland and gave the Tsar an opportunity to move into this territory. As a result of this long war, Russia obtained the lands along the Dnieper River, including the ancient city of Kiev. During this period, too, the power and wealth of the Boyars increased. They used their money to educate their sons in new ways, some of them along Western lines. Russia was beginning to move out of her Middle Ages and into a modern period of greater contact with the West.

The seventeenth century also produced one of the greatest of the Russian Tsars in Peter I (1682–1725). His desire to learn amounted almost to a passion. In 1697, he traveled extensively in Western Europe. What impressed him most was Western technology, especially the implements of war. He saw the great shipyards of Holland and England. He also sought the support of Western rulers for his program of Westernizing Russia and hired craftsmen to return to Russia with him. Later, when he founded his new capital at St. Petersburg as a "window on the West," he imported Western architects and builders so that the city would be constructed in Western style. As a result of his travels in the West, Peter attempted to introduce Western education and manners into Russia and to reform the Russian government along Western lines. He ordered the sons of officials and clergy to attend elementary school. Though the number of such schools and the available teachers were not sufficient to meet the demand, a small beginning was made in increasing the general level of education in Russia. Peter also planned to found an academy of sciences, but this project was left to his successors. The success of Peter's introduction of Western ways was greatest in those areas of his deepest interest, least in those where he attempted to influence the crude Russian aristocracy. His interest in military and naval technology led to the modernization of the Russian army and the founding of the first Russian navy. His greatest work was in the remodeling of the central administration of government along Western lines, following chiefly French and Swedish models. Yet he did not abandon the autocracy; rather, his reforms served to increase the wealth of the Tsar and to concentrate greater power into his hands.

Peter's wars are important not only for the territorial gains made but also for setting certain basic directions for future Russian expansion. To the south, he attempted to secure a warm-water port on the Black Sea at the expense of the Ottoman Empire. To the northwest, he attempted to wrest control of a portion of the Baltic shore from Sweden. His victory at Poltava in 1709 assured Russian dominance along the shore of the Baltic, though it was not until the Peace of Nystadt in 1721 that Sweden was forced to cede Livonia, Estonia, and the region surrounding St. Petersburg.

Although Peter merited the title "Great" for his conquests and his reforms, his rule did not basically alter the pattern of life in old Russia. He himself retained much of the barbarous streak of cruelty that had marred previous rulers. He put down the numerous rebellions against him without mercy for his opponents. He burdened his subjects with heavy taxes to pay for his military machine and pushed the Russian peasantry further down the ladder of serfdom. He tightened the control of the government over the Russian Orthodox Church, making it completely subservient to the state. His death in 1725 brought a swift reaction from the Russian nobility.

The years following the reign of Peter the Great were troubled by disputes over the succession and attempts by various factions to gain power. For ten years, a German princess, Anna of Courland ruled, having been brought to the throne on the condition that she would accept a limited monarchy. Once in power, Anna turned on her supporters and, with the support of the army and the lesser nobles, consolidated power in her own hands. Another palace coup, after the death of Anna, brought the Empress Elizabeth, daughter of Peter the Great, to the throne. She continued to favor the nobility, whose support was necessary to her continued rule. Throughout this period, though Russian power and prosperity continued to grow, the lot of the great mass of Russians, the agricultural serfs, declined. More and more, the free peasantry lost their lands and had to attach themselves to the estates of the nobility. Elizabeth even restricted the right to own land to the nobility. Russia was rapidly evolving into two societies: an elite minority educated in the Western manner ruling over a majority of uneducated and servile peasants.

In 1762, Peter III succeeded Elizabeth. His reign lasted less than a year. His bride, aided by a lover, murdered him and seized the throne. The Tsarina Catherine (1762–1796) had come to Russia as a stranger. Her education was largely French and she had fallen under the spell of eighteenth-century French culture. However, in spite of her personal admiration for the writings of the French critics of absolutism and some interest in reform, she ruled in the tradition of Louis XIV. Her ambitions, realized to such a large extent in her long reign, were the building of a strong Russian state and the extension of the Russian frontiers to their natural limits. She subordinated all other ends to these goals. Her reign was a lesson in the uses of power.

The first decade of Catherine's rule might well have been the last. Her continuation of her predecessors' policies of sacrificing the peasants to the nobles in return for the support of the latter aroused deep-seated animosity, which erupted in the Pugachev rebellion in 1773. Pugachev was a Cossack leader who pretended to be the murdered Tsar Peter III. For more than two years, he and his followers roused the peasantry in rebellion against the Tsarina. Only in 1775 was the revolt quelled and Pugachev executed.

But not even unrest at home had impeded Catherine's efforts to expand her empire. Between 1768 and 1771, Russian troops captured the Crimea and realized the Russian goal of a warm-water port on the Black Sea. In 1772, Catherine participated in the first partition of Poland, following this success with the later partitions of 1793 and 1795, which destroyed Poland. She also supported expeditions for the exploration and development of Siberia, as well as others aimed at establishing Russian trading posts from Alaska to California and at participating in the rich fur trade of Western North America. She was, more than any other ruler with the possible exception of Peter the Great, the founder of the Russian Empire.

Catherine consolidated her rule within Russia to preserve the autocracy. She built on the governmental institutions created by Peter the Great during the period of Western reforms, but retained the traditional Russian ruler's outlook on all institutions that smacked of broad political participation. She permitted the nobility a measure of control over their own affairs because it served the interest of the government to prevent them from joining rebellions against it. Her absolutism set the tone for the rule of her successors until the destruction of the Tsarist regime.

During the seventeenth and eighteenth centuries highly centralized, absolutist governments evolved in Central and Eastern Europe. Their subjects possessed little political sophistication and were unable to secure a significant voice in government. During the forthcoming period, the states of Western Europe achieved a worldwide dominance. In these states, control of political authority shifted from the old aristocracies to the leaders of industry and commercial enterprises. Increasingly, that power was shared with a politically awakened and increasingly better-led lower class. During this age of European leadership, the fact that power was no longer concentrated in the hands of the old aristocracies was important for its impact on the formation of the policies of the national state. Those policies must have a broader appeal and offer to more people a sense of national fulfillment. The failure of the old aristocracies and of the absolutist rule in the West was largely the result of major changes in Western economic, social, and cultural life during the eighteenth century.

PART III
The Age of Western Leadership

"Urania motusque poli scrutatur et astra."
"Urania examines the motions of the heavens and the stars."

14 The Scientific and Technological Basis

Historians have long used such terms as "scientific revolution" and "industrial revolution" to describe the momentous changes in these fields in the early modern period. More recently, the term "technological revolution" has been used to focus attention on the impact of the machine on the growth of modern civilization. All of these labels are useful in helping us to understand the nature of the changes which played such an important role in the formation of modern society. Yet it would be a mistake to accept the notion of "revolution" and to ignore the theme of "evolution" and fundamental development. Although the eighteenth century, somewhat like the thirteenth century, offered much that was apparently new and even strikingly different from the age immediately preceding, it provided a statement in a unified manner of many different themes. In the case of the eighteenth century, these themes became apparent during the seventeenth century, though their origins were earlier. Nevertheless, the achievement of a synthesis did unite diverse developments in science, industrial and commercial growth, technology, philosophy, art, letters, and politics into an "age of reason."

The eighteenth century also opened the way for Europe to dominate the whole earth. In part, this dominion was political and technological; in part, it was economic and cultural. The justification for it was partly the assumption of the superiority of European civilization to all others, an assumption that was seldom questioned before the twentieth century.

The Earth Seen from the Sun

The gradual acceptance of the heliostatic theory of Nicholaus Copernicus and the additional research of Johann Kepler and Galileo Galilei allowed men of science to view the sun rather than earth as the center of the universe. Similarly, the seventeenth-century advances in the scientific

Isaac Newton. Youth lingers on the meditative face of this genius, whose formulation of the law of gravity was the basis for a new interpretation of the dynamic principles behind the universe. (*The Bettmann Archive*)

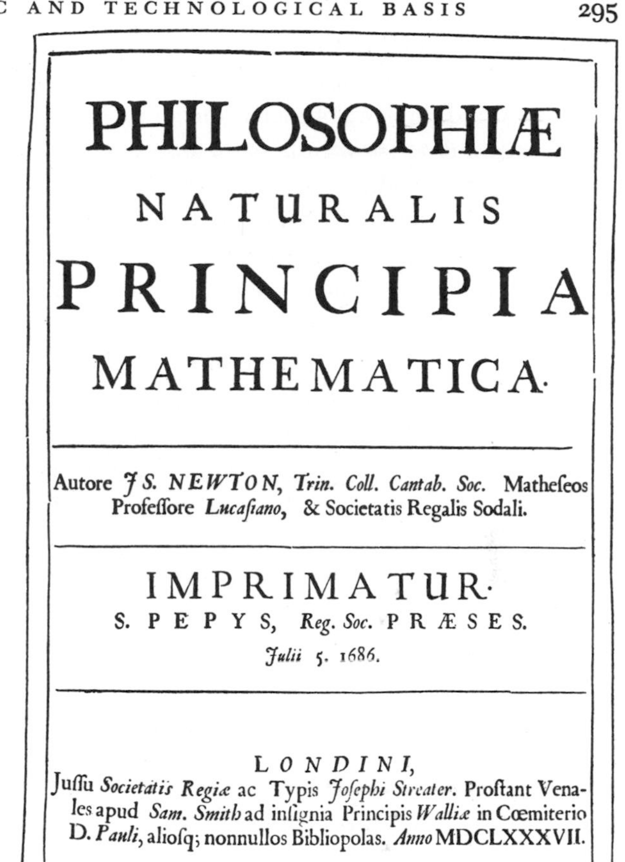

PHILOSOPHIÆ
NATURALIS
PRINCIPIA
MATHEMATICA.

Autore J. S. NEWTON, *Trin. Coll. Cantab. Soc.* Mathefeos Profeffore *Lucafiano*, & Societatis Regalis Sodali.

IMPRIMATUR.
S. PEPYS, *Reg. Soc.* PRÆSES.
Julii 5. 1686.

LONDINI,
Juffu *Societatis Regiæ* ac Typis *Jofephi Streater*. Proftant Venales apud *Sam. Smith* ad infignia Principis *Walliæ* in Cœmiterio D. *Pauli*, aliofq; nonnullos Bibliopolas. *Anno* MDCLXXXVII.

The Principia Mathematica, *title page of the first edition, 1687. This work launched an intellectual revolution. (Rare Book Room, Syracuse University Library)*

method from Bacon to Descartes provided a new framework for the development of knowledge, an emphasis on an empirical and inductive method as the foundation for future discoveries. The great scientific synthesis presented to the world at the end of that century by Isaac Newton was not merely the result of a great mind achieving a general statement of law governing the operation of the universe, but also the vindication of empirical methodology. The publication of Newton's *Principia Mathematica* (1687) heralded a new age in which science and reason, truth discovered by empirical study, would triumph over past superstition to create a new world for mankind. The age of reason had begun.

The achievement of Isaac Newton was, to put it simply, the discovery of the machinery of the universe. He explained motion in terms of gravity. Copernicus and Galileo had laid a partial basis. Copernicus had advanced the theory that the sun is the true center of the universe. Galileo had discovered the laws of inertia, according to which an object in motion would continue to move unless an opposing force stopped it. Kepler, a contemporary of Galileo, proved that the orbits of the planets were elliptical rather than circular. None of these theories contained any explanation of the dynamic force behind the machine of the universe. It remained for Isaac Newton to enunciate the principles of motion as general laws applicable to all bodies from the smallest speck of dust to the mightiest planets. Newton proved that gravity operates on all bodies in precisely the same fashion in inverse proportion to the square of their distances. For the next two hundred years, this theory held sway as the true explanation of the mechanics of motion in the whole universe.

The impact of Newton's *Principia* was greater than any other scientific work of the age. The chief reason for this fact was that Newtonian physics provided an inclusive framework for explaining the whole of the universe. It appealed to the philosopher as well as the scientist to stand in wonder at the mind of man which was able to comprehend so wonderful a design. But the work of Newton did not stand alone. As a matter of fact, it was all the more impressive because this age was deeply concerned with science and its advancement and paid special heed to its discoveries.

From the sixteenth century onward, as we have seen above (Part II, Chapter 12), there had been a tremendous increase in scientific knowledge. In part, the discoveries of new lands beyond the sea stimulated interest in botany and biology and led to the foundation of modern studies in these disciplines. Partly, too, an increasing concern with man led to advances in medicine. Even the advances made in warfare in the early modern period, particularly the invention of the cannon, pressed scientific knowledge further along by demanding new defenses against modern weapons. In the seventeenth century, the important advances made in mathematics—the invention of analytical geometry by René Descartes and of calculus by Newton and Leibnitz—were essential to further advances in the study of the laws of physics. That century also witnessed the founding of the first great learned societies for the study of science. King Charles II chartered the Royal Society for the Promotion of Natural Knowledge in 1662 and Louis XIV aided the establishment of the *Académie royale des sciences* in 1668. The members of these groups corresponded with one another and traded information about their observations and discoveries. They published papers read at their meetings to make the results known to other savants. These early journals offer much that is amusing and ridiculous in the light of modern science, for there was no area which these early scientists did not observe and report on. But amid the great mass of material, one discerns the presence of the scientific mind seeking to know by observation the nature of things.

The scientific attitude permeated all phases of life in the late seventeenth and eighteenth centuries. The desire to know led some men to question all that they had formerly accepted as an integral part of their society. Not, indeed, that they wished to destroy everything—they were generally not revolutionaries; rather they desired to examine all things from the standpoint of their use to society. The term applied to these thinkers is *philosophes,* from the fact that their movement developed in France. They were imbued with the spirit of science and convinced of their mission to inform mankind of the dawn of a new age.

The god behind the scenes was the spirit of Newton. His explanation of the laws of the universe seemed to some of the *philosophes* to call into question the whole Judaeo-Christian revelation about creation and redemption. They were especially critical of popular religious superstitions which appeared to them to shackle men's minds so that they were unable to search for the real truths about the world. They did not deny God, but they assigned to him a role in keeping with the new science. He was the designer of the world machine, the master clockmaker. The whole concept of providence, integral to Judaism and Christianity was scrapped. God had created a perfect machine which did not need His attention in order to function. Man had only to discover the laws of the universe and conform his actions to them to achieve his destiny, the making of a perfect world. Of course, the *philosophes* recognized that men were far from perfect creatures, but believed that they could become perfect if they followed the road of reason. The key to understanding the attitude of the *philosophes* is their conception of progress. Reason furnished man with the tool whereby he might overcome the darkness of his past and advance. Reason provided light for man to see the future. These religious views were summed up in deism, the natural theology created by the *philosophes* to reconcile Newtonian science and religion.

One of the most important of the *philosophes* was Denis Diderot (1713–1784). Diderot sprung from middle-class origins, but received a good education. As editor of a French edition of the Chamber's *Encyclopedia,* he produced an outstanding work reflecting the "enlightened" views of the *philosophes,* many of whom became contributors. In this manner, the *Encyclopedia* became a propaganda tool for their ideas. Their method was not a direct attack on the Church or other institutions which they believed anachronistic, but rather a sense of irony and a tendency to belittle that conveyed their disdain of the superstitious and outmoded past. But still more important was the selection of material for inclusion in the *Encyclopedia,* which contained articles on the new science and mathematics. The authors of these articles pointed out the importance of experimentation to the advancement of science and thereby made the reading public more familiar with the scientific method as developed by Bacon and his successors.

The *philosophes* considered themselves practical men and therefore devoted much of their effort to giving advice on practical matters. François Arouet, better known as Voltaire, spent several years at the court of Frederick the Great of Prussia and carried on an extensive correspondence. He offered that monarch his ideas on the principles of government, on the direction which reforms ought to take, on religious and political toleration, as well as clever criticisms of the existing order. Leibnitz, the great German mathematician spent some time in Russia, attempting to introduce Western ideas of limited government at that absolutist court. As the spirit of reason informed more intellectuals, they turned their attention to other areas beyond the political that needed reform. The Marchese di Beccaria (1735–1794) concentrated on prison reform. He believed that more effort should be made to prevent crime and he decried the too frequent use of capital punishment as a deterrent to crime, pointing out that a pickpocket (cut-purse) might as well kill his victim since he would hang anyway if the victim identified him. What made his work all the more valuable was his empirical approach, which relied on evidence he had collected about actual conditions of the treatment of criminals. In this sense, his work was scientific.

Similarly, in 1776, the Scots economist, Adam Smith (1723–1790), published *An Inquiry into the Nature and Causes of the Wealth of Nations,* an exhaustive study of the weaknesses of mercantilism that advanced the theory of an economy operating without governmental restraint. Smith was not the first to criticize the mercantile system. The French physiocrats, notably François Quesnay (1694–1774), argued that economic activities must follow the law of nature. The fundamental principle of this law was that each man should have the freedom to follow his own desires. The term *laissez faire* describes this attitude. However, the physiocrats were primarily interested in the agricultural sector of the economy rather than in industry or trade. They taught that the true wealth of the nation lay not in gold or silver or in labor, but rather in the land, which season after season provided man with sustenance. For this reason, the physiocrats believed that landowners were the real backbone of the nation. While Adam Smith believed in a free economy, he rejected the notion that land was the true source of wealth. His experience as a customs collector in Scotland had provided him with ample opportunity to study statistics on imports and exports. He believed the weakness of the mercantile system was its regulation, which prevented the natural growth of trade and therefore discouraged the increase of wealth. Real wealth, he believed, was the product of labor. Therefore, wealth might be increased both by increasing the productivity of labor and by providing the widest possible markets for the goods made. The mercantile system, with high-tariff barriers and numerous restrictions on shipping, resulted in each nation having a smaller market for its products. Removal of such barriers would, it was true, deprive sheltered and unprofitable industries of the protection under which they were able to exist, but their loss would be more than compensated for by the growth of those industries wherein the nation enjoyed an advantage because of superior resources. Since the natural law of supply and demand would operate freely without restrictions imposed by government, the nation would prosper because its citizens would prosper.

Smith never really considered the possibility that free enterprise might cause suffering for the working classes by keeping wages down in order to meet foreign competition and to increase sales. He taught that the market was safeguarded by an *invisible hand* which ensured an equitable distribution of the wealth. Smith believed that reason and self-interest would ensure to the working class their share in the bounty created by the pursuit of the free economy. It remained for later economic theorists to point out the effects of the operation of the law of supply and demand in the labor market.

But the primary concern of the thinkers of this age of reason or "enlightenment" was politics. In France, they were critical of the inefficiencies and corruption of the government. Absolutism, it seemed to some, merely perpetuated the worst features of the feudal system beyond their time and prevented needed reforms. Montesquieu's *Spirit of the Laws* looked with favor on the English monarchy after 1688. It presented the view that the English government gave greater guarantees of liberty than the French. The popularization of this view by other writers, including Voltaire, caused French political reformers to look upon England and its parliamentary system as an ideal form of government that might provide a model for France.

In political thought, the influence of the English philosopher, John

Locke (1632–1704), was great. His contract theory of sovereignty, in which real power reposed not in God but in the people, gained a considerable popularity in the course of the century. The most notable French writer to adopt a similar position was Jean-Jacques Rousseau (1712–1778). He observed that man is born free, "but everywhere is in chains." Yet it was within the natural right of man to regain his freedom from the tyrant. Rousseau was the greatest prophet of liberty of the age, but he was also the prophet of revolution. The contract theory formed the basis not merely for a political awakening but also the justification for revolution in defense of natural rights—the right to life, liberty, and property.

The concept of natural rights was only a corollary of the principles of natural law taught by the *philosophes*. The law of nature was written in all creation to be read and understood by man. When he learned it, he had in hand the key to the universe. Just as Isaac Newton had discovered the natural laws which all bodies in motion must obey, it was possible for others to discover the laws governing political relations, economic life, and all other spheres of activity. The tool placed by nature's God under the control of man to unlock these secrets was reason. By studying empirically all the phenomena man could arrive at a universal law. By following that law, he would avoid conflict with nature and thus achieve a better life in this world. At its best, such was the optimistic picture painted by the *philosophes* of man's capability for progress. They were, indeed, men endowed with a grand vision of a new world created by God but ruled by immutable laws. Man too, could hope to learn these laws. Would he then become like God?

Seldom has one age had a greater impact on its successors than the eighteenth century. The enthronement of reason by the *philosophes* shook their own society to its foundations. The synthesis which they had achieved in the new methodology became a hallmark of the modern world. There was a strong tendency in the nineteenth and early twentieth centuries to attribute to this period the founding of all modern scientific and technological advances, the emancipation of the human spirit, and the beginnings of progress.

Literature and Art in an Age of Reason

In the arts and letters of the eighteenth century reason meant an age of classical revival. This age reacted against the romantic elements of the baroque and sought in the discipline of the aesthetic teachings of classical authors of antiquity to discover the natural laws regulating the creation of beauty; its art and architecture are more impressive than attractive. It was also an age of realism, of investigation into the world of man in all its passion and degradation. This realism was closely related to the empiricism of contemporary scientists. It was an age of experimentation.

The eighteenth century saw the birth of the modern novel. This literary form drew more on the basic romantic stream in human nature than on the spirit of rationalism. The first novel in English, Samuel Richardson's (1689–1761) *Pamela,* was a discursive and disconnected adventure in sentimentality. *Tom Jones* by Henry Fielding (1707–1754) was more in

PAMELA:

OR,

VIRTUE Rewarded.

In a SERIES of

FAMILIAR LETTERS

FROM A

Beautiful Young DAMSEL,
To her PARENTS.

Now firſt Publiſhed
In order to cultivate the Principles of VIRTUE and RELIGION in the Minds of the YOUTH of BOTH SEXES.

A Narrative which has its Foundation in TRUTH and NATURE; and at the ſame time that it agreeably entertains, by a Variety of *curious* and *affecting* INCIDENTS, is intirely diveſted of all thoſe Images, which, in too many Pieces calculated for Amuſement only, tend to *inflame* the Minds they ſhould *inſtruct*.

In Two VOLUMES.

VOL. I.

LONDON:

Printed for C. RIVINGTON, in *St. Paul's Church Yard;* and J. OSBORN, in *Pater-noſter Row.*
MDCCXLI.

Pamela, *title page of the first edition, 1741. Samuel Richardson sets forth his high-minded purposes for writing this first novel. (Rare Book Room, Syracuse University Library)* tune with the currents of the age. Its realism and cynicism contrast strongly to the emotionalism of Richardson. Against a backdrop that reveals the follies and fancies of England's eighteenth-century squirearchy, Tom Jones moved toward his rehabilitation, but his amorous adventures do much to delay the process. Fielding's characters are real people rather than literary types. Their flesh is stuffed with appetites that reveal not merely their own personalities but also the class interests of a segment of the English aristocracy.

The literary and linguistic interests of the century resulted in the production of a number of outstanding works. The always brilliant, if somewhat cynical, mind of Samuel Johnson produced a great dictionary of the English language, noted for its scholarship as well as its originality. Among the greatest stylists in English was Edward Gibbon; whose *Decline and Fall of the Roman Empire* was the major historical work of the century. The *Decline and Fall* assumed the intrinsic merit of classical Roman civilization and proceeded to find the causes of its decline not so much in the decay of its political and social life as in the rise of Christianity, which sapped the vitality of paganism and made it unable to resist the onslaughts of the barbarians. Gibbon's erudition was tremendous. He was the master of his topic. His work was an expression of the ideals of his age, its secular and rationalist outlook as well as its rejection of formal religious institutions.

The poetry of this period was too much the creature of aesthetic principles and rules of form. While France produced some outstanding work by Racine under the constraints of classical rules, England and Germany offered little before the birth of the romantic movement later in the century in the work of Wordsworth and Johann Wolfgang von Goethe. The most important poetry inspired by classical norms was that of John Dryden (1631–1700) and Alexander Pope (1688–1744). Dryden perfected the heroic couplet, an excellent example of the subordination of art to the discipline of form. His most important work, "The Hind and the Panther," compared the hind of Catholicism to the panther of Anglicanism. The poem reflected the author's own conversion to the Catholic Church and had a polemic and didactic content that weakened its value as art. Pope was a master of intellectual satire. His "Rape of the Lock" drew its inspiration from the legendary incident of Roman history that led to the downfall of the last of the Etruscan kings, Tarquin the Proud. In reality, he was ridiculing a lovers' quarrel which had divided the families of some friends. His "Dunciad" was an attack on fools of his age as he saw them. It established his reputation as one of the sharpest tongued critiques of an age known for rapier thrusts of the pen. The poetry of Dryden and Pope possesses small appeal to modern taste. Though technically perfect, with lines that scan and rhymes that chime, it tends toward wordiness and superficiality. As art, it is definitely minor.

The satire of Alexander Pope did not equal that of his friend and contemporary, Dean Jonathan Swift (1667–1745), an ecclesiastic of the Church of Ireland. Swift is best known for *Gulliver's Travels,* in which he lampooned the men of his own day by making their intellectual shortcomings into physical characteristics. One of the best examples of this technique is the kingdom of the Lilliputians, inhabited by a tiny people with quite small brains. Its location on an island was no mere accident. Swift never lost sight of contemporary England. He also authored a *Modest Proposal to End the Famine in Ireland,* which recommended that the Irish consume their own children to solve the shortage of food. This work was as much a satire on the stupidities of English policies toward Ireland as an indictment of the Irish Roman Catholic peasantry and their priests.

For the most part, the age of reason was also an age of prose on the continent. Not until the closing decades of the century when the first waves of romanticism swept across Europe and captured Goethe, the greatest poet of the century, did there arise a figure whole talents were major. The best that the preceding century was able to produce did not begin to compare to him. The chief strength of eighteenth-century literature lay in its criticism of contemporary life. Whether the work was Daniel Defoe's *Moll Flanders* or Voltaire's *Candide,* the aim was similar. Whether the chief character was a prostitute or an innocent lad, the theme was the need of an imperfect world for a more perfect solution to its problems. There was no real conflict between the critic and the artist; indeed, criticism became a form of art.

The quest for realism, which in this period was the artistic counterpart of the spirit of criticism inherent in the writings of the *philosophes,* dominated the painting and sculpture of the age. The portraits done by Sir Joshua Reynolds show a cameralike fidelity to detail. This attention to detail as well as a strong traditionalism and fidelity to the ideal of aristocratic taste molded the work of many of his contemporaries. Classicism, which in the hands of the great figures of the Renaissance had served as the beginning of artistic inspiration, became the end of many of the painters of the eighteenth century. It was a sterile admiration for classical concepts of grace and beauty that offered the artist only an opportunity to imitate the great models of the past and not to innovate.

In architecture, the goal of the eighteenth century might best be

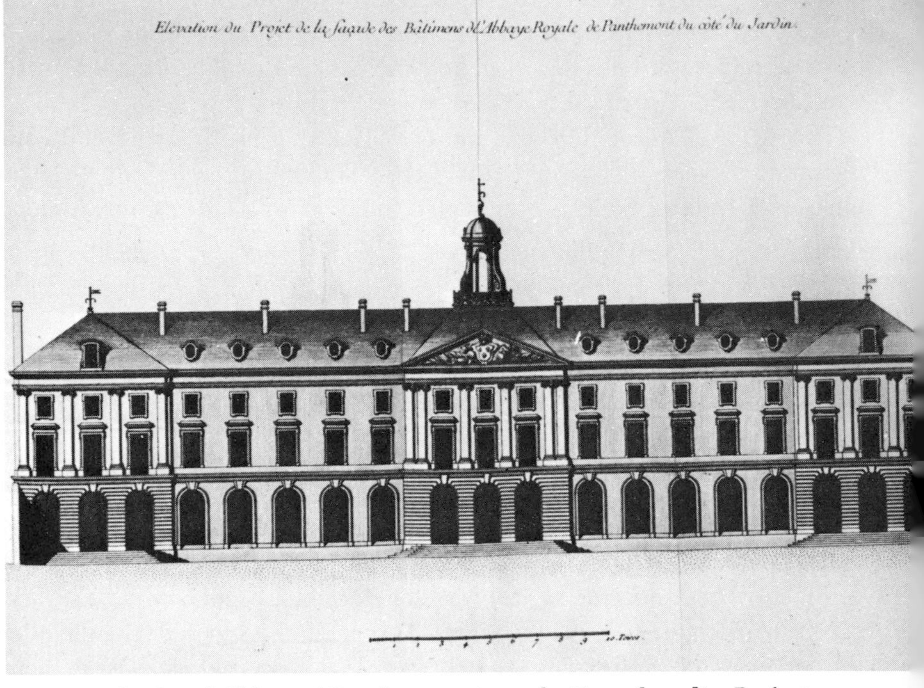

The Royal Abbey of Panthemont, from the Encyclopedie. *Perfect symmetry and classic simplicity mark this design. (Rare Book Room, Syracuse University Library)*

summed up in the notion of symmetry. The French became obsessed with the need to balance every part of their structures perfectly with every other. Their classical gardens and public buildings were laid out with utmost precision to achieve complete symmetry. Elsewhere, the revival of classical architecture, while falling short of the French ideal, produced imitations of ancient Greek buildings that caught the simple lines of the originals. This so-called Greek revival persisted into the nineteenth century.

The attempt to reduce music to a body of natural laws regulating harmony accorded well with the spirit of the age of reason, but failed to chain this most elusive of the muses in the prison of the intellect. Although classical music appeared near the middle of the century in the compositions of Franz Joseph Haydn and Wolfgang Amadeus Mozart, it was not tied to a narrow body of canons or rules. In large measure, the nature of music's appeal to the emotions prevented a full subservience to the cult of reason. Nevertheless, the classical composer did restrain his art by writing more for the concert hall than for the small and intimate salon

The Bibliotheque Sainte Geneviève, library of the University of Paris. Note the balance and classic lines, so typical of many public buildings in Paris. (*Author*)

and by attempting to limit his experimentation to fixed principles. However, the music of the age did not fall into the sterile classicism that characterized so much of the art of the period.

The relative lack of artistic and literary development within the eighteenth century points to one of the most significant aspects of the age: its overwhelming concern with the real world and its involvement with the immediate. Fascinated by advances in science and technology that were rapidly transforming it into a machine age, this era saw in these advances the hope for progress in the future and the possible means to realize its dream of a "heavenly city" on earth.

Industrial Beginnings and Technical Advances

After 1750, Europe entered the industrial age. In the next one hundred years, western Europe went through a technological and economic revolution. The foundations and causes for these changes are to be found in the expansion of the economy in the early modern period. This was the era of commercial capitalism, in which investors put their money to work in commercial enterprises. The volume of trade was increasing rapidly along with population and wealth. It was also an age of increased specialization of skills. The colonies of the New World played a very important role, furnishing gold and silver as well as raw materials. By the beginning of the eighteenth century, sugar, tobacco, and slaves were the most valuable articles in colonial trade. Europe was itself a great market for its own goods. It was this tremendous expansion that stimulated the "Industrial Revolution."

The sharpest change came in England and from there spread to the continent. This revolution continued throughout the nineteenth century and brought with it a whole host of other problems, most importantly the almost complete alteration of the social structure of European society before World War I. The industrial age brought misery to masses of factory workers and wealth to industrial capitalists, but it also made goods produced by its machines available to a larger body of people, and at a lower cost than ever before possible. This age helped to produce a higher standard of living for more persons than ever before. The impact of industrialism therefore profoundly affected the entire modern age.

One important aspect of the "Industrial Revolution" was the discovery of new sources of power. For centuries, man had relied on his own strength and skill and that of domestic animals to carry his burdens and to produce the goods he desired. Water and wind power were the only major improvements over this condition before the beginning of the age of steam. By using a waterfall, artificial as well as natural, one could harness the speed of the water to turn a wheel to grind corn or turn another wheel that would propel a machine. Wind power was similar but less dependable. In England, even before 1750, water power had been used to drive various kinds of machines used in the textile industry. After that date, the invention of the steam engine revolutionized the organization of industry.

The principle of steam power appears simple to us. Fire heats water. The water boils and turns to steam, which expands to fill a piston chamber. This presses the piston forward (or upward). The piston is usually attached to a wheel. The wheel turns. A system of valves releases the steam and the resultant vacuum permits the process to begin over again. In this way, the piston turns the wheel. Such simple engines, invented by Thomas Newcomen and James Watt were used first to drain water out of mine shafts and later were harnessed to machines in textile factories. Steam thus provided the power for the industrial age. But the new technology also had to provide machines that could perform functions formerly done by hand.

Major improvements in machinery in the textile industry may be traced as far back as John Kay's invention of the flying shuttle in 1733. The flying shuttle increased, in fact doubled, the efficiency of a weaver. It increased the demand for thread for the looms. In 1765, James Hargreaves invented the spinning jenny, which could spin several skeins of thread at the same

Steam engine invented by James Watt. Steam power was a basic factor in the Industrial Revolution. (The Bettmann Archive)

Coalman. One of the first industrial uses of the railroad. (The Bettmann Archive)

time. When Richard Arkwright invented the waterframe and Samuel Crompton brought out the "mule," spinners had machinery capable of producing thread much faster than weavers could use it. It was not until the early nineteenth century that the invention of a power loom using steam permitted the weavers to take advantage of the increased availability of yarn. Numerous other inventions aided in improved methods of production in the textile industry.

The machine age vastly increased the need for iron and steel. While most early machines were made of iron, the superiority of steel made its use desirable. However, steel remained in short supply because of the difficulty of producing it in large quantities. The first breakthrough of importance in the iron industry came in the 1780's with Henry Cort's invention of a method to make malleable iron by the puddling and rolling process. The removal of impurities in the iron by this process made iron available at low prices to the growing market. It was not until the mid-nineteenth century that Sir Henry Bessemer invented his process for converting iron into steel.

Steam also was applied to transportation. At the beginning of the nineteenth century, the American inventor, Robert Fulton, built the *Clermont*, a steam-powered vessel that sailed successfully on the Hudson River. George Stephenson was responsible for the first fully successful steam locomotive, constructed in 1814. In England, rail construction began with the line between Liverpool and Manchester in 1830. About the same time, a group of American businessmen backed the Baltimore and Ohio Railroad. The railroad revolutionized the rapid transportation of large quantities of goods and made it possible for travelers to go from one part of the country to another in relative comfort and at speeds greater than ever before.

The growth of industry between 1750 and 1850 was partly the result of these tremendous improvements in technology. To some extent, these improvements were related to the new science of the eighteenth century. These scientists were often practical men. Newcomen was a professor at the University of Edinburgh as well as inventor of the steam engine. Benjamin Franklin, a member of the Royal Society in London, submitted a number of plans to his colleagues for devices beneficial to mankind. Indeed, the Royal Society regularly considered reports on practical inventions.

The technological revolution was accompanied by significant changes in the organization of industry. During the late Middle Ages, the development of the "putting-out" system had permitted the use of the rural population to increase output of industrial goods. Rural industry had the advantages of cheap and plentiful labor and it was free of the restrictions established by the guilds in the towns. In the "putting-out" system, merchant-industrialists distributed raw materials among village households to be turned into finished products. This system flourished in England. However, despite its flexibility and its productivity, the "putting-out" system had its disadvantages because of the cost of transporting raw materials and finished goods, the lack of disciplinary controls over the workers, and the dishonesty of workers who used raw materials for their own profit. The new technology provided a solution by making the factory system feasible. The essential contribution of the factory was the discipline and control it gave the employer over its workers. The technological revolution made the factory system feasible by providing a central source of power. It was from these beginnings that the "Industrial Revolution" sprang.

The continent generally lagged behind England in industrial progress. Not until the Napoleonic period did France and Belgium make significant progress. In fact, small Belgium (it did not become a separate nation until 1830) industrialized more rapidly than France. The availability of coal in abundance and the ease of transportation in so small a country combined with the Belgians' long tradition in the textile industry to make the country an important center. France remained firmly committed to her agricultural economic base until well after the French Revolution. Although there were notable exceptions, the largest expansion in France took place after 1850. In the Germanies, only Prussia developed any significant industrial power in this period. Political disunity and the preponderance of agricultural interests over commerce and industry through much of the country were responsible for the slow rate of development until after 1870.

Industrialization took place in those areas where previous developments favored the growth of the new machine-powered industry. In England and Belgium, the long tradition of the textile industry had created a solid foundation for the development of the new machine age. Elsewhere progress was slower, save in occasional areas where a local industry of long standing made the transition to machines and power.

Industrialization was not an unmixed blessing. As it spread out over the land, the smoking stacks of industrial cities flung their soot against the sky. Dingy and dirty, these places were hardly fit habitats for the thousands who crowded into them. Poverty and filth went hand in hand. But, alongside these disadvantages came an unequaled progress in the standard of living for millions of people made possible by higher productivity and lower costs. By the mid-nineteenth century, the industrial age had spread to almost all parts of Western Europe.

15 The Political Revolutions

Just as the "age of reason" signified the achievement of a new synthesis in the intellectual life of Western man, the political revolutions of this era marked the transition from the territorial to the national state. While the chief mark of the territorial state was the uniting of a country under strongly centralized rule, usually in the hands of a king or prince, the distinguishing feature of the nation was a broadening of the base of power and the enlisting of elements from most strata of society in the service of the state. This change might be signalized in the difference between subject and citizen. The subject owes loyalty to a monarch; the citizen *offers* his loyalty to his country. In the French term *patrie,* the German *Vaterland,* and even in the English *Our Country,* there are elements of an emotional bond between the citizen and the nation. Because the nation-state presumed the existence of an emotional tie, linguistic, cultural, and religious similarities played an important part in its formation. One people meant a people sharing a common tongue and common loyalties.

In the eighteenth century, the long-forming forces of political expression reached their climax. The demand for fuller participation in government by the economically powerful but politically impotent middle class of property was an important factor in the revolutionary process that brought the nation-state into being. In England, the transition was gradual; in the American colonies and France an upheaval of the nation threw off the bonds of the old regime.

England and the American Revolution

Queen Anne, last of James II's Protestant heirs, died in August, 1714. By act of Parliament, George, Elector of Hanover, succeeded her as George I (1714–1727). The new king was a foreigner to English law and customs, an overweight pleasure-loving boor, who was more concerned about his native Germany than about England. The major value of his new kingdom was the support that he was able to draw from it to protect Hanover from the encroachments of France. Foreign policy rather than internal administration of the English government was his area of concern. But the period of his reign was relatively quiet; the conclusion of the War of Spanish Succession with the Treaty of Utrecht in 1713 and the death of Louis XIV made Europe pause momentarily to take stock of the change before launching off in a new war. The quiet was disturbed on the domestic scene by the bursting of the South Sea Bubble.

By the *Asiento* of the Treaty of Utrecht (1713), England had received the right to trade with Spanish America and particularly to furnish Negro slaves needed by the Spaniards. The arrangement promised to be very lucrative. A royal charter was granted to the South Sea Company, which undertook to pay part of the debt from the recent war through the sale of its stock and profits from the trade with South America. However, the attractiveness of the venture stimulated the spirit of speculation to such a point that the company could never have found it possible to return a sufficient profit on its stock. The stock was simply too expensive in terms of the promised return. Inevitably, the bubble burst. Many investors were wiped out. The government, which had supported the company, bore the brunt of the criticism and the ministers resigned. In 1722, the king summoned a new ministry; the leading figure in the new government was Robert Walpole.

The dominance of Walpole over the other members of the cabinet and his ability to control Parliament won for him the title of England's first prime minister (1721–1742). But, unlike the modern prime minister, Walpole and his fellow ministers had to concern themselves not merely with securing the passage of laws in Parliament but also with keeping the confidence of the king. For the king could dismiss them at will. Robert Walpole, however, identified his administration closely with the monarchy. One of his chief policies was the preservation of the Hanoverian succession against a possible restoration of the Catholic Stuarts. He was cautious and conservative about foreign affairs. He worked assiduously to prevent

English entry into the War of Austrian Succession. His major concern was to build public confidence in the shattered English financial structure. His caution, his close connections with members of the leading aristocracy, and his ability to secure loans covering the public debt at reasonable interest and for long periods were important elements in putting the country back on its feet. The Walpole policies generally benefitted England by strengthening her internally. Certainly, his leadership provided an atmosphere of unity about which the leading forces in political life could gather. But his caution alienated those who felt that England must play a more significant role in continental affairs, especially to prevent total French dominance. England must, in their view, preserve the balance of power in Europe.

The threat to the balance of power in the early seventeen forties lay in Eastern Europe, where the accession of Maria Theresa to the Austrian throne had aroused the cupidity of Frederick the Great of Prussia. France seized the opportunity to move against the Austrian Netherlands. Walpole opposed English entry into the war, but the growth of English sentiment favorable to an alliance with Austria against France mounted. In 1744, after Walpole had received the title Earl of Orford and withdrawn from political life, a new government under Lord Carteret led the country into war. England was of little help to Austria in the war on the continent. Her navy, after some setbacks, did assure her of command of the seas, but she was unable to turn this to decisive advantage in Europe. Only victories overseas, in particular the conquest of the French fortress of Louisbourg by New Englanders, saved the situation. The Peace of Aix-la-Chapelle, dictated by England and France to their allies, profited no one except Frederick the Great, who managed to hold onto Silesia. But this settlement was only a truce by way of prelude to a major military settlement in the Seven Years' War (1755–1763), a truly global war on a scale larger than the War of Austrian Succession.

Ostensibly, the focus of the Seven Years' War was European; in actuality, the European phase of the war was less important to the future history of the world than the fighting carried on in the forests of America, on the high seas, and in India and the East. The European phase settled nothing definitely about the balance of power; the global phase established England as the leading nation in North America and in the trade with the East. The Seven Years' War reached beyond the interests of the dynastic struggle between the European monarchies.

The growth of English power overseas had come late, after Spain and Portugal had already staked out Latin America. The first English colony in North America, at Jamestown, was planted in 1607, followed by further colonies in New England in the early seventeenth century. Expansion in the East followed. The founding of the English East India Company indicated increase of interest in the Eastern spice trade, still largely in Portuguese and Dutch hands throughout the seventeenth century. Not until the beginning of the eighteenth century and the reorganization of the East India Company did England undertake a more aggressive policy. By mid-century, England ruled over about fifteen million peoples around the globe, two million in the North American colonies alone. This vast colonial empire was in direct competition with French expansion. From the sixteenth century on, the French had increased their hold in North America from the valley of the St. Lawrence west to the Great Lakes and southward into the great watershed of the Ohio River. Voyageurs in swift canoes pushed even further inland to trade for the rich fur pelts that were the gold of the northland. The French also moved into the Far Eastern trade, setting up fortresses in India. Thus the scene was set for a titanic struggle for the leadership of Europe in the overseas empire.

The outbreak of the Seven Years' War in 1756 followed close on the heels of the diplomatic revolution, by which Maria Theresa of Austria had succeeded in drawing France into an alliance. England sought a connection with Frederick the Great. The first years of the war favored France. She was successful in her invasion of Hanover, while the addition of Russia to the Franco-Austrian alliance put Prussia at a great disadvantage. Frederick the Great found himself surrounded by enemies. Disillusionment with the conduct of the war caused public opinion to demand that the king appoint William Pitt as prime minister.

William Pitt (1708–1778) was the master critic of the government. He had spent most of his parliamentary career in opposition. But he was the popular idol and the mob now demanded his appointment. King George II was reluctant to appoint the unruly Pitt to office but feared the effect on the war of a failure to do so. Pitt became the chief minister of a king who did not want him. Nevertheless, the new minister tackled his office with vigor. He began the rebuilding of the British navy in conjunction with his announced intention of defeating the French and winning the war on the sea. He moved to support his ally Frederick the Great and laid plans for a new conquest of the great French North American fortress at Louisbourg. At this point, George II dismissed his unwanted prime minister from office. But the king and the enemies of William Pitt reckoned without the popular storm kicked up by their action. For a time, the country was on verge of a riot. George recalled Pitt to office. Now the new prime minister possessed a mandate to pursue his policies.

The first successes of the new policy were suitably enough on the sea. In 1759, in naval engagements at Quiberon Bay and Lagos, the rebuilt British navy destroyed the French Atlantic fleet and gained control of the seas. During the same period, Pitt was following his other objective: to win the war overseas. In India, the English gradually destroyed the bases of French power. In America, Louisbourg fell once again in 1758 and the French had to abandon Fort Duquesne, on the present site of Pittsburgh. The major victory came in September, 1759, when English forces under General James Wolfe stormed the plains of Abraham and took the massive French fortress city of Quebec, key to control of French North America. By these victories, England reached her major goals in the war, crushing the French colonial empire and destroying French naval power. Pitt had proved the value of his policies.

Many Englishmen were now tired of the war. They could not sympathize with Pitt's desire to remain in the war to aid Frederick the Great in his ambitions. When Pitt attempted to lead England into war with Spain to force that nation out of the alliance with France, the other members of the cabinet refused to go along. The very success that Pitt had achieved weakened his effort to persuade them to continue the war. Faced with defeat, he resigned. Thus the Treaty of Paris of 1763 was the work of the man who had supplanted William Pitt, who became Earl of Chatham as a reward for his great services to the empire. This treaty gave England Canada and the French territory east of the Mississippi River, in the lush region of the Ohio Valley. In India, the conquests made by Robert Clive were nullified and the British conquest of that great subcontinent had to wait until later. France's losses were great, but not irreparable. She not only retained her commercial interests in the Far East, but also controlled a share of the fisheries off the Newfoundland Banks. The first global war for control of the colonial empire had ended with many of the objectives set by the master strategists of the war lost at the conference table. However, England had emerged from the war as the leading European power; France had been humbled and awaited the opportunity to recover her losses.

The opportunity for which the French were waiting came from an unexpected quarter, as the result of a crisis within the British imperial possessions in North America. The thirteen coastal colonies between Canada and Florida renounced their loyalty to the crown in 1776 in the Declaration of Independence. This remarkable document from the pen of Thomas Jefferson laid the blame for the rebellion at the feet of the English King George III. In terms that owed a great debt to the writings of the English philosopher and political thinker, John Locke, Jefferson denounced George III as a tyrant and proclaimed the right and duty of the colonists to rebel.

The reputation of George III (1760–1820) has suffered from various directions. Historians writing in the Whig tradition viewed him as a threat to parliamentary rule in England. American historians long regarded him as a *bête noire,* determined to undermine the liberties of the colonists and to reduce them utterly to a role subject to the government in England. Although there is evidence to support both of these contentions, there is additional evidence that provides another picture of this much maligned monarch. Whig writers assumed that the royal ministers had succeeded in freeing themselves completely from royal control before the reign of George II and were party leaders subject to Parliament. Actually, their position was still ambivalent, and George, in taking the initiative in naming his ministers, was merely exercising the royal prerogative. Whether or not he was wise in his choice of his ministers was mostly a matter of his ability to maintain them in power against parliamentary opposition. Certainly, his early selection of Lord Bute as his chief minister aroused great opposition and caste him in the role of an arbitrary king. However, his subsequent ministries were more able to sustain themselves in power by securing some parliamentary support. In this light, it is hardly fair to charge George III with attempting to undermine parliamentary rule. As for his role in the American Revolution, the evidence charging his obstinacy and his support of bad ministers with triggering the rebellion ignores the long-standing causes of dispute between the colonists and the mother country. Many of these causes—we may cite the quartering of troops in the colonies and the increased taxes following the Seven Years' War, as well as dissatisfaction over the English navigation acts—could be put in a far different light by examining the needs of England and the services rendered by her in defending the colonies.

As a matter of fact, the early years of the reign of George III brought him a measure of popularity in the country. He stood for peace. Following his accession in 1760, he brought the peace negotiations at Paris to a successful, if somewhat disappointing, conclusion. True enough, his obvious preference for Tory ministers alienated the Whigs. But the major crisis of the early period of his reign arose from the growing tension between England and the thirteen North American colonies.

The Peace of Paris of 1763 removed the French threat to the English colonies, but raised new problems for them. English administration of the former French colonial possessions in North America did not mean a sudden shift in policy. In fact, the English tended to adopt the French attitude toward the preservation of the fur trade and preventing expansion of settlements into the western lands. Moreover, the attempt to get the colonists to pay part of the cost of the war aroused great animosities. Restrictions on colonial trade and efforts at strict enforcement of laws regulating it were most unpopular in the New England colonies. But the most unpopular measure of the period was the Stamp Act passed in 1765 and repealed the following year after it had united the colonies in opposition with the cry of "taxation without representation." During the early seventies the crisis increased in intensity climaxing in the "Boston Tea Party" in 1773, a protest against a tax levied on tea by the English parliament. In the following year, Parliament responded to this protest with the "intolerable acts," aimed at punishing Massachusetts for the tea party. The port of Boston was closed and Massachusetts had to accept British troops. Most of these measures hit hard at colonial merchants and planters who provided leadership to the revolution. Radical leaders like Samuel Adams of Massachusetts took the lead in uniting the colonies to resist the British.

The American Revolution was fought on the principles of Locke's *Treatises on Civil Government* to obtain the "rights and liberties" of Englishmen. But, after the passage of the Declaration of Independence in the Continental Congress, the colonists rejected the sovereignty of the mother country and decided to secure "life, liberty, and the pursuit of happiness" for themselves as an independent nation. This step was indeed daring. The colonists were willing to betray their loyalties to the Crown to secure those natural rights which they believed they did not possess under the English imperial system.

The rebellion of the thirteen American colonies attracted considerable attention in Europe. The colonists appealed for aid against England to various European powers and especially to France, where Benjamin Franklin was influential in securing the assistance of the French government. France first supplied limited military aid in the form of loans, but after the defeat of the British army at Saratoga in 1778, she decided to take the opportunity offered by the American Revolution to humiliate England. Thus, the war for American independence became part of a global struggle, the continuation of the rivalry between England and France for control of a vast overseas empire. The French forced Britain to divide her forces and supplied the Americans with materials and naval support that were basic to the winning of the war. The defeat of General Charles Cornwallis at Yorktown was largely the result of temporary French support.

Benjamin Franklin at the Court of France. The American diplomat made a deep impression on Paris society. (*The Bettmann Archive*)

The Treaty of Paris of 1783 brought France a moral victory over England but little in the way of compensation for her efforts. The most important result of the treaty was the creation of a new government in the American colonies, the United States of America. England retained possession of her colonial empire and even made gains in the Far East at French expense. France emerged from the war victorious, but on the brink of bankruptcy. England retained her leadership into the nineteenth century.

The American Revolution provided an example to Europeans, and especially to the French, of the working out of the philosophical concepts of John Locke and the French *philosophes*. The appeal made in the Declaration of Independence to natural rights as the basis for the overthrow of tyrannical rule was not lost on the growing body of critics of French absolutism. The success of the Americans in winning the right to govern themselves excited envy among those who felt their governments prevented them from exercising their rightful position in political life. To put the question succinctly, the American Revolution justified the French Revolution.

France in an Age of Revolution

The age of Louis XIV had marked the high point of French absolutism, but the rule of the "sun king" was a costly experience both for France and her monarchy. By the end of his reign, the country was heavily burdened by debt. Taxes, long in need of reform to meet the growing expenses of the state, did not yield sufficient income. The privileged classes of the clergy and nobility refused to accept any remedy that would deprive them of their special status. The parlement of Paris became the bastion of the conservative effort to force the king to accept the views of the aristocracy in the formation of government policies. Population, an important index of general economic health, had fallen about two million as a result of the wars of Louis XIV. In 1715, major measures were required to restore the nation; neither Louis XV nor his weak successor was able to overcome the limitations of their narrow outlook on government. They worked feebly to preserve the absolutism of the monarchy. Without providing a solution for the serious economic ills of the country and failing also to recognize the importance of demands by the middle class for a share in the political life of the kingdom.

Louis XV (1715–1774) was still a child when he inherited the throne. The first eighteen years of his reign were dominated by his regent, the Duke of Orleans, and the able Cardinal Fleury, last in the succession of French political cardinals. Orleans attempted to temper the absolutist complexion of the government by inviting nobles to share in its councils. He restored the right of the parlements, the noble judicial assemblies, to register the royal acts, thus giving the nobility a measure of control over the new laws. But the rule of Orleans foundered on his effort to reform the finances of the monarchy.

From 1723 to 1743, Cardinal Fleury guided France. His medicine was only temporary, but it enabled the shaky ship of state to stay afloat. He was fortunate in that expanding commerce and prosperous times within France eased the pressure of the economic problems somewhat, while he was wise enough to avoid taxing too heavily the limited resources available to him. However, there was no basic change in the structure of the French monarchy. The accession of Louis XV to full control of the government revealed very quickly his intention to follow the road of grandeur marked out by Louis XIV.

Louis XV had little to recommend him as the monarch of France save heredity, but that was sufficient to ensure his right to rule. He was a cynic. His intelligence was limited and he lacked even the tact to conceal this fact. He turned his government over to a succession of mistresses and favorites, while he enjoyed the position an accident of birth had conferred on him. The expenses of his court were enormous, especially in view of the negative impression it made on a country growing more conscious of its financial needs. His attempts to retain an empty absolutism without providing remedies for the mounting financial crisis simply aggravated the situation and drove the advocates of reform to seek aid elsewhere. Whether or not he made the famous remark "After me, the deluge," the description was too fitting to be lost. At his death in 1774, France stood at the verge of bankruptcy in desperate need of leadership.

The reign of Louis XVI (1774–1793) ushered in the end of the old regime in France. It began with a sincere effort to remedy the problems of the government, but, as it became more and more apparent that the needed reforms would result in major changes within both French government and society, the king vaccillated and turned to the road of temporary expedients.

Louis chose as his chief minister one of the leading economic thinkers of the period, Anne Robert Jacques Turgot, a physiocrat, who adopted policies aimed at heading off the imminent bankruptcy of France. This financial crisis was caused by the archaic tax structure of the country and not any economic weakness in the nation as a whole. In fact, France was the wealthiest and most prosperous country in Europe in the eighteenth century. The problem was not private wealth but public debt. Turgot's partial success in reducing the debt was based on the continuing prosperity of the era. However, his measure increasing the *vingtiéme* paid by the nobles aroused considerable opposition. This class, despite its privileges, resented its loss of political power to the monarch and hated the royal minister. Turgot simply gave it an added excuse for opposing his policies. Moreover, his efforts to reduce the control of the Church over education cemented an alliance against him among the leading nobles and the higher ecclesiastics. It was Turgot's misfortune to rise to power in France at the last moment and to find that the aristocrats had no real understanding of the nature of the crisis and were unwilling to tolerate any changes that would reduce their status or touch their wealth. This opposition persuaded Louis XVI to dismiss Turgot.

After the fall of Turgot, Louis turned to ministers who offered temporary solutions that would not disturb the *status quo*. Necker, a Swiss banker with excellent contacts, resorted to foreign and domestic borrowing of large sums at high rates of interest to meet the needs of the government. At the same time, he tried to curtail expenses by abolishing some of the many useless offices maintained by the Crown for the benefit of favorites. He also reduced the amounts of the pensions paid the nobility. Following in Turgot's footsteps, he attempted to launch provincial assemblies to decentralize the government, hoping thereby to obtain a measure of popular support for his measures. However, French loans and gifts to the American Revolution made his task virtually impossible. He resorted to clever accounting methods to show that the government was still solvent; in fact, it was operating deeply in the red. His successor, Calonne, hoped to stimulate the economy and create public confidence by a major spending program, but his ideas were poorly thought out and only served to heighten the crisis. Finally, in 1787, the king summoned an assembly of notables to advise him on possible solutions. The privileged classes who dominated this meeting believed they saw their opportunity to gain a permanent check on the royal government and demanded that the king summon a meeting of the Estates General, the medieval representative body of France that had not met since 1614. The king found himself facing a rising clamor for a meeting of the Estates. He saw no alternative to summoning it.

Aside from the basic weaknesses visible in the financial structure of the government and the decaying fabric of central authority, France had also to face the problems created by pressures against the existing social order within France. The nobility and the clergy no longer played significant roles in the political and cultural life of the country. Many bishops found the comforts of Versailles and the stimulating atmosphere of the Parisian salons preferable to the rather dull diocesan seats that were their legal residences. Since many were sons of nobles, they shared the outlook of that group and associated themselves in common cause with it. To support themselves, the clergy and the nobles drew their income largely from the land, from the great estates that they controlled, but also from special taxes and levies, such as the burdensome and unpopular tithe, a major source of ecclesiastical income. These classes were estranged from the rank and file in the population, including the wealthy members of the Third Estate, the lower clergy, and the peasantry. The Third Estate, which was composed of all non-noble elements of society, found its unity in opposition to the aristocracy. Not that the members of this estate objected to the notion that society was divided into different groups and that some possessed higher status and greater privileges than others. On the contrary, equalitarian ideas became popular only gradually and on a very limited scale in the late eighteenth century. Most men believed that all men of property should share the status of the aristocracy. The exclusion of the wealthy members of the Third Estate from the nobility created the foundation for a powerful and articulate opposition to the aristocracy.

But the disappointments of the middle class in its efforts to secure greater status within society did not form the basis for violence that was present in the mounting economic hardships suffered by the lower classes. Bread was a major issue with the poor. The depression which gripped France in the period just before the revolution accentuated the sufferings of the poor who depended on their pitifully small wages as day laborers for food and housing. The small peasant farmers were no better off in many cases. They found themselves caught in the squeeze between higher prices for their commodities and higher rents demanded by the lords, who technically owned the land they farmed and now attempted to increase rents to meet the expenses of life at court. Hardly a single group in France lacked reasons for hating the old regime; hardly anyone save the king and a relatively small group of supporters stood staunchly for the preservation of the existing order. Here matters stood when the Estates General met in May, 1789.

"The Tennis Court Oath" by David. A Romantic treatment of an important moment in the history of the French Revolution. (The Bettmann Archive)

Louis XVI's speech from the throne aroused the Third Estate by providing that each estate should vote separately and should cast only a single vote. Thus the Third Estate found itself swamped by the clergy and nobility. The reaction of the Third Estate came in the famed "tennis court oath" which declared that the Third Estate would not disband until it had prepared a constitution for France. Louis had to recognize the accomplished fact. In the weeks that followed, the king and queen began to plot with leading members of the nobility and with officers in the army to overthrow the new National Constituent Assembly, as the Estates General was now called. Troops from the provinces arrived in Paris and at Versailles in an obvious attempt to bolster the royal authority. The assembly demanded their removal. When Louis refused, a mob of Parisians sacked part of the city and attacked the fortress of the Bastille in search of arms. Louis once more backed down and came to Paris to appear in public wearing a red, white, and blue cap that had become the symbol of the revolution. But this gesture was empty. Marie Antoinette and Louis were simply playing for more time to bring additional troops from Flanders. When this plot was discovered, the Parisians reacted by escorting the king and queen from Versailles to Paris, where they would be under the vigilant eyes of the Paris commune. The discredited monarch had lost, by his participation in intrigue, any influence he might have had over the assembly and its work of creating a new constitution.

Meanwhile, the assembly had devoted itself to two major tasks; the destruction of the more odious aspects of the old regime and the writing of the constitution. On August 4, this body voted the legal destruction of all forms of feudal tenure, although it preserved the property of the nobility by turning it into private property. What was lost under one form was thereby regained under another. This act proved that men of property could work together. The assembly also issued the "declaration of the rights of man" setting forth the philosophical foundation of the revolution in terms of the theory of natural rights. It secularized Church property, taking over responsibility for payment of the clergy and demanding that all clergy take an oath to support this measure. Only a minority complied and the Church became a rallying point for opposition to the revolution. Finally, the assembly produced a constitution, which provided for a limited monarchy with a one-chamber legislature. The king had only a suspensive veto over legislation and no control over the military forces of the realm. The new chamber was to be elected by a body of electors so chosen that the propertied class would control it. Thus, the work of the National Constituent Assembly reflected the middle-class composition of that body and attempted to ensure the dominance of that class in political life.

The limited monarchy created by the Constitution of 1791 faced many obstacles. The nobility and the clergy who had refused to accept the revolution worked to undermine it and to restore the power of the monarchy. But the major responsibility for its failure rested with the king and queen. On June 20, 1791, Louis and his family disguised themselves and set out from Paris to the German border. However, they were recognized near the town of Varennes and escorted back to Paris. A pretence was made of preserving him as king for the next year, but he was actually a prisoner. His action had cost the limited monarchy considerable support and played into the hands of those who favored a republican government. Moreover, it appeared obvious to some that his continued presence was itself a danger to the revolution because his person formed the rallying point for the intrigues of émigrés abroad and of the conservative peasantry of the Vendée and Anjou, who desired a restoration. The outbreak of war against Austria in 1792 was largely due to fear of the radical left that she would lead a coalition to reestablish the royal absolutism.

Mounting pressures against the new constitution at home and abroad found their catalyst in the war. Each side looked to the war as a means for gaining the advantage in the struggle to control France. The king felt he had little to lose. In victory, his armies would make him a hero; in defeat, his Austrian relatives would force the return of his power. Many elements among the supporters of the revolution favored the war on the ground that it would strengthen the cause of national unity and cement the success of the revolution. Only a relatively small group on the radical left opposed the war for fear that it would lead to a military dictatorship.

Nevertheless, the war went badly for France during the opening months. The Marquis de Lafayette, hero of the American Revolution and leader of the French national guard during the revolution, met defeat on several occasions. The royal family cheered at the thought of an early Austrian victory that would result in a restoration of their powers. On July 25, 1792, the Duke of Brunswick issued a declaration that the victorious Austrians would restore the king to the "exercise of his legitimate authority." For all practical purposes, this announcement was the death sentence of Louis XVI. The growing determination to drive the foreign invaders from French soil was accompanied by the feeling that the king was responsible for the war. The French were in the process of forming a new army of citizens, dedicated to the defense of their fatherland. This army was to be the first in history founded almost entirely on nationalist principles. Its stirring anthem was the *Marseillaise*. During September, 1792, the French army achieved its first success at Valmy, defeating and turning back the forces of the Duke of Brunswick. Shortly after, the convention met and proclaimed a republic. In December, the king was tried and condemned to death by a single vote. He was executed in January, 1793.

The government of the National Convention had superseded the limited monarchy in the fall of 1792. Its major task was to achieve victory over France's foreign enemies. The dominant element in the convention through the early months of 1793 was the Gironde, so-named from the fact that its middle-class membership came largely from the department of the Gironde. The Girondins felt the revolution had gone far enough. They formed the right wing of the Jacobin Club, which provided much of the leadership for the revolution. The other important group was the Mountain, led by Danton and Robespierre. The Mountain was radical in its policies and gained its chief support from lower middle-class Parisians. The leaders of the Mountain supported the terror and were strongly behind the execution of the king. By mid-1793, the leaders of the Mountain joined forces with the Paris commune to drive out the Girondist deputies. But when Danton took a peace line, the radicals under Robespierre pushed him from power.

Meanwhile the war had proceeded well under the leadership of General Carnot. The first coalition against the republic, composed of Austria, Prussia, England, Holland, Spain, and Sardinia, broke up in 1795 when Spain and Holland were so hard pressed that they gave up and joined France as allies. These successes were due, in large measure, to the hard line followed at home. The convention had given extraordinary powers to the committee of public safety and the committee of general security. Using the terror as an instrument of policy, these committees put new backbone into the army and enforced a draft of all young men between the ages of eighteen and twenty-five for military service. But the committee found itself seriously divided. The moderates turned on the radicals, applying to them the machinery of the terror. Robespierre, who had dominated that body following his ouster of Danton, himself fell victim to the terror. Ironically, he was one of its last sacrifices. The country had grown sick of the bloodletting by the middle of 1794. But the terror had already achieved its purpose by instilling new spirit in the armies of France and the citizens at home.

The end of the reign of terror signaled the beginning of a new era in the revolution. The Gironde overthrew the convention. The government of the directory that replaced the convention in 1795 came to power with the support of the military and grew increasingly dependent on the army to maintain its power. But, in the four years of its existence, it proved itself unable to cope with the mounting problems of internal disorder and internal economic crisis. What some radicals had feared at the outbreak of the war against Austria now gradually occurred. The figure of one general, the brilliant and ambitious Corsican, Napoleon Bonaparte, emerged as a potential strongman in French politics. France moved toward military dictatorship.

The revolution produced profound changes in France. It wiped away the entire structure of the feudal regime, including forced labor services and dues. The peasants became proprietors of the soil. In this way, the foundation was laid for the development of a strong French peasantry, which has lasted to the present. The revolution also destroyed the guild system, which had been a major obstacle to the growth of industrial capitalism in France and had impeded free movement in the trades. Educational and legal reforms had destroyed the special position of the Church in these areas and strengthened the concept of the secular state as the supreme force in French society. Repudiation of the debt of the monarchy opened the way to fiscal solvency and financial reform. Most important, in the crisis of the revolution, France forged a nation. Its citizen army fought to protect the interests of home and hearth. It identified itself with the country. The spirit of nationalism was born.

The Age of Napoleon, 1799–1815

The rise of Napoleon to supreme power in France and throughout most of Europe revealed to Europeans the power of the new nation-state. For Napoleon capitalized on the revolutionary forces that had destroyed the old regime in France and created a nation with a citizen army capable of dominating the European continent. His great dream was the unification of Europe under French hegemony; the chief obstacle to its fulfillment was the naval power of England. Whether or not his advocacy of the ideals of the French Revolution was entirely sincere, he and his armies were responsible for the spread of these ideas in Central, Southern, and Eastern Europe. They also aroused the spirit of nationalism, the desire of a people for political unity to supplement unity of language and culture, in these same regions. In Italy, for example, the Napoleonic conquests favored liberal and reform elements who aimed at the unification of their country; in Germany, opposition to the Napoleonic armies created greater arguments for unification even as Napoleon's own conquests remodeled the map of that country, reduced its hundreds of territorial principalities to merely thirty-nine. But Napoleon was also the man who consolidated the position of the revolution within France. Dictator though he was, even under the guise of emperor, his revision of the civil law in the Code Napoleon, his founding of the Bank of France, his settlement of the religious question, and his reforms of education all followed lines laid down by the revolution. But all of these achievements may be summed up in his greatest accomplishment: the creation of the first truly modern national state.

To regard Napoleon's conquests merely as a continuation of the revolutionary wars of France is to fall into a trap laid by the accident of appearances. France fought the war of the first coalition to defend the revolution against the powers attempting to restore the monarchy and only secondarily as a war to free the oppressed peoples of Europe from their tyrannical rulers. Napoleon's great successes made the first objective a reality and went far to achieve the second. But Napoleon had simply taken over these goals of the revolutionaries without making them completely his own. His own concept of European unity under France was central to his aims. To some extent, he stood in this position as the heir of the policies of Richelieu and Louis XIV. But, under the impact of revolutionary thought, Napoleon conceived of his goals more in ideological than in dynastic terms. Not that he was entirely free of dynasticism. His efforts to secure crowns for his posterity and his relatives reveals the continued strength of this principle in political life. However, the greater motivating force behind the wars of Napoleon was the ideology of the French Revolution. His opposition to reactionary monarchy, the continuation of the old regime elsewhere in Europe, stemmed from his lack of respect for the old monarchy of France. His dream of unity was a further expression of the "fraternity" of the French Revolution. Within his new empire, property rather than birth was the true mark of nobility. He found allies in the middle-class businessmen in France and the conquered countries.

In 1799, France was still attempting feebly to recover from the effects of the revolution. Napoleon's first task was to build the nation. The constitution of that year, product of the *coup d'état* that brought Napoleon to power, was on paper a stronger document than any of the others that had come out of the revolutionary movement. Centralization of authority in a council of state dominated by Napoleon as first consul, was a device to ensure his and the army's voice in civil government. For all practical purposes, this constitution made Napoleon the real ruler of France. The machinery of local government was directed from Paris through a system

Napoleon I. Crowned with the laurel of the Roman emperors, the French ruler revives the idea of grandeur in France. (*Rare Book Room, Syracuse University Library*)

of appointed prefects, subprefects, and mayors. In the period following 1800, Napoleon embarked on a major program to reform many aspects of French life. A system of schools culminating in the University of France, which controlled the licensing of all teachers, was established. A major public works program, including the construction of about thirty roads leading outward from Paris, which were required by the army but were also valuable for the economic growth of the country, was undertaken. Systematic financial reforms emphasized the orderly process of administration. Napoleon was able to keep taxes relatively low, despite his wars, by seeing that their cost was borne by his "allies" and the conquered nations. Within France, honest collection and efficiency were the major marks of the regime. To restore the confidence of the middle class, the government undertook to pay its bills in gold and silver coin. Napoleon also founded the Bank of France, overcoming traditional French opposition to centralized banking systems in order to secure the advantages they offered for funding the national debt and encouraging increased investment in industry and commerce. Napoleon's religious settlement with the Catholic Church, embodied in the Concordat of 1801, laid the foundation for regularization of relations in this critical area. The antireligious campaigns of the radical revolutionaries had alienated many moderates and undermined support for the government. Napoleon wanted a united France and, although himself no ardent supporter of the Church, worked to secure a settlement that would ensure the support of Catholics for his regime. The concordat secured Church recognition for revolutionary confiscations of Church lands, but the government agreed to pay the salaries of the clergy. The Pope had the right to confirm bishops. While the government recognized Catholicism as the "religion of the majority" in France, the concordat preserved the revolutionary spirit of tolerance by ensuring the right of all to follow their religious beliefs. In this way, this revolutionary principle received indirect and limited recognition from the Church. The effects of these reforms should not be exaggerated. Their impact was gradual, some reaching culmination only after the fall of the Napoleonic regime.

Napoleon Bonaparte was, as is easily seen from his program, far more than a military dictator. Indeed, his image of himself was a combination of many roles, part dictator, part legitimate ruler and emperor—after his creation of the French Empire—and part law-giver. He thought of the Code Napoleon as the crowning achievement of his rule and attempted to promote its adoption wherever his armies and his influence reached. The Code Napoleon combined the traditions of old French law, based partly on Roman and partly on medieval Germanic legal principles, with revolutionary elements. It completed the dismantling of the feudal regime, abolished primogeniture, and established the equality of all citizens before the law. Marriage and other areas once under the ecclesiastical law came under control of the civil law. On the other hand, in accordance with the general views of the period, women remained in an inferior legal status. Nevertheless, the entire code was a monumental achievement and it remained the basis for French law after the overthrow of Napoleon, as well as influencing the modern legal development of Italy and parts of Germany.

To some extent, the Napoleonic wars were an outgrowth of the revolutionary wars of France; their aims, from Danton on, had partially paralleled those of the absolutist monarchy under Louis XIV. But Frenchmen now fought not for the king, but for the nation. They were "sons of freedom" and "citizens" in an army of the nation. Their goals were those of the nation in which all Frenchmen shared. Napoleon himself carefully identified the war aims of France with national aspirations: the winning of the frontiers of the nation, the glory of the nation, and the spread of the peculiarly French revolutionary ideas of "liberty, fraternity, and equality" to other nations.

By 1802, Napoleon had pursued the war of the Second Coalition—composed of England, Austria, and their allies—to a successful conclusion. In that year, England and the powers signed the Peace of Amiens and for the following year there was peace. But Napoleon took advantage of peace to further his own aims for continental Europe, particularly the reorganization of Germany. The growing realization that the French emperor intended to remake the map of Europe led to the formation of the Third Coalition under the initial leadership of Russia. But again the French ruler showed his great military skill. In three major battles, he removed the chief continental powers from the war. In 1806, the Austrians met a crushing defeat at the Battle of Austerlitz and the Battle of Jena in the following year forced the Prussians out of the war. A disastrous defeat meted out to the Russians at Friedland in 1807 convinced the Tsar of the advantages of withdrawal from the war and conclusion of an alliance with France. Only England remained to pursue the war. She remained all-powerful on the sea after Lord Nelson's victory over the combined fleets of France and Spain at Trafalgar.

French dominance on the continent provided the opportunity for drastic reorganization of Italy and Germany. In 1804, northern Italy became the Kingdom of Italy under the rule of Napoleon himself. Bonaparte installed his brother Joseph on the throne of Naples, later moving him to Spain and granting Naples to his brother-in-law Joachim Murat. Under Napoleonic administration, with which the Italian middle class found it no great difficulty to cooperate, Italy prospered and knew better government generally than had been the case under the lax but despotic rule of the Austrians in the north or the Spaniards in the south. In Germany, Napoleon's changes favored the greater states, especially the Catholic states to the west and south, at the expense of hundreds of petty principalities. When his remodeling was complete, there remained only thirty-nine states, the most important of which were raised to the status of kingdoms. Thus, the great duchies of Bavaria and Saxony became kingdoms at this time. In 1806, Napoleon founded the Confederation of the Rhine, composed of the German states on the east bank of the Rhine. The confederation formed a neat counterbalance to the power of both Prussia and Austria in the Germanies and thus accorded well with the traditional French policy of preventing a strong state from taking shape on its eastern frontier. At the same time, Napoleon feared the chaos of the petty German principalities almost more than he did a strong German state. The confederation gave hope for a solution to these problems.

The logical conclusion of this process of conquest and consolidation was provision for a more stable and enduring form of government than that inherent in the *de facto* dictatorship of the great general. Napoleon therefore attempted a solution to the difficult problem of legitimating his rule. His answer was the creation of the first French Empire with himself as emperor. Concern for the endurance of his policies and government led him to divorce his wife, Josephine Beauharnais, who had failed to bear him any children, and to marry into the Austrian Habsburgs. His new bride, the Archduchess Maria Louisa, bore him a son in less than a year and Napoleon conferred the title of King of Rome on him. Assured of a successor, Napoleon's other concerns were to build support for his dynasty among all elements of society in France. The empire revived titles of nobility as rewards for service. Increasingly, the emperor revealed his personal preference for the trappings of the old regime. But the solid foundation of his government remained in the bourgeoisie. Their support was important to its success, but the appeal was broader because it celebrated the moment of glory of the nation in the dominance that Napoleon's conquests brought to France.

Middle class support of Napoleon was bolstered by his effort to enforce the continental system, which cut off Europe from trade with England in an effort to destroy the economy of the island kingdom. The continental system was cleverly devised to deprive the English of their European markets and so to weaken the financial structure of the country so that she would have to give up the war. The theory was valid; in practice, Napoleon found it increasingly more difficult to enforce a complete embargo on British goods. However, the English blockade of continental ports had a detrimental effect on trade between neutrals and Europe. While the continent was still largely self-sufficient, the neutrals, particularly the United States, resented the search and seizure tactics of the British.

The first major chinks in the continental system appeared in Portugal, where the Braganza king had no desire to abandon the traditional Portuguese alliance with England. Napoleon decided to punish the Portuguese and demanded permission for his troops to cross Spain. Spain offered no real opposition. Her government was encrusted with the barnacles of reaction and corroded with the rust of corruption. King Ferdinand VII offered no resistance. But the Spanish populace soon found the French intolerable and began a revolt. Their guerilla tactics caught the French regulars off base. English support for the revolt under Wellington added to the problems of the French. Central and Eastern Europe also grew restive under the continental system. In Prussia, the Baron von Stein initiated a program of reforms aimed at building a national state. In Russia, Alexander II, partially influenced by his former tutor, La Harpe, had imbibed some of the ideals of the French Revolution and had introduced some of his liberal ideas into Russia. This grandson of Catherine the Great grew increasingly fearful, however, of Napoleon's policies in Central and Eastern Europe, especially his establishment of the Duchy of Warsaw. The continental system proved to be the last straw. Alexander decided to withdraw from the system. Despite his commitments in the Peninsular War, Napoleon decided to attack Russia.

War with Russia involved a serious risk of overextending French forces. But Napoleon counted on his military ability to minimize this possibility. He planned to force the Russians into a decisive battle, defeat their army, and so bring the campaign to a quick conclusion without jeopardizing his position in the West. However, his plans went awry. The Russians retreated before his army, burning and destroying their crops to make it difficult for his army to secure needed food. Finally, they even abandoned and burned Moscow itself without giving battle. Napoleon found himself facing greater unrest in Germany and Austria. He decided to retreat. The long retreat was disastrous. Harassed by Russian troops, unprepared for the bitter cold of the winter, and demoralized by defeat at the hands of an invincible enemy, the great Napoleonic army disintegrated.

Rebellion in Germany forced Napoleon to flee ahead of his troops to Paris, where he raised a new army to face the rebels. But these were not the soldiers of the grand army which had held all Europe at bay; they were green recruits and unequal to the task. In October, 1813, at Leipzig, in the Battle of the Nations, the Napoleonic army suffered a decisive defeat. No longer could there be any hope that a Napoleonic France might remain as a member of the European family. Victory at Leipzig meant the end for Napoleon.

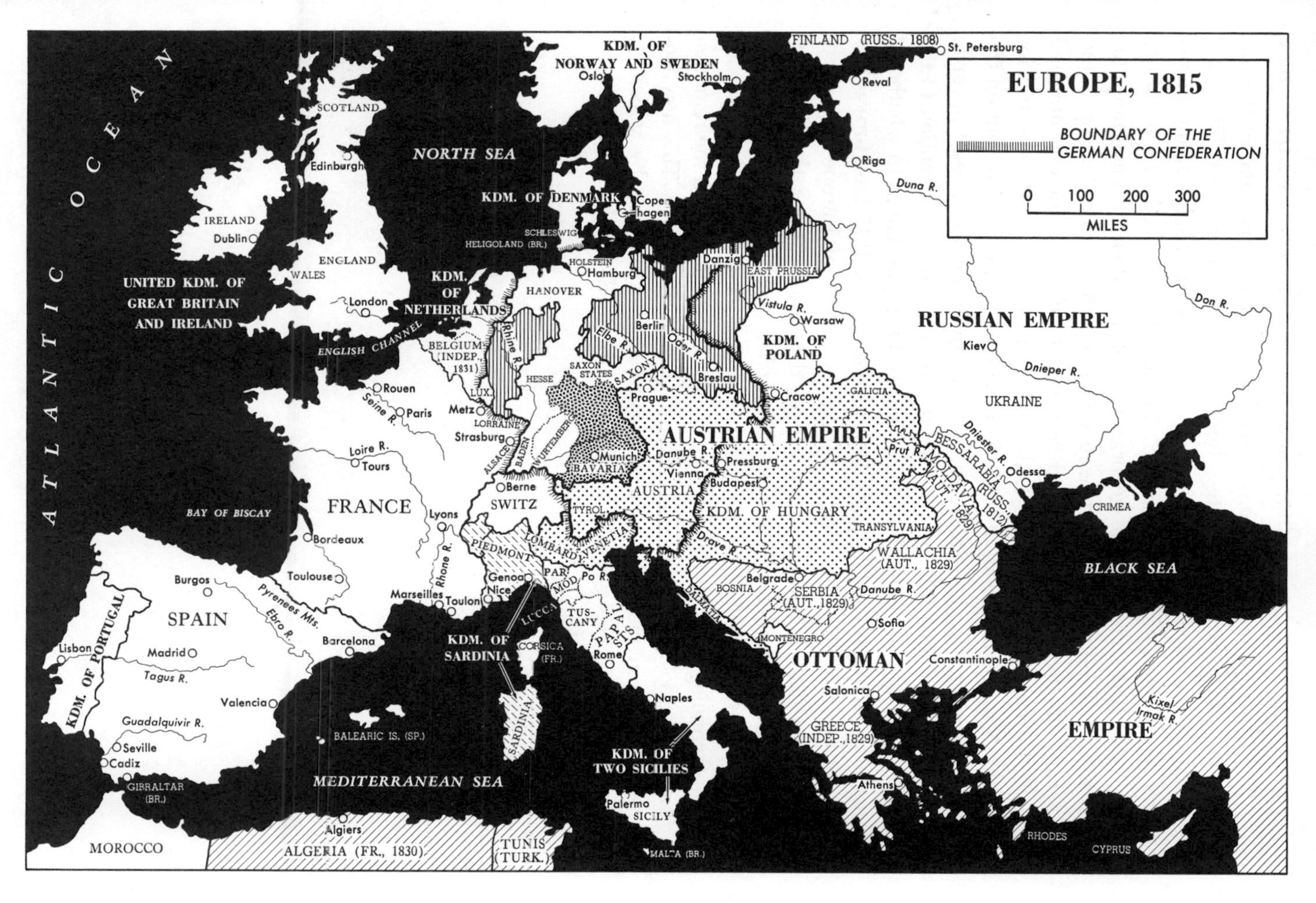
EUROPE, 1815
BOUNDARY OF THE GERMAN CONFEDERATION
0 100 200 300
MILES
ATLANTIC OCEAN
NORTH SEA
BAY OF BISCAY
ENGLISH CHANNEL
MEDITERRANEAN SEA
BLACK SEA
UNITED KDM. OF GREAT BRITAIN AND IRELAND
IRELAND
Dublin
SCOTLAND
Edinburgh
ENGLAND
WALES
London
KDM. OF NORWAY AND SWEDEN
Oslo
Stockholm
KDM. OF DENMARK
Cope-hagen
SCHLESWIG
HELIGOLAND (BR.)
HOLSTEIN
Hamburg
HANOVER
KDM. OF NETHERLANDS
BELGIUM (INDEP. 1831)
LUX.
Rhine R.
HESSE
SAXON STATES
SAXONY
Elbe R.
Berlin
Oder R.
Breslau
Danzig
EAST PRUSSIA
Vistula R.
Warsaw
KDM. OF POLAND
Cracow
FINLAND (RUSS., 1808)
St. Petersburg
Reval
Riga
Duna R.
RUSSIAN EMPIRE
Kiev
Dnieper R.
Don R.
UKRAINE
GALICIA
AUSTRIAN EMPIRE
Prague
Danube R.
Vienna
Pressburg
Budapest
AUSTRIA
KDM. OF HUNGARY
TRANSYLVANIA
Prut R.
MOLDAVIA (AUT., 1829)
BESSARABIA (RUSS. 1812)
Dniester R.
Odessa
CRIMEA
WALLACHIA (AUT., 1829)
Drave R.
Munich
BAVARIA
WURTEMBERG
BADEN
ALSACE
LORRAINE
TYROL
LOMBARDY-VENETIA
FRANCE
Rouen
Seine R.
Paris
Metz
Strasburg
Loire R.
Tours
Lyons
Bordeaux
Toulouse
Rhone R.
Marseilles
Toulon
SWITZ
Berne
PIEDMONT
Genoa
Nice
PAR.
MOD.
Po R.
LUCCA
TUS-CANY
PAPAL STS.
Rome
CORSICA (FR.)
KDM. OF SARDINIA
SARDINIA
Naples
KDM. OF TWO SICILIES
Palermo
SICILY
MALTA (BR.)
SPAIN
Burgos
Pyrenees Mts.
Ebro R.
Barcelona
Madrid
Tagus R.
Valencia
Guadalquivir R.
Seville
Cadiz
GIBRALTAR (BR.)
KDM. OF PORTUGAL
Lisbon
BALEARIC IS. (SP.)
MOROCCO
Algiers
ALGERIA (FR., 1830)
TUNIS (TURK.)
OTTOMAN EMPIRE
BOSNIA
DALMATIA
Belgrade
SERBIA (AUT., 1829)
Danube R.
MONTENEGRO
Sofia
Constantinople
Salonica
GREECE (INDEP., 1829)
Athens
Kixel Irmak R.
RHODES
CYPRUS

The Congress of Vienna, summoned to resolve the questions of the impending peace, was the greatest body of its kind ever held. Six ruling monarchs attended along with a numerous retinue. High-ranking ministers represented other governments. The congress moved at a desultory pace, but had laid down the general lines of a settlement when news arrived that Napoleon, who had been sent into exile to rule the tiny island of Elba off the Italian coast, had returned to France. For one hundred days, Europe waited until the Duke of Wellington quashed once and for all the Napoleonic dream at Waterloo (1815). Napoleon was sent on the long journey to desolate St. Helena off the South American coast never to return to France in this life. Europe was free to turn its attention to the building of a new society, but there was serious question as to whether it possessed the spirit for the task. Would the men of 1815 look forward or back? On the answer to that question the future of Europe depended.

Europe had changed dramatically in the century since the death of Louis XIV. The ideology of the *philosophes* and the age of revolution were not alone responsible for these changes, for the growth of science and technology had played an increasingly important role in the remodeling of the social and economic fabric of European society. This new Europe, based on industrial society, forged the instruments by which its leadership over the world was to be maintained for the next century.

16 The Impact of the Revolutions

The Congress of Vienna was the weathervane of Europe in the early nineteenth century. But it pointed no constant direction for the future of Europe. Its hopes for the future were largely cast in the vague uncertainties of diplomatic language, for each of the major powers had its own ideas about what that future should hold. None desired to repeal the immediate historical past in favor of the reestablishment of the old regimes. Restoration of legitimate rulers, a principle accepted by the congress, meant little in the practical context if those restored refused to adapt to the changed order. Vienna showed little desire to tamper too much with the Europe Napoleon had called into being. On the other hand, it also revealed little interest in changes wrought as a result of the political and economic revolutions of the age. Nationalism crept insidiously about the chambers without either finding a champion or an opponent. Its influence was felt chiefly outside the formal sessions.

The statesmen at Vienna attempted solutions based on a conception of Europe as it had existed, not as it was. Failure to comprehend the forces of industrialism, nationalism, and a growing liberal spirit led them to rebuild largely according to the old pattern of dynastic states. Within a few years it became apparent that the new Europe would not be another model of the old. The rise of the urban masses to a political role, the effort to create national states, and the desire to broaden the base of participation in government were significant factors in the transition from the old regime to an age of democracy.

Industrial Society

During most of the early modern period, the dominance of the old nobility had been challenged by the rise of commercial and landed middle class in most of the countries of Western Europe. The increasing wealth gained from trade made the merchants a powerful counterpoise to the nobility. In England, where younger sons of the nobles were regarded as commoners and often married with leading merchant families, the continued influx of new wealth not only strengthened the position of the aristocracy and lent greater status to the merchants, but also broke down the prejudice among the nobles against engaging in business. On the continent, however, even where the merchants had sometimes gained entry into the nobility during the later middle ages, rising barriers against permitting the merchants to become nobles forced a sharper cleavage between those who possessed privilege and those who drew their wealth from investments in business and the land. The marketplace was closed to the true noble. The French Revolution did much to alter this situation. With the destruction of much of the aristocracy of the old regime in France during the terror and the breakdown of old systems of landholding, including primogeniture, the bourgeois achieved dominance in France. Elsewhere in Europe, the process was more gradual, but the conquests of Napoleon did much to favor the leadership of the middle class.

The Krupp Works at Dresden, Germany. A vast modern industrial complex, the achievement of the industrial revolution. (*Brown Brothers*)

Thus, by 1815, almost everywhere in Western Europe, though hardly at all in Central and Eastern Europe, the middle class had gained supremacy in political life.

However, it would be a mistake to regard the middle class as static and unchanging throughout the early modern period. From its origins in the medieval towns, it had undergone numerous and significant transformations. Within itself, the tendency of the wealthiest merchant families of the towns to identify themselves more and more with the landed nobility by buying land and marrying into noble families was merely one aspect of the continuing process of differentiation between the leading members of the middle class and the majority, whose wealth raised them above the level of the masses but did not permit them to aspire to nobility. The term middle class should not obscure the fact that this group had its origins in the peasantry and lower classes, as well as in the nobility, and was constantly drawing new blood from these sources. Moreover the middle class was constantly changing under the impact of new developments in the economic order. Since its interests lay chiefly in business, it was more concerned about new methods and new inventions than either the nobility or the peasantry.

In the mid-eighteenth century, significant improvements in industrial technology rapidly accelerated the rate of industrial growth. The middle class, especially in England, where the beginnings of the industrial revolution were centered, took the lead in building factories and investing in industrial enterprises. Many members of this class were active in the technological revolution that made increased production possible. However, the large investments necessary for building factories were usually not available to a single individual. Usually, it was necessary to form a company. The investors then received a return on their investment, while the factory was put under the management of an entrepreneur whose interest in the concern might be small or even non-existent. The financial support for these enterprises came, however, both from the nobility and the lower classes.

Increasingly after 1800, the influence of Adam Smith and the classical school of English economists played a leading role in shaping the ideas and attitudes of middle-class industrialists. Smith had opposed all regulation of the economy by the state on the ground that natural law governed the operation of that sector. David Ricardo developed the famous iron law of wages, which maintained that wages would increase as the supply of labor diminished. He argued that nature regulated the supply and demand of the labor market. Prosperity brought a higher birth rate and therefore a greater supply of labor. The larger number of laborers reduced the wages and caused a decrease in the birth rate. Thus the cycle was continuous. Ricardo's theory condemned mankind to an eternal round of boom and bust, prosperity and misery in the name of nature. An Anglican clergyman, Thomas Malthus, studied the problems caused by an increasing population. He pointed out that population increased in geometric proportions (2, 4, 8, 16) while food increased only arithmetically (2, 4, 6, 8, 10). The population would outstrip the food supply and result in mass starvation unless man practiced continence. Other economists advocated free trade, removal of all restrictions on production and sale of goods; in brief, they believed that "that government governs best which governs least."

The great mass of men belonged not to the middle class of property but to the laboring class. In the early modern period, the old distinction between peasant and lord was swept away to be replaced by the landlord-tenant and master-employe relationships. In England, this transformation had taken place gradually as the landed aristocracy became more interested in money rents and investments in land. The rise of the gentry after the early sixteenth century saw the establishment of men of middle-class origins and attitudes on the soil in greater numbers than before. They sought to increase their incomes by making farming more profitable. With the increasing demand for grain to feed the growing populations of the rising industrial cities, they enclosed their land, eliminated many of the marginal peasant farms, and studied methods to make their operations more efficient. On the continent, the sudden and cataclysmic elimination of a large segment of the French aristocracy had laid the foundation for the rise of a middle-class peasantry, who remained on the soil and shared many of the views of their less wealthy neighbors. In Central and Eastern Europe, the transition was more gradual; the great landholders managed to retain their positions through most of the nineteenth century and even into the twentieth. In these lands, the status of the peasantry remained precarious.

The rise of industrial cities, especially in England in the second half of the eighteenth century, had a tremendous impact on the working classes. The factories demanded large numbers of relatively unskilled workers. Drawn from the surrounding countryside and even from afar, these former peasants found themselves cut off from their former life and forced to dwell in the slums that grew up adjacent to their factories. Their lot was worse than that of any other group in society.

In the period from the mid-eighteenth to the mid-nineteenth century, Europe took on the complexion of an industrial society. Agriculture, which had remained at the backbone of European economic and social life for its entire history, gradually was being pressed into a secondary role by the demands of industry. The shift in population from country to city was, of course, most noticeable in England, where industrialization developed more rapidly than on the continent. In France, the major shifts toward industrial cities took place only in the mid-nineteenth century; in Germany, somewhat later. The character of the new cities was considerably different from that of the medieval towns or the commercial centers of the later medieval and early modern period. The industrial city was situated near its raw materials and its chief sources of power as well as near good transportation facilities. It grew rapidly and in ugliness. Its purpose was not the life of its inhabitants; it seldom inspired civic pride. Rather it was functional. Its dirt and filth were prideful marks of the success of its industry. Since its growth was rapid, it frequently lacked the political structure of the medieval town and had little in the way of traditions or customs on which to base its actions. Without a past, it had to search for most elements that older cities took for granted. As a conse-

Slums of Wentworth Street, by Gustave Doré. Poverty and squalor were boon companions. (*The Bettmann Archive*)

quence, the industrial city represented a break with the past not merely in its attachment to technology, but also in its search for government.

The growth of industrialism was a major element in the creation of basic tensions in the social life of the nineteenth century. In large measure, the sources of these conflicts lay in economic inequalities. We have noted already the gap between the investor and the manager of industry. The chasm between the middle-class entrepreneur and the laborers was even greater. Social historians have pointed often to the suffering and hardships of the workers in the factories. Masses of evidence point to the exploitation of women and children in mills, mines, and factories. Misshapen bodies, broken spirits, accidental or lingering death were the lot of the poor. These images contrast sharply with the elegance and grace, the pleasure and opulence of life among the middle class in the eighteenth and nineteenth centuries. The French Revolution had lent some strength to the lower classes by providing articulate leaders able to state their demands for a greater voice in society. This theme was taken up in England in the nineteenth century as part of a demand for social and political reforms. The urban lower class aimed at securing the same influence in political life that the middle class had gradually won for itself.

The power of the industrial process to transform society sprang from the fact that it reorganized human labor along new lines. Factory replaced cottage; water power and steam replaced man and animal; the machine reduced the amount of skill required to complete a given task. For the first time in history, the lower classes suddenly acquired a position in control of the economic roots of society. Brought together in the cities, they were in a position to cooperate with one another in order to improve their lot as no peasants on the land had ever been. The element lacking was the realization that they possessed the power to transform society. In the course of the nineteenth century, the realization of this power in the hands of the lower classes was to result in the rise of both democratic and socialist movements.

It was against this background that the political settlement at Vienna in 1815 was made. Its attempt to preserve as much as possible of the old order was doomed from the very beginning by forces unleashed in the new industrialism. Failure to attune the political currents of Europe to these changes resulted in the failure of the peace settlement and the ushering in of a new age of political revolutions just fifteen years later.

From Vienna to Revolution, 1815–1830

If the Congress of Vienna was not merely a meeting of the powers designed to restore the old order in Europe, it was remarkably lacking in original answers to the problems facing Europe in 1815. The provisions of the treaty signed on June 9, 1815, reveal the housekeeping nature of many of the negotiations. In fact, the powers had agreed beforehand to avoid discussion of the major issues affecting their individual vital interests. Britain would not permit discussions of freedom of the seas; Russia would not discuss her plans for expansion into the Ottoman Empire. Even the brilliant suggestion of Talleyrand that the principle of "legitimacy" guide the deliberations of the members was meaningless in light of Napoleon's successful reorganization of Germany and Italy. Its meaning was simply restoration of the traditional houses of Europe wherever it was expedient to do so. Chiefly, this principle meant the restoration of the Bourbons in France with Louis XVIII, as well as in Spain and the Kingdom of the two Sicilies. Elsewhere, the principle bent where necessary. In Germany, not even the fact that the King of Saxony had supported Napoleon to the bitter end favored the legitimate princes seeking restoration of their domains at his expense. The naming of Napoleon's son, the Prince of Rome, as Duke of Tuscany recognized his position as son of the Archduchess Maria Louisa. Indeed, the most important fact about the Congress of Vienna was not its effort to restore the "legitimate" monarchs of the past, but its tendency to allow matters to remain much as they had been. France received no real punishment for her transgressions. Austria made no gains for her victory. Napoleon's declaration of the end of the Holy Roman Empire stood; the Austrian ruler was now an emperor of real domains in Central and Southeastern Europe, the beginnings of the Austro-Hungarian Empire.

The leading figures in the congress were men destined to play an important role in the European politics of the next decades. Perhaps the most commanding figure was the Austrian foreign minister, Count Klemens von Metternich. Conservative in outlook, he was extremely well informed and quite able. He saw Europe realistically and prior to the Battle of the Nations willingly acquiesced in a settlement that would have permitted Napoleon to retain the throne of France. Among the crowned heads at the meeting, Alexander II of Russia was to attempt a leading role in the years following. His mysticism caused most of his contemporaries to misunderstand him, but he was capable of deep insights into the meaning of political trends.

As a result of the settlement at Vienna, England remained the dominant mercantile empire of Europe and ensured her continued lead in industry by preservation of her command of the seas. Austria was the leading German state, but her commitments to Southeastern Europe drew her further from German affairs. Consequently, the importance of Prussia was enhanced by the congress, though Frederick William III was far from assertive of his country's position. Russia found herself drawn more closely into European matters. Finally, France, the defeated power, retained a position of equality with the victors.

The years immediately following the Congress of Vienna found Europe in the grip of a wave of reaction to the liberal ideas of the French Revolution. At most, the effort was to maintain the *status quo.* In the Quadruple Alliance, England, Russia, Austria, and Prussia bound themselves to preserve the peace of Europe and to settle all disputes by diplomatic means in periodic congresses. They were to be the policemen of Europe. Alexander II of Russia wanted to go still further. He proposed the Holy Alliance, which would require the rulers who signed to conduct themselves according to Christian principles. Louis XVIII of France was a party to the Holy Alliance. However, the Prince Regent of England and the Pope refused their signatures. The document was not taken seriously, but was set down as another example of Alexander's mysticism. However, from the Russian point of view, it served to bring France and Russia together and to divide the attention of Austria, thus allowing the Russians greater freedom in their diplomacy in Southeastern Europe. The Holy Alliance fitted well into the tenor of the period, which opposed the possible outbreak of revolutionary movements and attempted to ensure the stability of Europe.

However, the period between 1815 and 1830 was far from quiet. Failure of the Congress of Vienna to recognize the aspirations of national minorities within the larger states and its tendency to ignore deep-seated differences between peoples in establishing boundaries made it inevitable that there would have to be some adjustments in this period. Moreover, the reestablishment of the House of Bourbon in France proved impossible to maintain.

In spite of the Napoleonic wars, France was not badly off in 1815. The indemnity of seven hundred million francs demanded by the Congress of Vienna and the occupation of French territory were not crushing burdens. Louis XVIII was a moderate, mindful of the fate of his predecessor. His task was to create support for his rule in a nation that was still divided politically by the revolution. The liberals were heirs of the revolutionary tradition. They included both monarchists and republicans, in addition to supporters of Napoleon. Their support came from all segments of society, but was especially strong in Paris, and among the former soldiers of the revolutionary armies. The conservatives and reactionaries were members of the old nobility returned to France following the defeat of Napoleon, the majority of the clergy, and the monarchist peasantry of the Vendée and Brittany. The most conservative of these rallied behind the king's brother Charles in his desire to restore the old regime with its absolute monarchy. Against these forces of left and right, Louis attempted to steer a middle course. He gauged the relative sentiment of the country and decided to ally himself with the middle class.

The Bourbon restoration did not mean, therefore, a repeal of the acts of the revolution and Napoleon. The new government retained the Napoleonic Code as the foundation of French law. To have done otherwise would have been to open the door to utter chaos, for the laws of the old regime and the principles on which they were based would have been completely out of place in the new social order created by the revolution. The Code Napoleon recognized the position of the middle class as the class of property even as it provided for a strong central government. Another sign of Louis' alliance to the bourgeois was his retention of the Bank of France, which concentrated fiscal and monetary control in Paris. However, the king ran into major obstacles from his legislative branch. The new constitution provided for two houses, an upper house of peers (lords) appointed by the king, and a lower house of commons elected by a narrrow franchise based on wealth. The ultraroyalists managed to gain control of both houses and initiated a "white terror" against those who had supported the revolutionary confiscations of property from the nobility and the Church. Realizing that the policies of the ultras threatened the existence of the crown, Louis dissolved the chamber and ordered new elections. The return of moderates to power enabled him to stem the tide of reaction for the time being. But his death, in 1824, brought to the throne his brother, Charles X, acknowledged leader of the ultras.

Charles combined many of the graces of the good king, personal charms, courtesy, kindliness, and a deep religiosity, with a high sense of his position as God's chosen one. He subscribed completely to the principles of absolute monarchy and had no love for the revolution. In fact, he had been one of the very first to flee France during the revolution and, more recently, his own son had been murdered by a fanatical revolutionary. His attempt to restore the absolute monarchy cost him the support of bourgeois monarchists and drove him from the throne in 1830. His cousin, the Duke of Orleans, Louis Philippe replaced him. Louis accepted the invitation of the lower house to become "King of the French."

In the Germanies, the settlement at the Congress of Vienna left the advocates of a united Germany with feelings of frustration. Throughout the following years there were isolated incidents pointing to the desire for unification. Metternich responded with the Carlsbad decrees of 1819, which disbanded German nationalist organizations. He saw in these groups a threat to the dominance of Austria in German affairs. He also attempted to persuade the rulers of the South German States they had gone too far to meet demands from the liberals. However, they had begun to realize the value of popular support to the state and preferred to retain the constitutions they had granted as the basis for national rule. However, Metternich was able to repress such feelings in the territories of the Austrian Empire.

The restoration of Austrian rule in most of northern Italy, of Papal control of central Italy, and of the Bourbons in the Kingdom of Two Sicilies met with considerable and growing opposition from those who desired the unification of that country as one nation. Giuseppe Mazzini founded the Young Italy movement to prepare for that moment. Others flocked to the Carbonari, or charcoal burners, a secret society with considerable strength in the north. These liberals and patriots contrasted the relative efficiency and honesty of Napoleonic government with the corruption of the restored rulers. In the twenties and thirties, revolutionary disturbances swept through Naples and the Papal States, but Metternich was able to preserve the *status quo.*

The agitation that swept continental Europe in this period did not leave England undisturbed. The end of the war with Napoleon turned men's minds to domestic problems. On the one hand, a wave of conservative feeling typified in the writings of Edmund Burke, who abhorred the excesses of the French Revolution and predicted that they would result in the rise of a military dictator, had caught up many during the late eighteenth century. The war effort, led by the brilliant William Pitt the Younger, had strengthened the hands of the conservatives by the sedition acts of the 1790's that revoked *habeas corpus* and the combination acts of 1799 and 1800 that made it a crime for working men to combine into unions to secure higher wages. The war also increased the national debt, raised prices at home, and worked serious hardships on the poorer classes. Even the death of Pitt in 1805 brought no end to his policies.

At the conclusion of the Napoleonic wars, the conservatives were in control. The end of wartime prosperity brought a temporary but quite severe downturn in the economy with widespread unemployment. More than half a million men were released from the army in the summer of 1815 to add their numbers to the job seekers. Moreover, at a time when Europe was not yet ready to buy English manufactured goods, the domestic market had produced far more than it could consume. The Tories under the leadership of Lord Liverpool had no solution for these problems. Largely representative of the landed gentry, their major concern was to protect the interests of their class. Therefore, their chief legislation was a corn law that imposed high tariffs on foreign grains to protect English farmers. This aid to the farmers brought an almost immediate rise in the price of bread, the staple of life to the masses in the industrial cities. Although subsequent measures, including the government's resumption of payment of its bills in gold and silver, checked the inflation somewhat, suffering among the poor created an atmosphere of unrest.

Agitation against the ruling classes broke into the open as new leaders began to express demands for reform. Jeremy Bentham, the leading English radical thinker, published his *Catechism of Parliamentary Reform* in 1817. He maintained that reform of that body to make it more representative by including the industrial entrepreneurs and lesser men of property would promote the "greatest good of the greatest number." William Cobbett propagandized the working class and lower middle class in his *Weekly Register,* which sold for two pence and reached about fifty thousand readers. He inveighed against landlords, the established church, and the industrialists. The English poet, Percy Bysshe Shelley, advised the poor:

> Rise like lions after slumber
> In unvanquishable number
> Shake your chains to earth like dew
> Which in sleep has fallen on you—
> Ye are many—they are few.

Such revolutionary advice sounded a clarion for more direct action. The Peterloo massacre in which government forces charged a peaceful assembly gathered to hear the parliamentary reformer Henry Hunt resulted in eleven deaths and five hundred injured.

During the twenties, the Tories managed to maintain their hold on the government, but their new leaders were more responsive to demands for reform. Sir Robert Peel, son of a Lancashire industrialist, promoted major changes in the criminal law to reduce the number of capital crimes. He also established the metropolitan police force, called "bobbies" after him. William Huskisson worked for the repeal of the navigation acts to promote free trade. The accession of the Duke of Wellington as prime minister saw two further concessions to the reformers. The campaign of Francis Place, the little tailor of Charing Cross, to secure repeal of the combination acts restraining the formation of trade unions was finally successful. Reluctantly, too, Wellington supported legislation to remove disabilities against Roman Catholics. His action here was largely dictated by his fear of rebellion in Ireland.

England avoided outright civil strife in the twenties largely because ruling classes attempted to meet demands for reform with some type of compromise. It was possible for the Tories to follow a policy of compromise because some within their own ranks supported it. Property was never completely divided in England. No single voice was able to speak for either Tories or Whigs. Within each of the major political groups were advocates of many positions, most of them willing to bend a bit to reach a peaceful solution.

By 1830, the first cracks in the settlement at Vienna had become rather prominent. During that and the following year, there were outbreaks in Italy, France, the Germanies, Poland, and Belgium. Most were unsuccessful. In Poland, the revolt resulted in greater repression than had existed previously. In Belgium, on the other hand, the revolt was able to throw off the rule of the House of Orange and assert the independence of that country from the Netherlands. Generally, the forces of conservatism managed to weather the storm, even where they had to compromise as in England and France. But the winds of change had begun to blow. The desire to maintain the *status quo* was not as strong as the desire to change. Moreover, the powers were beginning to turn once more to their own interests and toward affairs outside of Europe.

The statesmen of Vienna had conceived of Europe as a concert of the powers. That image scarcely lived through the meeting itself; its validity by 1830 could not be maintained even by the most heady partisan of conservatism. The powers had gone their separate ways. However, the efforts to maintain the existing order did prevent the immediate realization of the goals of the revolutionary liberals. But the day of revolution could not be postponed indefinitely; in fact, it was more present with every tiny concession and more immediate after every measure of repression.

Nationalism

The contemporary world takes for granted the desire for men to form national states. The idea of nationhood permeates our modern educational systems and almost every aspect of public life. Yet, in the way historical developments are measured, the nation appeared only recently. Although incipient evidence of national feelings existed during the later middle ages, as for example, in the Hundred Years' War between France and England, the sense of a common identity born on the fields of Crécy and Agincourt was a far cry from the sense of identification that modern man feels with the nation-state. Nationalism is much more than a mere recognition of certain general similarities of race and language, culture and custom; indeed, the chief ingredient seems to be a compelling belief that these characteristics must be preserved within the framework of a nation-state, that is, a state dedicated to serving the interests of a group with such a common heriage.

Nationalism, therefore, has always been closely connected with the process of building the nation-state. For this reason, all forms of patriotic sentiment not directed to this aim are at most evidences of incipient nationalism. The first evidence of the development of the national state appeared in the early modern period. The England of Elizabeth I attempted to create a broad base for support and to build on national sentiment. But the Stuarts did not follow Elizabeth in this regard. Moreover, there are good reasons to doubt that Elizabeth herself, "mere English" as she was, was genuinely concerned with national feelings save in the limited sense that they might promote a temporary support for royal policy. The Virgin Queen remained committed to the ideals of the territorial or dynastic state. She was unwilling to sacrifice the royal prerogative in the interest of a broader or national consensus. Yet it is precisely on this point that the national state is founded. Whether democratic, monarchic, demagogic, or totalitarian, the modern national state is based on a consensus. The appeal of the ruler is not upward to God as sovereign but downward to the people, a significant part of the people, as the foundation of power.

It is virtually impossible to pinpoint the birth pangs of the national state with any hope of accuracy. But certainly the period of the American and French Revolutions present obvious examples of this phenomenon. If the winning of independence by the thirteen American colonies and their declaration of independence as the United States of America was not the charter of the first national state, its claim is as good as any. It was not alone that the American Revolution created a solidarity among the thirteen colonies and united them, though that was achieved in a limited fashion. What was more to the point was the development of a national system under the Constitution of 1789 and the strengthening of that system during the first years of the republic. In France the long history of the monarchy had only laid the foundations for national feeling even though it had provided a common governmental experience for the majority of Frenchmen. What the revolution and Napoleon brought was a sense of common cause, an identification with the fatherland, and feeling of direct participation in the life of the nation.

Nationalism was strongly reinforced by the ideals of the French Revolution. The French concepts of liberty, equality, and fraternity were carried throughout Europe by Napoleonic armies. But even more to the point was the revolutionary fervor of French troops fighting for the defense of their homes and country. The manner in which revolutionary leadership utilized the military draft to mobilize the nation revealed to all Europe a dramatic example of the strength of the national state. The secret of that power lay in its ability to reach down into the masses and to command a greater loyalty and sacrifice than any previous government in the history of Europe. The national state rested on a new conception of the subject; it raised him to the rank of citizen, gave him greater privileges, but demanded from him a deeper involvement, a greater participation, in political life.

The spread of nationalism during the Napoleonic period unleashed strong sentiments and desires for the achievement of true nationhood throughout Europe. In Spain, the reaction to Napoleon's invasions released an incipient nationalism that resulted first in the expulsion of the Bonapartes and the restoration of Ferdinand VII and then in a liberal revolution aimed at destroying the dynastic state of the Bourbon kings and establishing a national state in the republican tradition of France. As we have noted above, the period following the Congress of Vienna witnessed numerous nationalist-inspired uprisings in Italy, Germany, France, Belgium, and Poland. Although most of these were singularly unsuccessful, nationalism continued to gain strength throughout the early nineteenth century and its ultimate victory was assured. It was a moving force in the remaking of the English Constitution during the late eighteenth and nineteenth centuries, in the unification of Germany and Italy, and in the building of modern France.

By the time the national state began to come to the fore, Europe had already passed through a long development of feudal and territorial states. The machinery of the national state was therefore built on this foundation. What differed was the manner in which this machinery was employed. Its goal was no longer the aggrandizement of a dynasty or of a narrow aristocracy, but the glorification of the nation. The patriotic citizen paid taxes, served in the army, promoted his nation's economic good so that his nation would surpass others or, at least, maintain its position with respect to them.

The spirit of nationalism spread throughout Europe and into all the lands that came into contact with European civilization. Wherever it went, it carried with it the ideal of a state in the service of the nation. Throughout the nineteenth century and down to our own time, nationalism has been one of the major forces shaping the direction of historical development. Carried abroad by the fact of European domination of much of the world, it has, in the modern era, captured the minds of former colonial peoples in Asia and Africa.

The nation-state was the chief political accomplishment of Western civilization. It was the climax in a process of state-building that had begun in the tenth century under the Capetians of France and the Saxon kings of Germany. The achievement of the West in creating the nation-state may be estimated by the fact that the rising nations of Asia and Africa have imitated its structure and built on the spirit of nationalism.

17 Culture and Ideology in the Early Nineteenth Century

Since the early nineteenth century, European civilization has come under the influence of ideas more secular than religious. Nationalism has formed the reason for the existence of the state. Liberalism expressed, under several forms, the concept of the role of the individual in the nation-state and in industrial society. Socialism offered an alternative to the liberal ideology, emphasizing the role and the demands of the group rather than the individual. These concepts drew their inspiration only indirectly from the Judaeo-Christian ethical tradition; they owed much more to the growth of secular ideas among the philosophers of the eighteenth century. They reflected the disillusionment of that period with Christianity and the belief that reason and nature, or nature alone, contained the real answers to the building of a new society.

The beginnings of these ideas in the eighteenth century created a heady feeling of optimism, but the realities of the obstacles to making the ideal society brought frustration and even some measure of reaction. The social problems brought on by the growth of industrialism, the agonies of the French Revolution, and the naked power exercised in the name of revolutionary ideals by Napoleon impressed on writers and artists of the period the feeling that reason alone offered no sure guide to truth and justice. These romantics, as they came to be called near the mid-nineteenth century, sought many of the goals of the Enlightenment—freedom, for example—but rejected the mind as a guide in favor of the heart. As Gounod's *Faust* discovered, the higher law of love ruled reason. It was within this crucible of romanticism that the ideological framework of nineteenth-century society took shape.

Romanticism

The elements that went into the making of romanticism were not new. Indeed, they sprang from the innermost aspirations of man, from the emotional rather than the intellectual side of human nature, emphasizing the subjective and intuitive approach to reality. The romantics did not reject eighteenth century goals of tolerance and liberty. In fact, they felt these more strongly and struggled harder toward their realization. But they rejected the well-ordered path, the smooth way, the optimism that had characterized those who had popularized the Enlightenment. Their preserve was the fields of literature, philosophy, history, and the arts rather than science. Within these areas they found a kind of freedom of the spirit that they could not find, as yet, in the theorems of mathematics and the sciences. Art itself became the object of their striving, for it promised a new and deeper truth, one that lay behind the façade of scientific explanation.

The origins of romanticism are too varied to admit of simple treatment. The appeal to man's emotions lies at the root of literature, art, and music in every age. Yet there were strong currents of romanticism abroad in the late eighteenth century directly connected with the upsurge of this movement. The popularity of pietism, which emphasized the personal reliance of the soul on God rather than religious doctrines, was connected with the rise of such movements as Methodism, founded by John and Charles Wesley. Their rejection of the formalism of the Anglican Church in favor of a simple service with deep emotional appeal to the masses expressed the continuing search for new forms of religious expression. But romanticism was primarily concerned not with religious but with secular themes. Immanuel Kant (1724–1804) questioned the validity of the world order as objective reality. In his view, the immutable laws of natural science were merely the framework imposed on nature by men's minds. Science possessed no unique key to understanding man and the universe. Man could and should learn through his study of the arts and literature as well. Georg Wilhelm Hegel (1770–1831) saw the world as the result of a continuing dialectical process moving toward the absolute. Implied in this Hegelian dialectic was the denial or, at least, the subordination of reason to a form of idealistic determinism. The idealism of Kant and Hegel was, in part, a reaction against the natural law theories of the eighteenth century, but it was not a complete rejection of these theories. Rather, the idea of an immutable order on which all reality was based and to which it conformed was raised above the objective level of scientific phenomena to the level of a universal mind, an absolute that was the only true reality. In these philosophers, thought about the deep questions that have concerned men in every age resulted in a rejection of science rather than law. Romanticism in philosophy involved a quest for an absolute and immutable truth not found in science.

The romantic movement had its greatest impact in literature and the arts. In these areas, because of their direct dependence on creative minds, romantic feeling reacted against the formalism and façade of eighteenth-century classicism. One of the best indications of this new spirit is the rise of romantic poetry in the late eighteenth century. As we have noted earlier, the age of reason had not produced much outstanding poetry, and what did appear was straitjacketed by excessive formalism. The new poetry broke loose from rigid patterns and adopted more colloquial speech.

In England, romanticism took hold in the poetry of Samuel Taylor Coleridge (1772–1834) and held sway through the first half of the nineteenth century. Coleridge's work was marked by a deep appeal to the exotic and mystical element in human nature.

> In Xanadu did Kubla Khan
> A stately pleasure-dome decree:
> Where Alph, the sacred river, ran
> Through caverns measureless to man
> Down to a sunless sea.

His *Rime of the Ancient Mariner* pondered the question of the role of unseen and unnatural forces in directing the destiny of men. The albatross stood as the symbol of hope and fear that transcended the boundaries of scientific knowledge. In Coleridge, the absolute and immutable law of nature lies beyond the knowledge of man; he can only ponder its mystery. William Wordsworth (1770–1850), master of the lyric, was a leading romantic in his early period. He adopted a loose metrical style and tried to fashion his poems from the language of the streets and byways to give it greater simplicity and directness. He was deeply concerned not merely with the beauties of nature, but also with the concept of nature as the absolute—an idea that led him far in the direction of nature pantheism. Among the most dramatic younger figures of the romantic movement in English poetry were John Keats (1795–1821) and Percy Bysshe Shelley (1792–1822). They were attracted to the romantic aspects of the classical antiquity, idealizing the beauty of that age in much the way that historians of the period were raising up the nobility of the Greek ideal as a romantic standard for their civilization. George Gordon, Lord Byron (1788–1824) caught the theme of universal freedom from oppression in such poems as the *Prisoner of Chillon* and even attempted to carry it out in his own life; he died on his way to Greece to participate in the Greek war for independence from the Turks.

In prose, the novels of Sir Walter Scott (1771–1832) found in the Middle Ages a nobility and chivalry that contrasted sharply with the crass materialism and drab surroundings of their own industrial age. Other writers saw in the medieval period the beginnings of democracy. The American, James Fenimore Cooper (1789–1851), caught this spirit from the writings of Rousseau and the German historians. To him, democracy had its origins in the freedom of the Germanic tribes rather than in the absolutism of Rome.

On the continent, the dawn of the romantic age was prefigured in the poetry of Johann Wolfgang von Goethe (1749–1832). His *Faust* stood for the triumph of the human over the supernatural. Faust was the supremely self-sufficient man. His sins were the sins of man in the quest for knowledge of all reality. In this sense, therefore, Faust stood for a rejection of the Enlightenment, for he pointed to the dangers of knowledge without the guide of an absolute. In other poems, Goethe was deeply concerned with myth and the impact of the unknowable on man. In the *Erlkoenig*, he told the story of a race to preserve the life of a child against the mythical demon that would snatch it away. It is difficult to escape the conclusion that all men are seeking to escape the inescapable fate decreed for all. It was this concern that made Goethe a figure of such importance to the German romantics.

In France and Italy, the towering figures of Victor Hugo (1802–1885) and Alessandro Manzoni (1785–1873) dominated romantic letters. Hugo carried his romanticism even into his later and more naturalistic writings, the well-known *Notre Dame de Paris* and *Les Miserables.* The search for a beauty that transcended the evanescent shadows of form and figure and resided eternally in the soul of man was a major concern of his art. Manzoni, in *I Promesi Sposi* (*The Betrothed*), found the love of two rustics a force great enough to move the passions of the aristocrats of the age. In the true romantic tradition, he focused on the humble to reveal the nobility of the Italian soul. His message was national in that he identified himself with the cause of Italian unification.

Architecture and painting also reflected the shift to romanticism. In architecture, the influence of the classical revival spilled over into the nineteenth century. Indeed, some of the most notable examples of this style were the product of the early years of the century. In particular, the Empire style of Napoleon served to prolong the classic. However, as the century progressed, a full-scale revival of the Gothic was launched. The major figure was the architect Viollet-le-Duc, who was responsible for the restoration of Notre Dame in Paris and for replacing the façade of Santa Maria del Fiore in Florence. Imitation Gothic remained a paramount influence in architecture into the early twentieth century. Romantic painting became more interested in historical themes. In the period following the French Revolution, there was less emphasis on producing portraits of great nobles and more on recreating scenes from the history of the nation. David's *Tennis Court Oath* anticipated this trend in capturing a dramatic moment in the history of the revolution. Other themes were Magna Carta, and, in the new United States, the signing of the Declaration of Independence. The national hero, whether a Napoleon or a Washington, was the most fitting subject for portrait art.

Romanticism probably had its deepest influence in music. From Berlioz, whose dissonance and tense rhythms heralded the movement, to Richard Wagner (1813–1883), whose operas embodied the folk myths of the Germans, the romantic spirit dominated. The chief elements were the rejection of classical forms that had dominated eighteenth century music and a renewed spirit of experimentation. Under its

Ludwig von Beethoven. One of the great composers of the romantic period. (The Bettmann Archive)

influence, music, already the most subjective of the arts, became even more so, as the artist was allowed a wider latitude for the development of his themes.

Although so much of the romantic movement was intimately bound up with the literary and artistic productivity of the age, its influences beyond these spheres were important in providing an atmosphere in which nationalism, liberalism, and socialism grew. We have already noted some connections between the romantics and nationalism. For example, much of the art and literature of the period, while molded in the romantic framework, was in the service of nationalist ideals: the patriotic themes of some painters, the pervasive nationalist spirit in music, and the espousal of Italian and German movements for unification of these divided nationalities into states by romantic authors.

Liberalism, which was often closely tied both to romanticism and nationalism, promoted the movements for national freedom in Greece and for unification in Italy and Germany. It opposed the continuance of the old regimes in these countries and favored instead the establishment of constitutional governments modeled largely on that of England.

The relationship of socialism to the romantic movement may be seen from several points of view. The increased humanitarian concerns of the romantics were founded on their dislike of the "factory system" and industrial exploitation. "Utopian" socialists drew some inspiration from the gild system of the Middle Ages, which they idealized, as the foundation for unions of workers. "Scientific" or Marxian socialism drew on the determinism of Hegelian dialectic and the romantic quest for an absolute.

The romantics were pilgrims in search of an absolute in a society that had turned most of its attention to creating greater wealth and a more pleasant material world for those wealthy enough to enjoy it. They were members of a protest movement, whose influence far outweighed their numbers. They turned to emotion and sentiment for inspiration because their society appeared to place little emphasis on these values. They were, and in some cases the description is very appropriate, prophets in the tradition of Israel. Romantics could be found in the forefront of most political and social movements of their era.

Liberalism

No word in the English language invites controversy and misunderstanding more than liberal. Seemingly so simple, it has grown, historically, to mean many different things, unfortunately retaining its older meanings as it has acquired new ones. Yet, there is a sense in which all liberals, and all liberalisms, are united and share at their root a common definition. All liberals were concerned about freedom, but not all liberals were concerned about freedom in the same matters or in the same way. Nor, for that matter, did all liberals share a single consensus about how much freedom there ought to be and who ought to be free. Still, freedom does provide as good a starting point as any for a discussion of liberalism.

The origins of liberalism—we will use the small "l" when speaking of the term in its broadest sense—reach back to the later Middle Ages, where the development of representative institutions and machinery for presenting grievances provided a foundation for the advances made in England in the seventeenth century. However, it was not until the eighteenth century, especially in the writing of the French *philosophes,* that these ideas were given a current and popular meaning. The contract theory of sovereignty advanced by John Locke in his treatises on civil goverment then provided the impetus for the criticisms of the old regimes by men like Diderot and Voltaire. But the most influential thinker of the age was Jean-Jacques Rousseau, whose *Social Contract* advanced the doctrine of equality as the foundation on which all society rested. The spread of Rousseau's teachings was phenomenal. He was read popularly in America prior to the American Revolution. We have already noted the influence of these thinkers on the Declaration of Independence and on the French Declaration of the Rights of Man of 1791. But the *philosophes* had advocated not merely political freedom, but also ultimate freedom based on conformity to the natural laws of reason and the universe. In economics, for example, the physiocrats and Adam Smith had advocated the removal of governmental restrictions on trade. Smith had argued that each should follow his selfish interest since nature protected the good of all. Thus liberalism gave birth both to the political liberalism of the revolutionary movements and to the economic liberalism of the classical economists, the followers of Adam Smith.

Those who placed greatest emphasis on political ends were the so-called philosophical radicals led by the English philosopher, Jeremy Bentham. Bentham taught that the purpose of government was to secure the greatest good for the greatest number. As a Utilitarian, he applied but one criterion to test the value of any goal: did it contribute to the good of most of those whom it affected? Bentham's liberalism was subordinated to a moral judgment as to the good of each goal, though he clothed it in the guise of utility. Bentham and the Utilitarians were also concerned about securing the rights of the individual; they believed that freedom to pursue one's own interests was the basic principle for securing happiness. Enlightened self-interest was the hallmark of utilitarianism.

Liberal interest in political reforms centered in England on the demand for parliamentary reapportionment to abolish those electoral districts with relatively few voters and to give representation to the more populous industrial centers. However, the liberals did not want to enfranchise the working classes but only to distribute the vote more widely among the various groups composing the middle class. Likewise, their economic aims were directed mostly toward ensuring the prosperity of industrial England. They worked for the repeal of the corn laws to bring about lower domestic prices for grain and to remove tariffs on incoming raw materials. On the continent, liberals supported free trade within their own country, but favored government intervention in the form of high tariffs to keep out English manufactured goods.

This classic form of liberalism, sometimes called nineteenth-century liberalism, meant freedom chiefly for the middle class. More accurately, it was a movement to ensure the participation of that group in the making of policies regarding political and economic life. This liberalism continued to owe much to the eighteenth century for its ideological content and the arguments it employed, but certain new elements were coming to the fore. While the eighteenth century had recognized the importance of the individual, it had not had to deal with the rise of a powerful group of industrial entrepreneurs with the economic power to control a large segment of the economy of the nation. The liberal emphasis on the individual came to mean an unrestricted right to carry out one's will in the economic area with but the slightest legal restriction. Individualism was justified by the economic "law" of competition. The good businessman, whose industry was in the interests of the community, would survive. His less efficient and shoddier competitor would disappear. However, there was no evil in this process for the good product was sold for a lower cost and was within the reach of more buyers. Naive as this belief was, it has persisted as one of the economic truisms derived from economic liberalism.

The economic liberals believed that freedom in the market would bring prosperity to the majority, fair prices, and progress to the nation. They considered themselves as the mainstay of their society and believed that they were performing a valuable, even a necessary service, to their country. Their beliefs had a certain force of inner logic and gained general acceptance during the first half of the nineteenth century.

However, some voices were raised in dissent. For the most part, these criticisms were not so much directed at liberalism as at its failures. In fact, critics like John Stuart Mill (1806–1873) operated from liberal premises. Mill believed in the philosophy of freedom. However, he favored some controls on the freedom of the individual in order to support the good of the majority. Having grown up under the influence of his father, James Mill, and Jeremy Bentham, John Stuart Mill subscribed to many of the views of the Utilitarians. He was especially interested in enfranchising groups without property and he even supported a measure to grant women the vote. Where the philosophical radicals had supported some government regulation to secure proper policing of the streets and sanitation in the cities, Mill supported measures regulating hours and conditions of work. The liberal followers of Mill accepted more and more the democratic implications of the liberal view and advocated the broadest possible participation in government by the masses. Thus liberalism was divided within itself in the nineteenth century between the liberals of economic liberalism and the liberals of liberal democracy.

But the criticisms of liberalism came also from without, from those who refused to accept the tenets of liberalism as they had leapt forth from the eighteenth-century Enlightenment, or who found reason to quarrel with part of them. On the right, a strong traditional conservative movement persisted. Though the English Tories and the French monarchists of the old regime were not able to maintain their power during the early nineteenth century, they remained actively in opposition to the new ideas. Joseph de Maistre reveals the persistence of a conservatism imbedded in a feudal conception of society. On the other hand, the English conservative Edmund Burke (1729–1797) was more adaptable to change, less committed to tradition merely for the sake of tradition, and primarily an advocate of the need for order in government. Burke was not so much illiberal as unliberal. Important dissent from the liberal view also rose from below and from the thinkers who hopefully spoke for the masses. In the early nineteenth century, various forms of socialism and anarchism appeared, partially in an effort to fulfill the unrealized dreams of the revolutionary period and partially in reaction to the growth of industrial society and liberalism.

Socialism

Industrialism brought poverty and suffering to great masses of the poor, who were crowded into cities to work in the heat, stench, and squalor of the factories or who were sent down into pits from early ages to dig for coal. Their lot aroused sympathy from humanitarians, some even from among the older aristocracy and the newer middle class. Many of these were motivated by a desire to protect the poor. Among the old aristocrats, this desire represented, in some cases, a continuation of the feudal relationship which had existed between lord and serf, now transferred to a more general concern for the good of the poor. Romanticism also manifested itself in a reaction to filth and poverty and those who were responsible for them. But it remained for the socialists to attempt to formulate a total approach to the problems of industrial society.

Socialism accepted liberalism in order to reject it. That is to say, socialism generally accepted the liberal description of the economic world of the early nineteenth century along with liberal explanations of many of its problems as a basis for criticism of liberalism. But socialists were, at least for the most part, far from being liberals themselves. Some of them believed in freedom and progress within a constitutional framework, but all agreed in attacking the liberal attachment to property. Since the liberal regarded property as an essential human right guaranteed by the natural law, socialists were anathema to liberals.

The early socialists were, however, deeply influenced by the Enlightenment and romanticism. They believed that man could achieve a good society by his own efforts. Although a few advocated change by violent means, most were convinced that education and the gradual winning of greater political power for the masses would result in a more equitable distribution of the world's wealth. Far from abhorring the place of government in economic life, they believed that political controls were necessary to ensure justice for the weak and oppressed. Many of the early socialists looked forward to the creation of a near perfect society, a *utopia.*

These utopian socialists embarked on a number of experiments aimed at utilizing or harnessing the industrial behemoth to the welfare of the working classes. The followers of the Comte de Saint-Simon (1760–1825) believed that all society ought to be geared along technological lines to achieve the greatest benefits from industry. Their socialism consisted chiefly in their belief in centralized planning of production and expansion in order to reduce or destroy inefficient and ruinous competition. François Marie Charles Fourier (1772–1837) taught that workers must live in communities and share the products of their work. Other such communistic experiments were tried by Robert Owen (1771–1858), the Scottish industrialist, who paid his workers at New Lanarck well by contemporary standards and proved that he could still run a very profitable enterprise. Owen ran New Lanarck with an iron hand for the benefit of the workers as he saw it. The neat cottages and well-planned local government were a

Robert Owen's New Harmony. Vision of a Utopian community. (The Bettmann Archive)

strong case for factory reforms elsewhere. However, few of the utopian community experiments lasted for more than a short time. The effort to secure voluntary cooperation proved to be a major stumbling block as did the failure to take into account the strength of individual personalities.

More radical than the utopians were the anarchists, who believed that government was unnecessary and even evil. Deeply influenced by the assumption of some romantics that man was basically good, Pierre Proudhon (1809–1865) argued for the establishment of all society on a voluntary basis. Among the anarchists violence took root and flourished, thereby establishing the popular connotation that all anarchists advocated violence. In fact, such was not the case. Many anarchists were nonviolent and pacifist in their views. Those who adopted violent means simply obtained wider attention.

By the mid-nineteenth century, there were many different socialisms competing for the attention of the working classes and their leaders. At the same time, some strides had been made by humanitarians and democratic liberals in the direction of alleviating the condition of the workers.

However, not even the formation of the first labor unions or the regulation of wages, hours, and conditions of work in ships and mines was enough to solve the problems created by inadequate educational facilities, poor housing, low pay, continued insecurity, and filth. Some began to argue that only the most radical of revolutions could alter the cycle that seemed to lead inevitably from birth in a filthy bed to death on a filthy bed. After 1848, the leading voice of this group belonged to a scholarly and somewhat bookish man without any close experience of the plight of the working classes but with a conviction that his economic, social, and

Karl Marx. A familiar portrait of the founder of modern Communism. (The Bettmann Archive)

political theories would point the direction to the solution of the problems of the age. His name was Karl Marx (1818–1883). He was by birth German and Protestant—though his family had once been Jewish. However, he spent most of his mature life in England as a scholar and writer.

The tenets of Marxism—the word is more precise than communism, which refers to the system employed in various modern states—developed largely after 1850, though the *Communist Manifesto* appeared in 1848. Marxism is "scientific" socialism. What Karl Marx set out to do was to create an entire system within which man could achieve those goals that Marx regarded as the most essential of his nature. The basis for the system is philosophical, but it is not a mere abstraction. Rather it involves a fully developed philosophy of history in which the historical process is seen culminating in a new kind of society as the result of inevitable historical conflicts.

It is impossible to separate Marxism from its view of history. Karl Marx was a materialist, who rejected all historical causes that could not be directly or indirectly related to man's material needs. He believed that history was the story of man's efforts to meet those needs, that the conflicts of history arose because some men attempted to thwart others in their desire to attain satisfaction of those needs. This division of conflicting groups with opposing needs demanding fulfillment resulted in the creation of classes. These classes were unalterably opposed to one another—save where alliance might be necessary to achieve advantage over some other class. Thus members of the middle class might ally with the peasants against their common aristocratic or noble enemies. This conflict, based on the essential interests of each class and therefore inevitable, was the dynamic force creating change within civilization. For with the victory of each new class, a new society or even civilization came into existence. Ultimately, Marx argued, the industrial urban proletariat would become the dominant class as the result of a final class revolution. There would be no more classes for the simple reason that society had reached the stage of absolute equality. The new society, a communist society, would then meet the needs of each man in proportion to his labor. This historical framework is the materialist dialectic of Marx, founded partially on the idealist dialectic of Hegel, partially on the materialistic thought of Marx's contemporaries, and owing much to the utopian socialists and anarchists for its goals.

Marx was also an economic determinist. He believed that economic motives were the compelling force behind material man. Interestingly enough, Marx's greatest debt both for his economic thought and his determinism was to the classical economics of the nineteenth century. He accepted without any real questioning the motives and principles laid down by Adam Smith and his successors. Their views formed the foundation for his critique of capitalism in *Das Kapital.* Though radically different in its conclusions, *Das Kapital* had much in common with the *Wealth of Nations.* In two areas, we may point to special examples. The natural law theory of *laissez faire* capitalism has similarities with economic determinism. Both remove the control of the economy from the control of men and make it subject to a "higher" law. Moreover, the apparent freedom of "laissez faire" was restricted to those with the economic power to use it; in economic determinism, all power was a function of economic forces. Inevitably, too, Marx's criticism of industrialism relied on the concepts of the early nineteenth-century industrialists regarding prices and wages and regulation of production. His determinism tended to assume an unchanging capitalist adversary. As capitalism changed, Marx's critiques became dated and stereotyped. Yet, this fact in itself indicates how close was the relationship between Marxism and liberal capitalism.

Marx was, however, a powerful original economic thinker. By creating a systematic alternative to capitalism, he stimulated the development of economic thought. The attractiveness of his historical synthesis was an important influence in the growth of economic history. His philosophical system forced modern thinkers once more to come to grips with essential problems about the nature of man. For it was on this level that the real debate with Marxism has been waged. What is man? That question deserves an answer. Marx attempted an answer that captured the minds of many. Those who have lived in the post-Marxian age have had to ponder deeply the purposes of man and the source of his spirit.

In a work of this type, there is no room for anti-Marxist polemic or for attempted rebuttals of Marxism. Yet it is necessary to sketch the development of Marxism and its early impact, including the arguments marshalled against it. Marx founded the First International to spread the ideas of communism throughout the world among the working classes. For the most part, his movement attracted attention only among other socialist groups, particularly as the result of ideological conflicts between Marxists and others. Progress among the working classes was not merely slow but for a long time practically nonexistent. The workers were not ideologically inclined. Their conversion to Marxism, when it occurred, came as a result of their search for leaders in the struggle with their employers for tangible benefits. Only the few realized and came to grips with Marxism as an ideology. The opposition to Marxist ideas was chiefly the general opposition of the middle-class industrialists and men of business to radicalism. Little was known or understood about Marxist ideas themselves. During most of the nineteenth century, the most significant struggle was not between the forces of capital and those of "scientific" socialism as preached by the followers of Marx, but conflicts within the Marxist camp over the methods to be pursued in achieving the victory of the proletariat.

Marx had taught that the final revolution to create a classless society was inevitable, but he had also held that it was possible to pave the way for this coming by cooperating with the dialectical forces of history. The question that remained was to determine the nature of this cooperation. During the later nineteenth century, more and more Marxists came to accept the position that democratic evolution through the gradual winning of power at the ballot boxes represented the true Marxian approach to economic revolution. Others, however, more deeply influenced by the anarchist tradition so strong in Marx's opposition to the bourgeois state desired the violent overthrow of capitalist forms of government. The resultant split led to the formation of Social Democratic parties dedicated to the peaceful evolution of a Marxist society.

However, the major enemy of Marxism remained liberal capitalism. The growth of democratic liberalism in the countries of Western Europe during the last half of the nineteenth century had a profound impact on the future of Marxism. On the other hand, Marxism was a major factor in shaping the growth of the new nation-states of the same period, if not as the result of a conscious accommodation to Marxist ideas, then as a result of the spreading popularity of many of the tangible goals taken up by Social Democrats and transformed into political programs for the public welfare of the working classes.

18 The Rocky Road to Democratic Government

The winning of the political initiative by the middle class during and after the French Revolution proved to be the prelude to a much broader movement of political enfranchisement that swept across Western Europe later in the nineteenth century and even had some influences on political developments in Eastern Europe. Although, in a technical sense, full-scale democratic institutions did not appear anywhere until late in the century, the direction of the development may be marked as early as the thirties and forties. For the Revolutions of 1830 and 1848 were not without their democratic overtones; nor was English Chartism without important implications for the growth of democratic government. Ironically, the very years that saw the final achievement of the middle-class ambition to participate in and even direct the affairs of government witnessed the rise of the lower class to political prominence.

This widening of the base of European government occurred at the same time that European leadership was unquestioned around the globe. The climax in Europe's leadership in the twentieth century came largely as a result of trends that took shape in the nineteenth century. One of the most important was the growth of democratic government in Western Europe and the United States.

The English Way, 1830–1914

In the post-Napoleonic era, England had emerged as the major power in Europe if not, indeed, in the world. She was the leading commercial and industrial nation, the chief and first beneficiary of the industrial revolution. The setback dealt her imperial ambitions in the eighteenth century had had no deleterious effect on her economic growth, while she had succeeded in preserving the basis for a new empire in the East. Moreover, she had escaped the major revolutionary cataclysms that shook Europe in the age of the French Revolution and Napoleon. Not that she did not sometimes teeter dangerously near the brink of chaos, but each time the needed catalyst was lacking for the making of a revolution. On the other hand, as leader of the alliances against Bonaparte, yet separated from the continent by the English Channel, she stood staunchly for the forces of order without being driven by the winds of reaction caused by the presence of an occupying Napoleonic army. In England, the importance of the peace won at Waterloo in 1815 lay chiefly in the opportunity it provided for a shift in emphasis from foreign to domestic problems. The removal of the Napoleonic threat did not result in revolution but it did permit the country a time to examine its social, economic, and political problems on the domestic scene.

The late twenties and the thirties witnessed major changes in English politics. By 1829, the Duke of Wellington was able to secure legislation removing the civil disabilities against both Roman Catholics and Protestant dissenters; a similar measure granting the same status to Jews had to wait until the 1850's. The emancipation of Catholics was a major step not because it benefited any great numbers of English subjects—its benefits were felt chiefly in Ireland—but because it signaled the beginning of the breakdown of the eighteenth-century English political system. Already pressure was mounting for parliamentary reform, for the abolition of old and outmoded electoral districts, the rotten and "pocket" boroughs, and reapportionment of seats to reflect the rise of industrial wealth in the factory towns and elsewhere.

Parliamentary reform was carried by the Whigs. Their support of reform is not easy to explain. The Whigs were not a political party in the modern sense, but a loosely knit coalition of factions who had cooperated in controlling Parliament and were generally committed to enhancing the powers of that body. They drew their strength in part from the traditional source of political power in England, the old landed nobility and the gentry, but their search for political strength against the Tories, supporters of the monarchy, had led them into alliances with newer groups, particularly those of the industrialists who enjoyed the franchise and the philosophical radicals. The Whigs were, therefore, more influenced by liberalism than the Tories. They were attracted to the whole range of liberal political reforms. Yet they were far from united on these questions and many of the more conservative Whigs sought refuge among the Tories from the rising tide of radicalism. It was the victory of the Whigs in the elections of 1830 that paved the way for the reform of Parliament in 1832.

The Reform Bill of 1832, passed reluctantly by a Parliament that feared the consequences of its failure to act, was a far from revolutionary measure. Its major features included the abolition of those areas, the "pocket" boroughs, which no longer possessed sufficient electorate to entitle them to representation in Parliament and the assignment of seats to a number of industrial towns. The franchise remained in the hands of men of wealth and property. Indeed, the greatest significance of the act lay in its removal of the distinction between landed wealth and that made from industry. Wealth was no longer divided against itself in England. For more than a generation following the passage of the Reform Bill of 1832, men of property generally united to protect the settlement made in that bill. However, the Reform Bill opened the door to discussion of other questions besides Parliament. The reformed Parliament debated and passed some of the earliest measures for social reform as well as repealing the corn laws. It was not a radical body, but it paved the way for further advances toward democratic government.

A challenge to the *status quo* came from the philosophical radicals and from the rise of working-class movements aimed at securing a political role for the disenfranchised masses in the new industrial society. English radicals like John Stuart Mill (1806–1873) inclined toward democracy as the ultimate goal of liberalism. They did not reject the premises of the liberal movement but sought to carry them to what they regarded as their logical conclusions. The ideal of popular democracy received its most substantial support from the formation of the Chartist movement. The "People's Charter" set forth six fundamental principles for the reform of English government along democratic lines. These were: (1) universal manhood suffrage; (2) equal electoral districts; (3) removal of property qualifications for members of Parliament; (4) vote by secret ballot; (5) payment of salaries to members of Parliament; and (6) annual election of Parliament. The enactment of this program would have resulted in the immediate and revolutionary alteration of English government. With all in possession of the vote and all eligible to serve, many feared England would fall under the control of the rabble led by demagogues. Yet the advantage of a long hindsight makes it difficult for us to see the radicalism of the Chartist proposals. The gradual achievement of political democracy has destroyed for us the freshness of viewing these proposals as the vanguard of a radical movement aimed at destroying rule by an oligarchy. What made Chartism appear even more dangerous to the ruling class in the 1830's was the fiery oratory that whipped up the masses in the industrial cities of the north, Manchester, Leeds, and Birmingham. In 1839, the Chartists presented a monster petition with more than one million signatures in support of their program, but Parliament rejected it without consideration. This outcome caught the leaders of Chartism unprepared and without a program for further action. Indeed, the great weakness of this popular mass movement was its lack of a practical program aimed at applying pressure to force Parliament to meet its demands. In 1839, moreover, the Chartists split. The more radical elements embarked on a course of strikes and rioting; the majority remained committed to the peaceful search for a redress of grievances through the process of petitioning. Efforts in 1842 and 1848, however, failed to move the parliamentary leadership. As an attempt to mobilize the masses in support of democratic goals, Chartism had seemingly failed. Yet its failure was not complete, for the attitudes and grievances brought to light in the movement proved fundamental to the further social and political development of English society. What petitions had failed to win was achieved through a gradual social revolution.

During the forties, Chartism had more and more become submerged in the agitation for repeal of the corn laws, which kept the price of domestic grain high by regulating the price of imported. Naturally, the high cost of bread grains was important to the masses for whom bread formed a staple of life, but it was also important to the wealthy industrialists, who found the high cost of food an important factor in the popular demand for higher wages. It was they who took the lead in the formation of the Anti-Corn Law League, which agitated successfully during the forties for the repeal of this measure. Sir Robert Peel (1788–1850), leader of the Tories, split his party by his support of repeal of the corn law and his advocacy of free trade.

One of the most important developments of the early nineteenth century was the formation of modern political parties. The Whigs and Tories were traditional alignments of factions rather than political parties along modern lines. They had no stable leadership, no formal organization, no platforms, and no discipline. What loyalty they commanded from their followers sprang partly from allegiance to tradition and family, and partly from the popularity of various individuals. The thirties and forties saw these traditional alignments subjected to considerable stress under pressure of radical agitation and the propaganda of the anti-corn law and free trade movements. Just as Whig support of the Reform Bill of 1832 had alienated the support of some traditionally Whig noble families and driven them into the Tory party, Peel's advocacy of repeal of the corn law and his stand for free trade caused serious dissatisfaction among Tory farmers and landholders, many of them from the nobility. However, the Tories had no place to go. Peel had succeeded in capturing control of the Tory party and now turned his attention to building a Conservative Party. His program appealed not merely to those industrialists within his own party—his father had been one—but also to those among the liberals who were growing more concerned by the tendency of some liberals to listen to the demands of the lower classes for a voice in political life and their desires for social welfare and labor legislation. Conservatism also gained some support from the working classes through its support of social measures, though these were less sweeping than those carried by the liberals. The formation of a Liberal Party was also the product of shifts in the older system. Dissatisfaction with the Reform Bill of 1832 had driven many of the diehard nobility to the Tory camp. As a consequence, the relative power of the liberals within the party increased. During the forties and after, the Liberals gradually acquired the character of a modern political party.

With the decline of Chartism, the energies of lower class leaders went more and more to the organization of labor unions. The plight of the masses in the factories had begun to arouse not only sympathy but also remedial action. In 1842, Parliament passed the Mines Act, which excluded women and children from work underground. The Factory Act of 1844 was a milestone of regulation; it decreed a twelve-hour day for women and provided that children might work only twelve hours on alternate days—or six hours every day. What made the act important was the provision for inspectors to check on compliance. Previous legislation had been of no avail due to the impossibility of securing adequate enforcement. Earlier, Robert Owen had formed his Consolidated Trades Union. Though this body failed, the cause of unionization continued to advance with the founding of the Amalgamated Society of Engineers in 1851. The trade-union movement played an increasingly important role in alleviating the conditions of the industrial masses by securing better working conditions in the second half of the century.

The period between the collapse of the Napoleonic regime and the outbreak of World War I in 1914 was remarkably free of major wars. Throughout the age, the chief emphasis was on domestic politics. However, the fifties and sixties provided some distraction abroad. The chief figure was that of the Liberal Prime Minister, Viscount Palmerston (1784–1865). This controversial and aristocratic leader embodied the confidence of his age and the class whom he chiefly represented, the wealthy liberal industrialists. He conceived of England as a new Roman Empire, whose protection of its citizens would carry its flag throughout the world. In line with his liberal beliefs, he favored independence movements in various parts of the world, including support for the Confederacy during the American Civil War, a policy that was dictated partially by the feelings of his textile manufacturer supporters. But the major involvement of the period was in the Crimean War (1854–1856), in which England joined France in an attempt to restrain Russian ambitions against the Ottoman Empire. The defeat of Russia marked a turning

Benjamin Disraeli, 1878. Leader of the Conservatives and Prime Minister. (The Bettmann Archive)

point in international relations as Europe moved into a new age of imperialistic expansion. The harmony that had largely endured since the Congress of Vienna had gone; each power felt free to seek its own interests.

The latter half of the nineteenth century was known as the Victorian age. The youthful Victoria ascended the throne in 1837. Her reign was to be the longest in English history. During her rule, the monarch gradually learned her role in a limited monarchy. Victoria continued to exercise considerable power—she forced Lord Palmerston to resign from the cabinet in 1851, but, following the death of her consort, Prince Albert in 1861, she played a less active role and permitted the rising political parties to dominate the cabinet. She was the last ruler of England to wield power from the throne and the first to accept the complete dominance of Parliament.

As long as Lord Palmerston had retained his grasp on the prime minister's office, he was able to stave off all demands for a new and more far-reaching reform of Parliament. But, when he died in 1865, the time was already past for any more delay. The victory of the Conservatives brought to office the brilliant exponent of Tory democracy, Benjamin Disraeli (1804–1881). Under Disraeli's leadership, the Tories sponsored important social legislation in alliance with the radicals. In his first ministry the most important was the Second Reform Bill passed in 1867. As the leader of a party that drew its chief strength from the landed gentry and nobility, Disraeli met the demand for new reforms with a bill designed to grant a limited number of small property-holders the vote. However, Liberal amendments in the House of Commons added by William Gladstone turned the bill into a far more sweeping act than either party had anticipated. Beyond doubt, Disraeli had hoped that the Conservatives would gain the allegiance of the new voters, but the election of 1868 returned the Liberals to power under the leadership of William E. Gladstone (1809–1898).

Gladstone's first ministry set the tone for his subsequent administrations by pursuing the twin goals of peace and retrenchment. He was, to use a contemporary term, a "little Englander," whose interests were concentrated chiefly on the problems of the British Isles rather than the far-flung interests of England overseas. He addressed himself and the nation to the most pressing political, economic, and social problems of the day.

One of the most important questions facing England in the nineteenth century was the situation in Ireland. Although under English rule since the Middle Ages, the island had never been completely pacified. The Protestant Reformation had created a further cleavage, for the mass of

William E. Gladstone. The Liberal Party leader spoke at the introduction of the Home Rule Bill. (*The Bettmann Archive*)

Irish had remained Roman Catholics. William Pitt the Younger had attempted a solution to the problem by granting the Irish token representation in Parliament, but those elected were Protestants. During the thirties and early forties, Daniel O'Connell had mobilized Irish national sentiment in a demand for repeal of the Act of Union. However, England refused and successfully outlasted O'Connell. In the second half of the century, the Irish members had gradually come to form an anti-English block in the House of Commons. During the late sixties and seventies, Gladstone attempted various measures to win Irish support and possibly to solve the problem. In 1869, he secured the disestablishment of the Anglican Church in Ireland, since support of the church was odious to Roman Catholics. His land act of 1870 reimbursed tenants for the cost of improvements they made on the land. However, he did not abandon the traditional English policy of attempting to move the Irish by force.

Under the leadership of Charles Stewart Parnell (1846–1891), the Irish parliamentary bloc became a disciplined nationalist group. They generally supported the Liberals in return for their backing of the Irish demand for home rule, a position adopted by Gladstone in the eighties. The "Irish question" was one of the most important in English domestic politics, involving widespread anti-Catholic support for the Protestants in northern Ireland and fear that Ireland might support England's enemies. The solution of this problem came only after repressive measures had failed and England recognized the Irish demand for full independence after World War I.

More successful were the aspects of Gladstone's policy aimed at social and economic problems. The two major pieces of legislation of his first ministry were the Education Act of 1870 and the Trade Union Act of 1871. His education bill created a system of board schools, a system of public education available to the poor and also increased the support available to private education. The Trade Union Act removed one of the major barriers to the rapid growth of unions. Under the common law, trade unions had not possessed a corporate identity and were forbidden to sue in court. This bid allowed the union rather than individual members to assume responsibility and to defend actions at law. Union membership lost its legal liabilities. This law also gave unions the right to own property, which was basic to establishing their equality to employers in the eyes of the law. Both of these laws revealed the extent to which democratic influences were gradually winning support after the passage of the Reform Bill of 1867.

The seventies also saw a rising tide of interest in overseas colonies sweep England and much of Europe. Gladstone's "little England" stance paid little heed to the demands for government support of colonial ventures, but Disraeli's second ministry ushered in the era of the new imperialism. France and Egypt undertook the construction of the Suez Canal. Disraeli climaxed English dominance in the East by conferring the title of Empress of India on his sovereign. At the same time that steamships were rapidly reducing the time needed to travel to distant parts of the world, Europe was embarked on a new program of imperialistic expansion. Gladstone's second ministry (1880–1885) revealed the strength of that movement as it swept along the reluctant prime minister, whose chief interests remained fixed on the British Isles.

The Reform Bill of 1867 had doubled the size of the electorate to about two million by making the urban lower middle class and skilled laborer and shopkeeper eligible to vote. In 1884, Gladstone pushed through a further extension of the suffrage, granting the vote to agricultural workers. Though the vote remained a privilege for those who could prove that they were "responsible" elements by reason of their ownership of land or payment of taxes, the bill of 1884 was a further step in the direction of universal suffrage as advocated by the Chartists.

In the eighties and nineties, both the Liberals and the Conservatives supported programs for the improvement of social welfare programs, though Gladstone had increasing difficulty within his own party from the opponents of home rule for Ireland. His attempt to secure passage of a home rule bill caused the fall of his short-lived third ministry in 1886 and brought the Conservative Prime Minister Lord Salisbury to power. English conservatism was still largely under the domination of the rural classes. But the Tory Democrats, heirs of the Disraeli policies of the sixties and seventies, continued to work for social reforms. They secured legislation that almost completely abolished tuition in publicly supported schools and a bill forbidding labor in the mines by children over twelve. When Gladstone's last ministry fell on the issue of home rule, Salisbury's government passed the first English Workmen's Compensation Act. The opening of the twentieth century witnessed continued progress on the social and educational fronts in the direction of protection for the worker and universal free public education.

The new century also witnessed the rise of a new political force, the Labour Party, socialist in orientation and closely allied to the growing trade union movement. In the election of 1906, the Labourites obtained forty seats and became an important minority. In that same election, the Liberal government of Sir Henry Campbell-Bannerman won a decisive victory at the polls. The Liberals went far beyond the social measures passed by the Tory Democrats. Unions were further strengthened. Legislation establishing a minimum wage in certain industries heralded further government action in that sphere. The Children's Act of 1908 provided for free medical attendance at childbirth and free care of infants and young children. The government also passed an old age pension bill. England had embarked on the democratic road and had reached the point where it had to decide on the wisdom of its course. Time was ripe for a national debate.

The occasion for this debate was the whopping budget submitted by Chancellor of the Exchequer David Lloyd-George in 1911 to pay for the social programs just enacted into law. The debate arose because the House of Lords refused to vote the budget without amendments. The Liberal government demanded that the Lords pass the budget and turned to King George V for a solution to the impasse. The king agreed that, if the Liberals demonstrated national support for their policies, he would support them. The Lords backed down on the budget, but the Liberals determined to trim the power of the upper house. The struggle that ensued was constitutional, but its outcome was of utmost importance to the future of English democracy. By securing passage of the Parliament Bill of 1911, the Liberals carried to a logical conclusion the principles of control of government by representatives elected by the people. The Lords were left only with a two-year suspensive veto over legislation, a brake that would slow but not halt the march of the popular will as expressed in the House of Commons.

Even as England was passing through this major constitutional crisis, the world of the nineteenth century was passing rapidly away. The peaceful years of prosperity and trade expansion, of imperialistic ventures and internal social reform were giving way before the tensions created by the rivalries of newly industrialized European powers at home and abroad. The moment of climax arrived almost unobtrusively in 1914; World War I swept the remnants of the century away. But the new Europe of the twentieth century would not have been possible without the vast changes that had taken place in the preceding century not only in England, but also on the continent. Where England's course to democracy followed a gradual road with but occasional deviation, that of France was strewn with the wreckage of violence, as the French Revolution remained ever present on the political scene.

France: Experiments in Government, 1830–1914

The revolutionary spirit, which had played so large a part in the transformation of the French monarchy into a national state, had failed in its attempt to create a stable political order for that nation in the years before 1830. The dictatorship of Napoleon had given way to the Bourbon restoration, but the restoration had proved abortive. Charles X refused to bend from the old absolutism to meet the political demands of the bourgeoise, the class that had made a revolution. Once more France turned to a revolutionary solution to drive the Bourbon from the throne. In his place, the conspirators placed the middle-class monarch, the Duke of Orleans, Louis Philippe. Louis had supported the revolution and the middle class. His reign, from 1830 to 1848, tried to establish in France the concept of a limited monarchy based on the support of that class and committed to the principles of bourgeois liberalism.

The government of Louis Philippe was more noted for its ability to survive than for its talent at governing. Louis' chief minister, the historian Guizot, owed his position to royal support and worked to keep the sometimes turbulent forces of the legislature subservient to the crown. Though domestic prosperity aided the monarchy through a large part of the reign, the Orleanist government took no steps to ensure its continuance. Manipulation of the parliamentary opposition to prevent defeats of the government was Guizot's *forte*. However, since the government failed to address itself to pressing demands for an extension of the franchise to those groups in the middle class who did not possess the vote or to those critics who wanted to abolish corruption by preventing members of the Assembly from holding government posts, the usual and constitutional road to reform remained closed. There was no safety valve to drain off the excessive dissatisfaction of the protesters. Whereas, the English Parliament was never completely closed to the possibility of reform, the parliament of Louis Philippe was.

Moreover, the French internal political situation had never achieved stability in the post-revolutionary period. The revolt of 1830 had only served to further splinter the possible supporters of a moderately conservative royal government. Louis' ostensible support of liberalism and revolutionary principles cost him the loyalty of the clergy and those who supported them. The manner in which he had achieved power lost for the crown the aid of those monarchists loyal to Charles X and the Bourbons. Moreover, many Frenchmen could only contrast in sadness the tawdry escutcheon of the Orleanist king and the proud banner of Napoleon. In the choice between dullness and glory, even glory tinged with defeat, many Frenchmen preferred the glory. Finally, the radicals—leftists and socialists—as well as many moderates advocated the overthrow of this conservative regime and the establishment of a democratic republic.

Without hope of gradual and peaceful change, pressures mounted to shape a revolution in the France of the forties. The policies of the government protected the industrialists but offered nothing to the workers. During the later forties, agricultural depression drove up the prices of bread and other staples. Workers, like those in the silk factories of Lyons who was laboring fifteen to sixteen hours a day for eleven *sous,* rebelled rather than continue. They had no union to offer them advice or hope for a settlement so the riot was their only weapon. In Paris, the lower classes suffered heavily from rising prices and were ready for any leaders who would promise improvement of their condition.

The revolution that erupted in France in February, 1848, was part of a general outbreak of liberal and national sentiment that exploded across Europe in that year. The effort to preserve the *status quo* after the Congress of Vienna had shown the first signs of cracking in 1830. By 1848, deep cleavages had developed within the various countries of Western and Central Europe. Whereas in France, dissatisfaction with the regime of Louis Philippe centered chiefly on political and economic grievances, national sentiment formed around the desire for unification in Germany and Italy and for self-rule within the Hungarian part of the Austrian Empire. Everywhere revolutionaries demanded liberal constitutions that would permit the middle class a greater voice in government. In this way, liberalism was intimately connected with the attempt to create truly national states in Europe. The desire for constitutional government reflected the goal of liberals to broaden the base of participation in government so that it would be national in scope. In France, it was the constitutional effort to broaden the franchise and increase participation in government by these groups in the middle class who still did not possess political rights that paved the way for a new French experiment in the national state, the government of Louis Napoleon Bonaparte.

The opposition to Louis Phillipe, forbidden to organize, had carried on their antigovernment activities privately at parties in various Paris homes and salons. When Guizot attempted to prevent the holding of a monster banquet scheduled for February 22, 1848, the organizers went on with their plans. Attempts by police to restrain the opposition resulted in street rioting during the night of the twenty-second and the king called out the national guard. But the guardsmen refused to obey their officers. Louis' dismissal of Guizot on the following day came too late to prevent the revolution. Already the barricades were up in the street. When the army did not support the government against the mob swelling across Paris, Louis slipped quietly away to exile in England. France had no king. The mob now forced the proclamation of a republic with all male citizens eligible to vote. The new government, still provisional, made some concessions to the workers. The leading socialist of the day, Louis Blanc, became president of a commission to protect the welfare of the workers. The government also proposed the establishment of national workshops to provide work for the unemployed. However, there was little sincerity in these efforts. The government was simply playing for time. Its attempt to repudiate its promises to provide work led to the "June Days" outbreaks, which were put down by the army under the leadership of General Cavaignac. The Assembly, realizing the emergency, quickly proceeded to push through a new constitution and called for a presidential election for December, 1848. The candidates were Cavaignac and the nephew of Napoleon I, Louis Napoleon Bonaparte, who had returned from exile to run for office. The result was an overwhelming victory for Napoleon. The French had embarked on a new experiment.

It is difficult to find a term to describe the government of Louis Napoleon. The new president was no democrat and no liberal, but neither was he a conservative in any traditional sense. Politically, he was an opportunist, yet he appears to have had some definite goals for France. Beyond doubt, Napoleon was one of the most astute politicians of the age, endowed with an astounding insight into the psychology of the French political animal.

Napoleon's political sense aided him in formulating the policies he espoused on his inauguration. He wooed Catholics with his open support of the Papacy. In 1849, he despatched a mission to Rome to aid Pope Pius IX against the Italian rebels. He also supported the Falloux law, which gave control of education in France back to the clergy. Both of these steps were unpopular with radical and republican elements as well as many middle-class liberals, but Napoleon attempted to win their support in other ways. He promoted industrial expansion and took advantage of the return of prosperity to gain liberal support. He also instituted a plan of voluntary old age insurance to help the workers. His support of universal manhood suffrage retained for him some support from the left, especially when the more conservative National Assembly attempted to restrict it. However, these measures had the appearance of mere staging in prelude to the next steps undertaken by the new president.

Fear of threats to the republic from the right permitted Napoleon considerable latitude in his struggle with the National Assembly. Moreover, his support of universal manhood suffrage and his use of the methods of democratic government made the left less fearful of his policies. Yet he used these very democratic methods to undermine the republic and to establish a Second Empire with himself as Emperor under the title Napoleon III. His *coup d'état* received democratic approval on December 2, 1852, in a national plebiscite. Napoleon had demonstrated the way in which the tools of democracy might be employed to forge a different kind of national state.

The Second Empire stood for peace and prosperity. Napoleon III genuinely believed in the value of a peaceful policy to maintain confidence in his regime abroad. He also wanted prosperity, not merely for the middle class, but also for the working classes, for his government rested on the broad base of universal popular support. It was national because it drew its support from the nation. The transition from republic to empire did not mean any significant change in the policies and programs of the government. Napoleon still attempted to preserve the alliances with Catholics, liberals, and workers that he had made in the republican period.

The nineteenth century was the age of industrial growth in France. Napoleon III felt himself caught up in this movement in all of its aspects. His government espoused the doctrine of free trade and worked to lower tariffs and decrease the amount of government regulation of business. In 1860, France concluded a commercial treaty with England, providing for low tariffs and encouraging increased productivity in France. However, French businessmen were not completely satisfied because they feared English competition. They desired a partially protected market for their goods. Napoleon also supported a major program of railroad and road building as well as the replanning of the city of Paris. These activities not only provided work for the poor, but also stimulated prosperity and improved essential transportation facilities. As a direct result of Napoleon's plans for Paris, that city gained its wide boulevards and numerous parks. It became the most beautiful city in the world in the second half of the nineteenth century. Napoleon consciously identified himself with the working classes in his quest for their continued political support. One might find him riding in the cabs of a train with the engineer or sharing wine and cheese with a worker or peasant. He said that his was a government of cheap bread, public works, and more plentiful holidays. Although welfare and labor legislation in France lagged behind England, the regime did extend voluntary insurance to cover industrial accidents. Another law permitted workers to establish cooperatives for buying and selling their goods. The government was reluctant to give trade unions any legal rights beyond a simple right to exist. However, it did recognize the right to strike. Napoleon III led France slowly along the road of industrial growth and met some of the problems arising from it, but his approach was dictated more by political interest than by concern for economic development.

Napoleon also continued to appeal for the support of Catholics. Throughout his reign he kept troops in Rome to protect the Pope from Italian revolutionaries and the growing threat of the absorption of the city into a unified Italian state. The excellent reputation of his devout and charitable wife, the Empress Eugenie, also impressed Catholics and won them as friends for the emperor. His pro-Catholic policies were especially valuable in gaining the continued support of the peasants, most of whom had remained devoutly loyal to the Church and under the influence of the parish clergy. But Napoleon also cemented his relations with the peasants by working to increase the export sales of agricultural products and thereby maintain prices at a stable level.

The preservation of political popularity with groups of such varied interests proved increasingly difficult for the emperor in the fifties and sixties. His most thorny problems arose in the area of foreign policy. He maintained that his Empire meant peace, but found it difficult to avoid being drawn into conflict because of his ardent nationalism and his support for nationalist causes elsewhere in Europe. Moreover, foreign involvement served to unite the country behind the government in moments of crisis. However, it also raised the dangers that failures and policies unpopular with one or another group at home might cost the regime in the long run.

The most popular aspect of the Napoleonic foreign policy, and the most successful, was the drive to obtain colonial possessions in Asia and Africa. Napoleon annexed the whole of Algeria. When the pacification was completed in 1857 and permanent civil government established in 1858 under the leadership of Marshal MacMahon, it became the most promising of French territories. Its chief values lay in its agricultural wealth and its position on the Mediterranean, as well as the opening it provided for further expansion in North Africa. In the Far East, Napoleon joined England in forcing the Chinese to open their ports to foreign traders and missionaries. He also inaugurated French expansion in Indo-China and obtained a protectorate over Cambodia. His support of Catholic misionary endeavors in Asia and Africa lent an aura of Christian charity to these imperialistic activities.

In European affairs, Napoleon favored nationalist movements in Italy and Roumania at the expense of Austria, Russia, and the Ottoman Empire. His involvement in Italy reveals how difficult his position at home became because of his attempt to follow his inclinations to support Italian unification. Although support for Sardinia-Piedmont's efforts to oust Austria from Lombardy and Venetia in northern Italy was popular with French liberals, the danger that a centralized Italy presented to the Papacy aroused the opposition of French Catholics. As a result, Napoleon followed a halting policy, supporting Sardinia-Piedmont against Austria but withdrawing before the Italians could gain a decisive victory. In the late fifties he agreed to the annexation of papal territories by Sardinia-Piedmont so long as Rome remained in the hands of the Pope. There was little else that he could have done for he was not willing to fight a war to defend the Papal possessions. On the other hand, his support of Roumanian independence cast him in the role of the protector of minorities. It also served the practical end of preventing expansion of the Russian Empire into Southeastern Europe at the expense of the Ottoman Empire.

Napoleon's policy toward Russia had developed from his interest in the Near East. He joined with Britain to prevent further encroachment of Russia in the direction of the Ottoman Empire. When the Tsar demanded that the Sultan grant Russia the position of protector of all Christian minorities within the Ottoman Empire, Napoleon protested and, backed by Britain, joined Turkey in the Crimean War in 1853. Although the war revealed serious incompetence on both sides, in the end it was the Russians who were forced to ask for peace in 1856. France and Britain had succeeded in consolidating their positions as protectors of the integrity of the gradually weakening Ottoman Empire, the "sick man of Europe."

The Second Empire failed because there was internal disatisfaction with the regime as well as a failure in foreign affairs. The fact that the French were not strongly committed to the government of Napoleon III made it vulnerable to foreign attack. When Otto von Bismarck, the Prussian Chancellor, maneuvered France into war to secure the adherence of the South German States to a unified Germany, the moment of crisis had arrived. The capture of Napoleon and his army at Sedan (1870) spelled the end of the empire. The last moment of Napoleonic glory ended in a fizzle.

Military defeat put the founding of the Third Republic under a pall. The provisional government divided on the question whether to pursue the war or to accept German terms. With the fall of Paris in 1871, the question became academic, for France was rapidly losing the will to resist. The National Assembly elected in January, 1871, was heavily royalist in complexion. One of the leading figures was the former Orleanist minister Adolphe Thiers. The royalists favored peace and the restoration of the monarchy, but the division between the supporters of the Count of Chambord, heir of the Bourbon claim, and the Orleanists prevented them from succeeding in this endeavor. Thiers became a caretaker president.

In Paris, disillusion with defeat, suffering from the occupation, economic hardship, and republican aspirations were factors that provoked an

Napoleon III and Bismarck. The defeated emperor negotiated the surrender of his army. (The Bettmann Archive)

uprising and the establishment of the government of the commune. The Parisian rebels had little sympathy with the provisional government. Their action reflected the deep cleavage between Paris and the provinces. Politically, the capital had little in common with the country as a whole. It was the center of French radicalism; the provinces were the stronghold of a conservative peasantry. As a result of the revolt, Paris was cut off from the rest of the country. Thiers gathered an army at Versailles and launched an attack on the communards. After a stiff resistance, especially strong in the working-class districts of the city, the army destroyed the commune. The repression was costly both for the communards and their enemies. They executed hostages, including the Archbishop of Paris; the army killed thousands of defenders. Moreover, the government alienated the radicals, drove many of the workers in the direction of Marxist communism, and lost their support for the liberal movement. Although royalists and liberals had preserved the government, they had strengthened a basic cleavage between the middle and the lower classes in France.

With the royalists in the saddle, but unable to resolve their internal split, France moved in the direction of republican government by default. The new constitution, promulgated in a series of laws, provided for a president, whose powers were those of a limited monarch. There was also a senate and a chamber of deputies. The ministers of the government were responsible to the legislative rather than the executive branch of the government. The first president chosen under the new system was Marshal MacMahon, the successful administrator of North Africa under Napoleon III and a staunch monarchist, who used his office to promote a revival of the monarchy. But this effort foundered in the seventies and, in 1879, MacMahon resigned his office. The republic was established.

The instability of the Third Republic was largely due to the fact that it was always under attack from both right and left. Its survival through World War I was not so much a tribute to the success of its architects or to the talents of its leaders as it was to the inability of its enemies to deal it a decisive blow. France, during the Third Republic, was often on the brink of another revolution, yet none materialized. Nevertheless a sense of crisis pervaded its atmosphere.

The architects of the Third Republic were largely liberal republicans and monarchists. They paid little heed to the needs of the working class and answered their demands with repression. Their most impressive gains were made in the growth of industry, in the building of a network of public highways and railroads and in the field of education, where legislation required six years of schooling for all French children. It was only during the nineties and after considerable pressure from socialists and liberal Catholics that new legislation regulated the employment of women and children in factories, set up voluntary machinery for labor arbitration, provided for government supervision of hygiene and safety and for free medical care for workers and their families, and set up a workmen's compensation program to make awards to those injured on the job. But these laws fell far short of the demands of the socialists and were behind similar legislation in England.

The issues that posed the greatest threat to the republic came from the right and the left. The government's education laws and its anticlericalism alienated the more conservative Catholic elements along with the hierarchy. The attempt to ban members of religious orders from teaching in government schools and to substitute the teaching of civics for religion met with only limited success due to stubborn opposition. Liberal Catholics attempted to rally support for the republic. Pope Leo XIII called on all French Catholics to support their government. However, these efforts had only limited effects on the tension between Catholics and the government. After the turn of the century, the church-state issue grew even more intense with the expulsion of religious orders from France, breaking off diplomatic relations with the Vatican, and the expropriation of ecclesiastical property. However, with the achievement of their main objectives, the anticlericals were willing to accept compromise. Moreover, other issues arose to obscure the simple church-state controversy and the anticlerial block in the Chamber of Deputies split. The chief threat of a rightist takeover in this period arose from the Boulanger episode (1889). General Boulanger, a dashing and voluble military figure, attracted the support of conservatives and for a moment threatened to take over the government by force. But prompt action forced him to flee France. The ultraconservative forces lacked a leader with the ability and decisiveness to gain power.

Ironically, the incident that almost toppled the republic and did result in great loss of confidence in the moderate or liberal coalition that controlled it before 1905 was not political in its origins at all, and its major character was a very nonpolitical minded Captain Dreyfus, a dedicated officer in French military intelligence and a good husband and father. Dreyfus was hardly the person around whom to build a political crisis. That he was involved was due partly to the dishonesty of a fellow officer and partly to the blundering of the French military. With the aid of forged documents, a military court found Dreyfus guilty of passing information about the French defenses to the German Embassy. When a new commander of military intelligence discovered that some of the documents used in the conviction were forgeries and found that the real culprit was a certain Major Esterhazy, his superiors transferred him to North Africa to prevent the exposure. However, his information came into the hands of Dreyfus' brother, and through him, to the French novelist Émile Zola. Since Dreyfus was Jewish, the affair had begun to take on anti-Semitic overtones. Anti-Jewish elements in the press began to attack the loyalty of Dreyfus on the grounds that he was a Jew and to defend the military and the government that supported them on the grounds of patriotism and religion. Zola's exposure of the sordid affair in the press led to his prosecution on libel charges. Finally, the military had to consent to a new trial for Dreyfus. Refusing to recognize the evidence, ignoring the fact that the officer who had forged the documents committed suicide rather than testify, the court again found Dreyfus guilty. However, the president of the republic granted him a full pardon and a subsequent trial exonerated him. Ironically, Esterhazy was officially exonerated by the government and could not be tried in spite of his guilt; so far had the effort to cover up evidence gone that the guilty escaped with the innocent. As the Dreyfus affair progressed, the enemies of the government sought to embarrass it by revealing its failure and dishonesty in that affair. Thus the proceedings against Dreyfus became the political *cause célèbre* of the period. The discrediting of the conservatives in the army and many members of the government led to its fall.

After 1905, French concern focused more and more on foreign affairs as France became deeply concerned about her isolation on the continent with the growth of German power to the east. To offset this position, the French entered into agreements with Russia, England, and Italy in the years immediately preceding World War I. Yet, on the eve of the war, there was still no great sense of impending conflict in the country. War caught the French by surprise.

Through most of the nineteenth century, France moved slowly in the direction of democracy. Adoption of universal male suffrage in the late forties did not, however, swing the country radically toward the left. The political strength of the lower classes was not so great in France as in England, because the progress of industrialization was more rapid in that country. France had preserved a large and fairly prosperous peasantry that gave the country a more conservative outlook. Moreover, though Paris had developed into a major capital, it did not reflect the growth of the country as a whole. The cleavage between Paris and the provinces made for a difficult political climate. For the pressures of Paris on the central government were generally more radical than those exerted by the provinces and the danger that unrest in Paris would topple the government remained an important consideration in determining government policy. Because of the growing influence of Paris, the cause of the conservatives gradually lost ground, while that of the left improved. Yet, in the period before the war, no government was sympathetic to the needs of the lower classes. Repression was the answer to their demands for social and economic reforms.

The Americas: Testing Democratic Ideals

The late eighteenth and early nineteenth centuries had witnessed successful revolutionary movements that secured independence for many former English and Spanish colonies in North, Central, and South America. The English colonies, having won their independence, embarked on the course of national unification; the Spanish colonies each followed a different course toward nationhood. In the English colonies, the national state triumphed over local attachments only gradually and after a bloody civil war; in the Spanish colonies, localism had already triumphed and continued to triumph as the new governments remained under the control of local Spanish-speaking aristocracies almost everywhere in Latin America. On the one hand, the eagle came to symbolize the struggle of the nation to overcome decentralizing influences within the individual states; on the other, the man on horseback came to stand for the continuation of aristocratic dominance over the great mass of poor and partially educated or ignorant Indians.

The building of the United States into a unified nation began with the debates over the federal constitution during the Constitutional Convention of 1787. There the Federalists stressed the need for a strong central government while the anti-Federalists attempted to preserve the power of the individual states. The Constitutional Convention did not settle this question, however. In fact, it did no more than make such compromises as were needed to create the machinery of government. From the early years of the republic, the direction of its growth, toward greater centralization or toward broader jurisdictions for local authority, became a burning political and constitutional issue.

The strength of Federalism grew during the administrations of Washington and Adams as President, while John Marshall provided a Federalist interpretation of the Constitution from his seat on the United States Supreme Court. The powerful voice of Thomas Jefferson, which had advocated a weak central government, changed its tone somewhat with his election to the Presidency in 1800. His purchase of Louisiana from France revealed the depth of his national concern. However, the fear of a strong central power that would despotically deprive citizens of their rights was written into the first ten amendments to the Constitution, known as the Bill of Rights.

Issues in American political life have tended to polarize around the question of central versus local authority. During the pre-Civil War era, conservative Federalists and their Whig successors supported strong central government because it promised a greater stability. The anti-Federalists and the Democratic-Republicans supported decentralization as the best way of promoting a more democratic government. Andrew Jackson opposed a national bank and deposited federal funds with various state banks during his administration. A staunch supporter of the democracy, Jackson found support among small Western farmers and mechanics of the upper South and the Ohio Valley and his major opponents among the commercial and banking interests of the Northeast. This "sectionalism" was inevitable in a country so vast as the new United States and one with such varied resources from region to region. It became more intense with the growth of anti-slavery sentiment in the North, for slavery became the major sectional issue of the forties and fifties.

The anti-slavery campaign went hand in hand with the westward expansion of the new nation, which by the late fifties had reached the Pacific and consolidated its position in California. Gold, minerals, and land attracted Easterners across the continent to California, Oregon, Nevada, Texas, New Mexico, and other territories opened during this period. But expansion brought problems of another kind. One of these was the question of the westward extension of slavery; antislavery forces bitterly opposed the introduction of slavery into the new territories and threatened to block the admission of any new states that would permit the "peculiar institution" within their boundaries. The path of compromise proposed by Daniel Webster and Stephen Douglas succeeded temporarily in putting off a final decision by admitting some states as "slave" and some as "free." By the late fifties, however, the slavery issue had become inextricably bound up with the question of the right of the individual states to chart their own course regardless of the central government. States' rights emerged as a hard line position that could not be compromised. Drawing from the political ideas of John C. Calhoun, which permitted a state to "nullify" acts of the federal government, the Southern slave-holding states moved in the direction of secession.

The election of Abraham Lincoln of Illinois to the Presidency in 1860 marked the climax in the struggle over slavery and secession. Lincoln had taken the clear-cut position that the Union came ahead of the interests of the individual states. Though willing to be flexible on the slavery issue, he refused to bend on the question of secession. However, South Carolina took the lead in withdrawing from the Union. Soon, most of the other slave-holding states had also seceded. Lincoln faced a divided nation and the Civil War. He had not chosen the course of war, but willingly took up the task of preserving the Union. In his view, the Union rather than slavery was the chief reason for fighting. Speaking at Gettysburg, following one of the major battles of the war, he said: "Now we are engaged in a great civil war, testing whether that nation . . . can long endure. . . . It is rather for us to be here dedicated to the great task remaining before us . . . that this nation, under God, shall have a new birth of freedom. . . ." In the mind of Lincoln, freedom and the Union were one. Slavery must go, but its destruction would not ensure freedom. Only the Union could be the bulwark of freedom.

The Civil War settled the issue of slavery and weakened the strength of the states, but the tension between local and national government remained important in American political life. However, the decades following the Civil War were caught up in the process of railroad building and industrialization that swept America. The founding of a major American coal and steel industry and the rise of industrial leaders like Andrew Carnegie belong to this era. The railroads spanned the continent during the Civil War; in the postwar era, many additional lines were added to unite the nation by sinews of steel. Vanderbilt of the Central, Hill of the Northern Pacific, Stanford of the Union Pacific—these men were the heroes and villains who built the great railroad empires. With the rise of industry, the United States became more urban. Conflict between the captains of industry and the public interest drew the federal and state governments into the field of regulation with the formation of the Interstate Commerce Commission and the passage of antitrust legislation to curtail the growth of monopolies. Workers formed labor unions and fought to secure recognition of the right to strike and recognition of their union as bargaining agent for them. Words like scab entered the vocabulary to describe those who broke the labor code. Industrial growth brought with it a host of problems in the social order. Yet, in the United States, the existence of cheap land had always acted as a safety valve to channel these social pressures away. Not until the end of the century, when the last valuable agricultural land that could be obtained free for homestead was gone, did the United States have to face the prospect of narrowing opportunities. Even so, the rapid growth of industry and the cities attracted tens and hundreds of thousands of immigrants from Europe, who hoped to find a better life in the new land.

The late nineteenth century saw the United States begin to emerge as a world power. Through most of its history, it had remained somewhat aloof from the affairs of Europe and more concerned with internal development. But the nation was caught up in the imperialism of the eighties and nineties, culminating in the Spanish American War of 1898. The United States emerged from the war not merely as victor but with colonial possessions in Asia and a deep involvement in Latin America. The completion of the Panama Canal in 1903, during the administration of Theodore Roosevelt, indicated the increasing importance of its involvement in trade with the Far East. By the beginning of World War I, the American nation had gained status as one of the chief powers of the West.

The history of the Latin American republics differed substantially from that of the United States. Divided politically, the story of each still has many common elements. Agriculture rather than commerce or industry formed the economic base and, in most cases, the land continued to be held by a minority of the total population. The growth of democracy was virtually impossible without the existence of a numerous class of educated workers and farmers, so government remained long in the hands of the aristocratic elements. Political life was dominated by factions supporting various leaders of the ruling class, with occasional popular uprisings. Not until the twentieth century were there present those elements necessary to create a democratic society in a few countries. In Mexico, popular revolution overthrew the Díaz regime and put that country on the road to democratic government. In Argentina, the development of industry and commerce in Buenos Aires and the great cattle ranches of the pampas provided a base for economic development and the political growth. Brazil, the former Portuguese colony, remained under the control of aristocratic elements into the twentieth century.

The road to democracy in Western Europe and America was far from smooth. Although industrialization was generally accompanied by democratic movements, its failures often provided the seedbed for other ideas, some socialistic, others totalitarian. By the end of the century England, France, and the United States had emerged as the leading nations whose governments inclined toward democracy, yet, in each of these, political democracy had only begun to promote the economic and social betterment of the mass of the population. Democracy was still an ideal.

19 The Endurance of Conservatism

In Central and Eastern Europe, liberal nationalism did not generally gain the ascendancy in the nineteenth century. Instead, it generated considerable pressures against the conservative regimes of these nations in order to move them in the direction of national states. These pressures operated differently in the various countries. In Germany and Italy, the major concern was unification and the forging of the national tie among peoples whose particularism had been confirmed by centuries of living next to one another but separately. In Austria-Hungary, the chief effort was the making of a multinational empire. In Poland, it was the aspiration for independence. In Russia, it made itself felt partially in the demand for constitutional reform and partially in the movement to identify that nation with the West. On the surface, at least, democratic movements made little or no progress. Yet, by the end of the period under discussion, revolutionary movements in many of these countries revealed the strength of the demands of the masses for greater participation in political life. Still few of the countries of Central and Eastern Europe had succeeded in creating enduring democratic governments; rather, there was a tendency toward that aberration of modern democracy, totalitarian dictatorship. In part, at least, the long and even artificial endurance of conservative governments in these regions acted to retard the development of the political machinery of the democratic state so that few had either the experience or the commitment to liberal democracy necessary for it to work.

The Liberal Spirit in Germany, 1830–1869

Napoleon had called Italy a "geographical expression." Germany was hardly better off. These two countries shared a heritage of disunity and particularism from medieval times. True enough, the Napoleonic conquests had altered the map of Germany by reducing the number of German states and creating the Confederation of the Rhine; they had had less of an effect in Italy, where the restored Habsburgs and Bourbons shared the peninsula with the Pope. Only the House of Savoy, based in the Piedmont of the northwest and on the island of Sardinia, had any pretence to being a real Italian reigning dynasty and its pretensions were questionable, for the family had long been more French than Italian. The early nineteenth century saw the spread of national feeling in both countries and the beginnings of movements for unification and constitutional reforms. Yet the Revolutions of 1830 had failed to achieve any lasting effects in either Germany or Italy. Liberalism, which had furnished much inspiration to national movements, was not strong enough to carry the day.

In Germany, the disturbances of the 1830's created hardly a ripple in the vast ocean of conservativism. However, below the surface, some changes were taking place. After 1830 Austria showed a greater interest in her possessions in Southern and Eastern Europe than in German affairs. Prussia began to revive somewhat from the Napoleonic wars. The South German States, however, continued to incline more toward Austrian than Prussian leadership; both Catholicism and the rather relaxed attitudes of the Austrian Habsburgs assured them of the wisdom of this policy. Within these various states, the winds of change were also blowing. The German liberals agitated for constitutional reforms and, in some cases, for unification. They were composed of representatives of business and the professions and admired the constitutional reforms carried through in England and France. Some slight progress was made with the formation of a Zollverein (customs union) in 1818 under Prussian leadership. Its members were chiefly North German states already under Prussian influence. By 1834, seventeen German states belonged. Moreover, the Prussian King, Frederick William IV, had shown some signs of sympathy with liberal aspirations for constitutional reforms. A dreamy and paternal individual, he created a Prussian Landtag (assembly) in 1847, but failed to pay any attention to it. Nevertheless, the liberals continued to agitate for political reforms.

This was the picture when riots broke out in Berlin. Frederick William refused to believe that his loyal Berliners would ever revolt. He blamed the outbreaks on foreigners—some of the rioters were Polish workers. In fact, he was witness to another phase of the Revolutions of 1848, which had swept Louis Philippe from his throne in France, had wrung quick concessions from various Italian rulers, and driven the Austrians out of Hungary. Under the pressure of the riots, Frederick agreed to summon the Prussian Diet (a meeting of the nobility) and to press for a constitution. He also appointed a ministry composed of men with a liberal outlook on constitutional reforms.

Elsewhere in Germany, similar outbreaks had evoked somewhat the same responses. There was a growing demand that Germans should act in concert. This was an expression of the hope of the liberal nationalists for unification. It resulted in the meeting of the Frankfort Parliament in May, 1848. But the attempt to create a constitution for a united Germany at Frankfort failed. Royalists and republicans could not agree. Frederick William IV, offered the German crown by the parliament, refused to accept a crown from the "gutter." The assembly melted away and a restored Germanic Confederation restored the leadership of Austria in German affairs, largely because of the deferential attitude of Frederick William IV. Perhaps the view of Karl Marx was too harsh in maintaining that the assembly was in reality nothing but a "stage where old and worn out political characters exhibited their involuntary ludicrousness and their impotence of thought, as well as action, before the eyes of all Germany." Yet the fact remained that conservatism once more triumphed.

The unification of Germany, when it came, was not the result of a victory by liberal nationalism but the acceptance of the need for unity by German conservatives. The leadership was taken up by Otto von Bismarck, after 1862, Chancellor of Prussia. Bismarck (1815–1898) was a member of Prussia's ruling class, the conservative Junker aristocracy, who had served as officers in the Prussian army and officials in the government for centuries. He was fully committed to the idea of Prussian leadership in Germany and was willing to subordinate all else to the attainment of this important goal. Although he stood as the champion of a unified Germany, he was not a constitutionalist and met his greatest opposition from the liberal members of the Prussian Parliament pressing for constitutional checks on the monarchy. A measure of his success is that he proved to them the success of his approach and made them more nationalist then liberal in the future.

The first crisis of Bismarck's chancellorship arose over the military bud-

Otto von Bismarck. The "Iron Chancellor" struggled to get his way against the forces of decentralization in Germany. (The Bettmann Archive)

get. The chancellor and the king determined to strengthen the Prussian army. The parliament, led by liberals, refused to approve the budget needed to accomplish this aim. Bismarck simply ignored parliament and raised taxes without its approval. He proved that he would not allow constitutional niceties to stand in his way. In the long run, parliament went along, not because they yielded to pressure but because they came to see how successful the "Iron Chancellor" was in both diplomacy and war.

Bismarck's strategy for German unification began with strengthening Prussia's claim to leadership in Germany. Denmark provided the first opportunity. The Danes ruled Schleswig and Holstein, two duchies, whose populations were largely German speaking. Bismarck disputed the Danish claim and invited Austria to join him in a war to drive out the Danes (1864). As a result, Schleswig was awarded to Prussia, Holstein to Austria. But more important, Prussia had taken the initiative as defender of

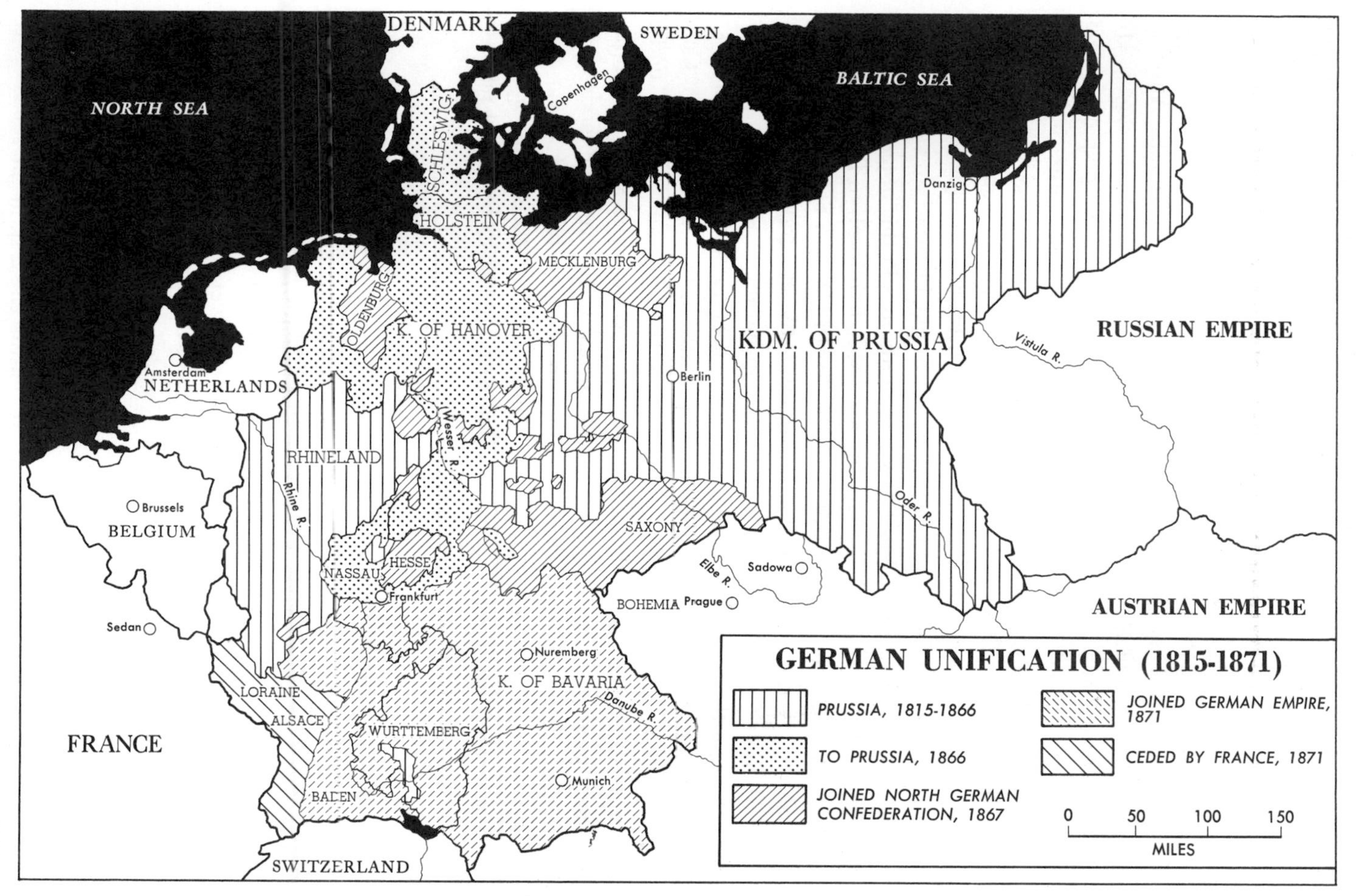
GERMAN UNIFICATION (1815-1871)
PRUSSIA, 1815-1866
TO PRUSSIA, 1866
JOINED NORTH GERMAN CONFEDERATION, 1867
JOINED GERMAN EMPIRE, 1871
CEDED BY FRANCE, 1871
0
50
100
150
MILES
DENMARK
SWEDEN
NORTH SEA
BALTIC SEA
Copenhagen
Danzig
SCHLESWIG
HOLSTEIN
MECKLENBURG
OLDENBURG
K. OF HANOVER
KDM. OF PRUSSIA
RUSSIAN EMPIRE
Vistula R.
Amsterdam
NETHERLANDS
Berlin
Wesser R.
RHINELAND
Rhine R.
Oder R.
Brussels
BELGIUM
SAXONY
HESSE
NASSAU
Frankfurt
Elbe R.
Sadowa
BOHEMIA
Prague
AUSTRIAN EMPIRE
Sedan
Nuremberg
K. OF BAVARIA
LORAINE
Danube R.
ALSACE
WURTTEMBERG
FRANCE
Munich
BADEN
SWITZERLAND

the Germans. Her prestige increased as a result of this action. However, Austria was still the traditional leader of the German states. Her ruler was the president of the diet. Even the Prussian king was reluctant to undertake any step that might alienate Austria. Bismarck suffered from no such sentiments. Taking advantage of supposed irregularities in the Austrian administration of Holstein, he ordered Prussian troops into the duchy. He had already seen to it that France would not come to the help of Austria and had secured Italy as his ally. The war was brief, lasting only seven weeks. At Sadowa (July 3, 1866), the Prussian army proved the wisdom of Bismarck's military policy by attaining a decisive victory. However, Bismarck had no desire to humiliate the Austrians. He wanted merely to break up the German Confederation and to put Prussia into command of a new Confederation of North German States and in this objective he was completely successful. Moreover, he also added Holstein to Prussian territory. Prussia was now the leader of the North German States. One major task remained to achieve full political unity: the integration of the largely Catholic states of the south into a German nation.

During the following years, Bismarck concentrated on two goals. First, he tried to forge closer ties between the states in the North German Confederation. Second, he sought the means to bring all Germany under Prussian tutelage into a unified state. The success of his wars and diplomacy promoted the first; therefore, he turned to the same methods to attain the latter objective. Bismarck saw in the possibility of a war with France the hope of persuading the South German States to accept Prussian leadership. Therefore, he set about seeking means to force France to attack. From victory would come unity.

The Unification of Italy

As Bismarck worked to build a unified Germany, he had the example of Italy, whose struggle for unification also began to meet success in the period following the Revolutions of 1848. There were many similarities between the experience of the two peoples. However, the Italian situation presented even greater obstacles because of the ancient traditions behind papal control of central Italy and the wide variations between northern and southern Italy. The north had participated fully in the commercial revolution of the later Middle Ages. Cities like Venice, Genoa, Milan, Florence, and Pisa had once been major powers in the Mediterranean world. They had a large and articulate middle class. If, in the seventeenth and eighteenth centuries, under foreign domination, northern Italy had ceased to play a paramount role in European politics, it remained an important center of European culture. Central and southern Italy, on the other hand, save for the capitals at Rome and Naples, had remained predominantly agricultural under the dominance of a numerous class of petty feudal landlords. While Napoleon's invasion of Italy had provided better administration to these regions than they had known in the previous several centuries, the basic pattern of economic and social life was unaltered. Restoration of the Bourbons in Naples returned the country pretty much to its former state. During the twenties there had been mounting pressure for unification of Italy. Thereafter, numerous proposals were made. Mazzini desired an Italian republic based in Rome. The Abbé Gioberti suggested a confederation of Italian states under the presidency of the liberal-minded Pope Pius IX. Others proposed that the King of Sardinia-Piedmont take the lead in uniting the country. The Revolutions of 1848 crystallized the concern of Italian nationalists and liberals and helped to put the country on the road toward the nation-state.

The outbreaks in Italy preceded those in Paris and elsewhere by several weeks. Riots in Naples frightened King Ferdinand II into granting a constitution on February 10, 1848. Charles Albert of Sardinia, acting on the advice of Count Camillo di Cavour, granted a *Statuto* on February 8, and, on February 17, the Duke of Tuscany promised a constitution. Pius IX had already begun to make concessions in the papal territories. However, the major focus soon turned from the demand for constitutional government to a war to drive the Austrians out of Italy. Milan revolted and drove out the Austrians. For a moment, it seemed that all Italy would unite against Austria. But that moment quickly passed. The reconquest of Milan by the Austrian Marshal Radetzky, while the forces of Sardinia-Piedmont refused aid, broke the back of the rebels. Pius IX and Ferdinand II quickly withdrew their forces. The war was over and so, too, was the revolution.

In the months that followed the defeat of Milan, the reaction set in. On May 5, 1849, Ferdinand II was allowed to reenter the city of Palermo. Pius IX, who had been driven from Rome by the forces of Mazzini in their effort to proclaim a Roman republic, returned with the support of French troops sent by the new French President, Louis Napoleon Bonaparte. Thereafter, Pius distrusted all change made in the name of reform. Only in Sardinia-Piedmont was a change made that bode well for the cause of Italy. The weak and hesitant Charles Albert, unpopular because of his failure to support Milan, stepped down in favor of his son, Victor Emmanuel II (1849–1878). It was this monarch who chose Count Camillo di

Cavour (1810–1861) as his chief minister. He chose, whether intentionally or not, the architect of Italian unification.

Cavour was ideally suited for the task to which he dedicated the remainder of his life. A member of the nobility, he was also active in business. He had a keen practical mind and broad experience of Europe gained partly by his travels outside of Italy. His liberal views were genuine, though his major concern was not so much with constitutional reform as with the achievement of the national goal. His newspaper. *Il Risorgimento,* became the voice of liberal nationalism in Sardinia-Piedmont. Cavour was also a successful and fairly important figure, whose views carried some weight in the government. His accession to the office of prime minister in 1852 provided him with the position from which to map and carry out his campaign.

As a strategist in the international politics of the mid-nineteenth century, Cavour proved himself and made gains for his cause. He led Sardinia-Piedmont into the Crimean War in 1855 to win a position at the peace conference, there to advertise the position of Sardinia and to seek for an ally against Austria. He scored well with Napoleon III, who was genuinely sympathetic with the Italian aspiration to nationhood. In 1858, Napoleon and Cavour entered a secret treaty against Austria, which stipulated that Napoleon would support Sardinia in a defensive war. For this aid, Napoleon was to receive Nice and Savoy. Sardinia would gain much more at Austrian expense.

Napoleon moved against Austria as he had promised as soon as Cavour had found a suitable excuse for opening hostilities. The French aid was sufficient to drive the Austrians out of Lombardy, but it suddenly ceased at that point. The reason for the French truce with Austria was Napoleon's belief—well founded, it turned out—that Cavour intended to take over part of central Italy that he had agreed would become an independent kingdom under Napoleon's brother. Still, the war had been a limited success. Sardinia-Piedmont had established itself as the dominant Italian state.

Cavour proved his ability as a master politician and strategist in dealing with the other leaders of the Italian unification movement. He used the radical republicanism of Mazzini to point up his own position as a responsible and conservative statesman interested in preserving the political stability of Italy and keeping it under conservative leadership rather than allowing it to fall into the hands of radicals. In 1860, he proved his ability to outmaneuver the dashing and heroic Giuseppe Garibaldi (1807–1882). In the past, this romantic figure had led ineffectual uprisings

ITALIAN UNIFICATION
0 50 100
MILES
Rhone R.
SAVOY
PIEDMONT
Turin
KINGDOM
OF SARDINIA
NICE
Monaco
Genoa
Magenta
LOMBARDY
Solferino
Villafranca
VENETIA
Venice
Adige R.
Po R.
PARMA
Parma
MODENA
LUCCA
Arno R.
Florence
SAN
MARINO
TUSCANY
Tiber R.
Castelfidardo
PAPAL STATES
Rome
CORSICA
SARDINIA
ADRIATIC SEA
KINGDOM OF
Naples
THE TWO SICILIES
TYRRHENIAN SEA
Palermo
Messina
Reggio
SICILY
Syracuse
MEDITERRANEAN SEA

Giuseppe Garibaldi. This romantic soldier and patriot dreamed of a united republican Italy and fought for that goal. (*The Bettmann Archive*)

against the Bourbons in Naples. In 1860, he once again launched a campaign from the Quarto dei Mille east of Genoa. At first, he planned to prevent the surrender of Nice to Napoleon, but Cavour diverted him to Sicily. The move was fortuitous. The Bourbon monarchy was attempting to quell a spreading revolt and was losing ground. Garibaldi and his thousand redshirts landed in Sicily and took Palermo, gaining control of the island and receiving some support from disaffected soldiers of the Bourbon army. Then the rebels crossed to the mainland and moved toward Naples amid mounting support. It was clear that Garibaldi would achieve the overthrow he had long desired. Cavour, however, had no intention of permitting the establishment of an independent republic under Garibaldi in the south. Using the pretext of riots in the Papal States—he had stirred them up, he moved from the Papal States into Neapolitan territory. There was little left for Garibaldi but to bow somewhat reluctantly and ungracefully to Cavour's *fait accompli.* Naples and

Sicily were preserved for the new Italian crown that was now proclaimed. The King of Sardinia-Piedmont became King of Italy (1861). But it was an Italy that still did not include Rome and its environs, where French troops in token force defended the Papal sovereignty, and Venetia, where Austria remained in control. But, before either of these objectives could be attained, Cavour died.

The completion of the work of unifying Italy went hand in hand with the task of building the political and other institutions of the new state. In fact, the acquisition of Venetia and Rome proved easier by far than the task of governing. The successors of Cavour played their foreign policy close to that of Bismarck and therefore benefited from his successes. Italy supported his brief war with Austria (1866) and received Venetia as its recompense. It remained aloof from the Franco-Prussian War, much to the disappointment of Napoleon III, and took advantage of the withdrawal of French troops from Rome to take control of that city, which now became the capital of the kingdom of Italy. Pope Pius IX, unwilling to make his peace with the upstart and somewhat anticlerical monarchy, withdrew behind the walls of the Vatican Palace next to the Basilica of St. Peter. Defense of the sovereign prerogatives of the Pope drove many Catholics into political inactivity. Thus Catholicism played no major part in Italian political life until the late nineteenth century, after Pope Leo XIII removed the restrictions on political activity. Yet even without the potential cleavage beween Catholics and anticlericals in the Italian Parliament, politicians found it difficult to build stable majorities on which to govern. The sixties set the style of temporary coalitions around leading personalities that was to characterize Italian political life during the following decades.

In neither Germany nor Italy was the achievement of political unity an end. The goal was the building of a modern national state. That task was hardly begun by 1870.

The State Achieved: Germany and Italy, 1870–1914

The forty-four years that separated the achievement of political unity in Germany and Italy and the outbreak of World War I were not a mere prelude to that war on the one hand or an era of major concern with foreign policy on the other. As a matter of fact, the immediate effect of unification on European foreign relations was slight. In large measure, the credit for this fact must go to Bismarck, who remained Chancellor of the German Empire until 1890. Having achieved his goal of unification, he had no desire to unsettle the politics of Europe and worked instead to create an alliance system that would ensure stability and peace in which the German nation might develop its power. War, to Bismarck, was an instrument of national policy. He was willing to resort to it in order to gain his purposes. But his goals were conservative. Once met, war could only threaten to destroy the very aims it had helped to achieve.

German unity was born in Paris; it was there that the German Empire was proclaimed in 1871. This proclamation came on the heels of the decisive victory of the Prussian army and her allies in the Franco-Prussian War. Bismarck had maneuvered Napoleon III into a war to defend the national integrity of France. He had doctored the famous telegram sent to the Prussian king by the French government to make it appear as an insult to the Germans. Napoleon himself had aided by pushing an army of 82,000 men into a position from which the only escape was surrender. The French cooperated by staging a revolution and by dividing on the question of continuing to fight the war. Bismarck took advantage of the swell of German national sentiment to lead the South German States into a new adventure, as part of the German Empire, with the King of Prussia as Emperor. Typically, the German title was Kaiser, Caesar, reminiscent of the Roman Empire and even more of the medieval Holy Roman Empire of the Germans that had been laid to rest in 1805 by Napoleon I.

The new German Empire was of unique design. Bismarck had recognized the impossibility of making a totally centralized state out of the various German principalities and kingdoms. He turned to federalism for a solution. In all, there were to be twenty-five states and the federal territory of Alsace-Lorraine, newly conquered from the French. Each state possessed considerable local autonomy. It controlled its own system of taxation, its own police and educational system, its own regulation of landholding, and its own health measures. The federal government, however, was far from weak. At its head was the Kaiser. Bismarck saw to it that he, as Chancellor, and the other imperial ministers were responsible to the Kaiser rather than to the German Parliament. That body was divided into two houses, the *Bundesrat* and the *Reichstag*. The *Bundesrat*, the upper house, was composed of representatives of the states. Prussia controlled two-thirds of the membership of this house, thus ensuring the emperor a veto in Parliament itself. The *Reichstag* represented all German citizens. It was elected by vote of all male German citizens of the age of 25. No law could take effect without the consent of both houses. The imperial government controlled foreign affairs, regulation of interstate commerce, the civil and criminal law, and relations between states. It also controlled the army and other military services. In this system, Prussia was not only the dominant member but the actual leader. States rights, an issue that continued to play an important role in imperial politics, were subordinate to national interest.

Between 1871 and 1890, Bismarck worked to make the new German Empire into a truly unified state. Here his interest was not merely political. He realized the need for uniformity in many areas in order to break down traditional German separatism. Uniform codes of law for the whole empire supplanted the law codes of the various states. In 1873, the creation of the Imperial Railway Bureau unified the railroads and coordinated them with the military, postal, and telegraph systems of the empire. This measure was of special importance in bringing the entire empire into an effective military posture. The new imperial German army was modeled on the Prussian army, including adoption of the Prussian tradition of universal military training. The Bank Act of 1875 transferred control of banking from the various state governments to the Bundesrat. In 1876, the *Reichsbank,* or Imperial Bank, was founded in Berlin, to serve as the chief financial arm of the government. Although the parliament technically had control of the budget, Bismarck succeeded in securing long-term provision for the military. He had wanted to make the military budget a permanent item, not subject to parliamentary debate; he settled for a five-year provision and later succeeded in getting this raised to seven years. Whenever the budget came up for consideration, Bismarck employed the war-scare technique to ensure that it would pass with a minimum of debate. But the powers in the hands of the imperial government were not the only reason for its domination of the states; part of the secret was Bismarck's political technique in dealing with the various parties in the parliament.

Bismarck, as was natural, relied on and received the support of the nationalists. The National Liberal Party, the voice of the industrialists and many liberal intellectuals was more nationalistic than liberal in its political views. It supported unification and industrial progress. The Free Conservatives represented the old Junker class of Prussia, to which Bismarck himself belonged. It commanded the loyalty of the army officer corps and most of the Lutheran clergy. These parties were chiefly Prussian in their membership. The opposition was divided, and during the first years, quite weak. The doctrinaire liberals, called Progressives, wanted a limited monarchy with a government responsible to an elected parliament. They were opposed to the constitution as it had been designed by Bismarck and the conservatives. During the seventies, there were relatively few socialists, but this picture began to change with the growth of German industry. Others in the opposition were members of relatively small splinter groups working for states rights. Many of these were Catholics, who feared the dominance of Protestant Prussia. Their fear gradually led to closer co-operation and the formation of the German Center Party, which became the voice of German Catholicism.

Bismarck's reaction to increasing criticism from Catholics in Parliament was the *Kulturkampf*. The term, which meant "struggle for civilization" depicted the anti-Catholic measures of the government as a struggle between German Protestant national feeling and foreign Catholicism. The Protestant majority in the *Reichstag* cast doubts on the loyalty of Catholics to the government. The essence of the program was contained in the "May laws," enacted in 1873–1874. This legislation required that every official of the Church had to be a German citizen, German educated, and had to receive authorization from the government to occupy his office. All seminaries were placed under control of the state. All preparatory seminaries, which trained students for the priesthood from their early teens until they began the study of philosophy, were closed. The laws also struck at non-national minorities. The requirement that religious instruction had to be given in German angered the Poles of Prussia. Catholic opposition stiffened as the Pope supported the German bishops and told them to disobey the laws. In an attempt to enforce the laws, the Prussian parliament issued a law that only authorized persons might hold services in a church. When the bishops and clergy disobeyed, they were jailed. By 1877, every German bishop and hundreds of priests were imprisoned or in exile. The government also was forcing Catholics out of the civil service. The Center Party became the focal point of the opposition. Working chiefly with the Socialists, it initiated a broad program of social reforms and attempted to embarrass the government on every possible occasion in Parliament. Bismarck, fearful of the Catholic-Socialist opposition, decided to relent. He reversed his field in the years following to gain the support of the Center Party against the rising tide of socialism. The May laws became a dead letter and were repealed almost in their entirety in 1886.

Bismarck's fear of socialism was based on the very rapid growth of the Socialist Party in Germany after 1875. Despite his efforts to apply repressive measures, including forbidding their meetings, the movement continued to attract more and more members from the increasing industrial proletariat of the cities. The appeal of socialism may be ascribed to a number of factors besides the mere increase in the number of workers.

The Socialists advocated a comprehensive program of welfare benefits before any other party. Theirs was a concrete appeal to the needs of the working class and one that was based on an understanding of its economic and social needs. Though the doctrinaire message of the Socialists was beyond the interest and comprehension of most working men, it found some support among the liberal progressives, some of whom believed that socialism was more democratic than the illiberal regime of Bismarck. The aging "Iron Chancellor" realized again that compromise was the better road. He relied on the support of Catholics and Conservatives—the National Liberal Party could not support him here—to pass a series of welfare measures. He secured laws to limit the working hours and conditions for women and children and to provide for compulsory old age insurance. In the latter measure, he was far ahead of his time. These and other welfare measures were important factors in winning the German working class to support the nation.

The accession of a new and youthful Emperor, William II (1888–1918), brought an end to the career of the man who had made Germany more than an expression. William desired to rule. Born to a nation, he wished to wield its power. Between 1890 and 1914, increasing emphasis was put on foreign affairs and imperialistic expansion. William assumed the lead over his ministers, making and unmaking them as necessary. He deserted Bismarck's policy of friends in the East in order to cultivate the Austrians. His favorable attitude toward Austrian expansion in Southeastern Europe cost him the Russian alliance. William and his ministers also worked to build the German navy and to expand German influence in the Near East, Africa, and the Far East. Their more aggressive policies brought Germany to the center of the international stage and into rivalry with both England and France. The stage for war was gradually set. Yet Germany was largely unaware of the meaning of the steps that were leading her in that direction.

While Bismarck had fallen back on the Prussian conservative tradition in politics to find a basis for building a united Germany, the Italians faced a crisis of leadership in the years following the death of Cavour. The problem was to find one national leader amid the many who put forward claims. That problem was never solved. Instead, the Italians turned to *trasformismo,* the practice of making temporary coalitions to enable a leader to form a government. With transformism went a considerable measure of political cynicism, the ignoring of lines of traditional party groupings, and a measure of outright corruption.

The Italians inherited the "liberalism" of Cavour, who had believed in the value of free political institutions for their encouragment of economic growth, but who had not hesitated to restrict freedom or to ignore parliament when he believed it was necessary to do so. This heritage was only partly liberal and far from democratic. Not more than two million Italians possessed the right to vote after the reform of 1881 broadened the franchise, far fewer than in any of the larger "democratic" states of the West or even than in Germany. Universal manhood suffrage did not come until near the beginning of World War I.

As the nineteenth century drew to a close, the government began to seek diversions abroad to cover its unspectacular achievements at home. Francesco Crispi (1819–1901), one of the major figures of the era, led his country in the direction of foreign expansion. A Sicilian and a former member of Garibaldi's redshirts, Crispi was more democratic in his thinking than many of his contemporaries. He pioneered significant social legislation. Yet he remained deeply committed to the notion that the chief strength of the government rested on the support of the monarch. He adopted the policy of Cavour without the ability of Cavour to mold parliament to his ends. Consequently, he turned to transformism as a way of remaining in partial control of the situation. But none of his domestic achievements won him overwhelming support. He found that the road to popularity lay along the byways of nationalism and it was into these paths that he turned. His imperialistic adventures in Africa, including the disastrous defeat of the Italians at Aduwa, Ethiopia, in 1896, were merely distractions from lack of success at home. The last distraction proved disastrous to Crispi's political career.

The turn of the century did seem to bring some promise of a better future for Italian democracy. Giovanni Giolitti, the liberal reformer and most practiced political figure of the day, skillfully combined a sincere interest in the welfare of the lower classes with a cynical approach to the problem of winning elections. He sponsored legislation to improve health care, to enforce requirements for education, to improve working conditions, and to extend the vote to all Italian male citizens. At the same time, he manipulated the electorate in a manner similar to that employed in the United States during the same period. His agents bought votes where possible and intimidated the illiterate peasant voters by the pressure of local landlords and politicians. Under this system, corruption became so widespread that many considered it a necessary corollary of public life. Such open violation of basic honesty at the period when the masses were beginning to enter the mainstream of politics was an important factor in confirming their cynicism about the possibility of achieving honest government. More and more Italians began to give their votes to extremist candidates, especially to the socialists, because they stood for a protest against the flagrant abuses existing in the present order. Thereby, protest became a major factor in the Italian voting pattern and has remained such until the present. Other problems also troubled the young republic, but none so grave or difficult to solve as the "southern question." The south, the region from Naples to the tip of Sicily, the former Neapolitan kingdom, was one of the most backward areas in Europe. A parasitic and noble class of landlords attempted to continue into the twentieth century the way of life they had known since the late Middle Ages. Low in natural resources, partially arid and considerably overworked, the soil of the south offered small rewards to its hardworking peasants. After unification, the major focus was on the north, where the relationship with Europe was strongest. The south, since ancient times, had its closest ties with Africa. In a sense, the decline of Africa had been its decline as well. In another sense, the centuries of foreign domination and poor government by a monarchy that never became aware of the industrial revolution or the commercial revolution that preceded it had prepared the south for its lot. Yet the problem of the south was a political powder keg, for civil unrest in that region constantly threatened the peace of the nation.

Though Germany, thanks largely to Bismarck's determined policies, had made significant strides in the direction of total unification by the beginning of World War I, Italy remained a land in search of a nation. North and south, Catholic and anticlerical liberal and socialist, idealists and cynics, all these elements and more divided the Italians into a prism of political disunity. The hope of Cavour for complete Italian unity was not realized prior to World War I.

The Old Regimes in Eastern Europe

The faint stirrings of the democratic pulse in the body politic in Germany and Italy found but slight echoes in Eastern Europe. The sprawling Russian Empire wrestled late with the problems of industrialization and liberalism, but its response was born out of its own autocratic tradition. Poland, partitioned in the late eighteenth century, revolted periodically against the Russians in hope of regaining her independence. Her struggle roused the sympathy of liberals throughout the West, but her cause attracted no solid political support. The multinational Austrian Empire worked to find a formula that would enable her to become a modern state. More advanced and less autocratic than Russia, Austria was a double symbol. On the one hand, she stood for the oppression of Slavic peoples in Southeastern Europe; on the other, she represented the hope for many of these same peoples to achieve a higher degree of culture and a better life within a large and somewhat laxly administered empire. In the Balkans, the fever of independence swept into Greece early in the century and from there traveled northward. But the Ottoman Empire yielded only reluctantly to demands for freedom, while Russia and Austria stood by with selfish interest to advance their own claims to territory in the region. The East and Southeast were backward compared to the West.

The Russian Empire lay across Europe and Asia like a huge barrier. Even in the nineteenth century, after Peter the Great had opened his window on the West and Catherine the Great had shared in the spoils of Europe, Russia remained a mysterious and forbidden land. In the course of the century, Western Europeans tended to bypass Russia rather than attempt to cross her vast reaches of steppes and mountains and forests and tundra. Instead of providing a bridge between Europe and Asia, Russia formed a land barrier and found herself pulled in both directions by geography and history.

The government of the Russian Empire made few concessions to the widespread changes in economic and social life that had so altered the pattern of states in the West. The Russian Tsars, autocrats of all the Russias, still ruled from St. Petersburg in the traditions of Ivan the Terrible and Peter the Great over a land where the mass of the population was still bound to the soil or to household serfdom, while the state and the nobility owned and controlled the land. What liberal ideas had entered the empire in the post-Napoleonic period had by and large taken root in Poland or the former German provinces along the Baltic shore and only gradually penetrated to St. Petersburg and Moscow. For brief moments in the century, it appeared that the Tsar might alter the course to favor the liberals, but the change was always temporary. Conservatism is perhaps too weak and too inaccurate a term to describe the Russian despotism. No ruler in the West had ever wielded the arbitrary power of the Russian Tsar.

Poland was the major Russian trouble spot. The real eastward sweep of liberal ideas from the West crossed Poland and found in that forlorn land men hungry for liberty. Though the Polish revolution of 1831 had but little connection with the revolutions that swept through much of Western Europe in that year, it attracted the widespread sympathy of Western liberals for the East.

With the death of Tsar Alexander I in 1825, Russia moved further to the right. Nicholas I (1825–1855) was a practical and hardheaded reactionary, whose chief answer to the liberals was the founding of the infamous "third section" or secret police. His sympathy with the old regime led him to dispatch troops to aid the Austrians in putting down the Hungarian Revolt in 1849. However, like most of the Tsars, he was a nationalist, perhaps better, an imperialist. His desire to see the expansion of Russia into Southeastern Europe led him to give support to the Slavophiles. He used them because their advocacy of a union of all Slavic peoples under Russian leadership fit in well with his own imperialistic foreign policy. The mystique of Holy Russia expounded by the Slavophile became a moral justification for Russian imperialism. Nicholas also attempted to champion the cause of Orthodox Christians under Ottoman rule. However, this move was countered by France and England, who feared the increase of Russian influence in that area. The Crimean War of 1853–1856 proved disastrous for Russian prestige and forced Russia to take a back seat while England and France took the lead in promoting the cause of independence among the various Balkan nationalities. Napoleon III supported the Roumanians. The British strengthened their ties with Greece by securing the selection of George I, a Danish prince, as King. They also prevailed on the sultan to withdraw the garrison that he was keeping in Serbia in 1867.

Domestic unrest increased rapidly during the forties and fifties. The most pressing problem was that of serfdom. Russia's rigid class structure kept the mass of Russian peasantry attached to the land. Yet, in the nineteenth century, serfdom was not economical. Most landlords were desperately in need of additional money. Still they had to support a growing number of serfs. Moreover, some desired to raise wheat and other money crops, using hired labor to plant and harvest. Serfdom prevented these changes. But even more persuasive than any economic considerations was the constant and real danger that the miserable serfs would revolt against their owners and spur on a general revolution as had happened during the Pugachev revolt under Catherine the Great. These were the considerations that motivated Alexander II's (1855–1881) emancipation of the serfs in 1861. In an effort to meet liberal demands for representative institutions and to provide for a more effective operation of local government, Alexander created provincial assemblies, the *zemstvos,* to discuss and decide matters relating to local public works, schools, prisons, poor relief, and public health. He also established a judicial system modeled on that of Western Europe. Trial by jury was provided for in criminal

Assassinated Tsar, Alexander II. Repression and terror often became fused in the minds of the revolutionaries in Russia. (*The Bettmann Archive*)

cases. The appeal of these measures to old reformers was great. Baron Rosen, who had participated in the Decembrist Revolt in 1825, repented his rebellion against a regime that could produce so enlightened a Tsar.

But Alexander II was no liberal. His motivation was chiefly the need to reform the cumbersome and inefficient Russian autocracy along more modern lines. When the Poles rebelled in 1863, he turned from his Western course and began to surround himself with reactionaries, chiefly Slavophiles. Yet he had proved himself an intelligent ruler. It was scarcely his fault that the long history of repression of reform in Russia caused the reformers to mistrust and even hate him. Sadly, this able ruler was assassinated in 1881.

Alexander III (1881–1894) came to the throne determined not to commit the grave mistake of his father in supporting the cause of reform. He remained a staunch reactionary until his death. His conviction of his mission was firm.

. . . the voice of God orders us to stand firm at the helm of government with faith in the strength and truth of the Autocratic Power, which we are called to consolidate and to preserve for the good of the people from every kind of encroachment.

No doubt, as he uttered these works, the Tsar could visualize his enemies, particularly the growing group of Intelligentsia.

The Russian intelligentsia consisted of those men of education, some nobles and some drawn from the sons of the clergy or the professions, who hoped to remake Russia along Western lines. Most were liberals, though the number of Marxist socialists increased considerably during the last decades of the century. Only a few were willing to resort to violence; it was they who made the bombs that threatened the life of the ruler. The total number of the intelligentsia was not large, yet their influence was considerable for they constituted the only real opposition to the regime. In spite of repression by the secret police and frequent sentences of exile to Siberia or escapes abroad, they kept up a steady stream of writing against the government in clandestine newspapers and smuggled books. They hoped to rouse the sleeping masses of Russia to an awareness of the need for political reform. But they had no real success in this attempt. When revolution came to Russia, it arrived in the wake of war and disaster.

Alexander III and his successor, Nicholas II (1894–1917), relied heavily on two ministers, Constantine Pobedonostsev and Viatcheslav Plehve. Pobedonostsev had been Alexander's tutor and became Procurator of the Holy Synod, the leading layman in the government of the Russian Orthodox Church. From this position he expounded a consistent philosophy of conservatism. He believed that democracy did not really work and would not work at all in Russia. He thought that democratic politicians were demagogues intent on deceiving the masses in order to maintain themselves in power. The Russian tradition, he argues, demanded a complete reliance on the autocracy of the Tsar and the religious message of the Orthodox Church. He supported the policy of total Russification attempted by Alexander III. In 1882, the Tsar forbade Jews to acquire land and restricted their admission to secondary schools and universities. In 1890, he decreed that all Jews in the interior had to emigrate to the western provinces. During these years, hundreds of thousands of Russian Jews fled the Tsarist persecution, many of them finding refuge in the United States. Viatcheslav Plehve was head of the secret police and minister of the interior under Nicholas II. He worked to promote the ideals of Panslavism and to repress the liberal and Marxist revolutionaries within the empire. During this period, too, some effort was made to introduce industry and build a modern communications network based on railroads. The moving figure behind these measures was Baron Sergei Witte. However, the Tsarist government was unwilling to commit itself to a total program of modernization for fear of the social and political consequences.

In the opening years of the twentieth century, Russia found herself ill-prepared to maintain her traditional position as one of the major powers. The Russo-Japanese War (1904–1905) served to demonstrate this fact to the world and to the Russians themselves. By the Treaty of Portsmouth (1905), Russia had to cede Port Arthur and the southern part of Sakhalin Island to Japan and to allow the Japanese to control Korea. She also turned Manchuria over to China. The disaster of the war was an important factor in the unrest leading to the Revolution of 1905. The regime succeeded in putting down that outbreak, but it was the last time. The next crisis, which came during World War I, proved too much. The despotism of the Tsars crumbled and fell.

Austria and Southeastern Europe

Throughout the nineteenth century, the rulers of Austria attempted to work out the problems rising from their sprawling multinational domain. Germans, Hungarians, Poles, Serbs, Croats, Czechs, and Italians were gathered together under the shadow of the Habsburg monarchy. In the eighteenth century, Maria Theresa and Joseph II had tried to weld these disparate elements into a modern state without spectacular success. The chief effort of their successors was the search for a formula that would contain the force of nationalism that threatened to tear the empire apart. The Revolutions of 1848 had come dangerously close to success in Austria, Hungary, and northern Italy. Thereafter, the wily Cavour had detached most of the Austrian territories in Italy, save Venetia, to add to his growing Sardinia-Piedmont. With the loss of Venetia in the sixties, Austria controlled only a few Italians in the Italian Tyrol. In Hungary, the pressures for independence from patriots like Louis Kossuth, who had fought in the American Revolution, resulted by 1867 in the *Ausgleich*, or compromise, that made Austria-Hungary a dual monarchy. Thereafter, the emperor faced the Hungarian Diet and the Austrian Diet on equal terms.

In the effort to placate all the varied forces in their empire, the Austrian rulers could not think of themselves as Germans. Previous attempts to Germanize the empire had ended in failure. Now, the German elements found themselves playing a smaller role in the empire. With the gradual recognition of the languages of the minorities in public life and education,

German tended to lose some of its distinctive position as the language of the empire and the Germans felt that they were in danger of inundation by Slavs. The unification of Germany by Bismarck during this period isolated Austria in a non-German world.

In the last decades of the century, the forces of disintegration began to gain the upper hand. The Viennese liberals lost out and turned to the arts as an outlet for their aspirations. In Bohemia and Hungary, strong independence movements continued to press for further separation from Austria. The Magyar aristocracy of Hungary demanded that the common imperial army be disbanded and only with difficulty did the emperor manage to stave them off. By the opening of World War I, the future of multinationalism was in the past; the Austrian Empire had failed. The question that remained was to determine what would replace it.

Even more desperate was the situation of the Ottoman Empire, whose European possessions at the beginning of the nineteenth century comprised much of the Balkans and at the end only a small strip of land in the vicinity of Istanbul (Constantinople). This empire, which had threatened all of Eastern Europe in the sixteenth and seventeenth centuries, was in its death throes. Its future rested with the great powers, who feared that the passing of the Ottoman sultan would destroy the equilibrium of the Near East and result in further gains for Russia and Austria. During most of this period, England and France tried to oversee the independence movements in the Balkans.

Attempts by the Sultans to reform their vast empire proved abortive. Mahmud II destroyed the power of the janissaries, the powerful army corps that had controlled the throne and prevented the reform of the empire. But this move, long overdue, came too late to arrest the spread of disintegration. Later reforms to grant equality to all non-Muslim subjects and to modernize the government also failed. Abdul Hamid II (1876–1909) went down in history as Abdul the Damned for his vicious efforts to put down revolts in Armenia and to root out subversives. By the turn of the century, a strong "Young Turk" reform movement advocated the westernization of their country.

The inability of the Ottoman sultans to hold onto their empire led to the gradual and bloody emancipation of most of the Balkans. This region, inhabited by Slavs, Greeks, Roumanians, and others was deeply fragmented. Not merely linguistic but also cultural and social cleavages divided its population. Intense hatreds between Greeks and Roumanians, Turks and Greeks, were characteristic of the area. As various of these peoples gained their independence from the Ottoman Empire in the course of the century, they translated their hatreds into national sentiments and directed them against their neighbors. But always a special dislike was felt toward the Turks and the Austrians, for there was a constant fear of being gobbled up into their empires.

By the eve of World War I, Eastern and Southeastern Europe had moved to the brink of tremendous internal changes. The old empires simply lacked the force or the will to maintain the position for which they had fought so long. The war provided just the right amount of force to cause the collapse of the old regime in each of these countries. Certainly in this part of Europe, it marked the end of the nineteenth century.

As this century progressed, Central and Eastern Europe had made some progress in the building of national states, especially in Germany. But the force of nationalism was only successful in much of Eastern Europe after World War I and largely as one of its results.

20 The Age of the Irrational

Reason is the peculiar ability of man to organize ideas to discover new concepts, patterns, and realities. From the Greeks through the early nineteenth century, man was chiefly concerned with the operation of reason and its exploitation to discover new veritics. In the eighteenth century, many thinkers became convinced that behind the whole order of the universe lay a rational plan that man might uncover. In reason, therefore, lay the key to all knowledge. This acceptance of natural rational ordering of all reality presumed the existence of a rational being to plan this order. God remained as the master-builder or architect of the universe in the thought of the Deists. In the mid-nineteenth century, certain theories and trends pointed to the importance of blind force as the directive element in the universe. This force did not operate from any moral grounds and did not exercise any rational choice in its development. It was irrational. From Darwin to Freud, thinkers worked to uncover the irrational elements in nature.

Preoccupation with the exploration of irrational elements has had a profound effect on contemporary civilization. The tradition that viewed man as a being of reason has had to give way to a more complex and, at times, diametrically opposed view. Needless to say, the new view of man has also influenced the interpretation of history. Modern scholars have largely rejected the theory of progress that influenced many historians of the eighteenth and nineteenth centuries. Under the impact of the irrational, the absolutes established by reason have suffered attack. This period, from 1850 to the opening of World War I marked a great shift in the history of Western thought.

The Impact of Evolution

Evolution means that change whereby something becomes different as a result of modifications of its own structure. In the idea of evolution, the new thing is always related to something that existed before. As applied in biology, evolution attempts to explain the development of more complex forms of life from simple ones. But the idea of evolution was never restricted to biology. The idea of change and the effort to understand the nature and causes of change had attracted the attention of thinkers at least since Heraclitus had maintained that "everything changes" in the seventh century, B.C. Evolution was in its origins, a philosophical rather than a scientific concept. However, during the early nineteenth century, some natural scientists had begun to explore the possibilities of a theory

Charles Darwin. Father of the theory of evolution. (Brown Brothers)

of evolution as an explanation for the existence of so many different varieties of life on earth. Jean-Baptiste Lamarck (1744–1829) and Charles Lyell (1797–1875) were pioneers in arguing that individual species change in such a way that entirely new species come into existence. But it remained for Charles Darwin to expound a fully developed theory of evolution in his *Origin of the Species* (1859).

Charles Darwin (1809–1882) was a careful scientist, who had collected mountains of data during his long voyage in the South Seas and on many other trips. He was the heir to a biology that had begun to develop a modern classification system in the mid-eighteenth century and was seeking the internal dynamic principles that produced the varieties of life. His contribution was to supply future scientists with an explanation of biological change. This theory maintained that evolution occurred because some

ON

THE ORIGIN OF SPECIES

BY MEANS OF NATURAL SELECTION,

OR THE

PRESERVATION OF FAVOURED RACES IN THE STRUGGLE
FOR LIFE.

BY CHARLES DARWIN, M.A.,

FELLOW OF THE ROYAL, GEOLOGICAL, LINNÆAN, ETC., SOCIETIES;
AUTHOR OF 'JOURNAL OF RESEARCHES DURING H. M. S. BEAGLE'S VOYAGE
ROUND THE WORLD.'

LONDON:
JOHN MURRAY, ALBEMARLE STREET.
1859.

The right of Translation is reserved.

The Origin of the Species, *title page. The appearance of this work revolutionized the science of biology. (Rare Book Room, Syracuse University Library)*

species were able to adapt to changing environmental conditions and thereby to survive while those less fit were destroyed. This "survival of the fittest" viewed the entire cycle of life from the view of the organism's essential needs to gather food and to protect himself against his enemies. Those that could escape or destroy their enemies and still obtain food thrived; the others died out. New species were the result of the survival of the strongest elements in older species. As Darwin posited the struggle for life, it was driven by a principle of natural selection: the fit should survive. Behind life lay not the ordered plan but the accident of physical force. In 1871, Darwin published his *Descent of Man,* in which he applied the theory of evolution to the development of man. His theory enabled biologists to study the world of living nature as part of a dynamically changing universe rather than as a static system of classification.

The immediate implication of Darwinian evolution appeared to some to be in the field of religion. Though Darwin himself had made no reference to God or creation, many felt that his theory was an attack on the validity of the account contained in the book of Genesis. Some, having accepted the extremely literal views of the Anglican Archbishop Ussher, believed that the world had been created in a week of seven days about four thousand years before the beginning of the Christian era. Other Christian thinkers were concerned about the theological implications of man's descent from lower animals. They believed that such teaching endangered the Christian position on the spiritual and distinctly human nature of the soul. Some also feared that Darwin's theory would provide the foundation for a materialistic explanation of the origin of man, a denial of the action of God in creation, and a rejection of Christian-based morality. The resulting conflict between science and religion, however, tended to center on the conflict between the account of creation contained in Genesis and the explanation offered by the theory of evolution. Some theologians fell into obsurantism and refused even to face up to the reality of scientific evidence; some scientists and popularizers, men like T. H. Huxley, often went to greater lengths to argue theology than to explain their scientific advances. In the long run, it was religion that had to reexamine its theological formulations in light of science. Theologians were able to argue that evolution did not really conflict with Genesis, because the author of that sacred work had intended to give a poetic interpretation of creation setting forth the role of God in making of the universe. However, this and other interpretations often fell on skeptical ears. They smacked of accommodation. Some religious sects, particularly among the Protestant fundamentalists, refused to accept evolution under any guise and attempted to prevent the teaching of the theory in the schools.

But the impact of Darwinian evolution on religion was, in a sense, merely one aspect of the conflict between religion and modern secular society. Since the Renaissance, Western society had been forging a secular foundation for its system of values. While the traditional moral principles of Christian ethics remained fundamental in this period, more and more thinkers were arguing that the foundation of morality did not lie in religious faith but in human integrity. By the nineteenth century, some romantic rebels like Byron had attempted to dramatize their rejection of religious morality. But the systematic development of a secular ethic based on social adjustment was the work of the French philosopher, Auguste Comte (1798–1857), whose philosophy of Positivism influenced many of the leading thinkers of the late nineteenth and early twentieth centuries and played an important part in the development of the modern social sciences. To Comte, science rather than religion was the true basis for morality, which was to be learned through the scientific investigation of society. Comte called this science of society, sociology.

The particular application of evolution to science served to stimulate thought about its meaning in other areas. The "survival of the fittest" was applied to society to justify the inequities of industrial civilization. Why should one man grow rich and command the labor of hundreds of others, while another was barely able to secure sufficient food and housing for himself and his family. Certainly, there was no question of justice or morality involved. The answer was that the rich man was both better endowed by nature and used those talents to their utmost advantage. In an age of imperialism, some Europeans argued for the supremacy of the white race over all others. Christian civilization and industrial society were the products of the native heritage of the white man. This racism was also directed against the Jews, who were looked down upon as inferiors within European society. The white race was born to rule the world. Thus Darwinism served as a justification for the European hegemony of most of the world established by the late nineteenth century.

The relationship between Darwinism and socialism is evident in the thought of Karl Marx. Darwin's theory of evolution offered a materialistic explanation of the origin and development of man. Since Darwin had emphasized the importance of environment in biological development, the socialists found justification for their argument on the primacy of economic considerations in society. "Moreover, where "scientific" socialism maintained that the dynamic force behind society was materialistic, that it was motivated by economics, Darwinian evolution set forth the force as natural selection. In neither case was reason the controlling agent; in neither was man the director. "Scientific" socialism shared in the irrationalism of evolution.

The leading thinker who championed the theory of evolution in its social implications was the English philosopher, Herbert Spencer (1820–1903). In his *Synthetic Philosophy,* Spencer attempted to set down a science of society along Comtian lines within the framework of evolution. An ardent supporter of industrial society, Spencer showed that the doctrine of evolution provided the true explanation for the growth of industrialism and the concentration of wealth. His popularizations were the vehicle whereby much of evolutionary theory became part of the stock in trade of the nineteenth-century liberal industrialists and their twentieth-century descendants.

The impact of Darwinism on the writing of history was strong. Yielding to an obvious temptation, evolution-minded historians saw the history of the nation—for they were mostly writing under the influence of nationalism, too—in terms of a continuing evolutionary progress that would ultimately result in the achievement of all the goals of the nation. The doctrine of the survival of the fittest was employed to justify national policies regardless of morality. The tremendous prestige of history in the nineteenth century gave to these works an aura of truth that sanctified their nationalistic contents.

In the industrial society of the second half of the nineteenth century, men labored under the tremendous impact of the machine. This inanimate and blind force brought home to them the great gap between the dictates of reason and the world in which they lived. Darwinism, applied in many different areas, offered a rationale for their society, explaining and justifying it to them by revealing the irrational elements underlying the development of life itself.

Literature, Art, and Music

Literature and the arts have always reflected the irrational element in a particular culture to a greater degree than most other disciplines. The creative writer or artist is introspective and subjective in his approach to external reality and hence tends to see it as an extension of his own identity. But in this period they focused on such irrational elements as the influence of environmental factors, the inability to grasp the world around them, and the desire to depict that world in a different light.

This age witnessed a democratization of culture. Cheap machine-printed books and newspapers combined with the beginnings of mass education to vastly increase the number of readers. The lower classes had little time for serious literature and found most of their entertainment in the papers, which often serialized melodramatic stories of workers and their children suffering at the hands of miserly landlords. The middle and upper classes not only had more time for literature, but also possessed better educational backgrounds that improved their tastes. Though often afflicted by snobbery, they read widely in the increasingly popular literary magazines and patronized the booksellers shops. If they preferred the poetry of Tennyson to that of Matthew Arnold and the novels of Thackeray and Dickens to those of Thomas Hardy, this preference reflected chiefly their love of the romantic even in a realistic setting. The fact is that art and literature were popular in both a good and bad sense. They had a wide appeal, but this appeal encouraged the publication of much that was inferior.

The major novelists of the period concerned themselves with the problems of the poor and the working class. Victor Hugo, famed for his romantic novels during the first half of the century, turned to a commentary on social conditions in *Les Miserables.* Honoré de Balzac described the social life of the French city and countryside in his novels. His characters suffer from the faults of the petty bourgoisie. In *Madame Bovary,* Gustave Flaubert related the story of the fall from virtue of young women of the middle class. During this same period, Russian literature came alive in the works of Leo Tolstoi, whose *War and Peace* may be viewed as one of the greatest tracts against warfare ever written. Fëdor Dostoevski explored the psychology of crime in *Crime and Punishment.* The leading English novelists were the popular William Makepeace Thackeray and Charles Dickens. Both wrote for the broad audience of the literary magazines. Both remained close to English experience in their writing. Dickens combined a romantic inclination with a penetrating vision of the social ills of contemporary England. No satirist, he nevertheless caricatured many of the leading types of his age. His heroes suffered grievously in hardly believable circumstances before gaining their victory at the end of the book; for Dickens much preferred the happy ending. Less popular and more profound was Thomas Hardy, whose *Return of the Native* relied heavily on environment and mood to recreate the tale of the tangled life of Eustacia Vye. His work plumbed deep into the psychological depths of his characters to find motives beneath the surface of reality in irrational factors that influence human behavior.

In poetry, the English poet laureate, Alfred, Lord Tennyson, wrote mostly of ages far removed from the grim present of nineteenth-century industrialism. He raised up the ideal of medieval chivalry captured in the image of Sir Galahad, the brave and pure seeker after the Holy Grail, in the *Idylls of the King*. "His strength was as the strength of ten, because his heart was pure." But Tennyson's escapism, if we may call it that, was something more. It represented the hope of his contemporaries for something that was worth more than the material world in which they were immersed. His poetry reminded them of values that could not be weighed or measured, of vicarious glories in which they might share by slaying dragons already dead, which was preferable to facing the realities of their present. The work of Robert Browning perhaps deserves more serious attention as literature than the poetry of Tennyson, but it is difficult to overlook the similarities between these contemporaries. Browning chose themes far removed from England. He spent many years in Italy and fell in love with the mystery of Italian aristocratic life. In technique, however, he was more inventive than Tennyson. His dramatic monologue—*My Last Duchess* is one of the best known examples—had the quality of a story told by a participant in figurative and poetic language. The poetry of Matthew Arnold pondered the central problem of the age. In *Dover Beach,* Arnold asked what had happened to reason and faith. He found little in the way of an answer. Force rather than reason and faith dominated the age as he saw it. ". . . we are here upon a purple plain, where ignorant armies clash by night."

Other writers, like the essayist John Ruskin and the socialist William Morris, sought escape from reality in aesthetics. Ruskin railed against the ugliness of factories. Like Morris, he attempted to show that true value came as the result of dedicated craftsmanship. He desired to see a restoration of the ideals of the medieval guilds. As a result of the harshness and bitterness of industrial life, Ruskin and others led a movement that romanticized the Middle Ages, holding them up as an ideal to the nineteenth century.

The chief playwrights of the age were the Swede, Henrik Ibsen, and the Irishman, George Bernard Shaw. Ibsen's *Doll's House* is a social and psychological study of the position of woman in a male-dominated society. Shaw, whose career lasted far into the contemporary period, was a master satirist and biting commentator on society. He laughed at men for trying to hold onto meaningless traditions of religion and morality, meaningless because they had lost all sense of their meaning. In Germany, playwrights like Alfred Sternberg satirized the strivings of the middle class for respectability and their complete lack of any really noble virtues. The greatest minds of the stage dedicated themselves to tearing down a social system they believed false.

This period produced some of the most outstanding painting and sculpture of any period since the Renaissance. Indeed, the painters were restless to create. During the fifties and for the next twenty years, realists like Jean François Millet and Gustave Courbet attempted to put on canvass the ordinary world of the common man. Millet's *Man with the Hoe* and *Angelus* caught essential aspects of the life of the peasants, their attachment to the soil and their loyalty to tradition. Realism did not try to explain what it saw, it simply questioned the mind by depicting scenes of everyday life. By taking these scenes out of context, the realist painters focused on the disparities between the life of the rich and that of the poor. But realism was not suitable for those painters who wished to escape or so enshroud their world that they would not have to face its rough edges. These impressionists wanted to paint reality as the eye saw it without study or meditation. They experimented with light and color in order to recapture the impression that the scene conveyed to them. Claude Monet produced landscapes in which the shadows echoed the scene depicted. Edgar Degas painted dancers alive with vital action. Auguste Renoir painted many different scenes but excelled in depicting the soft qualities of beauty in women and children. With Paul Cézanne, the artist forsook detail for broad expanses of geometric patterns, such as his famous studies of fishing villages. He loved to experiment with shadows cast by the sun across the varicolored roofs of houses. Vincent Van Gogh tormented his soul in the search for some reality within himself. Though he lived in poverty and drove himself to suicide, his painting achieved a quality that assured him of a place among the world's greatest artists. Gradually, painting became less concerned with realistic portrayal and more concerned about expressing the feelings of the artist. This tendency already existed in the work of Van Gogh, but came completely to the fore in the work of Pablo Picasso. Picasso rejected form almost completely in this period to portray his subjects under many different aspects simultaneously. Art moved toward cubism, which substituted geometrical forms greatly simplified and rearranged for the simple depiction of a subject. The artist was trying to see with his imagination rather than with his eyes and to depict what the imagination had come to rest on. Consequently,.art became more abstract.

While romanticism continued to exercise considerable influence on certain branches of music, particularly the opera, some composers experimented with the impressionist technique. Claude Debussy achieved extraordinary effects by ignoring the traditional rules of tonality and harmony. Igor Stravinsky and Arnold Schoenberg carried these experiments still further in the twentieth century.

The arts underwent dramatic changes during this period as they came to grips with industrial civilization. Characteristically, the response of the arts was more radical than in the fields of science and philosophy. The intuition of the artist sensed the profundity of the changes that were taking place and sought for radical answers. Consistent with the essentially irrational trend in late nineteenth-century intellectualism, the arts moved from realism toward a more subjective approach to reality. The eye no longer sufficed to experience what the artist wished to communicate; its role was now subordinated to emotion.

The Changing Dimensions of Man

Since the Renaissance thinkers had been striving for a secular interpretation of man. Drawing partly on Greek and Roman antiquity, humanistic writers of that period had exalted man's ability to achieve perfection through his own efforts. The Italians had coined the term *uomo universale* to describe those men endowed with *virtù,* the power to achieve perfection. This optimistic spirit about the possibilities of man dominated most of the sixteenth century, though the reformation cast long shadows over the humanistic notion of man, especially by asserting his utter dependence on God and by limiting the scope of free will. In the seventeenth century, however, the birth of new scientific and philosophical methodologies did much to restore human optimism. John Locke's essentially optimistic appraisal of human abilities provided a further stimulant to the thinkers of the eighteenth century. Despite the sometimes cynical outlook of thinkers like Voltaire in the *Candide,* most of the philosophers were firmly convinced that mankind was moving out of the shadow of superstition into the sunlight of reason. Rousseau and many of his contemporaries were optimistic that education would provide the true vehicle of human progress. Indeed, in this sense, the age of reason was essentially an educational movement aimed at teaching men to trust their own powers rather than seeking a solution in some divine mystery. The romantics did not reject this secular view of man or the theory of progress, but rather infused them with a new feeling. They emphasized the subjective elements in man's nature.

Ultimately the chief challenge to the acceptance of the theory of progress came from industrial society. The promise of a better life held in the invention of machinery had borne fruit in sweat shops, slums, poverty, and filth. The romantics had already rebelled against these conditions by attempting to escape from them or by proclaiming the answer in greater human liberty. But the gradual movement toward democracy had moved slowly to still the criticisms of the industrial age or to remedy the evils that accompanied it. In the last half of the century optimism and progress were put to the test and found wanting.

But what was man? Philosophy and psychology attempted to answer this question.

Friedrich Nietzsche (1844–1900) believed that man could still find the means to perfection but that they were within him. He also felt that there was no real achievement outside of the individual. His philosophy was basically existentialist in that it too denied ethical and social relationships the priority they had received in other philosophical systems and placed the integrity of the individual person at the center of its formulation. Nietzsche's "superman" was not a public person, part of a new elite or ruling class, but a man striving for perfection within his own being. Far from being the founder of any modern theory of a "master race," Nietzsche had no conception of a perfect political society as is implicit in the "master-race" theory. To Nietzsche, each man must be his own society.

Among the most significant advances made were in the development of an experimental psychology based on the study of human behavior. Since Aristotle had set down the definition of man as a "rational animal," psychology had concerned itself mostly with such questions as the nature of the soul and the manner in which man comes to know things outside of himself. As late as the seventeenth century, Descartes had made no further advance than to fall back on introspection as the ultimate basis for all knowledge. But experimental psychologists gave up what appeared to be a fruitless task of plumbing the secrets of man by introspection. They attempted to arrive at an understanding of his nature by studying his external activity. This quest was the starting point for the "behavioral" school of psychologists.

Pioneer work in psychology was carried on in both Europe and the United States. The chief figure in behavioral psychology in the United States was John Watson, whose work laid the foundations for a rapid advance of the discipline during the last decades of the nineteenth century. In Germany, Wilhelm Wundt was one of the earliest psychologists, but his work was overshadowed by the *Gestalt* movement, which argued that psychology must proceed from the study of the whole complex that was

Ivan Pavlov (center) and his staff. His studies of conditioned reflex in dogs were aimed at discovering patterns of human behavior. (The Bettmann Archive)

man. The Russian, Ivan Pavlov, performed startling experiments into conditioned reflexes. Using dogs as subjects, Pavlov got them accustomed to receiving food at the sound of a bell. Later, when the bell rang, the dogs salivated in anticipation of the food even though none was presented. His research was important in pointing out the basis for habits and for certain types of learning. The behaviorists viewed man not as a rational being but as a complex material being understandable in terms of reflexes and habits.

Departing from the techniques of experimental psychology, but employing the method of case study, Sigmund Freud (1856–1939) developed psychoanalysis for the treatment of mental disorders. Freud explored the mind to a depth that no other student of human psychology had even attempted. He maintained that man is largely motivated by unconscious drives and that reason as such plays only a minor role in human decisions. His emphasis on the importance of the sex instinct has led to popular distortion of his thought. Freud was not, for example, an exponent of free love or of unnatural sexual activities. Primarily, he was a scientist seeking to explain the system of controls operating in the person and to treat abnormalities. According to his view, each human person entered the world with certain basic drives that were still untrained. These reposed in the *id,* from the Latin term for "it," and were shaped by the organic structure of the individual. The child also develops an *ego,* the "I," the distinctive personality that results from the interaction of the person and his environment. He receives a *superego,* a body of rules or conscience, from society, his teachers, and parents. Freud believed that the *Ego* attempts to resolve conflicts between the *superego* and the *id.* The tensions between conscience and basic drives sometimes erupt in the form of mental illness. However, in the well-adjusted person, the *ego* sublimates or directs the drives of the *id* into other channels which have some social value. Freud therefore believed that the aim of psychoanalysis was to discover the conflict that caused the symptoms of an individual's illness and to work with him to understand and to sublimate his problem.

In general, the trends in philosophy and psychology, like those in science, literature, and the arts, pointed in this period to the importance of irrational elements in man, nature, and civilization. These discoveries had a very significant impact on modern thought. The rejection of pure rationalism has led many modern thinkers to seek an escape in some form of relativism, the position that truth is unknowable and that man can only hope for some temporary norms on which to base his action. In the early twentieth century, philosophers like William James and John Dewey advanced the idea of pragmatism, which tested the validity of means in terms of goals. The value of any act was judged by whether or not it worked. However, pragmatism was not amoral. Rather, in the hands of Dewey, it was molded to the democratic goals of American society. However, it contained much that was adaptable to other societies. Pragmatism dominated much of modern thought in the first half of the twentieth century.

Tho "irrational" aspect of man's being gained recognition throughout the second half of the nineteenth century. The discovery and exploration of this part of man has led to a deemphasis of reason and the influence of reason in almost every compartment of human life. The technical language of experimental psychology and psychoanalysis has created the clichés of contemporary speech. Yet the irrational was never limited merely to the realm of the arts and science. Nationalism and the national state possessed, in the view of Hegel, a dynamic force of their own. The materialistic dialectic of Marx revolted against reason and sought the explanation for historical development in the dynamics of material forces. The exploration of the irrational also opened up new dimensions in understanding man and inspired deeper study of his nature, being, and behavior.

21 The Climax of Western Leadership

Since the eighteenth century—and many historians would argue for a much earlier date, European dominance of the whole earth had moved rapidly toward reality. The cultural, scientific, and technological foundations for this dominance were laid early in the period and, as we have seen, their effects wrought significant changes in the society of Europe by the mid-nineteenth century. In another area, European dominance was potential rather than complete in 1850. Since the late fourteenth century Europeans had been deeply committed to the exploration and exploitation of the earth. However, during the late eighteenth century, the liberals began to argue against imperialism and in favor of free trade. It was not until after 1850, especially with the increasing competition in foreign trade from the United States and Germany, that interest in control over colonial possessions began to grow. The dominance of Europe over virtually all parts of the world became an accomplished fact by the beginning of the twentieth century. Yet the resultant tensions were a contributing factor that led Europe into World War I.

This war, global not merely by reason of the battles fought by Europeans in Asia and Africa, but also by reason of the involvement of non-Western powers, marked the climax of Western leadership. At the end of the war, Europe still was dominant, but the forces that would threaten to end that dominance had been set in motion.

The World as the West

During the last decades of the nineteenth century, many Europeans accepted as a matter of course the view that Europe had a mission to civilize the world. By that they meant the work of introducing the peoples of Asia and Africa to Western European culture. These unfortunate peoples should learn to wear Western clothes, to eat Western foods, to live in Western-style houses, to imitate Western manners, to speak Western languages, to think Western thoughts, and to aspire to the Western dream of a modern society. Of course, there were certain limitations, in practice if not in theory. It was usually accepted that these peoples had no ability to rule themselves, that their political institutions were archaic and valueless, and that they were not able to learn how to operate political systems according to the Western mode. Therefore, they had to be guided or, more bluntly, ruled by Europeans. Only the tasks of administration on the very lowest level could be permitted to the natives. Ironically enough, many Asians and Africans continued under the rule of their former governments because the Western powers found it easier to operate through such traditional forms. Still, these people came into gradual contact with Europe.

The motives behind European expansion in the second half of the nine-

Imperialism: the world's plunderers. This criticism of imperialism has an anti-English bias. (The Bettmann Archive)

teenth century were largely economic and national. Colonies meant markets in the atmosphere of the increasing competition of that age just as they had in the great era of the mercantilists. Though some historians have argued, with considerable evidence, that most colonies were not economically successful, the belief that they would be successful was of primary importance in arousing support from businessmen for colonial ventures. Yet the economic motivation has often been overstated while other factors have received less attention. The influence of nationalism was considerable. The strong feelings of identity with the nation that developed in the period carried over into all enterprises in which the nation was engaged. Nationalist politicians frequently used the arguments of imperialism to bolster their position on the domestic scene, a pattern laid down by Napoleon III and pursued by him with considerable success. Nationalistic jingoism aroused the masses to support imperialistic expansion on grounds of national honor and the sacred mission of the people. Rudyard Kipling spoke of the "white man's burden" in very much this sense. Beyond the solid economic reasons for expansion, there were also intangible and sometimes almost mystical appeals to the traditions of a particular people that transcended any economic motive and found their ultimate foundation in the growth of the national spirit.

Thus, it is impossible and even dangerous to attempt to separate imperialism from nationalism. Without the development of the national state, imperialism might have come in the form of economic rivalries between commercial and industrial powers for control of underdeveloped areas. But nationalism added the element of national pride and honor that intensified these rivalries and created an emotionally charged atmosphere from which statesmen and politicians found it increasingly difficult to extricate themselves or their countries. Nationalism provided a spark that could ignite these tensions into war.

Moreover, in still another sense, imperialism and nationalism must be examined together. The history of Europe's involvement in the non-Western world has shown that nationalism and imperialism traveled together into these lands. Wherever Western imperialism took root, the beginnings of national movements aimed at creating a new nation modeled on the Western nation-state began to develop. If imitation is the highest form of flattery, the West could feel flattered by the fact that fledgling nationalist movements sprang up in Asia in the late nineteenth century. The new nationalist leaders had learned from their European masters.

The expansion of the West during the last half of the century was foreshadowed not merely in the building of the first empires of the sixteenth and seventeenth centuries, but also in the continuing expansion of nations like Russia and the United States, which pushed their frontiers across continents as part of the growth of the nation itself. Also, there were numerous opportunities for imperialistic expansion in these years. In Africa, which still remained very much a mystery save for the North, and in Asia, which hung back from acceptance of Western technology, the West met opportunities to buy raw materials and to sell the products of their machines. However, it was not enough merely to buy and sell; the intense rivalries between industrial nations demanded a measure of control to assure the market for one's own nationals. Africa, although populous, was uncrowded by European standards. Some nations sought new lands to provide for their surplus populations. Nor can one ignore the political and economic instability in Asia and Africa that invited intervention in the name of maintaining order.

Early ventures by France and England in North Africa and the Near East were largely the result of their concern over the decline of the Ottoman Empire and their fear of the possible impact of this event on European diplomacy. Just as they had intervened in the Crimean War to prevent Russian expansion, so each of these powers kept watch on the other, lest one emerge as the leading power in that area. The most important results of this policy were the expansion of French power eastward from Algeria and the countermoves of England in Egypt and the Sudan to prevent total French dominance.

Egypt was nominally subject to the sultan, but its rulers (pashas) had gradually asserted their independence. Modernization began under Mohammed Ali (1805–1849). This effort began to meet with important results in the reign of Ismail (1867–1879). Unfortunately, the cost of modernization taxed the country far beyond its resources and the improvements could be carried out only by borrowing huge sums from European bankers. The French were especially influential. They planned and built railroads and took the initiative in the formation of the Suez Canal Company. However, overextension of the resources of the country resulted in virtual collapse. The Egyptians lost their important bloc of shares in the Suez Canal Company by sale to the English, but no measures were enough to prevent the country from going into financial receivership. When Ismail attempted to repudiate his debts, the English and French combined to force his abdication. His successor eventually had to agree to outside control of finances. Unfortunately for the French, whose interests were greater, the English managed to secure their position with the appointment of Lord Cromer as Egypt's financial adviser in 1883.

His administration put the country back on the road to solvency, but did little to remedy the basic economic problems of Egypt or to continue the task that Ismail had undertaken. This British action left a legacy of French bitterness that bubbled over as the British began to move into the Sudan and other parts of Africa.

By the outbreak of World War I, the map of Africa contained only two independent native states. Liberia, the only independent Negro ruled nation on the continent was founded by American Negroes, returned to Africa to find a new life of freedom. But they were foreigners and not well accepted by the Africans native to that region. Moreover, they had alienated the natives by their own behavior. Ethiopia, a Christian kingdom, whose ruler claimed descent from the Queen of Sheba, had defeated an Italian attempt at conquest in 1896 and preserved a measure of independence under increasing foreign influence. The remainder of the continent was explored, divided, and colonized during the last half of the century.

Western knowledge of African history and its social and economic life has long subsisted near the level of the Tarzan books created by Edgar Rice Burroughs. Tropical jungles, unknown dangers from wild animals of strange appearance as well as from cannibals and pygmies, and a level of tribal life similar to that of the North American plains Indians were part of the general impression. The facts were, however, far different. There was not one Africa, but at least two. The North and West extending even south of the Sahara into the wide belt of savannah north of the equator was predominantly Arab-speaking and Moslem in religion. The mingling of Negro and Semitic peoples in this area had gone on for centuries. But there were other racial traces, one of the most important being the Hamitic, which had existed in this region since the days of the early Egyptians. South of the savannah stretched tropical Africa and the great veldts or prairies of the South. Most of the peoples of this area were Negro, though the differences between individual peoples were often great. What is most remarkable about Africa south of the Sahara is not its lack of civilization, but rather the relatively high degree of political and social organization that did exist. Most Africans lived in villages and practiced agriculture. Though not highly developed from a technological point of view, African political society was far from primitive. The chief reason why it succumbed so rapidly to the Europeans was their possession of superior weapons.

The major European powers in Africa were England, France, Germany, Portugal, and Italy. The English moved south from Egypt into the Sudan and northward from the Cape of Good Hope. The French expanded their position from their base in Algeria into West Africa and eastward toward the Sudan. For a short time, it appeared certain that their eastward expansion would involve them in war with England. However, agreement between the two governments ended this threat. The Germans began to trade and colonize in both East and West Africa. The Portuguese gained control of Angola in West Africa and the island of Mozambique, while the Italians concentrated their efforts partly in North Africa and partly along the coast of the Red Sea. Their ill-fated effort to conquer Ethiopia in 1896 put an end to further expansion in that area until the coming of the Fascist regime. However, one of the major territories that came under European control did not belong to any government, but was the personal property of King Leopold of Belgium, who formed a private international corporation to run the Congo Free State. Although French and English administration has often been regarded as enlightened because of provision for health and limited educational and economic opportunities, little progress was made in any of these African colonies toward a full-scale economic, social, and political development until well into the twentieth century. What progress did come was largely reserved to the white minorities who constituted an economic and political ruling class.

The division of Africa was possible because that continent had remained in the hands of primitive peoples unable to offer any significant resistance to the determined efforts of the European powers. Asia presented an altogether different situation. The civilizations of Asia dated back thousands of years and had won the respect of the Europeans. Although frequently too weak to offer serious resistance to Western expansion, the governments of Asia were powerful enough to maintain some measure of political control over their territories and had traditions from periods when they wielded great power. Some, like the Chinese, looked down upon the European "barbarians" and attempted to prevent them from having direct contact with their venerable civilization. Others, like the Indians, who had succumbed early to rule by Portugal, France, and, later, England, had men of wealth and culture who were regarded by the Europeans as equals. The Japanese, who for most of the period from the sixteenth through the early nineteenth century had successfully limited Western trade and contacts, set a different pattern by deliberately attempting to imitate Western manners and to develop Western-style industry and trade. Thus, in Asia, the pattern of European expansion varied depending largely on local conditions.

China has often been termed the "sick man of Asia." The facts support this diagnosis. This sprawling nation of some three hundred million persons in 1850 was still attempting to live as it had for centuries. The Manchu or Ch'ing dynasty, which had gained power by conquest in the seventeenth century, was in the last stages of self-strangulation. Had no Europeans appeared, it would have eventually fallen in one of the periodic revolutions or invasions that marked the transfer of power in China. The Manchu lived remote from the Chinese people. They knew very little about the world outside. Suspicious of foreigners, they lacked either the intellectual curiosity or the political acumen to examine the strangers they found in their midst. Consequently, they consistently underrated the strength of the Europeans. The Manchu resolutely led China to submission without pausing to examine the alternatives. Their heady conservatism prevented them from recognizing until much too late the fact that the "barbarians" possessed superior military power and a culture that did much to promote aggressive action through the built in tensions within it. Since the Chinese generally failed to understand the men of the West, they came to fear and then to hate things Western. Throughout the second half of the century, the period during which the Western powers were most actively setting up spheres of influence for themselves, China reacted chiefly in waves of antiforeign demonstration. The most notable and last was the Boxer Rebellion of the early twentieth century, which enjoyed for a time the secret support of the empress dowager. However, since the Chinese were not strong enough to enforce their antiforeign policies, such outbreaks merely invited further advances by the European powers.

The major European imperialist powers in China each attempted to create separate spheres of influence in which their merchants and businessmen would enjoy the protection of their own law and of their own government. France had moved into Indo-China in the fifties and continued to expand into Yünnan Province during the remainder of the century. The English obtained Hong Kong and access to Canton and other major ports as a result of the Opium War in the early forties. The Germans, who did not arrive until after unification of their country, nevertheless made significant gains by obtaining concessions on the Shantung Peninsula, while Russia moved southward from Siberia into Manchuria and Port Arthur. However, the Russian advance met resistance from the Japanese, who pursued their own imperialistic ends in Korea and Manchuria. By 1914, China was dismembered, but was also beginning to awaken. One of the most important leaders of this awakening was the American-trained physician, Dr. Sun Yat Sen, an arch opponent of the

Manchu, who led his revolutionary movement to success in 1911–1912 and set up a nationalist republic. Sun's efforts to create parliamentary government were frustrated by the military. China found herself unable to create strong democratic government at home at the very moment when an aggressive Japan was beginning to make demands that amounted to placing her under a protectorate.

During the early part of the nineteenth century, the Japanese had continued to limit severely foreign contacts with their island empire. During the fifties, however, mounting pressure from the Western powers forced a reexamination of this policy. Many Japanese came to support the view that Japan had to take positive steps to modernize herself in the Western manner or she would follow the road already traveled part way by China. The chief opposition to the Westernizers came from the shoguns, the actual rulers of Japan. As a result, the Westernizers looked to the emperor as a rallying point. During the sixties, the Westernizers took advantage of the shoguns' increasing difficulties with foreign powers to overthrow their rule and reestablish the imperial authority. What followed was the Meiji period, an age of enlightenment, during which Japan rapidly copied Western military and industrial techniques, introduced a code of law based upon the French, and encouraged the adoption of Western manners and dress. Of course much of this process of Westernization was superficial, but the Japanese were able to understand the policies of the European nations and to adapt their own diplomacy in accordance with them. As a result, Japan became the chief military power in Asia and entered into the race to secure recognition of her place as the foremost Asian power. Her aggressive imperialism led her to assert her dominance first in Korea and then to challenge the Russian attempt to dominate Manchuria. The Russo-Japanese War, which broke out in 1905, revealed to the Western powers the success of the Japanese in modernizing their army and navy and brought her recognition as a world power.

The great Indian subcontinent was also an important area of imperialistic development in the Far East along with Southeast Asia. Since the sixteenth century, the Portuguese, the Dutch, and later the French and English, had extended their commercial interests in this broad area. In the seventeenth century, the Dutch managed to gain an edge in the rich spice trade of the East Indies and in the following century, England gradually ousted the French from their Indian trading posts and garrisons. However, in the nineteenth century, the tempo and quality of activity changed. The English government assumed responsibility for the rule of India from the British East India Company. Following the Sepoy re-

Perry in Japan. The Japanese decided that the policy of isolation might lead their country to subjection to the Western powers in the nineteenth century. (The Bettmann Archive)

bellion in the fifties, the English came to rely heavily on the native maharajahs for support in northern India while they administered the south directly. In 1867, Disraeli conferred the title "Empress of India" on Queen Victoria. India's development of native industry and her value as a source for raw materials made her the chief jewel in the English crown. But on the eve of World War I, an increasingly articulate and Western-educated group of Indian leaders began to press for greater independence.

Western dominance over most of the world was more than an economic and political hegemony. Important as these aspects were as vehicles of a superior technology, in the long run the most important factor was the impact of European culture, especially nationalistic concepts, on the non-Western world. This age of imperialism represented a real turning point in that Europe not only achieved hegemony but also planted seeds that were to lead to the gradual overthrow of European political power during the first half of the twentieth century throughout most of Asia and Africa.

The unleashing of nationalism proved to be the foundation of these independence movements, most of whose leaders had received Western educations. Some followed the road of liberalism and representative government, some took up the ideas of socialism and even Marxist communism, but all were true representatives of Western culture in their countries. They became the leaders of a great revolutionary movement to roll back the political and economic imperialism of the Western powers while benefiting from their technology and science. Thus, as World War I broke across the earth, Europe entered a new age of transition.

The Tensions Within the European State-System

Historians who have concentrated on the period prior to World War I and who have studied the causes of that war have almost all pointed to the developing tensions between the leading nations of Europe in the period from 1890 to 1914. Certainly, in comparison with the preceding decades, this period was one of tremendous diplomatic activity and one which saw numerous threats to the peace of the world. The rivalries of the powers in their quest for colonies led to frequent crises, some of a serious nature. Yet not all of the tensions within the European state-system are traceable to imperialistic factors. National honor and prestige were also at stake. Indeed, the future of man could depend on popular reaction to some insult to the nation. Moreover, underlying the entire climate of international affairs was the transformation of European society by the growth of industry and the accompanying social tensions. The great calm that had marked so much of nineteenth-century foreign affairs was drawing to a close.

On the surface, Europe was enjoying an almost unprecedented prosperity in the years just before the war. Even the working classes had more than at any other period in the past. The growth of social welfare programs, though far from universal, went a long way toward alleviating some of the more urgent ills of industrial society. But what was more important, there was promise of more to come. The future did not look so bleak as the past. Yet hope, which should inspire patience, has very often been the instrument of unrest. Although some progress had come and more was on its way, the ugliness of present reality pressed against the workers and their leaders to cause them to ask for that "more" immediately. Agitation increased in most of Europe in this period. England weathered the budget crisis and the reform of the House of Lords in 1911. France attempted to divert its workers with large doses of nationalism. In

Germany, the Kaiser ignored his parliament and the signs of increasing social unrest while he pursued the imperial will-o'-the-wisp. In Austria-Hungary, the old regime held on for dear life in hope that some better future might suddenly dawn. Southeastern Europe smoldered with unrestrained nationalistic feeling that threatened the peace of the area. Finally, the fearsome government of the Russian autocracy, shaken by internal revolution and the Russo-Japanese War of 1905 propped itself up with severely repressive measures and dreams of its invincibility. Under these circumstances, while it is correct to say that there was no real desire for war in any of these countries, it is even more correct to say that the leaders of the European powers were not unalterably opposed to war either. In fact, some even saw advantages that might accrue from war.

If internal social and political pressures created a climate favorable to the outbreak of war, these had significant help from the growth of nationalistic sentiments among the masses. The popular press, which had come into its own in the late nineteenth century with the spread of literacy, caught up the jingos and slogans of national honor and made these too often a substitute for responsible journalism. But the masses were receptive. The spread of universal military conscription created the idea of the citizen soldier. Pride in uniform and even some remains of medieval chivalric conceptions of warfare became part of the popular image of the army. Military parades became expressions of popular national feelings. There were few critics of militarism. Once the mighty behemoth of the popular will turned its hatred against another power and the whole machinery of nationalistic propaganda began to crank out messages exaggerating the insults to national honor and the dangers to national sovereignty, it traveled forward under its own power, grinding under all opposition and ignoring all messages of caution. In this sense, the democratic will became a dangerous instrument of nationalistic aggrandizement.

Before 1890, Bismarck had worked to preserve peace through an alliance of the powers of Eastern and Central Europe. England had remained aloof and France was therefore isolated. However, the diplomatic relations of the powers shifted dramatically following the dismissal of the "Iron Chancellor" by Kaiser William II. Germany moved closer to Austria-Hungary at the expense of her Russian ally; France took advantage of Germany's lapse to enter an alliance with Russia. When England and France settled their colonial differences in North Africa, these two powers found it expedient to work more closely together. Thus, the Franco-Russian alliance took on a new coloring as the British moved closer to France. Behind these shifts lay the story of the changing balance of power in Europe.

The idea of the balance of power was not new; England had worked to secure allies on the continent in the seventeenth and eighteenth centuries to counterbalance the French superiority. But through most of the nineteenth century, the English had held themselves aloof from continental affairs. Secure on their island with the most powerful navy in the world, they had not felt the need of continental allies. However, the unification of Germany and Italy materially changed the situation in Europe. Under Bismarck, Germany had emerged as the leading military power on the continent. However, as we have noted, his cultivation of peace, which had included a policy of friendship with England, combined with Franco-British rivalries elsewhere in the world to discourage the English from entering into any European alliances against the Germans. What altered this picture and pursuaded England to change her stance was primarily the increasing threat of Germany under the aggressive leadership of Kaiser William II and the growing conflicts between England and other industrial powers, especially Germany.

Under William II, Germany moved rapidly to assert her power. Where Bismarck had remained a reluctant supporter of imperialistic ventures, William anxiously pressed to secure a "place in the sun" for Germany. When the French, for example, moved to set up a protectorate over the independent sultanate of Morocco, William visited Tangiers and announced his support of the sultan. France had to back down. Again, in 1911, a German gunboat appeared in the Moroccan port of Agadir to protect German "interests." However, these interests were not in Morocco but in the Congo. The Germans were simply applying pressure to force the French to give them a strip of territory in West Africa. This time, England backed France and the Germans had to allow the French to establish the Moroccan protectorate in return for a token concession in West Africa. During this same period, the Germans were pressing their interests in the East, especially on the Shantung Peninsula in China. Concern about German activity in that area, plus the aggressive action of Russia, had led the British to seek an alliance with Japan. Thus, Britain moved into the new alliance structure in Europe, and in Asia, partially as a result of the aggressive imperialism of Germany.

But imperial rivalries represented only one side of the coin. The rapid industrialization of Germany and the tremendous increase in United States industry in the post-Civil War period radically altered the economic scene. The British had stood as the bastion of free trade during the mid-nineteenth century and into the eighties. However, during that time, they had encountered no serious threat to their hegemony as the greatest industrial and commercial power in the world. With the quick bid of the United States and Germany and the progress made in France under Napoleon III and the Third Republic, the English position faced a serious challenge. What made the problem more acute was the policy of protective tariffs aimed at restricting British imports that more and more countries adopted in the eighties and nineties. The English were slow to retaliate, but support for high tariffs against goods from the United States and the continent mounted under the leadership of the Liberal Joseph Chamberlain, who opposed Gladstone's "little England" policies. The adoption of high tariffs in England in retaliation for the actions of other nations was more a reaction to German industrial and commercial expansion than it was to France. Once more, England found reasons for drawing closer to the French.

Thus, England's rapprochement with France and the gradual formation of the Triple Entente of England, France, and Russia proceeded partly from German failure to continue a close alliance with Russia, partly from the removal of tensions between France and England, and partly because Germany had adopted an aggressive imperialistic policy that conflicted with the interests of both England and France in Africa and Asia. The resultant polarization pushed the countries of the Triple Entente closer together and separated them from the Central Powers, Germany and her chief ally, Austria-Hungary.

Yet when war came, it was only partly the result of the tensions we have described thus far. Nationalism, imperialism, high tariffs, jingoism—all of these factors were important. But the historian cannot ignore the accidental aspects of the problem. Indeed, modern scholars have become fascinated with the idea that World War I was an accident. Rather than attempting to fix guilt with one nation or even to distribute it according to its just proportions, these writers have taken the position that in an atmosphere of crisis brought on by the assassination of the Austrian Archduke Francis Ferdinand by a Serbian nationalist, European statesmen lost control of the situation. War ensued. It began in July and August, 1914.

War and Peace

The assassination of Francis Ferdinand was an act of terrorism by a Serbian nationalist. Suitably enough, therefore, the act that precipitated the crisis that led to war sprang from the spirit of nationalism. This fact was even more fitting than appearances might first suggest, for World War I was the first test of the national state, a war in which huge armies of conscripts struggled to defend the principle of nationhood. Behind all the slogans lurked the spirit of nationalism.

There was no immediate necessity for the war. Austria blamed the Serbs for the murder of Ferdinand and demanded satisfaction. The Austrian demands amounted to a surrender of sovereignty by the Serbs. Russia, from her position as the mother of all the Slavs, announced her support for the Serbs. Germany hesitated briefly before pledging aid to Austria. Yet the decision for war was not clear-cut. To enforce her demands, Austria mobilized. Russia also mobilized, though her leaders wanted only a partial mobilization to support their diplomacy. Germany responded with a demand for demobilization of Russia and, failing to receive assurances that her request would be heeded, declared war on Russia on August 1, 1914. The attack on Russia immediately brought France into the war. England remained neutral until August 4, when it was clear that she had no alternative. Then she announced that she was joining France because the Germans had invaded neutral Belgium in violation of international treaties guaranteeing Belgian neutrality. Italy remained outside the war until 1915, then declared war on Austria and Germany. Japan joined England and used the war as a pretext for taking over the German concessions on the Shantung Peninsula. The United States stayed neutral until 1917, then maintained that German submarine warfare was its reason for going to war. The Ottoman Empire, the Balkan countries, and many smaller countries chose sides in the contest. It was a world war.

At first, military initiative lay with the Germans. Following their planned strategy, they decided on a holding action on the Eastern front, while the main forces of their armies removed France from the struggle before England could come to her aid. The Schlieffen Plan, named for the general who originated it, was no sudden proposal. The Germans had built their roads and railroads with it in mind. They wanted a quick victory and a negotiated peace similar to the events of the Franco-Prussian War of 1870. The plan called for accurate timing and almost perfect coordination of Eastern and Western fronts. Unfortunately, its major weakness was its reliance on the Austrians to support their section of the line on the Eastern front. Before the Germans were able to achieve their telling blow at Paris, the Russians launched an offensive that broke the Austrian lines and pressed against the Germans in East Prussia; forcing the transfer of troops from the West to the East. This weakening of the

Western lines at the crucial moment gave the British time to land some of her forces in Belgium. The British lines held and the Germans were stopped. However, they were still the dominant military power; the delay might not have injured their cause for long. They had technological and logistical superiority during most of the early part of the war. But the Germans relinquished the initiative and permitted themselves to be drawn into a defensive war on Franco-British terms. This long delay—for four years the lines of trenches varied but little—allowed the French and English to build up their war machines and to deprive the Germans of their initial advantage.

During the second phase of the war—the longest in terms of time—the Western front settled down to trench warfare with periodic attempts by each side to break through the other's defenses. Tragically, the major battles of this period cost hundreds of thousands of lives and brought no major breakthrough. When Marshal Foch, French Commander at Verdun, declared "They shall not pass," he did so at a cost of more than half a million men, three-fifths of them his fellow Frenchmen. At the Battle of the Somme in 1916, total losses ran over a million. Yet most men hated the filth, disease, and boredom of the trenches even more than they feared the moment of battle. At least, for what may have been the last seconds

German soldiers going over the top. Such advances often gained nothing, while numerous lives were lost. (*The Bettmann Archive*)

or minutes of life they had escaped the rats, lice, fever, pneumonia, flu, dirt, and fellow human beings that made trench warfare so difficult.

On the Eastern front, the pace of this second phase was different. Opposition to the German armies was not serious; the only real problem was to avoid defeat at the hands of the terrible Russian winter. The German decision was to hold Poland and Roumania along with much of western Russia, but to make no sustained effort at total conquest. After all, the Russians themselves posed no threat to their armies. Russia was falling apart during the war. Before it would end, she would occupy herself with more important affairs at home; the making of a revolution.

World War I differed from previous wars in many ways. The numbers of men and countries involved, the geographical spread, the types of weapons, the strategy and tactics, the mobilization, the involvement of the homefront—all of these factors differed significantly from the Napoleonic wars and even from the Franco-Prussian War. The millions who fought at the front received direct support from the millions who worked in factories and foundries making weapons, trucks, tanks, and airplanes, or processing food. The war was global on land and sea. Terrible new weapons destroyed the enemy. The submarine slid through murky depths to deliver the deathblow to the unsuspecting merchantman. (A remaining trace of chivalry in some submarine commanders led them to surface and warn their victim before sinking his ship, but this practice was dangerous for the submarine, whose chief protection was concealment.) Machine guns and heavy cannon spewed out death. Airplanes and balloons spotted for the artillery, while the planes dropped bombs and engaged in the romantic dogfights that brought thrills into the heart of youth. But the life of the pilots was short. Trucks hauled men and supplies. Tanks were armored weapons carriers, moving forts. Railroads were the arteries of the armies. World War I was the last of the great fortress wars and the first of the mobile wars. Verdun signified defense; the Schlieffen Plan called for mobility. This war brought whole nations to arms and involved them in the war effort for the first time. Even the housewife found herself making bandages for the wounded or leaving the sanctuary of the home for the factory. World War I was almost totally different in the concern of the governments for propaganda and morale at home as well as on the front. It was a war of almost total involvement which eroded many of the long-standing moral positions on the right of nations to achieve their goals through military power. But, ironically, it was almost the last romantic war, fought in accordance with the belief that it would end all wars.

One weapon of World War I was so terrible that its use threatened the

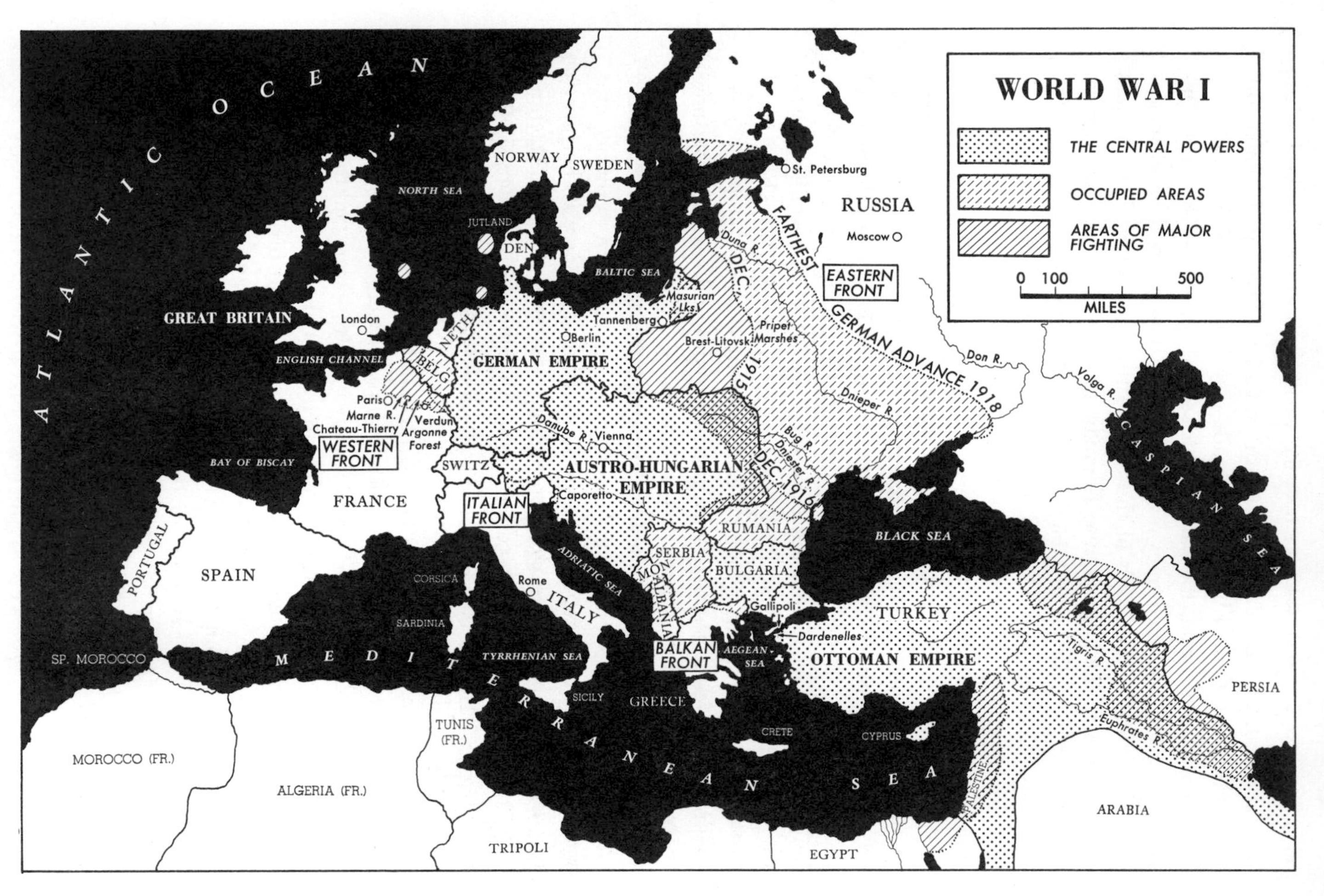
WORLD WAR I
THE CENTRAL POWERS
OCCUPIED AREAS
AREAS OF MAJOR FIGHTING
0 100 500
MILES
ATLANTIC OCEAN
NORTH SEA
NORWAY
SWEDEN
St. Petersburg
RUSSIA
Moscow
JUTLAND
DEN
BALTIC SEA
Duna R.
DEC.
FARTHEST GERMAN ADVANCE 1918
EASTERN FRONT
GREAT BRITAIN
London
Masurian Lks.
Tannenberg
Berlin
Pripet Marshes
Brest-Litovsk
NETH
ENGLISH CHANNEL
BELG
GERMAN EMPIRE
1915
Don R.
Volga R.
Paris
Marne R.
Chateau-Thierry
Verdun
Argonne Forest
Dnieper R.
Danube R.
Vienna
Bug R.
Dniester R.
WESTERN FRONT
BAY OF BISCAY
SWITZ
AUSTRO-HUNGARIAN EMPIRE
DEC. 1916
CASPIAN SEA
FRANCE
ITALIAN FRONT
Caporetto
RUMANIA
BLACK SEA
PORTUGAL
SPAIN
CORSICA
Rome
ADRIATIC SEA
SERBIA
MON
BULGARIA
ALBANIA
ITALY
Gallipoli
TURKEY
SARDINIA
Dardenelles
Tigris R.
SP. MOROCCO
MEDITERRANEAN SEA
TYRRHENIAN SEA
BALKAN FRONT
AEGEAN SEA
OTTOMAN EMPIRE
PERSIA
SICILY
GREECE
TUNIS (FR.)
CRETE
CYPRUS
Euphrates R.
MOROCCO (FR.)
ALGERIA (FR.)
PALESTINE
ARABIA
TRIPOLI
EGYPT

utter destruction of whole armies and raised questions about its morality. This weapon was gas. The invention of mustard gas, which burned and asphyxiated any who inhaled it, pointed up the role played in warfare by modern technology. Only the threat of full retaliation controlled its use.

The turning point of the war came in 1917. The inability of the Germans to break through the allied lines was the telling factor. As the war dragged on, initiative passed to the defenders. The entry of the United States into the war in support of England and France helped to turn the tide. The Germans made a gigantic effort to breach the allied lines in mid-1918. Though this second Battle of the Marne cost the allies alone about one million casualties, it netted the Germans nothing. Moreover, American supplies began to roll to the support of the allies in larger amounts. American food was especially important in removing the threat of starvation. Before the end of the summer, troops of the United States Expeditionary Force were arriving in France in large numbers. By early

German prisoners of war. Thousands dwelt in camps while the war raged on. (Brown Brothers)

September, 1918, Germany was on the verge of collapse. A last-ditch effort by the Kaiser to restore public confidence by appointing the liberal Prince Max of Baden Imperial Chancellor failed and the crackup of both the army and the homefront followed. Faced with revolution, the Kaiser resigned and fled to neutral Holland. On November 11, Germany agreed to terms for an armistice and accepted defeat. The war was over.

The end of World War I meant the beginning of an effort to build the peaceful order that the victorious leaders had promised. President Woodrow Wilson had issued Fourteen Points in January, 1918, aimed at establishing the foundation for a "just and lasting" peace. Many historians have condemned Wilson for presenting too idealistic a plan. Some of them have ignored the fact that the Fourteen Points was a unilateral declaration of an American President at a time when the prestige of the United States still did not carry great weight in European matters. But there is another point to consider. The Fourteen Points proved more realistic in the long run than the actual settlement of the Treaty of Versailles. Though not all points were attained, a surprising number of them have a note of prophecy. The fourth point, seeking a reduction of armaments, presaged the great "peace drive" of the twenties and thirties to limit navies and outlaw war. The fifth point permitted native populations a voice in settlement of colonial claims; the postwar period showed that it would not long be possible to prevent these people from taking an important role in their own affairs. Point Seven and Point Thirteen guaranteed self-determination to Russia and Poland. Twelve would have set up an independent Turkey; the Turks seized the initiative for themselves after the war. Indeed, the only idealism that might have appeared unreal was contained in the Fourteenth Point. It called for the establishment of "an association of nations" to guarantee territorial integrity and the political independence of great and small states. Thus, the aim of this league of nations was to protect the national state from self-annihilation.

In fact, however, Wilson's Fourteen Points did not form the basis for the peace settlement. The treaties that officially concluded the war were hammered out by the leaders of the great powers in the months between January and April, 1919. The chief figures at the peace conference were: Woodrow Wilson, President of the United States; David Lloyd George, Prime Minister of England; Georges Clemenceau, Premier of France; and Vincente Orlando, Premier of Italy. The Germans were not permitted to participate in the conference; they were handed the completed treaty and

The Big Four. David Lloyd George, Vincente Orlando, Georges Clemenceau, and Woodrow Wilson at a moment of relaxed tensions. (Brown Brothers)

asked to sign. The same was true for the other defeated powers. In all there were five separate treaties with the various enemies, the most important of which was the Treaty of Versailles.

In the period following the war the Treaty of Versailles became a symbol of degradation and of German defeat. During the thirties, some historians, including Americans and British, condemned the treaty on the grounds that it had been unduly harsh and had been based on the faulty premise that Germany alone was responsible for the outbreak of the war. These revisionists reacted against the notion that victory gives the conquerors the right to rewrite history. Certainly, there were harsh aspects to the treaty. It laid the guilt for the war on German shoulders. It surrendered Alsace-Lorraine to France and gave other territory to Denmark, Belgium, and Poland. The treaty forced Germany to surrender its colonies in Africa and Asia. It placed limitations on the building of a German army or navy. Finally, it set at a huge amount the "reparations" to be paid by the Germans to France and Great Britain. However, hard as these terms were, the allies had not drained Germany of her blood. She retained most of her European territories and would receive the industrially rich Saar region fifteen years after the war. She remained a unified state with all of the potential to become a major European power once again.

Germany did not suffer nearly so much as her Austro-Hungarian and Ottoman allies. The Austro-Hungarian Empire had fallen by revolution before the conclusion of the treaties, but the conferences in Paris made no attempt to breathe new life into the old body. Instead, they recognized an independent Austria, an independent Hungary, and created a number of new states, including Czechoslovakia and Yugoslavia, from the remnants of the empire. The Ottomans lost heavily. The last blow was the revolt of the Young Turks under Kemal Attaturk, that tumbled the sultan and established a modern, if not a democratic, government. This revolution succeeded in keeping Turkey out of the peace settlement and preserving her independence, while the remainder of the Ottoman Empire was divided among the victorious allies or put into trusteeship under the still to be formed League of Nations.

The one ray of hope that appeared to many after the Treaty of Versailles was the founding of the League of Nations. This protector of the weak and pacific force for international order would hopefully make the war worth the great sacrifices it had cost. Wilson had worked more than anything else for the creation of the League. His more cynical European colleagues bargained hard to obtain tangible gains and let Wilson have his way. But this victory of President Wilson went down the drain so far as his own country was concerned when the United States Senate refused to ratify the charter of the League of Nations. Without United States participation, the League never stood a chance of developing into an international peace-keeping body. The strong opposition of American isolationist and nationalist elements to the League was a victory for the forces of international disintegration.

World War I was the last act of the age of Western leadership and the beginning of an age of transition, an era of rapid and awesome change, of terrible wars and international crises, of the making of a new world still unborn. It was a nationalistic war that triggered the growth of new "isms" in the period of disillusion that followed. The new "isms" have dominated the twentieth century.

PART IV
Crisis, Change, and a New World

"Melpomene tragico proclamat maesta boatu."
"Melpomene cries aloud with the echoing voice of gloomy tragedy."

22 Revolt Against the West

The children of the twentieth century have wandered across a wasteland, have suffered barbarism, tasted despair, felt hope, enjoyed prosperity, and desired peace. Few centuries have known greater ferment before their years were half passed. If mankind had set out deliberately to wreck the theories of evolutionary progress that had optimistically impelled the men of the previous century forward, the task could not have been more thorough. For the wreckage of optimism has cluttered the waters of twentieth-century thought.

Even as World War I raged, revolution transformed the Russian Empire into the Soviet Union. In the aftermath of the war, Italy and Germany turned to fascist dictatorships in search of an answer to their disillusionment at the outcome of the war. The democracies first gave themselves over to an orgy of victory and then plunged into a death struggle for survival against the forces unleashed in the Great Depression. In the Far East, hope for democracy fell before triumphant militarism. The world prepared for another war. This time, Europe fought a war out of fear and reluctantly, as though there was an awareness that the old order could not survive another crisis. And it could not. The loosening ties of imperialism broke in the postwar period. European hegemony came to an end. A new world gradually unfolded, but so slowly that men at the mid-century still had no inkling of its nature. Struck down in awe before the dawn of the atomic age and raised up in wonder at space, they hovered between two worlds.

Communism in Russia

The collapse of the Tsarist regime in Russia came not with a roar or with a whimper, but like dust blown in the wind. There was a swirl and a stir and the old regime was gone. In most respects, the revolution of March, 1917, that destroyed the Tsarist government, was similar to that of 1905. Wartime disillusionment, the failure of Russian arms against the Germans, corruption and bungling, shortages and famine, fear, and the ever-present agitation of liberals and socialists against the regime were some of the chief factors behind the outbreak.

In March, 1917, workers in St. Petersburg rioted against the shortage of food. The troops in the city, mostly conscripts, threw in their lot with the workers and the revolution began to spread. Soon councils (soviets) of workers in other cities and groups of peasants were beginning to organize. Tsar Nicholas II returned from the front lines and was met with the demand that he abdicate. He stepped down in favor of his brother Michael, but it was already too late to attempt to preserve the regime. Power was no longer in the hands of the central government. The Duma, the elective assembly, set up a provisional government led by liberals and moderate socialists, but the new government did not control the soviets of workers, who were the major powers in the cities. The new government was further hampered because it had pledged to keep Russia in the war against Germany, but had received no support from the Allies in return. The workers and peasants wanted immediate reforms and an improved standard of living. The provisional government could only promise it would try to remedy these grievances in the future.

The leaders of the new government, men like the Socialist Alexander Kerensky (1881–), were believers in political democracy and reform. They were, for the most part, not militant revolutionaries. Rather they had had power thrust into their hands by the forces of events. But they did not really know how to handle power. They were unable to seize control of the situation and to manage it. Their hope was to gain the support of the West. However, the military situation continued to deteriorate. An attempted military coup d'état by the Russian commander-in-chief failed, but it was merely a prelude to the overthrow of democratic government in November, 1917, by the Bolsheviks led by Nicolai Lenin (1870–1924) (Vladimir Ulianov).

The Bolsheviks were militant Marxists. They embraced the idea of violent revolution. Lenin himself was a disciplined revolutionary. He had

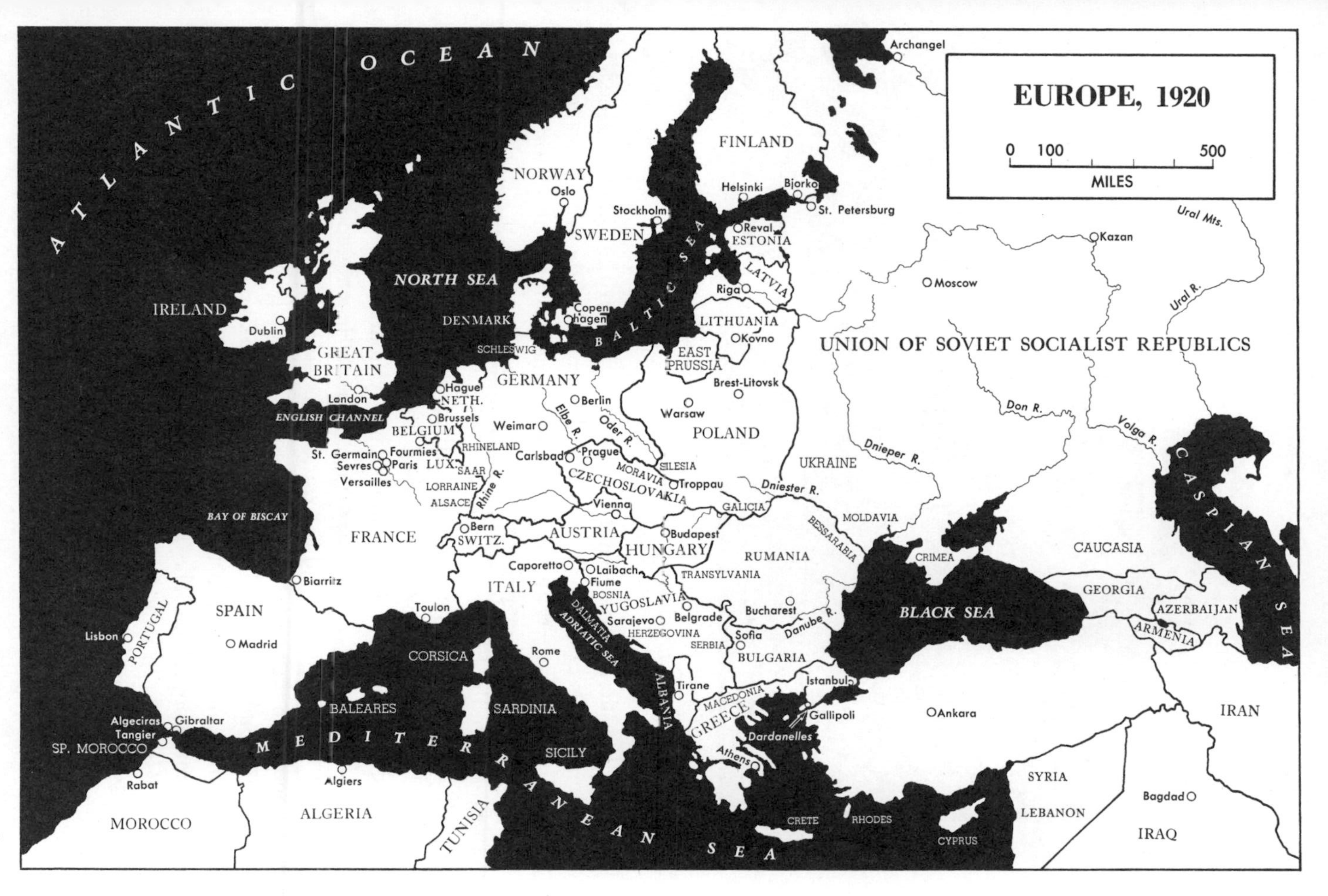
EUROPE, 1920
0 100 500
MILES
ATLANTIC OCEAN
NORTH SEA
BALTIC SEA
ENGLISH CHANNEL
BAY OF BISCAY
MEDITERRANEAN SEA
ADRIATIC SEA
BLACK SEA
CASPIAN SEA
UNION OF SOVIET SOCIALIST REPUBLICS
IRELAND
GREAT BRITAIN
NORWAY
SWEDEN
FINLAND
DENMARK
ESTONIA
LATVIA
LITHUANIA
EAST PRUSSIA
POLAND
GERMANY
NETH.
BELGIUM
LUX.
FRANCE
SPAIN
PORTUGAL
SWITZ.
ITALY
AUSTRIA
HUNGARY
CZECHOSLOVAKIA
YUGOSLAVIA
RUMANIA
BULGARIA
ALBANIA
GREECE
UKRAINE
CAUCASIA
GEORGIA
AZERBAIJAN
ARMENIA
IRAN
IRAQ
SYRIA
LEBANON
CYPRUS
RHODES
CRETE
MOROCCO
SP. MOROCCO
ALGERIA
TUNISIA
CORSICA
SARDINIA
SICILY
BALEARES
CRIMEA
MOLDAVIA
BESSARABIA
GALICIA
TRANSYLVANIA
SILESIA
MORAVIA
BOSNIA
HERZEGOVINA
SERBIA
DALMATIA
MACEDONIA
SCHLESWIG
RHINELAND
SAAR
LORRAINE
ALSACE
Archangel
St. Petersburg
Bjorko
Helsinki
Reval
Riga
Kovno
Brest-Litovsk
Warsaw
Stockholm
Copenhagen
Oslo
Berlin
Weimar
Carlsbad
Prague
Troppau
Vienna
Budapest
Hague
Brussels
Fourmies
Paris
St. Germain
Sevres
Versailles
London
Dublin
Bern
Caporetto
Fiume
Laibach
Sarajevo
Belgrade
Bucharest
Sofia
Tirane
Athens
Istanbul
Gallipoli
Dardanelles
Ankara
Bagdad
Moscow
Kazan
Toulon
Rome
Biarritz
Madrid
Lisbon
Gibraltar
Algeciras
Tangier
Rabat
Algiers
Ural Mts.
Ural R.
Volga R.
Don R.
Dnieper R.
Dniester R.
Danube R.
Oder R.
Elbe R.
Rhine R.

Nikolai Lenin. The Bolshevik leader was a master at arousing crowds. (The Bettmann Archive)

been in exile in Switzerland during the war, but the Germans aided his return to Russia via Finland because he supported the withdrawal of Russia from the war. With Lenin in Russia, the Germans also furnished this fiery orator and agitator with money to propagandize the workers and to strengthen the Bolsheviks. The success of Lenin's efforts culminated in the November Revolution, which overthrew the provisional government.

The Bolshevik Revolution spilled little blood in its overthrow of the Kerensky Government. Lenin immediately embarked on a program aimed at winning support for the new government. He entered into negotiations with the Germans to end the war and launched an all-out attack on those opposed to the revolution. Since there was little he could have done about it, he simply supported the peasants and workers in their appropriations of lands and goods. But the Bolsheviks soon found themselves facing considerable opposition. The Treaty of Brest-Litovsk, which they signed with the Germans to remove Russia from the war, was more than a blow to Russian national pride; it was a disaster. The Germans got the most industrialized and richest part of Russia with about twenty per cent of the total population of the country. Moreover, the Bolsheviks had begun to ride roughshod over the other political parties. Russia was on the verge of a new revolution, a counterrevolution.

From mid-1918 through early 1922, revolutionaries and counterrevolutionaries struggled for control of Russia. The Reds, as the Bolsheviks were called, faced the Whites, composed partially of former Tsarist army officers and partly of all the other opponents of the regime. The West remained largely aloof from the civil war, save to send expeditionary forces during the early twenties ostensibly to protect English and American property in Russia. This civil war was, in fact, the real revolution. It brought out all the deepest cleavages in Russian life and resulted in the deepest hatreds. Atrocities were the standard method of operation for both sides in the conflict as prisoners were shot *en masse* and civilians enjoyed no protection from the participants of either side. The victory of the Bolsheviks was largely the work of Leon Trotsky, who created the Red army and led it. As number two man in the new Soviet Union, Trotsky stood with Lenin in believing in the revolutionary mission of Russia to lead the workers of the world to revolt against their bourgeois governments.

However, the first order of business in Russia was the building of a socialist state. Lenin believed that Russia must first recover from the effects of the war and experience the type of industrial development that had occurred in Western Europe before it could build a real socialist society. In his New Economic Plan (NEP), he allowed for a semicapitalistic development of a private industrial sector to meet consumer needs. He also permitted peasants to benefit by increasing their holdings, thus strengthening the class of kulaks, or middle-class peasant farmers. Had Lenin lived, it is hard to say how long he would have permitted the continued growth of power in the hands of this artificially sustained middle class. His death dramatically changed the direction of Russian development.

The logical successor of Lenin was Leon Trotsky (1879–1940) when the great revolutionary died in January, 1924. But Trotsky had made enemies. He was a difficult man to get along with and ardently committed to the international mission of Communism. Many Russian communists wanted a leader who would concentrate on problems within Russia, especially the increasing bourgeois character of the Russian state under the NEP. However, neither logic not the desires of other Communist leaders played the significant role in the rise to power of Joseph Stalin (1879–1953). Stalin had been the party's banker during the revolution and had risen, in spite of Lenin's lack of confidence, to control the party secretariat. He used his position as party secretary to gain a complete knowledge of the key figures within the party and to cement ties that would help in his bid to succeed Lenin. He allied himself with Trotsky's enemies on the

Politburo, the party's committee for control of the government. Stalin opposed Trotsky's idealistic program for a world revolution with the concept of "Socialism in one country." By this position, he declared that he believed it more important to consolidate the revolution in Russia than to attempt its spread abroad. He also rejected the doctrinaire Marxist position that it was impossible to achieve a socialistic society without world revolution. Stalin used his control of the party to remove Trotsky from power and to drive him out of the Communist Party. He gradually achieved total control of the government, emerging as the dominant figure by 1928.

Stalin's major concerns during the thirties were developing basic industry within the Soviet Union and eliminating all possible opposition to his regime. The two aims went hand in hand. Stalin emphasized the need for basic industry in order to catch up with the capitalistic countries of Western Europe. His brand of Marxism put off the immediate problems of the working classes in order to solve the basic problem of the economic weakness of Russia. The worker therefore found himself the tool of the state in an ostensibly socialistic society dedicated to serve his needs. Yet the state of Russian industry in the twenties made Stalin's program necessary. Production of such basic materials as steel lagged far behind national needs. The transportation system was still primitive. The NEP was never designed to solve these needs. Rather it had permitted money that could be spent on heavy industry to flow into consumer channels. Stalin therefore moved against the NEP men and the kulaks during the thirties, because they posed a threat to his own series of five-year plans for the economic development of the Soviet Union.

In a state that aimed at the creation of a perfect society to fulfill man's economic and social needs, the cardinal sin is the pursuit of self-interest. The NEP represented selfish ends that must be destroyed if the state were to prosper. The ruthlessness of Stalin in reorganizing Soviet agriculture and industry was one of the worst aspects of his government. Employing methods learned from the Tsarist government, he and his secret police rounded up those suspected of resistance and sped them off to concentration camps. Many more, in fact, millions more, died from hunger and the results of the strife stirred up by party agitators. Not even Stalin had envisaged the effects of his plan and he tried to mitigate the effects and turned to less forcible measures to pursuade the peasants of the advantages of collectivization. In industry, state control brought labor conditions as bad as those in any capitalistic society. The infamous system of

Russian peasants. This prerevolutionary scene is typical of the life of the rural population in Imperial Russia. (The Bettmann Archive)

piecework used by industrial entrepreneurs to increase output and reduce unit costs found its counterpart in socialistic competition.

Finally Stalin worked to consolidate his position in the party and the state by eliminating his chief competitors. Beginning in 1936, the NKVD (secret police) rounded up many of the top party leaders, including those who had led the Revolution of 1917, and forced them to confess to crimes against the Soviet Union. Most of them died before the firing squad in these quasi-legal proceedings. However, the purges did not accomplish their purpose. Many Russians, especially in the Ukraine, began to have serious doubts and fears about the regime. They supported it only because no alternative presented itself to them. When the forces of Adolf Hitler's Nazi Germany attacked Russia in 1940, the first reaction among many of these dissidents was to look to the Germans for possible support against the Stalinist regime. However, German anti-Slavic policies soon left the Russians no choice but to support Stalin.

The reputation of Stalinist government in the West was always poor. One could hardly expect otherwise, since anticommunist sympathy made many Westerners champion even the Tsarist regime over communism, a position that offered the Russian people little in the way of hope. The fact was that most Western Europeans and Americans were poorly informed about the situation in Russia and desirous of believing the worst. However, bad as the realities of life under Stalin were, Russia did progress in the direction he had planned. The growth of heavy industry in the decade, 1930–1940, brought Russia to a position near its prewar status.

The Russian people under Stalin suffered much more than they had under Lenin. Shortages of foodstuffs and other consumer goods were aggravated by the shift to heavy industry and the effort to collectivize agriculture. Nor did they make any real progress in the area of political or civil rights. The Soviet Constitution of 1936 made much of "freedom," guaranteeing basic liberties of the individual. However, socialistic freedom meant that these rights could be exercised only when they did not threaten the security of the state. In theory, a man might worship. In practice, however, the enmity between the regime and the Russian Orthodox Church, indeed the hostility toward all religions, meant that this freedom was severely restricted. Socialism coupled freedom with obligation. Stalin coupled freedom with the needs of the state. The Constitution of 1936 was a mere façade behind which he maneuvered to establish one of the most powerful personal dictatorships in history.

Stalin subordinated the aims of Communism abroad, which tended to look to the Soviet Union for leadership, to the needs of the Soviet Union. He withdrew most of his support from the Chinese Communists in the thirties and gave little help to the parties of Western Europe and America. In fact, their need to justify the policies of the Soviet Government frequently cost them support in their own countries, particularly since Stalin seldom attempted to explain Soviet policy moves to anyone. To gain recognition from the Western powers for his regime, he disbanded the Internationale, the organization of Communism in all the countries of the world. He expected, even demanded loyalty, but gave little in return.

Disillusionment with the Russian Revolution within and without the Soviet Union increased markedly during the late thirties, yet no accurate summary of the period could omit the over-all success of the regime in holding the loyalty of the young and building a new "socialist" state. However, Russia had still to face it greatest crisis of the postrevolutionary period in World War II.

Fascism in Italy

Beside the image of the cold and efficient Stalin, the figure of Benito Mussolini (1883–1945) appears as a caricature. Yet, Mussolini was one of the ablest of the modern dictators, as well as one of the most unscrupulous. He was, in fact, the prototype for Adolf Hitler.

Italy emerged from World War I with some small compensations for her efforts. Chiefly, she gained control of the Italians in the Alps (Tyrol) along the Austrian border. However, her ambitious plans for expansion along the Dalmatian coast had come to nought. The creation of Yugoslavia blocked the Italian dream of a Balkan empire. Therefore, despite the fact that Italy was technically one of the victors, she felt cheated by the results of the war. National pride had suffered a serious setback.

But Italy was troubled by other problems, too. Her economy was shaky. She did not raise sufficient food to feed her population and had difficulty in selling enough abroad to meet her foreign obligations. Italian industry suffered from the disadvantage that the country had little in the way of raw materials and had to import most of the goods needed for manufacturing. The war had placed heavy strains on the economy and the return of peace did not bring prosperity. On the contrary, the influx of veterans of the war onto the domestic labor market created unemployment and unrest among the working classes. This period saw the continued growth of the socialist movement in Italy. The Italian government was not very adept at handling problems arising out of economic and social dislocation. Parliamentary democracy had never taken root in many parts of the country, where the old landed aristocracy continued to dominate, along with the clergy, the mass of illiterate peasants. Corruption had bred political cynicism. Politicians survived by making temporary coalitions to support one another in power without any real regard to political differences. Moreover, probably the majority of Italian politicians drew their support from those elements in society—men of business, aristocrats, and the higher clergy—who, as much as they might differ on other matters, were agreed each for its own reasons that government should not intervene too much in the life of its citizens. Thus, parliamentary weakness received additional support from the apostles of inaction.

Yet there were important activist elements in postwar Italy. The Socialists, despite serious internal splits, constituted the leading political party at odds with the government. They advocated the introduction of political democracy, reduction of the influence of the Church in public life, and reforms aimed at improving the status of both the peasants and the workers in industry. Their numbers were still relatively small but their programs instilled considerable fear in the hearts of the middle and upper classes. There was a very strong feeling that Italy might follow the road of Russia. But, when the takeover of democratic government—the term is loosely applied—came, the threat moved in from the right in the form of a new political force that combined ultranationalistic sentiments and antisocialism with totalitarian concepts of the organization of the state. The new creation was the rather misshapen political offspring of a former Socialist leader and newspaperman, Benito Mussolini. It took the name *Fascismo* from the bundle of reeds that symbolized the authority of the Roman imperial and republican governments. Fascism was a cult of authority first; its social and economic programs were added later.

Benito Mussolini (1883–1945) was born in the Romagna, northwest of Rome. His father was an old-line radical with anarchist sympathies; his mother was a devout woman of peasant background, who had received sufficient education to enable her to teach school. Mussolini himself was prepared for a career as a secondary school teacher, but never pursued it after a faltering start. Instead, he joined the socialists in Switzerland and became a journalist. After his return from abroad, he became one of the leaders of the Italian Socialist movement and eventually edited *Avanti* (Forward), the paper of the Socialist Party published in Milan. He broke with the Socialists on the issue of Italian participation in World War I. They opposed the war on the ground that it exploited the working class; he supported it on nationalistic grounds. On his return from the army, he founded a new paper, *Il Populo d'Italia,* and attempted to stir up Italian sentiment in support of the war. When the war ended, his popularity grew with the returning veterans, among whom he posed as one who understood their problems, their hopes for Italy, and their feelings of disillusionment that the peace had lost what they had fought to obtain. It was among these groups that Fascism appeared.

Any effort to discuss the theory of Fascism soon runs afoul of the fact that there is no genuine theoretical foundation underlying the movement. Although Mussolini and others attempted to create a theory, their effort was largely after the fact and had little bearing on the actuality of Fascist practice. Yet, in one sense, there is a theoretical foundation to the movement and that is in the sense that Fascism borrowed heavily from other ideologies for its own ideas and programs. Two ingredients were essential. The first was nationalism; the second, the concept of the authoritarian state. Nationalism provided both the dynamic force that propelled the movement to leadership of the state and the basis for much of its popular support. In Fascism, the exaltation of the state—a corollary of nationalism—resulted in the attempt to translate all democratic energies into support for authoritarian rule by creating institutional outlets for those energies and by channeling them into avenues useful to the state. Of course, such an effort was only theoretically possible; in fact, repression played an important role in keeping the authority of the state inviolable. Fascism also borrowed heavily from both the vocabulary and the methods of the socialist left. Although Mussolini rejected the Marxist conception of the class struggle in his subordination of all elements of society to the unitary state, he employed socialistic terms to describe the welfare and economic measures of Fascism. The movement also employed such customary leftist tactics as riots, mob action, and mass meetings. Most of the Fascists sprang from the ranks of the lower class or lower middle class, but their strong nationalism created the major tie binding them to the conservatives of the right and separating them from the left. Therefore, as the movement came into power, it found no real difficulty in accommodating itself to the existing power structure. Mussolini even accepted the monarchy.

The road to power for the Italian Fascists was made easy by the inability of the liberals and other supporters of constitutional government to work together to preserve parliamentary rule. Their mistrust and fear of socialism played into the hands of Mussolini. The deep cleavage between the right and center, which meant that the supporters of parliamentary rule could expect no support from that sector, further weakened efforts to oppose the popular leader. Mussolini himself was an able, if somewhat overcautious and even frightened, demagogue. He found himself at the head of a popular movement and was swept along with it. In a very true sense, he came to power in 1922 without really seeking to overthrow the government. The bankruptcy of democracy in Italy made it possible for him, the leader of a varied gang of veterans and small people to take what he had not had the nerve to demand. In history, this rise to power

Fascist youth in Italy. The Fascists attempted to mobilize all segments of society in the service of the state. (*Brown Brothers*)

was glamorized by the Fascists with the term "March on Rome"; in fact, the march was a straggling body of assorted types many of whom never got close to the city before giving up. But fear of possible revolution and paralysis born of ignorance caused King Victor Emmanuel III to ask Mussolini to form a government.

Mussolini's new government moved cautiously to win the support of right-wing elements in parliament in the initial months of its rule. Since the party had only a small fraction of the members of the Chamber of Deputies, Mussolini had to work for new elections that would give him control. To ensure his victory at the polls, he had to gain complete security to act. He secured emergency legislation and then proceeded to hold elections in which his bands of Fascists saw to it that the opposition got little opportunity for free exercise of the franchise. With his new majorities, he pummeled the opposition. He had one narrow escape in the popular reaction to the murder of the Socialist leader Giacomo Matteoti by Fascist thugs, but he rode out the storm and moved on to the next step. At the beginning of 1925, Mussolini outlawed all political parties save the Fascists and moved rapidly to make Italy a completely totalitarian state.

From that time until World War II brought the collapse of his government, he ruled without the hindrance of an effective opposition in Italy.

The dictatorship of Mussolini has sometimes gained a measure of respectability because it was not nearly so brutal as that of Stalin in Russia or of Hitler in Germany. The fact is that the credit for the failure of Italian Fascism to achieve the level of barbarism of the other dictatorships is largely due to the Italian people. They never allowed Mussolini to resort to the kinds of open persecution that characterized the other powers. Yet the Italian regime was oppressive. No achievements—and many of these were the creations of propaganda—could outweigh the destruction of human dignity and personal political and civil rights that went along with the Fascist dictatorship.

Mussolini was well aware of the need to work continually to improve the image of his regime in the eyes of the Italian masses. He realized that his power rested on the people and that he could ignore them only if they were happy. Therefore, he sought measures that would win their confidence. One of the most important was the rapprochement of the regime with the Catholic Church in the Lateran Accord of 1929.

The long estrangement between the Popes and the Italian government had worked to the disadvantage of both Church and state. Leo XIII, toward the end of the nineteenth century, had relaxed some of the restrictions on Cathoic participation in political life, but the Popes had continued to protest the seizure of their temporal estates by the Italian government. When Mussolini came to power, he inherited a situation that brought him enormous prestige with Catholics around the world, as well as in Italy, at no cost to himself. The previous government had all but concluded negotiations for a settlement with the Papacy. Mussolini brought them to a successful conclusion and reaped the credit. In fact, however, the regime was no friend to the Church. Pope Pius XI (1922–1939) and his successor, Pius XII (1939–1958), had continually to protest the mistreatment of Italian Catholics and violations of the concordat (treaty) between the Church and the government in matters of religious instruction and freedom of the Catholic Action movement.

Mussolini also attempted to gain support by his aggressive foreign policy. He conjured up the dream of the Mediterranean Sea as an Italian lake, recalling the grandeur of the Roman Empire. He even affixed a map of his new Italian Empire to the Colosseum in Rome. The grand moment of Mussolini's foreign policy was the conquest of Ethiopia in 1935–1936. This move, actually rather anachronistic, aimed at proving to the world that Italy, too, was a major power with a vast territory overseas. The con-

The League of Nations. The empty chairs are those of the German and Italian delegates. The Italians walked out when the League condemned their aggression in Ethiopia. (*Brown Brothers*)

quest also avenged the defeat of the Italians by the Ethiopians at Aduwa in 1896. But it merely strained the Italian economy without adding anything to compensate for the cost of the conquest.

On the home front, Mussolini strove to capture the popular imagination with propaganda and overdramatized efforts to increase agricultural and industrial production. By directing attention to the seeming efforts of the regime to solve these important problems, Mussolini was able to keep the majority of Italians from becoming too restive. However, not all of the accomplishments of the government were propaganda. Mussolini embarked on a large public works program to provide employment and to stimulate industry. His projects, not unlike those carried out by the PWA in the United States during the Great Depression, also gave many Italians a sense of pride and achievement in the building of their country. They created an air of optimism. Some strides were also made in increasing agricultural production. Mussolini's "battle of the wheat" raised productivity by increasing the amount of land under cultivation and by spurring the workers on to greater efforts. The most famous of the land reclamation projects was the draining of the huge and unhealthy marshes that had challenged the Italians since Roman times. However, much of the land put under cultivation to achieve the goals of the battle of the wheat was marginal. Use of such land over a protracted period proved uneconomical and even impracticable. Mussolini's military buildup stimulated the recovery of Italian industry. Such prosperity as there was, however, was the result of largely artificial stimulants; the economy itself underwent no basic change.

During the later thirties, Mussolini played a larger role in European politics and drew closer to the German dictator, Adolf Hitler. In 1936, Hitler and Mussolini formed the Rome-Berlin Axis. This alliance foreshadowed Italian participation in World War II.

The National Socialist Movement in Germany

A crippled and disillusioned Germany emerged from World War I. The Treaty of Versailles had cost it heavily in both wealth and prestige. Hundreds of thousands of Germans found themselves in Poland, Czechoslovakia, or under the control of France after the war. Billions of dollars in reparations burdened the German economy. Moreover, the country had greater than average problems in adjusting to peace. The last days of the war had witnessed the overthrow of the Hohenzollern dynasty and the end of the German Empire. Bismarck's proud Germany had lasted little more than a generation. Threatened by a socialistic revolution, the newborn Weimar Republic sought political stability amid chaotic conditions at the end of the war. The collapse of the empire was only one aspect of a broader weakness in German life. Industry was not able to absorb the returning veterans. Inflation threatened to destroy the entire economy. The Germans, with no real experience of parliamentary democracy embarked on a major political experiment during a period of great internal stress.

The weaknesses of the Weimar Republic were those of a government that had functioned only in a climate of authority and which now lacked the leadership on which it had depended. Although the political parties were not so numerous as in Italy, there was nevertheless a serious fragmentation that made it difficult to secure absolute parliamentary majorities. Given the depth of the crisis in which Germany found herself, the leaders of the Weimar Republic themselves began to undermine the democratic process by attempting to rule without Parliament, resorting to the old expedient used by Bismarck during the period immediately following unification. Thus these leaders played into the hands of the old conservative elements, who looked upon the republic as a creation of their defeat and were willing that it should pass away.

Yet the failures of the Weimar Republic do not account fully for the rise of the National Socialist movement in Germany. Historians have sought in many quarters for the roots of Nazism and have often found confirmations for a belief that Nazism was entirely consistent with the strain of German authoritarianism they traced in the history of that people. Still, the Germans were not unique in their strong commitment to the need for authority. In almost all countries in this period, there were movements that exalted the concept of loyalty to the state to a kind of surrender of the individual will to the collective will. As in Italy, so in Germany, the roots of Fascism are to be found in the strength of nationalist sentiments. Virulent nationalism had swept through Germany in the wake of unification and had increased in intensity during the era preceding World War I. The war had focused the hatred of many German nationalists on the Western democracies as enemies of a strong German state. With defeat, the most ardent of the nationalists were convinced that the war had been the result of a Western effort to destroy Germany. They could not support the Weimar Republic for they saw it as the tool of the Western powers for having accepted the Versailles Treaty, and as a scavenger on the bones of the empire. They sought a movement that would promise to restore the Germany that had disappeared. Nazism, in the first instance, appealed to the nationalists.

The founder of German Nazism was a former soldier in the German army, who had been born in Austria, but had become a believer in the unity of all German peoples. His name was Adolf Hitler (1889–1945). He had lived on the fringes of society in Vienna before the war and had found no real purpose for his existence. Disappointed in his hope of securing a higher professional education, he had drifted about aimlessly until the war gave meaning to his life by arousing his nationalistic sentiments. As a soldier, he compiled a creditable record, but was not conspicuous. Still, life as a soldier seems to have made him feel more important; at least, when returned to Munich, after the armistice, he sought the companionship of fellow veterans. During the early twenties, he haunted the beer houses and argued incessantly with his companions and anyone who would listen about German politics. Gifted with the ability to sway crowds, he also began to talk in public. His message was invariably the same. He employed the arguments of nationalism to show that Germany had been betrayed by enemies from within. His scapegoat was the Jews, whom he accused of an international conspiracy with the Western powers to undermine Germany. He also found the Jews the main supporters of socialism and laid the blame for the internal strife on the German home front during the last stages of the war at their door. By 1920, he had

Hindenberg and Hitler. The Nazi leader rose to power surrounded by a cloak of respectability. The leaders of the Weimar Republic were either too divided or too ambitious to prevent his rise. (*Brown Brothers*)

formed the National Socialist German Workers' Party, better known as the Nazi Party from the German pronunciation of the word *National*, the first word in the title of the party.

Many similarities between Nazism and Italian Fascism appeared, for Hitler had a deep admiration for Benito Mussolini, whom he regarded as the greatest political figure of the age. After Mussolini's rise to power, Hitler consciously modeled his tactics on those of the successful Italian. He formed the *Sturmabteilung* (SA), a body of brown-shirted Nazi bullies with which to intimidate his enemies and especially the socialists. The storm troopers posed as protectors of Germany against the threat of socialism. Hitler also copied Mussolini's techniques of propaganda, but improved upon them considerably after Dr. Joseph Goebbels (1897–1945) joined the movement.

The efforts of the Nazis to secure power in Germany during the twenties were such fizzles that many Germans who would have opposed Hitler's bid for power were lulled into believing that his movement represented no real threat. In fact, some Jews, disregarding his blatant anti-Semitism, lent him support in the early period because of his opposition to communism. In 1923, Hitler and a group of followers, including the aged World War I General von Ludendorff, attempted to take over the Bavarian state government in Munich. This "Beer-Hall *Putsch*" failed miserably. Hitler was sent to jail, where he spent his time writing *Mein Kampf,* in which he set down the aims of National Socialism in an autobiography.

After the failure of the Beer Hall *Putsch,* the Nazis concentrated on attempting to win popular support at the polls. However, here too their success was slight. In the election of December, 1924, theirs was the smallest representation of any political party in the *Reichstag.* In the election of May, 1928, they won even a smaller number of seats. All in all, it was difficult to take such a splinter movement seriously.

However, the situation in Germany had something to do with the seeming eclipse of the Nazis. After the terrible inflation of the early twenties, which had seen the price of bread rise to millions of marks, Germany regained a measure of prosperity. The problem of reparations was worked out according to the Dawes Plan so that Germany obtained from abroad the money needed to meet her obligations. The mark began to recover and German industry forged ahead once more. Although much of the comeback was apparent rather than real, Germany begain to share in a general prosperity that enveloped most of Europe in the twenties. Without the grave dissatisfaction that had played into their hands during the early part of the decade, the Nazis lost much of the status they had had and became another minor party. One might even have predicted for them a long and insignificant role as a party of protest for the extreme right.

What dramatically changed this situation was the new German economic crisis born of the Great Depression of 1929.

The worldwide depression of 1929 was a period of economic retrenchment brought on by too rapid expansion of industry and production after World War I and inadequate safeguards against unwise speculation by financiers and others. Germany was caught in an especially vulnerable position because her own economy had not made a genuine recovery from the inflation of the postwar period. Thousands were thrown out of work, most of them men who had served in World War I and many who belonged to the large German lower-middle income group. Especially hard hit were the small shopkeepers, owners of marginal business, which had depended on prosperity for existence. Some were forced into bankruptcy; others managed to survive in a kind of suspended animation. It was to these groups that Nazism had traditionally made a strong appeal. Now that appeal was heard. In the *Reichstag* elections of September, 1930, the Nazis won one hundred and seven seats to become suddenly the second largest political party in parliament. Only the Social Democrats (socialists) were larger. The Nazi gains came chiefly at the expense of the older right-wing parties, the Nationalists and the Peoples Party, indicating no massive support from the urban working classes. Hitler's movement appealed chiefly to Germany's respectable people.

With the turning of the tide at the polls, German political leaders suddenly found it desirable to deal with the Nazis. Chancellor Bruning tried to rule without relying on the Nazis or the Social Democrats, but was unable to muster sufficient support. His successors, men like the aristocratic leader of the Center Party, Franz von Papen, and General Kurt von Schleicher gave up the effort and openly conspired to secure Nazi backing. Now, however, Hitler saw that events were moving his way. In the presidential election of 1932, Hitler announced that he would oppose President Paul von Hindenberg, the old general, who had stood for stability in the Weimar Republic. The election was not close. Hindenberg won by about six million votes, but the Nazis did remarkably well in the elections to the *Reichstag* in July. Their two hundred and thirty members made them the largest party in the *Reichstag* and cut into the seats held by most of the other parties save the Communists. Still, the Nazis lacked a majority. Moreover, in the election of November, 1932, they lost considerable ground. However, no other government was able to achieve stability. The leaders of the right and center began to toy with the idea of a coalition with the Nazis to prevent a possible takeover by the socialists. President von Hindenberg resisted these efforts through the fall of 1932, while Hitler demanded that be become chancellor in any coalition government. Finally, Hindenberg yielded to the pressures and named the former corporal Chancellor of the German government, with Franz von Papen as Vice-Chancellor. The next step was the calling of new elections to obtain a parliamentary majority. In the elections of March, 1933, the Nazis won two hundred and eighty-eight seats, fifty-one short of a majority. The storm troopers had tried to drive the Socialists and Communists away from the polls and had intimidated as many of the electorate as they could, but their efforts were not enough. However, with the cooperation of the Nationalists and the elimination of eighty-one Communist members of the *Reichstag*, the coalition had a majority.

Hitler's next step was quite predictable. After the pattern of Mussolini, but with far greater confidence, he secured the passage of an act permitting the government to rule by decree for four years. With complete control of the legal machinery, Hitler now moved against the other political parties. He ordered them to dissolve and purged their members from the *Reichstag*. His erstwhile allies received virtually the same treatment as his opposition. No longer was it necessary for Hitler to observe the niceties of constitutional practice. The *Geheime Staats Polizei* (Gestapo) rounded up political undesirables and shipped them off to concentration camps with only the pretence of justice. Hitler also turned against the "tainted" elements in his own party in 1934. He purged the SA leadership and many men in the ranks, and also proceeded against former Socialists who had joined the Nazis in the belief that their goals included many of the aims of the Socialist Party. By the end of the summer of 1934, Hitler had consolidated his position and won the support of the most important elements in Germany, including that of the general staff, which agreed to take a personal oath of allegiance to their "fuehrer" (leader). Hitler also took over the presidency on the resignation of the aged General von Hindenberg.

Any evaluation of the Nazi regime must inevitably fall short of reality while losing most objectivity. It is difficult, even impossible, to conceive how any people, let alone the highly civilized and cultured Germans, could permit so much in the way of bestiality and barbarism. Yet the excesses of men, by their very nature, drive the majority of good men to hiding. Few really want to believe such crimes possible; many succeed in convincing themselves that they do not exist. The power of man to believe what he wills and to deny what he wishes reached an apex in Nazi Germany. In all truth, many Germans did not know what was happening in their country between 1933 and 1945; they had drawn a curtain over their minds to shut out reality and had forgotten that the curtain even existed.

Hitler's policies in the foreign and domestic fields aimed at redressing the "wrong" done Germany by the Treaty of Versailles and reestablishing German national pride. From his youth, Hitler had worshipped at the altar of Germany. As chancellor, he attempted to transform the German state into a divine being for all the German people to worship. He saw himself as a "salvation" figure, a messiah of the German *Reich*. Ultimately all of his practical measures got their significance from their relationship to nationalism.

Anti-Semitism sprang from many different sources in Germany and Eastern Europe, but for Hitler, the major source was his belief that Jews were non-Germans sharing the life of Germany and sapping its strength. Vividly, Hitler pictured the Jews as the enemy who had betrayed the *Reich* into the hands of the Jewish-dominated Western democracies. Thus, in the Nazi mind, the chief crime of the Jew was his disloyalty to Germany. The Jew became the scapegoat for all the disasters that had befallen the Germans. In Nazi terms, the distinction between German and Jew was racial. Germans were "Aryans," Jews were not. This blatant ignorance of basic science became the cult of the nation. No Jew could marry an Aryan and Jewish businesses were subjected to various kinds of discrimination. Finally, in the late thirties, the Nazis began full-scale persecution aimed at driving all Jews out of Germany. Their property was sold to "Aryans" for a fraction of its value and they had to wear the star of David as a yellow label on their clothes. By the beginning of World War II, the life of the German Jew was scarcely livable. Yet, none of the Western powers took any action to provide sanctuary for these victims of persecution.

Hitler's economic policies were more successful than those of Mussolini chiefly because Germany possessed a sound foundation for recovery. In modern terminology, Hitler employed the technique of pump priming to get business moving again. His finance minister made credit cheap and plentiful to attract borrowers. The government embarked on a large public works program to stimulate the recovery of basic industries and to reduce unemployment. However, these measures were short-term in their value. What sustained the momentum of the economy was Hitler's return to the traditional German policy of building a strong military force. Defense spending put more money into the pockets of the industrialists and the workers.

Most Germans appear to have accepted the regime without any great reservations. Opposition leaders of the old political parties were either abroad or in concentration camps. No new opposition could operate effectively in such a tightly controlled police state. Moreover, while there were reasons for individual Germans to complain, the sounds of progress drowned out the voices of the objectors. Probably the only center left for opposition to the government lay in the moral teachings of the churches and their leaders. Hitler worked hard to woo church leaders during the early years of his dictatorship. In 1933, he signed a concordat (treaty) with the Catholic Church. He posed as the protector of religion. However, his true colors soon came out. By the late thirties, persecution of the churches had resulted in the arrest of clergy and the closing of places of worship as well as restriction on religious instruction of youth in the schools. The Christian churches protested these actions and individual church leaders, like Pastor Martin Niemöller, fought against the regime. Bishop von Galen struck out at the government's euthanasia program and Bishop von Preysing protested the ill treatment of Jews. However, the churches avoided a complete break with the government and some clergy even gave the Nazis support from their pulpits. Though Pius XI condemned Nazism in his Encyclical "Mit Brennender Sorge" (With Burning Sorrow), many German Catholics reacted by taking the view that the Church was meddling. Some recent historians have criticized the churches for being too timid in their preaching of the moral code of Christianity and their leaders with fearing the wrath of the state. Certainly, there is evidence in some cases that supports these charges.

German foreign policy under Hitler proclaimed its aim as the revision of the infamous *Diktat,* the Treaty of Versailles and the incorporation of all Germans within the *Vaterland.* Between 1935 and 1939, Hitler pressed constantly forward to realize these goals. In the early years, some world opinion was sympathetic to German claims and Hitler was able to capitalize on the grain of truth in his demands to win further support. However, in the late thirties, his demands on Czechoslovakia and Poland threatened the stability of Europe and world peace. Only in the last phase did statesmen in the West clearly realize the extent of the Nazi menace. By then, it was too late. World War II had begun.

23 The Burdens of the Peace

The interlude between the Treaty of Versailles and Hitler's invasion of Poland in September, 1939, gave the Western democracies no respite from crisis. England and France faced the problems of economic readjustment. War debt and the return of the veterans combined with the transition from war to peacetime production to strain their currencies. During the war, the working classes had slowed the pace of their demands for a larger share of the profits of industry and more welfare legislation; the end of the war brought new agitation for progress in these areas at a time when other demands were already taxing the budgets of industry and government. Even the return of prosperity during the later twenties did not solve the imbalance between the life of the wealthy and the misery of the urban poor. When the Great Depression threw millions out of work in the early thirties, faith in democracy began to wane. Some looked to extremes of the left and right for solutions in much the same way as they did in Italy and Germany. Only the deep-rooted traditions of representative government, the stability of traditional political parties, and the strength of the liberal spirit slowed the movement toward dictatorship. Faced with a tragic lack of strong leadership through much of the period, the Western democracies yet managed to survive. In fact, this era was a testing time of democratic institutions. The examination revealed their vitality in spite of defects.

Yet the power of Europe over the world was on the wane. The confident leadership that had established the great colonial empires found no counterpart in the hesitant policies of the interwar period. The rise of nationalism in Asia and Africa took the initiative out of the hands of Europeans. This change is reflected in the greater concern shown for domestic problems and the failure to assess adequately the meaning of these changes for the future of Western civilization. Consequently, the democracies were caught off guard as the world moved toward a new global war.

After the War

In the American propaganda phrase, World War I had been fought to "make the world safe for democracy." However, the conclusion of the war brought home to many that there were more pressing concerns than the enforcement of the peace. As in so many cases, the confidence that sprang from victory assured the victors that they had no real need to pursue further their efforts. We have already witnessed the results of this policy in Germany, where it was a contributing factor to the rise of Nazism. In Western Europe and America its effects were perhaps more subtle, but they were just as real. The Western powers had worked for victory but they had not prepared for peace. Yet suddenly the world was no longer at war. Without time to plan, they moved from wartime emergency with its demands for millions of tons of arms and the paraphernalia of war to making baby bottles and roller skates. The transition was not easy.

The effect of peace on domestic politics was probably most dramatically pointed up in the elections held in the United States in 1920. Woodrow Wilson, who had led his nation into war and brought it peace once more, campaigned for his major achievement at the Paris Peace Conference. He wanted the United States to join the League of Nations. His Republican opponent, Warren G. Harding, faced with a divided party and fearful of losing support from isolationists in his party, straddled the issue. He chose as his campaign slogan "The Return to Normalcy." The electorate revealed its temperament in the vote it gave to Harding. The people wanted "normalcy," whatever that was. Although it is impossible to assert positively that a vote for Harding was a vote for American withdrawal from European concerns and for concentration on the all-important business of getting ahead, the Republican victory certainly had that effect. The boys were home again and that was that.

After a brief period of adjustment in the early twenties, the United States embarked on its grandest spree. While the bands around the nation played ragtime and the Charleston, American industry worked around the clock to fill the needs of millions of consumers, war-starved for their merchandise. Prohibition, enacted in 1918 by a Constitutional amendment, forbade the sale or manufacture of most wines, liquor, or beer. But speakeasies, often supplied by big-time mobsters, catered to the liquid needs of the population. On the surface, George Babbitt, hero of Sinclair Lewis' *Main Street,* was in full command of the situation and the nation had nothing to fear. However, just beneath that surface festered the problem of poor working conditions and low pay for factory workers in many industries as well as the failure of American agriculture to share in the prosperity. The twenties had lots of whoopie but not too much maturity.

In England, the end of the war brought the nation up against a harsh reality. In order to pay for the war the English government had liquidated most of the assets of its citizens overseas, chiefly in the United States. It had concentrated on military and naval materials and had neglected its merchant marine, long the mainstay of its position in overseas trade. It had lost much of its trade. These setbacks were crucial to England. Even before World War I, her position as the leading commercial power had been seriously threatened. For trade was her lifeblood. She depended upon it to exist. As the balance of payments from abroad became more unfavorable, the English economy approached crisis. After the war, this crisis was a reality because production and exports had not increased sufficiently to offset increased costs. Shipbuilding, coal, and steel, key industries in the English economy, aggravated this problem. Their poor recovery after the war handicapped England in its effort to secure a more favorable position in international trade. Although England did enjoy a brief recovery in the late twenties, the years between the wars were generally fraught with economic peril for the mistress of the empire on which "the sun never set."

England continued to move further in the direction of full democracy in this period. Although the war had put a stop to further welfare legislation, the impact of the broad franchise brought to the fore more and more political leaders from humble background. The growth of the Labour Party, which had just entered the political stage in a significant way after the turn of the century, pointed to the importance of the working classes in English politics. The extension of the vote to women after World War I—a step parallel to that in the United States—did not have the immediate and disastrous effects anticipated by male politicians, but did change the nature of political campaigns somewhat. During the thirties, in the atmosphere of economic crisis, the political party system gave way to a system of national governments designed to foster unity. The effort pointed up the rather critical absence of strong leadership in Parliament at this time.

Domestic crisis was never far off stage in England. In 1926, the coal miners struck in order to force the Conservatives to support their demands against the mine owners or leave office. Coal was a sick industry, hard hit by the lag in British steel's recovery. There were genuine difficulties in trying to meet demands for higher wages. Nevertheless, the miners called for a general strike of all industry and transport to enforce their demands. The strike lasted nine days and achieved nothing, partly because British labor leaders did not really support it out of fear of its effects on normal political life, and partly because volunteers were able to prevent the complete shutdown of vital services. The coal miners continued their efforts for several months, but finally had to return to work on the terms of the mine owners. The government had secured a victory. However, its policies must bear part of the responsibility for bringing the country quite close to violence and ignoring the demands of a large segment of the populace. Its victory came not because of its courageous leadership so much as because the workers lacked support to accomplish their goals.

A crisis of another kind arose over the succession to the throne following the death of King George V in 1936. England had preserved her hereditary monarchy, though the king's power was severely limited. When King Edward VIII, son of the late monarch, declared his intention to marry an American divorcee, Wallis Simpson, the government of Prime Minister Stanley Baldwin strenuously objected and eventually forced his abdication. This issue briefly threatened the stability of British government and could have precipitated a constitutional crisis. Only acceptance by the king of the government's demands prevented the situation from getting out of hand.

In major elements, France and England underwent a similar experience after the war. If the war had deeper effects on France, it was because that nation had borne the brunt of the battle on its soil and had suffered the greater losses on the battlefield. Fear of the possibility that Germany might rebuild had led the French to make stronger demands on them than the British, but, after all, France and Germany shared a common border. The similarities went to such matters as the lack of good leaders in government, inability to resolve economic problems, and desire to avoid deep international involvements.

France had entered World War I as one of the major powers of the world. She emerged in a state of shock that paralyzed her efforts to recover. Her great power status remained chiefly as a memory of the past and not as a reflection of reality in the present. During most of the twenties and thirties, the French atempted to play the role of major power. In an effort to protect themselves against a possible resurgence of Germany, they drew closer to Belgium and Poland. At Locarno, in the mid-twenties, the French began working toward a rapprochement with Germany that would give them a greater sense of security. The spirit of Locarno dominated French foreign policy for more than a decade.

Internally, the government of the Third Republic continued in much the same vane that it had before the war. The surplus of political parties made it almost impossible to secure clear-cut majorities. As a result, changes in government were frequent. However, the same faces usually appeared in each new government, merely shuffled about in order to secure the needed parliamentary majority. Political analysts have sometimes spoken of the "continuity" between the various governments to show that each change did not constitute an alteration of the direction of the policies of the state. On the whole, this analysis appears correct. However, it is also necessary to point out the weakness in such a system. No transitory political system could hope to solve the pressing social and economic problems facing the nation.

France had been hard hit by the war. She had lost considerable industry and had suffered a reduction in her agricultural production due to the occupation of part of her soil by the Germans. Although the end of the war permitted the resumption of manufacture of consumer goods and put an end to the German occupation, France came to bank heavily on German reparations payments to restore her economy. When Germany was unable to make these payments, the French had to stop payment of their own debts abroad and turn to other means to rebuild.

There were also deep cleavages in French social life. Labor was much more doctrinaire and more deeply influenced by Marxism in France than in England. Hatred and distrust of the bourgeoisie was rooted in the entire social experience of the workers. From childhood onward, the separation of Frenchmen into different social strata was the rule. Although universal free education was provided by the state on the primary level, secondary education was available only to those who could afford the tuition. Moreover, the strong classicism of the French secondary schools further encouraged social snobbery and class distinctions by making the gentleman one who was learned in the arts and humanities. The workers lived in separate districts and attended different forms of entertainment. There were two cultures in France to a much greater extent than in contemporary England or the United States.

These problems grew more serious during the thirties with the coming of the depression. Some of the middle class, fearful of the left, began to seek support in fascistlike organizations, many of which were anti-Semitic. In 1934, the rightists led an attack on the Chamber of Deputies. The riots lasted for several days and were put down with difficulty. The workers, on the other hand, supported the parties of the left, including the Communists. In 1936–1937, these parties formed the short-lived Popular Front government. However, the Popular Front showed no real talent for government and provided no solutions to the harsh economic realities of the depression. Hampered by its lack of control of the Senate and by the opposition of the French business interests, it fell. Its major contribution was that it disproved the theory that the left was attempting to overthrow the government and it brought the Communists into a parliamentary regime. French parliamentary democracy managed to survive the crises of the thirties on the domestic scene only to succumb to the German military machine in 1940.

In only one of the Western democracies did the thirties mark a significant change in domestic politics and the discovery of a great leader in the democratic political tradition. In the United States, the election of Franklin Delano Roosevelt as President in 1932, just as the country was suffering from the Great Depression, was an event of great consequence. Roosevelt, an aristocratic blueblood from New York and a distant cousin of the late President Theodore Roosevelt, tackled the problems of the depression with a will. During his first one hundred days in office, he secured from Congress a mass of important legislation to provide relief, increase expenditures for public works, regulate the stock exchange, aid agriculture, and a whole host of other projects. Roosevelt himself inspired confidence with his "fireside chats." Despite some setbacks at the hands of the courts, Roosevelt accomplished a "New Deal" for the American working classes and laid the foundations, by the Wagner Act, for collective bargaining on an industrywide basis. Although the depression struck hard at the American working class, the left secured only token support from that sector. Even in the depths of the depression, the majority of American workers remained committed to the traditional party system. Compared to France, the United States weathered the thirties well.

The Quest for Peace

The desire for peace enjoyed massive popular support in all of the democratic nations during the thirties. Looking back to World War I from the depression, many questioned the value of the war. It had claimed more lives than any war in history. Yet, what had it achieved?

Some questioned whether Germany had indeed been responsible for the war. They mistrusted their own wartime leaders and believed that they had been mere tools in an effort to limit German power on the continent. But the effort had failed. In the thirties, it appeared to some that Germany was better off than her conquerors. Hitler's resolute steps in dealing with the depression had brought a measure of prosperity to the country and at least ensured employment for the workers. In the United States, with more than ten million unemployed through the middle years of the decade, many persons of German descent began to think of their homeland as utopia. There was no question of disloyalty to the United States in their admiration for the German recovery, only a certain vicarious pride in being German. Others besides those of German background were sympathetic to German aspirations to regain lost territory and to recover lost prestige. Most people wanted peace and were willing to allow Germany almost anything so long as it might preserve that peace.

In the mid-thirties, both Germany and Italy emerged as aggressive powers. Late in December, 1934, an isolated incident along the common frontier between Italian Somaliland and Ethiopia gave Mussolini the pretext for a rapid conquest of that last independent native power on the African continent. Mussolini had determined that Italy would not be deprived of her rightful share of the vast African loaf divided among the European powers in the nineteenth century. His latter-day imperialism was as much motivated by his desire for a spectacular victory that would bolster his regime at home as by any particular interest in the Ethiopian highlands. The response of the Western powers was singularly feeble. The League of Nations took up the question of Italy's aggression and heard the pleas of the Emperor Haile Selassie. It recommended an embargo on Italy, but drew out the big teeth of this punishment by exempting oil. In the final analysis, it was obvious that peace was worth the price of Ethiopia in the minds of British and French statesmen.

Meanwhile, Hitler had begun his moves. Frustrated by Mussolini in an attempt to seize power in Austria in 1934, Hitler turned his attention to the Rhineland between France and Germany. He launched a strong propaganda campaign to justify his action and proceeded to march troops into the Rhineland in violation of the Versailles Treaty. His action was all the more daring in that he did not have the support of his own general staff. However, France made no effective moves against him and the troops remained. Hitler's prestige in Germany increased as a result of this success, handed to him by the French.

However, in fairness to Western statesmen, we must point to the general attitude in the West against interfering in what was thought of by many as Germany's private affairs. In the democracies, there was no popular support for intervention. On the contrary, the spirit of appeasement was in the air. Again disillusionment with World War I played an important part in molding public opinion, which played a decisive role in shaping the policy of appeasement. Sons who had listened from childhood to their fathers' bitter critiques on the failure of that war to achieve anything substantial either for the cause of peace or for aggrandizement had little desire to fight a new war. The peace movement swept the colleges in England and the United States. Students signed statements that they would never again go to war for their country under any circumstance. Interestingly enough, these acts were not confined to "radicals." In the United States, the peace movement found considerable support in American isolationism. The isolationists feared the consequences of American entry onto the international stage. Drawing heavily on support from the Midwestern "farm belt," they were instrumental in securing the passage of a series of neutrality acts in the years 1935–1937, aimed at preventing a recurrence of the submarine crisis preceding World War I. It is apparent that there was no support for the wise policy of nipping the aggressors in the bud.

Despite the strong desire for peace, its reality kept slipping further away. After 1935, events began to move so fast that it was hard to escape the air of crisis. Headlines shrieked out Spain, China, Czechoslovakia, Munich, Austria, one after another, to call attention to the current trouble spot.

One of the first areas of crisis was Spain. After the overthrow of the Spanish monarchy in 1931, Spain at last joined the ranks of republican nations. However, her experiment with democracy was short-lived. A large segment of the Spanish population was either indifferent or even opposed to the government. They included parts of the army and many of the leaders of the Church. The republicans themselves were divided. The regime was hard put to maintain itself in power. Yet, on balance, there was a large segment of the population that opposed the restoration of the monarchy and its conservative allies. There were also Catalonian separatists who supported the republic because it had met their demands for greater independence. There were moderate Catholics, who preferred a republican government with its greater freedoms. There were Basques, who desired some measure of independence. All of these, whatever their reasons, supported the republican government. The Civil War that broke out in 1936 pitted all of these groups against one another. Generalissimo

Francisco Franco, conservative of the old military class, but an able military leader, led the rebels. He received support not only from the supporters of the old regime, but also from Spain's budding fascists, the Falange. The war was one of the most bloody in history, with numerous atrocities committed by both sides. It also posed a threat to peace in the possible involvement of other nations. However, the Western powers adhered strictly to a policy of nonintervention despite utter disregard for the nonintervention agreement by Germany, Italy, and the Soviet Union. All of the leading powers had signed the pact, only the dictators ignored it. Spain thus moved to the right, very near the Fascist camp with the victory of the rebels and the accession to power of Franco.

The Nazis moved quickly in the late thirties to realize their announced goal, the creation of a pan-German state. In 1938, Hitler launched a campaign to annex Austria. The result was the *Anschluss,* by which Austria surrendered her independence to become part of a greater German state. Opposition within Austria was quickly stymied by the presence of German troops and Austrian Nazis loyally rallied the mob to Hitler. With Austria in his pocket, the German dictator demanded that Czechoslovakia "free" the large German population of the Sudetenland, part of western Czechoslovakia. His propaganda pictured these prosperous and generally happy Germans as oppressed subjects of an alien government and employed the techniques of nationalism to stir up opposition to the Czechs among the Sudetan Germans. Rallies, inflammatory speeches, and assurances of support from the fatherland put pressure on the Czechs. The determination of the Czechs, supported for the moment by the Soviet Union, France, and England, forced Hitler to delay his plans, but not for long. The French and English soon began applying pressure on the Czechs to agree to Hitler's demands. Prime Minister Neville Chamberlain of England, alarmed by the crisis and anxious to preserve peace joined the French in meeting Hitler at Munich in September, 1938, to settle the Czech crisis. There Mussolini acted the part of "honest broker" in an agreement that dismembered Czechoslovakia. Chamberlain returned to London to announce that the day was saved. There would be "peace in our time." Once more appeasement had prevented war. But the question that troubled many statesmen in 1938 was how long would the policy of appeasement succeed? There was an increasing realization that Hitler had to be stopped.

The quest for peace was failing in the West. It was also breaking down elsewhere in the world. Europe was moving to another war. No one really wanted to fight. But events kept pressing them into the conflict.

Munich. Mussolini, Hitler, and Chamberlain (far right) at the moment of crisis. Peace died here. (Brown Brothers)

The Democratic Reality

The development of political democracy was revolutionary in its impact on Western civilization. It has been a major influence in altering the structure of society, opening opportunity to more and more people. In the field of education, broader opportunities have meant not a sharing in older aristocratic conceptions of what knowledge has value but a new scale of democratic values. In the arts, democracy has inspired the artist to appeal to a new audience; it has also caused him to react against mass art forms. In science and technology, the concept of service to humanity in the democratic sense has brought a new sense of responsibility. The democratic experience has worked to transform industrial society by making ownership of productive property more responsive to the social needs of the masses. Thus in almost every area it is possible to see how democracy had played an important role in the creation of twentieth-century society in most countries of the West, of Western Europe and the Americas.

Yet the twentieth century has witnessed numerous critics of democracy. Marxist socialism has continued to view democracy as a fraud perpetrated upon the working classes to sustain the capitalistic economy. The fascist right ridiculed the ineffectiveness of democratic nations in dealing with their social and economic problems and their weakness in foreign affairs. Even within the pale of liberalism, conservatives have attacked democracy for putting power in the hands of the mob and for establishing the welfare state. On the left, some supposed supporters of democratic freedoms have proposed state regulation of almost every aspect of life. At no time has democracy been free from attack.

In the years between the wars, the democratic nations labored under continual stress. While the comparative strength of a particular nation's political institutions varied, the vitality of the democratic principle appears to have flourished in spite of adversity. In France, for example, attacks from the right and left did threaten to destroy the Third Republic, perhaps to replace it with some sort of totalitarian regime. What saved the republic was the coalition of moderates and leftists in the Popular Front that was committed to parliamentary rule. For a brief moment even the Communists deserted their traditional policies of harassment of constitutional government to make the Popular Front possible. In England, where there was somewhat more governmental stability in the thirties, the failure of the political parties to provide strong leadership raised the question of viability of democratic government. Some critics suggested that popular opinion had too great an influence on the molding of foreign policy, making it difficult to pursue successful negotiations with other countries in an atmosphere of reason. However, England continued along the democratic path without interruption. The United States raised the question of the role of the demagogue in democratic politics as opponents of Franklin D. Roosevelt saw his ability to sway popular majorities behind his programs. But, the constitutional framework of American government proved sufficiently flexible to permit the testing of new ideas without breaking. The United States Supreme Court continued its function as the watchdog of the constitutionality of legislation and the Congress provided a forum for dissent. In these countries, democratic government met the challenges of the thirties.

The most revolutionary changes in social organization occurred as one might expect in the United States, where the gap between the middle class and the worker became more and more blurred. In the Great Depression of the thirties, the United States experienced less of the conflict between classes and more a feeling of solidarity in face of a major economic disaster. In spite of the depression, opportunities for secondary education increased for the American workers and the development of a system of inexpensive state colleges and normal schools brought higher education within reach of many. Education was no longer the exclusive province of the sons and daughters of the middle class and those few worthy children of the poor able to secure scholarships. America made education a vehicle of democracy as the American philosopher John Dewey had recommended at the beginning of the century. Upward mobility provided a safety valve that enabled the potential leaders of the lower class to climb to a new freedom. But it was not a means of escape for them alone. Rather, it was a pathway for all who could follow their example. In the United States, too, the absence of any established aristocratic group made wealth the chief criterion for social advancement. The existence of broader economic opportunities meant that a larger portion of the population could enjoy a social status rivaling the old European nobility and the higher bourgeoisie. Democracy further broadened these opportunities by strengthening the voice of the lower classes in economic policy. In England and more so in France, the class structure was somewhat rigid. The impact of democracy on social organization was less and the tensions between the middle class and the workers were greater.

Democracy was the sire of the welfare state. The liberals of the nineteenth century had asked the state to abstain from interference in the operation of the economy. It should be a "passive policeman," offering protection with its armies and police, promoting good order, and preserving peace. Democratic liberals wanted a government that would promote the common good. They supported legislation to regulate conditions of labor, to set standards of health and sanitation, to prevent monopoly in industry, to provide for insurance for accident and old age, and acts that covered a wide range of human needs. They were concerned about education, public institutions for orphans and the elderly, and care for the poor. Thus, under democratic influences, the state grew more concerned about the broad welfare of its citizens. Although the charge of socialism sometimes slowed the progress of welfare legislation, the trend continued without major interruption.

But democracy has not been without fault. Its major weakness has been the slow pace of its progress toward the realization of its goals. Almost by its nature, because of its commitment to political gradualism, democracy has meant that the period between the recognition of a need and the furnishing of an adequate remedy is a long one. Impatience with this slow pace has frequently led to internal crisis including strikes and riots. A democratic process has also changed the nature of political leadership by encouraging the demagogue to use his powers of persuasion to run for office. In the United States, the practice of "bloc voting" by immigrant minorities like the Irish, Italians, Poles, and others, tended to negate the full effects of the democratic process by concentrating power in the hands of one party leader and his supporters in a particular city or state. Nor has the power of the ballot resulted automatically in a higher standard of political morality. Voters too often have developed predictable electoral habits that enabled politicians to become complacent in office. But, perhaps the most serious charge leveled at democracy is that it has established standards of mediocrity in all phases of life. The basis for the accusation lies in the tendency for the democratic society to develop mass approaches to art, literature, entertainment, and many other elements that form the culture of a society. Despite serious efforts to raise the level of public taste and to inculcate habits of good speech and writing, the gap between the masses and the educated and cultured minority has remained. The fear that the majority may succeed in destroying the concept of excellence by its control over government haunts those who desire their society to aspire to the highest goals.

Still, the achievements of democracy far outweigh any reservations we may be able to produce. Democracy offers man the freedom to explore further the best way to govern himself.

24 The Failure of Democracy in the Far East

The task of building democratic institutions along Western lines proved insurmountable in the Far East before World War II. Neither China nor Japan had traditions on which these institutions could be founded. They were imports from the West, advocated by a small number of intellectuals who had come under the influence of Europe and America and whose own liberalism was often a thin veneer over the alien political traditions of their own past. Not that the effort to create democracy lost through lack of their strong desire. On the contrary, their sincere attempts met constant frustration from warlords in China and from resurgent militarism in Japan. In the long run, it was the imperialistic expansion of Japan into China that dealt the death blow to any dream Chinese liberals might have had of establishing genuine parliamentary government. The Japanese invasion paved the way for the rise to power of the Chinese Communists.

The population of Asia and the great land mass of that continent were never historically brought into play in the shaping of world politics before the twentieth century, at least not since very early times. In the period following World War I, both China and Japan stepped onto the international stage. Japan was a modern industrial and military power. China still struggled to conclude the revolution that, having overthrown the empire, had become a struggle between various factions. Yet the potential power of China and the actual power of Japan only slowly made an impression on Europeans and Americans.

China: The Unfinished Revolution

The Chinese Revolution of 1911 toppled an imperial regime that had maintained its feeble grasp over the country only with difficulty in the face of the encroachments of European imperialism. It was no great task to overthrow the old empire; it proved very difficult to build a government in its place. One problem that faced the new government was the division among the revolutionaries themselves. Military dictatorship vied with the supporters of parliamentary government for leadership. The sheer difficulty of effectively ruling the vast land expanse of China with its numerous petty warlords and tendencies toward particularism put a major obstacle in front of the new regime. The continuing presence of Europeans and the need to formulate a policy aimed at preserving Chinese independence against their interference, real or suspected, made cooperation with any of them a dangerous policy. The indifference of the Chinese masses and their attachment to centuries-old traditions made the task of mobilizing the nation for a leap into the industrial age a constant frustration. The growing interest of Japan in Chinese affairs and the demand put by that nation to the revolutionary government of China endangered not merely its stability but even its existence. In the face of all these obstacles, the failure of the Chinese Revolution to achieve the goals of modernizing China does not appear so cataclysmic nor do the alternatives that present themselves seem simple. In fact, it is really not surprising that the Revolution of 1911 never ended at all, but was a continuing and unrealized goal until the fall of the Nationalist Government to the Chinese Communists in 1949.

The immediate heir to the power of the Manchu dynasty in China was General Yuan Shi K'ai (1859–1916), whose leadership of the rebel army had chiefly contributed to the fall of the old regime. Yuan established a military government with headquarters at Peking, where a new National Assembly designated him Premier of China. Despite this parliamentary façade, however, Yuan was no supporter of constitutional parliamentary government. In many ways, he was merely a greater version of the warlords who controlled various districts in China with their private armies. The opposition to Yuan came from Dr. Sun Yat Sen (1866–1925), who, having returned to China from exile in 1911, established a parliamentary government at Nanking. His regime was short-lived and he became the leader of the opposition to Yuan. During World War I, Japan, having seized the opportunity to advance her interests in the Far East under the guise of aiding her English ally, moved into China on a large scale. Her army invaded north China and the Shantung Peninsula, the German sphere of influence. Japan also took advantage of the involvement of England and the other European powers in the European war to demand an almost total recognition by China of Japan's position as the leading Asian power. The Twenty-One Demands, presented to Yuan in 1916, would have made China a dependency of Japan if accepted. Yuan's position was weak and he was unable to stand up to the Japanese. He had to accept the demands in part, despite the effects on the prestige of his leadership.

Yuan died in 1916. As the strong man of China, he had tried to unite the nation. With his death, his successors in the Peking government found it increasingly difficult just to maintain the fiction of rule. Dr. Sun Yat Sen led a separatist movement by setting up a new government in Canton. However, this division further weakened China in the face of the Japanese. At the end of World War I, Japan made good her conquest of the Shantung Peninsula at the Paris Peace Conference. China simply was unable to stand up to Japan. Divided politically and weak in industry, her leaders had to face the reality that she was prey to the aggressor unless they could transform this ancient land into a modern nation. China faced a new revolution, that would change her economic and social structure.

But China's weakness made the beginning of this task almost impossible. In the early twenties, taking advantage of the weakness of central authority, warlords took over much of the country. Dr. Sun Yat Sen had to flee Canton to escape one of them, who captured the capital. Sun turned to outside support from the only nation that appeared sympathetic to the plight of the Chinese people, the Soviet Union. In 1923, the Soviets began to send military and technical personnel to China to work with the Chinese. These advisers worked closely with the Chinese Communists to prop up the Canton government. Russian help was valuable in enabling Sun's regime to expand its control over a larger area of China. By the time the founder of modern China died in 1925, there was a glimmer of hope that his land would emerge from its long torpor.

Sun's successor was Chiang Kai-shek, Soviet-trained military commander and advocate of major internal reforms. Between 1925 and 1927, he worked closely with the Russians and the Chinese Communists to regain political and military control of north China. His success resulted in the capture of Shanghai and the establishment of the capital at Nanking. However, Chiang did a major about-face in 1927. He drove the Chinese Communists out of his government and rejected further Russian aid. He and the Kuomintang, the political organization formed by Dr. Sun Yat

Sen to oppose General Yuan, embraced nationalism rather than socialism as the key element in the creation of the new China. Chiang also moved his country closer to the Western powers during this period. He saw in their industrialization the direction in which China must move. In his bid for the support of the West, Chiang also worked to obtain the backing of China's powerful commercial and banking class, largely located in the cities along the coast. He soft-pedaled programs for land reform to obtain commercial support for industrialization. By 1930, China appeared certain to realize the goal of becoming a major power in Asia.

But once more, the hope of China was doomed to disappointment. Internally, opposition to the Chiang government came from the Chinese

Mao Tse-tung, leader of the Chinese Communists. Rejected by Moscow, he waited until victory came after World War II. (United Press International)

Communists, led by Mao Tse-tung. However, they were unable to pose a serious threat because Stalin had refused to support them after 1927. Without Russian aid, they were merely able to sustain themselves and little else. The real threat to China was external. Japan had not given up her imperialistic ambitions for leadership in Asia. During the thirties, she formulated these ideas into the plan for an "All Asia Co-prosperity Sphere" to appeal for Asian support for her program. At the same time, she began to step up her campaign against the Chinese in the north. It was the Japanese invasion of China in 1937 that played the decisive role in paving the way for the Communist takeover in China.

Japan the Aggressor

Modernization had brought Japan the respect of the Western powers. Victory in the Russo-Japanese War had taught them that Japan had ambitions of her own for the development of Asia not necessarily in agreement with those of the Europeans. Japanese entry into World War I had not received the enthusiastic support of England, who would have preferred to see Japan remain neutral in order to stabilize the political situation. England realized the nature of Japan's ambitions and had no desire to aid them. However, she was in too weak a position to prevent the Japanese from carrying out their decision.

The entry of Japan into World War I on the side of the allies was more than an opening toward possible imperial expansion. By this avenue, the Japanese secured further recognition of their position as a major power, indeed the only major power in Asia. She had gone far toward achieving equality to the Western powers in foreign relations. But the war also offered a safe opportunity for expansion in China at German expense. As a result of the war, Japan secured Germany's former sphere of influence on the Shantung Peninsula, a very significant key to the control of north China.

During most of the twenties, Japan pressed its advantage against China with economic rather than political weapons. Her government was dominated by the conservative interests of "big business," who had no desire to fight a war that might interrupt the lucrative Chinese trade. However, reluctance to fight did not mean relaxation of the tactics of harassment that had characterized the Japanese policy toward the Republic of China since its founding. The Twenty-One Demands presented to General Yuan during World War I still formed the basic text for Japanese policy toward China; the main features of this plan were economic domination and political subservience.

Democracy had made no progress in Japan before World War II. The Japanese Parliament had no real control over the ministers of the government. The emperor had been reduced, after 1931, to the position of a mere figurehead, with the real power in the hands of a group of top-level generals and admirals. In the process of industrialization, Japan had followed the continental European model and allowed the development of huge cartels or monopolies. As a result great wealth was concentrated in the hands of Japan's leading industrialists. With their emphasis on the growth of industry, the Japanese had permitted the industrialists a major voice in all phases of government policy. True, industry had prospered, but Japan remained a tightly controlled society ruled by a relatively small group of individuals. Under these circumstances, parliamentary government in Japan had never been anything but a façade. With the rise to power of the military, that façade remained.

The increasing militarism of the Japanese during the thirties paralleled the "tough" policy adopted by Hitler in Germany. It is hardly surprising, therefore, to find these two powers drawn closer during the years after 1935. The mounting criticism of Japan in Europe and America promoted the alliance of Germany and Japan.

The first big outbreak of Japanese aggression during the thirties occurred in Manchuria. This outer province of China lay along the Russia border and was only loosely controlled by the republican government. Japan took advantage of several minor incidents in 1931 to take over the area. In all probability, the Japanese had manufactured most of the incidents that led to their invasion. In place of the Chinese warlord who had ruled the region for China, the Japanese established a puppet Manchu emperor in Manchuria, now called Manchuchuo. This puppet regime hung over the Chinese as a threat of impending doom at the hands of Japan. The attack on Manchuria lasted but a few months. It aroused considerable public opinion against Japan in the West, but brought no sanctions. Neither the United States nor England pressed hard for effective measures to force Japan to return the territory to China. The League of Nations debated a resolution to condemn Japan for more than two years before finally voting to condemn the action. By that time, the League itself was in its death agony. Japan simply helped to hasten the demise of that unfortunate body by her withdrawal. Failure to censure Japanese invasion of Manchuria and effectively to control aggression there was a prelude to later failures in Ethiopia and in the withdrawal of Nazi Germany.

The League, which the American Senate had steadfastly rejected, had once promised the hope of world peace. By the mid-thirties, this slim reed was proving how poorly the victors of World War I had worked in their effort to create an institution for peace.

Japanese success in Manchuria opened the door to further incidents on Chinese soil. During most of the thirties, when the Chiang government was trying to build a modern Chinese state, it had to cope with continued Japanese harassment. In 1937, the Japanese gave up all pretence and invaded China. The first act of World War II had begun in Asia, though few at the time were willing to see the Chinese-Japanese War other than as a distant struggle between alien peoples.

The World in 1939

In 1939, Europe stood at the threshold of war. For the second time in the twentieth century, a struggle between Europe national states was to plunge the world into conflict. Again, nationalism was a significant factor. The extreme nationalistic bent of the Fascist powers, Germany and Italy, was a grotesque distortion of any true ideal of patriotism. It demanded utter subservience by the individual to the will of the state.

In face of this extreme view, Western Europe and the United States were gradually forced to reexamine their attitudes toward German aggression. The spirit of appeasement fell as Hitler showed that the concessions made in Munich would not stop his march. In 1939, he turned his attention to Poland and demanded that the Poles surrender the port city of Danzig, which they had acquired after World War I. His propaganda machine demanded the return of Danzig to the *Reich*.

Tensions mounted as the Germans moved to isolate the Poles diplomatically. Hitler's foreign minister, Joachim von Ribbentrop, flew to Moscow to discuss a nonaggression treaty with the Russians. The German aim was to prevent a Soviet-Polish alliance. Actually, the initiative for the meeting came from Stalin himself. The Soviet dictator feared that a German advance into Poland would be the prelude to an invasion of Russia. He had little respect for the Western democracies and desired to gain time to rearm. On August 23, 1939, von Ribbentrop and V. M. Molotov signed the nonaggression pact. This alliance was a significant blow to the Western powers. They were left to face Hitler alone.

While Europe moved toward war in the fall of 1939, the tenor of life in the United States was barely affected. President Roosevelt was increasingly alarmed by the prospect of war, but the dominant note through the

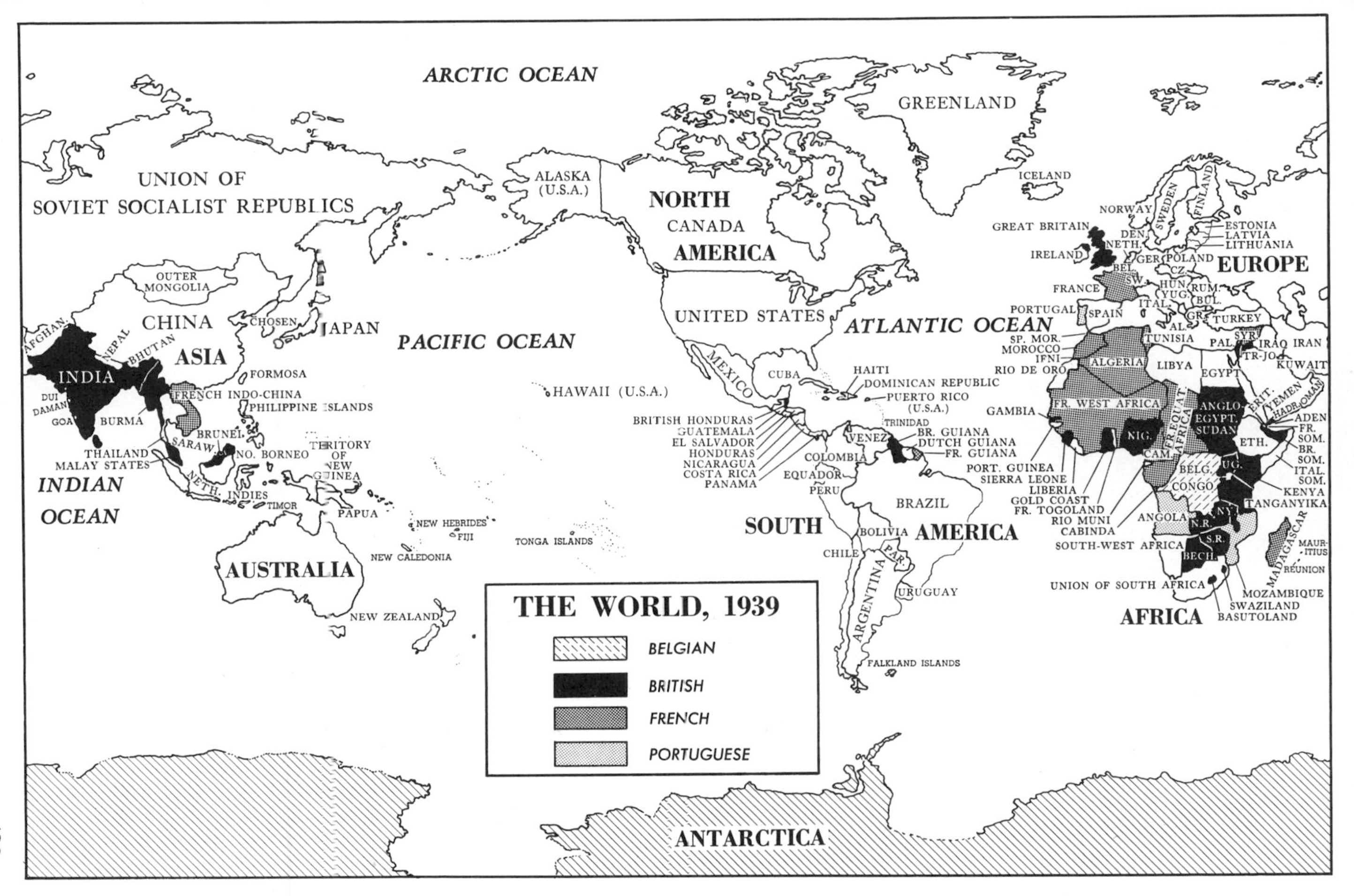
THE WORLD, 1939
BELGIAN
BRITISH
FRENCH
PORTUGUESE
ARCTIC OCEAN
PACIFIC OCEAN
ATLANTIC OCEAN
INDIAN OCEAN
NORTH AMERICA
SOUTH AMERICA
EUROPE
AFRICA
ASIA
AUSTRALIA
ANTARCTICA
GREENLAND
ICELAND
CANADA
ALASKA (U.S.A.)
UNITED STATES
MEXICO
CUBA
HAITI
DOMINICAN REPUBLIC
PUERTO RICO (U.S.A.)
HAWAII (U.S.A.)
BRITISH HONDURAS
GUATEMALA
EL SALVADOR
HONDURAS
NICARAGUA
COSTA RICA
PANAMA
TRINIDAD
BR. GUIANA
DUTCH GUIANA
FR. GUIANA
VENEZ.
COLOMBIA
ECUADOR
PERU
BRAZIL
BOLIVIA
PAR.
URUGUAY
CHILE
ARGENTINA
FALKLAND ISLANDS
UNION OF SOVIET SOCIALIST REPUBLICS
GREAT BRITAIN
IRELAND
NORWAY
SWEDEN
FINLAND
ESTONIA
LATVIA
LITHUANIA
DEN.
NETH.
BEL.
GER.
POLAND
CZ.
HUN.
RUM.
YUG.
BUL.
FRANCE
SW.
ITAL.
GR.
AL.
SPAIN
PORTUGAL
TURKEY
SYR.
PAL.
TR.-JO.
IRAQ
IRAN
KUWAIT
OMAN
HADR.
YEMEN
ADEN
SP. MOR.
MOROCCO
IFNI
RIO DE ORO
ALGERIA
TUNISIA
LIBYA
EGYPT
ANGLO-EGYPT. SUDAN
ERIT.
FR. SOM.
BR. SOM.
ITAL. SOM.
ETH.
FR. WEST AFRICA
FR. EQUAT. AFRICA
GAMBIA
PORT. GUINEA
SIERRA LEONE
LIBERIA
GOLD COAST
FR. TOGOLAND
NIG.
CAM.
RIO MUNI
CABINDA
BELG. CONGO
UG.
KENYA
TANGANYIKA
ANGOLA
N.R.
NY.
S.R.
BECH.
MOZAMBIQUE
MADAGASCAR
MAUR-ITIUS
REUNION
SOUTH-WEST AFRICA
UNION OF SOUTH AFRICA
SWAZILAND
BASUTOLAND
AFGHAN.
INDIA
NEPAL
BHUTAN
DUI
DAMAN
GOA
CHINA
OUTER MONGOLIA
BURMA
THAILAND
MALAY STATES
FRENCH INDO-CHINA
CHOSEN
JAPAN
FORMOSA
PHILIPPINE ISLANDS
BRUNEI
SARAW.
NO. BORNEO
NETH. INDIES
TIMOR
TERRITORY OF NEW GUINEA
PAPUA
NEW CALEDONIA
NEW HEBRIDES
FIJI
TONGA ISLANDS
NEW ZEALAND

country was antiwar. The chief concern of most Americans was the continuing depression, which had created widespread unemployment. Among the loudest voices heard was that of the Reverend Charles Coughlin, a Catholic priest of Detroit, who despite criticism, had an audience of millions. Father Coughlin denounced Roosevelt's "New Deal" and condemned what he called the "international bankers" and the Jews. He even spoke somewhat admiringly of the social programs carried out in Germany and Italy. He was an ardent defender of the Spanish rebel leader, General Franco. The radicalism of Father Coughlin certainly did not represent the thought of the mass of Americans, but it did indicate the troubled soul of a large segment of the country.

In 1939, there was a latent conviction among many Americans that Europe had embarked on a course of war. During the next year the debate over American entry into the war increased. However, the government of Franklin Roosevelt, while remaining technically neutral, gradually followed that body of public opinion that desired United States aid to England.

The Western democracies made little effort to prepare for the war. It was not until about a year before the actual outbreak that England began to rearm. The United States did not even introduce a military draft law until war had begun in Europe. France was torn by internal political dissension. The West was unprepared for a major war.

While last-minute preparations for war were being made in Europe, the Far East was already in turmoil. For almost two years, the Japanese had methodically driven the Chinese out of the major coastal cities and into the interior. Their conquests threatened the existence of that nation. Elsewhere in Asia, the major question was the persistence of colonialism. In India, Mohandas K. Gandhi led nonviolent protests against British rule. His hunger strikes won worldwide publicity for the cause of home rule for India. Other Indians demanded complete independence. In Southeast Asia, both the English and the French met opposition to the continuance of colonial rule from the small intellectual elites of these countries. In colonial Asia, the prospect of war appeared generally remote and the focus of concern was on the struggle for freedom from foreign rule. The coming of the war served merely to postpone the drive for independence in India and Southeast Asia.

Africa was still the dark continent. Most Americans and Europeans harbored romantic notions of jungles and pygmies, with naked savages eating boiled missionaries. Such information as trickled out of colonial Africa lent credence to this general picture of backwardness and sav-

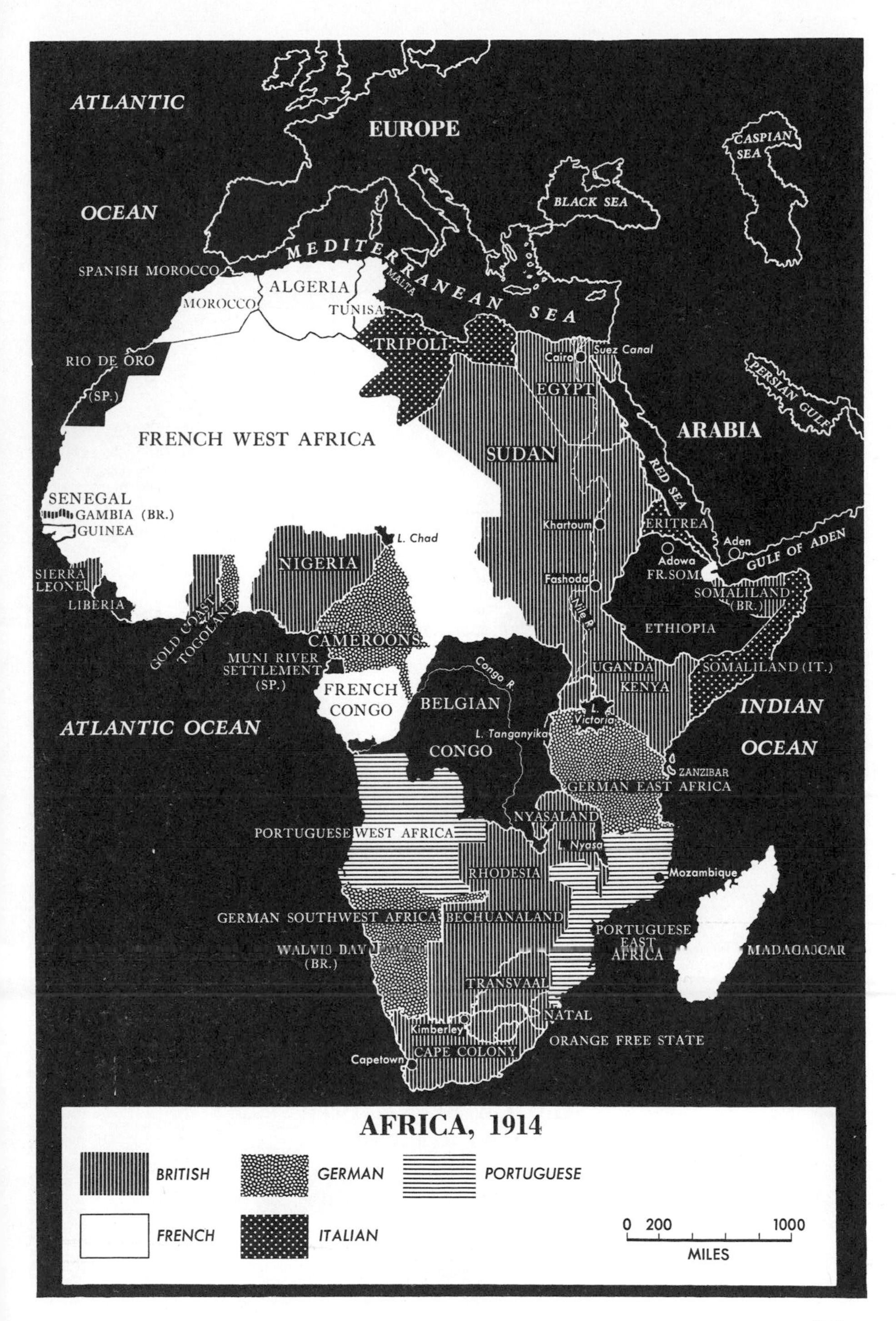
ATLANTIC
OCEAN
EUROPE
CASPIAN SEA
BLACK SEA
MEDITERRANEAN SEA
MALTA
SPANISH MOROCCO
ALGERIA
MOROCCO
TUNISA
TRIPOLI
RIO DE ORO (SP.)
Cairo
Suez Canal
EGYPT
PERSIAN GULF
ARABIA
FRENCH WEST AFRICA
SUDAN
RED SEA
SENEGAL
GAMBIA (BR.)
GUINEA
L. Chad
Khartoum
ERITREA
Aden
Adowa
FR.SOM.
GULF OF ADEN
SIERRA LEONE
LIBERIA
NIGERIA
Fashoda
SOMALILAND (BR.)
GOLD COAST
TOGOLAND
Nile R.
ETHIOPIA
CAMEROONS
MUNI RIVER SETTLEMENT (SP.)
Congo R.
UGANDA
SOMALILAND (IT.)
KENYA
FRENCH CONGO
BELGIAN CONGO
L. Victoria
INDIAN OCEAN
ATLANTIC OCEAN
L. Tanganyika
ZANZIBAR
GERMAN EAST AFRICA
NYASALAND
PORTUGUESE WEST AFRICA
L. Nyasa
RHODESIA
Mozambique
GERMAN SOUTHWEST AFRICA
BECHUANALAND
PORTUGUESE EAST AFRICA
MADAGASCAR
WALVIS BAY (BR.)
TRANSVAAL
NATAL
Kimberley
ORANGE FREE STATE
Capetown
CAPE COLONY
AFRICA, 1914
BRITISH
GERMAN
PORTUGUESE
FRENCH
ITALIAN
0 200 1000
MILES

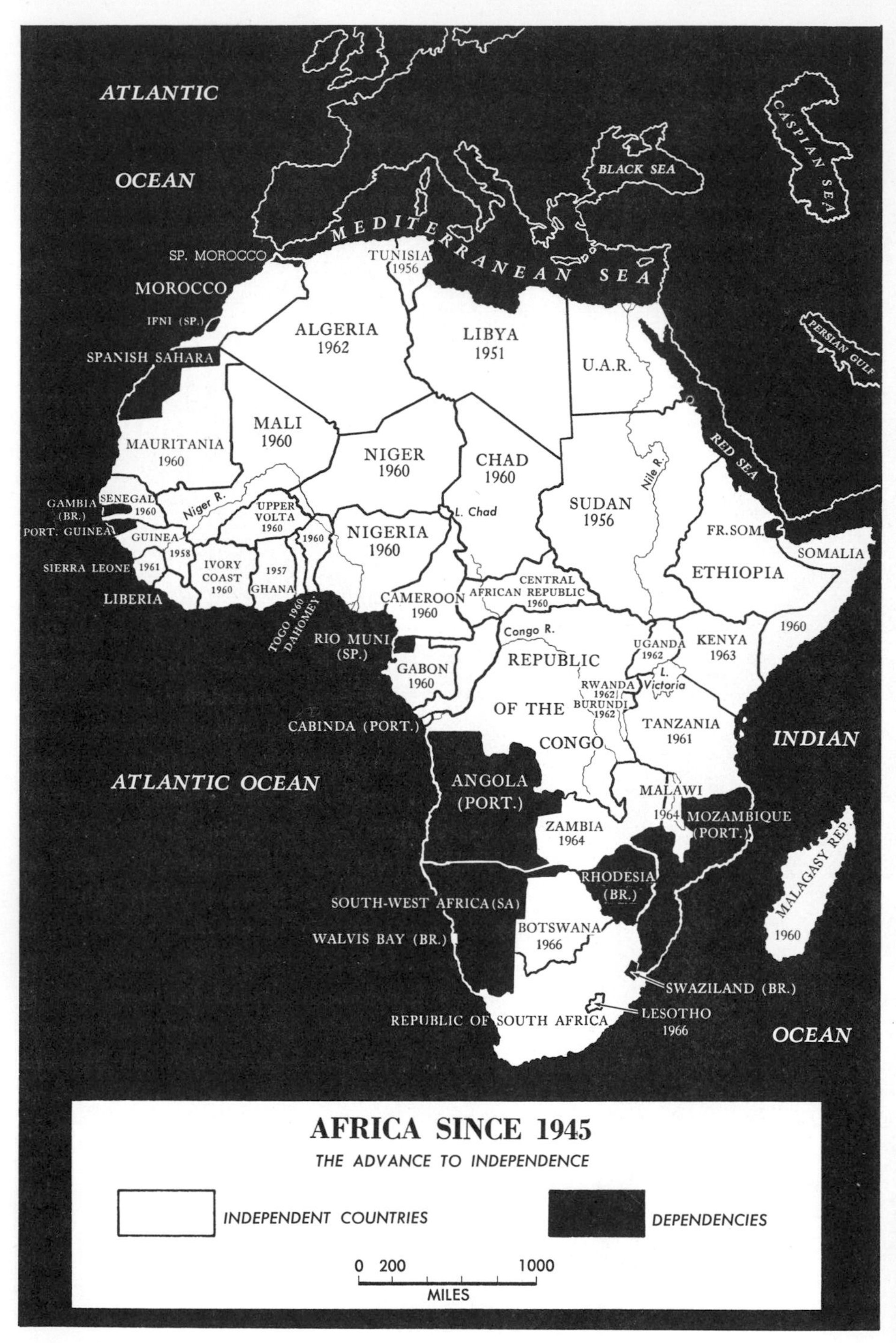
ATLANTIC
OCEAN
BLACK SEA
CASPIAN SEA
MEDITERRANEAN SEA
SP. MOROCCO
TUNISIA 1956
MOROCCO
IFNI (SP.)
ALGERIA 1962
LIBYA 1951
U.A.R.
PERSIAN GULF
SPANISH SAHARA
MALI 1960
MAURITANIA 1960
NIGER 1960
CHAD 1960
RED SEA
Nile R.
SUDAN 1956
GAMBIA (BR.)
SENEGAL 1960
Niger R.
UPPER VOLTA 1960
L. Chad
PORT. GUINEA
GUINEA 1958
1960
NIGERIA 1960
FR.SOM.
SOMALIA
SIERRA LEONE 1961
IVORY COAST 1960
1957 GHANA
CENTRAL AFRICAN REPUBLIC 1960
ETHIOPIA
LIBERIA
TOGO 1960
DAHOMEY
CAMEROON 1960
1960
RIO MUNI (SP.)
Congo R.
UGANDA 1962
KENYA 1963
GABON 1960
REPUBLIC OF THE CONGO
RWANDA 1962
L. Victoria
BURUNDI 1962
CABINDA (PORT.)
TANZANIA 1961
INDIAN
ATLANTIC OCEAN
ANGOLA (PORT.)
MALAWI 1964
MOZAMBIQUE (PORT.)
MALAGASY REP. 1960
ZAMBIA 1964
RHODESIA (BR.)
SOUTH-WEST AFRICA (SA)
BOTSWANA 1966
WALVIS BAY (BR.)
SWAZILAND (BR.)
REPUBLIC OF SOUTH AFRICA
LESOTHO 1966
OCEAN
AFRICA SINCE 1945
THE ADVANCE TO INDEPENDENCE
INDEPENDENT COUNTRIES
DEPENDENCIES
0 200 1000
MILES

agery. However, the winds of change had begun to blow across Black Africa. Modern sanitation and effective measures against the causes of malaria and sleeping sickness reduced the death rate, while better prenatal and natal care increased the percentage of live births. Through the efforts of governments and missionaries, some beginnings had been made in the field of education. A few Africans even made the long journeys to Oxford, Cambridge, Paris, and other European university centers to continue their education. These returned to their own countries very often to take up the cudgels against colonialism.

On the eve of the war, the world was on the brink of major changes that would change its entire structure and challenge Western European hegemony. The war served to postpone the realization of these changes in the sense that most colonial regimes remained intact until after the fighting, but it may also have hastened their demise by weakening the major colonial powers, England and France, in their ability and desire to maintain far-flung possessions. The age of European hegemony over the world was drawing to a close in 1939.

25 The Contemporary World

Perhaps at some future date, historians will write of World War II as one of the great turning points of history. Now it is too soon to do more than point to a few trends that have developed into major themes in world history since the war. The triumph of Communism in China has dramatically altered the history of that country. The growth of independent nations in former colonial possessions has already transformed the position of Europe in the world. The development of the United Nations Organization has not repeated the history of the old League of Nations and may point to a more important role in the future for international organizations. Since the war, conflict between the Communist nations and the Western powers has seen alternating periods of crisis and reduced tension, but no major breakthrough toward a settlement of differences. Though, in some ways, Europe has moved further from the nation-state, Asia has moved closer to it. Thus, hope of reduced national tensions has been frustrated by the high tide of nationalistic sentiment in the new nations.

At the end of World War II, the United States exploded the atomic bomb, ushering in the nuclear age. After the war, the Soviet Union and other nations joined the nuclear club and scientists developed a hydrogen bomb with even greater destructive force. Improvements in rocketry made possible the first probes of outer space and the launching of men into orbit. The space age had dawned. Technology thus held promise of a quest to explore the universe or the threat of annihilation.

World War II

On September 1, 1939, the German army invaded Poland. Thus began the lightning war, the *blitzkrieg,* as the Germans called it. The Germans made effective use of tanks and airplanes in overpowering the enemy. The Nazi invasion of Poland ended the hesitation of the French and British. France had pledged support for the Poles in event of war and war had come. But the French had planned basically a defensive war behind their impregnable fortresses along the Maginot Line. But the Germans did not invade and the French made no effort to launch an offensive. England sent her expeditionary force to France to await the Nazi invasion. From September, 1939, to May, 1940, the French and English experienced the "phony" war, when cafes in Paris still hummed with bright conversation while troops waited for an enemy who did not come. The Germans made short work of defeating Poland. By the end of September, they were in complete control and prepared to carry out the terms of their treaty with the Russians. Germany obtained most of Poland, almost the entire Polish population, while Russia got the East with its Ukrainians and Belorussians. The large Jewish population of prewar Poland lived in both areas, though probably more were in the East. Poland, whose brief freedom had begun at the end of World War I had its light extinguished at the very beginning of the war.

The long wait for the war to start in the West was partly the result of Hitler's desire to defeat Poland first and partly of poor weather conditions that would have hampered the operation of the German Panzer (Tank) Divisions. The Germans also wanted to consolidate the gains made by the army and to protect the German flanks. Concern about possible Anglo-French use of Norway to provide a base for harassment on the Baltic Sea led Hitler to invade that country and her Scandinavian neighbor Denmark early in 1940. By the middle of the year, Norway had fallen. In the meantime, Hitler turned his attention to France.

The French and English had expected the Germans to repeat the strategy of the Schlieffen Plan in World War I. They strengthened their line in Belgium and depended on the long Maginot Line to protect most of the Franco-German border. But Hitler moved his armies first against the Netherlands. He bombed the major cities heavily and rapidly occupied the country. Then, while the British and a large group of French and Belgians waited in Belgium, the Germans sent their tanks driving through the difficult terrain of the Ardennes Forest to the southeast and raced for the English Channel. Cut off by this maneuver, the English and their allies had to flee by every kind of craft they could beg, borrow, or commandeer. The evacuation of Dunkirk was one of those heroic moments that aroused tremendous patriotic sentiment, but it was a major defeat. The evacuation at Dunkirk took place early in June. The Germans had now bypassed the French defenses and headed for Paris, arriving on June 13, 1940. Before the month was out, France had surrendered. Hitler had succeeded where the armies of the Kaiser had failed.

With France out of the war, neutralized as a Nazi satellite under the government of the aged Marshall Petain at Vichy, England stood alone. She now faced the threat of a German invasion, while Mussolini's Italy took advantage of the German successes to invade the Balkans and Greece. The British expected an invasion at almost any time. The wartime prime minister of the national coalition, Winston Churchill, spurred on the flagging spirits of the British and told the world of England's plight. His words aroused deep sympathy in America for the cause of the English underdogs.

Through the remainder of 1940 and most of 1941, the war against England was an air war. German bombers returned again and again to rain down bombs on English cities. Londoners lived in the underground for days and nights, emerging valiantly to repair the damage caused by the blitz and to return to work. The indomitable spirit of the British rose to the occasion. British Spitfire fighters acquired an enviable reputation and their pilots won admiration for their courageous meetings with the Germans in the skies. Still, however, Hitler did not order the expected invasion. His reasons remain something of a mystery. England was no match for his superior air power and land forces in 1940. But the opportunity passed before the Nazis took it. England began to strengthen her defenses. The air war did not destroy her morale. Germany then turned to submarine warfare as in World War I. England depended on food and raw materials from abroad. Though the submarines bit deeply into these needed supplies, their effort was ineffective against the growing volume of materials flowing into England from her colonies, from Canada and the Commonwealth, and from the United States. For despite neutrality legislation, the United States early revealed its sympathy with the English cause. But the news of the war was far from encouraging to English newspaper readers. Faced with the "blitz" at home, they read how Field Marshall Erwin Rommel's *Afrika Korps* was pressing the British forces in North Africa across the desert of Libya toward Egypt. The picture looked bleak when suddenly the war took an entirely new dimension with the German surprise invasion of Russia in June, 1941.

To many historians, Hitler's attack on the Soviet Union appeared as the height of folly. Russia and Germany were protected from one another by the nonaggression pact. But Hitler had never regarded the treaty with the Soviet Union as permanent. His racial hatred for the inferior Slavs made war with the Russians a logical move in his drive to destroy Bolshevism, which had been one of the announced intentions of the Nazis.

The Germans had sufficient military forces available to give them a preponderance over the Russians. They also had an ally in Japan until, in April, 1941, almost three months before the German invasion, the Japanese concluded their own nonaggression agreement with the Russians. This treaty meant that Hitler was deprived of the possibly invaluable aid of Japan. Nevertheless, on June 22, 1941, the Germans began their *blitzkrieg*. The war started as it had in Poland and France. A demoralized Russia reeled under the powerful blows of the Panzers. Whole Russian divisions surrendered and many Russians simply retreated from the war entirely. The repressions of the Stalinist regime of the thirties had not won the undying loyalty of many Russians, especially in the Ukraine. There the antipeasant policies of the government had aroused a smoldering enmity. The German armies found themselves greeted as liberators in some sectors. But the tough anti-Slavic program of the Nazis, the barbarous treatment of civilians by SS detachments, and Hitler's refusal to allow German commanders to cultivate the local population soon alienated any misguided affection the Russians and Ukrainians felt for the incoming Germans. Moreover, Stalin relaxed his own policies in order to win more support. He secured the cooperation of the Russian Orthodox Church in the war effort and began to play on the ancient theme of the defense of the Russian homeland instead of the defense of Bolshevism. Aided by Hitler's mistakes in diverting troops for side excursions such as the invasion of the Ukraine and his failure to hold to his own timetable for the capture of Moscow, the Russians gained time to regroup their defenses. The Russian winter became a major ally of the Russian people in 1941 and 1942.

The final month of 1941 brought another major change in the war with the entry of the United States. The strong isolationist sentiments that had influenced American foreign policy so strongly in the thirties had begun to recede before the realities of American involvement in Europe and Asia. The United States simply could not cut herself off from her long-standing commitments in Asia. Nor could she ignore the significance of the war in Europe to her trade and industry. By the middle of 1940, mounting tensions with Japan and concern about preparedness led to passage of the Selective Service Act and alteration of America's neutrality stance. During 1941, the United States developed the Lend-Lease Program to provide strategic goods for England's war effort. Later, this program was extended to the Soviet Union. The United States also provided naval escorts for the materials. The issuance of the Atlantic Charter by Roosevelt and Churchill confirmed the American commitment to the defeat of the Nazis.

However, the United States entry into World War II resulted from her conflict with the Japanese in the Pacific rather than from deeper involvement in the Atlantic theater. The chief cause of the tension was the United States concern about Japanese imperialism in Asia. In 1941, Roosevelt and his advisers decided it was necessary to take strong action to protect American interests in the Pacific. They restricted trade with Japan. The Japanese continued to negotiate with the United States, but already they had decided on war. American intelligence intercepted a message from Tokyo to the Japanese Embassy in Washington detailing an attack on Pearl Harbor, but this information was too late to aid the American commanders in Hawaii. A major controversy has raged about the failure of the Chief of Staff, General George Marshall, to warn Pacific headquarters in time. The evidence in this dispute has often been contradictory, but most authorities now accept the position that Marshall made every effort to reach the Pacific commanders in time. His failure was due largely to the inadequacy of military communications at the time. Nevertheless, the failure was costly in men and lives. The bulk of the United States Pacific fleet was at Pearl Harbor on Sunday morning, December 7, 1941, when Japanese aircraft bombed and strafed the naval base, the harbor, and nearby Hickam Field, headquarters for the Army Air Force. The surprise attack was disastrous to United States naval and air power in the Pacific.

The United States responded with an immediate declaration of war on the Axis powers, Germany, Italy, and Japan. England and the Dutch, who held great possessions in the East Indies, followed the United States in declaring war on Japan. For the next year and more, however, the tide of the war ran in favor of the Axis. Japan followed Pearl Harbor with the capture of most of Southeast Asia and the Philippines. The Western powers, crippled by their initial losses could do little but fall back on New Guinea and Australia. General Douglas MacArthur evacuated the Philippines with only a few officers to lead the military operations in the Pacific.

In Europe, despite the setback from the Russian winter and the failure to invade England, Germany and Italy had made considerable progress in North Africa and were still in control of the military situation.

The turning point of the war came in 1942. The entry of the United States meant an increased flow of supplies to its allies. Following the decision to concentrate on the European theater and to pursue a naval war in the Pacific, the United States began the long task of massing men, planes, tanks, ammunitions, and other supplies in England. Large amounts of material went to the British Eighth Army facing Marshall Rommel's *Afrika Korps* at El Alemein. The British commander launched his offensive in late summer, 1942, and began to roll back the Germans and their Italian allies. Then, in November, partially to fulfill the demand of Stalin for a second front to relieve pressure on the Soviet Union, the United States and British launched an invasion of French North Africa, coordinated with the Free French forces under General de Gaulle and General Giraud. These forces joined up with Field Marshall Montgomery in Tunisia, where they cornered and captured the remnants of the *Afrika Korps.* The African Campaign presented the Western powers with their first clear-cut victory over the Fascists. Another major victory came in the

Ben Shahn's "1943, A.D." Symbol of the millions oppressed under Fascism. (Syracuse University Collection)

Soviet Union, at Stalingrad. There, in the early winter, General von Paulus, under personal orders from Hitler, fought until the Russians had completely cut off his escape before surrendering. The Russian offensive had begun and was to continue with mounting energy until the end of the war. The tide had begun to turn.

One of the crucial decisions made by the powers warring against Fascism was the rejection of any idea of stopping the war short of unconditional surrender. As the war progressed, this determination grew firmer. An important consideration in this decision was the nature of the Nazi system and its inhuman treatment of peoples under its control. There is little doubt, however, that this determination prolonged the war.

The Nazis carried their notion of the superiority of the Aryan "race" with them in their conquests. The SS and Gestapo were unstinting in their efforts to hunt out the hated Jews, who were dragged off to forced labor camps and then sent to the "final solution." During the last years of the war, millions of Jews and non-Jews, about twelve million in all, died as a result of brutal treatment and overwork in the slave camps. Many were gassed and cremated after the period of their usefulness was over. Experiments in sterilization and untried surgical techniques cost the lives and futures of others. Some who lived emerged from camps like Dachau and Buchenwald to cry vengeance against the entire German nation for its failure to stop the Nazis. The testimony of such barbarism was beyond human belief and only the liberation of these camps at the end of the war brought convincing evidence in the form of survivors and the pits of the dead.

As the tide of battle gradually changed, more news came about the underground in various occupied countries. In most countries of Europe, including Germany, anti-Nazi elements attempted to overthrow the Nazis. In France, under the leadership of General Charles de Gaulle, a stout resistance harassed the Germans and prepared for the day of the allied invasion of Europe. In Italy, partisans grew in numbers, drawing heavily from Italian Communists. Elsewhere, Communists joined the underground in large numbers. After the war, these partisans parlayed their brave war records into political popularity and even the road to power. One of the best examples of this was Tito of Yugoslavia.

The Yugoslav case indicates how the Communists gained from taking part in the resistance. Tito gradually edged out the representative of the Yugoslav government in exile, Colonel Draja Mihailovitch, by playing on the divisions between Serbs and Croats in that country. Tito gained enough support to transfer much of the military aid entering Yugoslavia

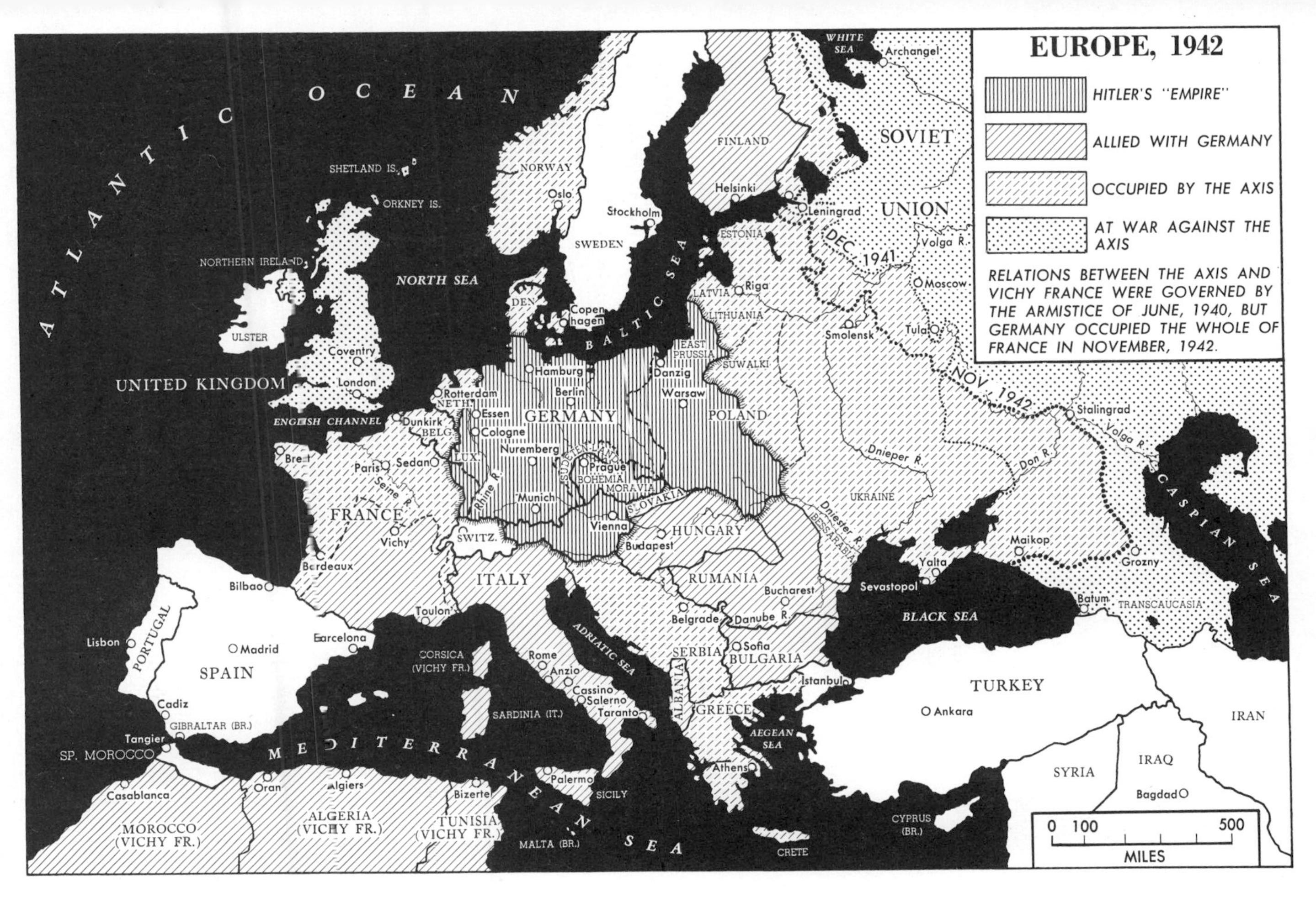
EUROPE, 1942
HITLER'S "EMPIRE"
ALLIED WITH GERMANY
OCCUPIED BY THE AXIS
AT WAR AGAINST THE AXIS
RELATIONS BETWEEN THE AXIS AND VICHY FRANCE WERE GOVERNED BY THE ARMISTICE OF JUNE, 1940, BUT GERMANY OCCUPIED THE WHOLE OF FRANCE IN NOVEMBER, 1942.
ATLANTIC OCEAN
NORTH SEA
ENGLISH CHANNEL
BALTIC SEA
WHITE SEA
BLACK SEA
CASPIAN SEA
ADRIATIC SEA
AEGEAN SEA
MEDITERRANEAN SEA
UNITED KINGDOM
SHETLAND IS.
ORKNEY IS.
NORTHERN IRELAND
ULSTER
Coventry
London
NORWAY
Oslo
SWEDEN
Stockholm
DEN.
Copenhagen
FINLAND
Helsinki
Leningrad
Archangel
SOVIET
UNION
DEC. 1941
NOV. 1942
Volga R.
Moscow
Tula
Smolensk
ESTONIA
LATVIA
Riga
LITHUANIA
EAST PRUSSIA
Danzig
SUWALKI
Warsaw
POLAND
GERMANY
Hamburg
Berlin
Rotterdam
NETH.
Essen
Cologne
Nuremberg
Munich
Rhine R.
LUX.
SUDETEN-LAND
Prague
BOHEMIA
MORAVIA
SLOVAKIA
Vienna
Dunkirk
BELG.
Sedan
Paris
Seine R.
Brest
FRANCE
Vichy
Bordeaux
SWITZ.
Toulon
ITALY
HUNGARY
Budapest
RUMANIA
Bucharest
Belgrade
Danube R.
SERBIA
Sofia
BULGARIA
ALBANIA
GREECE
Athens
Istanbul
UKRAINE
Dnieper R.
Dniester R.
BESSARABIA
Don R.
Stalingrad
Volga R.
Yalta
Sevastopol
Maikop
Grozny
Batum
TRANSCAUCASIA
TURKEY
Ankara
IRAN
IRAQ
SYRIA
Bagdad
CYPRUS (BR.)
CRETE
Rome
Anzio
Cassino
Salerno
Taranto
Palermo
SICILY
MALTA (BR.)
SARDINIA (IT.)
CORSICA (VICHY FR.)
Bilbao
Barcelona
Madrid
SPAIN
PORTUGAL
Lisbon
Cadiz
GIBRALTAR (BR.)
Tangier
SP. MOROCCO
Casablanca
MOROCCO (VICHY FR.)
Oran
Algiers
ALGERIA (VICHY FR.)
Bizerte
TUNISIA (VICHY FR.)
0 100 500
MILES

from Mihailovitch to himself. He also took the lead in driving out the last of the Germans. Acclaimed a public hero, he rode into power on a patriotic bandwagon.

The European war now moved to success from several directions. An allied landing in Sicily and Italy in 1943 encountered stern resistance, but succeeded in moving northward toward Rome. Meanwhile, the allied air forces had begun to soften up Germany for the second front. Whole German cities now realized what it had been like in London during the blitz. Air power was proving its decisive value by knocking out transportation centers and industrial facilities. It provided the punch needed to ensure the success of the allied landings in Normandy on June 6, 1944. Though the initial resistance was strong, the allies moved into France and freed most of the country within two months. A determined effort by the Germans in Belgium momentarily threatened to halt the allied advance in the Battle of the Bulge, but the superior forces and arms of the Western powers were too much. The allied advance moved eastward toward Germany facing less and less resistance in the early months of 1945. Meanwhile, the Russians had continued their drive and toward the middle of 1944 had reached the outskirts of Warsaw. Stout German opposition slowed the Russian advance as the Polish resistance forces in Warsaw broke into open revolt against the Germans. The Russians refused to press harder to bring relief and the Poles were forced to surrender. Stalin was the chief beneficiary of this destruction of the resistance, for it had been heavily anti-Communist. With this episode over, the Russians moved across Poland early in 1945.

The war in Europe was drawing to a close in the early months of 1945. The wartime allies met at Yalta in February to begin discussions about the disposition of Europe after peace. The major point of agreement was the founding of the United Nations, whose charter was signed in San Francisco later that year. However, it was obvious that the allies did not agree about many questions. Although, they decided to set up occupation zones in Germany, they were deadlocked on the question of Eastern Europe. Stalin was adamant that Russia should have the preponderant role in settling the affairs of this region. His support of the Communist-dominated Lublin government of Poland virtually forced Roosevelt and Churchill to accept it. Some have called Yalta a sellout to the Soviet Union in light of the growth of Communist power in Eastern Europe after the war. But the situation was very complex. Roosevelt was still looking forward to a long war with Japan and hoped for Russian aid to shorten it. Since Russia already held the upper hand in Poland, there was little he could do. He accepted the situation in order to get on with the business of the war.

By spring of 1945, Germany was on the verge of collapse. Adolf Hitler committed suicide in a Berlin bunker as the Russians were entering the city in March. The German military leaders surrendered their forces and the European war was at an end. Shortly after, the victorious allies met again at Potsdam. President Harry S. Truman had succeeded Roosevelt, who had died in April. The Potsdam Conference finished the work begun at Yalta. Once again, it proceeded to accept the existing situation as a basis for settlement, though the Russians and Poles pushed far beyond the limits of the agreement later in rearranging their boundaries.

The war in the Pacific remained. As the United States had gradually recovered from her losses at Pearl Harbor, the United States Navy had regained supremacy on the sea. Under General Douglas MacArthur,

The Big Three at Yalta. A tired Roosevelt attempted to secure aid from Russia to win the war in the Far East. (United Press International)

marines and army troops had recovered strategic island bases culminating in the retaking of the Philippine Islands in 1944. However, even as the Potsdam Conference was meeting, a dramatic development altered the entire picture of that war. The United States announced that it had succeeded in exploding an atomic bomb capable of destroying an entire city. This bomb had been developed in utmost secrecy by a group of scientists working on the Manhattan Project. The leading theoreticians were Albert Einstein, the famed German mathematician, and Enrico Fermi, the leading Italian nuclear physicist, both of whom had come to the United States to escape Fascism. The making of the bomb raised serious moral questions in the minds of some of its developers as to its use. However, President Truman ordered the bomb to be dropped on two Japanese cities in the hope that its effects would shorten the war. Early in August, American bombers dropped the first atomic bombs on Hiroshima and Nagasaki, killing more than one hundred thousand persons and leaving many others with radiation burns. The dawn of the atomic age inspired awe and fear at what man's technological skill had created.

But the bomb had done its job in another way. The Japanese emperor assumed direct responsibility of the government and announced his intention of surrendering. Within a few weeks, the terms of surrender were signed aboard the Battleship Missouri in Tokyo Bay. At last the war had ended.

The end of the hostilities was cause for great rejoicing in Europe and America. But the victors had learned one lesson from World War I. They were determined that the fruits of victory would not be lost through negligence. They had worked together to create the United Nations as a perpetual instrument for the preservation of international peace. Though already some cracks were appearing in the alliance between the Western powers and the Soviet Union, men looked at the United Nations with hope. The end of World War II did not see any dramatic return to normalcy despite the popular pressures for such a move. Though there was a letdown, though economic and social readjustments were necessary, the nations of the world generally proved more able to handle these problems than they had a generation before.

One World: A Dream Shattered

Since antiquity men have dreamed of a world united. Zeno and the Stoics had taught the concept of the brotherhood of man. Alexander the Great had promoted the unity of East and West in his empire. The

"Supplicant Persephone" by Ivan Mestrovic. As the war ended mankind hoped for a new world, united in peace. (Syracuse University Collection)

Romans had imposed the Pax Romana (Roman peace) on the Mediterranean world. St. Augustine of Hippo, writing in his corner of North Africa, had dreamed of a universal Christian society. The medieval emperors had often given thought to that dream as did the Popes. Thomas More in the *Utopia* and Voltaire in *Candide* saw the vision through a veil. Woodrow Wilson believed he might bring it into being in the League of Nations. Certainly many who participated in the making of the United Nations shared this hope. Yet the realities of the world in 1945 forced even the greatest dreamers to face up to the dangers that lay in the future. Born in hope, the United Nations early received its baptism of fire.

The immediate concern of people everywhere was fitting together the pieces of their existence in a peaceful world. At first, it seemed that the history of the post-World War I era might repeat itself. Even before the war with Japan was over, the English electorate rejected the bid of Prime Minister Winston Churchill to form a Conservative government to rule England in peacetime and chose instead the Labour Party, headed by the wartime Vice-Premier, Clement Attlee. The Attlee government immediately embarked on its program of nationalizing basic industry and transport, establishing a national medical insurance program, and increasing the commitment of the government in programs of social welfare. The French turned to their war leader General Charles de Gaulle for a time, but the resurgence of the old political parties indicated that the Fourth Republic would set up shop in the old stand abandoned at the demise of the Third Republic. In Italy, the king had acted at the last minute to dismiss Mussolini and to summon Marshall Badoglio to form a government. However, he had put off too long to save his throne. The monarchy was a last victim of the Fascist period. The new republic suffered from grave internal political divisions.

The question of the German settlement was a difficult one. The first matter on the agenda was the punishment of the Nazi war criminals. The allies agreed to try the German leaders, as well as Nazis in other countries, on the charge of crimes against humanity. Though no basis for such crimes existed in international law or custom, the victors believed that there was ample justification for their action. During late 1945 and most of 1946, these trials were held in Nuremberg, with representatives of the allied powers acting as judges and others representing the same powers serving as prosecutors. Of the twenty-two leading Nazis still alive or believed alive, twenty-one had been captured and brought to trial. The court sentenced twelve to death by hanging, but Hermann Goering, Nazi Luftwaffe Commander and Hitler's number two man, took poison, and

Martin Bormann remained at large. Three leaders were acquitted, including the aged Franz von Papen, long Germany's chief diplomatic troubleshooter. The trials did not concern themselves with the mass of Nazis and SS troopers; these were left to the "de-Nazification" courts set up by the powers in their own zones. It would be sententious to pass judgment on the value and legality of the trials from this vantage point. Yet it is worthy to note that Senator Robert Taft of Ohio felt grave concern about their legality and the possible future impact of holding such tribunals after a war. Perhaps the chief problem was and is that no one could really defend these Nazis because of the inhumanity of their acts. The war trials did appear to purge the German atmosphere somewhat and paved the way for the formation of a democratic West German Government in 1949.

Postwar Europe was very different from what it had been only six years before. A new spirit rose after the war. It was not so much antinationalist as unnationalist. Its hope was the creation of a European unity. The architects of this policy came from a number of political parties, but especially from the Christian Democratic parties that arose throughout

"Apprehension II" by Moses Soyer. Peace brought no certainty to the atomic age. (Syracuse University Collection)

Western Europe in the postwar period. These Christian Democratic leaders formed the leading bloc or influential minorities in France, Germany, Italy, Belgium, and Holland. They were less bound to the churches than older confessional parties, which had attempted to defend the position of religion in a secular world. They were also strongly committed to democratic political institutions as well as social and economic reforms. It was from this group that strong support came for European unification.

The remarkable economic recovery of Europe in the aftermath of World War II was due in part to the decision of the United States to maintain its strong European ties. General George Marshall, United States Secretary of State, proposed a massive program of economic assistance aimed at rebuilding the damaged economies of all the European countries in 1948. However, the chilling climate of relations between the Soviet Union and the West prevented the participation of Poland and other Eastern European countries. No doubt, Marshall had realized the possibility of a Soviet rejection; however, the United States launched the plan in Western Europe. Its great benefits won the admiration of most peoples in these countries and helped to prevent the spread of Communism in Italy and France.

The atmosphere of mistrust that interfered with normal relations between the East and West gradually deepened into the "Cold War" after 1946. In the words of Winston Churchill, an "iron curtain" had slammed down over almost the whole of Eastern Europe. Stalin had never really accepted the Western allies as true partners; with the war over, he suspected them of trying to build up an anti-Communist alliance. But the West was also concerned about the extension of Communist influence in Eastern Europe. By 1948, Poland, Bulgaria, Rumania, Yugoslavia, Hungary, Albania, and Czechoslovakia had regimes sympathetic to the Soviet Union. It became increasingly obvious in the West that these governments danced on the end of strings controlled in Moscow. There was no basis for these Soviet moves in the Yalta and Potsdam agreements, but there was little that the United States could do about them because technically the establishment of the new Communist governments was an internal matter, not subject to the United Nations. However, the United States did step up its efforts to prevent the spread of Communism in other countries. President Truman provided military and economic assistance for Greece and Turkey to prevent their loss to Communism in 1948. Later, the United States and Russia agreed to the neutralization of Austria, providing a buffer state between West Germany and the Communist nations in Southeastern Europe.

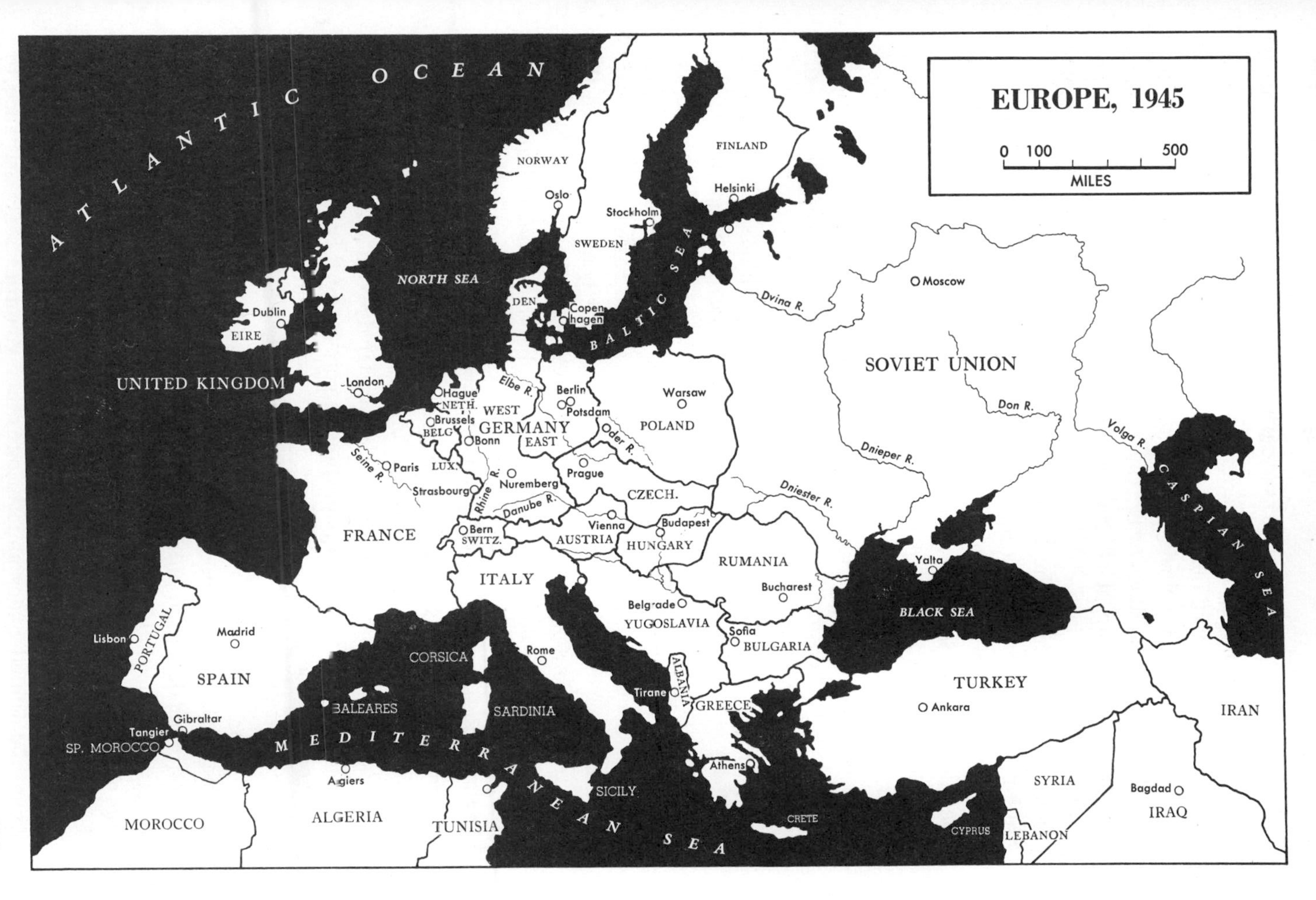
EUROPE, 1945
0 100 500
MILES
ATLANTIC OCEAN
NORTH SEA
BALTIC SEA
BLACK SEA
CASPIAN SEA
MEDITERRANEAN SEA
UNITED KINGDOM
EIRE
Dublin
London
NORWAY
Oslo
SWEDEN
Stockholm
FINLAND
Helsinki
DEN.
Copenhagen
SOVIET UNION
Moscow
Volga R.
Don R.
Dnieper R.
Dniester R.
Dvina R.
Yalta
POLAND
Warsaw
Oder R.
EAST GERMANY
WEST GERMANY
Berlin
Potsdam
Elbe R.
Bonn
Nuremberg
Danube R.
Rhine R.
NETH.
Hague
BELG.
Brussels
LUX.
FRANCE
Paris
Seine R.
Strasbourg
SWITZ.
Bern
CZECH.
Prague
AUSTRIA
Vienna
HUNGARY
Budapest
RUMANIA
Bucharest
BULGARIA
Sofia
YUGOSLAVIA
Belgrade
ALBANIA
Tirane
GREECE
Athens
CRETE
TURKEY
Ankara
CYPRUS
SYRIA
LEBANON
IRAQ
Bagdad
IRAN
ITALY
Rome
CORSICA
SARDINIA
SICILY
TUNISIA
ALGERIA
Algiers
BALEARES
SPAIN
Madrid
Gibraltar
PORTUGAL
Lisbon
Tangier
SP. MOROCCO
MOROCCO

The new Communistic governments of Eastern Europe were not so ruthless as the Nazis, but "reforms" touched a larger part of the population. Following the Soviet pattern, not merely the large estates but smaller peasant holdings were "collectivized." The governments assumed complete ownership of all but very small businesses. Control of finance was concentrated in the state-controlled banking system. Strict currency regulations prevented the deposit of wealth abroad. Restrictions on building prevented the use of construction materials for housing. Religion ran into government opposition on several points. Religious education interfered with the Communist program for indoctrinating the masses. The pulpit served as a possible center for criticism of the regimes. Identification of some church leaders with prewar governments provided sufficient reason for attacking them. In almost all of these countries, church leaders were jailed. Their major crime was their leadership of a competitor to the Communist state for control of men's minds.

In Asia, the Communist advance swallowed up China's millions in 1949. The government of Chiang Kai-shek had borne the brunt of the war against the Japanese and was unable to offer serious resistance to the Communists. The United States found herself in a dilemma. Only massive support could have propped up Chiang Kai-shek. Even then, there was no guarantee of success. The Chinese Communist controlled most of the northern part of China after the Japanese withdrawal in 1945. In the end, it did not require an American decision to abandon China to bring about communistic rule. Chiang withdrew to Formosa (Taiwan) with half a million men to lead free China with American support.

Through the late forties, the conflict between East and West became the major focus of international relations. The United States took the lead in the formation of the North Atlantic Treaty Organization and the Southeast Asian Treaty Organization to counter further Communist expansion. But the pressures of the Cold War continued to mount. In June, 1950, the army of the Communist satellite regime in North Korea crossed the thirty-eighth parallel and invaded South Korea. President Harry Truman asked the United Nations to intervene. The Security Council moved immediately to authorize a United Nations defense force and to demand an end to the hostilities. Since the Soviet delegate had been staying away from the meetings of the council to protest the failure of the United Nations to seat Communist China, he was not present to veto the action of the Security Council. In answer to the action of the United Nations, the United States and various other countries sent assistance to Korea.

The Korean War was the first of its kind. It was a limited military operation intended to deter aggression without creating a climate of complete international misunderstanding. The war was most unpopular with those elements in the United States who desired complete victory. The war was also frustrating to its military commanders. The brilliant and self-confident General of the Army Douglas MacArthur attempted to cut off the North Koreans by striking at their rear with amphibious landings in the north, but he lacked the troops to make this plan succeed. As the Red Chinese sent "volunteers" to aid their fellow Communists, MacArthur chafed under the restrictions that prevented him from bombing supply lines and military targets within China. After an inconclusive attempt to settle the differences between the military commander and the President, Truman removed MacArthur. His action was political dynamite, but necessary if the United States was to continue its limited objectives in Korea.

As the Korean War dragged on indecisively through the early fifties, the United States and much of the West sought for some break in the Cold War. But the cold shadow of Stalin continued to dominate the Soviet Union and the atmosphere of mutual suspicion continued.

From Cold War to Space Age

The fifties and sixties have witnessed a major shift in the direction of the Cold War and the opening of a new era in the conquest of space. While the threat of nuclear devastation has hung over the earth, men have continued to work in hope of peace. A new world has come into being in Africa and Asia, sovereign nations born into the greatest era of human technological development and an age of fear and mistrust. For the historian, this period has been marked with a sign of contradictions.

The Korean War did not result in victory for the United States, but in a negotiated peace that preserved the principle that aggression would not receive any reward. Its lessons were hard and not all learned. When President Harry Truman decided not to run for reelection in 1952, the Republican Party chose as its standard bearer, General Dwight D. Eisenhower, the hero of Europe. Eisenhower's victory came partly on his pledge to "go to Korea." His administration concluded the negotiations for the cease fire. However, the position of the Eisenhower government in foreign affairs was almost always ambivalent. His Secretary of State, John Foster Dulles, spoke of leading the nation to the "brink" to head off aggression, yet Republicans in Congress continued to criticize the involvement in Korea. When riots broke out in Poland, Hungary, and East Germany in 1956, the world waited for America to act. Successful revolt in Hungary installed the government of Imre Nagy, who appealed to the United States for aid. The weaknesses of the policy of "brinksmanship" and the "policy of liberation" were suddenly apparent. The United States could do nothing to aid the Hungarians in their hour of need. The world stood in shock while an uninvited Russian army brutally crushed the revolt. Almost simultaneously, England, France, and Israel joined in a brief war against Egypt, largely in retaliation for Egyptian nationalization of the Suez Canal. Not only did this outbreak distract attention from the Hungarian crisis, but it also threatened to split the Western alliance. However, rapid United States intervention in this instance resulted in a restoration of the truce. Suez had won nothing and had cost the Western powers considerable prestige.

Despite the harsh action of the Soviet Union in crushing the Hungarian Revolution, there were definite signs of change in its policies, both internal and external. Joseph Stalin had died in 1953. The West had grown accustomed to his cynical evaluations of their policies and learned what to expect from him as a response to their moves. He was in his last years a conservative and suspicious dictator, firmly committed to those goals he had set a generation earlier. But Russia had changed. The population had grown restive under the restraints of the security police and the chronic shortages of consumer goods. The new leaders were disunited. As they struggled for power among themselves, their grip on the world situation and the climate within the Soviet Union loosened somewhat. Not until the emergence of Nikita Khrushchev as the real power in the government in 1957–1958, after the Hungarian Revolt, did a Russian leader once more take the initiative. Khrushchev denounced Stalin's "cult of personality" and shifted the direction of Soviet foreign and domestic policies. Although he remained committed to Russian leadership of the Communist bloc, he spoke of the possibility of peaceful coexistence with the West. At the same time, he diverted part of Russia's capital expenditures to the production of additional consumer goods. Under his leadership, the standard of living increased. Despite several major crises in the late fifties and sixties, there seemed to be evidence of a new approach to the Cold War. Negotiation was taking the place of military threats.

In Western Europe, economic recovery was virtually complete in the early fifties and a basis for European unity was laid in the Common Market (1957). But France's Fourth Republic limped pitifully from government to government, while she faced military disasters in Indo-China and Algeria. Withdrawal from Asia in 1954 cost the republic prestige at home, but even more costly was the continuing drain of the Algerian War for independence. The demand of French colonists in Algeria for stronger support against the Arab nationalists put the government in the difficult position of choosing between greater commitment to an unpopular war and an equally unpopular withdrawal. The crisis came in 1958, with a threat of revolution. General Charles de Gaulle averted the civil war and proposed a new republic, with greater powers for the president to achieve greater political stability. Under de Gaulle's leadership, France worked to regain her position as the dominant European power with a major voice in world councils. He withdrew from Algeria and established a program for the independence of French colonies elsewhere. His opposition to American influence in European affairs was a major sore spot with that country, but he won reelection to another seven-year term in 1966.

Germany was a divided nation, but under Konrad Adenauer, the West Germans enjoyed a remarkable economic recovery, while pursuing a policy of close identification with the West. By the mid-fifties, suspicions of Germany had receded in France sufficiently to permit the inclusion of German forces in NATO. The new Germany, largely a product of the postwar period, is still regarded with mistrust in many quarters, but is a major bastion of Western policies in Europe.

The Conservative Party dominated English politics after 1950. When Churchill returned to power after five years of Labour rule, many thought his government would attempt to reverse the trend to the welfare state. Though the Conservatives did denationalize the steel industry, largely because of internal problems, they preserved the bulk of the Labour program. The nation had chosen the course of moderate socialism. In foreign policy, the Conservatives supported the Western alliance and tried to serve as middlemen in negotiations between the two blocs. On the domestic scene, periodic economic difficulties disturbed the otherwise booming economy. England's dependency on international trade forced her to watch carefully her expenditures overseas lest they exceed her exports and create an unfavorable balance of payments. The Conservatives weathered political scandals in the sixties, but finally succumbed to Labour in the narrow election of 1964, which brought Harold Wilson into office as Prime Minister. Labour has embraced a policy of domestic austerity, while attempting to promote the cause of peace between the East and West. In 1966, Wilson won a landslide victory and moved to nationalize the steel industry.

After the war, England gradually saw her great colonial empire gain its independence. In 1946, the Labour government supported independence for India, which became a republic within the Commonwealth. The divided state of Pakistan comprised most of the Moslem population of the Indian subcontinent. In the Near East, the British permitted the establishment of Israel. This Jewish state, born out of the desire for a homeland, struggled for its freedom against the Arab states until the United Nations succeeded in negotiating a cease fire in 1948. The Israelis accomplished a modern miracle in making the deserts bloom and introducing industry into their country. England's African empire was still working out the problems of independence in the sixties. Nigeria gave promise of stable government until a military revolt overthrew the prime minister. In East Africa, the whites in Rhodesia withdrew from the empire. The Labourites imposed strict economic sanctions in the hope of forcing the Rhodesians to negotiate. South Africa, the wealthiest of the former British colonies, followed the lead of its Afrikanner political rulers in establishing a policy of complete separation of the races, *Apartheid.* Negroes may not attend any function or work outside their reservations without permission of the government. Their educational opportunities are under strict government control. In spite of strong world opinion against *Apartheid,* the South African government has shown no tendency toward altering its policy.

In Asia, the major development of the fifties and sixties was the rise of Red China. Japan, under democratic leadership since the war, devoted her efforts chiefly to rebuilding her economic position. Her army remained small and most younger Japanese opposed anything that smacked of militarism. But China under Communistic rule quickly became the aggressive power in Asia. Her espousal of the cause of world revolution brought her into an ideological split with the Russians in the early sixties. In 1964, she exploded two atomic bombs, thus moving into the ranks of the nuclear powers.

The world of the sixties faced many pressing problems. The rapid growth of population during previous decades increased concern about a possible population explosion. Poverty and inequality aroused worry throughout the world. In the United States, Negroes struggled to achieve political, civil, and economic equality with the whites. Although advances in the peaceful uses of atomic energy gave promise of a great future, concern about the danger of an accidental war was a very important theme in the thinking of intellectuals and statesmen. Not even man's first conquests of space and the launching of rockets to Venus and the moon could keep the note of disquiet out of the air. Yet the men of the sixties continued to strive for peace. President John F. Kennedy dedicated his administration to the search for peace at his inauguration in 1960 when he pledged to travel anywhere to negotiate with the Communists. He raised up before mankind a high goal of service to their fellowmen that stirred the hearts of youth the world over. When he was cut down by an assassin's bullets on November 22, 1963, he bequeathed to them his dream of a world at peace.

26 The Twentieth-Century Intellect

Cultural life in this century has moved far from the traditional bases accepted in the West since antiquity. The rejection of traditional principles of aesthetics has paralleled important shifts in the underlying structure of the natural sciences. A similar development has appeared in recent philosophy. These searches have given the modern intellect the appearance of instability, and indeed the lack of stability is one of the major marks of modern thought. Because so much of recent work has been experimental, there has been a tendency to compare it unfavorably to the great works of the past. Only science, where concrete influences on modern technology have seemingly demonstrated its value, has gained acceptance of new fundamental approaches, as in the work of Albert Einstein. For the rest of the broad expanses of intellectual endeavor, this century has been a continuing quest for understanding. In that quest, contemporary thinkers have been deeply influenced by age of the irrational.

Science and Technology

The intellectual life of the twentieth century has drawn heavily on the scientific and technological advances of the previous two centuries. It has also emphasized those trends of the late nineteenth century toward exploration of the role of the nonrational forces of the universe. Although World War I and postwar disillusionment destroyed the facile theories of human progress through evolution, the impact of Freudian psychoanalysis increased as men sought to understand the inner motivations of man. In science, men began to fathom a dual sign in place of the symbol of optimism it had been in the eighteenth and even the nineteenth century. Under one aspect, science held promise of a better world; under another, it created anxiety and even threatened doom. Science, which the eighteenth century had viewed as the greatest creation of man, seemed almost to escape the control of its creator. The creature of reason was in danger of becoming the prophet of unreason.

In the physical sciences, the genius of Albert Einstein, whose theory of relativity opened up significant avenues of research in physics, created a new age. Einstein used mathematical computations to show that space and time were related to one another. Time became a fourth dimension. The importance of this theory is evident if one considers that time relationships become dependent entirely on the position of the observer. An observer in one system would have an altogether different time reference from an observer in a different system. Einstein also urged that mass and energy were related. This position was a direct attack on the traditionally accepted position that matter was substance that could not be created or destroyed. Yet, according to the formula $E = Mc^2$, matter might be converted into energy. Einstein's work also revealed the limitations of Newton's physics, which had explained the motion of the universe in terms of the universal law of gravitation. In Einstein's work, it became apparent that Newtonian physics was true only in a very limited sense. These revolutionary concepts challenged the entire traditional view of the universe and paved the way for important discoveries in various fields of science and technology.

The philosophical implications of Einstein's new physical theories were not lost. His work seemed to destroy completely the entire Aristotelian conception of Being, thereby denying the possibility of a metaphysical system. By revealing the relative nature of space-time relationships, Einstein's theory appeared to overturn the cause-and-effect relation fundamental to much of Western thought. Under these aspects, the impact of Einstein's ideas was to strengthen the tendencies toward the irrational in recent philosophy. These tendencies have influenced the development of philosophical analysis and existentialism.

But for the mass of men, science appeared as the partner of technology in its applications to human needs. In few areas was the advance so dramatic as in medicine.

The work of Louis Pasteur and others in discovering the existence of bacteria paved the way for exploration of the world of microscopic life.

Spectacular advances in instrumentation, particularly the invention of the electron microscope, made it possible to find still smaller living organisms, the viruses. Work with viruses produced some outstanding results. Alexander Fleming discovered penicillin in 1928. This mold proved effective in curing a wide range of virus-caused infections and led to the discovery of further antibiotics. In 1955, Dr. Jonas Salk produced a "killed virus" polio vaccine and Professor Albert Sabin soon after introduced a "live virus" vaccine. Development of electronic instruments such as the electrocardiograph provided physicians with aid in diagnosing heart disease. The electroencephalograph measured brain waves and gave new hope to those suffering from diseases and injuries to the brain. New surgical techniques improved chances for recovery from a wide range of diseases, particularly cancer.

One of the most difficult questions faced at mid-century was the problem of rapidly increasing populations around the world. China alone had six hundred million people and a growth rate of approximately two per cent per year in the fifties. The term "population explosion" described the alarming rate of increase and expressed also the concern that the basic necessities of life would be insufficient for the needs of the future. To many the solution appeared to be government or private programs of birth control. In Japan and India, such efforts were sponsored by the government. In the United States, government support was uncommon; most birth control clinics operated from private resources.

The techniques of birth prevention made important advances. Dr. John Rock of Harvard University developed a drug to control ovulation and thereby prevent birth. Others experimented with drugs to fix the time of ovulation and worked to make the "rhythm method" more predictable.

Major opposition to "artificial" birth control came from some religious groups, especially the Catholic Church. However, Popes John XXIII and Paul VI recognized the pressing problem of population growth and began a reappraisal of the traditional Catholic position in light of modern scientific advances. They also stressed the role of wealthier nations in aiding those that were poorer and the need for technological advances to increase food production.

The "population explosion" was, however, less impending than the threat of nuclear warfare. The exploding of the atomic bomb in 1945 had been merely the first stage in the development of larger and more destructive weapons. The hydrogen bomb threatened the existence of all living things on earth. Such terrible weapons raised questions of morality in the minds of many, including their inventors. Linus Pauling, one of the top

United States scientists, worked unceasingly for a halt to the nuclear arms race. Many theologians, including many attending the Second Vatican Council in the mid-sixties, condemned the use of nuclear weapons in war. In 1963, President John F. Kennedy of the United States secured agreement to a limited Nuclear Test Ban Treaty from all the atomic powers but France and Red China. Pope Paul VI made an impressive call on the nations of the world to settle their differences peaceably in an address to the United Nations in 1965. Science had provided the knowledge to develop the bomb; in the sixties, men continued to grope toward some way in which to control it.

While the threat of nuclear annihilation hung over the earth, man began his first probes of the sun, moon, and planets.

The Germans had done pioneering work in rocketry before World War II and had developed the V_1 and V_2 rockets as terror weapons during the war. Not until after the war, however, did rocket scientists working for the United States and the Soviet Union begin to build missiles for military purposes capable of carrying nuclear warheads to destinations thousands of miles away. Then, in 1957, came the major breakthrough, when the Soviet Union became the first nation to launch a man into space. In the sixties, scientific plans centered on the race to the moon.

Since World War II, there has been an increasing tendency among leading thinkers to reject the view that science can in itself provide solutions to all of man's needs. While recognizing the value of scientific and technological advances, they have pointed to the inadequacy of science in providing moral values as a basis for human action.

The Humanities

In philosophy, literature, and the arts, the quest for new cultural bases took on a personalist approach through much of the century. Introspection rather than observation of external reality was an important concern of many intellectuals. The influences of Freudian psychology and the discoveries of Albert Einstein provided new dimensions for the development of both philosophy and literature.

The revolt against rationalism that had characterized much of nineteenth-century philosophical thought carried over into the new century in the thought of men like Henri Bergson and William James. Though their thought contained little that was similar, both illustrated important tendencies in twentieth-century philosophy.

Bergson (1859–1941) taught at the University of Paris about the turn of the century. His *Creative Evolution* (1907) emphasized the importance of intuition rather than reason as the foundation for all human action. This rejection of the intellect was essential if man was to escape from the confines of scientific knowledge. Instinct is the true directing force of man for it is only by instinct that a man realizes the true life force of his being (*élan vital*). Despite his antirationalism, Bergson was no determinist. He believed in the force of will and human freedom. He wanted to free man from the limitations of a materialistic world.

William James (1842–1910) was the father of pragmatism. He believed that the only test of truth was in its functioning. If we believe something to be true, we act on it. If it works, it reinforces our belief and is therefore valuable and true. Pragmatism denied implicitly the existence of any objective standard of truth. Among the most important pragmatists was John Dewey, who attempted to build on it a philosophy for democratic society.

Various European thinkers moved in the direction of philosophical analysis. Bertrand Russell advocated the use of symbolic logic in order to escape the ambiguities and cloudiness of language. The Austrian philosopher, Ludwig Wittgenstein, was instrumental in the development of semantics as a branch of philosophy. These philosophers directly attacked the issues that had concerned philosophy through most of its history.

The most influential group of thinkers of the forties and fifties were the existentialists. They possessed no common philosophical system, but usually began with the conviction that life had no meaning apart from the simple fact of being. Some, like Jean-Paul Sartre, were atheists; others, like Gabriel Marcel, were Christians. Existentialism had a deep appeal to those who felt cut adrift in an alien world and who could find no meaning in reality.

Literature was in an almost constant ferment of experimentation. The two pioneers in new forms for the novel were Marcel Proust and James Joyce. Proust's *Remembrance of Things Past* was an autobiographical search for a human being's individuality. It was an effort to objectify introspection. Joyce began a lifelong quest for himself in his *Portrait of the Artist as a Young Man* and *Ulysses.* The difficulties of the language in *Ulysses* caused by obscure allusions to mythology and frequent symbolism made the work hard to read. Yet its influence on later writers was greater than almost any other recent novel.

The leading poets of the century were William Butler Yeats and T. S. Eliot. Yeats possessed a magnificent sense of imagery and deep lyricism. Eliot was at his best in commenting on his age. The *Waste Land* and the

Love Song of J. Alfred Prufrock pointed to the lacks of the modern machine age and the man it created. In *Murder in the Cathedral,* Eliot revealed his intense concern with the relevance of religion to modern society. In many ways, this century saw a poetic revival, which was accompanied by considerable experimentation in form. Although much of this verse was of inferior quality and barren in imagery, it revealed how the groping for new poetical forms had broadly influenced most persons with an interest in literature.

Drama became an increasingly popular art form through the medium of the movies and television, but most of the work shown in these media appealed to the mentality of a twelve year old. Ironically, serious drama found little support outside of a few major centers: London, Paris, and New York. The New York stage was largely concerned with successful musical comedies, although the drama of Tennessee Williams (*Glass Menagerie*) and Arthur Miller (*Death of a Salesman*) represented some relief from the general grind. More important were the works of the Irish playwrights of the period. John M. Synge's *Riders to the Sea* has become a classic. George Bernard Shaw continued to produce dramatic critiques of the foibles of his age during the interwar era. Since the war, Samuel Beckett has written existentialist drama. Much of this drama of the twen-

George Bernard Shaw. One of the most bitter commentators on the shortcomings of the modern world. (New York Times and Rare Book Room, Syracuse University Library)

tieth century exhausted itself trying to give meaning to the meaningless. Much stressed the ugly and sordid in the search for beauty.

Painters and musicians moved away from the forms that dominated their arts in the early part of the century. The cubism and expressionism of artists like Duchamp and Matisse yielded to a more existential art, less concerned about form than feeling. Arnold Schoenberg's twelve-tone scale was influential during the thirties and forties, but contemporary musicians have sought a more melodic mode of expression.

During the twentieth century, experimentation in literature and the arts was the counterpart of philosophy's quest for a meaningful synthesis. Though perhaps most philosophers would deny any intention of seeking a world view and though few in the arts have consciously striven to discover new principles—indeed, rejection of such principles had itself been a cardinal principle—the years since World War II have witnessed a yearning for cultural synthesis as exhibited in the popularity of the work of the historian-philosopher, Arnold Toynbee. Though all critics have pointed to the weaknesses in Toynbee's challenge and response theory of

"Margan, Vue d'Ensemble" by Maurice Utrillo. (Syracuse University Collection)

"Crucifixion" by Lebrun. A twentieth-century view. (Syracuse University Collection)

the development of civilizations, almost none have criticized the need for synthesis. In this trend, we may perhaps see the end of the age of the irrational.

Contemporary Problems

In the writing of this book, the author has tried to take the long view. Indeed, in a history of civilization any other approach would be almost meaningless. Yet there comes that moment when, at knife edge, past and future meet in the present. What can we say of this present? We are not gods. Historians interpret the past and seek thereby to throw light on the meaning of the present. But, as we noted in the introduction, the limitations imposed on the historian do make him pause at the threshold of today.

Perhaps all such books as this ought to end in the middle of a sentence, straggling off in a series of dots to indicate the unknowable character of the future. Yet, no historian could entirely admit that and still profess history. For is not the future related to present in the past? Is it not determinism to accept historical causality? The essence of the historical discipline itself demands this faith and the real relationship of past and future through the present.

The great problems of our day are not those we read about in the newspapers. Rather, they are those that have held thinking men captive since time began, since civilization was born.

The fundamental problem is man himself. Who is he? What is he? Whole civilizations have been founded on their conception of man. Our civilization is founded on the answers shaped within Western thought. As our view of man has changed, our society has also changed: From the rational humanism of the Greeks to the theocentric providential view of Christianity; from the God-centered to the secular view forged in the seventeenth and eighteenth centuries. The acceptance of the secular concept of man has led to a quest for the nature of secular man. Such were the efforts of Locke in the seventeenth century and William James in the late nineteenth century. From man the rational of Voltaire, the nineteenth century moved to the exploration of the irrational aspect of man. The impact of this shift on literature, art, and philosophy has been basic to the understanding of these fields.

In the development of the national state, a primary factor has been the

Apartments on the Janiculum, Rome. (*Author*)

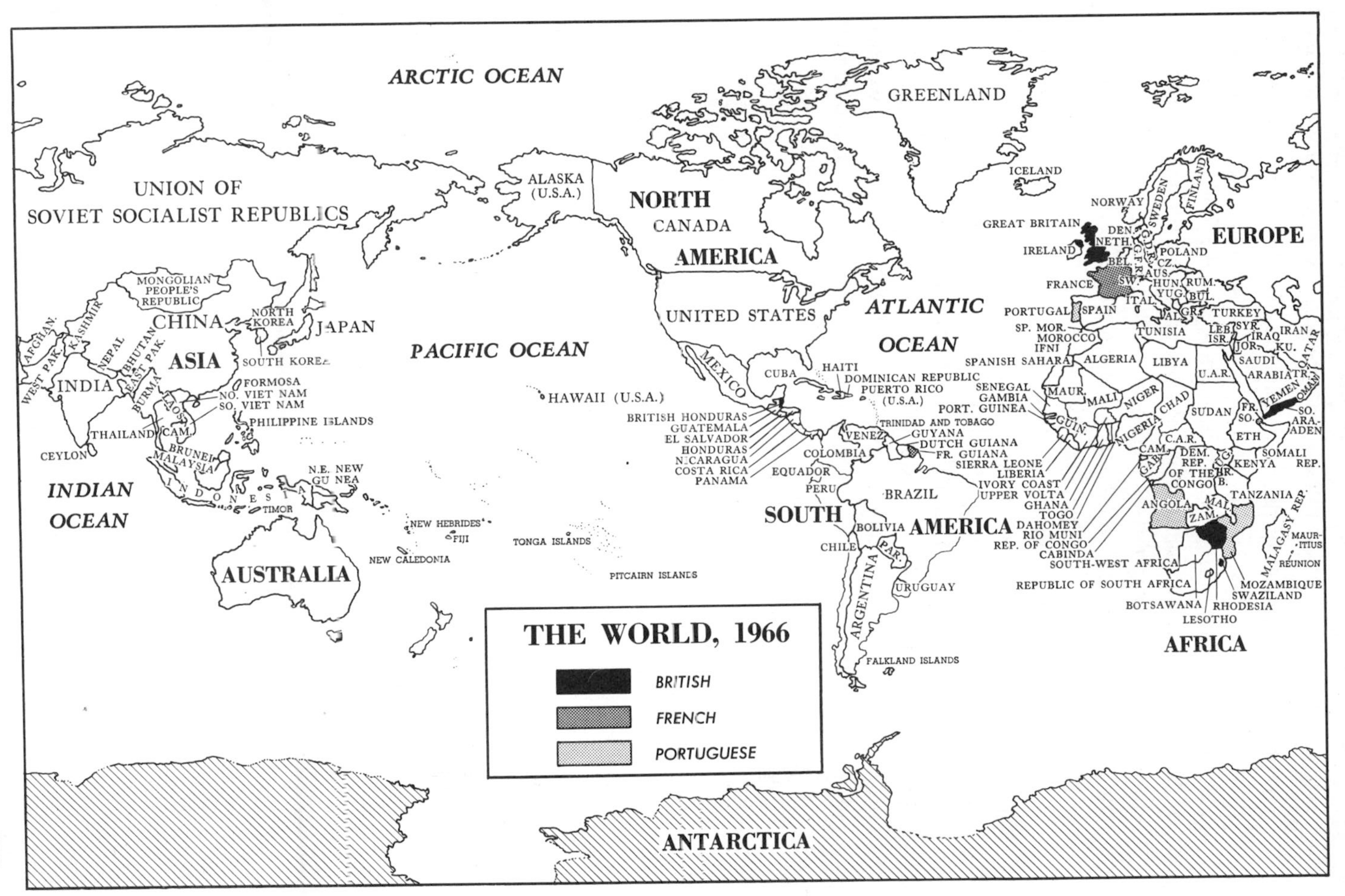
THE WORLD, 1966
BRITISH
FRENCH
PORTUGUESE
ARCTIC OCEAN
PACIFIC OCEAN
ATLANTIC OCEAN
INDIAN OCEAN
NORTH AMERICA
SOUTH AMERICA
EUROPE
AFRICA
ASIA
AUSTRALIA
ANTARCTICA
GREENLAND
ICELAND
CANADA
ALASKA (U.S.A.)
UNITED STATES
MEXICO
CUBA
HAITI
DOMINICAN REPUBLIC
PUERTO RICO (U.S.A.)
HAWAII (U.S.A.)
PITCAIRN ISLANDS
TONGA ISLANDS
NEW HEBRIDES
FIJI
NEW CALEDONIA
BRITISH HONDURAS
GUATEMALA
EL SALVADOR
HONDURAS
NICARAGUA
COSTA RICA
PANAMA
COLOMBIA
VENEZ.
ECUADOR
PERU
BOLIVIA
BRAZIL
PAR.
URUGUAY
CHILE
ARGENTINA
FALKLAND ISLANDS
TRINIDAD AND TOBAGO
GUYANA
DUTCH GUIANA
FR. GUIANA
GREAT BRITAIN
IRELAND
FRANCE
PORTUGAL
SPAIN
NORWAY
SWEDEN
FINLAND
POLAND
ITAL.
TURKEY
MOROCCO
ALGERIA
TUNISIA
LIBYA
U.A.R.
SUDAN
ETH.
SAUDI ARABIA
IRAN
SOMALI REP.
KENYA
TANZANIA
MALAGASY REP.
MOZAMBIQUE
SWAZILAND
RHODESIA
LESOTHO
BOTSWANA
REPUBLIC OF SOUTH AFRICA
SOUTH-WEST AFRICA
ANGOLA
CABINDA
REP. OF CONGO
RIO MUNI
DAHOMEY
TOGO
GHANA
UPPER VOLTA
IVORY COAST
LIBERIA
SIERRA LEONE
PORT. GUINEA
GAMBIA
SENEGAL
SPANISH SAHARA
IFNI
SP. MOR.
MALI
NIGER
CHAD
NIGERIA
MAUR.
UNION OF SOVIET SOCIALIST REPUBLICS
MONGOLIAN PEOPLE'S REPUBLIC
CHINA
JAPAN
NORTH KOREA
SOUTH KOREA
FORMOSA
NO. VIET NAM
SO. VIET NAM
PHILIPPINE ISLANDS
LAOS
CAM.
THAILAND
BURMA
EAST PAK.
BHUTAN
NEPAL
INDIA
CEYLON
KASHMIR
WEST PAK.
AFGHAN.
MALAYSIA
BRUNEI
INDONESIA
TIMOR
N.E. NEW GUINEA

acceptance by the mass of the view that the identity of the individual is bound to the identity of the nation. The weakening of this sense of identity to the nation in the West during the period following World War II has led to a greater questioning of the validity of the national state as the ultimate form of political institution. Whatever future forms man's political aspirations may create, his experience with nationalism will influence his attitudes toward his institutions.

In the history of Western civilization, the development of a secular outlook has been incomplete. The basic ethical framework has remained firmly imbedded in the Judaeo-Christian tradition. No secular world view in the modern era has offered the totality of conception of man's being and purpose offered by Stoicism in antiquity or by the Augustinian providential view of history in the early Middle Ages. Here we may suggest only that the full development of Western thought in the modern era is yet to come. What directions it may take, we can not say.

One may think it strange that a section on contemporary problems in history does not mention Vietnam or civil rights or any of the myriad of difficulties men face today. There is no denying the reality of these problems. Yet, their solutions are part of a broader picture that we have tried to sketch here. As Western man works out the problems of his own nature and seeks to perfect his society, he must build on the experience of the past.

Suggested Readings

I. Introduction:

* Bloch, Marc. *The Historian's Craft.* Vintage.
* Bury, John Bagnell. *The Idea of Progress.* Dover.
Carr, Edward Hallett. *What is History?* New York: Alfred A. Knopf, 1962.
* Collingwood, R. G. *The Idea of History.* Galaxy.
Einstein, Lewis. *Historical Change.* Cambridge: Cambridge University Press, 1946.
* Fromm, Erich. *Marx's Concept of Man.* Ungar.
Gardiner, Patrick (ed.) *Theories of History.* New York: Free Press, 1963.
* Hegel, G. W. F. *Lectures on the Philosophy of History.* Translated by J. Sibbree. Dover.
Namier, Lewis B. *Avenues of History.* New York: Macmillan, 1952.
* Stern, Fritz (ed.). *The Varieties of History: From Voltaire to the Present.* Meridian.

II. The Origins of the West:

MESOPOTAMIA

* Chiera, Edward. *They Wrote on Clay.* Phoenix.
* Frankfort, H. *et al. Before Philosophy.* Penguin.
* ———. *The Birth of Civilization in the Near East.* Anchor.
———. *Kingship and the Gods.* Chicago: The University of Chicago, 1948.
* Gordon, Cyrus H. *Hammurabi's Code: Quaint or Forward Looking?* Holt, Rinehart and Winston.
* Guerney, O. R. *The Hittites.* Penguin.
* Kramer, Samuel N. *History Begins at Sumer.* Anchor.

N.B. Paperback books are marked with an asterisk (*). For further information see *Paperback Books in Print:* R. R. Bowker, New York.

* ———. *Sumerian Mythology.* Torchbook.

McGovern, William N. *The Early Empires of Central Asia: A Study of the Scythians and the Huns and the Part They Played in World History.* Chapel Hill: The University of North Carolina, 1939.

* Moscati, Sabatino. *The Face of the Ancient Orient.* Anchor.

* Olmstead, A. T. *History of the Persian Empire.* Phoenix.

Pritchard, James B. (ed.). *Ancient Near Eastern Texts Relating to the Old Testament.* Princeton: Princeton University Press, 1955.

* Wooley, Leonard. *Digging Up the Past.* Penguin.

EGYPT

* Breasted, James Henry. *Development of Religion and Thought in Ancient Egypt.* Torchbook.

* Frankfort, Henri. *Ancient Egyptian Religion: An Interpretation.* Torchbook.

Glanville, S. R. K. (ed.) *The Legacy of Egypt.* Oxford: Clarendon, 1953.

* Wilson, John A. *The Culture of Ancient Egypt.* Phoenix.

HEBREWS

* Albright, Wm. F. *From Stone Age to Christianity.* Anchor.

* Driver, Samuel R. *An Introduction to the Literature of the Old Testament.* Meridian.

Gordon, Cyrus H. *World of the Old Testament.* New York: Doubleday, 1958.

The Old Testament. Revised Standard Version. New York: Nelson, 1955.

* Orlinsky, Harry M. *Ancient Israel.* Cornell.

GREECE

* Aristotle. *On the Constitution of Athens.* Hafner (and others).

* Barker, Ernest. *The Political Thought of Plate and Aristotle.* Dover.

* Cornford, Francis M. *From Religion to Philosophy: A Study in the Origins of Western Speculation.* Torchbook.

* Dickinson, G. Lowes. *The Greek View of Life.* Collier.

* Dodd, E. P. *The Greeks and the Irrational.* Beacon.

* Ehrenburg, Victor. *The People of Aristophanes: A Sociology of Old Attic Comedy.* Schocken.

* Farrington, Benjamin. *Greek Science.* Penguin.

* Freeman, Kathleen. *Greek City-States.* Norton.

* Fustel de Coulanges, N. M. *The Ancient City: A Study on the Religion, Laws, and Institutions of Greece and Rome.* Anchor.

* Grant, Frederick C. (ed.) *Hellenistic Religions: The Age of Syncreticism.* Liberal Arts Press.

* Graves, Robert. *The Greek Myths.* 2 vols. Penguin.

* Guthrie, W. K. C. *The Greeks and Their Gods.* Beacon.

* Hadas, Moses. *Ancilla to Classical Reading.* Collier.

———. *Hellenistic Culture: Fusion and Diffusion.* New York: Columbia University Press, 1959.

* HADAS, MOSES. *A History of Greek Literature.* Columbia.
* HERODOTUS. *The Persian Wars.* Penguin (and others).
* JAEGER, WERNER. *Paedeia.* 3 vols. Trans. by Gilbert Highet. Galaxy.
* KITTO, H. D. F. *The Greeks.* Penguin.
* LIND, L. R. (ed.) *Ten Greek Plays in Contemporary Translations.* Riverside Editions.
* LUCAS, F. L. *Greek Poetry for Everyman.* Beacon.

McKEON, RICHARD (ed.). *The Basic Works of Aristotle.* New York: Random House, 1941.

* NEUGEBACHER, OTTO. *The Exact Sciences in Antiquity.* Torchbook.
* ROBINSON, C. E. *Hellas: A Short History of Ancient Greece.* Beacon.
* ROSE, H. S. *Gods and Heroes of the Greeks.* Meridian.
* ROSTOVTZEFF, M. *Greece.* Galaxy.

———. *Social and Economic History of the Hellenistic World.* Oxford: Clarendon, 1941.

* SARTON, GEORGE. *Ancient Science and Modern Civilization.* Torchbook.
* TARN, W. W. *Alexander the Great.* Beacon.
* TARN, W. W. and GRIFFITH, G. T. *Hellenistic Civilization.* Meridian.
* TAYLOR, A. E. *Aristotle.* Dover.
* ———. *Socrates.* Anchor.
* THUCYDIDES. *The Peloponnesian War.* Penguin (and others).
* WEIL, SIMONE. *The Iliad or the Poem of Force.* Pendle Hill.
* ZIMMERN, ALFRED E. *The Greek Commonwealth, Politics and Economics in Fifth-Century Athens.* Galaxy.

ROME

* ADCOCK, F. E. *Roman Political Ideas and Practice.* Ann Arbor.
* BARROW, R. H. *The Romans.* Penguin.
* CARCOPINO, JEROME. *Daily Life in Ancient Rome.* Trans. E. O. Lorimer. Yale University Press.

CLARKE, M. L. *Studies in the History of Thought from Cicero to Marcus Aurelius.* Cambridge: Harvard University Press, 1956.

* CICERO. *Cicero's Selected Orations.* Translation Publishing Company.
* COWELL, F. R. *Cicero and the Roman Republic.* Penguin.
* DILL, SAMUEL. *Roman Society from Nero to Marcus Aurelius.* Meridian.
* GRANT, MICHAEL. *Roman Literature.* Penguin.
* ———. *The World of Rome.* Mentor.
* HADAS, MOSES. *A History of Latin Literature.* Columbia.
* HAMILTON, EDITH. *The Roman Way to Western Civilization.* Mentor.
* LIVY. *History of Rome.* Trans. B. O. Foster. 13 vols. Penguin.
* LUCRETIUS. *On the Nature of Things.* Penguin (and others).
* MACKAIL, J. W. *Latin Literature,* rev. by Harry E. Schnur. Collier.
* MARCUS AURELIUS. *Meditations.* Gateway Editions (and others).
* MARSH, FRANK BURR. *A History of the Roman World from 146 to 30* B.C. London: Methuen, 1953.
* PLUTARCH. *Lives.* Modern Library.

* ROSTOVTZEFF, M. *Rome.* Galaxy.
———. *Social and Economic History of the Roman Empire.* New York: Oxford University Press. Rev. by P. M. Fraser, 1957.
SCULLARD, HOWARD HAYES. *History of the Roman World from 755 to 146* B.C. London: Methuen, 1951.
* SUETONIUS. *The Twelve Caesars.* Penguin (and others).
* SYME, RONALD. *The Roman Revolution.* Oxford.
* TACITUS. *Histories and Annals.* Modern Library (and others).
* VERGIL. *Aeneid.* Anchor (and others).

FORCES RESHAPING THE WEST

* BAINTON, ROLAND H. *Early Christianity.* Anvil.
* BETTENSON, H. S. (ed.) *Documents of the Christian Church.* New York: Oxford University Press, 1947.
* BULTMANN, RUDOLF. *Primitive Christianity in Its Contemporary Setting.* Meridian.
* CHAMBERS, MORTIMER. *The Fall of Rome. Can It Be Explained?* Holt, Rinehart and Winston.
* COCHRANE, CHARLES NORRIS. *Christianity and Classical Culture.* Galaxy.
* DEISSMANN, ADOLF. *Paul: A Study in Social and Religious History.* Torchbook.
* DILL, SAMUEL. *Roman Society in the Last Century of the Western Empire.* Meridian.
DUCHESNE, LOUIS. *Early History of the Christian Church.* 3 vols. New York: David McKay, 1922–1947.
FISHER, G. P. *A History of Christian Doctrine.* New York: Scribner's, 1923.
* GIBBON, EDWARD. *The History of the Decline and Fall of the Roman Empire.* Modern Library.
GOODENOUGH, ERWIN R. *The Church in the Roman Empire.* New York: Holt, Rinehart and Winston, 1931.
* GOODSPEED, EDGAR J. *Paul.* Apex.
* GRANT, FREDERICK D. (ed.) *Hellenistic Religions: The Age of Syncretism.* Liberal Arts.
* HARNACK, ADOLF. *The Mission and Expansion of Christianity in the First Three Centuries.* Torchbook.
* HUGHES, PHILIP. *A History of the Church.* 3 vols. Image.
* KAGAN, DONALD. *Decline and Fall of the Roman Empire. Why Did It Collapse?* Heath.
* KATZ, SOLOMON. *The Decline of Rome and the Rise of Medieval Europe.* Ithaca, N.Y.: Cornell.
* LIETZMAN, H. A. *History of the Early Church.* 4 vols. Meridian.
* TACITUS. *Germania.* Penguin (and others).
WALLBANK, F. W. *The Decline of the Roman Empire in the West.* New York: Schuman, 1953.
* WEISS, JOHANNES. *Earliest Christianity, A History of the Period* A.D. *30–150.* 2 vols. Torchbook.

BYZANTIUM AND ISLAM

* ANDREA, TOR. *Mohammed: The Man and Faith.* Torchbook.
ARNOLD, THOMAS W. and GUILLAUME, ALFRED (eds.) *The Legacy of Islam.* Oxford: Clarendon Press, 1931.
* BAYNES, N. H. and MOSS, H. ST. L. B. *Byzantium.* Galaxy.
* BROCKELMANN, CAROL. *History of the Islamic Peoples.* Trans. Joel Carmichael and Moshe Perlman. Capricorn.
* BURCKHARDT, JACOB. *The Age of Constantine the Great.* Trans. M. Hadas. Anchor.
* CRESWELL, K. A. C. *Short Account of Early Muslim Architecture.* Penguin.
CROSS, S. H. *Slavic Civilization.* Cambridge: Harvard University Press, 1948.
* DERMEHGHEM, EMILE. *Muhammad and the Islamic Tradition.* Men of Wisdom.
DIEHL, CHARLES. *Byzantium: Greatness and Decline.* New Brunswick, N.J.: Rutgers University Press, 1956.
* GIBB, H. A. R. *Mohammedanism: An Historical Survey.* Mentor.
* GRUNEBAUM, G. E. VON. *Medieval Islam: A Study in Cultural Orientation.* Phoenix.
* GUILLAUME, A. *Islam.* Penguin.
* HITTI, PHILIP K. *The Arabs: A Short History.* Gateway.
* HUSSEY, JOAN. *The Byzantine World.* Torchbook.
* JEFFERY, ARTHUR (ed.). *Islam: Muhammad and His Religion.* Liberal Arts.
* JONES, A. H. M. *Constantine and the Conversion of Europe.* Collier.
* *The Koran.* Penguin (and others).
OSTROGORSKY, GEORGE. *History of the Byzantine State.* New Brunswick, N.J.: Rutgers University Press, 1957.
* RUNCIMAN, STEVEN. *Byzantine Civilization.* Meridian.
* TALBOT-RICE, DAVID. *Byzantine Art.* Penguin.
* URE, P. N. *Justinian and His Age.* Penguin.
* VASILIEV, ALEXANDER A. *History of the Byzantine Empire 324–1453.* Wisconsin.

THE BARBARIANS AND THE IMPERIAL DREAM

* AUGUSTINE. *Confessions.* Modern Library Series (and others).
* BARK, WM. C. *Origins of the Medieval World.* Anchor.
* BEDE. *The History of the English Church and People.* Penguin.
* BOETHIUS. *The Consolation of Philosophy.* Liberal Arts.
* DAWSON, CHRISTOPHER. *The Making of Europe.* Meridian.
* DUCKETT, ELEANOR S. *Gateway to the Middle Ages: Monasticism.* Ann Arbor.
* EASTON, S. C. and WIERUSZOWSKI, H. *The Era of Charlemagne: State and Society.* Anvil.
* EINHARD. *Life of Charlemagne.* Ann Arbor.
* FICHTENAU, H. *The Carolingian Empire.* Torchbook.
LAISTNER, M. L. W. *Thought and Letters in Western Europe, A.D. 500–900.* Ithaca: Cornell University Press, 1957.

* LOT, FERDINAND. *The End of the Ancient World and the Beginnings of the Middle Ages.* Torchbook.
* MARROU, HENRI. *St. Augustine and His Influence through the Ages.* Men of Wisdom Series.
* MCCANN, JUSTIN. *Saint Benedict.* Image.
* MOSS, H. ST. L. B. *The Birth of the Middle Ages, 395–814.* Galaxy.
* PIRENNE, HENRI. *Mohammed and Charlemagne.* Meridian.
* POPE, HUGH. *Saint Augustine of Hippo.* Image.
* RAND, EDWARD KENNARD. *Founders of the Middle Ages.* Dover.
SHOTWELL, J. T. and LOOMIS, L. R. *The See of Peter.* New York: Columbia University Press, 1927.
* SULLIVAN, RICHARD E. *The Coronation of Charlemagne. What Did It Signify?* Heath.
* ———. *Heirs of the Roman Empire.* Cornell.
* TAYLOR, HENRY OSBORN. *The Emergence of Christian Culture in the West.* Torchbook.
* WADDELL, HELEN. *The Desert Fathers.* Ann Arbor.
* WALLACE-HADRILL, J. M. *The Barbarian West: The Early Middle Ages, A.D. 400–1000.* Torchbook.

III. Europe as the West

FROM FEUDALISM TO FEUDAL MONARCHY

BARLOW, F. *The Feudal Kingdom of England 1024–1216.* New York: David McKay, 1954.
* BARRACLOUGH, GEOFFREY. *The Origins of Modern Germany.* Capricorn.
* BLOCH, MARC. *Feudal Society.* 2 vols. Phoenix.
BROOKE, CHRISTOPHER. *The Saxon and Norman Kings.* New York: Macmillan, 1963.
* BRYCE, JAMES. *The Holy Roman Empire.* Schocken Books.
* CAM, HELEN. *England Before Elizabeth.* Torchbook.
* FAWTIER, R. *The Capetian Kings of France.* St. Martin's Library.
* GANSHOF, F. L. *Feudalism.* Trans. Philip Grierson. Torchbook.
HASKINS, CHARLES HOMER. *The Normans in European History.* Boston: Houghton-Mifflin, 1915.
* HASKINS, GEORGE LEE. *The Growth of English Representative Government.* Perpetua.
KANTOROWICZ, ERNST. *Frederick the Second, 1194–1250.* New York: Unger, 1957.
* KELLY, AMY R. *Eleanor of Acquitaine and the Four Kings.* Vintage.
KERN, FRITZ. *Kingship and Law in the Middle Ages.* Chester, Pa.: Dufour Editions, 1948.
* LOPEZ, ROBERT S. *The Tenth Century: How Dark Were the Dark Ages?* Holt, Rinehart and Winston.
LUCHAIRE, ACHILLE. *Social France at the Time of Philip Augustus.* New York: Holt, Rinehart and Winston, 1912.

* MAITLAND, FREDERICK W. *The Constitutional History of England.* Cambridge University.
* PAINTER, SIDNEY. *Medieval Society.* Cornell.
———. *The Reign of King John.* Baltimore: Johns Hopkins, 1949.
* ———. *The Rise of the Feudal Monarchies.* Cornell.
* PETIT-DUTAILLIS, CH. *The Feudal Monarchy in France and England from the Tenth to the Thirteenth Century.* Torchbook.
POWICKE, F. M. *King Henry III and the Lord Edward.* 2 vols. London: Oxford University, 1947.
* SAYLES, G. O. *Medieval Foundations of England.* Perpetua.
* SOUTHERN, R. W. *The Making of the Middle Ages.* Yale University.
* STENTON, D. M. *English Society in the Early Middle Ages.* Penguin.
* STEPHENSON, CARL. *Medieval Feudalism.* Cornell.

MANOR AND TOWN

* ADELSON, H. *Medieval Commerce.* Anvil.
BALDWIN, SUMMERFIELD. *Business in the Middle Ages.* New York: Holt, Rinehart and Winston, 1937.
* BENNETT, H. S. *Life on an English Manor.* Cambridge.
* BOISSONNADE, P. *Life and Work in Medieval Europe.* Trans. Eileen Power. Torchbook.
* HOLMES, URBAN T. *Daily Living in the Twelfth Century.* Wisconsin.
* LAMB, HAROLD. *The Crusades: Iron Men and Saints.* Bantam.
* MUNDY, J. H. and RIESENBERG, P. *Medieval Towns.* Anvil.
* NEWHALL, RICHARD A. *The Crusades.* Holt, Rinehart and Winston.
* PIRENNE, HENRI. *Economic and Social History of Medieval Europe.* Harvard.
* ———. *Medieval Cities: Their Origins and the Revival of Trade.* Trans. Frank D. Halsey. Anchor.
* POWER, EILEEN. *Medieval People.* Anchor.
* RUNCIMAN, STEVEN. *A History of the Crusades.* 3 vols. Torchbook.
SETTON, KENNETH (ed.). *A History of the Crusades.* Vols. I and II. Philadelphia: The University of Pennsylvania, 1955, 1962.
* DE VILLEHARDOUIN, GEOFFREY, and DE JOINVILLE, JEAN. *Memoirs of the Crusades.* Penguin.
* WHITE, LYNN, JR. *Medieval Technology and Social Change.* Oxford.

THE MEDIEVAL INTELLECTUAL REVOLUTION

* ADAMS, HENRY. *Mont Saint Michel and Chartres.* Anchor.
* AQUINAS, ST. THOMAS. *Summa Contra Gentiles.* 4 vols. Image.
ARTZ, F. B. *The Mind of the Middle Ages, A.D. 200–1500: An Historical Survey.* New York: Alfred A. Knopf, 1954. 2d ed.
* BAINTON, ROLAND H. *The Medieval Church.* Anvil.
* BALDWIN, MARSHALL W. *The Medieval Church.* Cornell.
BALDWIN, SUMMERFIELD. *The Organization of Medieval Christianity.* New York: Holt, 1929.
* *Beowulf.* Penguin (and others).

CANTOR, N. F. *Church, Kingship, and Lay Investiture in England, 1089–1135.* Princeton: Princeton University Press, 1958.
* CHAUCER. *Canterbury Tales.* Penguin (and others).
* COPLESTON, F. C. *Aquinas.* Penguin.
* ———. *A History of Philosophy: Medieval Philosophy.* 2 vols. Image.
* CURTIUS, ERNST R. *European Literature and the Latin Middle Ages.* Torchbook.
* DAWSON, CHRISTOPHER. *Religion and the Rise of Western Culture.* Image.
* FREMANTLE, ANNE (ed.). *The Age of Belief: The Medieval Philosophers.* Mentor.
GILSON, ÉTIENNE. *History of Christian Philosophy in the Middle Ages.* New York: Random House, 1955.
* ———. *Reason and Revelation in the Middle Ages.* Scribner's.
HARVEY, JOHN H. *The Gothic World 1100–1600. A Survey of Architecture and Art.* London: Batsford, 1950.
* HASKINS, CHARLES H. *The Renaissance of the Twelfth Century.* Meridian.
* ———. *The Rise of the Universities.* Cornell.
* JARRETT, BEDE. *Life of St. Dominic (1170–1221).* Image.
* LEFF, GORDON. *Medieval Thought from St. Augustine to Ockham.* Penguin.
DE LORRIS, GUILLAUME and DE MEUN, JEAN. *Romance of the Rose.* Trans. Harry W. Robbins. Dutton.
* MCLAUGHLIN, MARY and ROSS, J. B. (eds.) *The Portable Medieval Reader.* Viking.
MOREY, CHARLES RUFUS. *Medieval Art.* New York: W. W. Norton, 1942.
* MORRALL, JOHN B. *Political Thought in Medieval Times.* Torchbook.
PACKARD, SIDNEY R. *Europe and the Church under Innocent III.* New York: Holt, Rinehart and Winston, 1957.
* PANOFSKY, ERWIN. *Gothic Architecture and Scholasticism.* Meridian.
* *The Poem of the Cid: A Prose Translation.* Trans. Lesley Byrd Simpson. University of California Press.
* POWELL, JAMES M. (ed.) *Innocent III: Vicar of Christ or Lord of the World?* Heath.
RASHDALL, HASTINGS. *Universities of Europe in the Middle Ages.* New York: Oxford University, 1936. Rev. ed.
* *The Romance of Tristan and Iseult.* Trans. Joseph Bedier. Anchor.
TELLENBACH, G. *Church, State and Christian Society at the Time of the Investiture Controversy.* Oxford: Blackwell, 1940.
ULLMANN, WALTER. *Growth of Papal Government in the Middle Ages.* New York: Barnes and Noble, 1955.
* VIGNAUX, PAUL. *Philosophy in the Middle Ages.* Meridian.
* WADDELL, HELEN. *Peter Abelard.* Compass.
* ———. *The Wandering Scholars.* Anchor.
* WULF, MAURICE DE. *Philosophy and Civilization in the Middle Ages.* Dover.

THE AGE OF HUMANISM

* BANNON, JOHN F. *The Spanish Conquistadores: Men or Devils?* Holt, Rinehart and Winston.

* BERENSON, BERNARD. *Italian Painters of the Renaissance.* Meridian.

* BREBNER, JOHN B. *The Explorers of North America, 1492–1806.* Meridian.

* BRUCKER, GENE A. *Renaissance Italy: Was It the Birthplace of the Modern World?* Holt, Rinehart and Winston.

* BURCKHARDT, JACOB. *The Civilization of the Renaissance in Italy.* 2 vols. Torchbook.

* BUTTERFIELD, HERBERT. *The Statecraft of Machiavelli.* Collier.

* CASSIRER, E., KRISTELLER, O., and RANDALL, JOHN H., JR. (eds.) *The Renaissance Philosophy of Man.* Phoenix.

* CELLINI, BENVENUTO. *Autobiography.* Bantam.

* CHEYNEY, E. P. *The Dawn of a New Era, 1250–1453.* Torchbook.

* DANTE. *Divine Comedy.* Viking (The Portable Dante) and others.

* ERASMUS. *The Praise of Folly.* Ann Arbor. (Orig. 1509.)

FERGUSON, W. K. *Europe in Transition, 1300–1520.* Boston: Houghton-Mifflin, 1962.

———. *The Renaissance.* Holt, Rinehart and Winston.

———. *The Renaissance in Historical Thought. Five Centuries of Interpretation.* Boston: Houghton-Mifflin, 1948.

* FERGUSON, WALLACE K. *et al. The Renaissance: Six Essays.* Torchbook.

* GILLMORE, MYRON P. *The World of Humanism, 1453–1517.* Torchbook.

HAMILTON, EARL J. *American Treasure and the Price Revolution.* Cambridge: Harvard University Press, 1934.

HART, HENRY H. *Sea Road to the Indies.* New York: Macmillan, 1950.

HIGHET, GILBERT. *The Classical Tradition: Greek and Roman Influences on Western Literature.* New York: Oxford University, 1949.

* HUIZINGA, JOHAN. *Erasmus and the Age of Reformation.* Torchbook.

* MACHIAVELLI. *The Prince and the Discourses.* Modern Library.

* MATTHEWS, G. T. (ed.). *News and Rumor in Renaissance Europe.* Capricorn.

* MEREJKOWSKI, D. *The Romance of Leonardo da Vinci.* Modern Library.

* MORE, SIR THOMAS. *Utopia.* Appleton.

* MORISON, S. E. *Christopher Columbus, Mariner.* Mentor.

* NOWELL, CHARLES E. *The Great Discoveries and the First Colonial Empire.* Cornell.

PARRY, JOHN. *Europe and a Wider World, 1415–1715.* London: Hutchinson's University Library, 1949.

* PATER, WALTER. *The Renaissance.* Mentor.

* PENROSE, BOIES. *Travel and Discovery in the Renaissance, 1420–1620.* Athenaeum.

* PRESCOTT, W. H. *The Conquest of Mexico.* Modern Library.

* ———. *The Conquest of Peru.* 2 vols. Dolphin.

* RABELAIS. *Gargantua and Pantagruel.* Penguin.

* ROEDER, RALPH. *The Man of the Renaissance.* Meridian.

* ROSS, JAMES B. and MCLAUGHLIN, MARY M. (eds.) *The Portable Renaissance Reader.* Viking.

* SANTILLANA, GEORGIO DE (ed.). *The Age of Adventure: The Renaissance Philosophers.* Mentor.

* SYMONDS, JOHN ADDINGTON. *The Renaissance in Italy.* 5 vols. Capricorn.
* TAYLOR, P. *The Notebooks of Leonardo da Vinci: A New Selection.* Mentor.

THE AGE OF REFORM

* BAINTON, R. H. *Here I Stand: A Life of Martin Luther.* Mentor.
* ———. *The Reformation of the Sixteenth Century.* Beacon.
BRANDI, KARL. *The Emperor Charles V.* London: Cope, 1939.
ELTON, GEOFFREY R. *England Under the Tudors.* London: Methuen, 1955.
GRIMM, HAROLD J. *The Reformation Era, 1500–1650.* New York: Macmillan, 1954.
* GRISAR, H. *Luther, His Life and Work.* Newman.
* HARBISON, E. H. *The Age of the Reformation.* Cornell.
* HARKNESS, G. *John Calvin, The Man and His Ethics.* Apex.
HOLBORN, HAJO. *A History of Modern Germany: The Reformation.* New York: Knopf, 1959.
JANELLE, PIERRE. *The Catholic Reformation.* Milwaukee: Bruce, 1949.
JEDIN, HUBERT. *A History of the Council of Trent.* 2 vols. London: Thomas Nelson, 1957.
MANSCHRECK, CLYDE L. *Melanchthon, The Quiet Reformer.* New York: Abingdon Press, 1958.
* MCFARLANE, KENNETH B. *John Wycliffe and the Beginnings of English Nonconformity.* Collier.
* MOLLAT, G. *Popes at Avignon, 1305–1378.* Torchbook.
* MOSSE, GEORGE L. *Calvinism: Authoritarian or Democratic?* Holt, Rinehart and Winston.
PARKER, T. M. *The English Reformation to 1558.* London: Oxford University Press, 1950.
* ROWSE, A. L. *The England of Elizabeth: The Structure of Society.* Macmillan.
* SMITH, PRESERVED. *The Age of the Reformation.* 2 vols. Collier.
* WEBER, MAX. *The Protestant Ethic and the Spirit of Capitalism.* Scribner's.
WILLIAMS, GEORGE H. and MERGAL, A. M. (eds.). *The Radical Reformation.* Philadelphia: Westminster Press, 1957.

EUROPE, 1648–1715

ASHLEY, MAURICE. *Louis XIV and the Greatness of France.* New York: Macmillan, 1948.
BRYANT, ARTHUR. *King Charles II.* New York: Longmans, 1931.
CADOUX, CECIL J. *Philip of Spain and the Netherlands; An Essay on Moral Judgments in History.* London: Lutterworth, 1947.
* DORN, W. L. *Competition for Empire 1740–1763.* Torchbook.
* FAY, S. B. *The Rise of Brandenburg-Prussia to 1786.* Holt, Rinehart and Winston.
* GARDINER, S. R. *Oliver Cromwell.* Collier.
* GERSHOY, L. *From Despotism to Revolution, 1763–1789.* Torchbook.
HOLBORN, HAJO. *A History of Modern Germany, 1648–1840.* New York: Knopf, 1963.
* LEWIS, H. *The Splendid Century.* Anchor.

* LOCKE, JOHN. *Two Treatises of Government*. Hafner (and others).
* MILTON, JOHN. *Areopagitica*. Croft Classics (and others).
* NEALE, J. E. *The Age of Catherine de Medici*. Torchbook.
* PACKARD, L. B. *The Age of Louis XIV*. Holt, Rinehart and Winston.
* ROBERTS, P. *The Quest for Security, 1715–1740*. Torchbook.
* SUMNER, B. H. *Peter the Great and the Emergence of Russia*. Collier.
* TANNER, J. R. *English Constitutional Conflicts of the Seventeenth Century*. Cambridge.
* THOMSON, G. S. *Catherine the Great and The Expansion of Russia*. Collier.

TREVELYAN, G. M. *England under the Stuarts*. 21st ed. London: Methuen, 1957.
* VERNADSKY, GEORGE. *History of Russia*. Yale.
* VOLTAIRE. *The Age of Louis XIV*. Everyman.

WEDGEWOOD, C. V. *The Great Rebellion*. 2 vols. London: Collins, 1955–1959.
* ———. *The Thirty Years War*. Anchor.
* WOLF, J. B. *The Emergence of the Great Powers, 1685–1715*. Torchbook.

IV. The Age of Western Leadership

THE EIGHTEENTH CENTURY

* ALDEN, JOHN RICHARD. *The American Revolution, 1775–1783*. Torchbook.
* ASHTON, T. S. *Industrial Revolutions: 1760–1830*. Galaxy.
* BECKER, CARL. *The Heavenly City of the Eighteenth Century Philosophers*. Yale University.

BELL, ARTHUR E. *Christian Huygens and the Development of Science in the Seventeenth Century*. London: Edward Arnold, 1947.
* BRINTON, CRANE. *The Anatomy of Revolution*. Vintage.
* ———. *A Decade of Revolution, 1789–1799*. Torchbook.
* BRUFORD, W. H. *Germany in the Eighteenth Century: The Social Background of the Literary Revival*. Cambridge: Cambridge University Press, 1935.
* BRUNN, GEOFFREY. *Europe and the French Imperium*. Torchbook.
* BURTT, E. A. *The Metaphysical Foundations of Modern Science*. Anchor.

BUTTERFIELD, HERBERT. *George III, Lord North and the People, 1779–1780*. London: Bell, Harcourt and Brace, 1949.

———. *The Origins of Modern Science, 1300–1800*. New York: Macmillan, 1951.
* DAMPIER, W. C. *A Shorter History of Science*. Meridian.

FARMER, PAUL. *France Reviews its Revolutionary Origins*. New York: Columbia University, 1944.
* *Federalist Papers*. Liberal Arts Press (and others).
* FIELDING, HENRY. *Tom Jones*. Modern Library.
* GERSHOY, LEO. *The Era of the French Revolution*. Anvil.
* GEYL, P. *Napoleon: For and Against*. Yale.
* GIPSON, LAWRENCE H. *The Coming of the Revolution*. Torchbook.

HAMMOND, D. L. and BARBARA. *The Town Labourer 1760–1832*. London: Longmans, Green, 1918.

* HAZARD, PAUL. *The European Mind (1680–1715)*. Meridian.
* ———. *European Thought in the Eighteenth Century*. Meridian.
LANDES, DAVID S. *The Rise of Capitalism* (Main Themes in European History). Macmillan.
* LEFEBVRE, GEORGES. *The Coming of the French Revolution*. Vintage.
* LOCKE, JOHN. *Two Treatises of Government*. Hafner.
* MALTHUS, T. R. *An Essay on the Principles of Population as It Affects the Future Improvement of Society*. 2 vols. Everyman.
* MANUEL, FRANK E. *The Age of Reason*. Cornell.
* MONTESQUIEU. *The Spirit of the Laws*. Hafner.
MORGAN, E. S. *American Revolution: A Review of Changing Interpretations*. Macmillan.
* ———. *The Birth of the Republic, 1763–1789*. University of Chicago Press.
MOWAT, R. B. *The Age of Reason*. Boston: Houghton Mifflin, 1934.
* NUSSBAUM, F. L. *The Triumph of Science and Reason, 1660–1685*. Torchbook.
ORNSTEIN, MARTHA. *Role of Scientific Societies in the Seventeenth Century*. Chicago: University of Chicago, 1928.
* PALMER, R. R. *Twelve Who Ruled: The Committee of Public Safety During the Terror*. Athenaeum.
ROGERS, CORNWELL, B. *The Spirit of Revolution in 1789*. Princeton: Princeton University Press, 1949.
* ROUSSEAU. *Social Contract*. Hafner.
* SMITH, ADAM. *The Wealth of Nations*. Modern Library.
THOMPSON, J. M. *Napoleon Bonaparte: His Rise and Fall*. Oxford: Blackwell, 1952.
———. *Robespierre and the French Revolution*. Collier.
* DE TOCQUEVILLE, ALEXIS. *The Old Regime and the Revolution*. Anchor.
* USHER, ABBOT. *A History of Mechanical Inventions*. Beacon.
* WAHLKE, JOHN C. (ed.). *The Causes of the American Revolution*. Heath.
* WALLACE, WILLARD M. *Appeal to Arms: A Military History of the American Revolution*. Quadrangle.
WATSON, J. STEVEN. *The Reign of George III, 1760–1815*. New York: Oxford University Press, 1960.
WESTFALL, RICHARD S. *Science and Religion in Seventeenth Century England*. New Haven: Yale University Press, 1958.
* WHITEHEAD, ALFRED N. *Science and the Modern World*. Mentor.
* WRIGHT, LOUIS B. *Atlantic Frontier: Colonial American Civilization (1607–1763)*. Cornell.
* ———. *Cultural Life of the American Colonies*. Torchbook.

THE NINETEENTH CENTURY

ALBERTINI, L. *The Origins of the War of 1914*. 2 vols. London: Oxford University Press, 1952–1953.
* BARZUN, JACQUES. *Darwin, Marx, Wagner: Critique of a Heritage*. Anchor.
* BERLIN, ISAIAH. *Karl Marx: His Life and Environment*. Galaxy.
* BINKLEY, R. C. *Realism and Nationalism, 1852–1871*. Torchbook.

* BRIGGS, ASA. *The Age of Improvement, 1783–1867*. Torchbook.

BROGAN, D. W. *France under the Republic*. New York: Harper and Row, 1940.

CECIL, ALGERNON. *Queen Victoria and Her Prime Ministers*. London: Eyre and Spottiswoode, 1953.

* CLAPHAM, JOHN. *The Economic Development of France and Germany, 1815–1914*. Cambridge University Press.

COLE, GEORGE D. H. *A Short History of the British Working-Class Movement, 1789–1947*. London: Allen and Unwin, 1948.

———. *Socialist Thought: The Forerunners 1789–1850, and Marxism and Anarchism 1850–1890*. Vols. I and II. *History of Socialist Thought*. London: Macmillan, 1954–1955.

CRATTWELL, C. R. M. F. *A History of the Great War, 1914–1918*. Oxford: Clarendon Press, 1936. 2d ed.

* CURIE, EVE. *Madam Curie: A Biography*. Pocket Books.

* DARWIN, CHARLES. *The Origin of the Species and the Descent of Man*. Modern Library.

* DE VOTO, BERNARD. *Across the Wide Missouri*. Sentry.

DILL, MARSHALL, JR. *Germany, a Modern History*. Ann Arbor: University of Michigan Press, 1961.

ELTON, GODFREY. *The Revolutionary Idea in France, 1789–1871*. London: Edward Arnold, 1931.

ENSOR, R. C. K. *England, 1870–1914*. Oxford: Clarendon, 1936.

* EYCK, ERICH. *Bismarck and the German Empire*. Norton.

* FREUD, SIGMUND. *An Outline of Psychoanalysis*. Norton.

GASH, NORMAN. *Politics in the Age of Peel: A Study in the Technique of Parliamentary Representation 1830–1850*. London: Longmans, Green, 1953.

GRAY, ALEXANDER. *The Socialist Tradition: Moses to Lenin*. London: Longmans, Green, 1946.

GUÉRARD, ALBERT. *Napoleon III*. Cambridge: Harvard University Press, 1943.

* HARDY, THOMAS. *The Return of the Native*. Pocket Books.

* HAYES, CARLTON, J. H. *A Generation of Materialism, 1871–1900*. Torchbook.

* HEILBRONER, ROBERT L. *The Worldly Philosophers, the Lives, Times, and Ideas of the Great Economic Thinkers*. Simon and Schuster.

* HOBSON, J. A. *Imperialism: A Study*. Ann Arbor.

HOFSTADTER, RICHARD, AARON, DANIEL, and MILLER, WILLIAM. *The American Republic*. 2 vols. Englewood Cliffs, N.J.: Prentice-Hall, 1959.

* IBSEN, HENRIK. *Ghosts; An Enemy of the People; a Doll's House: The Master Builder*. Modern Library.

* JASZE, OSCAR. *The Dissolution of the Habsburg Monarchy*. Phoenix.

* KARPOVICH, M. M. *Imperial Russia, 1801–1917*. Holt, Rinehart and Winston.

MCBRIAR, A. M. *Fabian Socialism and English Politics, 1884–1918*. Cambridge: Cambridge University Press, 1962.

MARX, KARL and ENGELS, FREDERICH. *Communist Manifesto*. Gateway.

MAY, ARTHUR J. *The Hapsburg Monarchy, 1867–1914*. Cambridge: Harvard University Press, 1951.

* Meinecke, F. *The German Catastrophe.* Beacon.
* Meyer, A. G. *Marxism Since the Communist Manifesto.* Macmillan.
Miliukov, Paul. *Outlines of Russian Culture.* 3 vols. Philadelphia: University of Pennsylvania Press, 1943.
* Mill, J. S. *On Liberty; Representative Government; Utilitarianism; Autobiography.* Liberal Arts.
Moon, P. T. *Imperialism and World Politics.* New York: Macmillan, 1936.
* Mumford, Louis. *The Story of the Utopias.* Compass.
Nicolson, Harold. *Peacemaking 1919.* London: Constable, 1933.
* Owen, D. E. *Imperialism and Nationalism in the Far East.* Holt, Rinehart and Winston.
* *Philosophers Speak for Themselves: Berkeley, Hume, and Kant.* Edited by T. V. Smith and Marjorie Grene. Phoenix.
Plamenatz, John. *The Revolutionary Movement in France, 1815–1871.* London: Longmans, Green, 1952.
* Pringle, Henry. *Theodore Roosevelt.* Harvest Books.
* Robertson, Priscilla. *The Revolutions of 1848: A Social History.* Torchbook.
* Rosenberg, Arthur. *Imperial Germany: The Birth of the German Republic, 1871–1918.* Beacon.
* Schlesinger, A. M. Jr., *The Age of Jackson.* Mentor.
* Scott, Walter. *Ivanhoe.* Pocket Books.
* Seton-Watson, H. *The Decline of Imperial Russia, 1855–1914.* Praeger.
* Shafer, Boyd C. *Nationalism: Myth and Reality.* Harvard.
* Slade, R. *The Belgian Congo.* Oxford.
* Somervell, D. C. *English Thought in the Nineteenth Century.* Tartan.
* Taylor, A. J. P. *The Course of German History.* Capricorn.
———. *The Habsburg Monarchy, 1809–1918.* Torchbook.
* Tuchman, Barbara. *The Guns of August.* Dell.
* Turner, Frederick Jackson. *The Frontier in American History.* Holt, Rinehart and Winston.
* Wallbank, T. W. *India: A Survey of the Heritage and Growth of Indian Nationalism.* Holt, Rinehart and Winston.
Woodward, E. L. *The Age of Reform, 1815–1870.* Oxford: Clarendon, 1938.

V. Crisis, Change, and a New World

* Allen, Frederick L. *Only Yesterday.* Bantam.
* Barth, Karl. *The Word of God and the Word of Man.* Torchbook.
* Bohannan, Paul. *Africa and Africans.* American Museum Science Books.
* Bullock, Allen. *Hitler: A Study in Tyranny.* Torchbook.
* Carter, Gwendolen M. *Independence for Africa.* Praeger.
* Churchill, Winston. *The Gathering Storm.* Bantam.
* Deutscher, Isaac. *Stalin: A Political Biography.* Vintage.
* Dickens, Charles. *David Copperfield.* Modern Library.
Ebenstein, William. *Fascist Italy.* New York: American Book Company, 1939.

EINZIG, PAUL. *The World Economic Crisis, 1929–1931.* London: Macmillan, 1932.

* FAIRBANK, JOHN K. *The United States and China.* Compass.

FARMER, PAUL. *Vichy: Political Dilemma.* New York: Columbia University Press, 1955.

FEILING, KEITH. *The Life of Neville Chamberlain.* London: Macmillan, 1947.

* FISCHER, LOUIS. *The Soviets in World Affairs.* Vintage.

* FLORINSKY, MICHAEL T. *The End of the Russian Empire.* Collier.

* FRAZER, SIR JAMES. *The Golden Bough.* Macmillan.

GEDYE, G. E. R. *Betrayal in Central Europe: Austria and Czechoslovakia, The Fallen Bastions.* New York: Harper and Row, 1939.

* GRAVES, ROBERT and HODGE, ALAN. *The Long Week-end: A Social History of Great Britain, 1918–1939.* Norton.

GRINDROD, MURIEL. *The Rebuilding of Italy: Politics and Economics, 1945–1955.* London: Royal Institute of International Affairs, 1955.

GROSSER, ALFRED. *The Colossus Again: Western Germany from Defeat to Rearmament.* New York: Praeger, 1955.

* HITLER, ADOLPH. *Mein Kampf.* Sentry.

HOLBORN, HAJO. *The Political Collapse of Europe.* New York: Alfred A. Knopf, 1951.

HOSKINS, HALFORD L. *The Middle East.* New York: Macmillan, 1954.

HUGHES, H. STUART. *Contemporary Europe: A History.* Englewood Cliffs, N.J.: Prentice-Hall, 1961.

* HUNT, R. N. CAREW. *The Theory and Practice of Communism.* Penguin.

HUTCHINSON, KEITH. *The Decline and Fall of British Capitalism.* New York: Macmillan, 1957.

* KENNAN, GEORGE F. *Russia and the West Under Lenin and Stalin.* Mentor.

* KNAPTON, E. J. *France Since Versailles.* Holt, Rinehart and Winston.

* LÖWITH, KARL. *Meaning in History: The Theological Implications of the Philosophy of History.* Phoenix.

* LUETHY, HERBERT. *France Against Herself.* Meridian.

* MCNEILL, WILLIAM. *The Rise of the West.* Mentor.

* MOOREHEAD, ALAN. *The Russian Revolution.* Bantam.

* MULLER, HERBERT J. *The Uses of the Past.* Mentor and Galaxy.

* NEHRU, JAWAHARLAL. *Toward Freedom.* Beacon.

* DU NOÜY, LECOMTE. *Human Destiny.* Mentor.

* POPPER, KARL R. *The Open Society and Its Enemies.* 2 vols. Torchbook.

SALVEMINI, GAETANO. *Under the Axe of Fascism.* New York: Viking, 1936.

* SCOTT, DEREK, J. R. *Russian Political Institutions.* Praeger.

SETON-WATSON, HUGH. *Eastern Europe Between the Wars, 1918–1941.* Cambridge: Cambridge University Press, 1945.

* ———. *From Lenin to Khrushchev.* Praeger.

SETON-WATSON, ROBERT W. *A History of the Czechs and Slovaks.* London: Hutchinson, 1943.

SHAPLEY, HARLOW and others (eds.). *A Treasury of Science.* New York: Harper and Row, 1958.

* SHERWOOD, ROBERT E. *Roosevelt and Hopkins.* 2 vols. Bantam.

* SHIRER, WILLIAM L. *Berlin Diary*. Popular.
* ———. *The Rise and Fall of the Third Reich*. Crest.
* SHUB, DAVID. *Lenin*. Mentor.
STAVRIANOS, LEFTEN S. *The Balkans Since 1453*. New York: Holt, Rinehart and Winston, 1958.
* THOMAS, HUGH. *The Spanish Civil War*. Colophon.
THOMPSON, DAVID. *Democracy in France*. London: Oxford University, 1946.
* TOYNBEE, ARNOLD. *A Study of History*. Galaxy.
TREADGOLD, DONALD W. *Twentieth Century Russia*. Chicago: Rand McNally, 1964. 2d ed.
VERMEIL, EDMOND. *Germany in the Twentieth Century*. New York: Praeger, 1956.
VERNADSKY, G. *The Russian Revolution, 1917–1931*. Holt, Rinehart and Winston.
WALTERS, FRANCIS P. *A History of the League of Nations*. 2 vols. London: Oxford University Press, 1952.
WHEELER-BENNET, JOHN W. *Wooden Titan, Hindenberg, in Twenty Years of German History, 1914–1934*. New York: William Morrow, 1936.
WHITE, THEODORE H. *Fire in the Ashes: Europe in Mid-Century*. New York: William Sloane, 1953.
WILLIAMS, PHILIP. *Politics in Post-War France; Parties and the Constitution in the Fourth Republic*. London: Longmans, Green, 1958. New Edition.
* WOLFE, BERTRAM. *Three Who Made a Revolution*. Delta.
WOLFF, ROBERT L. *The Balkans in Our Times*. Cambridge: Harvard University, 1956.
WRIGHT, GORDON C. *Raymond Poincaré and the French Presidency*. Stanford: Stanford University Press, 1942.

Index